THE SCHOOL OF MONTAIGNE IN EARLY MODERN EUROPE

The School of Montaigne in Early Modern Europe

Volume 2: The Reader-Writer

WARREN BOUTCHER

OXFORD
UNIVERSITY PRESS

OXFORD
UNIVERSITY PRESS

Great Clarendon Street, Oxford, OX2 6DP,
United Kingdom

Oxford University Press is a department of the University of Oxford.
It furthers the University's objective of excellence in research, scholarship,
and education by publishing worldwide. Oxford is a registered trade mark of
Oxford University Press in the UK and in certain other countries

© Warren Boutcher 2017

The moral rights of the author have been asserted

First Edition published in 2017

Impression: 1

Published in the United States of America by Oxford University Press
198 Madison Avenue, New York, NY 10016, United States of America

British Library Cataloguing in Publication Data
Data available

Library of Congress Control Number: 2015938319

ISBN 978–0–19–812374–3 (Volume 1)
ISBN 978–0–19–873966–1 (Volume 2)
ISBN 978–0–19–873967–8 (Set)

Printed in Great Britain by
Clays Ltd, St Ives plc

To Rossella Brambilla and Stella Maria Boutcher
With love

Contents: Volumes 1 and 2

VOLUME 1

1. THE PATRON-AUTHOR

Acknowledgements

When John Florio began his translation of Montaigne in the late 1590s he had Lady Anne Harrington and the Countess of Bedford breathing down his neck. One cold dawn in Twickenham in April 1984 my mother Alma and I huddled over a typewriter completing the typescript of my final-year undergraduate dissertation on Florio's work. At a similar hour seven years later in Cambridge, my wife Rossella supervised the laser-printing of what she insisted was the final draft of my doctoral dissertation on Florio's Montaigne and humanism in Renaissance England.

Shortly afterwards, Kim Scott Walwyn† of Oxford University Press, the most inspiring academic publisher I have ever met, exhorted me to move on to a monograph. As Commissioning Editor, Jacqueline Baker drove it through with sure judgement in the final stages—offering me the benefits of a very generous and helpful response on the part of OUP's anonymous reviewer. Sophie Goldsworthy, Andrew McNeillie, Ariane Petit, Jenny Townshend, and Rachel Platt have at various stages taken up the reins and supported the project with dedication.

I have needed these and many further encouragements to complete the current study, which descends only indirectly from long-gone first attempts. I am grateful to everyone who has kept faith with me and waited patiently for 'the book'. I have been supported by a number of funding bodies and institutions over the years, all of which have likewise shown great patience: the Arts and Humanities Research Council (when still the AHRB), the Leverhulme Trust, The British Academy, Queen Mary University of London, and the School of Advanced Study, University of London. I thank them all for their generous support.

The School of Montaigne is based on post-doctoral research but it does aim to account for the things that fascinated and intrigued me about reading Florio and the French *Essais* together as an undergraduate in the 1980s, and it does owe much to my own teachers and my own experience of literary and general education. I would like to remember here: Jack Hurst (Haberdashers' Aske's School), the greatest language-teacher I have ever met; Stewart Eames (University of Cambridge), who taught me to love Florio's Montaigne; and Marie Axton† (University of Cambridge), who taught me to take account of the fact that Florio's Montaigne, and all the other books I was reading, were objects.

Florio was rather ill-equipped for his task. I sympathize. He was more fluent and better read in Italian than in French, and he needed help with his Latin. His English was a bit verbose. So he sought aid from Matthew Gwinne and Theodore Diodati, two men of superior scholarship. I did the same.

George Hoffmann and John O'Brien have been extraordinarily generous in helping and supporting an interloper in their field. For more years than I care to remember they have tolerated my inaccuracies and over-ambitious arguments, gently steering me in—I believe—better directions. George has been in constant touch with suggestions and responses, and found time to read drafts of individual chapters with great acuity. In London in 2007–8, John led a seminar on 'Early modern freedoms' that profoundly influenced my thinking. I benefitted, in particular, from the contributions made by Richard Scholar (whose book on *Montaigne and the Art of Freethinking* is complementary to my own), Isabelle Moreau, Hugh Roberts, and André Tournon.

I have also benefitted constantly from the support of three other great Montaigne scholars of earlier generations: Terence Cave, Michael Screech, and Ian Maclean. I shall always be grateful for the advice and encouragement all three have unfailingly offered me over the years. Their classics—*The Cornucopian Text*, *Montaigne and Melancholy*, and *Montaigne philosophe*—were by my side every step of the way as models of scholarship and argument, which is not to say I have been able to live up to them.

Terence invited me to participate in a very important project at the University of Oslo entitled 'Dislocations: Practices of Cultural Transfer' (2005–9), which influenced my thinking greatly. I should like to thank in particular Kathy Eden, Kristin Gjerpe, Gro Bjørnerud Mo, Kirsti Sellevold, Trond Kruke Salberg and Vibeke Roggen. I was also galvanized in the final stages of writing-up by Terence's Balzan project 'Literature as an Object of Knowledge', based at the St John's College Research Centre, Oxford.

Even from his retirement, Mike sent me encouraging messages to keep me going. Ian's Lyell lectures on the Latin book trade of the late Renaissance, delivered in Oxford in May 2010 and published by Harvard University Press in 2012, were an inspirational source of ideas and information in the final stages of the research.

Many other members of the international community of specialist Montaigne scholars freely offered their support. I would like to reserve a special mention for Philippe Desan, whose dynamism has single-handedly driven the revival in Montaigne studies, both in Europe and America. His important new work on Montaigne's political biography (*Montaigne: une biographie politique*, Paris, 2014) unfortunately came out too late to be taken fully into account in the current study. My thanks also to: Daisy Aaronian, Katherine Almquist[†], Joanna Barker, Cathleen Bauschatz, Concetta Cavallini, Philip Ford[†], Virginia Krause, Alain Legros, Michel Magnien, Catherine Magnien, Richard Regosin[†], Bruno Roger-Vasselin, Richard Scholar, Michel Simonin[†], Ingrid De Smet, Laura Willett, Michael Wyatt. It was a particular joy to discover the work of William Hamlin, who has transformed the study of Florio's Montaigne with his research into extant copies of the three seventeenth-century editions, and who generously shared his knowledge in correspondence.

Friends and colleagues in other fields and other professions to whom I am extremely grateful include: Duccio Belsito, Anna Bettoni, Peter Burke, Stephen Clucas, Anne Coldiron, Virginia Cox, Simon Ditchfield, Roberta Filippi, Irene Fosi, Angus Gowland, Neil Kenny, Jill Kraye, Jeannine De Landtsheer, Jan Machielsen, Paul Nelles, David Norbrook, Jan Papy, Andrew Pettegree, Francesco Piccione, Mita Pippa, Suzanne Reynolds, Maria Adele Rubino, Lorenzo Scarpelli, Fred Schurink, Sarah Alyn Stacey, Nick Wells.

My picture researcher Susan Neale went well beyond the call of duty in turning my inchoate list of desired images into the illustrations that appear in these pages. Alex Gray helped very ably and patiently with the editing. Terence Cave, John O'Brien, Ingrid De Smet, William Hamlin, Neil Kenny, Jan Machielsen, and Tom Hamilton all took the trouble to read drafts of chapters in the final stages, and to correct errors. The many errors that doubtless remain are my own responsibility.

Insofar as this study is interdisciplinary in scope, it owes much to two institutions I found myself in at particular moments. The first was Trinity Hall, Cambridge, during the 1980s, under its Master and Mistress, Sir John and Lady Danielle Lyons. In this great college, fellows from different disciplines were actually heard talking to one another about their work. Peter Holland and Jonathan Bate were important mentors there during my first encounters with Montaigne.

The second is the Faculty of Humanities and Social Sciences, Queen Mary University of London. The project began to assume its current shape during the Spring 1993 interview which both secured my post in the Faculty's School of English and Drama and sowed the seeds of Volume 1, Chapter 1. I found myself in a highly stimulating intellectual environment, initially shaped by Lisa Jardine[†] and Jacqueline Rose, and energized in medieval and early modern studies by a steadily accumulating group of scholars either employed by or regularly visiting the School and the Faculty: Alan Stewart, Lorna Hutson, William Sherman, David Colclough, Jerry Brotton, Julia Boffey, Evelyn Welch, Kevin Sharpe[†], Graham Rees[†], Maria Wakely, Quentin Skinner, James Shapiro, Laura Ashe, Rosanna Cox, Chloe Houston, Andrea Brady, Mary Flannery, Tamara Atkin, David Wootton, Miri Rubin, Kate Lowe, Michael Moriarty, Trevor Dadson, Adrian Armstrong, Ruth Ahnert, Gwilym Jones, Joad Raymond, Claire Preston.

Successive Heads of School and of English have supported the project, especially Julia Boffey, Morag Shiach, Paul Hamilton, Michèle Barrett, and Chris Reid. With characteristic dynamism and selflessness, Evelyn Welch directly facilitated its completion when serving as my appraiser, while Morag Shiach, Virginia Davis, Simon Booy, Chris Cramer, June Ryde, and Marta Timoncini did everything they could to make it possible for a Dean to carry on with research and writing. David Colclough helped enormously by doing his job and providing support in all weathers.

Eleven scholars who took doctorates with me during this time also contributed much to my thinking: Jason Scott-Warren, Ana González, Raya Al Jadir, Katherine O'Mahoney, Matthew Finch, David Barnes, Tom Parkinson, Eleanor Merchant, Clare Whitehead, Judith Atty, Lydia Zeldenrust. I am indebted in particular to their illuminating discussions of, respectively, gift-books, 'conversation', service, female agency, *lieux de mémoire*, literature and cultural politics, the relationship between manuscript and print, reformed humanist education, the court drama of the early Jacobean years, translation and Elizabethan poetry, translation and rewriting. I am also indebted to the excellent doctoral work of Tom Hamilton (on Pierre de L'Estoile), and of Felicity Green, now published with Cambridge University Press as *Montaigne and the Life of Freedom*.

I am also very grateful to all those who between 1993 and 2014 invited me to give the papers and publish the studies in which I worked out my argument. The seminars and conferences in which I gave the papers are too numerous to mention. Some of the chapters include substantial reworking of material that has been tried out in a different form in previous publications: *The Cambridge Companion to Montaigne* (1.1, 1.3); *Montaigne Studies* (1.2); *Montaigne politique* (1.4); *Michigan Romance Studies* (1.7); *The changing face of Montaigne* (2.3); *Montaigne et Shakespeare* (2.3); *Reassessing Tudor Humanism* (2.3); *Nouveau Bulletin de la Société Internationale des Amis de Montaigne* (2.5). Two chapters contain lighter reworkings of material published in *Montaigne and the Low Countries* (2.4), and *EMF: Studies in Early Modern France* (2.6).[1]

The images in this study are reproduced with the kind permission of the following colleges, archives, and libraries: Abbot Hall Art Gallery, Kendal (Illus. 2.3.4); Archive of the Congregatio pro Doctrina Fidei, Rome (Illus. 1.7.1); Archivio Storico Capitolino, Rome (Illus. 1.7.2, 1.7.3); Biblioteca Universitaria Alessandrina, Rome (Illus. 1.3.3); Bibliothèque Municipale de Bordeaux (Illus. 2.5.9, 2.5.10); Bibliothèque Municipale de Reims (Illus. 2.5.8, 2.5.11); Bibliothèque nationale de France (Illus. 2.1.2, 2.1.3, 2.1.4, 2.1.5, 2.1.6, 2.1.7, 2.1.8, 2.2.1, 2.5.1, 2.5.2, 2.5.3, 2.5.4, 2.5.5, 2.5.6), The Bodleian Libraries, the University of Oxford (Illus. 1.4.1, 1.4.2, 1.4.3, 1.5.1, 1.5.2, 1.6.4, 2.2.2, 2.2.3, 2.2.6, 2.3.1, 2.3.2, 2.3.3), The British Library Board (Illus. 1.1.1, 1.1.2, 1.1.3, 1.1.4, 1.1.5, 1.1.6, 1.1.7, 1.1.8, 1.1.9, 1.1.10, 2.4.1, 2.4.2, 2.4.4, 2.4.6, 2.4.7), Philippe Desan, Bibliotheca Desaniana (Illus. 1.6.1, 1.6.2, 1.6.3, 1.7.4, 2.1.1, 2.5.7), Folger Shakespeare Library (Illus. 1.4.4), Anna Fox (Harshlight) (cover illustration Volume 1, Illus. 1.3.1), Musée d'art et d'histoire, Geneva (cover illustration Volume 2, Illus. 1.1.11,

[1] Warren Boutcher, 'Montaigne's Legacy', in U. Langer (ed.), *The Cambridge Companion to Montaigne* (Cambridge: Cambridge University Press, 2005), 27–52; Warren Boutcher, 'Schooling America: Donald Frame, Pierre Villey, and the Educational History of the *Essais*', *Montaigne Studies*, 20 (2008), 117–28; Warren Boutcher, '"Le pauvre patient": Montaigne agent dans l'économie du savoir', in P. Desan (ed.), *Montaigne politique: Actes du colloque international tenu à University of Chicago (Paris) les 29 et 30 avril 2005* (Paris: Honoré Champion, 2006), 243–61; Warren Boutcher, '"Le moyen de voir ce Senecque escrit à la main": Montaigne's *Journal de voyage* and the politics of science and *faveur* in the Vatican Library', *Michigan Romance Studies*, 15 (1995), 177–214; Warren Boutcher, '"Learning mingled with nobilitie": Directions for reading Montaigne's *Essais* in their institutional context', in Keith Cameron and Laura Lee Willett (eds.), *Le visage changeant de Montaigne/ The changing face of Montaigne* (Paris: Honoré Champion, 2003), 337–62; Warren Boutcher, 'Marginal Commentaries: The Cultural Transmission of Montaigne's *Essais* in Shakespeare's England', in P. Kapitanak and J. M. Maguin (eds.), *Montaigne et Shakespeare: vers un nouvel humanisme* (Montpellier: Société Française Shakespeare, 2003), 13–27; Warren Boutcher, 'Humanism and Literature in Late Tudor England: Translation, the continental book and the case of Montaigne's *Essais*', in J. Woolfson (ed.), *Reassessing Tudor Humanism* (Basingstoke: Palgrave Macmillan, 2002), 243–68; Warren Boutcher, '"Fadaises domestiques": Montaigne marchand bourgeois bordelais lu par un marchand bourgeois rémois', *Nouveau Bulletin de la Société Internationale des Amis de Montaigne*, IV, no. 2 ('Numéro spécial: Montaigne et sa région'—also 8th series no. 48) (2008), 401–18; Warren Boutcher, 'From Father to Son: Van Veen's Montaigne and Van Ravesteyn's "Pieter van Veen, his Son Cornelis and his Clerk Hendrick Borsman"', in P. J. Smith and K. A. E. Enenkel (eds.), *Montaigne and the Low Countries (1580–1700)* (Leiden: Brill, 2007), 263–303; Warren Boutcher, 'Awakening the Inner Man: Montaigne Framed for Modern Intellectual Life', *EMF: Studies in Early Modern France*, 9 (2004), 30–57.

2.4.5—detail), Musée du Louvre/Gérard Blot, Paris (Illus. 2.4.3), Biblioteca Apostolica Vaticana (Illus. 2.2.4, 2.2.5), Andrew Wee (Illus. 1.3.2).

The book also owes much to the great libraries in which it was put together, and to the staff who run them. Most of the work was done in the Rare Books Room in the British Library, a great institution supported in difficult times by wonderful, dedicated staff. The staff in the *Salle des manuscrits* in the Bibliothèque nationale de France provided an excellent service during a period of upheaval. I would also like to make particular mention of Hélène de Bellaigue at the Bibliothèque Municipale de Bordeaux, Madame Quéreux-Sbaï and her colleagues at the Archives de Reims, Colin Beney in the Queen Mary University of London library, David Pearson in the University of London Senate House library, the staff in the Biblioteca Apostolica Vaticana and the Biblioteca Alessandrina in Rome, and in the Biblioteca Marciana in Venice.

One figure, more than any other, lies behind the emergence of a distinct and interdisciplinary field of early modern intellectual and cultural history in Britain in the last quarter of a century. Quentin Skinner has single-handedly and unstintingly shaped the conditions in which practitioners of the history of early modern ideas both outside and inside History departments all work, and made acceptance and publication of their research possible. I, like so many others, have benefitted for decades from this support—support without which this study would never have been finished or published. As holder of a visiting professorship at Queen Mary in 2007–8, he generously agreed to act as reader of draft chapters when already overwhelmed with requests from several different departments. He persisted in the task over several years, commenting in detail, making corrections, and never complaining about the burden it imposed. I could not have finished the work without the constant encouragement he provided.

I must acknowledge two other, equally profound intellectual debts. The first is to Jean Balsamo, whose historical and textual scholarship on Montaigne has changed the field, and whose redescription of the *Essais* as a 'livre noble', along with Armando Petrucci's notion of the 'free literate', provides the foundations for this study. The new Pléiade *Essais*, which Jean edited with Michel Magnien and Catherine Magnien, is the most important edition to be published since the Édition Municipale of the Bordeaux copy. His work influences what I write on almost every page.

The second is to Lisa Jardine[†], who supervised the original thesis and who with Anthony Grafton—another key supporter—founded an informal school of intellectual history in the late 1980s. Lisa was an inspiration to me in print or in person at some point in every working week for a quarter of a century. This study is in many ways a tardy response to her work on humanism and Gabriel Harvey (with Anthony Grafton), and on Desiderius Erasmus. She was also Director of what was Queen Mary's and is now UCL's Centre for Editing Lives and Letters (CELL), which provided a highly stimulating and stylish environment during my Senior Visiting Scholarship there in 2003. It also provided a mission: to make the conjunction of archival research and digital technology more central to the practice of early modern intellectual history. My thanks to CELL's staff and researchers—Jan

Broadway, Alison Wiggins, Eleanor Merchant, Annie Watkins, Harriet Knight, Robyn Adams, and Patricia Brewerton—for the wonderful hospitality they extended. I had great fun while working, and I hope you did too.

Neither my parents nor my wife, if truth be told, hold much store by professional intellectuals and their literary education. Montaigne welcomed them into his house with less reverence than his father did. This is probably why I have made the *Essais* the focus of my life as a paid researcher and teacher of literature. Montaigne's book stops you from falling too helplessly into the hands of the pedants and the literati. As a child at home I was not immersed in the traditional liberal arts like the young Michel and like the boy in the painting on the cover of Volume 2, and this did not change when I moved in with my wife Rossella, who concentrated on improving my wardrobe. But in both households I have enjoyed the best education a person could wish for.

List of Illustrations: Volumes 1 and 2

VOLUME 1

Chapter 1

Chapter 3

Chapter 4

Chapter 5

Chapter 6

Chapter 7

VOLUME 2

Chapter 1

Chapter 2

Chapter 3

Chapter 4

Chapter 5

Abbreviations

ACDF	Archivio della Congregazione per la Dottrina della Fede, Vatican City
ARTFL	'American and French Research on the Treasury of the French Language' (a project of the Laboratoire ATILF (Analyse et Traitement Informatique de la Langue Française) of the Centre National de la Recherche Scientifique (CNRS), the Division of the Humanities, and the Electronic Text Services (ETS) of the University of Chicago), available at <http://artfl-project.uchicago.edu/>
ARTFL EB	The ARTFL Project, The Montaigne Project, 'Les Essais de Montaigne d'après l'Exemplaire de Bordeaux', available at <http://www.lib.uchicago.edu/efts/ARTFL/projects/montaigne/index.html>
ASF	Archivio di Stato di Firenze, Florence
BAV	Biblioteca Apostolica Vaticana, Vatican City
BIU Santé	Bibliothèque interuniversitaire de Santé, Histoire de la santé, Bibliothèque numérique Medic@, available at <http://www.biusante.parisdescartes.fr/histmed/medica.htm>
BL	British Library
BmR	Bibliothèque Municipale de Reims
BnF	Bibliothèque nationale de France, Paris
Boase	Alan M. Boase, *The Fortunes of Montaigne: A History of the Essays in France, 1580–1669* (London: Methuen, 1935)
Bordeaux 1580	*Essais de Messire Michel Seigneur de Montaigne*, 2 vols. (Bordeaux: Simon Millanges, 1580)
BVH	Les Bibliothèques Virtuelles Humanistes, available at <http://www.bvh.univ-tours.fr/index.htm>
BVH Bordeaux 1580	*Essais de Messire Michel Seigneur de Montaigne*, 2 vols. (Bordeaux: S. Millanges, 1580), copy of the Musée de Sologne Romorantin, Fonds Emile Martin, pressmark Brom_1, published online at <http://www.bvh.univ-tours.fr/Consult/index.asp?numfiche=235>
BVH Bordeaux 1582	*Essais de Messire Michel, seigneur de Montaigne* (Bordeaux: Simon Millanges, 1582), copy of the Bibliothèque municipale, Bordeaux, pressmark PF 6927 Rés.coffre, published online at <http://www.bvh.univ-tours.fr/Consult/index.asp?numfiche=1227>
BVH Bordeaux 1588	*Essais de Michel seigneur de Montaigne* (Paris: Abel L'Angelier, 1588), copy of the Bibliothèque municipale, Bordeaux, pressmark D 11632 Rés.coffre, published online at <http://www.bvh.univ-tours.fr/Consult/index.asp?numfiche=1228>
BVH Paris 1595	*Les Essais de Michel de Montaigne* (Paris: Abel L'Angelier, 1595), copy of the Cambridge University Library, pressmark Montaigne_Essais1595, published online at <http://www.bvh.univ-tours.fr/Consult/index.asp?numfiche=862>

DB	Dezeimeris, Reinhold and Barckhausen, Henri Auguste, (eds).: *Michel de Montaigne, 'Essais' de Michel de Montaigne: texte original de 1580 avec les variantes des éditions de 1582 et 1587* (Bordeaux: Féret & Fils, 1870–3)
DBI	*Dizionario biografico degli italiani*
Dictionnaire	Desan, Philippe (ed.), *Dictionnaire de Michel de Montaigne* (second edn., Paris: Champion, 2007)
DLF	Michel Simonin (ed.), *Dictionnaire des lettres françaises: Le XVIᵉ siècle* (Paris: Fayard, 2001)
DMF	'Dictionnaire du Moyen Français (1330-1500)', 2012 version (Analyse et Traitement Informatique de la Langue Française, Centre national de la recherche scientifique and Université de Lorraine), available at <http://www.atilf.fr/dmf>
Du Cange	Digital edition of Du Cange, et al., *Glossarium mediæ et infimæ latinitatis* (Niort: L. Favre, 1883–7), available at <http://ducange.enc.sorbonne.fr/>
EB	Exemplaire de Bordeaux ('Bordeaux copy' of Paris 1588 with additions and corrections in Montaigne's hand, Bibliothèque municipale de Bordeaux)
EDIT 16	EDIT 16, Censimento nazionale delle edizioni italiane del XVI secolo, Istituto centrale per il catalogo unico delle biblioteche italiane e per le informazioni bibliografiche, online edn., last updated 31 December 2012, available at <http://edit16.iccu.sbn.it/web_iccu/ihome.htm>
EM	Édition Municipale: Montaigne, *Les 'Essais'…publiés d'après l'Exemplaire de Bordeaux*, eds. Fortunat Strowski, François Gebelin, Pierre Villey, Grace Norton, 5 vols. (Bordeaux: Imprimerie nouvelle F. Pech & Compagnie, 1906–33)
ESTC	English short title catalogue, British Library, online edn., available at <http://estc.bl.uk/F/?func=file&file_name=login-bl-estc>
F	Michel de Montaigne, *The Complete Works: Essays, Travel Journal, Letters*, trans. Donald M. Frame (Stanford: Stanford University Press, 1957)
Ferrara 1590	Michel de Montaigne, *Discorsi morali, politici, et militari…. Con un discorso se il forastiero si deve admettere alla administratione della republica*, trans. Girolamo Naselli (Ferrara: Benedetto Mamarello, 1590)
Frame	Donald M. Frame, *Montaigne: A Biography* (London: Hamish Hamilton, 1965)
Gallica	Gallica, Bibliothèque numérique, Bibliothèque nationale de France, available at <http://gallica.bnf.fr/>
GLN15–16	'Bibliographie de la production imprimée des 15e et 16e siècles' (Geneva, Lausanne, Neuchâtel, Morges), Jean-François Gilmont and Bibliothèque de Genève, 2006–13, available at <http://www.ville-ge.ch/bge/gln/>
ILE	*Ivsti Lipsi Epistolae*, A. Gerlo et al. (eds) (Brussels: Paleis der Academiën, 1978–)
Jadart	Jean Maillefer, *Mémoires de J. Maillefer, marchand bourgeois de Reims, 1611–1684, continués par son fils jusqu'en 1716*, ed. Charles Henri Jadart (Paris and Rheims: Alph. Picard and F. Michaud, 1890)

Journal Henri IV	Pierre de L'Estoile, *Journal pour le règne de Henri IV*, eds. Louis-Raymond Lefèvre and André Martin, 3 vols. (Paris: Gallimard, 1948–60)
Leiden A [Geneva] 1602	*Les Essais de Michel Seigneur de Montaigne* (Leiden [Geneva]: Jehan Doreau, 1602)
Leiden B [Geneva] 1602	*Les Essais de Michel Seigneur de Montaigne* (Leiden or Cologny [Geneva]: Jean Doreau, 1602)
LEME	'Lexicons of Early Modern English', Ian Lancashire (ed.), University of Toronto Library and Press, 2014, available at <http://leme.library.utoronto.ca/>
London 1603	Michel de Montaigne, *The essayes or morall, politike and millitarie discourses*, trans. John Florio (London: Valentine Simmes for Edward Blount, 1603)
Lyon 1593	Michel de Montaigne, *Livre des Essais* (Lyon: Gabriel La Grange, 1593)
Lyon [Geneva] 1595	Michel de Montaigne, *Les Essais* (Lyon [Geneva]; François Le Febvre, 1595)
Millet	Olivier Millet, *La première réception des Essais de Montaigne (1580–1640)* (Paris: Honoré Champion, 1995)
NNBW	*Nieuw Nederlandsch biografisch woordenboek*, eds. P. C. Molhuysen and P. J. Blok, 10 vols. (Leiden: 1911–37)
NP	New Pléiade: Montaigne, *Les Essais*, eds. Jean Balsamo, Michel Magnien, and Catherine Magnien (Bibliothèque de la Pléiade; Paris: Gallimard, 2007)
NUL	Nottingham Univerity Library, Department of Manuscripts and Special Collections
ODNB	*Oxford Dictionary of National Biography*, Oxford University Press, 2004; online edn, Jan 2008, available at <http://www.oxforddnb.com/>
Paris 1588	*Essais de Michel Seigneur de Montaigne* (Paris: Abel L'Angelier, 1588)
Paris 1595	*Les Essais de Michel de Montaigne* (Paris: Abel L'Angelier, 1595)
Perseus	Perseus Digital Library, ed. Gregory R. Crane, Tufts University, available at <http://www.perseus.tufts.edu/>
R	Michel de Montaigne, *Journal de Voyage*, ed. François Rigolot (Paris: Presses Universitaires de France, 1992)
RIECH	'Répertoire des imprimeurs et éditeurs suisses actifs avant 1800', Bibliothèque cantonale et universitaire de Lausanne, available at <http://dbserv1-bcu.unil.ch/riech/intro.php>
S	Montaigne, *The Complete Essays*, trans. M. A. Screech (Harmondsworth: Penguin, 1991)
Sayce and Maskell	R. A. Sayce and David Maskell, *A descriptive bibliography of Montaigne's 'Essais' 1580–1700* (London: The Royal Bibliographical Society, 1983)
SCETI	Schoenberg Center for Electronic Text & Image, The University of Pennsylvania Libraries, available at <http://sceti.library.upenn.edu/>
SCETI London 1603	Michel de Montaigne, *The essayes or morall, politike and millitarie discourses*, trans. John Florio (London: Valentine

	Simmes for Edward Blount, 1603), copy of the University of Pennsylvania Rare Book and Manuscript Library (Horace Howard Furness Shakspeare Library), pressmark Folio PQ1642.E5 F6 1603, published online by SCETI at <http://sceti.library.upenn.edu/sceti/printedbooksNew/index.cfm?textID=montaigne&PagePosition=1>
Sources	Pierre Villey, *Les sources et L'évolution des Essais de Montaigne*, second edn, 2 vols. (Paris: Librairie Hachette, 1933)
UoV Paris 1571	University of Virginia copy (pressmark Gordon 1572.X45) of Étienne de La Boétie, *La mesnagerie de Xenophon. Les regles de mariage de Plutarque. Lettre de consolation, de Plutarque à sa femme... Ensemble quelques vers latins & françois, de son invention. Item, un Discours sur la mort dudit seigneur de La Boëtie, par M. de Montaigne* (Paris: Federic Morel, 1571), published online at <http://search.lib.virginia.edu/catalog/uva-lib:1017844>
USTC	Universal Short-Title Catalogue, St Andrew's University, online edn., 1997–2012, available at <http://www.ustc.ac.uk/>
Van Mander	K. Van Mander, *Lives of the illustrious Netherlandish and German painters, from the first edition of the Schilder-boeck (1603–1604)*, ed. H. Miedema, 6 vols. (Doornspijk: Davaco, 1994–9)
VD16	'Verzeichnis der im deutschen Sprachbereich erschienenen Drucke des 16. Jahrhunderts', available at <http://www.bsb-muenchen.de/16-Jahrhundert-VD-16.180.0.html?L=1>
Venice 1633	Michel de Montaigne, *Saggi..., ouero Discorsi, naturali, politici, e morali*, trans. Girolamo Canini (Venice: Marco Ginammi, 1633)

Note on Texts, Terms, and Conventions

The edition of reference for the current study is the new Pléiade of 2007, which contains Montaigne's *Essais*, annotations from his books, and the inscriptions from his library.[1] This choice requires justification for two reasons. First, the new Pléiade differs from most editions published in the last hundred years in taking the first posthumous edition, prepared by Marie de Gournay, and not the Bordeaux copy as its copy text.[2] The text that was standard until recently—Villey-Saulnier—is based on EB and is now accessible online.[3] Second, digital facsimiles of Bordeaux 1580, Paris 1588, Paris 1595, and the Bordeaux copy are also available online. These make it perfectly possible to refer the reader with web access directly to the text of the early editions, and to particular pages of the Bordeaux copy itself.

The relation between EB and Paris 1595 is an ongoing matter of scholarly debate. The Bordeaux copy has additions and revisions in Montaigne's hand, and a few in Gournay's hand. Many of the former are written in a fair, legible hand, but some (perhaps those made after EB had ceased to have the status of a fair copy) are more difficult to decipher. The pages have been trimmed and some of the writing lost. Editors of EB therefore have to seek assistance from Paris 1595. But Paris 1595 also presents numerous variants relative to EB. These include a few passages which appear in EB but not in Paris 1595, many more which appear in Paris 1595 but not in EB, including a passage praising the editor of Paris 1595, Marie de Gournay.[4]

Paris 1595 displaced 'Que les goust des biens et des maux depend en bonne partie de l'opinion, que nous en avons' from I 14 (as it was in Paris 1588) to I 40, which meant that chapters I 15 to I 40 as they were numbered in Paris 1580 and Paris 1588 were all renumbered downwards (by one). As twentieth-century editions were based on EB, they did not respect this renumbering. They also modernized orthography, introduced paragraphs, and used a system of symbols for denoting

---

[1] Michel de Montaigne, *Les Essais*, Jean Balsamo et al. (eds.) (Bibliothèque de la Pléiade; Paris: Gallimard, 2007) (henceforward abbreviated as 'NP'). The previous Pléiade, published in 1962, comprised the *Œuvres complètes*.

[2] Michel de Montaigne, *Les Essais*, Marie Le Jars De Gournay (ed.) (Paris: Abel L'Angelier, 1595) (henceforward abbreviated as 'Paris 1595'). The Bordeaux copy (henceforward abbreviated as 'EB') is a copy of Michel de Montaigne, *Essais* (Paris: Abel L'Angelier, 1588), with corrections and additions in Montaigne's hand (held at the Bibliothèque Municipale de Bordeaux).

[3] The ARTFL Project, The Montaigne Project, 'Les Essais de Montaigne d'après l'Exemplaire de Bordeaux', available at <http://www.lib.uchicago.edu/efts/ARTFL/projects/montaigne/index.html> (ARTFL EB). This online edition uses colour-coding to distinguish the three layers of composition, but users should be aware that the coding does not accurately reflect the layering of the text as it is marked in Michel de Montaigne, *Essais*, Pierre Villey and V.-L. Saulnier (eds.) (Paris: Presses Universitaires de France, 1965). More useful is the linking of the online text of Villey-Saulnier to an online digital facsimile of EB. It is therefore possible, by going to this site, to check all 'C' additions directly on the Bordeaux copy itself.

[4] NP xlviii.

XXX Note on Texts, Terms, and Conventions

the latest possible date of composition of the first version of any passage (a = 1580, date of the first edition in two books; b = 1588, date of the first major revised edition, with third book added; c = 1592, date of Montaigne's death).

This whole set of editorial choices and practices was challenged from two different perspectives during the 1990s. On the one hand, André Tournon emphasized that the Bordeaux copy was not, strictly speaking, the copy text of the standard Villey-Saulnier edition, or of any other scholarly edition. He set out to prepare the first edition to use EB as copy text. His 1998 edition for the Imprimerie Nationale restores the outline of Montaigne's punctuation from the Bordeaux copy—a revolutionary editorial move—but it also introduces modern orthography and adapts some of Montaigne's punctuation marks in idiosyncratic ways.[5]

On the other hand, a group of French scholars built upon arguments that had originally derived from the application of the principles of the British tradition of textual bibliography to the case of the *Essais*. They explained the considerable variants between Paris 1595 and EB, and remarks made by Gournay at the end of her 'Preface', by arguing that Montaigne had prepared a further copy (not extant) with revisions ulterior to those contained in EB, and that Gournay had received a transcription of this (not extant). For these scholars, Paris 1595 is closer to the final authorial text than EB. Two scholarly editions of the 1595 text have subsequently been published.[6]

At the time of writing in 2013, scholars and general readers were left, on the one hand, with a standard edition of the Bordeaux copy (Villey-Saulnier) which was no longer felt to be satisfactory, but which was available on the internet (with the a-b-c layers in different colours) with corresponding pages from the Bordeaux copy (in a good digital facsimile); and, on the other hand, new editions of both the Bordeaux copy and the 1595 text, none of which had yet had time to establish themselves as the vulgate for scholars, and none of which were available online.

Furthermore, as I have already mentioned, good online facsimiles of the early editions are now available. The Bibliothèque de France's resource 'Gallica' offers facsimiles of various early editions of the *Essais*, though the quality of the reproductions was not high at the time of writing. Much better are the digital facsimiles available via 'Les Bibliothèques Virtuelles Humanistes' (BVH), the University of Virginia's Gordon Collection, and the Schoenberg Center for Electronic Text and Image (SCETI) at the University of Pennsylvania (for London 1603). Towards the end of the writing-up of the present study an ambitious new project, 'MONtaigne à L'Œuvre' (MONLOE) at the Centre d'Études Supérieures de la Renaissance (Tour), connected with BVH, began to gather an online corpus of all Montaigne's documentary remains.

This study is about the *Essais* as written, read, and produced in a variety of forms by a variety of people in the early modern and modern periods. I therefore refer to

---

[5] Michel de Montaigne, *Essais*, ed. André Tournon, 3 vols. (Paris: Imprimerie nationale, 1998).
[6] Michel de Montaigne, *Les Essais*, Jean Céard et al. (eds.) (Paris: Livre de Poche, 2001); NP.

different editions and copies, including the Bordeaux copy, at different points, depending on the context. For two reasons it seemed appropriate to include references and direct hyperlinks to facsimiles of these editions, where possible, rather than cite editions that note the 'layers' of the text for the reader. First, the editions that derive from the Bordeaux copy and use the a-b-c notation only give a rough sense of how each 'layer' of the text read. Much better to go directly back to the texts that early modern readers actually saw, the texts of editions such as Bordeaux 1580 and Paris 1588.

Second, a good proportion of the research for the current monograph was undertaken digitally. It is published in a parallel online edition (Oxford Scholarship Online). It is therefore possible to include hyperlinks to specific pages of online digital facsimiles of various editions of the *Essais*, as well as to other digital resources. These links include page numbers that will enable the reader of the printed edition to access the online editions manually, or to access the relevant pages of copies of the relevant edition in rare books libraries. Hyperlinks to other sources, available on Gallica and elsewhere, are provided on a more sporadic basis.

None of this obviates the necessity for reference to both a single critical edition of the *Essais*, and to a standard translation, in printed form. The text needed to be that which most early modern people encountered: Paris 1595 and its derivatives. Of the two authoritative editions of Paris 1595 currently available, one (ed. Céard) introduces modern orthography. The other, in the Bibliothèque de la Pléiade, stays closer to the original orthography and records for the first time all the textual variants between 1595 and all the relevant early editions, including the Bordeaux copy itself.[7] This is therefore the edition of choice. One consequence is that even when I refer to Bordeaux 1580 and Paris 1588 I give the chapter numbers as they were re-arranged in Paris 1595 and in all subsequent editions until the early nineteenth century.

The choice of modern translation is more difficult. There is no authoritative modern English translation of the *Essais* that consistently uses only a text derived from Paris 1595. I give references to page numbers in M. A. Screech's translation, as it includes more readings from 1595 than Donald Frame's translation.[8] But the English versions I give draw on both translations and on my own understanding of the French text.

References to the *Essais* in the footnotes therefore take the following form: 'I 20 NP000/BVH Paris 1595, p. 000 [000]/S000', where: I 20 = 'De la force de l'imagination' (and not 'Que philosopher, c'est apprendre à mourir', as it is in Bordeaux 1580, Paris 1588, and in all editions based on the Bordeaux copy); NP = Michel

---

[7] The 'Notes et variantes' for each chapter also include page numbers for the chapter as published in 1580, 1588, 1595, 1598, the Villey-Saulnier, and Céard editions, as well as Michel de Montaigne, *Les Essais. . . . Publiés d'après l'exemplaire de Bordeaux, avec les variantes manuscrites & les leçons des plus anciennes impressions, des notes, des notices et un lexique*, Fortunat Strowski et al. (eds.), 5 vols. (Bordeaux: Imprimerie nouvelle F. Pech & Compagnie, 1906–33) (henceforward abbreviated as 'EM').

[8] Michel de Montaigne, *The Complete Essays*, trans. M. A. Screech (London: Penguin Books, 1991)—henceforward abbreviated as 'S'.

de Montaigne, *Les Essais*, ed. Jean Balsamo et al., 'Bibliothèque de la Pléiade' (Paris: Gallimard, 2007); BVH Paris 1595 = the online digital facsimile of the University of Cambridge's copy of Paris 1595 in 'Les Bibliothèques Virtuelles Humanistes' (page numbers in square brackets are the actual page numbers, in cases where the numbers in the edition are erroneous); S = Michel de Montaigne, *The Complete Essays*, trans. M. A. Screech (London: Penguin, 1991). The page numbering in Paris 1595 restarts for book III, so I indicate the book number only when the reference is to a chapter in that book.

Likewise, where the reference is to Bordeaux 1580 rather than Paris 1595, it takes the following form: I 20 NP000/BVH Bordeaux 1580, vol. II, p. 000 [p. 000]/S000, where: I 20 still refers to 'De la force de l'imagination' (even though it is numbered I 21 in Bordeaux 1580); BVH Bordeaux 1580 = the online digital facsimile of the Musée de Sologne's copy of Bordeaux 1580 in 'Les Bibliothèques Virtuelles Humanistes'. In the case of Paris 1588 references take the following form: 'I 20, NP000/BVH Paris 1588, p. 000/S000', where I 20 still refers to 'De la force de l'imagination' (even though it is numbered I 21 in Paris 1588), and BVH Paris 1588 = the online digital facsimile of the Bibliothèque municipale de Bordeaux's copy of Paris 1588. There are also a few references to BVH's online facsimile of Bordeaux 1582.

References to London 1603 take the following form: 'SCETI London 1603, p. 000)', where SCETI London 1603 = the online digital facsimile of the University of Pennsylvania Libraries' copy (the Furness Collection) of London 1603, hosted by the Schoenberg Center for Electronic Text and Image. As the SCETI facsimile's dropdown menu refers to 'pages' I always give the page number rather than the signature, putting the correct page number in square brackets where the numbering is wrong in London 1603, for example 'p. 558 [538]'. Where SCETI does give the signature as the page reference, I give the reference as follows: 'p. A1r'. Links and references are also provided on occasion to individual pages of The Montaigne Project's online facsimile of the Bordeaux copy.

References to the *Journal de voyage* take the following form: 'R000/F000', where R = Michel de Montaigne, *Journal de Voyage*, ed. François Rigolot (Paris: Presses Universitaires de France, 1992), and F = Michel de Montaigne, *The Complete Works: Essays, Travel Journal, Letters*, trans. Donald M. Frame (Stanford: Stanford University Press, 1957).

In order to avoid confusion, I use roman numerals for the book number in references to chapters from the *Essais* and arabic numerals for references to the chapters of the two volumes comprising this study (e.g. 'I 2' for Montaigne's chapter 'De la Tristesse' and '1.2' for *The School of Montaigne*, volume one, chapter two). Where arabic numerals are used to refer to a numbered illustration rather than to a chapter section, they are always prefixed by 'Illus.'.

In order to avoid large sections of unbroken text, which would be particularly difficult to digest for users of the online edition, I have introduced more frequent paragraph breaks than are normal in an academic monograph. To avoid the proliferation of footnotes I sometimes group references in a single footnote after a sequence of two or more paragraphs.

Terminology derived from the work of the anthropologist Alfred Gell is used throughout: 'index', 'nexus', 'prototype' (the object represented), 'recipient' (the reader or user), 'abductive inference', 'patiency' (the opposite of 'agency'), and so on. But I have tried not to use these terms too insistently and to find alternatives where possible. One can, for example, convey the point that a work of art 'indexes' a particular action by saying that it gives rise or testifies to it. A 'nexus' is a concrete social context: the social relations of agency in which a literary or verbal artefact is embedded in a particular instance (according to a description that a participant-observer might give). An 'abductive inference' is an inference about the intentions or capabilities of another person, an inference of the kind we make equally from a smile or a work of art. The reader can find a short introduction to Gell's theory, and to further literature on it, in the 'General preface', along with practical examples of its application in Chapters 1.1, 1.2.6, and 2.6.7.

Gell's work is important because the central issue in this study is the description of the agency relations in which copies and editions of the *Essais* become involved. I therefore try to be as careful as possible in describing such relations in the course of my own analysis. It is all too easy to say 'Montaigne' or 'Montaigne's work' when one means inferences about the authorial *persona* that are made from a text or copy of the *Essais*. But on many occasions, to avoid ungainly phrasing, I use these simpler expressions, which after all reflect a widespread and important habit of attributing agency to the people who write books. It will nevertheless hopefully be clear to the reader throughout that to speak of 'Montaigne' in the early modern period is largely to speak of the history of a book, and of the authorial *persona* inferred from that book and its text by readers.

Some of the more ordinary terms I use, though current in modern English, have different or stronger senses in early modern vernaculars or Latin. There is a difficulty with the terms 'art' and 'artist', which I use in their modern senses when drawing on Gell's theory, but which appear in some of the passages I cite in their different, sixteenth-century senses. In the latter cases, 'art' is more akin to 'method' or 'skill' (anything from writing to physiognomy), and an 'artist' is someone schooled in the liberal arts in general.

I italicize '*persona*' to indicate that I am not using it in the weak modern sense of an aspect of personality, but in its early modern sense, derived from the Latin for a theatrical mask, of 'a manifestation, or realisation and representation of a character, or type' such as a slave or a free man. I italicize the term '*patron*' where it means a 'pattern' or 'model'—sometimes in addition to its meaning of 'a social protector or supporter'.[9] For the situation in which the *patron* is the author—in the sense of originator, commissioner, first cause—of a work of art or philosophy, I have coined a compound term: 'patron-author'.

Though I choose not to use italicized Latinate forms (*officium*, *officia*) for the vocabulary of 'office', it should be understood throughout not in the restricted modern sense of an administrative or political role but in the sense of the duties

---

[9] Conal Condren, *Argument and authority in early modern England: the presupposition of oaths and offices* (Cambridge: Cambridge University Press, 2006), 6–7.

which are attached to a particular *persona*, whether that of a magistrate, a philosopher, or a father.[10] I use the italicized *'familia'* to denote both a group of people—not just 'family' in the modern sense—associated with a particular household (including, for example, servants), and a group of people united by shared literary texts and education, and led by particular humanists or intellectuals.

Quotations are given in English translation. For selected key phrases and words I include the original text in italics in square brackets within the quotation. Where I give all of the original text, inverted commas and round brackets rather than italics and square brackets are used. Classical works are normally cited with their English titles, except when I am respecting the form given in a primary source. I have transliterated Greek terms. Proper names are given in their most common and recognizable forms, whether vernacular or Latin (so 'Andrea Alciato', but 'Justus Lipsius'). In transcribing Latin and modern languages I have not attempted a diplomatic transcription. Except in the titles of works, the following conventions apply: contractions are silently expanded; 'u' is regularized as 'v'; '&' as 'et' or 'and'; long 'ʃ' as 's'; 'i' as 'j' (e.g. 'ie' changes to 'je').

---

[10] Condren, *Argument and Authority*, 29.

VOLUME 2

THE READER-WRITER

Introduction
Volume 2

In Paris in early 1609, as he began a new volume of his *registres*, Pierre de L'Estoile adapted Varro's Latin to describe his existence evading the effects of melancholy in private: 'So I fashion a life reading and writing' ('Sic legendo et scribendo Vitam Procudo').[1] He was no monk or scribe, but a layman keeping a personal archive of what he heard and read—including extracts from Montaigne's *Essais*.

In Volume 2 we switch focus from the patron-author to the reader-writers of the *Essais* across Europe. These are seventeenth-century descendants of the free literate of the late medieval period.[2] The *Essais* become a context for their works, instead of vice versa. The primary objects of study are less, now, nexuses involving Montaigne and his collaborators than those involving various commentators, imitators, promoters, translators, and their networks of friends and family. We are concerned less with Montaigne's book than with their books—whether printed, manuscript, or a hybrid of both, whether literary works or personal records.

The early modern printed book was less protected, less fixed, more open to changes in form and use, from edition to edition, from copy to copy, than its modern counterpart. Early modern individuals who took advantage of this openness displayed a whole range of behaviours when they interacted with books in circulation. On the one hand, anyone from individual readers and translators to publishers and official censors could take what would now be considered extraordinary liberties with the published and unpublished writings of others. They could correct and expurgate or prohibit them, fragment and re-use them without acknowledgement, republish them without permission.

These dangers grew more severe once a greater variety of regulatory authorities were put in place after 1560. Any text, the *persona* of any author, could be subverted for confessional or commercial reasons when they circulated through international centres of differing religio-political hues, from Paris and Lyons, to Geneva, Frankfurt, and Rome. The instruments that could be used to protect against this, from royal privileges to friendly epistolary networks, were not guaranteed to work, as Jacques Auguste de Thou discovered after the first publication of his universal history in 1604 (see 2.1.5).

---

[1] See 2.4.5 and Illus. 2.5.2.
[2] For Armando Petrucci's notion of the 'free literate' see the 'General Introduction' to both volumes, in Volume 1.

In the case of new works by relatively unknown authors, users and publishers could, without acknowledgement, appropriate and reproduce parts or all of the work, with account taken neither of the meanings of the text in its original context nor of authorial intentions. The fate of La Boétie's most famous text in the hands of Huguenot propagandists (see 1.6.13) is a case in point: they disguised its true intentions (from Montaigne's point of view) by setting it amongst texts of a rebellious nature.

On the other hand, everyone from correctors in the printshop to readers in the marketplace could be described as intervening to help make a book what it had to be in order to survive unscathed.[3] From this perspective, they could be said to be participating in the composition and revision of rounded moral, intellectual, and social stories about the making and transmission of a work (see 1.1.12). A simple example of such a story would be the enfranchisement of its writer with the *persona* of a noble author of good faith, by means of rhetorical praise. This could mean placing the work in meaningful relation to other works and *personae* in ways that shifted its understood significance as it moved from location to location.

The third chapter of Volume 1 (1.3) began with an analysis, in these terms, of the first printed response to the publication of Montaigne's book and of an anecdote concerning Henri III's reception of the work. The final chapter (1.7) featured another occasion upon which a specific copy of Montaigne's book was received as a *recommendation* of the memory of its author: the author's stay in Rome in 1580–1, and the return of the copy seized for examination at the gates.

Together, the two occasions suggest an outline of the kind of judgemental and anecdotal framework within which an elite consumer or patron might have been expected to place Montaigne's book, of the kind of inferences that might conventionally have been made. In both cases, a certain kind of story is told—by a royal bibliographer (La Croix du Maine), by papal authorities—about the author and what the book is doing for his public reputation. The book is received as an index of Montaigne's performance in the conversation of the time, as it centred on great contemporary patrons such as the King of France and the Pope, and on great classical *patrons* such as Plutarch and Seneca.[4]

Volume 2 will ask what other stories were told with the *Essais* by early modern reader-writers in different locations across Europe. It mines some of the richest veins of evidence concerning the participation of the *Essais* in others' projects, for the fully evolved *Essais* were intended to facilitate sustained private *commerce* with the author on the part of a diverse public ('divers visages') of friends and family, of *honnêtes hommes* and *dames* who would frequent his book—as they might have frequented him in person—in their cabinets.[5]

---

[3] Anthony Grafton, *The culture of correction in Renaissance Europe* (The Panizzi Lectures 2009; London: British Library, 2011), 139–42, 200–2.

[4] For the use of 'index' and other terms derived from the anthropological theory of Alfred Gell, see the 'General Preface' to both volumes in Volume 1, 1.1, 1.2.6, and the 'Note on Texts, Terms, and Conventions' in this volume.

[5] I 39, NP256/BVH Paris 1595, p. 149/S283; III 9, NP1026/BVH Paris 1595, bk. III, p. 136/S1109; III 5, NP889/BVH Paris 1595, bk. III, p. 42/S956.

Putting to one side (with the exception of Charron) the frequently studied philosophical texts of well-known public philosophers from seventeenth-century France (Descartes, Malebranche, Pascal), I assemble a sample public of reader-writers from across Europe. It is only a sample. With still more space, more might have been included about, for example, Spanish and neo-Latin contexts of reception and transmission. Nevertheless, as will become clear in the concluding chapter (2.7), the selected case-studies do provide a set of historical coordinates by which to plot a reading—against the grain of more abstract modern interpretations—of the *Essais'* place in wider cultural history.

So, the chapters in Volume 2 address: the most important early *elogia* of Montaigne, and readings of his text, by *parlementaires* in France; the three most important early vernacular translations in Italy and England (Naselli, Florio, Canini); the early Genevan editions, including Goulart's corrected text of 1595; the three manuscript journals with the best evidence of private readers' use of Florio's *Essayes* in England and the *Essais* in France (Slingsby, Yorkshire; Maillefer, Rheims; L'Estoile, Paris); the two copies (Van Veen, The Hague; Maillefer, Rheims) which offer the richest evidence of the text's use as a personal instrument of self-study or practical philosophy over a lifetime; the set of printed *Discorsi* (by Flavio Querenghi) that best reveal use of Naselli's translation as a vade mecum in Italy; the printed work which systematized the text as an instrument of practical philosophy for the seventeenth century (Charron's *De la sagesse*); the seventeenth-century account of the *Essais* (in Bishop Camus's *Diversitez*) which, along with Gournay's preface, offers the most telling insights into its relationship to the contemporary culture of reading and writing.

In each case there is enough documentary evidence to reveal the social networks and conditions that shaped individuals' use of the *Essais*, as well as the purposes and outcomes involved.

The first chapter is complementary to the final chapter of Volume 1; together they comprise the core of the two-volume study. Chapter 1.7 was about how Montaigne's self-portrait in print worked in conjunction with his person in Rome. Chapter 2.1 is about how it worked in Paris and across the parliamentary network of intellectuals centred on the capital, with people who knew him—or of him—personally. We follow Montaigne on his trip to Paris in 1588, this time with the copy text for the new quarto edition of the *Essais*.

In Rome in 1580–1 there proved to be a close relationship between Montaigne's reception in his physical person by the curial elite and the reception of his book. But in this case the physical encounter is less immediately significant. It emerges that Montaigne, in his *persona* as the author of the *Essais*, did not properly 'arrive' in Paris, as far as the parliamentary elite were concerned, until the posthumous publication of Paris 1595. And even then he was not accorded the position of a patron-author, which was held only by great lawyer-scholars such as L'Hospital. His *persona* and his text were re-written for the early seventeenth-century purposes of a whole community of *parlementaires*.

Indeed, until the 1600s, he was very much in the shadow of the friend whose works he had edited and addressed to *parlementaires* in the early 1570s: La Boétie.

When he did arrive (by means of Paris 1595, and the subsequent octavos), he was welcomed in terms that were complementary to but different from those used by Gournay, and which retrospectively inserted the author and his book into a *politique* context. The similarities and differences in ethos and fortunes between the *Essais* and that truly *politique* book, de Thou's *Historiae*, are explored, especially with respect to the latter book's own fortunes in the same two cities of Rome and Paris.

Montaigne and de Thou represent opposite ends of a range of choices available to free literates wanting to keep records of personal or historical matters. The important point is that de Thou and the other *politiques* understood Montaigne's book to witness to a certain kind of free discursive behaviour, which they rooted in the author's noble *persona* as an ex-*conseiller* and private court mediator who was amenable to peace, and who saw the true causes of the wars of religion (not religion, but aristocratic factionalism).

The comparison between the circulation of Montaigne's and de Thou's books across France and Europe leads naturally to a broader consideration of the *Essais*-in-transmission across various countries and cities. The second chapter uses the English poet Samuel Daniel's famous description of the cross-border 'intertraffique' of the mind to ask whether the 'franchise' of Montaigne's worth was indeed recognized in cities from Geneva in Switzerland to Ferrara, Padua, and Venice in north-eastern Italy.

The official and unofficial culture of correction had an important role to play in all these locations, as 'negotiated censorship' (Ingrid Jostock's phrase) resulted in different outcomes in different cities. In Geneva, we need to attend to the relationships between ecclesiastical censors and *libraires*, and between the book trades in Paris and Lyon, to account for the fact that the *Essais* were first published in a heavily censored edition, before appearing unexpurgated—both times with false title pages.

Despite his activity as a censor, it is Simon Goulart who prepares us for the later chapters by revealing the market of free literates for whom Montaigne was judged to be writing. His 1595 edition combines with other evidence to show how one of the most significant early reader-writers of the *Essais* (Goulart himself) corrected and used the work.[6] Scaliger received the edition as part of the *œuvre* of Goulart, and of the city of Geneva he served. There are some parallels with the first Italian translation, which was also published in the period following the poorly distributed edition of Paris 1588, and which we can also see as part of the *œuvre* both of its translator, Naselli, and of the Ferrarese court.[7]

As we move to Padua-Venice we again find secular and regular clerics active in the mediation of the informal, 'academic' culture of practical philosophy. They become involved via courts, academies, and bookseller-publishers with the articu-

---

[6] Michel de Montaigne, *Les Essais* (Lyon [Geneva]: François Le Febvre, 1595)—henceforward abbreviated as 'Lyon [Geneva] 1595'.

[7] Michel de Montaigne, *Discorsi morali, politici, et militari ... Con un discorso se il forastiero si deve admettere alla administratione della republica*, trans. Girolamo Naselli (Ferrara: Benedetto Mamarello, 1590)—henceforward abbreviated as 'Ferrara 1590'.

lation of philosophical *personae* for themselves and their elite patrons. In the late 1620s and early 1630s, clerics called upon the *Essais* to assist in the fashioning of *virtù civile* and models of the philosophico-religious life for the noble elite of the Veneto. Flavio Querenghi used Naselli's translation not in his public lectures on moral philosophy, which he delivered ex-officio, but in his *discorsi*, which draw on his private reading and writing in the settings of the *accademia* and other forms of *amicizia*.

The third chapter analyses the English school of Montaigne. For most of the seventeenth century, this derived in large part from the way John Florio and his associates, especially Samuel Daniel, enfranchised the essayist as a participant in the aristocratic culture of private learning in late Elizabethan–early Jacobean noble and royal households—especially the female sphere of these households (including Queen Anna's court).

The *Essais'* arrival in England is associated in modern historiography with an abstractly conceived rise of scepticism, individualism, or self-consciousness. At the time, however, it was associated more with the ambivalence surrounding the role and outcome in elite social and cultural reproduction of this free, family-based style of noble schooling and learned leisure—which extended to theatrical entertainments.

This type of *schola* was based on practical experience and on reading and writing fed by recent European vernacular literature (including romances in prose and verse), as much as by standard humanist tuition in the Graeco-Roman classics. Though designed to enfranchise those not training to be schoolmen from enslavement to both scholastic and humanistic couplings of grammar and logic, its outcomes and applications were uncertain, even undesirable (especially in the case of women), in many critics' eyes.

Florio's translation originated in a manuscript version of Montaigne's chapter on the 'institution' or education of a young nobleman, addressed to the Countess of Bedford. The first edition (1603) was dedicated to six noblewomen, and the second (1613) to Queen Anna of Denmark. It consequently became a kind of sophisticated breviary for the institution and learned entertainment of the Jacobean gentry and nobility, especially for witty critique of the tyrannies of custom and fashion. This fact was brilliantly lampooned in Ben Jonson's stage caricature of a 'would-be' politic Lady who uncritically follows all court fashions, including the reading of Montaigne and other non-curricular continental texts. By relating this to the use of Florio's text in Samuel Daniel's *The Queenes Arcadia* (performed 1605), we gain a better understanding of the context of Shakespeare's use of the same text in *The Tempest* (1610–11).

The fourth and fifth chapters explore the relationship between the European transmission of the *Essais* and non-institutional cultures of record-keeping. What kind of book was in practice dedicated to what Montaigne describes (in 'Au lecteur') as a domestic and private end? Villey established the relationship between the *Essais* and printed miscellanies of 'readings' or *leçons*. Chapters 2.4 and 2.5 complement this by exploring—in the vicinity of the *Essais*—the relationship between reading and various kinds of miscellaneous private writing and self-accounting.

In 2.4.2, a Yorkshire gentleman caught up in the late 1630s in the beginnings of the British wars of religion starts to keep a book of personal commentaries modelled on Florio's English Montaigne. In the second half of the chapter we switch to the religious wars in the Low Countries in the 1580s, where Pieter van Veen's copy of the *Essais* first becomes a 'Memoire' of its owner—as it still is in the 1620s. It is a memoir not only in the specific sense that he writes a narrative of his life in the back, but also in the more general sense that it is designed to be an index of a son's active remembrance and perpetuation of his father's character and virtues. Van Veen's extraordinary copy reifies an early modern understanding of the *Essais* as a work of art made for friends and family.

Chapter 2.5 begins with Pierre Huet's early-eighteenth-century description of the school of Montaigne, which he says has been flourishing for more than a century. He denounces the *Essais* as 'the breviary of urbane loafers and ignorant pseudointellectuals', of undisciplined, over-free literates who do not want to pursue proper scholarship and knowledge. The chapter goes on to offer two further case-studies of such free literates in early modern France. Both read Montaigne's work while writing paper journals to domestic and private ends; both combined reading and writing in books with the keeping and reviewing of personal records.

Ultimately, I aim to persuade the reader of this study that the manuscript records of L'Estoile and Maillefer, when combined with those of Slingsby and Van Veen, have as much to tell us about the historical meanings and uses of the *Essais* in early modern Europe as the printed philosophical responses of Descartes, Pascal, and Malebranche.

The final two chapters are complementary to the first two chapters of Volume 1. In 2.6, we return to the subject of 1.2: modern scenes of reading, teaching, and translation analogous to the early modern scenes described in the intervening chapters. It features two modern reader-writers of Donald Frame's American English translation of the *Essais* (Gore Vidal and David Denby).

We consider a range of related intellectual contexts for Frame's *Essays*: modern, pedagogical versions of 'human philosophy'; the educational goals of elite institutions such as the École Normale Supérieure and Columbia University; the legacy of Pierre Villey's work in twentieth-century Montaigne studies; and 'Frame's Montaigne' as a composite product consisting of biography, translation, and critical study. We see how, in the twentieth century, generations of humanists in America and Europe called up the real person 'Montaigne' from behind his text and made him explain that text's value to idealist programmes of general literary education. In Frame's day, these programmes aimed to protect humane values against the reductive forces of 'progressive' modern society, to enfranchise the inner man.

The 'Epilogue' (2.7) picks up the discussion from the 'General Introduction' (in Volume 1) and the 'Prologue' (1.1) and extends it across a broader historical canvas. I ask how the case-studies in previous chapters, and new ones in this chapter of Bishop Camus and Pierre Charron, might revise the sketch of the *Essais* offered in Erich Auerbach's *Mimesis*. The history of Montaigne's text and *persona* is related to the wider, post-Reformation battle over the enfranchisement of the unofficial reader-writer, the person who in particular circumstances is freed to use literary materials for their own purposes, in their own way.

I argue that the fundamental issue at stake in the early modern making and transmission of the *Essais* is the issue that is explicitly raised by Marie de Gournay in her preface of 1595, and, in a different style and context, by Charron's use of Montaigne in *De la sagesse* (1601, 1604): how best to preserve and regulate the well-born individual's natural *liberté* of judgement, their *franchise* or frankness, through reading and writing, in an age of moral corruption and confessional conflict.

2.1

Montaigne at Paris and Blois, 1588
La Boétie, the *Essais*, and the *Robins*

In the last chapter of Volume 1, we saw that both the book (*Essais*) and the person (Michel de Montaigne) could act on their travels as a free agent who, on the one hand, might invite suspicion from all parties in the French and European religious wars but who, on the other hand, might equally inspire trust on all sides as a non-partisan Catholic nobleman and private moderator or 'wise man'. From the start, Montaigne's work was designed to travel, whether via the Bordeaux publisher Simon Millanges's commercial network or in the luggage of the author.

In 1580, as part of a seventeen-month journey accompanying Charles d'Estissac, Montaigne entered a Rome suspicious of Frenchmen and French religion, with copies of his 1580 *Essais* and of other books inviting censure, and emerged unscathed, with full recognition of his credentials, and a significant noble title to boot. In 1588, as part of an eleven-month trip on which he initially accompanied Matignon's son Odet de Thorigny, he entered Catholic League-controlled Paris with his revised book. What recognition did author and book get in the French capital?

2.1.1 MONTAIGNE AT PARIS AND BLOIS, 1588

Once again, on this trip Montaigne is carrying the *Essais* with him. He is burdened with the copy text for L'Angelier's new edition, and charged, as part of the entourage of Matignon's son, with an unofficial task of diplomatic mediation.[1] Both as a courtier and as an author, his reputation is beginning to form. He is known not as a writer isolated in a tower-library but as a wise man with powerful patrons who participated in a publicized literary friendship (with La Boétie). The English ambassador to France, Edward Stafford, writes in a missive letter to Principal Secretary Walsingham of Montaigne's arrival at court. He portrays him as 'a very wise gentleman of the king of Navarre', who is 'a great favourite' of Diane

---

[1] On this trip and its political context, see Donald M. Frame, 'New light on Montaigne's trip to Paris in 1588', *Romanic Review*, 51 (1960), 161–81; Donald M. Frame, *Montaigne: a biography* (London and New York: Hamish Hamilton and Harcourt, Brace & World, 1965), 270–84 (henceforward abbreviated as 'Frame'); Amy Graves, 'Crises d'engagement: Montaigne et la Ligue', in Philippe Desan (ed.), *Montaigne politique, actes du colloque international tenu à University of Chicago (Paris), les 29 et 30 avril 2005* (Paris: H. Champion, 2006), 329–52, 339–51; Richard Cooper, 'Montaigne dans l'entourage du maréchal de Matignon', *Montaigne Studies*, 13 (2001), 99–140, 132–6.

d'Andoins de Gramont (comtesse de Guiche or Guissen), mistress to Navarre and lady-in-waiting to Catherine de Bourbon.[2]

Stafford makes no mention of Montaigne's authorship of the *Essais*. But his understanding of Montaigne's political affiliations does correspond to the epistolary dedication of La Boétie's sonnets to his patroness Diane d'Andoins (in *Essais* I 28), and in general to Montaigne's dedications of various chapters to noblewomen of the entourage of Navarre's wife, Marguerite de Valois.[3]

Montaigne gets some publicity as an author later in the same year, but in the Low Countries, and in a very particular context. A dedicatory letter by Dominicus Baudius, a professor of Leiden University in the reformed Low Countries, appears in print there at the head of Adrien van Blijenburg's *Poemata*.[4] The context is the praise of statesmen such as Michel de L'Hospital who were successful as both jurists and poets.

Baudius invokes Montaigne as someone of celebrated wisdom and judgement whose opinion on the contribution of poetry to his great friend La Boétie's reputation carries weight. The opinion is expressed in the same chapter of the *Essais* (I 28) and in his edition of La Boétie's neo-Latin poetry (dedicated to L'Hospital). Baudius cites Lipsius's nomination of the author of the 1580 *Essais* as the French Thales, and explains that Montaigne is a man of very sharp judgement ('vir . . . judicii acerrimi').[5]

As we saw in 1.6.3, Lipsius's nomination had been made in a familiar letter printed in his 1586 *Epistolae* (Illus. 1.6.4), and he was about to write again to Montaigne in praise of his judgement, in letters that would be published in 1590. By printing these letters Lipsius sought publicly to enfranchise the author of the 1580 *Essais* as a noble and illustrious citizen of the European republic of letters.

There follows the publication of the first authorized Parisian edition, in quarto (1588). Montaigne subtly gives himself the credit for this success. He says that his enterprise's strangeness and novelty, which tend to give value, are his best hope of an honourable outcome; the fact that it is so fantastic, and has a face so far from common usage, may enable it to pass ('que cela luy pourra donner passage')—as his face enabled him to pass in the two instances reported at the end of III 12.[6] But the success of the work in moving from Bordeaux to Paris was due as much to its publishers, the connections between them, and the literary field and readership they created as to its innate merits.

The enterprise of Simon Millanges, in particular, enabled this strange new book to pass. Montaigne started writing around the time the printer-bookseller set up business at Bordeaux—surely no coincidence. Millanges's *politique éditoriale* came

[2] Frame, 271.

[3] Jean Balsamo, 'Un gentilhomme et ses patrons: remarques sur la biographie politique de Montaigne', in Desan (ed.), *Montaigne politique*, 223–42, 233–7.

[4] USTC 422666.

[5] Olivier Millet, *La première réception des 'Essais' de Montaigne: (1580–1640)* (Paris: Champion, 1995), 56 (henceforward abbreviated as 'Millet'); Olivier Millet, 'Dominicus Baudius lecteur de Montaigne', in Paul. J. Smith and Karl A.E. Enenkel (eds.), *Montaigne and the Low Countries (1580–1700)* (Leiden: Brill, 2007), 119–39, 119–21.

[6] II 8, NP403–4/BVH Paris 1588, f. 358 [158]/S432.

to focus even before the publication of Montaigne's work on 'tasters' ('essais') or trial publications of first literary works by new authors. His close connections with the Parisian book market, especially with Abel L'Angelier, enabled distribution of copies for sale in the capital.

More significantly still, many of the authors whose works appeared first with him migrated to *libraires* in Paris, with L'Angelier again prominent in such arrangements. Other authors who migrated from first works in Bordeaux to fuller editions in Paris included Brach, Raemond, Joubert, Du Bartas, de Thou, and Monluc.[7] So de Thou tried out his first major poetic project (*Hieracosophon*) at Bordeaux with Millanges in 1582, embedding it in the network of the Parisian *noblesse de robe*, before reaching out to a more international community of scholars with the fuller Parisian edition of Mamert Patisson in 1584.[8]

By 1588, then, the *Essais* had been travelling to Paris and beyond via commercial networks for several years, and Montaigne would have been aware of this fact.[9] There had already been an unauthorized Parisian edition in 1587.[10] It had never been a strictly local book, designed only for a provincial market.

L'Angelier's edition was nevertheless a new departure relative to Millanges's editions of 1580 (Illus. 1.6.1) and 1582: a grand quarto with an extravagant title page that spoke of status and intellectual prestige (Illus. 2.1.1). Montaigne now had a contract as an author with a big Parisian publisher and did not have to part-finance publication himself (as he did in 1580). Whatever the preface 'Au lecteur' still said, the expanded work now reached more confidently for Parisian readers and for L'Angelier's national and European clientele; it spoke intimately to a broad public accessed through the *boutique* of a famous bookseller.[11]

The Parisian presses were awash with partisan propaganda in this period.[12] In the midst of this print battle, L'Angelier produced a book (the *Essais*) that purported in many of its newly added passages and chapters to be authored by a non-partisan figure, a figure who was at peace with himself even in the midst of the tumults that possessed both his own region and the capital. And both he and the book are very aware of their forthcoming appearance in the capital.

As we heard in 1.7.7, III 9 celebrates the universal and common bonds associated with Rome. But the chapter is careful to balance this with the 'national bond'

---

[7] George Hoffmann, 'Millanges, Simon (Mille-Millanges, 1540–Bordeaux, 1623)', *Dictionnaire*, 764–6, for this and the previous paragraph. '*Dictionnaire*' is henceforward the abbreviation for Philippe Desan (ed.), *Dictionnaire de Michel de Montaigne* (2nd edn., Paris: Champion, 2007).

[8] Ingrid A. R. De Smet, *Thuanus: the making of Jacques-Auguste de Thou (1553–1617)* (Geneva: Droz, 2006), 52–63. Throughout this chapter I am heavily indebted to Ingrid De Smet's excellent studies of de Thou.

[9] On Millanges's wide distribution network see Paul Nelles, 'Stocking a library: Montaigne, the market, and the diffusion of print', in Philip Ford and Neil Kenny (eds.), *La librairie de Montaigne: Proceedings of the tenth Cambridge French Renaissance Colloquium 2–4 September 2008* (Cambridge: Cambridge French Colloquia, 2012), 1–24, 17–23.

[10] Sayce and Maskell 9–11, though this edition may also have been the result of an agreement between Millanges and the publisher Richer.

[11] NP xxv; Jean Balsamo, 'Montaigne's noble book: book history and biographical criticism', *Journal of Medieval and Early Modern Studies*, 41 (2011), 417–34, 419.

[12] D. Pallier, *Recherches sur l'imprimerie à Paris pendant la Ligue, 1585–1594* (Geneva: Droz, 1975).

ESSAIS
DE
MICHEL SEIGNEVR
DE MONTAIGNE.

Cinquiefme edition, augmen:
tée d'un troifiefme li:
ure: et de fix cens
additions aux
deus premiers.

A PARIS,
Chez ABEL L'ANGELIER,
au premier pillier de la grand
Salle du Palais.
Auec Priuilege du Roy.

1588

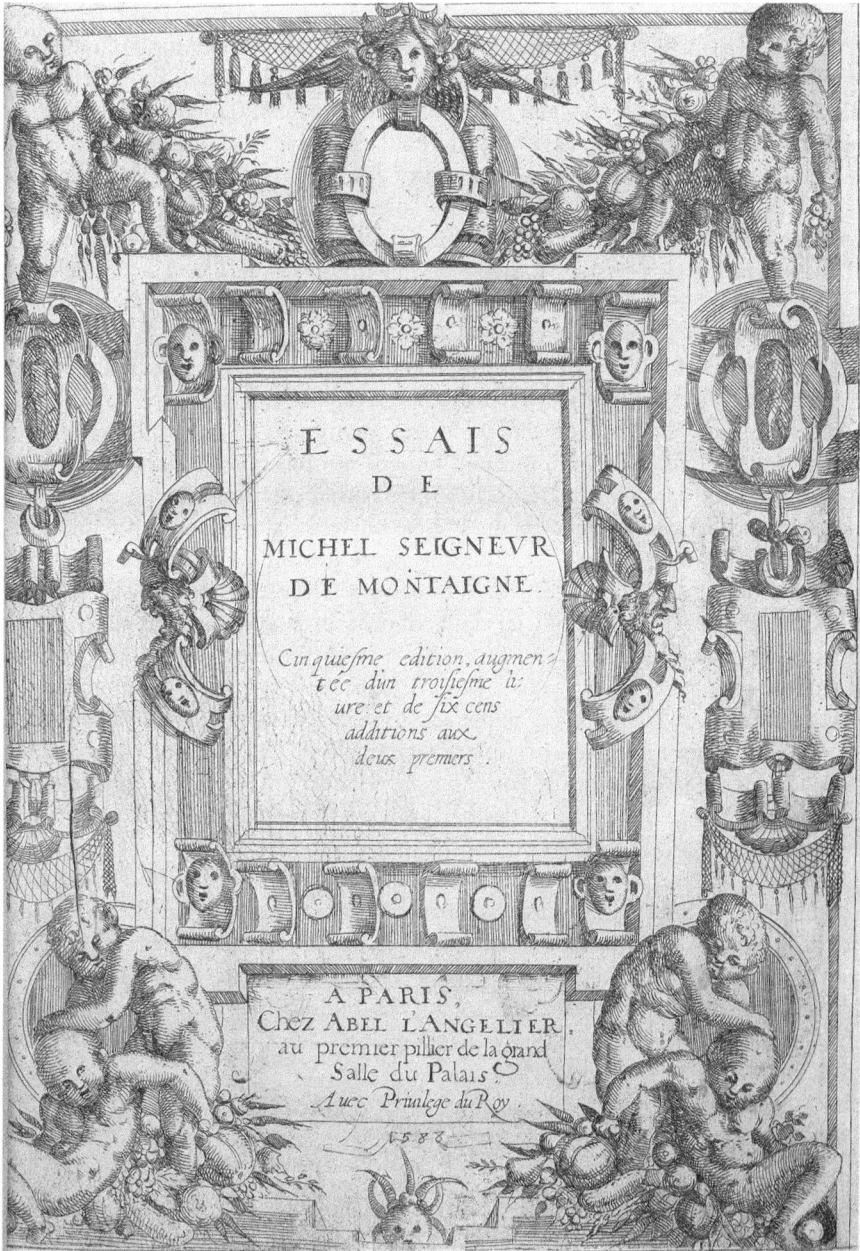

Illus. 2.1.1. Philippe Desan, *Bibliotheca Desaniana, Catalogue Montaigne* (Paris: Classiques Garnier, 2011), *Les Essais de Montaigne* (Paris: 1588), title page (second state). Courtesy of Philippe Desan.

('lyaison nationale') that is rooted in Montaigne's affection for Paris, which he fervently hopes will remain clear of 'our divisions'—a strikingly topical and committed statement in the circumstances of the later 1580s.[13] *Essais* III 10 describes his conduct of the mayoralty and his character in a manner designed to ensure that he would be known on the national stage neither as a partisan of the League nor of the Huguenots, nor as an enemy of any party. And one could go on. The audacious third book offered very free reflections on current moral and political topics along with what Étienne Pasquier later described as a history of Montaigne's morals and actions ('une histoire de ses [Montaigne's] moeurs et actions').[14]

As we heard in 1.6.1 and 1.6.2, the text contained an extraordinarily confident declaration of the uniqueness at one and the same time of the Book ('un Livre de bonne foi') and of the author and his *bienheureuse franchise*. He was now, on the title page, just 'MICHEL SEIGNEUR/ DE MONTAIGNE'. The author's dignities and offices were no longer mentioned (Illus. 2.1.1). He would add after 1588 that he communicated himself not by some 'peculiar extraneous mark' ('marque speciale et estrangere') such as that of a 'Jurisconsulte' or *parlementaire*, but by his 'universal being' ('estre universel'), that of a gentleman tied only to his fief and estates—as if nobility were not only a social status but 'an attribute defining his essence'. The message was clear. Authorship of this book does not depend upon any official status of professional knowledge, scholarship, or style: '[o]nly one quality authorizes his words, guarantees his book: the production of his own name'.[15]

The title page's reliance on name recognition explains the fear Montaigne expresses of finding himself in a place where the production of his own name does not secure free passage (II 5).[16] On the trip itself, in early 1588, Montaigne was charged with a delicate and unofficial mission—probably to mediate between Navarre and Henri III. There were suspicions on all sides. He was seized first by Protestants under the Prince de Condé's command, in reprisal for recent holdups by the League, then by Leaguers in reprisal for the arrest of a Leaguer by Henri III in Rouen. In both cases his name was produced and recognized by powerful patrons (Condé, Catherine de' Medici, Henri de Guise, Villeroy). He was released quickly both times, just as he was on the two occasions of danger

---

[13] Géralde Nakam, *Les 'Essais' de Montaigne, miroir et procès de leur temps: témoignage historique et création littéraire* (Paris: Librairie A.-G. Nizet and Publications de la Sorbonne, 1984), 232–9; III, 9 NP1017/BVH Paris 1588, f. 428v [436v]/S1100: 'And I do not want to omit that I am never such an enemy of France that I fail to look kindly on Paris: Paris has had my heart since boyhood. And as happens with all incomparable things, the more beautiful the other towns I have seen the more the beauty of Paris gains power over my affections. I love her for herself, more when left alone than overloaded with extra ornaments. I love her tenderly, warts, stains and all. That great city alone makes me a Frenchman, a city great in citizens, great in its happy choice of site, but great above all and incomparable in the variety and diversity of its attractions; it is the glory of France and one of the world's great splendours.'

[14] Millet 146/Étienne Pasquier, *Les lettres*, 2 vols. (Paris: Laurent Sonnius, 1619), vol. 2, sig. 2A6r.

[15] III 2, NP845/BVH Paris 1595, bk. III, p. 12/S908; NP xxxvi; Balsamo, 'Montaigne's noble book', 428–9.

[16] See the 'Conclusion' to Volume 1.

described in the book manuscript (at the end of III 12) he was carrying with him for publication.[17]

When it came to securing release from captivity, Montaigne's 'name' was good in very high places on his journey to Paris. But did this reception extend to, or was it extended by, the 1588 *Essais de Michel Seigneur de Montaigne*? Did the named author and his work quickly find friends who recognized their quality and ensured their free passage? Pierre de Brach was by Montaigne's side and wrote privately to Justus Lipsius after Montaigne's death to describe his constancy during a severe illness he suffered during his 1588 Parisian stay, relating it to his constancy in his writings. The letter was never printed.[18]

One remarkable encounter that year did become part of the story of the book for evermore, though it involved not a Parisian intellectual but a thitherto unknown young woman from the provinces. It was told in the eulogy of Gournay at the end of the Paris 1595 text of II 17, in Gournay's preface and in her *Proumenoir* and elsewhere: how Marie, alone in the provinces with a copy of the book, was able to judge the true quality of the author of the *Essais* and conceive such a vehement love for him that she sought him out in person; how she became his *fille d'alliance* and invited him back to Picardy the same year, where they began working together on a copy of the 1588 *Essais*; how, upon his deathbed, he sent her a tender adieu via his brother and bequeathed her his literary studies; how she crossed France to join Madame de Montaigne and her daughter in grief; and how she brought his final text to press in Paris in late 1594 with the help of Brach and Madame de Montaigne.

The impact of this story on *robe* readers of the book is only too apparent in Pasquier's letter, where he recalls that while Montaigne was making a long stay in 1588 in the town of Paris, she (Gournay) came expressly to visit him ('faisant en l'an 1588. un long seiour en la ville de Paris, elle [Gournay] le vint expres visiter').[19]

But where are the *éloges* of the book's other friends in the capital? As we heard in 1.6.4, Gournay contrasted her story, which is entwined with Lipsius's and his associate Baudius's public eulogies of Montaigne and the *Essais* in the Low Countries, with the 'cold reception given to the *Essais* by our men' ('froid recueil que nos hommes ont fait aux Essais').[20] She is very conscious in 1594–5 that a book that first appeared in Paris six years previously is now reappearing in a new folio edition with only a preface from an unknown gentlewoman from Picardy to guarantee its noble authority—hence the space taken up by her self-apology.

For Gournay cannot document a wide reception for this great patron-author; the private letters of Arnaud d'Ossat—whose approval, we shall see in 2.1.4, was

[17] Frame 273–6; Géralde Nakam, *Montaigne et son temps: les événements et les 'Essais'* (Paris: Nizet, 1982), 184–6. See 1.6.11 for the anecdotes at the end of III 12.

[18] Justus Lipsius, *Epistolae*, eds A. Gerlo, M. A. Nauwelaerts, and Hendrik D. L. Vervliet (Brussels: Koninklijke Academie voor Wetenschappen, Letteren en Schone Kunsten van België, 1978–), vol. VI, 93 02 04 (references to this edition will henceforward be abbreviated as follows: 'ILE VI 93 02 04').

[19] For this and the previous paragraph see II 17, NP701/BVH Paris 1595, p. 439/S751–2; Millet 148/Pasquier, *Lettres*, vol. 2, sig. 2B1r.

[20] NP4/BVH Paris 1595, f. a2.

important to de Thou—have gone missing. She cannot even document his 'famous' death, a crucial part of any *éloge*, as there appear to be no witnesses willing or able to confirm the particulars.[21] There is good evidence for one partial explanation of this lack of a reception for Paris 1588, at least until the success of Paris 1595 encouraged L'Angelier to distribute his remaining stock of the earlier quarto, late in the day. The rebellion of the League and the siege of Paris severely hampered the book trade between 1588 and the return of peace in 1594.[22]

Nevertheless, the context of the remark concerning the 'froid recueil' makes it clear that Gournay is referring to the whole period since the *Essais*' first publication in 1580, and that she is primarily drawing attention to the lack, in France, of any printed, public eulogies of Montaigne to compare with those of Lipsius and herself. What significant *éloges* had in fact appeared in print in France in the years between 1580 and 1594? As we have already heard, Pierre de Brach's letter was not printed. Claude Expilly's sonnet was probably written into his copy of Paris 1588 before 1594, but was not printed by L'Angelier until 1596.[23]

Perhaps only two *éloges* qualify, and we have already encountered them both, though without noting the role of Millanges and L'Angelier in their publication: La Croix du Maine's entry on the Gascon in the *Bibliotheque* of 1584, published by L'Angelier; and Florimond de Raemond's digression in the 1594 edition of *Erreur populaire de la papesse Jane*, published by Millanges.[24]

In La Croix du Maine, Montaigne is indeed presented as *un homme de bonne maison, de crédit et de qualité*, the son-in-law of an illustrious *robin* of the region, who has been presented at court to Henri III and who has successfully imitated Plutarch in his book. This is 'faint praise' in Gournay's terms. Raemond's fulsome *éloge* of the *sage* from Bordeaux is less easy to see as faint praise, but for some reason she never acknowledged it—perhaps because she knew it was orchestrated by Brach in advance of the 1595 edition.

A noble and wise captain in the ancient mould has arrived on the Parisian scene, playing the part consummately in his book, but no one aside from Lipsius has 'visited' him (in person or in print) to recognize and praise his true noble quality. The expectation informing Gournay's disappointment is the one lightly parodied by Rabelais in the figure of Thaumaste, who appears in *Pantagruel* (*c*.1531). Thaumaste declares that if the very *image* of *science* and *sapience* appeared bodily to human eyes, the whole world would be excited in admiration. Rumour would spread knowledge of this appearance to all *philosophes*, who would neither sleep nor rest until they had run to the place to see 'la personne' in whom *science* had

---

[22] Jean Balsamo and Michel Simonin, *Abel L'Angelier & Françoise de Louvain (1574–1620): suivi du catalogue des ouvrages publiés par Abel L'Angelier (1574–1610) et la veuve L'Angelier (1610–1620)* (Geneva: Droz, 2002), 81–8.
[23] On Expilly, see later in this section: 2.1.1.
[24] Millet 52–4, 76–9. There were brief and minor praises of Montaigne printed in Bouchet's *Les Sérées* of 1584, Saint-Julien's *Meslanges* of 1588, Tabouret's *Les Touches* of 1588, and in the *Chonique Bourdeloise* of 1594 (Millet 51–2, 62–3, 75–6).

established her temple and promulgated her oracles. This is exactly what has brought Thaumaste to Paris from England to see Pantagruel.[25]

In the same way, Gournay has run to the place—Paris—to see the philosophical 'personne' of Montaigne, for there is one section in her 'Preface' that makes it clear that the scene in question is indeed Paris 1588. Gournay moves from the 'censeurs' of the *Essais* to another kind of impertinent judge—those who damn with faint praise ('mediocres loüeurs'). They are heard to pay the work some minor compliments. But if they had truly recognized the grandeur of the soul behind the book, they would either have run from every direction to be in Montaigne's presence, or invented and printed *éloges* equal to his merit to praise and proclaim him as one of the illustrious greats—as Lipsius had done.[26]

Could they have been suspicious that the book was all borrowings from elsewhere, and failed to honour him for that reason? No, says Gournay: it is obvious that the chapters are 'all by the same hand; a book with a new air' ('tout d'une main: livre d'un air nouveau'). So why didn't these 'personnages', these faint praisers, seek out 'ceste grande ame'?:

> My Father, wishing to goad me one day, told me he judged that there were thirty men in our great city [*nostre grande ville*], where he was at the time, with as powerful an intellect as himself [*aussi forts de teste que luy*]. One of my arguments in countering this was that if there had been one, he would have come to greet him and, I was fain to add, idolize him; and that so many people received him for being a man of good family, of credit, and of noble birth [*un homme de bonne maison, de credit et de qualité*]: none for being Montaigne.[27]

We saw above that the title page of the 1588 *Essais* precisely asks for recognition from the customer in L'Angelier's *boutique* of the unique quality of being 'Montaigne' (Illus. 2.1.1).

The implication is clear. The author 'Montaigne' was received via his book in the Paris of 1588 as a generic gentleman from Guyenne, of noble extraction, of the kind described in La Croix du Maine, not as a great philosophical *patron*, a great noble soul of the ancient stamp. For the singular 'quality' of the book is identified by Gournay with those essential and personal qualities which should be recognized as the true 'condition' of the author, the *condition* beyond that of a generic 'man of good family, of credit, ... of noble birth'. The intellectual elite of the city appear not to have agreed that a philosophical giant such as Pantagruel had arrived in the city. They neither rushed to his side nor rushed into print with *éloges* of this wondrous author, unmatched (according to Gournay) in fourteen or fifteen centuries.

In the course of this chapter, we shall consider two vital pieces of evidence that appear to relate to Montaigne's and his book's conversation with the Parisian intellectual elite, when he travelled to Paris and on to Blois in the same year of 1588. I say 'appear' because they actually reveal that the noble *persona* 'Montaigne', the author of the *Essais* (as opposed to the *conseiller* who edited La Boétie's works), only

---

[25] François Rabelais, *Œuvres complètes*, eds. Jacques Boulenger and Lucien Scheler (Paris: Gallimard, 1955), 248.
[26] NP17–18/ BVH Paris 1595, f. e3v–e4.   [27] NP19/BVH Paris 1595, f. e4v.

'arrived' in the city posthumously in 1594–5, only began to receive significant praise as a *vir illustris* amongst members—at least amongst those beyond Gournay's milieu—of the parliamentary, office-holding elite in the early 1600s, and only became a touchstone in printed, public intellectual conversation towards the end of the 1610s.

Our focus on this parliamentary elite shall make it more appropriate to consider the parallel case of the posthumous association made in print in 1606 between Montaigne and the priest and theological teacher Pierre Charron, and between their respective works (the *Essais* and *De la sagesse*), in a later section of this study (2.7.5).

In 1588, the historical person Montaigne stayed in the capital after the Day of the Barricades, then followed the king's court to Chartres and Rouen. He was accompanied by Jacques Auguste de Thou, who reported a conversation they had later in the year at the Estates General of Blois. The report (made in de Thou's *Vita*) includes no explicit mention of the *Essais*, but I shall argue that we should understand it to be informed by Montaigne's post-1594 reputation as the author of that work, for it was not composed until 1614 and not published until 1621. It turns out to be an act of retrospection designed to welcome 'Montaigne', the author of the mature *Essais,* into the *politique* conversation of the 1610s, not a record of his entrance into the same in the late 1580s. It was closely associated with two Latin *elogia*—one by de Thou himself, one by Scévole de Sainte-Marthe—that were composed in the early 1600s.

Exactly the same is true of the other piece of evidence. This includes mention of a copy of the *Essais* which—to recall the events described in 1.7.5—did not fall into the hands of customs officials at the gates of Paris, but which was censured as a Gascon work on behalf of the Parisian legal intelligentsia. The censor was someone who considered himself to be an intimate friend of Montaigne's: Étienne Pasquier. Like the censors at Rome, he proposed corrections, which he expected to see included in the next edition. Like de Thou, he described a private conversation he had with Montaigne at Blois in 1588. The letter containing the description is marked in other ways by Montaigne's and his book's appearance at Paris the same year.

But, again, it proves to be an act of retrospection. It is difficult to date with any precision the original redaction of the letter, especially as it may never have actually been sent, and may have been revised before publication up until Pasquier's death in 1615. It must have post-dated the publication of Marie de Gournay's edition in late 1594, so its composition and subsequent revision certainly fall within the period which followed Henri IV's abjuration (1593) and his retaking of Paris (1594), and which pivoted around the king's internal and external moves to establish peace in 1598–9 and his assassination in 1610. There are other circumstantial indications that place its original redaction in the middle decade of this period: 1598–1608.

When Gournay addressed 'les Censeurs des Essais' and the 'mediocres loüeurs' in her preface of 1595, she clearly had Pasquier, de Thou, and his ilk—the office-holding, parliamentary network centred on Paris—in mind. They are the dominant, elite, literary 'public' whose reaction makes sense of her preface. They provide what is at one and the same time a rival and a complementary way of praising the author of the *Essais*, and of understanding the moral behaviour indexed by the book.

Together, the two groups—on the one hand, Gournay and her collaborators (including L'Angelier for a brief period and some *robins*), and, on the other hand, the group including de Thou, Pasquier, and other *robins* beyond Gournay's milieu—define a range of ways of describing the nexus of the mature *Essais* as they were first successfully published at Paris from 1595. These descriptions ultimately centre not on literary-critical appreciation, but on the way the author is praised in eulogistic portrayals.

Towards one end of the range, Montaigne is already a patron-author, an instant classic—like Pantagruel for Thaumaste. He is a great captain and philosopher who has lived the most exemplary life in Europe. The *Essais* rise above the contemporary troubles to conduct a frank conversation about the classical art of living and of judgement. The author is *Thales Gallicus*, and only other sages from antiquity to the present can relate to him.

Towards the other end, the author Montaigne is an ex-counsellor, ex-mayor of Bordeaux, unofficial court mediator, and one-time friend to a more illustrious sage in the ancient mould (La Boétie). The *Essais* are noteworthy for the extraordinary variety and freedom of the discourses they offer; they provide moral *sentences* and *traits* directly relevant to the troubles, especially the wars of the League and of the royal succession. The author is a man of free spirit, alien to factions, who can relate to other such men—including *parlementaires* of *politique* inclinations. But, relatively speaking, he is a bit-part player in the intellectual history of the revival of letters amongst the *parlementaires*.

In general terms, a good proportion of the documented early reception of the *Essais* relates to members of this parliamentary network, and much of it is indeed 'faint praise' by Gournay's standards.[28] The main exceptions amongst the *robins*— Raemond, Expilly—were those who were consciously composing *éloges* in tune with Brach's, Gournay's, and L'Angelier's plans for the new edition of 1595.[29] There is, furthermore, a more particular correspondence between the criticisms she attributes to these censors, especially the first one concerning Montaigne's language, and those of the *robin* Pasquier. Of the six principal criticisms listed by Gournay in her 1595 preface, one clearly derives from the censorial process of 1581 (Montaigne's irreligion, as evidenced by the fact that he listed a heretic

---

[28] See Millet 51–2 (Guillaume Bouchet, 1584), 54–5 (Étienne Tabourot, 1585), 75–6 (Gabriel de Lurbe, 1594).

[29] On Expilly and L'Angelier, see Shanti Graheli, 'Building a library across early-modern Europe. The network of Claude Expilly', paper given at 'International Exchange in the European Book World', University of St Andrews, 21 June 2013, forthcoming in *International exchange in the European book world* (Leiden: Brill, 2016). Raemond was the editor of Jean de Sponde's self-apology, published with L'Angelier in 1594–5 (USTC 3054, which dates it 1595; dated 1594 by Balsamo and Simonin, no. 244), and of Monluc's *Commentaires*, published by L'Angelier and other booksellers in 1594 (USTC 5209).

among the leading poets of the time, and other points), while the other five appear in Pasquier's letter.

Gournay is highly conscious throughout that, as a noble 'captain', a *noble d'épée*, writing in the vernacular, Montaigne would be judged alongside the likes of Monluc and La Noue, and potentially found wanting in his lack of fame as the author of great noble deeds on the battlefield. Pasquier's letter in judgement on the *Essais* again makes sense of this apologetic stance. For, as we shall see in 2.1.7, it is paired with another letter in judgement on Monluc, a great noble captain who wrote up his deeds as *Commentaires* (edited by another *robin*, Raemond) analogous to those of Caesar. Pasquier indeed treats the two authors in very different ways.

The point is not that Gournay saw an early draft of this letter, but that Pasquier was summarizing a mode of judgement of the *Essais* that had been around for some time in *robe* circles.[30] He was speaking on behalf of a whole parliamentary network of office-holders and scholar-magistrates. Besides Pasquier and de Thou, and individuals already encountered in this chapter and in Volume 1 (Brach, Raemond, Lancre, Expilly) the key individuals to engage with Montaigne and the *Essais* in this network were Scévole de Sainte-Marthe, Antoine Loisel, Antoine de Laval, Antoine Séguier, and Pierre de L'Estoile.[31]

Many of these men have since been characterized as Gallicans and *politiques*, but not all. Two were *nobles de robe* of high rank and office (de Thou; Séguier, a *Président à mortier* and ambassador to Venice). At least two expressed the views of more orthodox Papists (Raemond, Lancre). Two of them were on the *chambre de justice* sent to Guyenne in 1581 (de Thou, Loisel), while Montaigne was mayor. Four were with the Gascon at the ultimately disastrous Estates General of Blois in late 1588 (Pasquier, de Thou, Laval, Sainte-Marthe), some in an official capacity, others as observers (serving their own or others' private interests).

After the assassination of the Guises, many of them became, like Montaigne, potential enemies in the eyes both of the Catholic League and the Huguenots. Four claimed him in print as a friend (Pasquier, de Thou, Raemond, Loisel), one in private letters (Brach), and one in a private annotation (Laval). Nine definitely owned copies of the *Essais* (of which five definitely bore annotations), while Brach had some role in editing the text, and Lancre clearly read it closely. Two used his book as a vade mecum (Pasquier and L'Estoile).[32]

---

[30] See Frame 311–12.

[31] For other owners of copies of the *Essais* amongst *parlementaires* and office-holders in Paris see Lyndan Warner, *The ideas of man and woman in Renaissance France: print, rhetoric, and law* (Farnham: Ashgate, 2011), chapter 7. See 2.7.7 for a brief discussion of Bernard de La Roche Flavin, a *parlementaire* from the Bordeaux area.

[32] For this and the previous paragraph see Marie Houllemare, *Politiques de la parole: le parlement de Paris au XVIe siècle* (Geneva: Droz, 2011), 263–70, 595–607 (on Séguier); Catherine Magnien, 'Étienne Pasquier "familier" de Montaigne?', *Montaigne Studies*, 13 (2001), 277–313; Ingrid A. R. De Smet, 'Montaigne et Jacques-Auguste de Thou', *Montaigne Studies*, 13 (2001), 223–40; Catherine Magnien, 'Raemond, Florimond (Agen, v. 1540–Bordeaux, 1601)', *Dictionnaire*, 993–4; George Hoffmann, 'Croiser le fer avec le Géographe du Roi: l'entrevue de Montaigne avec Antoine de Laval aux Etats généraux de Blois en 1588', *Montaigne Studies*, 13 (2001), 207–22; Balsamo and Simonin, *Abel L'Angelier & Françoise de Louvain (1574–1620)*, 242 (de Thou's copy of 1588), 268 (Sainte-Marthe's and Laval's annotated copies of 1595).

The documentation relating to the posthumous introduction of the *Essais* and the *persona* of their author into *robe* networks is thus various. It consists not only of epitexts, but also of extant copies with annotations, narratives about non-extant copies, transcriptions of annotations, and *extraits* in non-extant copies. Each document relates to a specific nexus of transmission. Séguier copied and adapted various *traits* from his copy of the 1580 *Essais* into his personal register at the height of the troubles in 1588–9. Raemond both praised and cited Montaigne in print, and annotated his work in private, providing glosses that identified figures and events alluded to in the *Essais*. His copy (not extant) made it a bolder work, as the reader could see in the margins the names of the great patrons whose morals Montaigne was discussing so freely.[33]

The copy of Paris 1595 acquired in 1597 by Antoine de Laval, and annotated in the decade that followed by him and his great-nephew Charles de La Mure, is extant, but in private hands. Laval, who has already been studied in detail, is at the censorious end of *robe* opinion, the one who, along with Lancre, was most inclined to tax Montaigne's *liberté*. The annotations mark many of Montaigne's comments on the subject of religion as dangerously *risqué*. But his 1605 *Desseins de professions nobles*, which feature Montaigne's cousin in a dialogue set in the year of Henri IV's triumph (1594) and which provide a kind of model of the *robe* culture of the Henrician intellectual elite, are akin in some respects to the *Essais*.[34]

We can already sense here the outline of a process of negotiation amongst French parliamentarians and office-holders concerning the gentleman from Gascony not dissimilar from the one amongst the curia at Rome about the gentleman from France. They are joined in public debate, in the 1610s and 1620s, by clergy such as Bishop Jean-Pierre Camus and François Garasse, S.J. The negotiation is mindful of Gournay's role and is conducted by means of rhetorical praise and blame of the qualities of the author—a rhetoric that is highly nuanced and potentially ambiguous. Is, for example, someone who calls the *Essais* the breviary of the *gentilshommes* praising or blaming the author?[35]

In the end, there are those, such as Lancre and Laval, who judge that Montaigne's *liberté* is more like *licence*, and that his nobly free authorial *persona* disguises his true intentions. Others grant the author and his work his liberties, but not before corrections and censures are mooted—as at Rome. In what follows, we shall complement our discussion of Lancre in Volume 1 (1.5.4) with a look at the documents relating to four *parlementaires* who shared the *politique* mentality: de Thou, Sainte-Marthe, Pasquier, and L'Estoile. Two feature as authors of *éloges*, two as

[33] Houllemare, *Politiques de la parole*, 264, 607 (I have not verified the dating of these annotations with reference to the manuscript, BNF MS Lat. 14218, f. 121–6); Pierre Bonnet, 'Une nouvelle série d'annotations de Florimond de Raemond aux *Essais* de Montaigne', *Bulletin de la Société des Amis de Montaigne*, 3rd series, 10 (1959), 10–23; Alan Boase, 'Montaigne annoté par Florimond de Raemond', *Revue du seizième siècle*, 15 (1928), 237–78.

[34] Hoffmann, 'Croiser le fer'; George Hoffmann, 'Laval, Antoine Mathé de (Crémaux, 1550–Moulins, 1632)', *Dictionnaire*, 660–2; 'Laval (Antoine Mathé de)', *DLF*, 700–1; Millet 129–30, 142–3. The annotations in the Laval and Raemond copies are included in the editors' notes to the text of NP (see p. XCVIII).

[35] Millet 194–5 (Lancre).

reader-writers of the *Essais*. These documents tell a coherent story about a moment in the first two decades of the seventeenth century when the *Essais* became a breviary for *robins* seeking to moralize the times and fortify their ethos as men of free spirit, alien to factions.

Montaigne certainly shared an experience of the civil wars and a literary culture with these men. They are undoubtedly part of the audience of readers his book envisages. We heard in 1.5.7 how Lancre inadvertently accredited Montaigne's book with being the touchstone for a whole readership of *parlementaires* and judges who privately share a certain ethos, a disinclination fully to commit to belief in and prosecution of 'impossible' crimes such as transvection (witches' flight to sabbats). The *Essais* appropriate, in more natural vein, a *parlement*-style rhetoric of citations modelled on Amyot's Plutarch. They draw on legal modes of glossing and argumentation, and take justice and the venality of offices as one of their main themes.[36]

And Montaigne must surely have known that the 1588 edition would reach the *parlementaires* such as Pasquier who frequented L'Angelier's shop in the *Palais de Justice* in Paris.[37] One copy was directly dedicated by Montaigne himself to Antoine Loisel, *avocat du Roi*, in recompense for 'labeurs' he had previously received from Loisel. The letter implies Loisel would be able and inclined to judge whether the work was getting stronger or weaker as the new edition appeared.[38] And readers such as Loisel would, like Raemond, have been able to identify, or at least guess, the contemporary events to which Montaigne was tacitly reacting and the contemporary figures he invokes but often fails to name.

But Montaigne does not publicly honour his relations with *parlementaires* in Bordeaux, Paris, and elsewhere in his new edition of 1588. He does not dedicate the *Essais* directly to one or more of them, in the way he did his edition of La Boétie (who they saw as one of their own). The most important difference is that— unlike de Thou, L'Estoile, and Pasquier—he does not directly engage with contemporary political events when compiling his texts. He does not, unlike them, directly memorialize or write histories of the religious wars—most probably because he was obeying the royal injunction, repeated in the edicts of pacification from 1563 onwards, against reviving the memory of the troubles, whether in print or in acts of commemoration.[39] This is not to say, of course, that the experiences of the wars do not mark the *Essais* profoundly.[40]

---

[36] Marc Fumaroli, *L'Âge de l'Éloquence: rhétorique et 'res literaria' de la Renaissance au seuil de l'époque classique* (3rd edn.; Geneva: Droz, 2002), 444–5, 474.

[37] NP xxv; Étienne Pasquier, *Choix de lettres sur la littérature, la langue et la traduction*, ed. D. Thickett (Geneva: Droz, 1956), 11–12; Étienne Pasquier, *Lettres familières*, ed. D. Thickett (Geneva: Droz, 1974), 242–6. On the relationship between L'Angelier and the readership of the *Palais de Justice*, and between both and Montaigne, see Warner, *The ideas of man and woman*, especially chapters 6 to 8.

[38] Michel de Montaigne, *Œuvres complètes*, eds Maurice Rat and Albert Thibaudet (Paris: Gallimard, 1962), 1396–7.

[39] Philip Benedict, 'Shaping the memory of the French wars of religion. The first centuries', in Erika Kuijpers et al. (eds.), *Memory before modernity: practices of memory in early modern Europe* (Leiden: Brill, 2013), 111–25.

[40] Nakam, *Les 'Essais' de Montaigne*; Nakam, *Montaigne et son temps*.

The 1588 edition generally preserves the appearance of a text composed in private with minimal interference from patrons and correspondents. No new letters, preliminary verses, or tributes by approving members of the regional or national intellectual elite are added—as would have been normal. There is no additional apologetic preface, as there would be in 1595. The book is still presented as it was when published in Bordeaux in 1580: embedded in relations with the Roman Catholic aristocracy of southwest France, and with La Boétie, Amyot, and Pierre Eyquem's Sebond.

The author might even be said to have disguised his identity as a one-time magistrate and legal scholar, and as friend to *parlementaires* from Raemond and Laval to Pasquier and de Thou. Indeed, if he converses with the group to which they belonged (scholarly *robins*), it is—as Pasquier suggests—to distance them, to rile them for their officiousness and pseudo-learnedness. It is insistently presented as a book by and for gentlemen-at-arms, not lawyers and scholars.[41]

But from Pasquier's and Séguier's readings in the mid- to late 1580s (using the 1580 text) through to L'Estoile's use of the full text between 1606 and 1610, the *Essais* nevertheless provided resources for reading and writing the experiences of the wars of the League and their aftermath. The *robins* saw in Montaigne's text a philosophically rich gestation of their own experiences of division and civil war on the part of someone whose career had put him in touch with events, both in Gascony and at the court.[42]

This is apparent, for example, in the sonnet 'Sur les essais de messire michel de Montagnes' that Expilly wrote on his copy of Paris 1588, *c.*1592–3, before peace had been restored and before news of Montaigne's death reached him. It was later published in a volume of his poems by L'Angelier (1595); it then served as a paratext in Paris 1602, and copies of Lyon [Geneva] 1595 were re-issued with the poem included *c.*1602.[43]

Expilly was in tune with Brach, Raemond, and Gournay in inferring a great soul from the literary work, but he also hears its contemporary relevance. The book provides a masculine language ('masle langage') and reasonings capable of fortifying the weakest spirits in defiance of the vicissitudes and storms of the times ('raisons...Capable d'enhardir, les plus lasches espris/ A defier du temps l'inconstance et l'orage!'). In his courageous essays ('braves essais'), his faithful witnesses ('fidelles tesmoings'), Montaigne shows that he knows how to trample underfoot the cares that devour *us* ('le soin qui *nous* devore'; my emphasis)—alluding to the *curae edaces* ('voracious cares') dispersed by Bacchus in Horace, *Odes*, 2.11.18.[44]

---

[41] Millet 145.

[42] Jean Balsamo, 'Des *Essais* pour comprendre les guerres civiles', *Bibliothèque d'Humanisme et Renaissance*, 72 (2010), 521–40.

[43] Alessandra Preda, ' "Les siècles à venir te loueront à bon droit": Montaigne et Claude Expilly', *Montaigne Studies*, 13 (2001), 187–205, 192–3 (this article contains the text of the sonnet, as discussed in the following paragraph here). The copy is Bibliothèque municipale de Grenoble, Fonds ancien, pressmark Rés. V. 2856. Expilly must have picked up 'Messire' from the title pages to earlier editions as it does not appear on the title page of the copy in which he wrote the sonnet.

[44] My thanks to Ingrid De Smet.

This is a book by a knight—Messire Montaigne—whose discourse, whose everyday conduct, in the midst of profoundly troubled times, teaches 'us', the *robins*, how to speak, live, and die in troubled times of religious division. As Lipsius had done for the international republic of letters, Expilly is self-consciously opening the gates of praise for the *robe* elite—'the centuries to come will give you your just praise' ('les siécles à venir te loueront à bon droit').[45] Not many were to rush through with the same degree of enthusiasm.

Nevertheless, from the appearance of Raemond's eulogy with Millanges in 1594, Loisel's dedication with L'Angelier in 1595 (see the end of this section), and Expilly's sonnet with L'Angelier in 1596, the *robins* started to compose and print epitexts that gave the book the relational context it fails itself to offer (with the exception of the advertised friendship with the *parlementaire* La Boétie).[46] Such epitexts retrospectively embed the *Essais* in a collective attempt—in which publishers such as L'Angelier participated—to fashion a pre-history and a moral philosophy for the fragile Henrician concord. The participants were seeking to define *personae* and offices for themselves and others in public and private life. They were seeking enfranchisement as noble professionals, as members of a civic and moral magistracy dedicated to active peace-making and peacekeeping: men of free spirit, alien to faction.

They were, in other words, retrospectively bringing together a community of lettered *politiques* across the decades of the civil wars.[47] It is in this context that the noble authorial *persona* of Montaigne was enfranchised by the *robins*—if in a more muted fashion than he was by Lipsius and Gournay, and in relation to a more concrete political career. The most important sign of this is that around the turn of the century he became the subject of *éloges*.

One could not become an illustrious author of credited literary works at this time unless one was the subject of *éloges*, for the language of criticism was largely the language of praise and blame of an author's qualities as a *vir illustris* in life and death. This is the setting for Montaigne's project of self-portraiture: the kind of literary portraits others might have been expected to make of him, and therefore of his book. In 1.3.1, we heard about the international revival of Plutarchan and other forms of biographical writing between the 1520s and the 1550s, which was part of a general rediscovery across various media of Roman-style portraiture of *viri illustres*. The distinctively natural and free image already offered in the 1580 *Essais* entered an environment saturated with literary and visual *imagines* of the noble-minded and the great-souled.

Later in the century, in France, a prosopographical literature would seek to make the newfound tranquillity of the state depend upon the shared ethos of the magisterial classes and the *noblesse de robe*. This included a *robe* redefinition of the values to be admired in the *noblesse d'épée*, especially the *valeur* and *clemence*

---

[45] Preda, 'Les siècles à venir te loueront à bon droit', 193.   [46] Millet 76–9, 128–9.
[47] Mario Turchetti, 'Une question mal posée: L'origine et l'identité des politiques au temps des guerres de religion', in Thierry Wanegffelen (ed.), *De Michel de L'Hospital à l'édit de Nantes: politique et religion face aux églises* (Clermont-Ferrand: Presses Universitaires Blaise-Pascal, 2002), 357–90, 386.

of the conquering peacemaker, King Henri IV.[48] By the early 1600s, as the Henrician concord took hold, a *robe* practice of literary portrait reading and writing was thriving in France, both in print and manuscript. This included active reader participation in the supplementing (with drawings and text), cross-referring, and cutting-and-pasting of series of portraits.[49]

Group biographies and other moral portraits of men of letters were used to promote a collective identity amongst *gentilshommes* seeking enfranchisement as noble professionals via learning and office.[50] This biographical literature created a new pantheon of recent *robe* heroes and authors. It constituted a network of mutually reinforcing significance within which texts associated with or authored by these heroes and authors could be read and recirculated.[51] The moral *personae* of the authors, as portrayed and contested in various texts, were fundamental contexts for reading and writing. This is only too clear in the later *registres-journaux* of L'Estoile, which are studded with obituaries, death scenes, and eulogies that relate to the reputation and authority of the texts whose circulation he tracks and facilitates.[52]

Literary prosopography was part of a broader *robe* culture of oratorical eloquence with roots in the early Reformation and the revival of classical letters under François I. These parliamentary and scholarly networks were constituted by multiple nexuses in which texts were read ethically and pragmatically, both in relation to the problem of religious and political reunification caused by the Reform, and to the problem of the conservation of Gallican liberties caused by the papal Counter-Reform.

This in turn depended on the formation of private collections and the editing, circulation, and copying of printed books, manuscripts, and *libelles*. L'Estoile is, again, an excellent if extreme example. His ethical reading focused on portraits (including his own self-portrait) of *personae* whose morals were conducive to peace and reunification; his pragmatic reading focused on the accumulation of authorities as weapons for Gallican polemics against the Jesuits and other parties hostile to Gallican liberties.

The corresponding writing produced within these networks blended oratory (Loisel's *Remonstrances*), dialogue (Laval's *Dessein*), public and ecclesiastical history (de Thou's *Historiae*, Raemond's *L'Erreur*), letters (Pasquier's *Lettres*), biography (Sainte-Marthe's *Elogia*), philosophy and theology (Lancre's *L'Incredulité*), and more private forms of writing such as the marginal annotation (Laval's notes in his

[48] Amy Graves, 'L'art du portrait chez Jacques-Auguste de Thou', in Frank Lestringant (ed.), *Jacques-Auguste de Thou (1553–1617): Écriture et condition robine* (Paris: Presses de l'Université Paris-Sorbonne, 2007), 127–42, 137.
[49] Katherine MacDonald, 'Un exemplaire illustré des *Elogia gallorum doctrina illustrium* (1602) de Scévole de Sainte-Marthe et l'iconographie de Joachim Du Bellay: un portrait inconnu?', *Bibliothèque d'Humanisme et Renaissance*, 64 (2002), 79–95.
[50] Katherine MacDonald, *Biography in early modern France, 1540–1630: forms and functions* (London: Legenda, 2007), 5.
[51] Jean-Marc Chatelain, 'Heros togatus: culture cicéronienne et gloire de la robe dans la France d'Henri IV', *Journal des savants*, nos. 3–4 (1991), 263–87.
[52] Pierre de L'Estoile, *Journal pour le règne de Henri IV*, eds Louis-Raymond Lefèvre and André Martin, 3 vols. (Paris: Gallimard, 1948–60), vol. 2, 193ff. and vol. 3 *passim* (henceforward abbreviated as '*Journal Henri IV*').

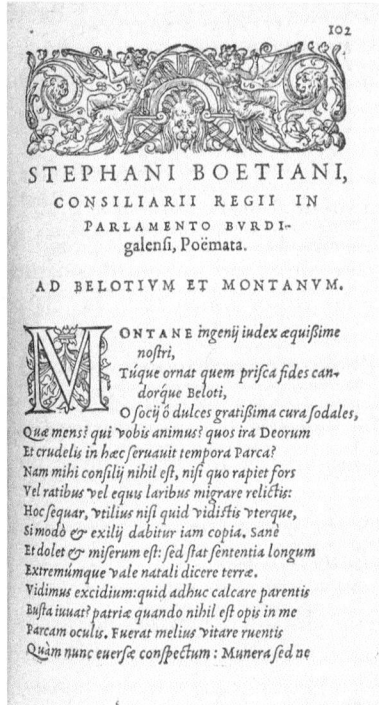

Illus. 2.1.2. La Boétie, *Mesnagerie*, ed. Montaigne (Paris: Fédéric Morel, 1571), Bibliothèque nationale de France, pressmark Z Payen 511 (1), fol. 102r (La Boétie's poem to Belot and Montaigne). Reproduced by permission of the Bibliothèque nationale de France, Paris.

copy of the *Essais*) and the personal manuscript *registre* (L'Estoile's 'Registres-journaux', Séguier's notebooks or 'livres d'extraicts').

Montaigne, or rather 'Montanus', entered the literary world in passive mode in the late 1550s and early 1560s by means of this erudite, parliamentary culture. The senior magistrate La Boétie invoked his neo-classical friendship with the younger man in three long neo-Latin poems. The very first poem in his *Poemata* pairs 'Montanus' with another *conseiller*, Jean de Belot or 'Belotius', who Montaigne describes visiting the moribund La Boétie on his deathbed.[53]

The poem begins: 'Montane, ingenii iudex æquissime nostri,/Tuque ornat[e] quem prisca fides candorque, Beloti…' ('O Montaigne, most equitable judge of our character / and you Belot, endowed with the faithfulness and frankness of the ancients'; Illus. 2.1.2). This roots Montaigne's ethos as a judge of human nature, associated with values of faithfulness and candour, in the parliamentary milieu from which he is seen to emerge in these early publications.

---

[53] Montaigne, *Œuvres complètes*, 1358. Most of the works mentioned in the previous paragraph are discussed in this or the first volume. The others are: Antoine de Laval, *Desseins de professions nobles et publiques* (Paris: Abel L'Angelier, 1605); Florimond de Raemond, *Erreur populaire de la papesse Jane* (Bordeaux: Simon Millanges, 1587).

121

EXTRAICT D'VNE LETTRE
que Monſieur le Conſeiller de Montaigne
eſcrit à Mõſeigneur de Montaigne ſon pere,
concernant quelques particularitez qu'il re-
marqua en la maladie & mort de feu Monſieur de la Boetie.

Vant à ſes dernieres paro-
les, ſans doubte ſi homme
en doit rendre bon conte,
c'eſt moy, tant par ce que
du lóg de ſa maladie il par-
loit auſſi volontiers à moy
qu'à nul autre : que auſſi
pource que pour la ſingu-
liere & fraternelle amitié que nous nous eſtions
entreportez, i'auois treſcertaine cognoiſſance des
intentions , iugemens & volontez qu'il auoit eu
durant ſa vie, autant ſans doute qu'homme peut a-
uoir d'vn autre : & par ce que ie les ſçauois eſtre
hautes, vertueuſes, pleines de treſcertaine reſolu-
tion, & quãd tout eſt dit, admirables: ie preuoyois
bien, que ſi la maladie luy laiſſoit le moyen de ſe
pouuoir exprimer, qu'il ne luy eſchapperoit rien
Q

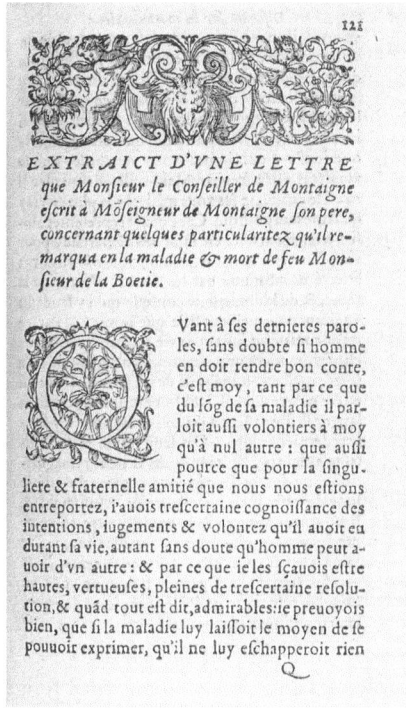

Illus. 2.1.3. La Boétie, *Mesnagerie*, ed. Montaigne (Paris: Fédéric Morel, 1571), Bibliothèque nationale de France, pressmark Z Payen 511 (1), fol. 121r (Montaigne's letter to his father regarding the death of La Boétie). Reproduced by permission of the Bibliothèque nationale de France, Paris.

The 1571 volume culminates in La Boétie's neo-Latin poetry and in Montaigne's first major, original composition in print: 'Extraict d'une lettre que Monsieur le Conseiller de Montaigne escrit à Monseigneur de Montaigne son pere' (Illus. 2.1.3), which contains the matching reference to Jean de Belot just mentioned. In that 1571 volume he was 'Monsieur le Conseiller de Montaigne', not 'Michel Seigneur de Montaigne', as on the title page to the 1588 *Essais*.

It is in this broad cultural context that an important provincial *parlementaire*, Sainte-Marthe, was to publish a new Latin eulogy of Montaigne in print in 1602, and an internationally renowned—and infamous—historian and president of the Paris *parlement*, de Thou, was at the same time to write Montaigne's death and a portrait of his life into a public history of the religious wars in Europe. Together, these *elogia* offer a related but distinct discourse of praise to that inaugurated by Lipsius and Gournay, and, as a consequence, a related but distinct way of conversing with Montaigne's book and *persona*.

In both cases (Sainte-Marthe's and de Thou's), and in Pasquier's, the portrait of Montaigne's *franchise* and *liberté* appears in a diptych with a portrait of an associated or parallel figure. None of these *éloges* were to gain a mention in the later texts of Gournay's preface, or in *L'Ombre*, which saw no modification of her stance on Montaigne's cold reception. She continued to maintain that no one had praised the great soul of Montaigne to the rhetorical degree it deserved.

All four of our principal figures have been described in modern historiography as Gallicans and *politiques*. The meanings and utility of both terms are still disputed in contemporary historiography. The second term is a vexed one as it was primarily used from the mid-1580s by Catholic Leaguers to abuse opponents who were accused of subordinating religious belief to political opportunism. It is rarely used in the more recent historiography as it once was: to denote a definable and durable political party that emerged in the council of Catherine de' Medici in the early 1560s before rallying the nation around Henri IV's efforts to lay what early twentieth-century scholars had anachronistically identified as the foundations of the modern, tolerant, secular state. But the term ('politique') still provides a focus for discussion of distinct attempts, made by specific groups in differing circumstances from the early 1560s to the 1590s, to formulate practical strategies for survival and peaceful mediation in the wide and open frontier between the militant, ultra-Catholic, and ultra-Reformed camps in the civil and international wars of religion.[54]

Mack P. Holt summarizes recent trends by describing these intellectuals not as heroic early advocates of modern concepts of religious toleration and of the primacy of a separate state over the church, but as heroic survivors in the midst of cacophonous religious polemics and the real dangers of religious violence. We have seen that Montaigne publicizes his and his book's capacity to survive, to enjoy an innate freedom in such perilous times. The passage that closes II 15 (discussed in the 'Conclusion' to Volume 1) presents the book as public witness to the survival through thirty years of civil war of an independent nobleman who never armed his house, who remained open to all comers.[55]

But does this make the *Essais* a *politique* book, especially if we compare it with an unambiguously *politique* book such as de Thou's *Historiae*, which directly addresses the causes and events of the religious wars? Modern historians, critics, and biographers have themselves oriented Montaigne's literary work and authorial

[54] Christopher Bettinson, 'The Politiques and the Politique Party: a reappraisal', in Keith Cameron (ed.), *From Valois to Bourbon: dynasty, state and society in early modern France* (Exeter: University of Exeter, 1989), 35–49; Nancy L. Roelker, *One king, one faith: the Parlement of Paris and the religious reformations of the sixteenth century* (Berkeley: University of California Press, 1996), 325–8; Turchetti, 'Une question mal posée'; Mack P. Holt, 'L'évolution des "Politiques" face aux Églises (1560–1598)', in Wanegffelen (ed.), *De Michel de L'Hospital à l'édit de Nantes*, 591–607 (594–5). For an argument that the term can still be used to denote a shared political sensibility across the whole period of the civil wars in France, see Arlette Jouanna, 'Les ambiguïtés des Politiques face à la Sainte Ligue', in Wanegffelen (ed.), *De Michel de L'Hospital à l'édit de Nantes*, 475–93.
[55] Holt, 'L'évolution des "Politiques" face aux Églises (1560–1598)', 595 ('ils sont héroïques pour une toute autre raison: non pour avoir préconisé des vues modernes et avancées, mais simplement pour avoir survécu au milieu de la cacophonie du débat polémique et du danger réel de violence religieuse'). See also Marie-Luce Demonet, 'Le politique "nécessaire" de Montaigne', in Philippe Desan (ed.), *Montaigne politique*, 17–37 (20–1).

persona in relation to Gallican, *politique*, and parliamentary currents of thought and practice.

Some assimilate the *Essais* to the pre-history of modern ideas of toleration and secularization and position their author as the radical philosopher who cleared the ground for modern liberal institutions and ideas.[56] Others do no more than associate him with intellectuals whose politics revolved around 'one faith, one law, one king'—restoration of public order and adherence to the legitimate royal succession and the Catholic religion of France (as defined by its traditional liberties)—and whose personal ethos was one of natural *liberté* and, where compatible with due respect for royal authority, clemency.[57]

Here, I am making two interrelated arguments. The first is that this association was a 'context' actively put in place at the moment (*c.*1595–1605) when a long-standing *politique* party was being retrospectively assembled in texts composed and/or published *after* the publication of L'Angelier's and Gournay's 1595 edition, and when the belated diffusion of unsold stock of Paris 1588 and the flurry of Parisian and Genevan octavo editions (1598–1602) gave the author of the mature *Essais* an illustrious name on the national stage for the first time.

The second is that this authorial *persona* was seen in parliamentary circles to have originated not with Montaigne's publication of the 1580 *Essais* but with his 1570–1 edition of La Boétie's surviving works and his public role as *conseiller* in the Bordeaux *parlement* and private role as friend to the more senior parliamentarian (Illus. 2.1.4).

La Boétie's works had been explicitly addressed from Paris to high-ranking *parlementaires* by 'Monsieur le Conseiller de Montaigne' and were given equal billing, even in the early 1600s, with the *Essais*. In these circles, Montaigne was in the background as the maker of a portrait of La Boétie and of a literary friendship in regional parliamentary circles, before he moved more into the Parisian and national foreground as the maker of a noble self-portrait.

And he was attributed, as he was not in Gournay's preface, with a political career that took him, like his book, from Bordeaux to Paris. This attribution shaped a shared *robe* understanding of the kind of conversation that gave rise to the book, and to which it could give rise in turn. The *parlementaires* did, in other words, what some recent scholars have done: they inserted the *Essais* into Montaigne's quasi-professional but ultimately failed 'career' as a parliamentary magistrate (later

[56] John William Allen, *A history of political thought in the sixteenth century* ([S.l.]: Methuen, 1928), 372–3; Alan Levine, *Sensual philosophy: toleration, skepticism, and Montaigne's politics of the self* (Lanham, Md.: Lexington Books, 2001).

[57] Most influentially, perhaps, in Nakam, *Montaigne et son temps*, pp. 171 ('Montaigne parle alors en Politique'), 173, 195–7, 224 ('Montaigne sert la monarchie aux côtés des Politiques. Il partage les idées du conseiller Paul de Foix, du conseiller Henri de Mesmes, de Loisel, de de Thou'). For more recent discussions, see Philippe Desan (ed.), *Montaigne politique*; Biancamaria Fontana, *Montaigne's politics: authority and governance in the 'Essais'* (Princeton: Princeton University Press, 2008), 8–9, 81–3. On Montaigne's affiliations to Gallican thought, see Jotham Parsons, *The church in the republic: Gallicanism & political ideology in Renaissance France* (Washington, D.C.: Catholic University of America Press, 2004). On Montaigne's *persona* and its ethos of clemency, see David Quint, *Montaigne and the quality of mercy: ethical and political themes in the 'Essais'* (Princeton: Princeton University Press, 1998).

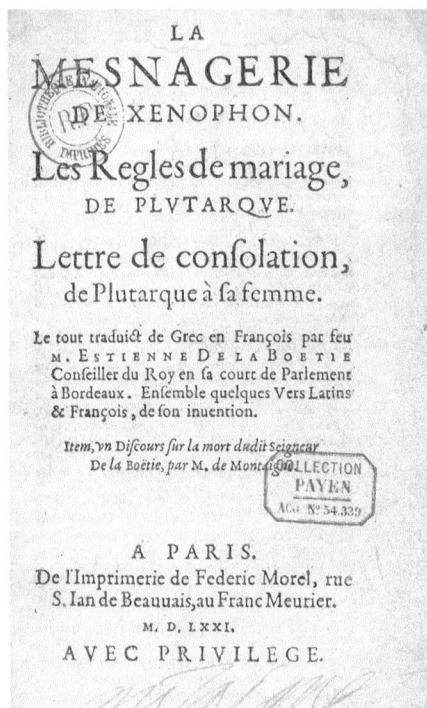

LA
MESNAGERIE
DE XENOPHON.
Les Regles de mariage,
DE PLVTARQVE.

Lettre de confolation,
de Plutarque à fa femme.

Le tout traduict de Grec en François par feu
M. ESTIENNE DE LA BOETIE
Confeiller du Roy en fa court de Parlement
à Bordeaux. Enfemble quelques Vers Latins
& François, de fon inuention.

Item, vn Difcours fur la mort dudit Seigneur
De la Boëtie, par M. de Montaigne.

A PARIS.
De l'Imprimerie de Federic Morel, rue
S. Ian de Beauuais, au Franc Meurier.
M. D. LXXI.
AVEC PRIVILEGE.

Illus. 2.1.4. La Boétie, *Mesnagerie*, ed. Montaigne (Paris: Fédéric Morel, 1571), Bibliothèque nationale de France, pressmark Z Payen 511 (1), title page. Reproduced by permission of the Bibliothèque nationale de France, Paris.

mayor) who symbolically 'retired' as a landed nobleman, but who continued until 1588 or so to pursue noble honours and diplomatic offices at the courts of Henri III, Henri de Navarre, and Pope Gregory XIII.[58]

But, again, this was done retrospectively, *c.*1600. Neither Montaigne nor his book were recognized as prominent actors in events before that date and no significant portraits—beyond Gournay's—were printed. Once the *Essais* gave Montaigne posthumous prominence as an author, he became more prominent, in retrospect, in events, by means of literary portraiture. So whereas de Thou makes no mention at all of Montaigne in his early works or in his private correspondence of 1582–92,

---

[58] The groundbreaking study in this respect was George Hoffmann, *Montaigne's career* (Oxford: Clarendon Press, 1998). For the notion that Montaigne's works betray his pursuit of a political career on the model of a *politique* such as Paul de Foix, see Philippe Desan, 'Montaigne: *Politicus Aquitanicus*', *Nouveau Bulletin de la Société des Amis de Montaigne*, IV, no. 2 ('Numéro spécial: Montaigne et sa région'—also 8th series no. 48) (2008), 345–58. For the argument that Montaigne did not really have what would now be described as a political career, and that his works are distinct from his conduct of his public life, especially after 1580, see Balsamo, 'Un gentilhomme et ses patrons'; Jean Balsamo, ' "Le plus grand bien que j'atande de cete miene charge publique": Montaigne, entre vie publique et vie privée', *Nouveau Bulletin de la Société des Amis de Montaigne*, IV, no. 2 ('Numéro spécial: Montaigne et sa région'—also 8th series no. 48) (2008), 359–75.

he goes on in his writings of the late 1590s and early 1600s first to endorse Montaigne's remarks on the reception of the *De la servitude volontaire*, then to narrate key moments in his career as a friend to the *politiques*.[59]

This had consequences for a whole community of reader-writers, including the relatively extreme case of the meticulous chronicler Pierre de L'Estoile. The research of Tom Hamilton is beginning to show that L'Estoile was not an isolated figure. He was well connected in parliamentary circles, and took his cue in his reading from more eminent *parlementaires*.[60]

This perhaps explains why the *Essais* did not come to L'Estoile's attention until after de Thou and Sainte-Marthe had 'discovered' them. In his entries for 1592 and the years following, he completely failed to register news of Montaigne's death and of the circulation and reception of the *Essais*. In the years between 1606 and 1610, he regularly invoked the Gascon essayist's name and work with reverence in his *registres-journaux*. Similarly, in 1584, Loisel printed and circulated some of the *remonstrances* he delivered during the sittings of the king's *chambre de justice* in Guyenne (1582–4).[61] He privately offered mayor Montaigne a manuscript copy of his closing speech to the opening session, in which he paid a compliment to notable families of the region (including Montaigne's). But he did not print the speech.[62]

However, the *remonstrances* were republished separately in 1595 by the very house—L'Angelier's—that in the same year produced Gournay's edition of the *Essais*. This time the closing speech is printed, with a dedication to the now deceased dignitary 'Monsieur de Montaigne'. But the *persona* addressed by Loisel is subtly different from the one invoked by Gournay's 'Preface' and indeed by the *Essais*. He is a man knowledgeable about the customs and history of the Bordeaux region; he is Mayor and one of the first Magistrates of Bordeaux ('Maire et l'un des premiers Magistrats de Bordeaux'), one of the principal ornaments of Guyenne and of France.[63] This, in Gournay's terms, is still faint praise.

By appearing in L'Angelier's shop in 1595, the *Essais* had already become part of a *politique éditoriale* that interpreted the experience of the civil wars for a readership

[59] De Smet, 'Montaigne et Jacques-Auguste de Thou', 229.

[60] Tom Hamilton's University of Oxford thesis is currently entitled 'Pierre de L'Estoile and his World in the Wars of Religion, 1546–1611'. I am grateful to Mr Hamilton for sharing details of his work with me in advance of submission. For L'Estoile, see 2.1.8.

[61] USTC 12211, USTC 12212 (*De l'oeil des rois et de la justice. Remonstrance faite en la ville de Bordeaux*), and USTC 29104.

[62] USTC 12212 contains neither the speech nor the dedication to Montaigne.

[63] The three separate editions of 1595 are USTC 6499, USTC 24010, and USTC 48630 (*De l'oeil des rois et de la justice*, in which the dedication to Montaigne appears, according to Balsamo and Simonin, at sig. K3v, dated from Agen, 1.11.1582). See Balsamo and Simonin, *Abel L'Angelier & Françoise de Louvain (1574–1620)*, 265–6; Antoine Loisel, *La Guyenne... qui sont huict remonstrances faictes en la Chambre de Justice de Guyenne sur le subject des Edicts de Pacification* (Paris: Abel L'Angelier, 1605), sig. E1; Catherine Magnien, 'Loisel, Antoine (Beauvais, 1536–Paris, 1617)', *Dictionnaire*, 660–2; De Smet, 'Montaigne et Jacques-Auguste de Thou', 229n.21. I have used the collected, 1605 edition of these *remonstrances* as I was unable to gain access to a copy of the 1595 edition in the BnF ('hors usage'). Magnien states that in the 1605 edition Loisel's dedication to Montaigne was switched to another *remonstrance*, but in fact it was simply switched to a position after the same *remonstrance* (all the dedications in this volume follow rather than precede the discourses to which they refer).

who aspired to continued peace under Henri IV.[64] The impact of the publication of this edition at this moment, with the accompanying and belated diffusion of previously undistributed copies of 1588, and the octavo editions of 1598–1602, is what is registered at the end of Pasquier's letter, and in Sainte-Marthe's 1602 *elogium*: 'the great reputation for learning and wisdom that he acquired even in foreign nations by means of the publication of this very beautiful work' (alluding to the Bull of Roman citizenship printed in 1588 and 1595). From *c.*1594, Montaigne and the *Essais* moved from the deep background where Gournay found them in 1588 to somewhere a little closer to centre stage by the early 1600s.

2.1.2 DE THOU AND MONTAIGNE

Consider the history of a book that entered the city of Rome with pretensions to liberty of judgement a quarter of a century after Montaigne's: de Thou's *Historiae*. Montaigne began writing around the same time de Thou began collecting materials for his great work. The eminent magistrate may even have been one of those who encouraged him to follow the same course, to write the affairs of his time, 'reckoning that I see them with eyes less vitiated by passion than others do and that I have a closer view than they, since Fortune has given me access to the various leaders of the contending parties'.[65]

The suggestion carries some weight because de Thou later described Montaigne at Blois doing what he does not do in the *Essais*: using the access fortune had given him directly to assess, without passion, the motives of Guise and Navarre in the wars of religion (see 2.1.6). Whether offered by de Thou or not, Montaigne ignored the advice, most likely because he was obeying the royal injunctions against memorials of the events of the civil wars—he was never directly to mention or condemn the St. Bartholomew Day's massacre in print. In the same passage Montaigne distances himself from philosophers of exact and exquisite conscience, such as de Thou, who might choose to write such a public history. Indeed, the *Essais* define themselves against any attempt to publish 'universal' truths from the point of view of an 'official' authorial *persona* such as a magistrate-historian.

Put alongside the *Essais* and their fortunes, de Thou's work and its fortunes help us describe a spectrum of possible strategies and outcomes for widespread circulation, from Paris to Rome, of free-thinking books that are consubstantial with their authors and that purport to tell the truth in 'good faith'. The *Historiae* are no less an extension of the *persona* of de Thou than the *Essais* are of that of Montaigne. The two books share an ethos but behave in very different ways. Both are written in the *personae* of laymen with no office to teach or preach in university or church (even though de Thou had taken minor orders in obedience to his father). Both

---

[64] Balsamo, 'Des *Essais* pour comprendre les guerres civiles', 527.
[65] I 20, NP106/BVH Paris 1595, p. 53/S118.

insist they claim no doctrinal authority, submitting themselves to official theologians in that respect.[66]

But one behaves like an official charged by the King publicly with negotiating
and keeping the peace (de Thou, who was such an official), while the other behaves
like a gentleman who discourses in private. De Thou's more private discourse is
confined to his letters, some of his poems, and the *Vita*.

They thus represent two related but very distinct attempts to enfranchise the lay
reader-writer: one as a judge-philosopher with international status, writing a grand
public history of the religious wars for the Latin trade, a history that claimed the
authority of a Tacitus or a Sallust and that was addressed to scholars and princes
across France and Europe; the other as a gentleman knight, with no name in
national or international scholarship, writing a strange kind of miscellaneous personal memoir in the vernacular, circulating—despite Marie de Gournay's best
efforts—in the margins of the Latin trade, addressed to family and new friends
such as a young gentlewoman from Picardy.[67] The complication is that the gentleman knight and his book gain a relatively minor place in the gallery of portraits
that partly comprise and legitimize de Thou's work; they are reportrayed in the
background of the portrait of the author of the history.

Each nexus of enfranchisement tells a different story. But the stories under consideration in this section have a common theme: the capacity of a book to carry
and win acceptance for a noble ethos of moderated liberty of judgement. De Thou's
book asked to be judged, and was judged, in exactly the ethical terms employed by
Montaigne at the end of II 10 in relation to the tradition of noble memoirs and
histories compiled by the likes of the Du Bellay brothers (terms which we argued
in 1.3.9 were to be applied in a different way to his own book). Both drew on the

[66] Jacques Auguste de Thou, *Historiarum sui temporis libri CXXXVIII*, ed. Thomas Carte, 7 vols.
(London: Samuel Buckley, 1733), vol. 7, pt. I, 4 ('Je n'en parle en Theologien')/MS Dupuy 409, fol.
79v; Barbara B. Diefendorf, *Paris city councillors in the sixteenth century: the politics of patrimony*
(Princeton: Princeton University Press, 1983), 130–4. In what follows I frequently cite volume 7 of
the 1733 Buckley-Carte edition of de Thou's *Historiae*, which offers *pièces justificatives*. Alfred Soman's
critique of this volume makes it advisable to identify the original manuscript sources and to verify
quotations against them (as I have done, where possible). However, the extent of Carte's editorial
distortion of the manuscript sources needs further examination. Soman only offers two examples and
the second one is questionable. If Carte were principally concerned to introduce evidence of the
Bourbon dynasty's identification with de Thou as a proto-enlightenment hero, why did his allegedly
fraudulent interpolation (into de Thou's letter to Dupuy of 14 November [1605]) contain evidence of
de Thou's willingness to negotiate discreetly so that a lightly expurgated edition could be published in
Rome? Much of the allegedly interpolated passage concerns other matters covered elsewhere in the
correspondence. There are, furthermore, pen strokes in the original hand (as Soman acknowledged) at
the point in the manuscript where the 'interpolation' occurs in the printed text. These may indicate
that the passage was written on an inserted sheet since lost. See Alfred Soman, 'The London Edition
of De Thou's History: A Critique of Some Well-Documented Legends', *Renaissance Quarterly*, 24
(1971), 1–12; Thou, *Historiarum sui temporis libri CXXXVIII*, vol. 7, part I, 6/BnF, MS Dupuy 409,
fol. 82v.

[67] On de Thou's *Historiae* and the Latin trade, see Ian Maclean, *Scholarship, commerce, religion: the
learned book in the age of confessions, 1560–1630* (Cambridge, Mass.: Harvard University Press,
2012), 30–7, and Samuel Kinser, *The works of Jacques-Auguste de Thou* (The Hague: Martinus Nijhoff,
1966). The *Essais* were listed in Frankfurt catalogues once in 1581 and once in 1612. See Nelles,
'Stocking a library', 19–21, and Balsamo and Simonin, *Abel L'Angelier & Françoise de Louvain
(1574–1620)*, 83.

Tacitean programme to write 'without anger or zeal' ('sine ira et studio'; *Annals* 1.1), without partiality and 'without hatred' ('sine odio'; *Histories* 1.1). For the *Historiae* purported to be not a partisan but a truthful account of the affairs of the time, produced by a noble actor in the events themselves, without 'hatred, favour or vanity' ('haine, faveur ou vanité'), with 'the unfettered judgements he makes of the greats' ('libres jugemens des grands'), with 'good faith' ('bonne foi') and 'a shining frankness and freedom in writing' ('la franchise et liberté d'escrire').[68]

The attempted social enactment of such virtues by means of the composition and circulation of memorial writings was common to both the *Historiae* and the *Essais*. It was an important condition of writing in this period that it had to claim to be non-partisan, truthful, free, and authentic, while almost invariably being identified as partisan by someone, somewhere. The claim was most usually made in relation to the quality of the named authorial *persona*. The question was whether the quality was recognized in the right terms on the writings' travels.

The crucial difference between the two projects is that Montaigne's book took the liberty of telling the truth only about himself, de Thou's about the religious wars of his time—thereby contravening the royal injunctions contained in the edicts of pacification. The ethos of Montaigne's authorial *persona*, with its apologetic function, is immediately declared in the brief, evasive preface to the *Essais* and prevails over all other subject matter throughout (at least from the editions of 1588 and 1595).

De Thou's long and direct preface, by contrast, boldly goes to the heart of the most controversial argument in his work: that violent opposition to and censorship of religious dissenters is not the best way to restore the unity of the church and conserve peace in the state.[69] And in de Thou's case, the apologetic authorial *persona* is portrayed for the most part after publication of the principal work in separate correspondence and memoirs, even if it is already apparent in the preface that he is speaking in the office and with the conscience and qualities of an impartial magistrate or judge.[70]

The case of de Thou is particularly important, then, for three reasons. First, as we have just seen, the *Essais* explicitly measure themselves against the whole noble tradition of memoir and history writing that de Thou sought to inhabit as a scholar-magistrate known to members of the Republic of Letters everywhere. Second, the choices made by de Thou in producing his book, and the fate it suffered,

---

[68] II 10, NP440/BVH Paris 1595, p. 269/S470–1. As a representative expression of this ethos see de Thou's letter to Cardinal Sforza, 1 May 1606, in Thou, *Historiarum sui temporis libri CXXXVIII*, vol. 7, pt. I, 16–17. On de Thou's *parrhesia*, or commitment to *veritas* and *candor*, see De Smet, *Thuanus*, 260, 266.

[69] Thou, *Historiarum sui temporis libri CXXXVIII*, vol. 1, 'Auctoris præfatio ad Henricum IV' (this volume does not use a uniform, continuous method of pagination); De Smet, *Thuanus*, 259–61.

[70] Thou, *Historiarum sui temporis libri CXXXVIII*, vol. 1, 'Auctoris præfatio ad Henricum IV', 2 ('Quod igitur boni judices facere debent, cum de capite et fortunis hominum consultant, idem et nos fecimus, cum hanc historiam scribere sumus aggressi, nostram saepius conscientiam interrogantes, an ullius rei acriore sensu tangeretur, quae nos in opere instituto a recta via transversos ageret').

provide an important perspective on the contrasting choices made by Montaigne and the contrasting fate of his book.

Where de Thou offered tasters of his work across the European republic of letters, in order that collective correction by a community of scholars and censors might make the work safe, Montaigne purported disingenuously to produce nothing but tasters ('essais')—tasters that eschewed the whole culture of correction (or attempted to).[71] The outcomes of the two distinct but related strategies were different in the short to medium term, but similar in the longer term.

De Thou may have made the *persona* of Montaigne, as witnessed by his book, part of the background context for his own work. But the Gascon's vernacular miscellany spoke freely from Paris in a complete edition (from 1595), met neither expurgation nor prohibition at Rome, and circulated relatively uncorrected and unobstructed across both northern and southern Europe in the early seventeenth century—even if it did not 'break' the major European publishers of the Latin trade, as Gournay intended.

Furthermore, the *Essais* found a new lease of life in the 1620s, around the time de Thou, Pasquier, and others portrayed their author in print. In 1625, Gournay's grand quarto edition of the *Essais* appeared with many publishers at Paris, and inaugurated a whole series of triumphal quarto and folio editions that ended with the 1657 folio, twenty years before Montaigne's book was finally placed on the Index at Rome in 1676.[72]

By contrast, the historian de Thou complained in a poem published with his *Vita* that, for having defended *libertas* and *veritas*, 'I am defamed everywhere, at Rome, and at the court of France' ('Et Romae et nostra passim traducor in aula').[73] The grand neo-classical history fell foul of troubles home and abroad, was not published in full at Paris, and was prohibited at Rome. A full edition first appeared, along with the *Vita* (with a separate title page, dated 1621), in a semi-dissimulated and toned-down edition published in Geneva in 1620, then disappeared after a few editions of the 1620s at Geneva and Frankfurt.[74] The *Historiae* were in demand via the Latin trade, but supply could not meet the demand.

In the longer term, of course, Montaigne's work was to suffer a similar fate. Indeed, where it initially managed, to a certain degree, to transcend the bifurcation between the southern and northern circuits of European print culture, it was forced northwards after *c.*1670. Placed on the Roman Index for the first time in 1676, the *Essais* were not published unabridged in France between 1669 and 1724. Both Montaigne's and de Thou's works would then re-emerge in monumental editions at the same moment in the London of the 1720s and 1730s: Pierre Coste's 1724 edition of the *Essais*, and Samuel Buckley's 1733 edition of the *Historiae*— though Italy and Spain were not to regain the *Essais* for two centuries.

---

[71] On Montaigne's *Essais* as a false or disingenuous *édition à l'essai*, see Michel Simonin, *L'encre & la lumière: quarante-sept articles, 1976–2000* (Geneva: Droz, 2004), 737.

[72] Sayce and Maskell, 95–153.

[73] Jacques Auguste de Thou, *La vie de Jacques-Auguste de Thou = I. Aug. Thuani vita*, ed. Anne Teissier-Ensminger (Paris: H. Champion, 2007), 872.

[74] Kinser, *The works of Jacques-Auguste de Thou*, 26–45, 50–2, 54–6.

Third, and most importantly for the argument of this study, the case of de Thou underlines the point that emerged in the discussion of the case of Lancre in 1.5.4: the principal significance of Montaigne's book amongst the *robins*—especially the expanded book as it first appeared in 1588 and 1595—was its successful produc-tion and communication of a noble ethos of *liberté* across divided religio-political terrain in both France and Europe. This is true for de Thou, Saint-Marthe, Pasquier, and L'Estoile. They understood the book to index a certain kind of free discursive behaviour, which they rooted in Montaigne's noble *persona* as an ex-*conseiller* and private court mediator who was amenable to peace.

In some respects they found it *too* free (at least in its style and morals), and they could not see in the author a hero of official, pragmatic peace-making and of schol-arly neo-Latin letters. Lancre regretted the seductive effect Montaigne's ethos had on his intellectual master Delrio; de Thou praised Montaigne, but gave him noth-ing like the prominence or status he gave great scholar-magistrates such as L'Hospital. None of the *robins* beyond Gournay's milieu recognized the author Montaigne's quality in the grandiose, quasi-spiritual terms she required. But, like her, they did understand that it was intended to be a 'noble book'. They recognized that the point of the book was to communicate and preserve particular noble qual-ities in the circumstances created by the civil and religious wars in France and Europe. If 'Montaigne' was not a great noble sage, he was a gentleman author who talked freely of everything—who was 'extraordinarily' free and sincere, to recall the terms used in the 'Vindication'—and who was free of faction.

Both men and both works, then, were fundamentally concerned with the prob-lem of communicating the ethos of a freeman in the circumstances of the late six-teenth and early seventeenth centuries. How could one behave and speak as a freeman, with liberty of judgement, in the environment created by religious dis-sensions and the conflicts that followed from them?

One tackled this as a matter of private moral conversation between a gentle-man and his *politique* friends, mostly on commonplace topics not recent histori-cal events, the other as a matter of public speech and political action on behalf of the French nation. In both spheres, a book, like a person, might prove to have the ethical qualities required to make and keep peace without compromising truth and liberty. Equally, a book in circulation across France and Europe might fail to surmount the difficulties of a person attempting to negotiate his way across the middle ground between the factions in the civil and international wars and the various powers and authorities who regulated human behaviour in different juris-dictions. It might even give rise to new troubles, new scandals, new disturbances of the peace.

2.1.3 SAINTE-MARTHE AND DE THOU

The publication in print of Scévole de Sainte-Marthe's *elogium* of Montaigne (1602) was the key event in the retrospective, public introduction of the author of the *Essais* into the circles of the *robins*, for Sainte-Marthe told the story of

Montaigne's enfranchisement as a noble author from a *robe* point of view—rather different from Gournay's. His was the first important public eulogy other than Gournay's to refer to either of the major expanded editions (Paris 1588 and Paris 1595). It distilled the *Essais* into an *imago* of various learning and of speech characterized by *ingenuitas* and *libertas*, the broad Latin equivalents for Montaigne's *franchise* and *liberté*.[75]

Sainte-Marthe explicitly linked the granting of Roman citizenship at the papal court with Montaigne's international reputation as author of the *Essais*. This aligned him with other subjects of *elogia* who were described by Sainte-Marthe as having received the same honour in connection with particular works of learning (Longueil, Philandrier, Muret), even though the text of the generic Roman bull delivered to Montaigne did *not* make the connection—it was made by Montaigne himself when he incorporated it into his published book (see 1.7.6 and 1.7.7).[76]

However, it is important to realize that the praise of Montaigne is subsidiary to the praise of his friend La Boétie, with which it is joined in a single entry. Montaigne–La Boétie was one of only seven combined portraits contained in the 1602 edition. The others comprised family relations (fathers and sons, brothers) or scholars from the same neighbourhood or university. The whole volume is, however, concerned with the tracing of families or dynasties of learning and office-holding, including the de Thou and the Sainte-Marthe families themselves, in ways that lend them some of the prestige of the *noblesse d'épée*.[77] So Montaigne is there as a

[75] See the beginning of 1.5 for the translation of 'vir libertatis ingenuae' as 'extraordinary *Free and Sincere*' man, and 'franchise' as 'generous Temper' in the 1711 edition of Cotton's translation. The two Latin terms do not translate distinctly and precisely into French as 'liberté' and 'franchise'; *ingenuitas*, for example, might be translated as 'integrity' or *honnêteté*, and *franchise* in French might be translated into Latin as *libertas*. But the pair of Latin terms cover a similar range of meanings to 'liberté et franchise', a catch-all phrase for the noble frankness and honesty of someone who is free-born. Robert Estienne's 1552 *Dictionarium Latinogallicum* (ARTFL) defines *libertas* as '[l]iberté et franchise de parler, et vivre comme on veult', and *ingenuitas* as '[l]' estat et condition de liberté. C' est aussi l' honnesteté et noblesse qu'ont les personnes franches et libres, Ingenuité'. In Thomas Thomas's 1587 Latin-English dictionary *ingenuitas* is, similarly, '[t]he state of a free and honest man: freedome: an honest, and liberall, or free nature or condition'; *libertas* is '[l]ibertie, freedom, leave, boldnes in speaking, admonishing, or reprehending: also, an unbridled lust or licentiousnes: also an honest, liberall, or free nature and condition' (LEME). In early modern French dictionaries the term 'franchise' appeared to be broadly equivalent to 'liberté' and *libertas* (ARTFL, Jean Nicot, 1606). But in late medieval French, and in chivalric contexts, 'franchise' could denote the '[i]dée de noblesse (la noblesse supposant par nature le non-asservissement) ou de qualité associée à la noblesse (noblesse de coeur, de conduite, générosité, loyauté)' (DMF). It was also linked in some contexts, through false etymology, to the 'Franks', the French nation, and their innate freedoms. See Timothy Hampton, *Literature and nation in the sixteenth century: inventing Renaissance France* (Ithaca: Cornell University Press, 2001), 2. So, of the two equivalents in French, 'franchise' is arguably closer to denoting the moral integrity of a freeman (*ingenuitas*) than 'liberté', which is more often the term for freedom of speech, judgement, and movement. On Montaigne's 'liberté et franchise' see Felicity Green, *Montaigne and the life of freedom* (Cambridge: Cambridge University Press, 2012), 177–84.

[76] Scévole de Sainte-Marthe, *Gallorum doctrina illustrium, qui nostra patrúmque memoria floruerunt, elogia* (Poitiers: Jean Blanchet, 1602), sigs. A4r–v ('Christopherus Longolius', for Latin eloquence, including in his printed *oratio* in praise of the French); K2v–K3r ('Marcus Antonius Muretus', after the production of his first books of *variae lectiones*), R2v–3r ('Gulielmus Philander', for his commentaries on Vitruvius). For the case of Longolius or Longueil, see 1.7.6.

[77] Neil Kenny, 'Patrilinear transmissions of literature and learning: The example of early modern France', paper given at The Warburg Institute, 14 May 2014. For a comprehensive study of Sainte-Marthe's

noble d'épée who becomes heir to La Boétie's studies and who briefly pursues a career in the same parliamentary court.

The placement of the joint *elogium* of the two friends is one indication that the life and death of La Boétie is the main event. The 1598 edition, which contained just book I, ordered the *elogia* in chronological order, by date of death; it started with Jacques Lefèvre d'Étaples (d. 1536) and ended with Florent Chrestien (d. 1596). The 1602 edition retains book I without insertions (but with a few changes of order) and adds a new book II, also in chronological order, by date of death, starting with Philippe de Commines (d. 1511). It is the date not of Montaigne's but of La Boétie's death (1563) that determines the combined entry's place in the sequence in book II. The opening to the following *elogium* of Arnoul de Ferron (d. 1563) links Ferron with La Boétie as another scholar-*conseiller* of the Bordeaux *parlement* and another translator of Plutarch—Ferron would later acknowledge La Boétie's assistance in emending a Greek text from the *Moralia* that he turned into Latin.[78]

This is not, however, the only indication (it might have seemed natural, in any case, to place the entry according to the earlier of the two dates of death) of the primacy of the senior man. As we shall later in this section (2.1.3) Sainte-Marthe gave La Boétie higher praise as a truly philosophical and scholarly figure; he better fitted the pattern of a *vir illustris*.

The *Elogia* evolved through single editions at Poitiers in 1598 (63 entries in 1 book), 1602, 1606 (with other Latin works), and as part of the *Opera* of 1616 (Paris), and the posthumous edition of 1630, until they comprised 137 entries in 5 books. Though ostensibly a collection of portraits of Frenchmen deemed illustrious for letters and learning, it has, from the first edition on, strong *politique* associations.[79]

The 1598 edition is dedicated in neo-Latin verses to state counsellor and president of the Paris *parlement*, Jacques Auguste de Thou, and praises loyal supporters of both Henri III and Navarre/Henri IV, whether Roman Catholics or Huguenots. It ends in an epistle to the reader with news of the death of Pierre Pithou (d. 1596), who, in the next edition (1602), would be extravagantly praised as the philosopher—historian, textual critic, jurist—whose wise advice had been directly instrumental in defeating the ruses of the Spanish faction and resecuring Paris for Henri IV in 1594.[80]

Indeed, the purpose of the whole work as it expands through editions is to define the kind of noble, scholarly *persona*—wise, eloquent, learned, politically

---

text and its evolution, see Jean Brunel, 'Rhétorique et histoire dans les *Elogia* de Scévole de Sainte-Marthe', in Gilbert Schrenck (ed.), *Autour de l'Histoire universelle d'Agrippa d'Aubigné: mélanges à la mémoire d'André Thierry* (Geneva: Droz, 2006), 121–59.

[78] Sainte-Marthe, *Elogia*, sigs. Q4v–R1v/Millet 138–42; 'Arnoldus Ferronus' follows on sig. R2r. For La Boétie's philological work for Ferron see Michel Magnien, 'La Boétie traducteur des anciens', in Marcel Tetel (ed.), *Étienne de La Boétie: Sage révolutionnaire et poète périgourdin: Actes du Colloque International Duke University, 26–28 mars 1999* (Paris: Honoré Champion, 2004), 15–44, 23–4.

[79] Brunel, 'Rhétorique et histoire dans les *Elogia* de Scévole de Sainte-Marthe', 128, 145–8.

[80] Scévole de Sainte-Marthe, *Virorum doctrina illustrium, qui hoc seculo in Gallia floruerunt, elogia* (Poitiers: Jean Blanchet, 1598) [USTC 110487]; Sainte-Marthe, *Elogia*, 1602, sigs. Z3v–5r.

active, but moderate—needed actively to secure the unification of the kingdom under one monarch (Henri IV), one law (the French constitution as upheld by the monarch and his *parlements*), and one faith (Roman Catholicism in matters of doctrine and discipline). Montaigne is placed in the background as the noble friend to such a *persona* in the form of La Boétie.

Neither man, of course, was a professional man of letters, and as such one might ask why either was included. The early editions of Sainte-Marthe's work feature a majority of professional humanists, scholars and poets, such as Jacques Lefèvre d'Étaples, Adrien Turnèbe, and Pierre de Ronsard. Some of these, such as François Douaren and Charles du Moulin, were jurists associated with the protection of Gallican liberties. But the selection ranges beyond figures known strictly for learning, especially once the chronological order takes the reader though to the period of the civil wars.

Pasquier was somewhat reprovingly to note in a published letter that many of those included were noteworthy mainly for the *robe longue* and for the *charges* they had undertaken in the royal administrations of the French kings from François I to Henri IV.[81] These men were typically counsellors, lawyers, and office-holders trained in jurisprudence, literature, and philosophy, though some were churchmen.

Amongst those included towards the end of the first edition, and associated by later historians with *politique* attitudes, are: Michel de L'Hospital, Christophe de Thou (Jacques Auguste's father), Guy du Faur de Pibrac, Paul de Foix, Arnaud du Ferrier, Barnabé Brisson, and Henri de Mesmes. Later editions make this emphasis still more apparent, adding further *parlementaires* such as Christophe de Harlay, François Olivier, Michel Hurault de L'Hospital (1602), Jacques Faye d'Espesses, Jacques de La Guesle (1606), and moderate bishops such as Jean de Monluc (1606), Jean de Morvilliers (1606)—both of Catherine de Medici's council—and Pontus de Tyard (post-1606).

Sainte-Marthe ends the 1606 edition by telling us that the death of Cardinal d'Ossat in 1604, as he was completing the work, gave him occasion to extend it further. As we shall in 2.1.4, this news probably came from de Thou, along with a direct request that he write an *elogium* of the cardinal. In the resulting text, d'Ossat is praised as the individual responsible for reconciling Henri IV with Rome.[82] The last portrait added to the final book is that of Pasquier.

Sainte-Marthe's collection of portraits of Frenchmen deemed illustrious for the profession of letters increasingly becomes a *politique* history of the Henrician concord, comparable in this respect with other works of prosopography and historiography—such as de Thou's chronicle, Pasquier's letters, Loisel's *Remonstrances*, and L'Estoile's more private *registres-journaux*—that retrospectively incorporated the author 'Montaigne' into a *politique* narrative of the wars of religion. To gather the authors of a national 'literature', as Sainte-Marthe did, was to

---

[81] Pasquier, *Les lettres*, vol. 2, sig. 2D8.
[82] Scévole de Sainte-Marthe, *Poemata et Elogia, collecta nunc in unum corpus, & ab auctore partim aucta, partim recognita* (Poitiers: Apud viduam Joannis Blanceti, 1606), sigs. R1–2r.

gather the national network of learned administrators and intellectuals and noble patrons who had contributed most to the restoration of the peace—which meant respect for legitimate royal authority and the traditional liberties of the Catholic Church of France.

The *elogium* which most obviously marks this conception of the project in the first edition is that of 'Michaelus Hospitalius'.[83] For Sainte-Marthe, as for so many other *politique* intellectuals of the later sixteenth century, Michel de L'Hospital is the originary *patron* of the judicial philosophical *persona* trained in *bonae litterae* and equipped for counsel and pragmatic peace-making.[84] He is the model of the major literary and political figure. In Sainte-Marthe's hands, L'Hospital is the Horace of contemporary neo-Latin poetry and the Aristotle of contemporary practical philosophy—than which there could be no higher praise.[85]

The predominance of L'Hospital and his legacy in the work as a whole, as it expands through editions, explains what Sainte-Marthe does with the story of Montaigne's *œuvre* and *persona* when he adds it for the second, 1602 edition. He draws on his knowledge of Montaigne's earlier political and literary career. He reverses the story up to its origins in the parliamentary milieu of Bordeaux, which engendered Montaigne's literary friendship with Étienne de La Boétie and his role in the editing and promotion of La Boétie's works.

Though Sainte-Marthe's is a portrait of two friends, it incorporates an implicit description of an evolution in the literary and political career of the surviving friend (Montaigne): from 'Monsieur le Conseiller de Montaigne', illustrator of the reputation of the philosophical paragon La Boétie, to 'Michel Seigneur de Montaigne', author of the mature *Essais*.

Indeed, Sainte-Marthe's double portrait is based almost entirely on his borrowings and inferences from books edited and authored by Montaigne: on the one hand, the two-volume 1570–1 edition of La Boétie's surviving manuscripts, together with *Essais* I 27 and I 28; and, on the other, the 1588–95 *Essais*. In the praise of La Boétie, he draws directly upon, and endorses, everything Montaigne says about La Boétie and his works, both in the letter concerning his death and in *Essais* I 27—including Montaigne's reasons for not publishing the 'sensitive' text *De la servitude volontaire*. La Boétie's life and works, and Montaigne's discourse about them, are more prominent than the *Essais* themselves.

With the hindsight of posterity, we might ask: how this could be? The answer: because La Boétie fits the *Elogia*'s model of a patron-author more than Montaigne.

---

[83] Sainte-Marthe, *Elogia* [1598], sigs. H1v–2v.

[84] See Wanegffelen (ed.), *De Michel de L'Hospital à l'édit de Nantes*; Marie-Dominique Legrand, 'L'éloge de Michel de L'Hospital d'après Scévole de Sainte Marthe, Guillaume Colletet et Estienne Pasquier', in F. Argod-Dutard (ed.), *Histoire et littérature au siècle de Montaigne: mélanges offerts à Claude-Gilbert Dubois* (Geneva: Droz, 2001), 157–70. For L'Hospital's as one of a number of judicial philosophical *personae* available in the period, see David Saunders, 'The judicial *persona* in historical context: the case of Matthew Hale', in Conal Condren, Stephen Gaukroger, and Ian Hunter (eds.), *The philosopher in early modern Europe: the nature of a contested identity* (Cambridge: Cambridge University Press, 2006), 140–59, 152–6.

[85] Sainte-Marthe, *Elogia* [1598], sig. H2r–v. A new edition of volume 1 of L'Hospital's *Carmina* was published with Droz as the current study went to press.

In the milieu of Sainte-Marthe and his friend de Thou, the routes to recognition as a major *vir illustris* were L'Hospital's combination of neo-Latin letters, practical philosophy, and political action in the cause of peace, and Monluc's combination of Caesar-like narrative ability and great military deeds in the service of the King.

La Boétie's image as a counsellor, philosophical jurist, and neo-Latin poet, which is taken by Sainte-Marthe from Montaigne's paratexts for his friend's works, fits the model of the *politique* philosopher-orator and counsellor, derived as it is from the *patron* L'Hospital. Thanks to Montaigne's dedications and his letter on his friend's death, La Boétie's reputation as someone who *would have* gone on to achieve an illustrious career in the mould of André Tiraqueau or Aymard Ranconnet was secured. Sainte-Marthe (in both 1598 and 1602) recounts how the jurist Tiraqueau was plucked from Poitou by François I to serve as a *conseiller* in the Parisian *parlement* and to be commended in a Latin poem by L'Hospital; Ranconnet likewise went from being a *conseiller* at Bordeaux to a *président* in the Parisian *parlement*.[86]

Montaigne had addressed his edition of La Boétie to high-ranking *parlementaires* connected with Catherine de' Medici, and entrusted them with the defence and illustration of the memory of his friend (Illus. 2.1.5, 2.1.6). Three of the dedicatees who receive La Boétie's works in Montaigne's edition also feature in the *Elogia*: Paul de Foix, Henri de Mesmes, and Michel de L'Hospital himself. In the letter Montaigne includes regarding his friend's death, which Sainte-Marthe mentions before the *Essais*, La Boétie asks his great friend if he is refusing him *une place*.[87]

The place he actually gains by means of these three letters, and a fourth dedicatory letter to Lansac, is amidst the privy council of Catherine de' Medici and her son, which, in the final years of La Boétie's life, led by L'Hospital, had sought to forge peace by political means.[88] In the letter offering the neo-Latin poetry to L'Hospital, Montaigne states that that there was no man in whose milieu La Boétie would more willingly have been lodged than L'Hospital's (Illus. 2.1.6).

The overall theme of the letter is the importance and the difficulty, for someone in L'Hospital's position, of finding and knowing the right people to fulfil the offices of the state. The particular message delivered to the chancellor is that La Boétie would have been one of the men to whom he would have given offices ('hommes de vos charges'), if only L'Hospital had known his qualities in the way he can now by means of his Latin verses.[89]

This fashioning of La Boétie's reputation, by means of Montaigne's edition of his surviving texts, had an undoubted impact across the national parliamentary network that brought together figures such as Sainte-Marthe, de Thou, and Claude Dupuy. A note in the 1619–20 edition of the *Chronique Bordeloise* (published by Millanges) refers to Montaigne's Parisian edition of La Boétie, 'of which will be found a number of copies in the libraries of the right honourable members of

---

[86] Sainte-Marthe, *Elogia*, (1602), sigs. E1r–3r.
[87] Montaigne, *Œuvres complètes*, 1359.
[88] Jean Balsamo, 'Lettres de Montaigne', *Dictionnaire*, 671–5, 672.
[89] Montaigne, *Œuvres complètes*, 1365, 1363.

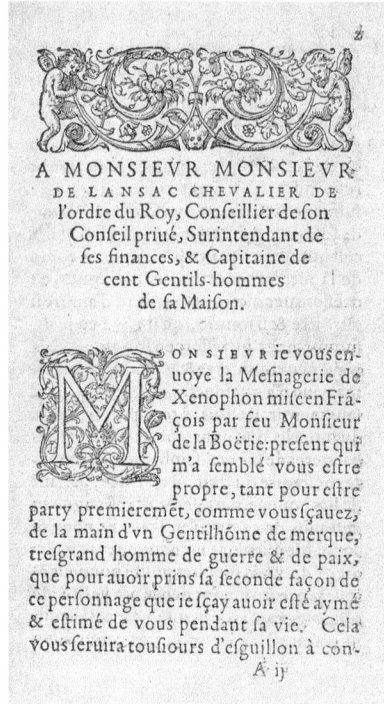

A MONSIEVR MONSIEVR
DE LANSAC CHEVALIER DE
l'ordre du Roy, Conseillier de son
Conseil priué, Surintendant de
ses finances, & Capitaine de
cent Gentils-hommes
de sa Maison.

ONSIEVR ie vous en-
uoye la Mesnagerie de
Xenophon mise en Frã-
çois par feu Monsieur
de la Boëtie: present qui
m'a semblé vous estre
propre, tant pour estre
party premieremēt, comme vous sçauez,
de la main d'vn Gentilhõme de merque,
tresgrand homme de guerre & de paix,
que pour auoir prins sa seconde façon de
ce personnage que ie sçay auoir esté aymé
& estimé de vous pendant sa vie. Cela
vous seruira tousiours d'esguillon à con-
A ij

Illus. 2.1.5. La Boétie, *Mesnagerie*, ed. Montaigne (Paris: Fédéric Morel, 1571), Bibliothèque nationale de France, pressmark Z Payen 511 (1), fol. 2r (Montaigne's dedication of La Boétie's *Mesnagerie* to M. de Lansac). Reproduced by permission of the Bibliothèque nationale de France, Paris.

Parliament' ('dont se trouveront quelques exemplaires ez librairies de Messieurs de Parlement').[90] It was a book intended for and collected by *Messieurs de Parlement*.

When Claude Dupuy listed the edition of La Boétie's *La mesnagerie* as one of the books he was sending Pinelli via Frankfurt in March 1575, nearly thirty years before Sainte-Marthe's *elogium*, he added a note to indicate the reputation (of La Boétie) that the book was carrying across Europe: 'this was a noble personnage, one who promised much of himself' ('c'estoit un gentil personage et qui promettoit beaucoup de soi'). There is no mention of the editor Montaigne's name.[91]

When Dupuy's library was inventoried the year after his death (1595), it contained a copy of the same work by La Boétie.[92] The copy was bound with other

[90] Millet 76.
[91] Gian Vincenzo Pinelli and Claude Dupuy, *Gian Vincenzo Pinelli et Claude Dupuy: Une correspondance entre deux humanistes*, ed. Anna Maria Raugei, 2 vols. (Florence: L. S. Olschki, 2001), vol. 1, 164; Étienne de La Boétie, *La mesnagerie de Xenophon. Les regles de mariage de Plutarque. Lettre de consolation, de Plutarque à sa femme … Ensemble quelques vers latins & françois, de son invention. Item, un Discours sur la mort dudit seigneur de La Boëtie, par M. de Montaigne* (Paris: Federic Morel, 1571).
[92] See the magisterial work of Jérôme Delatour, *Les livres de Claude Dupuy: une bibliothèque humaniste au temps des guerres de religion: d'après l'inventaire dressé par le libraire Denis Duval (1595)* (Villeurbanne: Enssib, 1998).

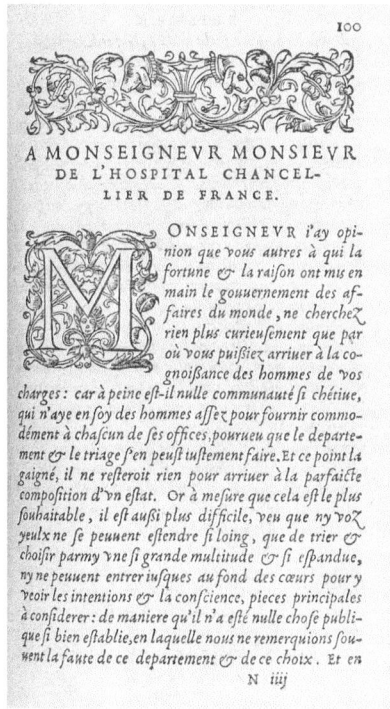

100

A MONSEIGNEVR MONSIEVR
DE L'HOSPITAL CHANCEL-
LIER DE FRANCE.

ONSEIGNEVR *i'ay opi-*
nion que vous autres à qui la
fortune & la raiſon ont mis en
main le gouuernement des af-
faires du monde , ne cherchez
rien plus curieuſement que par
où vous puiſſiez arriuer à la co-
gnoiſſance des hommes de vos
charges : car à peine eſt-il nulle communauté ſi chétiue,
qui n'aye en ſoy des hommes aſſez pour fournir commo-
dément à chaſcun de ſes offices,pourueu que le departe-
ment & le triage ſ'en peuſt iuſtement faire.Et ce point la
gaigné, il ne reſteroit rien pour arriuer à la parfaicte
compoſition d'vn eſtat. Or à meſure que cela eſt le plus
ſouhaitable , il eſt auſſi plus difficile, veu que ny voz
yeulx ne ſe peuuent eſtendre ſi loing , que de trier &
choiſir parmy vne ſi grande multitude & ſi eſpandue,
ny ne peuuent entrer iuſques au fond des cœurs pour y
veoir les intentions & la conſcience, pieces principales
à conſiderer: de maniere qu'il n'a eſté nulle choſe publi-
que ſi bien eſtablie,en laquelle nous ne remerquions ſou-
uent la faute de ce departement & de ce choix . Et en
N iiij

Illus. 2.1.6. La Boétie, *Mesnagerie*, ed. Montaigne (Paris: Fédéric Morel, 1571), Bibliothèque nationale de France, pressmark Z Payen 511 (1), fol. 100r (Montaigne's dedication of La Boétie's neo-Latin poetry to M. de L'Hospital). Reproduced by permission of the Bibliothèque nationale de France, Paris.

publications of the royal printer Fédéric Morel (the elder) from the years 1562–73. After the *Mesnagerie* (with Montaigne's letter included) came the companion volume of La Boétie's *Vers latins & françois*, then a series of *politique* discourses including Pierre de La Place on moral philosophy (1562), dedicated to L'Hospital while Chancellier, and several works by Le Roy, including his exhortation to peace (1570; dedicated to the King), his considerations on French history (1571; dedicated to the Queen Mother), and his discourse on the troubles (1573).

The volume's spine bears the legend 'DE LA BOETI[E]/ETC.' and it provides further confirmation of the frame—here derived from the *politique éditoriale* of Morel—within which the likes of Dupuy and de Thou received his work (Illus. 2.1.7). The library also contained a manuscript of La Boétie's *De la servitude volontaire*, in Claude Dupuy's own hand. But upon his death in 1594 it contained no copy of the *Essais*, even though he had sent a copy to Pinelli in the early 1580s.[93] The *Essais* were not yet *de rigueur* in the libraries of *Messieurs les Parlementaires*.

[93] Delatour, *Les livres de Claude Dupuy*, 91, 192 (catalogue no. 509). There is no indication that this collection of Morel texts was bound together after Claude's time by the Dupuy brothers. The constituent works are classified separately by the BnF as Rés. R-2119–2124. The texts of *La*

Illus. 2.1.7. La Boétie, *Mesnagerie*, ed. Montaigne (Paris: Fédéric Morel, 1571), Bibliothèque nationale de France, pressmark Res R 2119, spine (collection of Morel imprints from the library of Claude Dupuy). Reproduced by permission of the Bibliothèque nationale de France, Paris.

What exactly was La Boétie perceived to have promised of himself, with his editor and friend Montaigne's help? Anne-Marie Cocula has argued that La Boétie was actively engaged with the lieutenant of the King of Navarre, Charles de Coucys ('seigneur de Burie'), in a mission of pacification in Guyenne in 1560–3, part of the ultimately failed attempt to deliver L'Hospital's policy. She has described Montaigne's transcription of La Boétie's deathbed speech to the converted protes-tant Thomas de Beauregard (Montaigne's brother), which pleads in 1560s *politique* style against the formation of 'a band and body apart' ('de bande et de corps à part') and for a new *concorde* of all parties under the umbrella of a reformed Catholic Church, as an exhortation compatible with L'Hospital's policy at the time.[94]

---

mesnagerie, *Les regles de mariage*, and the *Lettre de consolation* (Rés. R-2119) have ink underlinings throughout, but no marginalia. Claude Dupuy's copy of *De la servitude volontaire* is BnF MS Dupuy 239. On the copy for Pinelli see 2.2.1.

[94] Montaigne, *Œuvres complètes*, 1356. Cocula's argument leads her to contest La Boétie's authorship of the extant manuscript 'Mémoire touchant l'édit de janvier 1562' (which a number of modern scholars have identified with the 'quelques mémoires sur cet edict de Janvier' named by Montaigne as a work of La Boétie), and to propose that the speech to Beauregard may be a more reliable guide to the contents of this work. It is clear, however, neither that the manuscript 'Mémoire'

In the 'Mémoire', La Boétie states that his whole proposal for concord depends upon the selection of 'capable men who are lovers of peace and union' ('hommes sufisans et amateurs de paix et de concorde') who can effect the policy.[95] The fact that the paratexts to Montaigne's edition of his surviving works describe La Boétie as a paragon of such men (even though he was never called to serve at national level) makes it unsurprising that Sainte-Marthe gives this portrait and its maker (Montaigne) a place in his collection—the *Elogia*—of *hommes suffisans et amateurs de paix et de concorde.*

As I mentioned earlier in this section, Sainte-Marthe is aware of the way in which the self-portrait offered in the later editions of the *Essais* moves away from the mould provided by La Boétie's promising but stunted career. In Gournay's terms, his is another instance of faint praise, for Sainte-Marthe does not find in the book the qualities and conversation of a great noble soul, an all-round, exemplary philosophical sage. The book is neither the effect nor the cause of grand, peace-making actions. He recognizes Montaigne as a gentleman of noble extraction who has enhanced his personal name as a knight by means of the publication of a book in which he speaks freely, candidly, and learnedly. He has gained glory—in *robe* fashion—by means of a naturalized display of letters and learning (hence his inclusion in a collection of *viri illustres*).

In Sainte-Marthe's eyes, the Gascon published forth by these later editions is a kind of caste hybrid: a *noble d'épée* still exhibiting the culture of a *conseiller* in the *parlement*. For there is continuity in the means by which he seeks glory. Montaigne, says Sainte-Marthe, initially neglected the glory of his family's military heritage in favour of study and entrance into the Bordeaux courts. But he then willingly abdicated from his magistracy to institute a quite different form of noble life—that of his birth as a titled, landed nobleman. Nevertheless, he did not fail to honour the alliance he had contracted with the Muses (i.e. with learning) in his previous incarnation wearing the *robe*.[96]

Sainte-Marthe sees the *Essais* as a testament to this continued contract, and to the combined qualities of natural liberty of expression and variety of learning that go with it. In what follows, he continues with the theme of titles and glory, first by saying that Montaigne gave his work a modest title when it was worthy of a glorious

in question was written before the event, in order to prevent registration in the Bordeaux *parlement* of Catherine's and L'Hospital's January 1562 edict, nor that it is incompatible with the broad aims of that edict and with the views at the time of other *politiques* such as de Foix, du Ferrier, and Harlay. The attribution to La Boétie remains likely, though not completely secure. See Anne-Marie Cocula, 'Michel de L'Hospital, Étienne de La Boétie et Michel de Montaigne: histoire d'une filiation', in Wanegffelen (ed.), *De Michel de L'Hospital à l'édit de Nantes*, 565–73 (569–72); Sylvie Daubresse, *Le Parlement de Paris, ou, La voix de la raison: (1559–1589)* (Geneva: Droz, 2005), 92–3. For a lucid exposition of the issues surrounding the authorship and dating of the manuscript 'Mémoire' attributed by various editors to La Boétie, see Géralde Nakam, 'Estienne de La Boétie, Mémoire sur la pacification des troubles', *Bulletin de l'Association d'étude sur l'humanisme, la réforme et la renaissance*, 20 (1985), 62–6.

[95] Étienne de La Boétie, *Mémoire sur la pacification des troubles*, ed. Malcolm Smith (Geneva: Droz, 1983), 85.

[96] Sainte-Marthe, *Elogia* [1602], sig. R1r/Millet 138; Nakam, *Montaigne et son temps*, 123.

one, then by pointing out that the author could not later desist from decorating them with a glorious title (in another sense): the Bull of Roman citizenship.[97]

So Montaigne's authorial *persona* is welcomed into Sainte-Marthe's collection, and by extension into the Gallican and *politique* milieu of the late sixteenth and early seventeenth century, under the aspect of their particular relationship with the model parliamentary sage La Boétie and of their residual relationship to the *robe* culture of letters. Does the *elogium* also hint that the book tracks Montaigne's social and intellectual career by evolving from a modest show of learning on the part of La Boétie's junior friend into a more vainglorious display on the part of a titled *noble d'épée*?

Whatever the tone of Sainte-Marthe's epideictic rhetoric may be, the crucial point is his understanding, first, that Montaigne made a noble reputation for himself, transnationally, by means of the publication of his book, and, second, that Rome took the initiative in awarding him the citizenship in recognition of this. The producers of the 1603 London edition shared a similar understanding at exactly the same moment in the early 1600s (see 2.2.2).[98] We heard in 1.7.6 that it was in fact Montaigne who took the initiative, and that the award of the citizenship was not explicitly tied by the authorities to his reputation as author of a book. Sainte-Marthe is making inferences from the publication of the charter in *Essais* III 9.

In Sainte-Marthe's milieu, Montaigne's name spread posthumously via L'Angelier's second publication of the book in 1594–5. The book does not reveal the deeds or the exceptional scholarship or philosophical personality of a grand political peacemaker, but it does witness to the author's noble *ingenuitas* and *libertas* of discourse, which derived from his time wearing the *robe*. If it also testifies to his *constantia* in putting up with the pain of his renal colic, this is still far from enough to make him the noble sage celebrated by Gournay.

2.1.4 DE THOU ON LA BOÉTIE AND MONTAIGNE

At the same moment as he entered Sainte-Marthe's public record of illustrious men of learning, in the shadow of La Boétie, Montaigne found a place in the manuscript of de Thou's public history of the European religious wars and subsequent peace. The writing, circulating, and collecting of *éloges* and of *histoires* were closely related activities in this milieu.[99] In the case of our two works (by Sainte-Marthe

---

[97] Sainte-Marthe, *Elogia* [1602], sig. R1r–v/Millet 138–9.

[98] Sainte-Marthe, *Elogia* [1602], sig. R1v/Millet 139: 'Quantam porro sibi pepererit ex illius pulcherrimi operis editione vel apud exteras nationes eruditionis et sapientiae opinionem tum patuit, cum ipsa illa Roma, quae inter omnes totius terrae civitates principem sibi locum vendicat, eum ultro in civium suorum numerum allegit atque cooptavit.'

[99] This is particularly apparent in the correspondence between de Thou and Christophe Dupuy. See Alfred Soman, *De Thou and the index. letters from Christophe Dupuy, (1603–1607)* (Geneva: Droz, 1972), 38, 48, 88–91. See also De Smet, *Thuanus*, 206–7; Thou, *Historiarum sui temporis libri CXXXVIII*, vol. 7, pt. 1, 1/BnF, MS Dupuy 409, fol. 76r–v.

and de Thou), and of the two authors and their families, the association is particularly strong.

If Sainte-Marthe was writing a group of eulogistic obituaries of learned, *politique* men of concord that integrated elements of a history of the religious wars, de Thou was writing a history of the religious wars that integrated (at the end of each year's narrative) eulogistic obituaries of learned, *politique* men of concord—including men 'of the Religion' such as Scaliger (a major bone of contention at Rome).

So, for example, the *ingenium* and *natura* of François de La Noue make him, in de Thou's narrative, equally admirable to both parties during his attempts to mediate peace between the Huguenots and the royal army at La Rochelle. De Thou refers to these obituaries in one letter as a kind of separate work-within-the-work: 'les Eloges des hommes de Lettres'. After his death they were excerpted and collected in separate publications.[100]

It is in this broad context of portrait- and history-making that Sainte-Marthe and de Thou jointly used and related to the *Essais* as an extension of the *persona* of Montaigne as friend to La Boétie and as retired magistrate. Grouped moral portraits had instrumental functions in this milieu; they shaped the conditions for shared intellectual and political action in history.[101]

One could go further and suggest that Sainte-Marthe and de Thou co-ordinated their eulogies of the two Gascons. More research is needed on the extent to which the choice of subjects for Sainte-Marthe's *elogia*, especially for the second book in 1602, was a collaborative one. In a letter to Sainte-Marthe of February 1594, de Thou had announced his own project of a history culminating in the retaking of Paris by Henri IV that very year. In January 1598, de Thou was involved in negotiations with the Protestants near Poitiers, and wrote to Sainte-Marthe, who had played a major peace-making role in keeping that town loyal to Henri IV. He told him his project had reached 1562—just before the year of La Boétie's death (1563)—and asked him for a written account of the siege of Poitiers (1562). He also asked for biographical information on Guillaume Pellissier, whom he was sure Sainte-Marthe had not forgotten in his *Éloges*—perhaps a leading suggestion that he *should* include him, as indeed he did in the next edition (1602).[102]

In the same year (1598), Sainte-Marthe published the first edition of the *Elogia* and associated the work explicitly with the unpublished work of his friend in his dedication to de Thou. In April 1600, Sainte-Marthe wrote privately to de Thou in light of a communication from his twin sons. Louis and Scévole II de Sainte-Marthe, who were now employed as scribes by de Thou, told their father that de Thou had mentioned the *Elogia*. Sainte-Marthe was encouraged by this to

---

[100] Thou, *Historiarum sui temporis libri CXXXVIII*, vol. 7, pt. 1, 12/BnF, MS Dupuy 409, fol. 94r; Graves, 'L'art du portrait chez Jacques-Auguste de Thou', 129–30; Kinser, *The works of Jacques-Auguste de Thou*, 301–4. Graves makes a strong argument that moral portraits of the various protagonists are integral to de Thou's historiography.

[101] Graves, 'L'art du portrait chez Jacques-Auguste de Thou', 133–4.

[102] Jacques Auguste de Thou, *Choix de lettres françoises inédites*, ed. Paulin Paris (Paris: Société des Bibliophiles, 1877), 46–9; Sainte-Marthe, *Elogia*, 1602, sigs. P2v–3v.

continue his work on the new pieces for the second edition, which he promised to show de Thou the next time he was in Paris.

It is therefore probable de Thou saw Sainte-Marthe's joint *elogium* of La Boétie and Montaigne even before they were published in 1602, and possible that he suggested them as a subject. De Thou was certainly thought not only to have access to Sainte-Marthe's writings, but also to have influence over their subject matter. In April 1604, a servant of the just deceased Cardinal d'Ossat travelled to see de Thou in Paris with the intention of exchanging his late master's notes on the *Historiae* for an *éloge* of d'Ossat to be procured by de Thou from Sainte-Marthe.[103] This was probably the origin of Sainte-Marthe's obituary for the cardinal, and of his intention to extend the work still further.

Meanwhile, by March 1603, de Thou was sending Sainte-Marthe the earliest printed gatherings of what will become the first 1604 edition—printed in late 1603—of the first part of his *Historiae*, which covers events from 1546 up to 1560.[104] This edition, containing material first composed in the mid-1590s, already offers significant evidence that de Thou shared with Sainte-Marthe a joint relationship to the *personae* and early works of La Boétie and Montaigne, for one passage does exactly what Sainte-Marthe's 1602 *elogium* of La Boétie does. It draws directly upon the *Essais* (though without mentioning either the work or its author) as a defence and illustration of the *persona* and work of La Boétie.[105]

In his annals for 1548, de Thou gives considerable space to the salt tax (*gabelle*) revolt in Guyenne, which was caused by royal encroachment on the region's customary commercial liberties. The horrific slaughter of Moneins, the king's lieutenant, by a rebellious mob is central to the narrative (as it is to *Essais* I 23), and prefigures the violence of the civil wars that would start in 1562. But de Thou is as amazed by the rapidity with which La Chassaigne (Montaigne's future father-in-law) and the other parliamentary magistrates peacefully (for the most part) regained their authority on behalf of the King as he is horrified by the violence and cruelty of this rebellion.

Before he goes on to recount the violent and cruel punishments subsequently meted out by Montmorency's troops, de Thou pauses to reflect upon the fact that La Chassaigne and his fellow governors, as representatives of royal authority, could so quickly and easily reduce a passionately rebellious crowd to willing servitude. This is exactly the kind of frank moral reflection upon the events of history that the work as a whole is concerned to authorize.

It is this reflection, de Thou adds, which La Boétie has taken up in *De la servitude volontaire*, a text which powerfully expressed the personal ethos of innate *liberté* and variety of learning shared by *parlementaires* in mid-century Bordeaux.

---

[103] For this and the previous paragraph see Jean Brunel, 'Jacques-Auguste de Thou et ses amis poitevins', in Lestringant (ed.), *Jacques-Auguste de Thou (1553–1617)*, 53–71, 67–8; Soman, *De Thou and the Index*, 38.

[104] Kinser, *The works of Jacques-Auguste de Thou*, 81–2.

[105] For this passage, discussed over the next four paragraphs, see Jacques Auguste de Thou, *Historiarum sui temporis pars I*, 2 vols. (Paris: Ambrose and Jerome Drouart, 1604), vol. 1, lib. IV, sigs Aa8v–Bb1r; Thou, *Historiarum sui temporis libri CXXXVIII*, vol. 1, 187.

By placing La Boétie's text in this context—loyal royal officials pacifying troubles—he is joining Montaigne in attempting to make it and its author's reputation safe. He is directly endorsing Montaigne's own insistence, at the end of I 27, that this reflective text was emphatically not intended to stir up sedition.[106]

La Boétie's *liberté de jugement* was moderated by his loyalty to the throne of France and the cause of national peace and unity. De Thou includes a brief eulogy of the magistrate from Sarlat and goes on to specify that *De la servitude volontaire* has since been used against the author's original intentions to stir up a popular revolt (of the kind just described in Guyenne in 1548) in the wake of the St Bartholomew Day's massacre. Both de Thou's praise of La Boétie and the detail of his apology for his most famous text might seem gratuitous in this context until we consider that Montaigne would have been the source for both—and also in all probability for the narrative of the salt tax revolt.[107]

Why would the defence of La Boétie's intentions have been so important to de Thou? Because, as his friend Sainte-Marthe's *elogium* makes clear, La Boétie was considered in retrospect to be one of their 'party', wedded to their cause of pacification and officially charged with its realization. Furthermore, the distinction between legitimate free-thinking or *liberté de jugement* of the kind he and de Thou as counsellors were exercising in relation to the salt tax revolt in historical and moral writing, and illegitimate or licentious free-thinking of the kind exercised by those who used La Boétie's text to stir up rebellion, was crucial to de Thou's whole enterprise as a *politique*.

It corresponded to the distinction, on the religio-political level, between legitimate Gallican liberties that did not threaten the existence of the Roman Catholic Church and illegitimate new liberties taken by Reformers founding new churches. He was, furthermore, to repeat the reference. Still closer in content and spirit to Sainte-Marthe's obituary for the two friends is de Thou's obituary for La Boétie (d.1563), again composed in the late 1590s, and first published in the following, 1606 edition. There, the story of La Boétie's qualities of *prudentia* and *eruditio*, and of a promising but failed career, is exactly the one told in the paratexts to Montaigne's edition of his works, which is again mentioned. The failure of the Huguenot propagandists who published *De la servitude volontaire* to reflect the true intentions of the author is reiterated.[108]

The important point is that de Thou has so far not mentioned the *Essais* in their own right. They feature only as implicit backup to a shared defence, in the parliamentary milieu, of La Boétie's reputation as a promising, *politique* counsellor and as author of a free-judging text that was later 'distorted' by Huguenots as a call to rebellion, and therefore (wisely) not republished.

[106] I 27, NP201/ BVH Paris 1595, p. 113/S218–19.
[107] Étienne de La Boétie, *De la servitude volontaire, ou, Contr'un...Avec des notes additionnelles de Michel Magnien*, eds Malcolm Smith and Michel Magnien (2nd edn., Geneva: Droz, 2001), 8–9.
[108] Jacques Auguste de Thou, *Historiarum sui temporis tomi secundi*, 2 vols. (Paris: Ambrose and Jerome Drouart, 1606), vol. 1, lib. XXXVI, sigs. 2P8v–2Q1r; Thou, *Historiarum sui temporis libri CXXXVIII*, vol. 2, 380.

This, I argue, is how Montaigne's literary works were received in the *robe* milieu of the 1570s and 1580s. However, around the same time as he was sending Sainte-Marthe gatherings of the 1604 edition of his *Historiae*, de Thou was writing his eulogistic obituary of Montaigne for book 102, which includes the events of the year 1592 (not printed until 1620). By then he would certainly have seen Sainte-Marthe's *elogium* of the essayist. Within just a few months, the Sainte-Marthe brothers were to copy this and the surrounding books into manuscripts intended for their own library.[109]

2.1.5 DE THOU'S *HISTORIAE* AT ROME

What is the importance of all this for the history of the *Essais*? The conjunction of the 1602 printed *elogium* and de Thou's composition of an obituary of Montaigne for an internationally renowned—and infamous—history of Europe constitutes a watershed moment in the history of Montaigne's *persona* and book. Though this has not been recognized in modern accounts of the fortunes of the *Essais*, it was clear to early modern editors and critics.

Pierre Coste's selection of judgements and criticisms of the *Essais* ('Jugements et critiques sur les *Essais* de Montaigne') begins with Sainte-Marthe's and de Thou's *elogia*, then offers the passages from de Thou's *Vita* and the entirety of Pasquier's letter, before including the relevant extracts from Lipsius's *epistolae*.[110] For Coste, whose edition canonized Montaigne as a free-thinking Enlightenment *philosophe*, these passages of praise defined the Gascon's place and the meaning of his book in posterity.

De Thou's obituary, and two matching passages in the *Vita*, were printed for the first time in the same edition at Geneva in 1620–1, four years after Sainte-Marthe's *elogium* was printed at Paris for the first time, a year after Pasquier's epistolary sketch of the Gascon, and two years before Lancre's attack and Father Garasse's defence (against Pasquier—see 2.1.7).[111]

Indeed, de Thou's biographical texts would become more important than Lipsius's comments in the reception of Montaigne in the later seventeenth and early eighteenth centuries because of de Thou's more enduring status as a master of European Latin letters. When a full 'Defence of the Author' was added to the fourth edition (1711) of Cotton's English translation of the *Essays*, the principal

[109] There is evidence that de Thou had completed book 100 by the middle of 1603, and that he may have been writing books 104–8 by February 1604. For the dating of the composition of these books and of the Sainte-Marthe brothers' copies, see Kinser, *The works of Jacques-Auguste de Thou*, 81, 121–3.

[110] Michel de Montaigne, *Les Essais*, ed. Pierre Coste, 3 vols. (Paris: Par La Société, 1725), vol. 1, liii–lix.

[111] Jacques Auguste de Thou, *Historiarum sui temporis ab Anno Domini 1543 usque ad annum 1607 libri CXXXVIII*, 5 vols. ([Geneva]: de la Rovière, 1620); Scévole de Sainte-Marthe, *Opera* (Paris: P. Durand, 1616); Pasquier, *Les lettres* [1619]; Pierre de Lancre, *L'incredulité et mescreance du sortilege plainement conuaincue* (Paris: Nicolas Buon, 1622); François Garasse, *Les recherches des Recherches et autres œuvres de Me Estienne Pasquier* (Paris: Sébastien Chappelet, 1622).

source was Charles Sorel's section on Montaigne in the *Bibliotheque françoise* (1667). But the clinching testimony, not found in Sorel, is that of 'the incomparable *Thuanus*'.

The writer includes de Thou's eulogy of the essayist in English and comments that this '[t]estimony of *Thuanus* is sufficient to justify the Memory of our Author, for no Body will believe that a Man of that Integrity would have been so great a Friend with so vicious a Man as *Malbranche* has represented *Montaigne*'. He then adds an English text of de Thou's report in the *Vita* of Montaigne's private remarks at Blois in 1588 as evidence of 'the Reason why *Montaigne* meets with a more favourable Entertainment in *England* than in his native Country': 'an author who talks freely of every thing, is not suitable to the Temper of a servile Nation [France], that has lost all sense of Liberty'. Centuries later, the passage by de Thou still had an important place in Montaigne's biography.[112]

The author of the 'Defence' or 'Vindication' understands very well how the eulogy and the passages from the memoirs dovetail. De Thou's obituary departs, like Sainte-Marthe's, from his friendship with La Boétie, and goes on to describe the *Essais* as testifying to the nature of their author as 'vir libertatis ingenuae'. But it also supplies Montaigne with an illustrious political career that is continuous with this friendship and its milieu, and that provides a context for the literary career as it evolved between the La Boétie edition and the mature *Essais*—which in turn situates the author and his works as part of the context for the *Historiae*.

Montaigne goes from being a most dignified counsellor ('assessor dignissimus') with La Boétie in the Bordeaux *parlement*, to being elected mayor of Bordeaux while in Venice (in fact he was in Rome), to counsellor to the king's lieutenant in Guyenne, Matignon, during the civil wars. To further bolster this career, de Thou pairs the Gascon—in the gallery of moral portraits of learned men which ends his narrative for 1592—with a political counsellor to Phillip II. Fadrique Furiò Ceriol (1527–92) is praised as a kind of Spanish *politique* who made every attempt to pacify the troubles in the Low Countries.[113] In his annals for 1575, de Thou had described the treaty Ceriol drafted to negotiate a settlement between the Dutch rebels and the Spanish, around the time of the breakup of the conference at Breda.[114]

De Thou further claims in the obituary that when he was with Montaigne both in Guyenne (in the early 1580s) and later at the court and in Paris (corresponding, as we shall see, to the two passages in the *Vita*), they were brought together by the conformity of their studies and dispositions ('studiorum et voluntatum consensione conjunctissimus').[115] He is not testifying here in disinterested fashion to the facts of Montaigne's life. For apologetic purposes that will become more apparent

---

[112] Michel de Montaigne, *Essays*, trans. Charles Cotton, 3 vols. (4th edn., London: Daniel Brown et al, 1711), vol. 1, sigs. B6r–7r; Frame 140–1.

[113] Thou, *Historiarum sui temporis libri CXXXVIII*, vol. 5, 180/Millet 195–6. The 1733 edition's version of this passage contains phrases from an early manuscript (BnF MS Lat. 5977) that do not appear in the early printed versions. See De Smet, 'Montaigne et Jacques-Auguste de Thou', 223 and n.1.

[114] Thou, *Historiarum sui temporis libri CXXXVIII*, vol. 3, 392–3.

[115] Thou, *Historiarum sui temporis libri CXXXVIII*, vol. 5, 180/Millet 195–6.

in the *Vita*, he is drawing on the *persona* behind a book that *c.*1602–4 (when he wrote the passage) had begun to achieve a successful career, that had itself moved from a first edition in Guyenne to successive editions in Paris without being censored at Rome. Thanks to Gournay's 1595 edition and the belated distribution of copies of 1588, Montaigne's noble fame has been growing by means of his expanded book.

In what did this retrospectively claimed *consensio* consist, and how did it serve to reinforce the ethos of the author of the *Historiae*? As we have heard, de Thou ascribes the same noble qualities to Montaigne as Sainte-Marthe: *ingenuitas* and *libertas*.[116] It is to these qualities that the discourse of the *Essais*—dignified with their own Latin title ('Conatus')—testifies. They are also the qualities de Thou will ascribe to himself as a *noble de robe* in the opening to his apologetic *Vita*, and to which his *Historiae* testify. In the manuscript version, de Thou complements Sainte-Marthe's reference to the Roman citizenship by citing Lipsius's naming of the Frenchman as the French Thales, though this was probably taken out in the printed version due to the rising antipathy towards the Dutch humanist in France.[117]

We shall turn shortly to the close relationship between this obituary, composed *c.*1604, and de Thou's later references to Montaigne in the *Vita*, composed *c.*1614. Before this, we need to consider the fortunes of de Thou's book in the interim, which provide an important foil for the fortunes of the frank and free *Essais* at Rome. Remember once again that de Thou's collaborator Sainte-Marthe had in 1602 praised the *Essais* in print for their free-minded liberty of speech ('ingenua loquendi libertate'). The successful, unimpeded publication and circulation across Europe of a book that testified to this and other virtues had gained the author a great reputation in foreign nations. The clearest measure of this had been the fact that Rome, which claims first place among all cities on the earth ('inter omnes totius terrae civitates principem sibi locum vendicat'), took the initiative of electing and naming Montaigne amongst its citizens.[118]

By *c.*1602, thanks largely to Gournay and L'Angelier, 'Montaigne' is beginning to be known as the noble authorial *persona* who has produced a successful book. The greater ambition of book III, and his posthumous achievement in gaining recognition in Paris and Rome for a free-judging, openly published work, drives Sainte-Marthe's and de Thou's retrospective praise of his character and actions.

Furthermore, de Thou was himself about to seek recognition for his work in Rome. There is no evidence that he coveted Roman citizenship. But his plan in 1602–3 was certainly to publish a public history that would gain him a reputation for free-minded liberty of speech and truthfulness across France and Europe, and provide a narrative foundation for the peace that he was charged, in his official *persona*, by Henri IV with negotiating and keeping. The engraved frontispiece of the second edition (1604) features prominent representations of these two virtues.

---

[116] On these two Latin terms, which do not translate precisely into their broad French equivalents *liberté* and *franchise*, see 2.1.3 and the first footnote there.

[117] De Smet, 'Montaigne et Jacques-Auguste de Thou', 223n.1; De Smet, *Thuanus*, 97–9.

[118] Sainte-Marthe, *Elogia*, sig. R1r–v/Millet 138–9.

A key part of the plan was personally to send copies to Rome, the first among cities on earth, in order to gain recognition there. He was already doing this in late 1603 and lining up Christophe Dupuy as his agent in the shaping of his work's favourable reception at the court of Rome.[119]

But his fellow *robins* were worried from the start, as they understood that the receptions of the work in Paris and in Rome would be linked and would be subject to political circumstances. According to L'Estoile in early 1604, everyone feared that, de Thou's book having been sent to Rome, if it were then to be censored, the King would appease the Pope by not protecting the work—as indeed happened.

They also questioned de Thou's decision to release the work in parts. This was a common strategy as it allowed the author to test the work on a relatively controlled audience of friends, and to incorporate corrections and other suggestions in the follow-up parts and editions. But was it prudent in this case? Had de Thou published the whole work straight off, everywhere, then it would have been so well received that the censures of the envious would have been in vain, and it would have found *contre-censeurs* and *bon avocats* to defend it.[120] Perhaps this was Marie de Gournay's strategy when she sent corrected copies of Paris 1595 to all the famous printing-houses of Europe.[121]

De Thou believed that if he got copies into the hands of friends in Rome who could 'introduce' it, then it would be better treated than if he just let it be carried there by other booksellers or individuals.[122] He sent two copies of the one-volume folio edition of the first part, covering events from 1546 to 1560. They reached Rome in early 1604.[123]

These were quickly followed by copies of the two-volume octavo edition of the first part, which already contained some authorial corrections designed to appease Roman censors. From the start, de Thou was briefing Dupuy and sympathetic Cardinals by letter with the arguments that might be used to protect the work at the Roman court—arguments closely related to those he had already printed in the preface to Henri IV. Principal amongst them was an argument from ethos: that he self-evidently wrote without any hate or partiality ('haine', 'partialité'), and with the sincere freedom ('franchise', 'liberté') that had been needed to secure peace in the circumstances of the French troubles, and that he should be allowed at Rome on those grounds. In return he offers statements of his good faith in obeying the doctrine and discipline of the Holy See, and in countenancing corrections as long as they do not compromise the truth of History or the honour of France.[124]

Initially, there was the prospect that booksellers in Rome would also stock and sell copies more widely. But in 1605 the Master of the Sacred Palace seized and retained seven or eight copies that arrived as part of a consignment of books from

---

[119] Anthony Grafton, *The footnote: a curious history* (Rev. edn.; Cambridge, Mass.: Harvard University Press, 1997), 133–4; Kinser, *The works of Jacques-Auguste de Thou*, 7–11; Soman, *De Thou and the Index*.

[120] Grafton, *The footnote: a curious history*, 133–4; *Journal Henri IV*, vol. 2, 126, for this and the previous paragraph.

[121] Sayce and Maskell, 32.

[122] Thou, *Historiarum sui temporis libri CXXXVIII*, vol. 7, pt. I, 28/BnF, MS Dupuy 409, fol. 112r.

[123] Thou, *Historiarum sui temporis libri CXXXVIII*, vol. 7, pt. I, 3/BnF, MS Dupuy 409, fol. 77r.

[124] Thou, *Historiarum sui temporis libri CXXXVIII*, vol. 7, pt. I, 2/BnF, MS Dupuy 632, fol. 9r.

France destined for a Roman bookseller. The Master passed three or four on to Cardinals, and the formal process of examination began. In 1606 De Thou hesitated about sending copies of the second part, covering events from 1560–72, as he was not sure how the efforts of his patrons to take control of the censorial process were going, and he feared the second part would just stoke the flames. In the event, many of the copies he did send were lost or damaged in transit, with one ending up in a ditch.[125]

Nevertheless, he was still following the same strategy in 1608. He sent copies of the last section of the second part, which dealt with the last few years of Charles IX's reign and the St Bartholomew's Day massacre, and asked for Cardinal Sforza's approval to publish further books that would take the narrative right up to 1584. He stated firmly that he would keep the other forty books for a better time, when one would be freer to think what one likes, and to write what one thinks ('plus libre de penser ce que l'on veut, et d'escrire ce que l'on pense')—a phrase de Thou had used in his 'Preface'.[126]

In the event, as far as the history of de Thou's book is concerned, this time did not really come until well into the eighteenth century. The books to 1584 duly appeared in a folio edition in 1609. But the other forty did not appear in de Thou's lifetime, and appeared posthumously only at Geneva and Frankfurt in editions of the 1620s. For the rest of the seventeenth century, de Thou's *Historiae* appeared in no more than extracts and fragments.[127]

The crucial point concerns de Thou's understanding that the fortunes of his book amongst potential enemies both at home in Paris and abroad in Rome would themselves serve either to extend the prudent action of pacification, or to reignite the troubles—depending on who got control of the process. There was no distinction between the ways he and others acted by means of his book and the ways they acted in political situations to further or oppose the cause of peace.

So his apologetic preface asks potential opponents prudently to recognize the liberty he has taken to praise and blame protagonists from all parties to the wars according to his own judgement, and not along party-religious lines. This liberty arises both from his own nature as a freeman, and from Henri IV's pacification of the realm by law. It is exercised in the specific context of the religious troubles in France, as a way of conserving the state and the ancient beliefs of the church.[128] We shall see that de Thou shows Montaigne exercising exactly this liberty at Blois in 1588—but in a private conversation.

---

[125] Soman, *De Thou and the index*, 46; Thou, *Historiarum sui temporis libri CXXXVIII*, vol. 7, pt. I, 15–16/BnF, MS Dupuy 409, fols. 98r–99v; Thou, *Historiarum sui temporis libri CXXXVIII*, vol. 7, pt. I, 31.

[126] Thou, *Historiarum sui temporis libri CXXXVIII*, vol. 7, pt. I, 34–5/BnF, MS Dupuy 409, fols. 118r–119v; Thou, *Historiarum sui temporis libri CXXXVIII*, vol. 1, 'Auctoris præfatio ad Henricum IV', 2 ('quibus unicuique sentire quae velit, et quae sentiat eloqui, licet.'); Kinser, *The works of Jacques-Auguste de Thou*, 14–15, 19.

[127] Kinser, *The works of Jacques-Auguste de Thou*, 19–20, 26–45, 54–6, 300–9, 312–13.

[128] Thou, *Historiarum sui temporis libri CXXXVIII*, vol. 1, 'Auctoris præfatio ad Henricum IV', 12–14.

The crucial issue then becomes whether this liberty of judgement will be prudently allowed at Rome and the book permitted to circulate freely, thereby extending the politics of pacification described in the preface, or whether those conspiring
to end the Henrician concord will do violence by means of the book (i.e. get it
censored), thereby reigniting the troubles. In other words, the reception of the
book directly indexes the reception of what are simultaneously personal (in the
persona of a senior French magistrate) and national (French) liberties at Rome. This
is not least because the work contained textual monuments of French *libertés* and
franchises, such as the *Arrest de Tanquerel*, that could not be removed.[129]

How was this likely to turn out? From 1605–6 De Thou is doubtful that his
liberté and *franchise* in telling the truth at a particular moment during the past
conflicts in France will be acceptable at the papal court in the early 1600s. He does
offer to trade corrections for conditional permission for the work to circulate there.
But in addressing his protectors via letters to Dupuy he also raises the stakes by
claiming that the Henrician peace was under attack and that God himself was
protecting his work against the enemies of the truth. Those at Rome who wanted
completely to take away the honest and legitimate liberty of speech and writing
risked causing the opposite of what they desired: an outbreak of unbridled licence.

As early as late 1605, when the initial report was put in the hands of the Jesuit
Cardinal Bellarmine (who indicated immediately that the 'Preface' was a sticking
point, especially given its placement at the very beginning of the work), de Thou
suspected that the reception of his book in Rome would be used by the order to
disturb the hard-won public peace in France, which the Jesuits would not dare to
do except by such indirect means. He feared that the Bourbons would in turn take
this attack on his book personally and retaliate against Rome—though, as it turned
out, in this he was mistaken (Henri IV distanced himself from de Thou and his
work).[130]

Montaigne had taken a copy of the *Essais* to Rome personally, though not with
the intention of getting his book approved; de Thou sent copies of his book with
that very intention. Montaigne's was seized at the gates of Rome and held by the
Master of the Sacred Palace for examination; copies of de Thou's *Historiae* were
sequested by the same official, for the same purpose. Both men fashioned an ethos
of *franchise* and *liberté* as part of their apology for their book on its travels. The
outcome in Rome, however, was very different in each case. This was at least partly

---

[129] Thou, *Historiarum sui temporis libri CXXXVIII*, vol. 7, pt. I, 26/BnF, MS Dupuy 409, fol. 108r
(re the *Arrest de Tanquerel*). On the case of Tanquerel (a student forced to retract his claim that the
Pope could remove rebellious Princes from their thrones), registered by de Thou's father Christophe,
see Daubresse, *Le Parlement de Paris*, 87.

[130] For this and the previous paragraph see Thou, *Historiarum sui temporis libri CXXXVIII*, vol. 7,
pt. I, 5–7 [this letter should be dated 14 November 1605, as it clearly responds to Soman no. 10,
dated 18 October 1605]/BnF, MS Dupuy 409, fols. 82r–83v; Thou, *Historiarum sui temporis libri
CXXXVIII*, vol. 7, pt. I, 11 [I was unable to locate this letter of de Thou's to Dupuy, dated 29
November 1605, in BnF, MS Dupuy 409]; Thou, *Historiarum sui temporis libri CXXXVIII*, vol. 7,
pt. I, 11–12/BnF, MS Dupuy 409, fols. 93r–v; Thou, *Historiarum sui temporis libri CXXXVIII*, vol. 7,
pt. I, 12–14/BnF, MS Dupuy 409, fols. 94r–96v; Thou, *Historiarum sui temporis libri CXXXVIII*,
vol. 7, pt. I, 30/BnF, MS Dupuy 409, fols. 115r–116v (re 'license effrenée de parler et d'escrire');
Soman, *De Thou and the Index*, 55–6 (no. 10, 18 October 1605).

because de Thou's *persona* was that of an official reader-writer of histories of the religious wars which publicly represented not just his own, but his nation's liberties. His private *persona*—unlike Montaigne's—emerged in writing that was only published after his death.

2.1.6 MONTAIGNE IN DE THOU'S *VITA*

The *Vita* is a belated attempt to intervene in the fortunes of the *Historiae* by putting proof of the private ethos of the author on the written record. It begins in 1614 with the author—and by extension his book—enveloped with the flames of the worst animosity 'in his own country, then soon abroad, in Rome...and later in Spain'. This refers to the criticism the work received from the very first publication in 1604, its placement on the Roman Index in November 1609, and the long list of corrections commissioned by the Spanish Inquisition in 1612. Corrections were also produced by the Congregation of the Index in Milan in 1612—though these may have been the result of another aborted attempt, initiated either in 1607 or in 1609–11 (when de Thou was seeking to resurrect his career), to rehabilitate the project of an expurgated version of the work.[131]

As the text opens in the authorial manuscript version, we find de Thou doing what he has been attempting to do in person and in his writings all his adult life: pacify the latest troubles (the rebellion of Condé and other nobles), by means of negotiation, on behalf of the king's government. In the midst of these negotiations, a bookseller of Frankfurt brings him a copy of a work of *Notationes*, by the Frenchman Machault (under the pseudonym of 'Joannes Baptista Gallus'), printed at Ingolstadt (1614), that ferociously attacks the *Historiae* and the author's morals. The book later enters Paris, but is quickly prohibited by the Parisian authorities.

---

[131] ACDF, Indice, Protocolli Y, fols. 400–5v (with two further blank leaves fols. 406–7). This 'correttione' was completed on 9 May 1612 by theologians appointed by the Congregation in Milan, under the supervision of Antonio Olgiati, prefect of the Ambrosiana library (fol. 404v). The edition used is the two-volume 1606 Drouart edition. It does not appear in vol. 7 of the 1733 edition of de Thou's works, and is not taken into account by Soman. It is inserted in the volume in the midst of another document (which therefore jumps from fol. 399 to fol. 408), and appears to have pages out of their correct order. It begins with five general cautions about the work, which mainly concern the way de Thou speaks favourably of heretics and unfavourably of Cardinals and Popes. It then lists passages that need to be deleted if an expurgated edition is to be published (which it never was). Under the arrangements brought in by the Congregation responsible for the implementation of the Clementine Index, which hinged on the creation of local congregations, historical works were meant to be sent to Milan. This may suggest that the impetus for this new attempt to expurgate rather than prohibit de Thou's work came from Rome, which had indeed re-opened negotiations with de Thou in 1609–11, via the Jesuit father Louis de Richeome and Cardinal de La Rochefoucauld. However, de Thou had sent a copy in the summer of 1607 via Antonio Olgiato to Cardinal Federico Borromeo, who acknowledged its receipt and then wrote to declare his support (in March 1608). See Gigliola Fragnito, 'The expurgatory policy of the church and the works of Gasparo Contarini', in Ronald K. Delph, Michelle M. Fontaine, and John Jeffries Martin (eds.), *Heresy, culture, and religion in early modern Italy: contexts and contestations* (Kirksville, Missouri: Truman State University Press, 2006), 193–210, 198–200; Soman, *De Thou and the index*, 26, 101–2; Thou, *Historiarum sui temporis libri CXXXVIII*, vol. 7, pt. I, 32, 34, 38–43.

Nevertheless, with such calumnies in circulation, the fictional narrator of the *Vita* (really de Thou himself) resolves to put the author's true character in writing, so that future generations can learn of the morals and the private life of the author whose mind and good faith ('ingenium et candorem') they will always be able to judge from his writings. The *Vita* is the journal of everyday notes that de Thou himself might have written to complement his public histories ('in ephemeridem sive rerum cottidianarum commentarios'). The reader is exhorted to believe these writings about a friend 'whose noble liberty, harmful to no-one, has left everyone with complete freedom to judge him and his morals' ('cuius *ingenua* ac nemini noxia *libertas* plenam de se ac moribus suis *censendi libertatem* omnibus fecit'; my italics).[132]

Here is the core narrative of enfranchisement that is meant to shape both the relations that determine the fortunes of de Thou's book, and the relations that determine whether peace will endure amongst the potentially opposed parties in divided France and Europe. The book is transparently made with an *ingenua libertas* that is evidently 'harmful to no-one'—and therefore conducive to peace—and that leaves everyone with *censendi libertas* (freedom of judgement).

Just as de Thou claims a liberty in his historical work freely to praise and blame the morals of protagonists in the civil wars, regardless of their party and status, so his book extends this liberty to others in relation to itself—within controlled conditions. He circulates copies of early editions of the *Historiae* with a view to receiving criticisms from all over Europe that can inform corrections in later editions. Dupuy's function is to let him know the diverse judgements of his book; he would be blameworthy if he could not endure the very freedom of speech which he had asked readers of his histories to endure.[133]

All of de Thou's efforts to shape the fortunes of his text in correspondence, and in his apologetic memoir, adhere to this conception of the work and its fortunes. The problem is that it foundered in practice at Rome and elsewhere. His *ingenua libertas* was only considered harmless as long as his friends held sway with the Congregation of the Inquisition, and the liberty of judgement the Congregation exercised ex-officio was way beyond what he envisaged—not a list of manageable corrections, but total prohibition.

For the other interesting point about this passage is of course the difference between what de Thou is causing in person (the pacification of troubles by negotiation) and what the extension of his person (his book) is causing (renewed troubles between factions). He and his book are not consubstantial in this respect (at least from his own point of view). If he is a man whose temperament is alien to factions, his book becomes a site of international struggle between Gallican Paris and papal

---

[132] For this and the previous paragraph see Thou, *Vita*, ed. Teissier-Ensminger, 188, 190, 192. The opening passage under discussion appears in the original authorial manuscript of the *Vita* (BnF, MS Lat. 5979), and was almost certainly composed by de Thou himself, but it was deleted from the first, Genevan edition of the text. See Kinser, *The works of Jacques-Auguste de Thou*, 168–72. The whole text is written in the third person, as if by a friend of de Thou, but is securely attributed to the author of the *Historiae* himself.

[133] Thou, *Historiarum sui temporis libri CXXXVIII*, vol. 7, pt. I, 4/MS Dupuy 409, fol. 79v.

Rome in the prolonged theological–political crisis of the early seventeenth century.[134]

Just as censors attack and prohibit his book in Rome, so do their counterparts in Paris attack and prohibit his opponents' books. In 1607 Jacques Séguier talks of a continual war in Rome between the supporters and the detractors of de Thou's book, and of his own contestation with the brilliant anti-Protestant polemicist Caspar Schoppe (or Gaspar Scioppus). L'Estoile tells us that on 4 December 1609 the *grande salle* of the Palais was full of *légistes* saying that the Roman censure of de Thou's *Historiae* (just published along with that of other works) should in turn be censored and physically torn apart ('lacérée')—as was the standard punishment—by the *Parlement*.[135]

In fact, Machault's was not the only book attacking de Thou to be prohibited by the Parisian authorities: they burned Schoppe's *Ecclesiasticus* in 1612, even as its praises were being sung in Rome.[136] Meanwhile, after an olive branch was briefly extended by a Jesuit priest to de Thou in 1610, the Parisian *parlement*'s prohibition of a work by Cardinal Bellarmine was interpreted by Jesuits in Rome as de Thou's personal vengeance for the placement of his own work on the Index in 1609, and as the beginnings of a new schism.[137]

By this point, the reception of the *Historiae* has become a matter of partisan politics. The *Vita* is not an immediate, polemical response; it remained unpublished until after de Thou's death. The text tries to pacify these book-related troubles not by answering Machault and Schoppe point-by-point, and thus feeding the flames, but by revealing in private writing how unpartisan the author is in his speech and behaviour, and by inviting free judgements of his morals. This means revealing the 'web of connections, both past and present', that have shaped the book.[138]

It means showing the author in his relations with *viri illustres* across the religio-political spectrum, friends who are both reliable sources for and correctors of his work, and bearers of shared virtues of independence and good faith that are witnessed in their own works. One of these, amongst a whole crowd in the background, is Montaigne. The Gascon features as an unpartisan authority not only for the affairs of Guyenne around the time of the salt tax revolt, but for the beginnings of the war of succession, in 1585—the war which shaped the *parlementaires*' use of the *Essais* and of the *persona* of their author.

As we turn to the passages in which de Thou discusses his relations with the essayist we must recall an important premise of the argument so far: that 'biographical' anecdotes of this kind, like more formal *éloges*, are intended to shape, and are shaped by, the fortunes of texts in circulation. This is true of the anecdotes

[134] Sylvio Hermann de Franceschi, *La crise théologico-politique du premier âge baroque: antiromanisme doctrinal, pouvoir pastoral et raison du prince: le Saint-Siège face au prisme français (1607–1627)* (Rome: École française de Rome, 2009), 226–30, 232–3, 237–9, 241–3, 295, 305, 328, 474–5.

[135] Thou, *Historiarum sui temporis libri CXXXVIII*, vol. 7, pt. I, 33; *Journal Henri IV*, vol. 2, 561.

[136] De Smet, *Thuanus*, 266n.12, 274.

[137] Thou, *Historiarum sui temporis libri CXXXVIII*, vol. 7, pt. I, 42–3.

[138] De Smet, *Thuanus*, 156.

about de Thou across the *Vita* as a whole, which aim to show the kind of private conversation that gave rise to the *Historiae*, and to which they in turn can give rise.

And it is true of the anecdotes about Montaigne, which must be read in conjunction with de Thou's comment in his *elogium* that the *Essais* witness to the author's noble qualities as *vir libertatis ingenuae*, as an officeholder and a private mediator. These passages give us de Thou's Montaigne, the Montaigne *politique* he needs both as a source for and friend to his book, and as a correlative to a topical reading of the *Essais*.

So, on the one hand, these passages draw on book III to embed the *Essais* in Montaigne's political 'career' as a magistrate, mayor, and courtier who mediated privately between opposed parties in the civil wars, and to embed them, by extension, in the libraries of *parlementaires* who share similar experiences and attitudes. On the other hand, they serve to embed the making of the *Historiae* in networks of scholars, officials, and seigneurs who, like Montaigne, exercise free and independent judgement in their lives and works, and rise above partisan politics of the kind peddled by Guise.

In general terms, the *consensio* of studies and dispositions lies in their shared background as humanistically trained *conseillers*, as cultured travellers to Italy, as loyal kingsmen.[139] But it lies more particularly in the fact that the author Montaigne is one 'whose noble liberty, harmful to no-one, has left everyone [by means of his book] with complete freedom to judge him and his morals'. The *Essais* offer a precedent for a book in de Thou's milieu that rises nobly above partisan religious politics—in a way that, in the event, de Thou's book was unable to do.

This becomes still clearer when we realize just how well the two passages in the *Vita* complement the obituary offered in the *Historiae*, which explicitly links the qualities of Montaigne's personal discourse to the publication of a text designed to witness to them in writing. The first passage concerns their meetings in Guyenne and ties Montaigne to de Thou's studies, but no reported speech is involved. The second passage puts a testimony to Montaigne's personal discourse—parallel to the *Essais* themselves—on the record. It shows the author Montaigne sharing de Thou's own disposition to liberty of judgement, and concerns the later meetings during 1588, when they were together at court at Paris, before following the King to Chartres and Rouen, and converging once more at the Estates General of Blois later in the year. In both passages it is important to understand that Montaigne is included as part of a group: in the first case of *parlementaires*, in the second case of *politiques*.

The first reference occurs in the context of de Thou's narrative of the delegation from the *Parlement* of Paris that, as required by the conference of Fleix, toured Guyenne to dispense justice in the early 1580s. The importance of this moment for de Thou's whole enterprise is apparent from the fact that he mentions it when he addresses Henri IV in his preface to the *Historiae*. In Guyenne, religious divisions

---

[139]   De Smet, 'Montaigne et Jacques-Auguste de Thou', 235–8.

had made the troubles more violent, and judgements were correspondingly partial, driven by favouritism or hate.[140]

In between sessions of the court, Jacques continued to pursue his studies, and to seek to frequent people who would be useful to his projected histories. He learned by applying his judgement to things which he remembered reading or hearing spread around, but which were thrown into doubt or recounted in a different way by others. He learned much in this respect from three seigneurs and officials of Bordeaux whose judgements, it is implied, were reliably impartial: Jacques Benoît de Lagebaston, Montaigne, Geoffroy Malvyn de Cessac.

Here, Montaigne is far from being the stand-alone philosophical example he is in Gournay's account; he is one of a group with shared values, associated with the *Parlement*. De Thou learned much from Montaigne, a man of free spirit, alien to factions ('ingenii liberi homine, et a partibus alieno'), who was fulfilling the extremely honourable function of mayor of Bordeaux, and who had profound knowledge of 'our affairs', especially of those of Guyenne.[141] The first half of this sentence draws upon Montaigne's character and credentials as described in *Essais* III 10 (which deals with the mayoralty), while the second half provides specific authority for the passages on Guyenne in the *Historiae*.

The second passage is more important, as it reports Montaigne's conversation on the subject of his attempts to mediate between Navarre and Guise, and aligns him and his work still more explicitly with de Thou and his work. In the *Historiae*, de Thou deals with the public speeches and politics at Blois—including a bold public intervention by his friend Sainte-Marthe—and the background of military conflict in the nation at large.[142]

In the *Vita*, he deals with the private backdrop, and it is there we find Montaigne. The context is the growing power of Guise in pursuing his war against Navarre and the heretics, and the weakening authority of the King. Montaigne is now given much more status, as he is one of a series of four actors in high political events whose discourse with de Thou during the Estates General at Blois is reported verbatim. This is Montaigne *politicus Aquitanicus*.[143] However, the other three are of much higher rank in terms both of *noblesse* and of offices held. Montaigne is there as a private gentleman without office whose enhanced status, whose presence in this exalted company, implicitly derives from his authorship of a noble book that later (in relation to the date of the events described) became famous.

---

[140] Thou, *Vita*, ed. Teissier-Ensminger, 398, 400, 408; Thou, *Historiarum sui temporis libri CXXXVIII*, vol. 1, 'Auctoris præfatio ad Henricum IV', 17.

[141] For this and the previous paragraph see Thou, *Vita*, ed. Teissier-Ensminger, 414, 416. On this passage and its narrative context see the important discussion in De Smet, 'Montaigne et Jacques-Auguste de Thou', 226–30, which notes that the phrase quoted above in parenthesis appeared in the autograph manuscript version (BnF, MS Latin 5979) as an addition between the lines (226–7n.9). On the European, humanistic provenance of the notion of the man who is alien to faction or to controversy, see José María Pérez Fernández, 'Andrés Laguna: translation and the early modern idea of Europe', *Translation & Literature*, 21 (2012), 299–318, 309.

[142] Thou, *Historiarum sui temporis libri CXXXVIII*, vol. 4, 623–47.

[143] Thou, *Vita*, ed. Teissier-Ensminger, 656, 658, 660, 662; Desan, 'Montaigne: *Politicus Aquitanicus*', *passim*.

On his way to Blois, de Thou called in at the château of his brother-in-law Philippe Hurault de Cheverny, who is lauded in Sainte-Marthe's *Elogia* for having held the highest office available to a *noble de robe*—Chancellor of France. Having just been sent into retirement by Henri III, Cheverny prophetically foresees that the King, far from continuing to shrink before the steadily augmenting power of Guise, would strike at him with desperate courage.

Later in his account of Blois, de Thou cites a section of a public discourse given by Cheverny's cousin, Renaud de Beaune, Archbishop of Bourges, on the need to reform expenditure on luxuries such as coaches. The section, which praised de Thou's mother for her moderation in this respect, was omitted from the version of the discourse that was printed in the public acts of the Estates General—hence its inclusion in the *Vita*. Finally, de Thou reports his conversations with Charles de Balzac, seigneur de Dunes, governor of Orléans, who shared with de Thou his plans for securing the city against the attacks of Guise and the Leaguers, and making it a haven for good Frenchmen, servants of the King, and good Catholics.[144]

In the midst of these discourses by major actors in events—a Chancellor, an Archbishop, and a grand *noble d'épée* and governor—de Thou reports the remarks of Montaigne.[145] Most literary historians approach the passage without reference to its narrative context, and with a view to establishing the biographical facts—exactly when, and in what circumstances, Montaigne carried out the private intermediary function to which de Thou alludes. No consensus has been reached.[146]

But it is more fruitful to read it in the apologetic context of the *Vita* itself. As we have heard, everything in that autobiographical text is ultimately designed to contextualize, legitimize, and justify the *Historiae*. The anecdote about Montaigne at Blois performs this function on several different levels. On one level, as we have already seen, it takes its place in a series of discourses by noble individuals who both share a *politique* understanding of the causes and likely outcomes of events, and who speak and act freely to defeat the *factiosi* and shore up the authority of the King.

On another level, de Thou is claiming Montaigne the author as a reliable source for part of his account towards the beginning of *Historiae* lib. 81 (covering 1585) of the origins of the wars of the League in the rebellious machinations of Guise. While Anjou was alive, Guise had courted Navarre as a rival claimant to the throne. But in encouraging these approaches, Navarre had duped Guise, as became apparent when he fled the court and declared himself protestant. Guise dissimulated his vengeful reaction to this until Anjou died (1584), when he became Navarre's open enemy. In the *Vita*, de Thou reports that Montaigne gathered this intelligence

---

[144] Thou, *Vita*, ed. Teissier-Ensminger, 656, 662, 664, 666, 668, for this and the previous paragraph.

[145] Thou, *Vita*, ed. Teissier-Ensminger, 658, 660. Once again, the first manuscript draft varies from the 1733 printed text in a few particulars. See D. Maskell, 'Montaigne médiateur entre Navarre et Guise', *Bibliothèque d'Humanisme et Renaissance*, 41 (1979), 541–53, 548, and n.1; De Smet, 'Montaigne et Jacques-Auguste de Thou', 234.

[146] Maskell, 'Montaigne médiateur entre Navarre et Guise', follows on from Frame's discussions, but proposes no definitive solution.

when he and Guise were at court at the same time, and when he was serving as an intermediary between Guise and Navarre—possibly in the spring of 1586.[147]

But de Thou is also aligning the ethos and discourse of the author of the *Essais* in the private political sphere with his own. The key liberty he takes in his historical work is freely to praise and blame the morals of protagonists in the civil wars, regardless of their party and status. This is exactly what he now reports the author of the *Essais* as doing in a private conversation at Blois in late 1588, just before the catastrophe that was about to unfold.

Immediately before the meeting with the Gascon we gather that de Thou, without any official charge, has been frequenting the Bourbon brothers to assist them in their affairs. He used his familiarity with Anne d'Este, mother of both the Guises and the Leaguer Nemours, to attempt a private mediation between the Bourbons and the Guises. At this point in the narrative, his mind naturally turns to a gentleman who was very experienced in such private mediations: Montaigne. After a brief passage in which the Gascon offers to facilitate de Thou's succession to and tenure of the ambassadorship of Venice (which never materialized), we get to Montaigne's discourse on the causes of the troubles ('de caussis horum motuum'), and his account of the falling-out of Guise and Navarre.[148]

Montaigne goes on to reveal that in both cases religion was no more than a pretext for the hostilities that followed: Navarre would have returned to the Catholic fold but for fear of losing his supporters; Guise, if he could have risked it, would not have been averse to following the Lutheran Confession of Augsburg. Meanwhile, back in the present at Blois, Guise was openly soliciting all and sundry to his faction, by selling honours and dignities. He duly approached de Thou. But de Thou, who had no sympathy for any faction ('a factione omni alienus'), did not welcome the approach, and frankly indicated why—he saw few good citizens in Guise's entourage, while the Duke constantly pursued altercations with the King. He was not prepared to pay the price of entering relations with such people in order to pursue a brilliant career under Guise's wing.[149]

In this passage, then, a vignette of the author of the *Essais* takes its place in a series of vignettes of *politique* noblemen. The series in turn provides the setting for a key moment in the self-portrait of the author of the *Historiae*: his bold statement of independence from 'faction'—that is, from Guise. As a minor, unofficial intermediary, Montaigne is out of his depth in the company of a Chancellor, an Archbishop, a Governor; he is there as the famous noble author of brilliant

---

[147] In the spring of 1586, there was a rumour of a potential rapprochement between Guise and Navarre, and Guise and Montaigne could have been together at court. See Maskell, 'Montaigne médiateur entre Navarre et Guise', 549–52. Maskell prefers 1578 on the grounds that the historical documentation of the rumours of the potential rapprochement in 1586 reveals them to be without foundation. But the key point here is the strong relationship between what Montaigne is reported as saying in the *Vita*, and the relevant passage in the *Historiae* on the causes of the wars of the League. See Thou, *Historiarum sui temporis libri CXXXVIII*, vol. 4, 255.

[148] Thou, *Vita*, ed. Teissier-Ensminger, 658, 660. On these passages, and on the variants between manuscript and printed versions, see De Smet, 'Montaigne et Jacques-Auguste de Thou', 234 and nn.52–3.

[149] Thou, *Vita*, ed. Teissier-Ensminger, 660, 662.

discourses that offer a thesaurus of frank and balanced judgements to the *robins* in the 1610s.

It is the author of that book (the *Essais*) who tells the truth during the wars of the League and the ascendancy of Guise, and who provides frank moral support at a difficult moment both for de Thou and for *politique* supporters of the King in general. He speaks in de Thou's episode as the *vir libertatis ingenuae* that he evidently is in his book. He fortifies de Thou in not pursuing a brilliant career as a creature of a grand patron such as Guise. In short, we should read the episode as an account of the *Essais*' role as a truth-telling book in the *politiques*' moral conversation, in the form of the record of an event in the life of the historical person Michel de Montaigne, and not as a disinterested biographical anecdote.

Except that de Thou puts into the mouth of Montaigne a much more direct and candid assessment of the motives of two of the named *chefs* in the war than is to be found in the *Essais*. The assessment is suspiciously close to de Thou's own and has the effect of aligning the *Essais* with a *politique* point-of-view. For de Thou was the principal source of a new historiographical view of the religious wars, distinct from the martyrological and self-justificatory traditions of the opposing Protestant and Catholic parties. The conflicts were now to be seen as arising neither from the seditious and sacrilegious actions of the Protestant heretics nor from genuine Roman Catholic zeal, but from factious rivalries between the great noble houses of the day, and from the Guises' machinations in particular.[150]

This is where the generic and ethical differences between the two works must be reaffirmed. For the most part Montaigne does not in his book take the particular liberty of judgement that got de Thou's *Historiae* into trouble, least of all in the opening preface. He keeps within the limits set out in the royal injunctions (in the successive edicts of pacification) against reanimating controversial memories of the events of the wars. The *Essais* offer a vigorous general critique of the use of religious pretexts in the civil wars, and of the situation of the individual who is caught in the middle, neither Guelf nor Ghibelline. But they do not name names and events in the explicit way de Thou's Montaigne does at Blois.

Of course, this does not mean they do not invite—on the part of reader-writers of the *Essais*—explicit applications to current events. Like Florimond de Raemond in his annotations, de Thou's account of the conversation at Blois effectively applies Montaigne's published moral *sentences* and *traits* to specific figures and junctures in the civil wars. At the same time, the larger passage embeds the author, and by extension the *Essais* themselves, in a network of noble *politiques* who were alien to factions, and to war-mongering counsels, and who were working in various ways in the background and foreground at Blois to further the cause of peace and secure the authority of the King.

De Thou even associates Montaigne with the independent republican politics of Venice.[151] He is of the party of the King, and has followed the court out of Paris;

---

[150] Benedict, 'Shaping the memory', 119–20.

[151] Renaud de Beaune, the archbishop of Bourges, is 'ab omni factione et consiliis turbulentis alienus', and Charles de Balzac is 'regiis partibus addictum et a factione omni semper alienum'. See

like de Thou, he speaks with freedom of judgement, but without hate and partiality, of the leaders and followers of other parties. The author of the *Essais* is, from de
Thou's retrospective viewpoint of the 1610s, a *politique* in his private discourse, if
not in his public life and action.[152]

2.1.7 PASQUIER'S *ESSAIS*

In the other account we have of Montaigne's conversation with a *robin* at Blois, it
is much easier to see that he is being received in retrospect as the author of a
free-talking, free-judging book:[153] the moment Pasquier sees him in the courtyard
at Blois, and they take a walk together, he reproves Montaigne for having 'forgotten' to communicate his work to his friends for corrections before publication—as
de Thou later did. He then leads Montaigne to his chamber, where he shows him
a manually corrected copy of what was most probably an early Bordeaux edition of
the *Essais* (1580 or 1582), published by Simon Millanges, or (less likely, in my
view) the recently published 1588 Paris edition of Abel L'Angelier.[154] Like his

---

Thou, *Vita*, ed. Teissier-Ensminger, 662, 670. On de Thou, Montaigne, La Boétie and Venice see De
Smet, 'Montaigne et Jacques-Auguste de Thou', 237–8.

[152] For de Thou's retrospective application of this term to those who embraced the religion of the
forefathers and kept away from disturbances and factions, especially from that of the Lorraines, see De
Smet, *Thuanus*, 240–1.

[153] Pasquier, *Les lettres*, vol. 2, sigs. 2A5r–2B1r/Millet 143–9. There is also an edited and annotated
text of the letter in Magnien, 'Étienne Pasquier "familier" de Montaigne?', 309–13.

[154] Michel de Montaigne, *Essais*, 2 vols. (Bordeaux: Simon Millanges, 1580) (henceforward abbreviated as 'Bordeaux 1580'); Michel de Montaigne, *Essais* (Bordeaux: Simon Millanges, 1582); Paris
1588. It is impossible to be certain which edition Pasquier showed Montaigne. As a literary artefact
that has been polished for posthumous publication over a decade after the events it purports to
describe, the letter should not be read as a scrupulously factual account. Catherine Magnien states it
to be a copy of Paris 1588 and does not consider the alternative possibility. It is true that by the time
Pasquier came to compose the letter for publication he was referencing a copy of Paris 1588 (he
describes, for example, II 12 as a chapter of about eighty folios). But was this necessarily the copy he
showed Montaigne at Blois in late 1588? He did in theory have time to obtain a copy of L'Angelier's
edition before he left Paris around 12 October for the official opening of the assembly at Blois on 16
October 1588, as we know (a) that the 1588 edition was published some time after mid-June 1588
(the *privilège* is dated 4.6.88 and Montaigne's preface 12.6.88), and (b) that Pasquier frequented
L'Angelier's *boutique* and knew the bookseller well. But there was a political crisis on and few copies
were in circulation (Balsamo and Simonin, *Abel L'Angelier & Françoise de Louvain (1574–1620)*, 85).
Would he have had time to mark it up in detail in these circumstances? There is clear evidence elsewhere that he had been studying the 1580/82 text in the period before 1586, when he published the
first edition of his *Lettres*. At least two of these 1586 letters imitate chapters in the 1580/82 *Essais*,
though neither acknowledges the source (letter III 3 imitates *Essais* II 12 and letter X 1, *Essais* I 30).
Another letter (II 12) shows that he had already noted and planned to re-use (in his *Recherches*) at least
one Gasconism (as Pasquier believed it to be) from the 1580/82 *Essais* (see Magnien, 'Étienne Pasquier
"familier" de Montaigne?', 303–5 and 304n.144). Is it not therefore more likely that the copy he
showed Montaigne was the one in which he had been making notes for a number of years? Furthermore,
all of the words and locutions to which Pasquier says he drew Montaigne's attention at Blois were
present in the 1580/82 editions and none appeared for the first time in Paris 1588 (see Magnien,
'Étienne Pasquier "familier" de Montaigne?', 310–11 nn.9–15). Indeed, in the letter as a whole, most
of the references Pasquier makes are to passages that appeared for the first time in 1580 (only five are
to passages that appeared for the first time in 1588). Pasquier appears, furthermore, to be talking at
the Blois interview about the first publication of the *Essais*, in 1580, for he remarks to Montaigne that

fellow *parlementaire* Antoine Séguier in the same period, he had certainly been reading an early edition and writing out adapted *sentences* from the text for re-use.[155] Whichever edition was in his hands at Blois, it is clear from the letter as a whole that Pasquier at some point compared in detail his copies of both the editions he owned and used (1580/82, 1588) and a copy of Paris 1595, and that his initially quite hostile use of Montaigne's text modulated into a more open and generous interaction with the expanded work.

The account appeared in a letter at the beginning of book XVIII of the second edition of Pasquier's *Lettres*, published in 1619. To the ten books of letters published in 1586, which covered the *premiers troubles* (especially books IV and V, in letters addressed to the seigneurs Fonssomme and d'Hardivilliers), this edition added all the letters Pasquier had written, as he put it in a 1594 letter to L'Angelier, 'since the last troubles [*derniers troubles*]'—that is, since about 1585 and the beginnings of the wars of the League.[156] The title page advertised them as offering 'excellent subjects and discourses on French state affairs, including the civil wars' ('belles matieres et discours sur les affaires d'Estat de France, et touchant les guerres civiles'). Books XI through XIV cover the troubles from 1585 to 1593, while book XV has letters dated both 1594 and 1595. In book XVI Pasquier describes the return of peace and the retaking of Paris (1594).

So although the letter about Montaigne is not dated, the reader of the volume in which it appeared would have discerned a rough chronological sequence that places it after *c.*1605. Book XVI ends with a letter to Sainte-Marthe thanking him for a gift copy, sent via his son, of the 1598 *Elogia* of men with reputations

---

he neglected to communicate his work to friends before publishing it. The result was that no one could help but notice the uncorrected Gasconisms, which Pasquier proceeds to point out using, I suggest, a copy of that first publication, the 1580 Millanges edition (Pasquier, *Les lettres*, vol. 2, sig. 2A6v/Millet 145–6). The passage in which he states that the corrections were not incorporated is quite difficult to interpret: 'However, not only did he not do it [correct the Gasconisms], but also, as it fell out that he was overtaken by death, his adopted daughter had it reprinted exactly as it was; and told us in her preliminary epistle that Madame de Montaigne had sent it to her in the exact form in which he intended to republish it' (Pasquier, *Les lettres*, vol. 2, sig. 2A6v–7r/Millet 146). The most natural interpretation of this is that Pasquier knew he had suggested corrections too late for the Paris 1588 edition (whether or not he first made them in a copy of Paris 1588 or, as I believe, in a copy of Bordeaux 1580 or 1582), that the next authorial edition (Paris 1595) reprinted the text without these corrections, and that this was not because Montaigne simply did not manage to effect them before his death or because his executors did not have his last wishes (as he had left his wife with a copy in which his intentions for a new edition were clear). The force of the grammatical construction used is: 'not only did he neglect to do it, he clearly had no intention of doing it'. The important points are (a) that Pasquier knew, used, and compared in detail copies of Bordeaux 1580 (or possibly Bordeaux 1582) and Paris 1588; and (b) that he noted that the corrections he offered Montaigne in person were not corrected in 1595, which he appears to have seen (he knows what Gournay says about the *copie* in the preface) but which he did not use for citations.

[155] Séguier appears to have read his copy of Bordeaux 1580, and copied extracts (adapted) into his notebooks in 1588–9. Houllemare dates Séguier's reading notes to 1588 and transcribes an inscription as follows from the end of the notes themselves: 'cadoni 1589 flagrantae aestu rer[um] pub[licarum] et privat[arum]' (the expansions are mine). Though I am unable to translate 'cadoni' and have not consulted the manuscript (Houllemare's work came to my attention too late) the inscription clearly points to the raging commotion of private and public events in 1589 as the context of Séguier's reading. See Houllemare, *Politiques de la parole*, 264, 607. My thanks to Tom Hamilton.

[156] Pasquier, *Lettres familières*, 244 (letter XV 10).

for 'bonnes lettres' in France. Pasquier reciprocates with a copy of his own 'Congratulation sur la paix generale, faicte au mois de mars 1598', presented to Henri IV in 1599.[157]

Book XVII then consists of four further letters to Sainte-Marthe that recount the events leading up to the deaths of the *robin* Barnabé Brisson in 1592 and of Marshal Biron in July 1602. These are more like a historical *registre* than familiar letters. The letter about Montaigne is paired at the beginning of book XVIII with another that mentions a work by Florimond de Raemond published by L'Angelier in 1605. In the former letter, Pasquier is responding to a request from his friend and fellow *robin* Claude Pellejay for his judgement of the *Essais* of Montaigne, a common friend of both when alive.[158] The latter letter—also to Pellejay—immediately follows.[159] Therein, Pasquier places Montaigne in the context of a group of Gascon authors, and offers his judgement of another of these, Blaise de Monluc. Until 1604, Pellejay was 'conseiller du Roy et Maistre en sa chambre des Comptes de Paris' and, like his friend Sainte-Marthe (both were from Poitiers), frequented the milieu of the des Roches.[160]

Pasquier's letter self-consciously captures a moment in the early seventeenth century when the *robins* were collectively forming their judgement of Montaigne and the *Essais*, and beginning—after a period of relative neglect—to illustrate and honour his memory. In this respect, it is complementary to the *elogia* of his friend Sainte-Marthe and of de Thou.

In all three cases, the description and praise of Montaigne's life and work is situated amidst histories of the civil wars—especially the wars of the League from 1585—and amidst series of portraits of protagonists and victims in those wars. Pasquier is, furthermore, equally clear that this is a 'noble book'. The story extends in Pasquier's account to the memorable history of the 'Damoiselle de Jars' (Gournay), who he specifies belonged to several grand noble families of Paris, and whose personal honour was enriched by the reading of good books, especially the essays of the seigneur of Montaigne.[161]

As an *avocat*, Pasquier describes how the free-ranging discourses of this *gentilhomme* and *noble d'épée* sound to 'us', office-holders and lawyers. The crucial link he makes is the one also made by Sainte-Marthe and de Thou. The *liberté* Montaigne gives himself to jump from one *propos* to another, as his *esprit* took him, and to use unaccustomed words, derives from 'a personal liberty that he was born with' ('une liberté particulière qui estoit née avec luy'). That is to say, it derives from his particular nature as a well-born gentleman, a 'bold character' ('personnage hardy'), who takes pleasure in displeasing, even mocking 'us'—namely, scholarly *robins* such as Pasquier and Pellejay. Pasquier returns again and again to the question of whether this *liberté particulière* of the noble author degenerated at points into

---

[157] Pasquier, *Les lettres*, vol. 2, sigs. Q7r–8r.
[158] I am heavily indebted in what follows to Magnien, 'Étienne Pasquier "familier" de Montaigne?', a brilliant study.
[159] Pasquier, *Les lettres*, vol. 2, sigs. 2B1r–7r.
[160] Magnien, 'Étienne Pasquier "familier" de Montaigne?', 278.
[161] Pasquier, *Les lettres*, vol. 2, sigs. 2A8v–2B1r/Millet 148.

licence, especially when later in life, in his third book, he digressed too much into self-apology.[162]

It is difficult not to hear gently ironic retorts throughout Pasquier's letter. When this cocksure gentleman undertook to defend Sebond in the *Apologie*, the least part concerned Sebond, while the rest concerned 'our Montaigne', who does not neglect to mention his honours. These mentions distance him as far as possible from a mere *chiquaneur* or *practicien*—that is, jobbing lawyer—as his profession was completely different: that of a *noble d'épée*. Yet Pasquier points out that he nevertheless uses expressions associated with legal practice, such as 'Item' (in I 49), in order to seek *gloire* from having affronted 'us'. Pasquier is only too aware that the author of this book is emphasizing his nature as a well-born gentlemen, in order to distance *avocats* such as himself, at every turn. He warns Pellejay not to be seduced by Montaigne's 'Courtizanie'.[163]

In the copy shown to Montaigne at Blois, Pasquier's corrections consisted of annotations on a whole series of words and locutions that he considered to be too redolent of Gascon parlance. Here, Pasquier is fulfilling his self-granted office as public censor of the language, institutions, and history of Gallican France. The office enfranchises him with liberties of judgement appropriate to a *politique* historian who remonstrates with and counsels the King in discourses such as the 'Congratulation'.

Had Montaigne followed the normal practice and showed his work to friends before publication, Pasquier felt, these locutionary errors would never have made it into print. He roots this normal practice in classical antiquity by referring to Asinius Pollio's role as corrector of the Paduan provincialisms of Livy's Latin histories. It was also normal practice in contemporary terms, as we have already seen in the later case of de Thou (2.1.5). The whole process of creating, printing, publishing, revising, and reprinting works allowed for corrections at all stages; it was even possible for a small print-run to be destined solely for 'friends' charged with making such corrections, before publication per se. Michel Simonin has described this general type of edition as 'l'édition à l'essai'.[164]

Pasquier clearly considered that a work with such a tentative title, addressed to friends and family, was positively inviting correction. At Blois in 1588, like Gournay in the same year, he was implicitly offering himself as an editor and corrector of the book for the L'Angelier editions to follow. The specific nature of the corrections—to make the book less redolent of Gascon speech ('manieres de parler de Gascogne') and more full of elegant and bold touches of French style ('beaux traits François et hardis')—was very much in tune with his associate L'Angelier's editorial campaign to defend and illustrate the French language.[165]

Pasquier had clearly expected that this ex-*conseiller* and ex-mayor, editor of La Boétie, would have handed his work over to his friends amongst the scholarly

[162] Pasquier, *Les lettres*, vol. 2, sigs. 2A5v–6r/Millet 144–5.
[163] Pasquier, *Les lettres*, vol. 2, sigs. 2A5v–6r/Millet 144–5.
[164] Simonin, *L'encre & la lumière*, 736.
[165] Pasquier, *Les lettres*, vol. 2, sig. 2A7r/Millet 146; Balsamo and Simonin, *Abel L'Angelier & Françoise de Louvain (1574–1620)*, 101.

parlementaires. He had been surprised at the apparently uncorrected state of 1580 and was piqued at the subsequent refusal to incorporate his own corrections in the still bolder and freer edition of 1595. Indeed, the letter also indicates that Pasquier might even have proposed other, still more drastic corrections to the expanded text of 1588, before he surrendered with some lingering reluctance to its pleasurable liberties:

> if someone had deleted all the passages he devoted to speaking of himself, his family, his work, his *œuvre* would have been shortened by a good quarter, especially in his third book, which seems to be a history of his morals and actions—which I attribute somewhat to the liberty of his old age, when he composed it.[166]

Pasquier would have wished a degree of 'abridgement' (*retranchement*)—he did not know what exactly—in chapters such as III 5 and especially III 11, in which Montaigne seemed to have exchanged his *liberté* for an extraordinary *licence*.[167]

Nevertheless, the letter does ultimately become an *éloge*, complete with an account of Montaigne's religious death—lest there should be any doubts about his good faith as a Roman Catholic. Half way through the letter, Pasquier takes off his disguise (like Montaigne's captor in III 12) as a professed enemy of the author, and reveals himself as a close friend who considers the *Essais*—like Gournay—to be 'Chefs d'oeuvre'.

Just as Gournay recommends, he always has the book to hand as a touchstone of practical philosophy—another Seneca 'in our language'. For, playing Montaigne's advocate now, he opposes all those Gasconisms with an infinity of bold French elegancies ('beaux traits François et hardis') or *pointes* to be found in the *Essais*. And, he says, 'I cannot still be offended, when he gives himself free rein to talk of himself.' There follows a list of classical-style moral *sentences* or aphorisms from the *Essais* similar to those copied out and adapted by Séguier (in the latter case, entirely from the 1580 text). In the end, Pasquier's response is remarkably in tune with that of the captors who, in the III 12 anecdotes, seize the author, then read the qualities in their captive's face and ultimately find themselves persuaded to release him, and to reveal themselves to him.[168]

But this is less of a personal encounter between Pasquier and Montaigne than it appears to be; it is shaped by a commercial and political geography of publication. On behalf of the *robin* network, centred on Paris, Pasquier is welcoming and por-traying a whole group of authors from the provinces in a manner that is consonant both with Sainte-Marthe's project and with his own historiographical and political enterprise. The group includes both militant and moderate Catholics and a Huguenot. At the beginning of the second letter to Pellejay, Pasquier expresses amazement that noble French authors such as the Seigneurs Monluc, Montaigne, Raemond, and Du Bartas could have emerged together from a provincial back-water like Gascony to excel in, respectively, the narration of heroic deeds and in

[166] Pasquier, *Les lettres*, vol. 2, sig. 2A7r/Millet 146.
[167] Pasquier, *Les lettres*, vol. 2, sig. 2A8r/Millet 147–8.
[168] For this and the previous paragraph see Pasquier, *Les lettres*, vol. 2, sig. 2A7r–v/Millet 146; Houllemare, *Politiques de la parole*, 595–607. See 1.6.11 for the III 12 anecdotes.

military discipline, the development of an infinity of beautiful and rich discourses, the historiography of religious reform, and the exaltation of the works of God.[169]

This remark, and the pair of letters as a whole, is shaped by the commercial relationship between two publisher-booksellers in different locations: Simon Millanges in Bordeaux and Abel L'Angelier in Paris. Their names have recurred throughout this chapter. Both Millanges and L'Angelier published works by all four of these authors, and specific works by three of them passed from one to the other—from an edition in Bordeaux to an edition in Paris.

The *Essais* went from a 1580 Millanges edition to 1588, then to 1595 L'Angelier editions; Raemond's edition of Jean de Sponde's response to Bèze went from a 1595 Millanges edition to L'Angelier editions in 1595–6; and the *Commentaires* (edited by Raemond) from a 1592 Millanges edition to a 1594 L'Angelier edition (shared with many other publishers).[170] When, at the end of the second letter, Pasquier includes an epitaph in Latin on Monluc, he is making a contribution to the *Tumulus* of epitaphs included by the editor Raemond in both the Millanges and L'Angelier editions.[171]

Pasquier's letter on the *Essais* is in many respects broadly complementary to Gournay's 1595 preface, which first appeared in L'Angelier's 1595 edition. It outlines *censures* similar to the ones she enumerates, and then rejects them. On one level, Pasquier is participating in the publicity surrounding the transfer of these noble Gascon authors from a provincial to a national stage, and claiming them for the *politique* French nation that had first gathered precariously around the reconverted Catholic Henri IV in the early 1590s. His letters are self-consciously fashioned as epitexts in tune with the paratexts in the editions he was using. What he does with his copies is shaped, to a greater or lesser extent, by the stories the volumes have been made to tell by their authors and editors/correctors: Marie de Gournay and Florimond de Raemond.

However, for Pasquier himself, the activity of judging these authors involves not just reading and receiving their texts. As a reader-writer, he authors his own copies of these works; he marks them with corrections; he considers larger *retranchements*; he marks up key 'sentences' that might inform writing and behaviour on his and others' parts; he composes new epitexts that rival and complement the official paratexts.

In the case of Monluc, however, this process is more straightforward, less conflicted. The moral and intellectual story told by the book—by Monluc and by his editors and correctors—is clearer, more conventional, and more easily assimilable to Pasquier's semi-official epistolary and historiographical project. There is no sign of the controversy surrounding Monluc's actions as a militant, royalist Catholic. In the hands of the editor and corrector Raemond, Monluc is an exemplary, office-holding *noble d'épée* who was loyal to the French monarchy and who

---

[169] Pasquier, *Les lettres*, vol. 2, sig. 2B1r.

[170] USTC 3676; USTC 3054; USTC 15026; USTC 2763; USTC 5209.

[171] Pasquier, *Les lettres*, vol. 2, sig. 2B7r. The *Tumulus* was less complete in the 1595 L'Angelier edition. See Balsamo and Simonin, *Abel L'Angelier & Françoise de Louvain (1574–1620)*, 259.

excelled in both arms and soldier-like letters (registering his actions in writing each night).[172]

In Pasquier's eyes, Monluc's *liberté* as a noble Gascon soldier justified—without any ambivalence—the Gasconisms in his style.[173] This perhaps suggests that his objections to the Gasconisms in Montaigne's style were due to the fact that the *Essais* purported to excel not in the narration of heroic deeds, but in the development of beautiful and rich discourses. By 1619, literary circles in Paris were becoming less and less tolerant of regionalisms, and more and more in favour of a classicizing style.

The title page of the Millanges 1592 edition of the *Commentaires* promises 'diverse instructions, which should not be unknown to those who aim to achieve honour through arms, and to conduct all acts of war wisely' ('diverses instructions, qui ne doivent estre ignorées de ceux, qui veulent parvenir par les armes à quelqu'honneur, et sagement conduire tous exploits de guerre'). Following Monluc himself, and Raemond in the epistle to the Gascon nobility, Pasquier gives these instructions the authority of the classical commentaries by the greatest Roman captain, Caesar. Just as the great princes described by Xenophon and others were 'patrons and models for becoming a Prince' ('patrons et exemplaires de l'accomplissement d'un Prince'), so Monluc was the same for the profession of arms.

Using the commonplace method, Pasquier writes out twenty-nine extracts or 'good military instructions' ('belles instructions militaires') from the first book of the *Commentaires*, so as to entice the reader to continue the same process for the rest of the volume.[174] While the selection of some of these extracts is guided by the printed marginalia in the Millanges edition, the majority are selections made by Pasquier himself. The text of these extracts is edited and redacted by Pasquier (like Séguier's extracts from Montaigne), and the printed marginalia that accompany them are largely new.

He follows a similar procedure in the preceding letter, copying out eighteen *sentences* of Montaigne, which, in line with Gournay's promotion of her author, he declares to be as beautiful as any in antiquity.[175] To reduce the *Essais* to *sentences* may now seem reductive, but in the terms of the day this is high praise indeed. Paquier is equating Montaigne with a wise man of antiquity who gains a reputation for moral and political *sententiae*.[176]

But they are not accompanied by printed marginalia, and they do not combine as axioms for the formation of the perfect captain, for Montaigne's role is different in kind from those of Monluc, Raemond, and Du Bartas. They make contributions on particular, formative subject matters—military discipline, religious history,

---

[172] Barbara Sher Tinsley, *History and polemics in the French Reformation: Florimond de Raemond, defender of the Church* (Cranbury, NJ, London and Mississuaga, Ontario: Associated University Presses, 1992), 50–2.

[173] Pasquier, *Les lettres*, vol. 2, sig. 2B2r.

[174] Pasquier, *Les lettres*, vol. 2, sigs. 2B2r–v, 2B3r–B6v, for this and the previous paragraph.

[175] Pasquier, *Les lettres*, vol. 2, sig. 2A8r/Millet 147.

[176] See the remarks by Thomas Hobbes cited in the 'General Preface' to this study.

religious devotion. Montaigne shows *how* to invent and judge discourse on all topics in a new, compellingly free way that derives from his particular nature, not from his profession.

Pasquier writes out a selection from this abundance of moral *sentences* on everything from *amour* to judicial torture, and says that, were he to continue, he would end up making a book, not a letter ('faire un Livre, et non une lettre'). But in this 'meadow cultivated in pell-mell fashion, without art' ('prairie diversifiée pesle-mesle et sans art') one can also find oneself nodding off to sleep, or wandering into licentious territory, especially when it comes to the third book and chapters such as III 5 and III 11. Most of the *sentences* Pasquier extracts are from the first two books, and a majority of those taken from the third book are from III 2.[177]

Pasquier's letter is very important for the argument of this study because it clearly shows him hesitating, in his reading and writing of the *Essais*, between his own *personae* as a free, private literate who would appreciate and follow Montaigne's abundant *liberté*, and as a professional lawyer-historian and semi-professional corrector who would reduce the book to a more appropriate form for publication in L'Angelier's *boutique*, alongside other works of French literature.

The letter could certainly seem ambivalent in the period itself. The Jesuit polemicist François Garasse repeatedly felt the need to defend Montaigne against Pasquier, such as when he attacked the latter's *Recherches* in print in 1622.[178] For Garasse, it was Pasquier who was the *glorieux* and the *libertin*, because he had censured the Roman Catholic Church and the kings of France in print. It was Pasquier who had taken quite ludicrous liberties of judgement in addressing various grand personages while praising himself and his works. Against this *glorieux*, this *libertin*, Garasse re-asserts Montaigne's status in a significant, double-pronged manner.

Garasse says that Pasquier's apparent *éloge* is in fact an attack on Montaigne similar to his notorious attacks on Jesuit writers. As evidence, he cites the passage in which Pasquier declares he would expurgate a quarter of Montaigne's book. Garasse retorts that Pasquier will only become worthy of comparison with Montaigne when his thick volumes of letters and researches have been sold, sought after, distributed, and printed as many times as the *Essais*, and when his legal and historical observations have earned him the title of Roman citizen; the honour of a knight, a mayor, and a royal counsellor; and the other excellent qualities that witness to the genius, virtue, and merits of a Michel de Montaigne.[179]

In other words, Garasse metaphorically tears the book and the authorial *persona* from the hands of the *parlementaires* and the *politiques* and claims them for the ongoing rapprochement between the French monarchy and Catholic Church and the Society of Jesus. But he concurs with them in identifying the increasing commercial success of the book in the first two decades of the seventeenth century

---

[177] Pasquier, *Les lettres*, vol. 2, sig. 2A8r/Millet 147–8; Magnien, 'Étienne Pasquier "familier" de Montaigne?', 311–13.

[178] Garasse, *Les recherches des Recherches et autres œuvres de Me Estienne Pasquier*. The relevant passages are conveniently collected in Millet 197–200.

[179] Millet 200.

with the particular noble qualities of the gentleman author. Montaigne's novel authorial strategy had worked.

Even though the book becomes momentarily the site of controversy between a Jesuit and a *parlementaire*, the two parties are vying to praise it as 'one of ours'. And in Garasse's eyes, the intertwined publication and life histories of the book and its author, gave 'Montaigne' more independent authority, more right to liberty of judgement, than free literates such as Pasquier and de Thou who adopt the *personae* of more 'official' public intellectuals.

2.1.8 MONTAIGNE AS L'ESTOILE'S CONFESSOR

What kind of book would Pasquier have made out of the *sentences* he took from his vade mecum, the French Seneca? There is no specific evidence for this, but there is some in the case of his near contemporary and fellow *parlementaire* Pierre de L'Estoile—though L'Estoile does not avoid Montaigne's Gasconisms and does not extract and isolate morally and stylistically correct aphorisms in the way Pasquier does.

We heard in 2.1.1 that neither Montaigne nor the publication of the *Essais* got on the record of the *troubles* kept by L'Estoile until *c.*1606—which was around the time Pasquier, Sainte-Marthe, and de Thou were composing their *elogia* of the Gascon. L'Estoile does indeed make books incorporating *traits* from Montaigne, in the process giving the *Essais* the status of other classic books—by the likes of Plutarch, Tacitus, Polybius, Augustine, and Lipsius—that he uses as philosophical touchstones for the times.[180]

The books are his three-volume 'Tablettes', which are distinct from his earlier books of record, and which open with the entry for 2 July 1606.[181] Onto the inside cover and preliminary leaf of the first volume he at some point wrote a description of the form and purpose of the new type of records he had decided to keep (Illus. 2.1.8). He names them *registres-journaux* or *registres*, similar to those described by Montaigne in *Essais* I 34, but more similar still to the *Essais* themselves. Montaigne provides the moral authority for a private book that will testify to L'Estoile's *naturel* as someone who is marred by a vain curiosity and liberty—a vain curiosity and liberty upon which his life and health, as someone who is extremely free, nevertheless depends.

So L'Estoile takes us one step beyond Sainte-Marthe, de Thou, and Pasquier, whose *mentalité* as a *parlementaire* and a *politique* he broadly shares. L'Estoile not only sees in the *Essais* a book witnessing to the nature of a *vir libertatis ingenuae*; he makes an analogous book to witness to his own nature as the same. Like Pasquier,

---

[180] *Journal Henri IV*, vol. 2, 26–7, 499, 520, 526–7, 547, 563–4; vol. 3, 191–2.

[181] BnF, MSS Fr. 10300, 10301, 10302. In the printed edition they begin at *Journal Henri IV*, vol. 2, 193. See 2.5.3–5 for the place of these three volumes in L'Estoile's larger project. Where it has been possible to identify corresponding passages in the manuscripts, references will be given to these as well as to *Journal Henri IV*. In these cases, transcription is also from the manuscript, and not from the printed source.

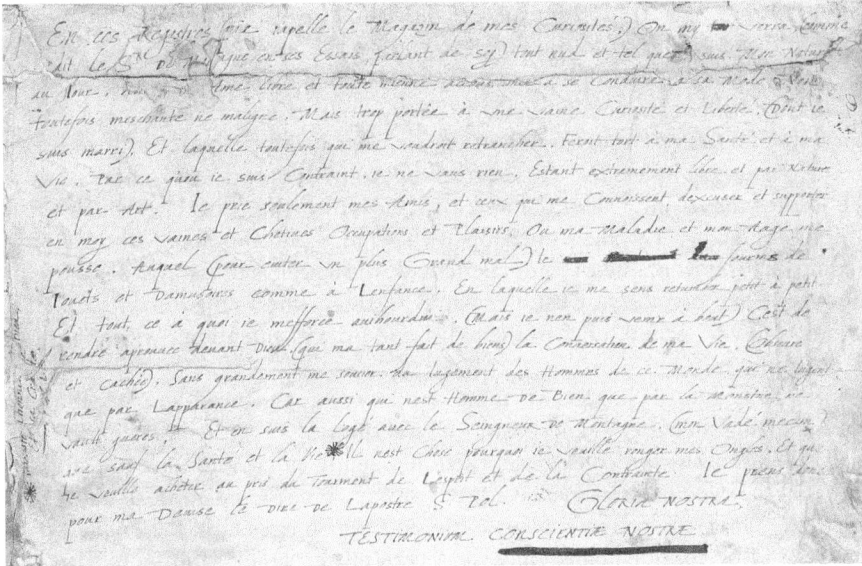

Illus. 2.1.8. Bibliothèque nationale de France, MS Fr. 10300, inside left-hand cover (Pierre de L'Estoile's 'Registre' from July 1606 to January 1609). Reproduced by permission of the Bibliothèque nationale de France, Paris.

however, in rewriting Montaigne he is inclined to correct him. In the first instance, he wrote out Montaigne's *trait* more or less verbatim: 'apart from health and life, there is nothing over which I am willing to chew my nails' ('sauf la Santé et la Vie, Il n'est Chose pourquoi je veuille ronger mes Ongles'). Going over the passage afterwards he inserts an asterisk and in the margin writes: '✻ to which I add the honour and fear of God' ('✻ jajoute l'honneur [de] Dieu Et sa Crainte') (Illus. 2.1.8). This is the first clue that L'Estoile will put Montaigne's truth-telling in a more explicitly confessional context.

In the pages of the *registres* that follow, L'Estoile occasionally picks up a *trait* from the *Essais* in order to adapt and apply it to particular protagonists in events as they unfold. So, in the entry for May 1608, L'Estoile is recounting the refusal of Mlle de Mercœur to marry M. de Vendôme. The young lady tells a *demoiselle* friend of L'Estoile's that she is determined to retire to a Franciscan convent rather than consent to the marriage. L'Estoile assimilates and adapts a Montaignean *trait* as his own opinion concerning the difficulty of keeping chaste (for women), before explicitly quoting his source:

> Also for my part I hold that no attaining so bristles with difficulties as does this abstaining, principally for /[continues in margin]/ the young ladies and gentlewomen of the court. In this, I am following the opinion of Montaigne, who says in his Essays, that he finds it easier to keep on a suit of armour all his life than to keep a maidenhead.[182]

---

[182] Bnf MS Fr. 10300, fol. 190v/*Journal Henri IV*, vol. 2, 339 (direct quotations from Montaigne in italics): 'Encores que pour mon Regard je tienne *qu'il n'y à point de faire plus Espineux quest ce non*

Similarly, writing his *registre* for July 1609, L'Estoile extracts a *trait* from the beginning of III 12—'Our society has been prepared to appreciate nothing but ostentation: nowadays you can fill men up with nothing but wind and then bounce them about like balloons'—and applies it to the political hot air generated across two days about a putative royal mobilization of troops for war against Spain and then about the king's displeasure at the retreat from court of the prince of Condé. Again, he absorbs the second half of the *trait* into his own writing, then cites the first half from Montaigne. The men filled up with wind, bouncing about like balloons (compared unfavourably by Montaigne with the simple and natural discourse of Socrates) then become in L'Estoile's hands all those who vainly discourse of state affairs, and who would judge of the kings' and princes' intentions, with respect to peace and war.[183]

The procedure is similar when he applies a Montaignean *trait* to himself. Summarizing the miseries and misfortunes of the year 1609, half praying to God, half talking to his own conscience, L'Estoile silently enters into dialogue with his *vade mecum* about his tendency secretly to save money and to lie about it. He turns the statement into an explicit confession, which it is not in the *Essais*: 'I have always laid by considerable savings for a man of my station (and more than was thought), having only ever spoken of my money to lie, I confess it'. Only in the next sentence does he reveal that 'le S^R de Montagne' calls this 'a ridiculous and shameful prudence' ('une ridicule et honteuse Prudence'), a *prudence* which L'Estoile nevertheless defiantly says has served him well. Having conversed in the course of his prayer with Montaigne he then moves on to Augustine.[184] He is using both authors as confessors.

It is not, however, until L'Estoile's entries for the summer of 1610, in the period after the assassination of Henri IV (14 May 1610), that we get a clear insight into the circumstances in which Montaigne is facilitating this ongoing confession of an *homme extrêmement libre*. After the defeat of the Catholic League, orthodox Roman Catholicism was fighting back within the establishment in France. The Edict of Rouens in September 1603 outlined the terms on which the Society of Jesus was to be welcomed back after its expulsion in 1594. The King funded the opening of a new Jesuit college at La Flèche, and ordered that his heart be buried there. L'Estoile noted every sign of the Jesuit advance in his *registre*, and opposed it with venom.[185]

In his entries for July 1610, L'Estoile describes the rapid rise to prominence of the fiery Jesuit preacher, Father Gontery. M. de la Varanne presented Gontery,

---

faire principalement pour /[continues in margin]/les Filles et Damoiselles de la Cour. Estant en ce de lopinion de Montagne, qui dit en ses Essais, qu'il trouve *plus aisé de porter une Cuirasse toute sa vie qu'un Pucelage.*' Compare III 5, NP904/BVH Paris 1595, bk. III, p. 52/S973.

[183] BnF MS Fr. 10301, fols. 79v–80r/*Journal Henri IV*, vol. 2, 487–8; III 12, NP1084/BVH Paris 1595, bk. III, p. 174/S1174.

[184] BnF MS Fr. 10301, fol. 229r–v/*Journal Henri IV*, vol. 2, 570–1 (direct quotations in italics): '[J]'en ay eu toujours *Reserve* asses *notable selon ma Condition,* (et plus quon na pensé,) naiiant parlé de mon Argent *qu'en mensonge,* Je le Confesse'. For the source in Montaigne see I 40, NP274/BVH Paris 1595, p. 161/S68.

[185] Parsons, *The church in the republic*, 107; BnF MS Fr. 10301, fol. 231r/*Journal Henri IV*, vol. 2, 572.

with an *éloge*, to the prince himself on the very day that *président* Pierre Séguier separately exhorted his royal highness to continue the deceased king's support for the Jesuits. In his entry for Sunday 18 July 1610, L'Estoile records that Gontery continued his 'bloodthirsty' preaching at Saint-Estienne-du-Mont, and that on this occasion he delivered a strongly seditious and scandalous sermon. This was according to the highest-ranked Catholics, those who are 'not seditious like him, but good people, lovers of public peace and quiet' ('non Seditieux comme lui, mais Gens de bien, Amateurs de la Paix et Repos publiq').[186]

This makes it only too clear that the divisions which de Thou, Pasquier, and L'Estoile saw opening up in French Catholicism in the 1580s—between militant, war-mongering Roman Catholics and *politique*, Gallican, peace-loving Catholics— were still wide open in the wake of the king's assassination in 1610. In a previous sermon, eight days before, Gontery's gospel of division and sedition ('Evangile de Desunion et Sedition') had extended to pointing out that the party of 'good catho- lics' outnumbered the party of the Huguenots, whom he estimated at 900,000, by a factor of five or even six or seven to one, as if calling the people to arms for another St Barthélemy.[187]

L'Estoile records that the powerful aristocratic patron of the Jesuits, M. d'Espar- non—Jean-Louis de Nogaret de La Valette, duc d'Épernon—had attended Gontery's seditious and scandalous sermon. He had indulged in populist displays of piety to show the zealousness of his faith, just as his late master Henri III had done—though without doing himself much good.

The same morning, L'Estoile had been passing his time reading Montaigne's *Essais* I 29, 'De la Moderation', and, after a *sentence* from the Bible, had found a Montaignean *trait* about great men who harm their reputation for religion by showing themselves more religious than any of their sort: 'I have seen one of our great noblemen harm the reputation of his religion by showing himself religious beyond any example of men of his rank.'[188]

Modern editors believe Montaigne was probably thinking of Henri III. But, as usual, Montaigne does not name names, which leaves his readers free to apply the *trait* more widely. So the *politique* reader-writer L'Estoile takes the liberty of filling in the name of a particular *grand*. And this time he reveals the process whereby such *traits* get into his *registre*:

> The passage [*Le Traict*] does not seem to me to apply badly to this lord— and having stumbled across it, this morning, as I was passing the time reading the said Essays, which I love and usually have to hand, I transcribed it, after lunch, on this paper and applied it to this subject [*acommodé à ceste Matiere*].[189]

[186] BnF MS Fr. 10302, fols. 65v–66v/*Journal Henri IV*, vol. 3, 148–9. On Gontery, see Alfred Soman, 'Press, pulpit, and censorship in France before Richelieu', *Proceedings of the American Philosophical Society*, 120, no. 6 (1976), 439–63, 449.
[187] BnF MS Fr. 10302, fol. 67r/*Journal Henri IV*, vol. 3, 149–50; Philip Benedict, *The Huguenot population of France, 1600–1685: the demographic fate and customs of a religious minority* (Philadelphia: American Philosophical Society, 1991), 76.
[188] I 29, NP203/BVH Paris 1595, p. 114/S222–3.
[189] BnF MS Fr. 10302, fols. 66v–67r/*Journal Henri IV*, vol. 3, 149.

Here is another description of a particular nexus of reading and writing, which consists of the application of an extracted *trait* to a particular historical individual. It offers a precise account of how L'Estoile's private recreational reading, in the books he ordinarily has to hand, feeds into his writing in his private *registre*.

First L'Estoile 'notes' the passage in the morning, most probably by marking it in his copy of the printed *Essais*, then he transcribes it in the afternoon into his ledger of ephemeral and daily records, his *journal-registre*. The *Essais* are a source of *sentences* and *traits* which he can extract in writing and apply or accommodate to events and protagonists as they present themselves. The book can play this role because the author Montaigne had recently been welcomed posthumously into the community of *gens de bien* or *amateurs de la paix et repos publique*, and because it had been composed to provide a free and moderate voice amidst the cacophony of partisan, extremist voices dominating the pulpits and the press from the 1580s and the rise of the League.

Using extracts from his own reading, Montaigne had documented the follies of his time, and of himself, and had found a moral, truth-telling voice to comment 'privately' and unofficially on both. As a free literate, L'Estoile was seeking to do the same in the related circumstances of the early seventeenth century.[190]

In May 1609 L'Estoile had considered the books from the last Frankfurt fair and described it as replete more with *fadaises* than with good books. He had described how the ill-turned *esprits* of the time nourished and fed themselves with 'calumnies, slanders and vanities' ('calomnies, médisances et baguenades'), and how this fed a market that everyday produced new *fadaises* for sale. His response was to acquire and archive the 'abundant trifles, invectives, and insults of all factions' ('fadezes, invectives, et injures d'une part et d'autre') as a witness to the vanity of the times. He would later write that the inanities and *fadaises* to be found in the resulting *registre* could be communicated to no one except himself.[191]

The *Essais* represented a rare good book that rose above this 'factional' literature, and that he could keep ordinarily to hand as a vade mecum—exactly, in other words, what they were represented to be around the same time in London, in Samuel Daniel's preliminary poem to London 1603. L'Estoile had a number of books he used in this way, as supplements to the counsels he could receive from doctors and priests. Some were secular, some were religious. Shortly after the passage about Frankfurt, on 24 June 1609, he calls another unspecified book given him by M. Convers (or a particular Latin prayer extracted from it) his 'Vade mecum', by which he means a text ordinarily to hand that is useful for repelling bad thoughts, temptations, and conceptions in his mind.[192]

---

[190] For a brief but perspicacious commentary on the relationship between Montaigne's and L'Estoile's texts, see Margaret McGowan, ' "La conversation de ma vie": la voix de L'Estoile dans les *Registres/Journaux*', *Travaux de Littérature (T.L.)*, 3 (1990), 249–59. My thanks to Mark Greengrass.
[191] *Journal Henri IV*, vol. 2, 459 (May 1609); BnF MS Fr. 10302, fol. 87r/*Journal Henri IV*, vol. 3, 165; Roelker, *One king, one faith*, 102.
[192] *Journal Henri IV*, vol. 2, 464. My thanks to Tom Hamilton.

By September 1610 things were coming to a head for L'Estoile. Towards the end of the previous month, the Jesuits had received letters patent from the Queen Regent for the reopening of their college in Paris, though it was opposed by the University of Paris (and would not open until 1618).[193] L'Estoile himself fell gravely ill and, fearing the end, confesses both on the page in his *registres-journaux* and in person to a priest.[194] As we shall see, however, the confession in person before the priest is displaced in a very interesting way by his confession in writing to himself, facilitated by the secular confessor Montaigne—exactly the kind of *office sans nom* Montaigne imagined himself fulfilling with his patrons and readers. The *Essais* describe themselves as displacing 'private and auricular confession' with an open, public confession on paper.[195]

It is during this extended piece of confessional writing that L'Estoile most clearly presents his soul 'free and all my own' ('libre et toute mienne') and most obviously claims his *liberté* against the forces of tyranny and constraint, which are clearly identified with militant Roman Catholicism. Towards the end of this written confession he self-consciously echoes his invocation of Montaigne's 'Au lecteur' from the opening of the first volume of his 'Tablettes': 'One thing I will record here, since I too portray myself whole and wholly naked . . .'; 'in everything that I scribble down here, I have set myself no other end than a domestic and a private one'.[196]

But the most telling passage occurs in his account of his private confession and *conférence* with a Jacobin priest, Father des Landes, whose preaching L'Estoile had found more pure than others.[197] Father des Landes wanted to extract a protestation that L'Estoile would die in the faith of the Catholic, Apostolic, and Roman church. L'Estoile's reservations, as what we now call a Gallican, did not permit him in all conscience to do this, but he did not rule it out in the event that he could be persuaded over certain points of Roman ceremony and doctrine, for he was also resolved not to leave the Roman Catholic Church.[198]

Later in his confessional discourse, L'Estoile recalls the ascendancy of the Catholic League in the late 1580s and early 1590s, when he lived under tyrannous constraints ('la tirannie et contrainte') with respect to religious conscience and ceremony. As we have seen, this appears to have become, in retrospect, a formative moment for the relationship between the *parlementaires* and the *Essais*.

---

[193] BnF MS Fr. 10302, fol. 100v/*Journal Henri IV*, vol. 3, 177.

[194] BnF MS Fr. 10302, fols. 106r–110v/*Journal Henri IV*, vol. 3, 182–7.

[195] III 5, NP888/BVH Paris 1595, bk. III, p. 41/S955; Virginia Krause, 'Confession or parrhesia? Foucault after Montaigne', in Zahi Anbra Zalloua (ed.), *Montaigne after theory, theory after Montaigne* (Seattle and Washington: University of Washington Press, in association with Whitman College, 2009), 142–60. On Montaigne's book and *offices sans nom*, see 1.4, and 1.4.2 in particular.

[196] BnF MS Fr. 10302, fols. 110r, 112r/*Journal Henri IV*, vol. 3, 186–7 (direct borrowings from Montaigne's 'Au lecteur' in italics): 'Une Chose enregistrerai je ici (puisqu'aussi bien je m'y *peinds tout entier et tout nud* . . .)'; 'ne mestant *proposé* en tout que je Griffonne ici, *aucune fin que Domestique et Privée*'.

[197] *Journal Henri IV*, vol. 3, 125. On this passage, and on L'Estoile's relationship to the confessions of Rome and Geneva, see Thierry Wanegffelen, *Ni Rome ni Genève: des fidèles entre deux chaires en France au XVIe siècle* (Paris: H. Champion, 1997), 464–77.

[198] BnF MS Fr. 10302 fol. 107r–v/*Journal Henri IV*, vol. 3, 183–4.

However, Father des Landes appears at first not to force the issue, and is happy to grant L'Estoile a temporary liberty of conscience:

> In conclusion, I have enough with which to content myself with the patience of this good Father (that I will love and honour always) for having kindly suffered me in my illness and in taking such liberty in my speech in this last scene (as I thought at the time, but God disposed things otherwise) between Death and myself, where, as Montaigne says in his Essays, there is no more feigning, we must speak straightforward French, we must show whatever is good and clean in the bottom of the pot. This is why if he had not given me this liberty, I would have taken it, because my nature is such that it always leans more towards open malice than towards [hypocrisy]. (However, may God protect me from both the one and the other.)[199]

Here, L'Estoile draws on Montaigne to associate speaking freely with the national candour of the French people and language (*franc, franchise, français*). However, L'Estoile subsequently discovers that the Jacobin priest has not in fact sustained him in taking this *liberté*. For he has concluded that L'Estoile holds heretical opinions that are incompatible with the faith of the Catholic, Apostolic, and Roman church, and that this is partly caused by his possession and study of a large number of heretical books.

In what follows, L'Estoile extends his confession in writing, revealing his innermost conscience in matters of faith—sustained, now, not by Father des Landes, but by his secular confessor Michel de Montaigne. For here L'Estoile draws not only on a particular *trait* from the highly pertinent chapter I 18 ('Qu'il ne peut juger de nostre heur, qu'après la mort'), but also on the whole ethos of the *Essais* as testament to the speech and behaviour of a *vir libertatis ingenuae*. It is that book which fortifies him in his hour of death to refuse any disguise—*masque* in Montaigne's French, *persona* in Lucretius's Latin (cited by Montaigne in the relevant passage)—and to speak straightforward French to the Roman Catholic priest, 'to reveal what is good and clean in the bottom of the pot' in writing in his personal *registre*.[200]

The fact that Montaigne himself signed up with much greater readiness than L'Estoile, in print, to the Catholic, Apostolic, and Roman church, and that he opposed personal liberty of judgement in religion, is not important. The *Essais* were written by a man of free spirit, alien to faction, a man who had lived through the tyranny of the League, like L'Estoile, a man whose praises were being sung—if too faintly for Gournay—by *politique* intellectuals twenty years after he first arrived

---

[199] BnF MS Fr. 10302 fol. 108r/*Journal Henri IV*, vol. 3, 184: 'Pour Conclusion, j'ay bien dequoi me Contenter de la Patience De ce bon Moine, (que j'aimerai et honnerarai tousjours) pour m'avoir doucement supporté en mon Infirmité et liberté de parler en ce dernier Rolle (que j'estimois, mais Dieu en à disposé autrement,) de la Mort et De moi, Ou; comme Dit Montagne en ses Essais; il n'y à plus que faindre, Il faut parler Francois, et monstrer ce qu'il y à de bon et de net dans le Fond du Pot. Cest pourquoi quand il ne men eust pas donné la liberté, je leusse prise, Car mon naturel est tel qu'il tourneroit tousjours plus tost à la Meschanceté aperte qu'a [l'hypocrisie], (Toutefois Dieu me Garde de lun et de lautre.)' The manuscript reads 'l'hreocrisie' or 'l'hieocrisie' where the printed edition reads 'l'hypocrisie'.

[200] BnF MS Fr. 10302 fol. 108r/*Journal Henri IV*, vol. 3, 184. For the passage in the *Essais* see I 18, NP81/BVH Paris 1595, p. 35/S87.

in Paris with his book. They displaced the official confessor and became a vade mecum for L'Estoile, as he wrote his free, personal testament in the spirit his father had bequeathed to him.

2.1.9 DANGERS FOR BOOKS IN CIRCULATION

So far in this two-volume study, we have for the most part been recovering the story told publicly by Montaigne and his friends about his book, and about the ideal reader-writer or 'free literate' in whose hands it hopes to find itself. Though Montaigne himself does not appear publicly to have elected *parlementaires* such as L'Estoile and Pasquier as wished-for recipients of his book, they jointly delineate the culture of reading and writing prevalent amongst L'Angelier's clientele.

And perhaps we can say that, under one aspect, Pasquier fits the bill of the ideal reader-writer and that he self-consciously joins the school of Montaigne. He knew the author in life and frequents and studies the book intensively when at leisure across half an adult lifetime. In the book, he discovers and is compelled by a free and natural process of discursive invention and judgement.

Some of the same points also hold for L'Estoile, even though he did not know Montaigne and even if the period in which he studied the book intensively, and wrote extracted *traits* into his private *registre*, appears to have been shorter. L'Estoile, still more than Pasquier, was—in relation to the keeping of his *registres-journaux*— precisely the kind of private reader-writer, freely collecting and assessing the 'presse of writings' outside formal study or the exercise of a public office, that we have been identifying as central to the early modern history of the *Essais*.

But the stories told by the author and by friends such as de Thou, Pasquier, and L'Estoile also point up dangers of the kind which Montaigne experienced with La Boétie's text, and which he encountered personally in Rome, and vicariously and posthumously via his book in Geneva. He describes them in quasi-allegorical terms in the anecdotes that end III 12.

In the post-1560 period, these dangers were part of the territory for any text going into broader circulation, as they were part of the territory for any person travelling through areas in which they were liable to be detained or captured as 'suspect', in confessional or religio-political or just moral terms—though, as the first III 12 anecdote indicates, they could equally reach one at home (L'Estoile was identified as 'suspect' by his own confessor in his own house, partly because of his reading). Texts looking to be frequented and sympathetically transformed in the corner of a library did so in an environment where they risked being censored, ransacked, pirated, or appropriated to ideologically hostile ends.

L'Estoile claimed Montaigne as a companion in his infirm old age. But he also followed de Thou's and Sainte-Marthe's lead in enlisting him to a parliamentary, Gallican, *politique* faction. He used him as a resource for anti-ultramontane senti-ment—something the book itself, it could be argued, attempts to preclude. From the perspective of the current chapter, the *Essais* would appear to be the result of a deliberate choice *not* to produce a scholarly, *politique* book in the style of a *robin* such as de Thou, and to use the *persona* of a *noble d'épée* to produce a different style of book altogether, a book that would be safer and freer on its travels. The choice of Gournay—and not a *robin* like Pasquier—as editor is part of this deliberation.

From the perspective of the *parlementaires* themselves, however, this could perhaps have seemed a disingenuous set of choices. The *Essais* so evidently share many elements of their literary, ethical, and political culture. One cannot ultimately prove that de Thou's account of their conversation at Blois was confected to justify his own work by association with the author of the *Essais*. Montaigne might have made such statements in private, and not included them in the *Essais*. The *parlementaires* felt justified in rewriting both the book—as they copied extracts out— and the *persona* of the author, reducing the latter to his roots in the literary milieu of the Bordeaux *parlement*, and in the friendship with a senior, superior figure (La Boétie), a hero who (unlike Montaigne, they might have said) stuck his head above the parapet and acted to keep the peace, while at the same time pursuing proper studies, scholarly studies.

There were, we saw above, two aspects to even a friend such as Pasquier's use of the work. On the one hand, he was compelled, in his private office as a friend, to grant Montaigne—in the form of a free, uncorrected text—his *liberté* and to begin to copy and amplify his startlingly original moral *sentences* in familiar letters to other friends. On the other hand, he was inclined, in his quasi-public office as a *politique* historian of France and censor of its language, to correct and expurgate the author's moral and stylistic *licence*. In the next chapter, we follow Montaigne's book still further afield, beyond the reach of his friends and family, into the hands of others who would exercise their liberty of judgement to correct his work, whether in private or public.

2.2

Safe Transpassage
Geneva and Northeastern Italy

In a treatise printed at Basel in 1560, the Tudor intellectual Laurence Humphrey declared that the European nobility needed to know its faults. But how could they be told of their faults when their ears were only open to flattery, not to counsel and truth? Commonly, they could not see their own diseases until they were 'openly printed' ('publice traducantur'), so that they could read, and by reading understand them of written books, which 'frely roame and wander eche where, and abashe not to tell the truthe' ('ex libria scriptis qui vagantur passim, et libere obambulant, ac verum dicere non erubescunt').[1]

Around the same time, the literary career of a Gascon counsellor and nobleman got underway. First published twenty years later, Montaigne's *Essais* advertised themselves as a book unabashed to tell the truth to the well-born reader, a book that could travel everywhere without disguising its author's nature and loyalties.

But could books still roam freely across France and Europe in the late sixteenth and early seventeenth centuries? Commercial networks linked publishers in provincial and national centres across the continent, facilitating the efficient exchange and distribution of stock. Intellectual networks promised to provide safe routes of transmission and translation for texts needing friends in new places. But both were vulnerable to the effects of war and disease, and, by the 1580s, of regulation and censorship, controversy, and piracy.

After 1560, all the major confessions in Europe began more systematically to control the access of lay reader-writers to literature, and to enlist intellectuals officially and unofficially to select and correct the books they did have access to. The faultlines of confessionalization became wider after the St Bartholomew Day's Massacre of 1572, and the markets of Italy and of Northern Europe grew more distinct. When routes were open, some books and genres—classical literature such as Aesop's *Fables* and emblem books such as Alciato's—could still, for the most part, circulate above the fray in Latin and all the major vernaculars, providing a tranquil refuge from the troubles.[2]

---

[1] The treatise was republished in English three years later in London. See Laurence Humphrey, *The Nobles: or, of Nobilitye: the original nature, dutyes, right, and Christian institution thereof three bookes* (London: T. Marshe, 1563), sig. a4v; Laurence Humphrey, *Optimates, sive de nobilitate eiusque antiqua origine, natura, officiis, disciplina, et recta ac Christiana institutione libri tres* (Basel: Oporinus, 1560), vol. 1, sig. c5v. My thanks to Eleanor Merchant.

[2] Maclean, *Scholarship, commerce, religion*, 223, 236–9, and *passim*; Andrew Pettegree, *The book in the Renaissance* (New Haven: Yale University Press, 2010), 199, 225, 246–8, and *passim*; Ingeborg Jostock, *La censure négociée: le contrôle du livre à Genève, 1560–1625* (Geneva: Droz, 2007), 201–2.

But what about new, argumentative books that were not abashed to tell the truth? Could they find publishers in different places and circulate peacefully across countries and continents? Afford their readers liberty of judgement and be widely credited with telling the truth in an impartial and independent way? Or was every such book destined to cause trouble somewhere, to be seized by municipal authorities, to be declared partisan or abused in partisan fashion, pirated by foreign publishers or 'corrected' by private individuals?

We heard in 1.1.9 of the rapid transnational dissemination of King James's *Basilikon dōron*, which offered a few home truths about kingship. But de Thou would write in June 1607 that 'truth has scarcely any friends these days'. In Rome, the Cardinal de la Rochefoucauld was still trying, in 1609, to have his *Historiae* reduced to a state—with de Thou's consent—which would allow such a beautiful work *liberté* 'to go everywhere' ('qu'elle puisse aller par tout'; 'pour mettre en plus de liberté un si bel œuvre'). He knew that it was in the Church's interest, if at all possible, to secure an edition of the work acceptable both to de Thou and the Parisian *parlement*, and to Rome.[3]

But he failed. The case of de Thou, studied in 2.1, and those of other authors of the sixteenth century such as Castiglione, Machiavelli, and Erasmus, all suggest that new works could not easily travel everywhere in the same form and be equally well received in the late Renaissance period. The religious conflicts across Europe had driven, and had been driven by, the expansion of the European book trade since the 1520s. Books divided people and disturbed the peace as much as they did anything else. As Paolo Sarpi said after the Venetian Interdict (1606–7), the substance of books may just be words, but from words come the opinions of the world, 'giving rise to factions, seditions and ultimately to war'.[4]

Rome was of course not alone in attempting to exercise official controls and to turn strangers' intellectual commodities to its own advantage. Any book entering a city, court, or community could arouse suspicion and needed friends to smooth its path. But friends could be hard to come by. Many people in post-Reformation Europe, not just official censors, feared that books and writings were at least as likely to cause schism and sedition, licence and atheism, as they were to protect against them.

After Luther, as Montaigne says at the beginning of II 12, anyone might feel free to form their own judgements in their search for truth. Liberty of judgement and what is now called censorship were two sides of the same coin, and could be variously exercised by any reader-writer in both unofficial and official capacities. Montaigne himself is on the one hand a champion of noble liberty of judgement, but on the other hand someone who judges that his great friend's most famous text should not appear in print. Though not an official with any institutional role in the

---

[3] Thou, *Historiarum sui temporis libri CXXXVIII*, vol. 7, pt. I, 28/BnF, MS Dupuy 409, fol. 111v; Thou, *Historiarum sui temporis libri CXXXVIII*, vol. 7, pt. I, 40 (letters dated just 29 January and 26 May, most likely of 1609, as the Cardinal says the *Historiae* are not yet on the Index).

[4] Pettegree, *The book in the Renaissance*, 203–25; Filippo de Vivo, *Information and communication in Venice: rethinking early modern politics* (Oxford: Oxford University Press, 2007), 1 (citing Sarpi's 'Sopra l'officio dell'inquisizione', 1613).

regulation of the book trade, he effectively prohibits publication of the manuscript. Pasquier (2.1.7) and Baudius, Goulart, Perrot, Naselli, and Canini (to be discussed in 2.2) all 'approve' Montaigne's book in one sense or another while also advocating or effecting corrections.

One person's liberty was another person's licence; one city's attempt to protect its citizens from disturbances of the peace, by means of censorship, was an international scandal to another. More people could see and be confused by the resulting diversity of judgements thanks to the handpress and the copyists. Public controversies played out in print, factions formed, and intellectual dissensions gave rise to—or were used as a pretext for—violent conflicts.

2.2.1   CENSORING THE *ESSAIS* ON THEIR TRAVELS

In 1.7.3 we saw how Montaigne's negotiation of liberty of conscience for himself, as a noble layman in debate with regular clergy at Rome, left its mark on future editions of the book. In conceding this liberty (within certain conditions), and in praising Montaigne in person, the Master of the Sacred Palace grouped the *Essais* with works by counter-reforming authors whose reputations as ecclesiastical nobles had not been damaged by the censorial process—even as he was still expecting Montaigne to effect some recommended corrections.

In 2.1, we saw the author painted into group portraits of *amateurs de paix*, and of loyalist Gascons of diverse confessional hues converging on Paris to help build a national French literature for sale in L'Angelier's *boutique*. The authorial scenario at Rome was replicated in the case of Montaigne's reader L'Estoile, who privately invoked the Gascon's work when maintaining his own liberty of conscience against the exhortations of his clerical confessor.

In 2.2.2 we shall consider in more detail how John Florio and Samuel Daniel tell a story about the French author's 'transpassage' to England, how networks of pastors and *libraires* in Geneva (in 2.2.3) facilitated his transpassage back from Geneva to France and to other foreign markets, and how clergy in northeastern Italy used him to teach the virtue of self-knowledge to the nobility of the Veneto (in 2.2.8).

In the adverse circumstances created by the civil and international conflicts that arose from religious dissensions, the *Essais* attempt to lay the ground for such acts of enfranchisement in distant locations—acts anticipated at the beginning of I 56 and figured at the end of III 12. As Montaigne's book and consubstantial *persona* travel via networks from city to city and household to household, their uses and credentials are re-assessed; they become the property and the work of users who collect, correct, reproduce, and assimilate them, or aspects of them, in new relational and confessional settings.

Montaigne and his friends attempt to regulate this process by promoting the book as a 'self-portrait' of a frank and natural kind. The *Essais* attempt to make a particular kind of noble virtue of the 'openness' of the book. The book does not disguise itself or its true intentions (or so it claims), which will be recognized by all parties, whatever their confessional and political allegiances are. For it can produce, wherever it goes, the noble qualities of the *persona* of the named author: *bonne foi, santé, franchise, liberté de jugement, oisiveté*. These are tied to his qualities, in the other sense, as a titled knight, mayor, citizen of Rome—as we heard Garasse confirm in 2.1.7.

It is a book, furthermore, which has been composed on a principle of non-correction. The whole point of it, from one perspective, is that the author is not only unabashed but naturally compelled to tell the truth about himself and his opinions. Even as he submits to the authority of Roman Catholic censors over his actions, writings, and thoughts, he claims personal jurisdiction over the registration and *contrôle* of the public record of his *fantasies*, which themselves partly arise from the judgement of others' writings. And 'contrerolle' in this case does not mean correction, for Montaigne's claim in III 2 that he rarely repents corresponds to his claim that he does not correct—in the sense of change or delete—judgements that he has already published.[5]

The book subjects itself to the authority only of the official Roman Catholic corrector, and only on points of doctrinal Roman Catholic truths—upon which the author, in any case, claims to have made no independent judgements. Montaigne was only too aware that many authors corrected their own works through editions—sometimes in response to direct pressure from censors (he himself made at least one major such correction in Paris 1588).[6] But in principle, none of the judgements he does make can be corrected by him or by others because they are offered as his honest opinions at given moments—which means none of them can be said to have been made in error by himself at a later date or by some superior correcting authority.

Or so he successfully argued in person with learned clergy at Rome, and at various points in his text. And as we begin to examine how well the book fared in this respect when travelling without the physical author-in-person, we can anticipate the answer by briefly considering whether other books of the period carry their apologetic authorial *persona* with them quite so efficaciously. No editions appeared in Germany or the Low Countries, but relatively uncorrected editions and translations of the *Essais* did appear in many of the major publishing centres of western Europe—Paris, Lyon, Geneva, Venice—as well as at London, between 1580 and 1640. These editions were of course adapted for local markets in various ways, but only one (Lyon [Geneva] 1595) could be described as having been 'confessionalized' (for a Calvinist, anti-papal readership).

During this sixty-year period the book was subjected to some kind of official censorial review five times (Rome 1580–1, Ferrara 1600, Geneva 1595 and 1602, Spain 1640). On none of these occasions was outright prohibition the prescribed outcome—though in one it was the effective outcome, as the *Essais* were placed on

⁵ Steven F. Rendall, 'The principle of non-correction', in Marcel Tetel and G. Mallary Masters (eds.), *Le Parcours des 'Essais': Montaigne, 1588–1988: colloque international, Duke University, Université de la Caroline du Nord-Chapel Hill, 7–9 avril 1988* (Paris: Aux Amateurs de livres, 1989), 253–62, 260.

⁶ Alain Legros, 'Montaigne face à ses censeurs romains de 1581 (mise à jour)', *Bibliothèque d'Humanisme et Renaissance*, 71 (2009), 7–33, 27–8.

the Spanish Index of 1640, *donec corrigatur* ('until corrected'), then left uncorrected until prohibited outright in 1790.

A correction in the form of a manuscript translation commissioned from an ex-Carmelite theologian (Diego de Cisneros) by an inquisitor, Don Pedro Pacheco, was undertaken in Spain 1634–7, but never completed (only a translation of chapters from the first book is extant) or printed. Only twice, then, in 1602 in Geneva and in Spain in 1640, did the circulation of the book become a public scandal, to the extent of motivating action by a regulatory authority. In one case it was ineffective (Geneva); in the other case (Spain), it was highly effective—Montaigne was not translated and printed in Spanish until the turn of the nineteenth and twentieth centuries.[7]

At other moments, and in other places, Genevan pastors and Italian monks alike granted this nobleman a free passage. What other authors of Montaigne's era had achieved the relatively unhindered and unchallenged circulation that he had, *c*.1640? Certainly not de Thou, Pasquier, or Charron.

Lipsius willingly participated in a fairly extensive correction of his own *Politica* to ensure their safe and legal circulation in Roman Catholic territories; the resulting expurgation was widely disseminated throughout the seventeenth and eighteenth centuries. He also revised the *De constantia*, in response to criticisms from his friend Laevinus Torrentius (who would become bishop of Antwerp) and others. But Lipsius's defence of this text (in a new preface) was more successful; it circulated across countries and languages in a relatively uncompromised form.[8]

As we have begun to trace the book's encounters with the world of people and places beyond Montaigne's closest collaborators and friends, we have found that these encounters were to a certain extent both anticipated and incorporated in the book as it evolved. If Montaigne's work from 1588 envisages interactions not only with his immediate 'friends and family', but also with friendly strangers in foreign

[7] Otilia López Fanego, 'Contribución al estudio da la influencia de Montaigne en España', *Bulletin de la Société des Amis de Montaigne*, 5th series, 22–3 (1977), 73–102; Otilia López Fanego, 'Quelques précisions sur Montaigne et l'Inquisition Espagnole', in Pierre Michel et al. (eds.), *Montaigne et les 'Essais', 1580–1980: actes du Congrès de Bordeaux (Juin 1980)* (Paris: Champion-Slatkine, 1983), 368–78; Jean-Robert Armogathe and Vincent Carraud, 'Les *Essais* de Montaigne dans les archives du Saint-Office', in Bruno Neveu, Jean-Louis Quantin, and Jean-Claude Waquet (eds.), *Papes, princes et savants dans l'Europe moderne: mélanges à la mémoire de Bruno Neveu* (Geneva: Droz, 2006), 79–96. It is debatable whether the Genevan expurgation of 1595 was the result of an official censorial review. As López Fanego says, it is reasonable to assume that the Spanish manuscript translation and its prefatory discourse (testifying to contemporary enthusiasm but pointing out Montaigne's lack of orthodoxy) may have led directly to the prohibition *donec corrigatur*—given that it was undertaken for an inquisitor. One other Spanish manuscript translation of all three books of the *Essais* (no. 18, 'Ensayos y Preuvas de miguel de montaña Traducido de frances en español = y son tres Libros primera segunda y tercera parte') is listed in the 1626 inventory of the library of Ruy Gómez de Silva, III Duque de Pastrana. The Duque possessed many prohibited books. See Trevor J. Dadson, *Libros, lectores y lecturas: estudios sobre bibliotecas particulares españolas del Siglo de Oro* (Madrid: Arco/Libros, 1998), 359, 173.
[8] Justus Lipsius, *Politica: six books of politics or political instruction*, ed. Jan Waszink (Assen: Koninklijke Van Gorcum BV, 2004), 120–1, 173–86, 193. On the *De constantia* see J. De Landtsheer, 'Justus Lipsius (1547–1606) and Publius Clodius Thraseus Paetus', *Humanismo y pervivencia del mundo clásico*, 3 (2002), 1283–8, 1286, and Justus Lipsius, *Concerning constancy*, ed. R. V. Young (Tempe: Arizona Center for Medieval and Renaissance Studies, 2011), xx–xxi. My thanks to Natasha Constantinidou-Taylor.

cities such as Rome and Leiden, and with participants in the broader French and European republic of letters, it becomes increasingly difficult to see where the circle of 'family and friends' ends and the extended 'public' readership of free literates begins.

The furthest afield we have travelled so far is to view the specially bound copy of Paris 1602 in the Duke of Urbino's library of counter-reformation scholarship—which most probably arrived via a Venetian bookseller with contacts in France (see 1.3.10). In this case, the copy had been repackaged on the spine as *Discorsi*, ruled in red ink, and shelved with political literature. It testifies to the agency relations between a collector, a bookseller, a binder, and a librarian in transporting and disposing the work in that form in that place.

What happened to other copies in foreign cities and households? How did strangers import, tax, and repackage the intellectual goods—especially the 'truth'—the *Essais* had to offer? What new works did they make? Copies of the *Essais* were certainly travelling rapidly across the continent from their earliest appearance.

Some were advertised for sale in the bookseller Georg Willer's Frankfurt fair catalogue for the autumn of 1581, though Willer gathered information from various printers and booksellers, making it difficult to know who sourced the copies from Millanges and shipped them to the fair. In September 1581, Claude Dupuy sent a copy of Bordeaux 1580 to Gian Vincenzo Pinelli in Padua, bundled with a number of other books. It was in one of two bundles he entrusted to Parisian booksellers Sebastien Nivelle and Denis Duval for transfer at the Frankfurt fair to a Venetian bookseller, either Francesco Ziletti or Pietro Longo, who would convey it to Pinelli. The exchange of stock via Frankfurt between Parisian and Venetian booksellers was probably the principal route by means of which copies of the French *Essais* reached Italy in the early decades after their first publication.[9]

In 1590, the town clerk of Leiden, Jan van Hout, and the Leiden university humanist, Janus Dousa, solicited the Leiden bookseller Franciscus Raphelengius to obtain copies of Paris 1588 on their behalf from Jan Moretus in Antwerp.[10] In 1595 Marie de Gournay sent corrected copies of her edition to major publishing houses across the continent, some (sent via Lipsius, but not sent on) to printers in Basel and Strasbourg, others to Plantin and unspecified famous printing houses.[11] This was in line with her strategy of launching the book, via Lipsius's recommendation, as an instant classic, a mirror of the most exemplary life in Europe.

However, the book's chief recommender did not in the event facilitate its publication with any of these houses. Lipsius's famous comment concerning the 'French

---

[9] Nelles, 'Stocking a library', 19–21, and notes 71–2; Angela Nuovo, *Il commercio librario nell'Italia del Rinascimento* (2nd edn.; Milan: F. Angeli, 2003), 91–4. I consulted the British Library's incomplete collection (for 1577–97, not 1577–80, as the Library's catalogue says) of the rival Portenbach and Lutz catalogues (pressmark C.107.bb.3). The catalogues list very few books in the Italian and French vernaculars. The sections of 'Libri peregrini idiomate conscripti' contain no mention of the *Essais*, but do list works by Machiavelli and Lipsius (a French translation of *De constantia*).

[10] Paul. J. Smith, 'Introduction: Montaigne and the Low Countries—synopsis and new perspectives', in Paul. J. Smith and Karl A. E. Enenkel (eds.), *Montaigne and the Low Countries (1580–1700)* (Leiden: Brill, 2007), 1–15, 8.

[11] Sayce and Maskell, 31–2.

Thales' was published in 1586 and referred to the *Essais* of 1580–2 (see 1.6.3). He was never to print an equivalent eulogy of the expanded *Essais* of 1588 and 1595, which of course included an additional book with bold new chapters such as III 5 and III 11.

By 1595, the Dutch humanist was striking a different note in private letters— letters that he did not include in his printed collections—to friends of the southern Netherlands moved by his example to admire the Frenchman's work. He wrote privately to one such friend, Remaclo Roberti, declaring that the expanded *Essais* could not be printed in the southern Netherlands. Even if the printers attempted it, theologians and book censors would not approve. There is much in the book, Lipsius says, that is too strong and raw, not to say too wise, for the stomach of the vulgar. Intended for men (and manly women such as Marie de Gournay) who will take it the right way, it is a book for other, simpler, less mistrustful times.[12] In other words, the *Essais* could not circulate openly and uncorrected in the southern Low Countries—they would invite too much suspicion.

Editions did appear with the imprint of Leiden, in the northern Low Countries, in the early seventeenth century, but they were Genevan editions in disguise—as we shall see in 2.2.5.[13] And Baudius, another friend of the book in its early days and a student of Lipsius's on the other side of the religious divide, publicized significant reservations from Leiden in 1607. They occur in the context of author- ial commentary on a neo-Latin eulogy addressed to the heroic virago Marie de Gournay.

The poem begins with an invocation of the 'celebrated Montaigne, whose august name thrives in the mouth of Fame'—more for the love Gournay showed him than in his own right. The authorial gloss at the back of the volume on 'Montanus ille' is significant for the present study as it offers a detailed and authoritative assess- ment of the school of Montaigne by an intellectual of international repute.[14]

Baudius describes Montaigne's as a free-spirited but flawed genius which cannot be contained—as his critics' can—within the limits of the arts and scholastic precepts ('intra terminos artium et scholasticarum praeceptionum'). His *ingenium, stilus,* and *judicium* are praised to the skies by some, denigrated as an intemperate abuse of *otium* and *litterae* by others. Even while praising Montaigne's genius, however, Baudius joins Pasquier in starting to talk like a corrector and censor. Montaigne's use of metaphor is excessively bold. He is vainglorious in seeking to enhance his repu- tation by pretending that he has had no help from the arts and sciences. Baudius is particularly indignant at Montaigne's absurd claims to have a weak, non-existent memory and at his affected vanity in saying he cannot remember his servants' names

---

[12] ILE VIII, 95 08 09R (unpublished), Lipsius (Leuven) to Remaclo Roberti [Brussels], lines 5–10: 'Ipsi typographi non facient ob caussas a te dictas et si volent, nolent illi quorum arbitratus hic est, theologi et librorum censores. Multa en eo libro robustae et adhuc crudae, ut sic dicam, sapientiae, quae non transmittant stomachi popularium iudiciorum. Viro ad illum virum dextre capiendum opus est, sed et temporibus aliis, simplicibus magis et minus suspiciosis.'

[13] Philippe Desan, 'Les éditions des *Essais* avec des adresses néerlandaises aux XVIIe et XVIIIe siè- cles', in Paul. J. Smith and Karl A. E. Enenkel (eds.), *Montaigne and the Low Countries (1580–1700)* (Leiden: Brill, 2007), 327–60.

[14] Millet 151–8.

(because there are so many of them). Baudius convicts him of a desire for glory (*gloriae cupiditas*) all the more manifest for his attempts to hide it. He thinks so highly of himself that he insists on registering every sordid action and domestic detail, down to the hour at which he tended to take his siesta.[15]

This was a common theme in professional intellectuals' reactions to the *Essais*, from Pasquier and Baudius right up to Huet in the 1720s (see 2.5.1). Baudius's paradoxical apology for Montaigne ends by stating, first, that inquisitors looking for heresy would find matter to expurgate in the text with their severe pens; and, second, that, nevertheless, the author was not unworthy of the title (French Thales) awarded by the Belgian Thales, Lipsius.[16]

2.2.2 SECURE COMMERCEMENT

Florio and his collaborators in London are particularly helpful when it comes to assessing the *Essais'* early fortunes as a commodity—a whole storehouse of commodities—in the international traffic in truthful self-knowledge, for it is they, above all, who bring out the story of the book that is being recovered in this study. On 4 June 1600, Edward Blount entered Florio's translation in the Stationers' Company register under the hands of the Warden and the secretary and chaplain to Archbishop Whitgift, Abraham Hartwell, himself a translator from French and Italian.[17]

But there is also an unofficial process of perusal and allowance. The preliminary and dedicatory materials to London 1603 textually enact the social process that we saw the author and his book go through officially in person in Rome in 1.7.3, and unofficially in Paris and Blois in 2.1. For, as we began to see in 1.4.1, the paratexts to London 1603 assess the credentials of the noble stranger Montaigne, then enfranchise him as a citizen in England.

Humanist prefaces often used metaphors of hospitality, conviviality, and trade to describe the ways in which books could mediate intellectual transactions amongst scholars and patrons, especially in international contexts. Translations were personified as foreigners entering England and seeking to become denizens with the help of native friends.[18]

---

[15] Millet 152–4.   [16] Millet 154.

[17] Edward Arber, *A transcript of the registers of the Company of Stationers of London, 1554–1640 A.D*, 5 vols. (London: Privately printed, 1875–94), vol. 3, p. 59v; Cyndia Susan Clegg, *Press censorship in Elizabethan England* (Cambridge: Cambridge University Press, 1997), 60–3; Mark Bland, *A guide to early printed books and manuscripts* (Chichester: Wiley-Blackwell, 2010), 191; Christina DeCoursey, 'Society of Antiquaries (*act.* 1586–1607)', *ODNB*. Only a certain proportion of the books printed in the late Elizabethan period were entered in the Register, and only a certain proportion of these carried ecclesiastical authorization. See Clegg.

[18] Paul White, 'From Commentary to Translation: Figurative Representations of the Text in the French Renaissance', in Tania Demetriou and Rowan Tomlinson (eds.), *The culture of translation in early modern England and France, 1500–1660* (Basingstoke: Palgrave Macmillan, 2015), 71–85; A. E. B. Coldiron, 'Commonplaces and metaphors', in Gordon Braden, Robert Cummings, and Stuart Gillespie (eds.), *The Oxford history of literary translation in English: Volume 2 1550–1660* (Oxford: Oxford University Press, 2010), 109–17, 112.

But in the case of London 1603, the metaphors point to immediate social realities: the noble households in which Florio was working both employed learned strangers (such as himself) to mediate foreign tongues and books, and welcomed foreign dignitaries—even princes—for 'trade or traffike', regardless of their confessional allegiance.[19] So to import and translate this French book is to welcome a Roman Catholic nobleman from the Parisian court, 'Lord Michaell de Montaigne, Knight of the noble Order of St Michael, and one of the Gentlemen in Ordinary of the French king, Henry the third his Chamber' into his aristocratic patrons' households, and to see him, also, set up with his own house in England.

But, as in Rome and Paris, strangers and strange intellectual goods have to be carefully assessed upon entry and taxed if necessary. The customs dues and impositions applied to goods entering and leaving cities and territories were a fact of economic life and a key instrument of state policy and revenue generation. Daniel and Florio think in these terms when they welcome Montaigne and the intellectual goods he brings with him to England. Books were, after all, imported like other commodities.

But what information did they have to go on? When Florio became involved in the mid-1590s in the whole enterprise of translating and publishing a new work by an unknown author just over from France, he did not have the benefit of four centuries of critical appreciation and bibliographical investigation. He offers an invaluably practical sense of how someone based in England would set about assessing the credibility of a new import from Paris in the age of confessionalization.

Apologizing for the faults of his own edition, Florio refers to 'the falsenesse of the French prints, the diversities of copies, editions and volumes (some whereof have more or lesse then others), and I in London having followed some, and in the countries others; now those in folio, now those in octavo'.[20] This confirms that English booksellers were importing multiple copies of different editions of the *Essais* for noble customers in London and the country. But Florio suspects some of these prints of 'falseness', and finds the diversity of different editions confusing.

And as the son of an Italian protestant refugee, he voices other doubts—doubts about the author's moral and intellectual credibility. We considered some of these in 1.4.1. Why are the only virtuous women Montaigne manages to find in the whole of antiquity all suicides? What has his Roman Catholic 'Paris preacher' been telling him—alluding, perhaps, to the possible influence of Leaguer fanatics? Why does he write in such an extravagant way about himself? With so little apparent coherence? Is he overtaken by some 'humour', some imbalance in his temperament? Why does he not just tell us the sources of all the borrowed materials incorporated in his text, instead of pretending that he does not remember them?[21]

To resolve these doubts Florio compares all the texts and decides that the full 1595 text as presented and defended by its editor Marie de Gournay is the most

---

[19] Michel de Montaigne, *The essayes or morall, politike and millitarie discourses*, trans. John Florio (London: Valentine Simmes for Edward Blount, 1603), sig. 2R2r (SCETI p. 2R2r)—henceforward abbreviated as 'SCETI London 1603', with page number references only. On strangers in these households see the beginning of 2.3 and 2.3.1.

[20] SCETI London 1603, p. A6r.   [21] SCETI London 1603, p. 2R2v; p. A5v.

credible. He calls witnesses to give evidence about the author's good faith. He collects, first, the evidence that he understands Montaigne himself to be giving in the text. He cites, of course, the author's prefatory acknowledgement that 'it is de bonne foy, then more than that c'est moy'. He calls on the 1595 prefatory verdict of Gournay, Montaigne's 'fine-spoken, and fine-witted daughter by alliance', which he says she need not have recanted (as she did in the 1598 edition, which Florio had clearly seen). But he also looks throughout the text for further 'prefatory' materials. He cites one of the embedded dedicatory letters, the 'discourse' in II 8 to the Lady of Estisaac, in which Montaigne proves '[h]ow rightly it [the book] is his, and his beloved'. He refers the reader to the page numbers of Montaigne's own replies to critical objections to his work.[22]

He leans particularly heavily on the judgement of Montaigne's most important English friend, Sir Edward Wotton, who had just become a Privy Councillor (in late December 1602) and who had effectively vouched personally for the qualities of Montaigne's wit and judgement by commissioning the translation of the one chapter. Wotton's own judgement is described as the 'staydest censure of as learned a wit as is amongst you', as 'the counsel of that judicious worthy Counsellor'.[23]

Wotton in 1595 had also become publicly known in literary circles as a friend of the most revered of learned English gentlemen, Sir Philip Sidney—he was mentioned as 'E.W.' in the first line of *The defence of poesie*. Sidney had translated other French works associated in Florio's circles with the *Essais*. Florio uses these relations to insinuate a family resemblance between the *Essayes* and the *Arcadia*.[24] Florio, in short, had not met the author in person, but he was able to put together enough knowledge about the book's relations in France and England, its original and new mises en scène, to make it appear trustworthy reading produced by an honest Roman Catholic.

The key point is that Samuel Daniel's epistolary poem combines with his brother-in-law's dedications to tell a story about the European circulation of the book since its first publication. This is a book coming out of Paris, only recently pacified by Henri IV after the terrors of the League, which has been approved in Rome and Geneva. Despite the fact that it is written by a nobleman in a Gasconized French, and not by a scholar in Latin, and despite the fact that the Parisian learned book trade had been largely cut off during the religious wars, both Daniel and Florio are clear that the book—against the odds—has already achieved a free transnational circulation.[25] Both are also clear that this is largely due to its status as a noble book, destined in England for noble readers in the school of Philip Sidney, and for a wider readership aspiring to the values of his school.

What are the specific qualities that have carried it through customs in different places, of rival confessions, to find an appreciative audience everywhere? While readers are oppressed with the uncontrollable 'presse of writings', Daniel writes,

[22] SCETI London 1603, p. A2r; p. A5v.   [23] SCETI London 1603, p. A5v.
[24] Philip Sidney, *The defence of poesie* (London: William Ponsonby, 1595), sig. B1r [USTC 512995/ ESTC 119205]; SCETI London 1603, p. R3r.
[25] On the Parisian learned book trade in this period, see Maclean, *Scholarship, commerce, religion*, 196, 226.

choicer books such as this show true liberty of judgement. The 'Prince' Montaigne
has adventured more of his own estate than anyone has previously dared, in order
to discover in writing the 'doubtfull *center of the right*'.

There are extravagant aspects to the book; many are inclined to 'taxe' Montaigne's
confused and 'troubled frame' (i.e. his stylistic and compositional freedoms). But
these potential censors are referred by Florio to the passage in III 9 where Montaigne
does refer both to his predilection for confusion and to the frame of his work.
He himself informs us that if he 'stragle[s] out of the path...it is rather by licence,
then by unadvisednesse', the 'licence' in question coming from classical authorities
such as Plato, Terence, and Plutarch. Florio acknowledges there are errors in the
book: 'if of matter, the Authours; if of omission, the printers: him I would not
amend, but send him to you as I found him: this I could not attend'. He enjoins
the reader to 'peruse', 'to correct as you reade; to amende as you list', for the printers lacked a 'diligent Corrector'.[26]

Daniel's poem draws on the post-Reformation, humanist trope of a transnational
learned community that defines its values against those of the Turkish despot who
enslaves his subjects. This is not, now, a universal Christian empire, but a secularized,
multilingual cultural unity put together by networks of humanists, diplomats, and
publishers who facilitate the circulation and translation of texts across borders.[27] So,
the heroic reader-writer—Montaigne—is represented as a knight-adventurer on the
international scene who makes bold sallies out upon the mighty tyrant 'Custome',
personified as an Ottoman sultan keeping us all in subjection.

But the metaphor is as much mercantile as chivalric—it seeks to harmonize
the double identity of the book as a commodity and as an act of mind. In the same
way that a merchant, in a contemporary phrase picked up by David Quint, hazards
his estate 'amongst men of all nations' in the hope of franchises and profits, so
Montaigne freely ventures his self-knowledge before the intelligentsia of all nations,
only to find himself a person of worth, with property in foreign lands:[28]

> Here at his gate do [I] stand...
> ...
> T'applaude his happie setling in our land:
> And safe transpassage by his studious care
> Who both of him and us doth merit much,
> Having as sumptuously, as he is rare
> Plac'd him in the best lodging of our speach.
> And made him now as free, as if borne here,
> And as well ours as theirs, who may be proud
> That he is theirs, though he be every where
> To have the franchise of his worth allow'd.
> It being the portion of a happie Pen,
> Not to b'invassal'd to one Monarchie,

---

[26] SCETI London 1603, p. [para]1r–v; pp. A5v–6r, for this and the previous paragraph.
[27] Fernández, 'Andrés Laguna', 308–11.
[28] David Quint, *Epic and empire: politics and generic form from Virgil to Milton* (Princeton:
Princeton University Press, 1993), 265.

> But dwell with all the better world of men
> Whose spirits are all of one communitie.
> Whom neither Ocean, Desarts, Rockes nor Sands
> Can keepe from th'intertraffique of the minde,
> But that it vents her treasure in all lands,
> And doth a most secure commercement finde.

This is a book able to travel because it is a noble freeman, not 'invassl'd' to the French monarchy. Wherever it goes there are those whose 'studious care' ensures its 'safe transpassage'—agents, shippers, promoters, and patrons who see the potential worth of the book in a particular market and circumvent the physical and regulatory obstacles in the transnational communications circuit. It is freed of taxes and impositions entering and leaving the ports.[29]

We saw in 2.1.5 how de Thou sought to enlist the assistance of such agents and patrons in the transpassage of his book to Rome. In the case of England, Florio is the agent who has provided this care, placing the visiting nobleman in the best lodging, enfranchising him as an English citizen. This 'rare' book—rare for its intellectual qualities—deserves the most sumptuous speech (Florio's elaborate, euphuistic language) and, implicitly, the fine folio format provided by the publisher Edward Blount.

The metaphors point insistently to the fact that intellectual exchange depends upon merchants and merchandise achieving 'secure commercement' across linguistic, geographical, and religio-political hazards—hence 'intertraffique of the minde'. For transporting intellectual goods from one place to another is a risky enterprise requiring collaboration between agents at both ends. Freedoms of passage have to be negotiated on all stages of the journey: Montaigne has to escape vassalage to the French monarchy and free himself and his readers from subjection to custom; Florio and his collaborators have to ensure that he is not overtaxed or amended upon entry and is allowed the liberties of a native citizen, provided with the best language and form.

These famous lines have often been cited and discussed but their connection to specific statements by Florio about the history of Montaigne and his book elsewhere in the dedications to London 1603 has not been noted. Daniel says not only that Montaigne has been enfranchised as a citizen of England, but that he everywhere has the 'franchise of his worth *allow'd*' (my italics). So his worth is recognized and his freedom, in the sense of his immunity from taxation or subjection, is granted in all countries, not just in England. Florio tells us exactly what this means and who the agents involved have been. He points to the book's proof of noble descent, in the form of the 'letters testimoniall of the Romane Senate and Citty' printed at the end of III 9, referring like Sainte-Marthe to the charter of Roman citizenship awarded to Montaigne during his visit to Rome.[30]

He also informs us that,

in the judgement (beside others, yea even of the precise Genevians he hath so bin judged, and amongst them *allowed* to be printed) of your most learned wise and

---

[29] Maclean, *Scholarship, commerce, religion*, 171–210.
[30] SCETI London 1603, p. A2r. On Sainte-Marthe, see 2.1.3.

honourable kinsman, sir Edward Wotton... there are in it so pleasing passages, so judicious discourses, so delightsome varieties, so perswasive conclusions, such learning of all sortes, and above all, so elegant a French stile... (my italics).[31]

Florio goes on to call Montaigne the 'Prince' of French eloquence, 'his worth being so eminent'. He is echoing Daniel and informing us that 'the franchise of his worth' has been allowed in Geneva, in Rome, and now in London—informally— by a Privy Councillor. And for the son of a protestant refugee from Italy, assisted in his translation by the son of another such refugee whose family settled in Geneva (Theodore Diodati), the judgement of the 'precise' Genevans is probably of greater significance than that of the Roman senate. Florio also alludes to the fact that an edition has been published in Italy (1590) by using its title as his sub-title: 'Morall, Politike and Millitarie Discourses' (from Naselli's 1590 *Discorsi morali, politici, et militari*).

So this book has found 'secure commercement' with friendly strangers every-where. In what follows in the rest of this chapter, and in the next three chapters (2.3, 2.4, 2.5), the primary tasks will be recovery of such strangers' agency, and assessment of the claim that the franchise of his worth is everywhere allowed.

For it is not just Florio's translation that tells a story of 'intertraffique', of dealings between Montaigne and his friends, and other parties in other places. All copies and editions tell more or less complex versions of such stories, in which negotiations between various parties enable the book to circulate from place to place, assume new appearances, new sets of friends and relations. And as we have already seen, the prospect or the actuality of taxation in the form of 'correction' has a role to play in a majority of them, not just those involving official censors, for clergy, officials, publishers, and private individuals alike both claim and grant liberties or privileges of judgement in relation to the circulation of this book.

In some cases, the signs of this are public and visible in the book itself. Florio, for example, claims in a paratext to have exercised his judgement in sending Montaigne on as he finds him, unamended.[32] In other cases, the clues are harder to find. The story of those judgements made by Genevan friends and relations who trafficked the book between Geneva and France via Lyon around the turn of the seventeenth century has to be pieced together from various sources as there are no paratexts in the relevant editions. The principal authors of the Genevan Montaigne turn out to be ecclesiastical censors and correctors working closely with *libraires*. In the case of northeastern Italy, we have to look at printed publications of the 1640s to find the story of the transmission of the *Essais* in the 1610s and 1620s.

Once again, we find members of the regular and secular clergy closely involved— with the partial exception of England (the book was allowed by clergy). As the *Journal* shows, Montaigne sought *conférence* with members of religious orders wherever

---

[31] SCETI London 1603, pp. R2v–3r. This must demonstrate knowledge gleaned via international networks by Florio himself (most probably via Theodore Diodati) for although unlicensed, unexpurgated editions and one licensed, expurgated edition were published at Geneva (see 2.2.5) no contemporary copy advertised this fact. See Sayce and Maskell, 21–4 and F. Giacone, 'Gli *Essais* di Montaigne e la censura calvinista', *Bibliothèque d'Humanisme et Renaissance,* 48, no. 3 (1986), 671–99.

[32] SCETI London 1603, p. A5v.

he went, and showed great interest in their rules and confessional identities. The *Essais* engage with the spiritual models of the orders, and with the arguments of theologians of all kinds throughout. He had particular love and admiration for the Feuillants of Bordeaux, to whom the Bordeaux copy was entrusted by his widow.[33] Small wonder, then, that we find clerics interacting with the book—and not just as censors—almost everywhere it goes; the book invited and prepared for such interaction.

In Elizabethan parlance 'allowance' denotes a permission granted once a work has received official scrutiny.[34] But in what sense were the *Essais* 'allowed to be printed' by the Genevans, or the author enfranchised, as if born there? As we shall hear in more detail in 2.2.3, a heavily corrected edition of the *Essais* was printed at Geneva in 1595, but with a false place of publication (Lyon). This hardly represented full, open enfranchisement. Unsold stock of this edition was distributed during or after 1598, or possibly during or after 1602, with new, inserted leaves offering preliminary materials published in the interim by L'Angelier.

In 1602, two editions of the *Essais* (Leiden A and Leiden B in Sayce and Maskell) that were not officially allowed by the *Compagnie* or the *Conseil* appeared at Geneva with the false imprint of 'Leiden: Jehan Doreau'.[35] Pyramus de Candolle was held responsible for at least one of these. As we shall see, there are clear references in the Genevan records to at least two distinct printings of the *Essais* that year, and the balance of probabilities is that these references correspond to the extant editions, Leiden A [Geneva] 1602 and Leiden B [Geneva] 1602. The one indication that the earlier edition (Lyon [Geneva] 1595) was probably allowed comes in a fleeting reference in a record of 1602 to the 'correction' already printed at Geneva.

The story, then, is much more complicated than Florio implies, and difficult to tell with any certainty.[36] But several elements are clear enough to make it a fascinating tale, worth telling at greater length in the following sections. First, the false title pages tell us that the early Genevan editions of Montaigne were produced to enter in *concurrence* ('competition') with a *contrefaçon* published at Lyon in 1593, then with L'Angelier's octavos (published from 1598) on French and other foreign markets, by slipping past customs checks (of the kind carried out on Montaigne's own books when he entered Rome) in transalpine Europe. They may also have

---

[33] Alain Legros, 'Feuillants (monastère)', *Dictionnaire*, 455–7; Alain Legros, 'Jésuites ou Jésuates? Montaigne entre science et ignorance', *Montaigne Studies*, 15 (2003), 131–46.

[34] Clegg, *Press censorship in Elizabethan England*, 11–12.

[35] Michel de Montaigne, *Les Essais* (Leiden [Geneva]: Jehan Doreau, 1602a)—henceforward abbreviated as 'Leiden A [Geneva] 1602'; Michel de Montaigne, *Les Essais* (Leiden or Cologny [Geneva]: Jean Doreau, 1602b)—henceforward abbreviated as 'Leiden B [Geneva] 1602'.

[36] It has been told with variations by the following: Giacone, 'Gli *Essais* di Montaigne e la censura calvinista'; Desan, 'Les éditions des *Essais* avec des adresses néerlandaises aux XVIIe et XVIIIe siècles', 334–48; Jostock, *La censure négociée*, 259–60. There are, however, significant problems of interpretation in matching the various references in the registers of the *Conseil* and the *Compagnie* to the extant Genevan editions Leiden A [Geneva] 1602 and Leiden B [Geneva] 1602. The main new points I make here are that Candolle, Berjon, and Rouvière were associated, and that it was more likely to have been Candolle's brother-in-law Jean Vignon who revealed Perrot's role in the publication of the *Essais*, which in turn (combined with evidence of the association between Perrot and Candolle) makes it likely that Perrot authorized Candolle's edition.

fooled some Catholic readers who would otherwise have been suspicious of anything printed at Geneva, but they would not have fooled those in the know in the
European republic of letters.

The falsification of the place of publication was standard practice even amongst
reputable *libraires* who wished to get their books past suspicious customs officers
in France, and especially in Lyon itelf. The inventory taken of Pyramus de
Candolle's business in 1623 reveals that a large proportion of his merchandise went
through agents and partners, including *libraires marchands*, in Lyon. In 1609,
Candolle was even charged by the *Conseil* of Geneva with lobbying for 'the free
commerce of books through France' ('le libre commerce des livres par la France')
at the court of Henri IV. He obtained letters of patent from the King approving the
subterfuge of Genevan *libraires* in putting specific false places of publication (e.g.
'Colloniae Allobrogum') on the title pages of books in the humanities published in
Geneva, in order that they might pass customs in cities such as Lyon and Paris
more easily.[37]

Second, the pastor Simon Goulart, who corrected the *Essais* for publication
at Geneva in 1595, was himself reading and excerpting a copy of the full, unexpurgated text in the years that immediately followed, probably once L'Angelier's
octavos started arriving in numbers (1598 onwards).[38]

Third, the *marchand libraire* (Candolle) principally responsible in 1602 for
securing the commercement, in clandestine fashion, of copies of a relatively uncorrected text of the *Essais* between Geneva and markets in France, Germany, and
England, was the same *marchand libraire* who a few years previously had been
entrusted by the pastors of Geneva with distributing Genevan bibles abroad.[39]
This should not surprise us. It was fairly common practice amongst Genevan
libraires to print books that had not been officially allowed, perhaps because they
treated the fines they were liable to incur from the *Conseil* as a kind of acceptable
tax, and because they trusted that the more severe punishments occasionally meted
out—such as imprisonment—would not fall upon them.

Finally, the senior pastor and treasurer sent by the *Compagnie* in April 1602 to
condemn the Genevan edition of the *Essais* to the city's *Conseil* turned out to be the
crypto-Catholic pastor (Charles Perrot) who was subsequently reprimanded by the
same *Conseil* for unofficially allowing its printing, and who posthumously was
found to have produced heretical manuscript writings. Even official censors could
take extraordinary liberties.

In the next section we turn first to the corrected edition of 1595. The culture of
correction was habitual across Europe in the late Renaissance.[40] It originated in the
classical custom invoked by Pasquier and revived by de Thou and many other

[37] Jean-Pierre Perret, *Les Imprimeries d'Yverdon au XVIIe et au XVIIIe siècle* (Lausanne: Librairie de
Droit, 1945), 46–7; Eusèbe-Henri Gaullieur, *Études sur la typographie genevoise du XVe au XIXe siècles
et sur l'introduction de l'imprimerie en Suisse* (first published 1855; Nieuwkoop: B. de Graaf, 1971),
219 (citing a letter of Candolle's from Paris, 1609); Jostock, *La censure négociée*, 307, 356.
[38] On Simon Goulart, see above all Cécile Huchard, *D'encre et de sang: Simon Goulart et la Saint-
Barthélemy* (Paris: Champion, 2007), and the bibliography of Goulart studies at 608–9.
[39] Jostock, *La censure négociée*, 248.
[40] Grafton, *The culture of correction in Renaissance Europe*.

authors—the submission of a work to a friend's judgement before circulation. But it incorporated a whole range of individuals and of practices, from official censors expurgating texts and correctors proof-reading in printshops to private readers correcting their own copies and translators making adjustments for their markets. Even Florio's edition removes a reference to the execution of Mary, Queen of Scots, and omits translations of sexually explicit Latin poetry.[41]

As I began to argue above, it is more productive to think in terms of a single range from less secure to more secure 'commercement', including various degrees and kinds of correction, both unofficial and official, both lay and clerical, than categorically to distinguish 'faithful' from abusive receptions of Montaigne's book.

2.2.3 SAFE TRANSPASSAGE FROM GENEVA TO FRANCE

When Florio aligns the judgement of the Genevans with that of Wotton in finding the *Essais* to offer pleasing passages and judicious discourses in so elegant a French style, he may be recalling the title page of Lyon [Geneva] 1595, which offers a 'rich and rare treasure of many beautiful and noteworthy discourses, couched in the purest and most ornate style to be found this century' ('un riche et rare thresor de plusieurs beaux et notables discours couchez en un stile le plus pur et orné qu'il se trouve en nostre siecle').

As we shall see in 2.2.4, Goulart published other *trésors* of miscellaneous discourse and examples around the same period, including translations of Seneca and Camerarius, and a compilation of his own. The use of this term on the title page of the corrected *Essais* helps us understand, then, what he and the publisher Le Febvre thought they were giving their readers in France and across northern Europe. They were giving ordinary, decent, Christian reader-writers a safe treasure of beautiful and noteworthy discourses for their own use, in a compact, cheap duodecimo format. It is in this respect that we shall consider the edition as part of Goulart's *œuvre*. More broadly, we shall consider it as part of Geneva's *œuvre*.

What evidence (beyond the mention in 1602 of the previously printed 'correction') warrants such an attribution and such an approach? There is no doubt that Le Febvre, though a native of Lyon, produced his books at Geneva from about 1588.[42] Goulart would be a prime candidate for the work of correction even without further circumstantial evidence. He published expurgated versions of a number of texts, whether by official commission, or on his own initiative. But there is one important piece of direct evidence that he corrected Montaigne. It occurs in the later table-talk of Joseph-Juste Scaliger, which was written down *c.*1604–6 by Jean de Vassan and printed as the *Secunda Scaligerana* later in the century.[43]

---

[41] I 18, NP80/BVH Paris 1595, p. 34/SCETI London 1603, p. 29; William M. Hamlin, 'Sexuality and censorship in Florio's Montaigne', *Montaigne Studies*, 23 (2011), 17–38.

[42] RIECH.

[43] Jérôme Delatour, 'Pour une édition critique des *Scaligerana*', *Bibliothèque de l'École des Chartes*, 156 (1998), 407–50.

There is no substantial reason to doubt the validity of this evidence. Scaliger and Goulart met when the former was in Geneva in the early 1570s. Scaliger reportedly described him as an *amicus conjunctissimus*. They corresponded over a quarter of a century, with many of the extant letters dating to the 1590s and 1600s, when Scaliger also began a correspondence with Goulart's son (another Simon).[44] Some of the things he is recorded as saying in 1604–6 in the *Secunda Scaligerana* correspond to letters we know he was receiving at the time from the Goularts. Even if Jean de Vassan was remembering and mediating in retrospect what Scaliger said, he himself was in correspondence with Goulart's associate Perrot and would constitute a good source for the attribution.[45] There is, furthermore, an important connection between what Scaliger is reported as saying about Montaigne and a remark made by Justus Lipsius in an unpublished letter of 1595.

In his remarks as they appear in the article on Goulart in the printed *Scaligerana*, Scaliger's theme is that he became a good Latinist despite starting late, and that he is a 'gentil personnage' and a very clear preacher. He indirectly refers to his lifelong friendship with Goulart by alluding to his stay in Geneva in the early 1570s. He also refers in the present tense to Simon Goulart junior's successful ministry in Amsterdam (attested by Simon Goulart senior *c.*1605).[46]

Scaliger selects for mention just three of Goulart senior's works. The first is his French translation of Osorius's *Histoire de Portugal*, published at Geneva in 1581; the second, and most important, is his edition of St Cyprian, published at Geneva in 1593 and dedicated to the reformed churches of Holland and Zeland, which Scaliger says he read through; the third is his correction of Montaigne's *Essais*: 'Mr Goulart corrected the works of Montaigne; what boldness with another's writings!' ('Mr Goulart a fait chastrer les œuvres de Montaigne; quae audacia in scripta aliena!').[47]

So the edition pointed Scaliger to a remarkable liberty or boldness of corrective judgement on Goulart's part. The article on Montaigne supplements this with a related comment: 'His father sold herring. The great banality of Montaigne, who wrote that he preferred white wine. M. du Puy used to say, "what the devil do we care what he preferred". Those Genevans were certainly impudent to take out more than a third' ('Son Pere estoit vendeur de harenc. La grande fadaise de Montagne, qui a escrit qu'il aymoit mieux le vin blanc. M. du Puy disoit, que diable a-t-on à faire de sçavoir ce qu'il ayme. Ceux de Geneve ont esté bien impudens d'en oster plus d'un tiers').[48]

---

[44] Leonard Chester Jones, *Simon Goulart, 1543–1628: étude biographique et bibliographique* (Geneva and Paris: Georg Éditeurs and Librairie Ancienne Honoré Champion, 1917), 4–5n.2, 304, and the letters to Scaliger from both Goularts in the 'Pièces annexes'.

[45] Léon Dorez, *Catalogue de la collection Dupuy*, 2 vols. (Paris: Ernest Leroux, 1899), vol. 2, BnF MS Dupuy 699, containing letters from Perrot to Jean de Vassan.

[46] Pierre Des Maizeaux (ed.), *Scaligerana, Thuana, Perroniana, Pithoeana, et Colomesiana* 2 vols. (Amsterdam: Cóvens and Mortier, 1740), vol. 2, 354–5; Jones, *Simon Goulart, 1543–1628*, 185.

[47] Des Maizeaux (ed.), *Scaligerana, Thuana, Perroniana, Pithoeana, et Colomesiana*, vol. 2, 354–5; USTC 7267/GLN15–16 2888; USTC 451372/GLN15–16 3607; Lyon [Geneva] 1595.

[48] Des Maizeaux (ed.), *Scaligerana, Thuana, Perroniana, Pithoeana, et Colomesiana*, vol. 2, 457–8.

However, it is important to understand at this point that there are no 'articles' in the text as originally written out by Jean de Vassan. The printed *Scaligerana* present the remarks in a completely different way to the manuscript. The manuscript was compiled as a journal, a running record of remarks de Vassan heard in conversation with Scaliger between 1604 and 1606. But the printed version collects remarks on particular topics and authors from different leaves in this journal and turns them into discreet but often incoherent articles with headings. This means one can only really understand the context and the chronology of a given remark by returning to the manuscript. Also, it is easier to see in the manuscript how certain key topics and figures are recurrent throughout.

So, for example, it is more apparent in the manuscript version just how regularly Scaliger talks of Geneva and the Genevans—including Goulart. He is constantly on the lookout for what 'ceux de Geneve' are doing, whether it is building bridges, finding ways to augment their meagre revenue, punishing miscreants over-severely, converting Roman Catholics to Calvinism, or printing books.

This is hardly surprising. Not only had Scaliger fled to Geneva after the St Bartholomew Day's Massacre, but his interlocutor and scribe, Jean de Vassan, had come from Geneva to Leiden to study with him. And we know that during the relevant period (1604–6) Scaliger was in regular correspondence with Goulart in Geneva. Jean de Vassan records him saying at one point that Goulart has written to him to say that the licentious pursuit of pleasure is greater in Geneva than in France ('Monsieur Goulart m'a escrit que la licence de paillarder est plus grande à Geneve qu'en France').[49]

When replaced in their contexts in the manuscript journal, Scaliger's remarks about Lyon [Geneva] 1595 situate it as one of a whole series of Genevan publications, and republications of Parisian and other French editions, that are exported to France and the Low Countries. His friend Goulart is involved in many of these as editor, translator, commentator, and intermediary.

Scaliger sometimes betrays a certain ambivalence in what he says about these publications. So, some time between late June and September 1605, he reminisces about his father's sympathy for those 'of the Religion' in the early days of the religious conflicts. People say that all the written evidence of the trials of heretics is burnt. But there is always someone around like his brother, who gathered and sent the evidence of one such trial to Geneva, where they put it in 'the "book of Martyrs" which is a very good book but printed on poor paper—sold here in a bound copy for eleven francs'.[50] Complaints about the quality of Genevan publications—the paper, the lack of proof correction, and so forth—were common, and the authorities were only too aware of how it affected their city's reputation abroad.[51]

But this is nevertheless, for Scaliger, a good book, and the likelihood is that by the early seventeenth century he associated it with his friend Goulart. Jean Crespin's

[49] Charles Seitz, *Joseph Juste Scaliger et Genève* (Geneva: Georg et Compagnie, 1895); Des Maizeaux (ed.), *Scaligerana, Thuana, Perroniana, Pithoeana, et Colomesiana*, vol. 2, p. 342; BnF MS Fr. 2388, p. 119 (this manuscript has page numbers rather than folio numbers).
[50] BnF, MS Fr. 2388, p. 138.
[51] Jostock, *La censure négociée*, 42, 63, 252–4, 316–17, 344–5, 348–9, 351–2, 358, 360–2.

Livre des martyrs was first published at Geneva in 1554, but appeared in various guises in Latin and French (*Actes des martyrs, Receuil des martyrs, Actiones et monimenta martyrum*) throughout the 1550s and 1560s. Then, in 1582, Goulart re-edited it, adding two entire books and various narratives and annotations. His became the standard edition, reissued with Vignon and others in 1597, 1608, 1609, and 1619.[52]

Following straight on from this in de Vassan's manuscript journal—though not in the printed version—is Scaliger's comment on the Genevan edition of his father's *Poemata*, and once again Goulart is involved: 'It was badly done at Geneva to omit the Divæ et Divi from my father's poems. Monsieur Goulart wanted them printed; Commelin has now printed them' ('On fit mal à Geneva de omettre ès poemes de mon pere diva et divi Mr Goulart vouloit qu'on les Imprimast, [Com]melin les a imprimez maintenant').[53]

Editions of J. C. Scaliger's *Poemata* were published at Geneva in 1574, 1591, and 1600. The edition appearing under the name 'Commelin' (Commelin himself had died in 1597), which restored both the 'Divi' (poems addressed to male figures) and the 'Divæ' (to female figures), had indeed just appeared with the *héritiers de Commelin*, who were based in Heidelberg but collaborated closely with Genevan printers.[54]

It is not clear from Scaliger's remark exactly when, and in relation to which edition of the *Poemata*, Goulart made or attempted to make his intervention, but the train of thought is clear. It continues in the remark that immediately follows in de Vassan's manuscript journal: 'Mr Goulart corrected the works of Montaigne; what boldness with another's writings!'[55] The restoration of this remark to its context in a series of remarks about Genevan publications in which Goulart had been involved makes the attribution of the corrections in Lyon [Geneva] 1595 still more solid. It also makes the agency of Goulart in using the handpress to shape Geneva's reputation on the international stage, for better or for worse, the primary consideration, not the reception of the *Essais* per se.

We can thus add an important dimension to our overarching discussion of the claiming of liberties of judgement on the part of both individuals and authorities in this age of confessionalization. On the one hand, Scaliger is reproving the author of a particular text, the *Essais*, for publicizing in print his preference for white wine, and for other trivial judgements. On the other hand, he is judging what Geneva is doing by scrutinising the books they produce, by comparing those products with previous or rival editions, by discovering what liberties they have taken in omitting material.

---

[52] USTC 6414/GLN15–16 1978; USTC 41080/GLN15–16 1579; USTC 41081/GLN15–16 1980; USTC 2949/GLN15–16 2925; Huchard, *D'encre et de sang*, 51–8.

[53] Des Maizeaux (ed.), *Scaligerana, Thuana, Perroniana, Pithoeana, et Colomesiana*, vol. 2, p. 555; BnF, MS Fr. 2388, p. 138. The manuscript reads 'omettre' where the printed version reads 'mettre'.

[54] These two groups of poems appear in the second part of Julius Cæsar Scaliger, *Poemata in duas partes divisa* ([Heidelberg/Geneva]: in Bibliopolio Commeliniano, 1600) [USTC 668503/VD16 S 2087], but are missing from Julius Cæsar Scaliger, *Poemata in duas partes divisa* ([Geneva]: [Jacob Stoer for Gaspard de Hus], 1574) [USTC 450676/GLN15–16 2523]; Julius Cæsar Scaliger, *Poemata in duas partes divisa* ([Geneva]: [Jacob Stoer] for Pierre de Saint-André, 1591) [USTC 450529/GLN15–16 2264].

[55] BnF, MS Fr. 2388, p. 139.

The same is true of Scaliger's other reference to Lyon [Geneva] 1595. Later on in the same period between June and September 1605, Scaliger is back on the theme of what 'ceux de Geneve' are doing in print. They have printed the *Epistolae* of Petrarch (Samuel Crespin, 1601). But they are 'great bowdlerisers', for they 'took the best part out of the index of the Paris Cyprian' ('Ceux de Geneve sont de grands detronquers et ils ont osté de l'indice de Cyprian de Paris de plus beau').[56]

Scaliger is here referring to Goulart's Cyprian of 1593, which mediated the standard Catholic edition for reformed readers.[57] First published at Antwerp in 1568, edited by Paolo Manuzio and Guillaume Morel, and annotated by Jacques de Pamèle, this edition of St Cyprian's *Opera* had indeed migrated to Paris by 1574, where it was published by Sebastien Nivelle.[58]

The edition was particularly noteworthy for the indices it offered of biblical citations, of topics, of the contents of Pamèle's commentary. The most important intervention made by Goulart when he republished this edition at Geneva in 1593 was the interjection of 'responses' to many of the points made in Pamèle's annotations that tended to confirm Papist dogma. Scaliger very much approved of this work, which he praises three times in the *Secunda Scaligerana*—on one occasion for the respectful tone of Goulart's ripostes to Pamèle.[59]

But although Goulart includes many of the paratexts from the Antwerp–Paris edition, he does substitute two of them with new and slighter paratexts of his own. The 'Index in tres D. Cypriani Operum tomos' and the 'Index rerum ac vocum in adno[t]ationes explicatarum' give way to Goulart's own index disposed by the 'scholastic method' and a table referring the reader to all the interventions he has made in Pamèle's commentary. These are the changes that lead Scaliger to call 'ceux de Geneve . . . de grands detronqueurs'.[60]

The manuscript record of Scaliger's remarks goes straight from this to another example of the Genevans as *grands detronqueurs* and of Goulart's mediation of Catholic literature: Lyon [Geneva] 1595. It appears a later editor made the decision to attribute one of the remarks to Dupuy, as it is not so attributed in the manuscript: 'The great banality of Montaigne, who wrote that he preferred white wine. What the devil do we need to know for? The Genevans have certainly been impudent to take out more than a third' ('La grande fadaise de Montaigne qui

[56] Des Maizeaux (ed.), *Scaligerana, Thuana, Perroniana, Pithoeana, et Colomesiana*, vol. 2, 343; BnF MS Fr. 2388, p. 157.

[57] USTC 451372/GLN15–16 3607.   [58] USTC 401366; USTC 170225.

[59] Pierre Petitmengin, 'De Théodore de Bèze à Jacques Godefroy. Travaux genevois sur Tertullien et Cyprien', in Irena Dorota Backus (ed.), *Théodore de Bèze (1519–1605): actes du colloque de Genève (septembre 2005)* (Geneva: Droz, 2007), 309–37 (317–21); Des Maizeaux (ed.), *Scaligerana, Thuana, Perroniana, Pithoeana, et Colomesiana*, vol. 2, 287, 326, 484.

[60] Saint Cyprian, *Opera* (Geneva: Ioannes le Preux, 1593); Saint Cyprian, *Opera* (Antwerp: Apud viduam & hæredes Ioannis Stelsii, 1568). The two indices in question are the last two before the main text begins at the front of the Antwerp 1568 edition [USTC 401366], and the last two at the very end of the Geneva 1593 edition [USTC 451372/GLN 15–16 3607]. The Paris edition has the same indices as the Antwerp edition. See, for example, Saint Cyprian, *Opera* (Paris: Apud Sebastianum Niuellium, 1603).

escrivoit quil aimoit mieux le vin blanc que diable a on [?faute] de le scavoir Genevenses ont esté bien Impudens d'en oster plus d'un tiers').[61]

After the publication of the *Secunda Scaligerana*, later in the century, Pierre Huet picked up and expanded this comment of Scaliger's concerning Montaigne's *fadaise*, making clear that it referred to the long section in 'De l'experience' in which the Gascon described his *forme de vie*, including the minutiae of his tastes and his domestic routine (see 2.5.1).

At one and the same time, Scaliger suggests that the expanded *Essais* represented a book that needed some correction, and that the Genevans were impudent to reduce it by a third. We have seen that other intellectuals were itching in private to correct or expurgate the mature *Essais*. Pasquier did correct a copy and expressed an inclination to make much larger cuts, especially in book III. Baudius stated in print that the censors would find much to object to. Later, the Spanish began the official process of expurgating the *Essais* in manuscript, and banned them until corrected. But the Genevans were the only ones who went ahead—boldly or impudently—and actually printed an expurgated copy. Indeed, in their corrected edition, Goulart took out the precise passage referred to by Scaliger, containing remarks on Montaigne's preferences in wine, together with many other passages from his long description of his domestic *forme de vie*.[62]

It appears that the most famous critic on the other side of the confessional divide in the Low Countries broadly agreed with Scaliger's sentiment. Despite rating the book on a personal level, Lipsius saw the mature *Essais* as unsuitable for vulgarization because they offered strong truths that ordinary people could not be trusted with in such raw form. In his unpublished 1595 letter to Remaclo Roberti, discussed in 2.2.1, Lipsius uses a tellingly similar phrase (in Latin) to Scaliger's. Having opined that the *Essais* were too raw to be published in the southern Netherlands, he goes on to deplore the act of the Genevans in publishing an expurgated version. Echoing Scaliger's French phrase, he expresses amazement at the impudence of the Genevans ('Vah impudentiam Genevensium...') in expurgating

---

[61] BnF MS Fr. 2388, p. 157.

[62] Michel de Montaigne, *Livre des Essais* (Lyon: Gabriel La Grange, 1593), second part, sigs. y5v–6v ('ma resolution. Quand j'ordonne...(car comme Epicure ieusnoit...)')—henceforward abbreviated as 'Lyon 1593'/Lyon [Geneva] 1595, sig. 2r11r ('ma resolution. Epicure ieusnoit'). The passage here cut from Lyon 1593 (upon which Lyon [Geneva] 1595 is based) includes Montaigne's comment concerning his changing taste from white wine to claret, then back from claret to white wine. For other cuts in this section see Lyon 1593, second part, sig. x2r–v ('inegalité de vie. Quoy que....ruyne sur eux. Et plain plusieurs')/Lyon [Geneva] 1595, sig. 2r3v ('inegalité de vie. Et plains'); Lyon 1593, second part, sig. x3r ('à l'indiscretion. Parquoy je...ne nous trouble. je ne juge donc point')/Lyon [Geneva] 1595, sig. 2r3v ('à l'indiscretion. je ne juge donc point'); Lyon 1593, second part, sigs. x3v–4r ('de la vie. Et sain...*Barba meæ*. Les Medecins')/Lyon [Geneva] 1595, sig. 2r4r ('de la vie. Les Medecins'); Lyon 1593, second part, sig. y2r–v ('mouvement: je m'esbranle...que le siege. Il n'est occupation')/Lyon [Geneva] 1595, sig. 2r9v ('mouvement: Il n'est occupation'); Lyon 1593, second part, sigs. y3r–4v ('se rendre gendarme. Je suis n'ay de...pour se coucher. Si j'avoy des enfans')/Lyon [Geneva] 1595, sig. 2r10r ('se rendre gendarme. Si j'avoy des'); Lyon 1593, second part, sigs. y6v–z1r ('ainsi contrains: l'extreme fruict...corrompre ses regles. Quand je voy')/Lyon [Geneva] 1595, sig. 2r11v ('ainsi contraints: Pour nos occupations...mieux en veillant. Quand je voy'). This last example shows the care Goulart took: he cuts four and a half pages' worth of *fadaise* but finds one morally worthy paragraph in the middle, and retains it!

the work, in taking out all signs of, all references to, ancient religion and piety—namely, the Catholic faith ('notas et testimonia detraxerunt religionis et pietatis antiquae').[63]

These comments by the leading humanists of Catholic and Protestant Europe suggest that in the European republic of letters of the late 1590s and early 1600s, Lyon [Geneva] 1595 was widely understood and judged as a work authored by 'the Genevans', who had impudently taken liberties in cutting the text. When discussing the pros and cons of censorship of books dangerous to good government Paolo Sarpi warned in this period that it was neither honourable nor safe to expurgate books and 'have it thought that in Venice books are castrated, as is slanderously claimed of some other cities'.[64]

The fact that the Genevans had reprinted Montaigne's work in heavily corrected form indeed caused something of a scandal. For scholars were aware very quickly after its publication that it had been heavily and impudently expurgated—a shared sentiment that points to the status accrued by Montaigne's book in the republic of letters between *c.*1595 and *c.*1605. With his inside knowledge, Scaliger placed it in the context of a series of editions officially or semi-officially produced by Goulart on behalf of 'the Genevans' as a response to the scholarly and historiographical literature of Catholic Europe—a series about which he showed some ambivalence.

2.2.4 BOOK IN ONE HAND, PEN IN THE OTHER

In studying Lyon [Geneva] 1595, scholars have understandably concentrated on the way in which a canonical text was bowdlerized. In this respect, the key point for us about the chapters and longer passages that are cut is that the severity and comprehensiveness of the corrections corresponds to the *Compagnie*'s judgement in 1602 that the full, unexpurgated text was a profane and cynical book forming men in atheism.[65] Goulart systematically takes out all the 'choses non convenables à nous'—the shameful profanities that threatened public order in Geneva. He also systematically takes out—as Lipsius noted—all positive and personal references to the Roman Catholic faith.

So, for example, the omission of I 34 ('D'un defaut de nos polices'), an otherwise innocuous chapter, must be due to the mention of the translator Sébastien Castellion as one of the two central examples of great personalities who have not received their due rewards—Castellion was chased from Geneva by Calvin. The praise of Roman politics, contemporary papal Rome, and the charter of Roman citizenship which form the closing section of III 9 ('De la vanité') are

---

[63] ILE VIII, 95 08 09R (unpublished), Lipsius (Leuven) to Remaclo Roberti [Brussels], lines 17–18.

[64] Rodolfo Savelli, 'The censoring of law books', in Gigliola Fragnito (ed.), *Church censorship and culture in early modern Italy* (Cambridge: Cambridge University Press, 2001), 223–53, 252–3 (citing Sarpi, *Scritti giurisdizionalistici*).

[65] See 2.2.5.

also missing.[66] As corrected, Montaigne is no longer an identifiably Roman Catholic author who deplores the Lutheran innovations, and he no longer talks indecently and profanely of sexual and other risqué matters.

But there is a further question that follows from Scaliger's location of the edition as one of a series of Genevan works authored by Goulart. What, exactly, did Goulart see in Montaigne's text, and why did he invest so much time in preparing a safe, corrected edition? Some clues can be gathered by following the movements of Goulart's pen across his working copy of Lyon 1593, in order to see not just how he cuts, but also how he nuances and rewrites the chapters and passages he chooses to retain—a task some scholars have already begun to undertake.[67] It is certainly possible, for example, to glean that the corrector behind Lyon [Geneva] 1595 has a demonstrable interest not only in the memorable historical examples assembled by Montaigne, but in the way they are being judged or presented.[68]

We also need, however, to consider clues in other works Goulart published. As we heard in 2.2.3, he had worked before with Genevan *libraires* to quickly produce safe, cheaper Genevan versions of texts that had just appeared at Paris or Lyon. There are many other examples of this not mentioned by Scaliger. When in 1576 Claude Juge requested permission from the Genevan *Conseil* to print an edition of the French translation of Jean Bodin's *Six livres*, which had just appeared in Paris, they granted it on condition that it was 'reviewed' by Goulart. There is no documentary evidence that the correction of the *Essais* originated in the same, official fashion.[69]

In the case of Bodin's work, with the author still very much alive, Goulart anticipated that the edition would be compared to the original and judged *as* a correction, so he published a prefatory justification of the changes made. He categorizes the changes as 'things [that] have been cut, corrected, or taken out altogether' ('choses ont esté retranchees, corrigees ou ostees du tout'). He imagines the author and perhaps some readers bringing a formal complaint that he has done them wrong in handling Bodin's book in this way—just as he was in the habit of going to the *Conseil* in Geneva and complaining on behalf of the *Compagnie* that things in books published in the city had done them wrong.

Goulart claims to have redisposed the matter in accord with the truth, and not to have shown any passion or desire to 'monitor' the author, who is simply badly informed in certain matters ('ragençez à la verite, sans aucune passion n'y desir de controller l'auteur, mal informé en cela'). This is quasi-friendly correction, in other words, not outright censorship. Goulart is defending the liberties he has taken in judging the behaviour shown by Bodin in accessing and handling his own sources, in the context of imagined tribunals of opinion. He knows that people will alight

[66] Lyon 1593, second part, sig. p2r/Lyon [Geneva] 1595, sig. 2n7v. In Lyon [Geneva] 1595, III 9 ends with the Latin citation 'Quo diversus abis?'

[67] Alain Legros, 'Ce qui gênait Simon Goulart dans le chapitre "Des prières" (Montaigne, *Essais*, I, 56)', *Bibliothèque d'Humanisme et Renaissance,* 67 (2005), 79–91; Daisy Aaronian, 'La censure de Simon Goulart dans l'édition "Genevoise" des *Essais* (1595)', *Bulletin de la Société des Amis de Montaigne,* 8th series, 27–8 (2002), 83–97.

[68] See 2.2.7.   [69] Jostock, *La censure négociée,* 208–9.

quickly on the changes he has made and turn them potentially into an international 'scandal', just as Lipsius was inclined to do when he saw Lyon [Geneva] 1595.[70]

So why republish Bodin's book at all, even in a corrected version? Because it contains many things that are freely and usefully said ('beaucoup de choses dites librement et qui peuvent servir'). This is a free-speaking text, and, when re-aligned with 'the truth' in some particulars, Goulart does wish to disseminate it further to the lay reader. He thought it would please the French to provide them with this text in a smaller and cheaper format, especially as he had understood that the Parisian *libraire* had been prohibited from reprinting it immediately.[71] A commercial opportunity blends with an opportunity to correct an important text for ordinary French readers.

A similar opportunity presented itself when someone brought to Goulart in Geneva a copy of Lyon 1593, a *contrefaçon* based on L'Angelier's ill-fated 1588 edition.[72] La Grange's edition, the first to contain tables of the principal matters and most memorable things ('choses plus memorables') in the book, was most probably the form in which the fuller 1588 text first reached Geneva and many other cities across Europe. For it is crucial to note that La Grange was taking advantage of the gap in the market caused by the crisis in Paris, which had prevented widespread distribution of L'Angelier's 1588 edition. Just a few years later, from 1598, L'Angelier would close the gap with a series of octavo editions, rendering both Lyon 1593 and Lyon [Geneva] 1595 obsolete.[73]

La Grange's tables, furthermore, presented the text in a particular light. The provision of a good alphabetical index made it more like the miscellaneously ordered collections of commented extracts that were so popular at exactly this time, and that were based on ancient precedents such as the *Attic Nights* of Aulus Gellius.[74] As Goulart says in the dedication to the second volume of the *Thresor*, this manner of writing by *récits divers* is far from being unprofitable.[75]

The *Essais* became a 'treasure of beautiful and noteworthy discourses', a consultation-ready miscellany of examples from ancient and modern histories, intertwined with Montaigne's particular 'spin' and his associated commentary on key topics and authors. The table occasionally reveals a clearly protestant perspective, as in the entry for Montaigne's discussion of the Spanish in III 6, which hints at a providential punishment: 'The Spanish, their great avarice, their cruelty against the King of Peru, their other instances of bad conduct in the West Indies, their

[70] For this and the previous paragraph, see Jean Bodin, *Six livres de la republique* ([Geneva]: [Claude Juge], 1577), sigs. ¶8v–*1r [USTC 1425/GLN15–16 2614].

[71] Bodin, *Six livres de la republique*, sig. *5r–v.

[72] Michel Simonin, 'Les contrefaçons lyonnaises de Montaigne et Ronsard au temps de la Ligue', in François Moureau (ed.), *Les presses grises* (Paris: Aux Amateurs de Livres, 1988), 139–59.

[73] Sayce and Maskell, 18–20; Balsamo and Simonin, *Abel L'Angelier & Françoise de Louvain (1574–1620)*, 82–5, 87–8.

[74] Ann Blair, *Too much to know: managing scholarly information before the modern age* (New Haven: Yale University Press, 2010), 126–31.

[75] Simon Goulart, *Thresor d'histoires admirables et memorables de nostre temps*, 4 vols. (Geneva: Samuel Crespin, 1614–20), vol. 2, sig. 2Mr. This text also appears in the Houzé 1610 edition of volume two. Crespin published volumes 3 and 4 in 1614, and volumes 1 and 2 in 1620. I give references in what follows to this edition of the complete work.

pillaged goods mostly absorbed by the sea'.[76] The table hardly refers the reader at all to the many passages about the author himself—who is not therefore treated as a 'principal matter'.[77]

The principal clues concerning the nature of Goulart's interest in the *Essais* are to be found in two other publications that first appear at Paris in 1600, and at Lyon in 1603, and that both contained alphabetical tables of the principal matters similar to those in Lyon 1593, Lyon [Geneva] 1595, and the Leiden B [Geneva] 1602 editions of the *Essais*: Goulart's own *Histoires admirables et memorables de nostre temps*, and his translation, with interpolations, of *Les meditations historiques de M. Philippe Camerarius*.[78]

These publications were both miscellanously arranged works that used unsystematic headings together with alphabetical indexes. Goulart's own collection was closer to a cento. But he does frequently tie his extracts together with authorial commentary and personal examples, in the manner (bar, of course, the frequently devotional tone) of Montaigne's earlier and shorter chapters. His translation and adaptation of Camerarius was closer to a miscellanous commentary or work of *variae lectiones* as it included more authorial judgements and more complex chapter titles or headings.

As we heard earlier in this section, there is one French word for 'miscellany' that groups these works. Both the *Histoires admirables* and the *Meditations historiques* were described by Goulart as 'thresors' in their paratexts, and both included extracts (in the case of the *Meditations* added by Goulart) from that other *trésor* Goulart had published: the *Essais*. All three were 'living libraries'.

In the dedicatory preface to the third volume of his translation and adaptation of Camerarius, Goulart helps us understand the broad and fluid category of literature to which he was contributing, and the market for which he was catering. He says he has added his own observations here and there to Camerarius's text, with the French nation in mind, who desire diversity in their reading ('desireuse de diverse lecture'). He then describes the genres of miscellaneous writings by ancient and modern authors that meet this desire:

> Medleys of natural history, antiquities, novels, lessons, collections, pandects, treasuries and theatres of examples, anthologies, philological studies, researches, discourses, miscellanies, daily exercises, evening exercises, banquets, table-talks, discourses, essays, hoards, observations, and other works.[79]

---

[76] Lyon 1593, second part, sig. z8v/Lyon [Geneva] 1595, sig. 2*1r.

[77] There is no entry in either table for 'Michel de Montaigne', and only a few isolated references to him elsewhere (e.g. 'Autheurs Latins plus agreables au S. De Montaigne', 'Actions de l'autheur durant sa Mairie en la ville de Bordeaux', 'Physique de l'Autheur').

[78] On these two works see Huchard, *D'encre et de sang*, 110–12. The *Meditations* first appeared at Lyon in 1603 (with further editions in 1608 and 1610), the *Histoires* at Paris in 1600 (volume 1 is USTC 74130, with volumes 2 and 3 following in 1601, then further editions in 1604, 1606, 1607, 1610, 1612, 1614, 1618, 1620, 1628). See Leonard Chester Jones, *Simon Goulart, 1543–1628*, 630–2, 635–6. I have used the Lyon 1610 edition of the *Meditations*.

[79] Philippus Camerarius, *Les meditations historiques... Nouuelle édition, reueue sur le Latin augmenté par l'auteur, & enrichie d'vn tiers par le translateur; outre la nouuelle & entiere version du troisiesme volume*, ed. Simon Goulart, 3 vols. (Lyon: Widow of Antoine de Harsy, 1610), vol. 3, sig. 2¶2r: '[H]istoires naturelles et meslees, des antiques, nouuelles, leçons, des recueils, pandectes, thresors et theatres

This list adapts and vernacularizes the neo-Latin genres of miscellaneous writing described by Conrad Gessner in the *Pandectæ* as 'varia et miscellanea', which included, for example, Plutarch's *Symposiaca* ('Propos de table' or 'Tabletalk') and collections of *varia historia* and *mirabiles narrationes*.[80] The new genre of *essais* takes its place in a broad tradition of miscellaneous literature from reference works to dialogues, from *histoires mêlées* to *leçons* and *trésors et théâtres d'exemples*. This literature was thriving at the end of the sixteenth century and the beginning of the seventeenth century, thanks to a taste for *diverse lecture*.

So we can triangulate the three *trésors* as a single Genevan enterprise to enfranchise—within, as ever, certain protestant limits—the individual, private reader-writer in Francophone territories with the materials and capacity for *diverse lecture*. It assimilates and adapts Montaigne's own enterprise, which, on the model of Amyot's Plutarch, also aims to enfranchise the reader-writer within certain limits.[81] The key principle of adaptation is the notion that reading should give rise to a sense of vocation, which usually in Goulart's milieu meant a personal calling towards devotion to God.

In another paratext, Goulart states that there is no way of life less sad and uncommodious than that of the man who holds the book in one hand, the pen in the other, to ruminate in reading what concerns his vocation, and to procure by means of his writings that some good comes to him, and to others, from his frequent meditations ('l'homme qui tient le livre d'une main, la plume de l'autre, pour considerer en la lecture ce qui convient à sa vocation, et procurer par les escrits que quelque bien reviene à lui mesme, et aux autres, de ses frequentes meditations').[82] This describes both Goulart's activity as a reader-writer correcting and inserting his observations into others' works, to make them his own, and the activity of the public for whom he prints and summarizes his publications.

Who are his models for this activity, for the *triage exquis* of memorable histories for self and others? Aulus Gellius provided the general model for miscellanies that followed the haphazard order of reading notes.[83] But Plutarch and Seneca were more immediately relevant as authors of *œuvres mêlées* or 'histoires naturelles et meslees'. Goulart had published both as *trésors* of moral and natural philosophy, re-editing Amyot's French text and offering his own French translation of Seneca. He added his own prefatory summaries, including guidance on how the Christian, *débonnaire lecteur* should read the text, as well as extensive indices of the principal matters that were very similar to those offered in the other volumes we have been

---

d'exemples, des anthologies, Philologies, recerches, discours, diversitez, journees, Serees, banquets, propos de table, discours, essais, amas, Observations, et autres pieces'. I provide the full French text as these terms for miscellaneous literary collections are very difficult to translate with precise English equivalents.

[80] Jean-Marc Mandosio, 'La miscellanée: histoire d'un genre', in Dominique de Courcelles (ed.), *Ouvrages miscellanées et théories de la connaissance à la Renaissance: actes des journées d'études organisées par l'École nationale des chartes (Paris, 5–6 avril 2002)* (Paris: École des chartes, 2003), 7–36, 18–25, 28–36.

[81] See 2.7.11 for further elaboration of this point.

[82] Camerarius, *Les meditations historiques*, 1610, vol. 1, sig. 2*1r.

[83] Blair, *Too much to know*, 127; Mandosio, 'La miscellanée: histoire d'un genre', 8–12.

considering.[84] Goulart enlisted Plutarch as a pagan ally in his polemics against the contemporary atheists and epicureans who, he claimed, denied the signs of God's Providence.[85]

Goulart's edition of Amyot's translation of Plutarch's *Moralia* or *Morals* was, along with his edition of the *Vies*, his most important contribution to secular literature. It was, indeed, a publishing phenomenon that showed how his so-called 'pirated' versions of French publications could capture a lion's share of the market, and how *libraires* in Paris (especially Abel L'Angelier) and Geneva could effectively share the production of particular works. It first appeared at Geneva in 1581–2, with L'Angelier distributing some stock in Paris; L'Angelier then published his own edition in 1584; thereafter it appeared in regular editions in both cities until the 1640s. Many of these were handy octavos, but some, such as Chouet's 1627 edition, were prestigious folios.[86]

Goulart explains that the *œuvres mêlées* in the second volume—which include miscellaneous texts such as the 'Propos de table', 'Les opinions des philosophes', and 'Collation abregee d'aucunes histoires'—are defined not by their content but by their avoidance of the style of the formal philosophical schools (Aristotelian and Platonic). In them, Plutarch favours a more 'Academic' style ('parler Academiquement'). Goulart says something very similar of Seneca's style in the preface to the third volume of his translation, where he contrasts it with the 'methode exacte' of Aristotelian philosophy. He aligns his French translation of Seneca with his edition of Amyot's translation of Plutarch's *Morals* by giving it the same title.[87]

A style of philosophy more suited to a non-scholastic, vernacular market is being offered across several publications here. It is being offered to readers who were themselves writing miscellaneous, non-methodical philosophical works based on their reading and experience.

The more recent models for *variae lectiones* included Pedro Mexía, Caelius Rhodiginus, and Erasmus.[88] But Montaigne and Camerarius specifically appealed as writers of modern 'œuvres morales et meslees'. They were 'representers' of miscellaneous *histoires naturelles et mêlées*, histories gathered from reading in

[84] USTC 83256/GLN15–16 2891, with further editions in various cities in 1582, 1584, 1587, 1588, 1594, 1595, 1597, 1603, 1607, 1613, 1615, 1616, 1621, 1627, 1645; USTC 57423, with further editions in 1604 and 1606. See Jones, *Simon Goulart, 1543–1628*, 582–5, 619–20. Goulart's translation and edition of Seneca was described as 'ce Thresor de Philosophie Morale et Naturelle' on the title page, while he described his edition of Amyot's Plutarch as a *trésor* throughout his prefatory materials, especially his preface to volume 1. The indices to Goulart's works of Seneca stretch to nearly 150 pages and include, besides the main index of principal matters, separate sections on the cited authors, paradoxes, 'tableaux' of vices and virtues, similes, and apophthegms. I used the Lyon 1615 edition of the Plutarch and the Geneva 1606 edition of the Seneca.

[85] Cécile Huchard, 'Histoire et providence dans l'oeuvre de Simon Goulart', *Bulletin de la Société de l'Histoire du Protestantisme Français*, 152 (2006), 221–44, 221–4.

[86] Balsamo and Simonin, *Abel L'Angelier & Françoise de Louvain (1574–1620)*, 199–200, 227, 286–7, 330–1, 362; Jones, *Simon Goulart, 1543–1628*, 582–5.

[87] Plutarch, *Les Œuvres morales et meslees*, ed. Simon Goulart, 2 vols. (Lyon: Paul Frelon, 1615), vol. 2, sig. §2r–v; Lucius Annaeus Seneca, *Les œuvres morales et meslees*, 3 vols. ([Geneva]: J. Arnaud, 1606), vol. 3, sig. 3A2v; Marie-Dominique Couzinet, 'Les *Essais* de Montaigne et les *Miscellanées*', in Courcelles (ed.), *Ouvrages miscellanées et théories de la connaissance à la Renaissance*, 153–69, 163–5.

[88] Blair, *Too much to know*, 126–31.

books, from oral report, and from personal experience. Montaigne's work was described in 1602 by Sainte-Marthe as 'Miscellaneorum libri' and later by Sorel as a 'mélange'.[89]

Philipp Camerarius was a scholarly, pious counterpart to Montaigne. The younger son of Joachim Camerarius, he held the lifelong position of the first Pro-Chancellor of the Altdorf Academy, on behalf of the City Council of Nürnberg. Goulart's prefaces indicate that Camerarius retreated in his later years, like the Gascon, to the cabinet of the muses, in order to offer successive editions of the fruits of his reading and meditations (1591, 1601, 1609). But many of the academician's chapters in fact derive from informal little orations that followed the more serious and useful offerings of the Dean at graduation ceremonies.[90]

As we shall see, it was more often Camerarius that Goulart shadowed when offering the fruits of his spare-time reading in successive editions of his collections of histories. As orchestrated by Goulart, all three volumes provide contemporary materials, models, and guidance—complementary to the ancient resources provided by his editions of Plutarch and Seneca—for reading and rewriting histories and memoirs in relation to moral-philosophical and natural-philosophical topics, within a protestant spiritual framework.

In this respect it is important to stipulate, however, that by the time Goulart was compiling and publishing the *Thresor* and Camerarius, the text of the *Essais* he was normally using was not his own protestant-friendly edition of 1595, but the full text first published in that same year by L'Angelier, and first published in Geneva in 1602 by Pyramus de Candolle, with whom both Charles Perrot and Goulart were associated (as we shall see in 2.2.5 and 2.2.6). Goulart's corrected Montaigne had not captured the market in the way some of his other re-editions had done, for Parisian octavo editions of the full text began to circulate freely from 1598. For a decade after that, Paris and Geneva vied for control of the market for the full, unexpurgated *Essais*.

2.2.5 THE GENEVAN EDITIONS OF 1602

An entry under 19 February 1602 in the registers of the *Compagnie* reveals a series of shocked discoveries on the part of the pastors: that Pyramus de Candolle has just printed Montaigne's *Essais* 'unabridged' ('tous entiers'), not 'based on the correction' ('selon la correction') that had already been printed (i.e. Lyon [Geneva] 1595); that the book is 'cynique' and contains 'things that are not appropriate for us' ('choses non convenables à nous'); and that this print-run went ahead without permission, even if it was distributed in its entirety 'hors d'ici' (i.e. in France and beyond). 'Cynique', here, is more likely to mean 'shameful' or 'outrageous', in the

[89] Millet 138; Couzinet, 'Les *Essais* de Montaigne et les *Miscellanées*', 161.
[90] Frederick John Stopp, *The emblems of the Altdorf Academy: medals and medal orations, 1577–1626* (London: Modern Humanities Research Association, 1974), 84–5.

manner of ancient Cynics such as Diogenes and Epicurus, than 'cynical' in the modern sense.[91]

The reference to an implied prior judgement of the book, connected in the record to this condemnation, is important. The pastors do not commission someone to review this book—as they frequently do on other occasions—because they already know it and have a shared judgement of it. It appears that the previous 'correction' had at least—if it had not been officially commissioned by the *Compagnie* (and/or by the *Conseil*)—not been disallowed and had corresponded to a shared judgement on the part of the members. Indeed, this reference to it in the records may be the first official acknowledgement of its status, for a scandalous book could be published if the scandalous things in it were taken out. Lyon [Geneva] 1595 had been considered acceptable because it had removed the shameful and indecent material that threatened to damage the reputation of Genevan ecclesiastical society.[92]

Geneva did not follow Rome in issuing an index of prohibited books that classified the entire *œuvres* of identified authors as heretical. The book and the things it contains are the focus. But the goal, as at Rome, is to maintain moral and public order in the city, which the *Compagnie* felt was constantly under threat during the wars and agitations suffered by Geneva during this period.[93]

If we compare the Genevan process with the Roman process revealed in 1.7.3, a difference of emphasis emerges. In this case, there is no evidence that the noble *persona* 'Montaigne', supposedly carried with the book, is an agent in the assessment of the book. Here, it is not the author and everything he stands for that is being judged, as at Rome, but the things in the book (instances of scandalously immoral and irreligious behaviour that cannot be permitted 'before' the church in Geneva) and the *libraire* who threatened public order by printing them and distributing them from a Genevan location.

The *Compagnie* resolves to advise 'Messieurs' on the *Conseil*, the civil authority, to summon and punish Candolle, so that nothing adverse to or indecent for this church ('contraire et mal decent à ceste Eglise') is hereafter printed, and to reaffirm the legislative principle that a copy must always be deposited prior to publication, so that nothing can be published without their permission.[94]

The fact that the *Compagnie* has to send representatives to the *Conseil* to request censorial action reveals the constitutional feature for which the city was praised by Jean Bodin. The ministers of the church act as spiritual police but have no civil

---

[91] Gabriella Cahier and Matteo Campagnolo (eds.), *Registres de la compagnie des pasteurs de Genève: tome VIII, 1600–1603* (Geneva: Droz, 1986), 130; Hugh Roberts, *Dogs' tales: representations of ancient Cynicism in French Renaissance texts* (Amsterdam: Rodopi, 2006), 132–3.

[92] Though, strictly speaking, we can deduce from the 1602 entry neither that Lyon [Geneva] 1595 was allowed officially by the *Conseil*, nor that the *Conseil* and *Compagnie* would in 1602 have allowed a correction to be published. In 1577 Goulart's corrected edition of Bodin's *Six livres* was allowed, but in 1585 the whole work was prohibited as contrary to piety and good order. See Jostock, *La censure négociée*, 37; Corinne Müller, 'L'édition subreptice des *Six Livres de la République* de Jean Bodin (Genève 1577). Sa génèse et son influence', *Quaerendo*, 10 (1980), 211–36, 235.

[93] Jostock, *La censure négociée*.

[94] Cahier and Campagnolo (eds.), *Registres de la compagnie des pasteurs de Genève: tome VIII, 1600–1603*, 130.

jurisdiction. They are, in a sense, the victims of immoral behaviour who remonstrate with the *Conseil* to act to restore their reputation and the reputation of the city. So complaints about particular 'scandals' drive the development of regulatory policy, as when Jean Calvin and Théodore de Bèze remonstrate with the *Conseil* in 1563 because an abcedary has been printed with a passage implying that Jesus Christ was not God. Conversely, the civil authorities actively commission senior ministers of the church, along with their own members, to examine and correct copies on their behalf.[95]

Ingrid Jostok describes the censorial process at Geneva as 'negotiated censorship', though the concept might also be applied to the manner in which the works of Montaigne and de Thou were dealt with at Rome, and even to unofficial processes of judgement such as Pasquier's.[96] Official censorship in practice was a series of debates, arrangements, and compromises between the institutions and the personnel involved, and it overlapped with unofficial censorship in various ways.

There was no overall clarity as to who held the ultimate power or liberty of judgement and what the reach of that judgement would be. At Rome in this period, three censorial authorities were engaged in internal debates and conflicts: the Master of the Sacred Palace, the Congregation of the Index, and the Congregation of the Inquisition.[97]

Even when judgements were reached and registered in the record, they were not necessarily enforced, and they did not necessarily prove to be definitive; they could quickly be overtaken by new commercial or political circumstances. This is what happened when Lyon [Geneva] 1595's position in a relatively uncrowded marketplace was overwhelmed by L'Angelier's new octavo editions of 1598 and 1600—even the corrector of the first Genevan edition would use the much fuller texts available from 1595, and especially from 1598.

We can see evidence of this ongoing negotiation in the document under consideration. The publication of an uncorrected edition of the *Essais* is clearly considered by the pastors to be a scandal for the church, and it prompts them to make a larger intervention. The *Compagnie* are not just aiming to condemn one *libraire*, they are expressing an intention to remonstrate with the *Conseil* on a more general political principle: their own 'liberty' of judgement, which is granted and controlled by the civil authorities. They wish to defend their privilege to judge whether each and every book—not just every theological book, but *every* book, even a literary miscellany—published via Geneva is appropriate to 'us', the ministers of the reformed church.

---

[95] Jostock, *La censure négociée*, 37, 43, 101–2; Müller, 'L'édition subreptice', 220–3, 233. The Genevan edition of this work, corrected by Simon Goulart, changed some of the details of Bodin's account and removed parallels with Rome, but retained his basic account of the operation of censorship in the city.

[96] Clegg, *Press censorship in Elizabethan England*, xii: '[E]ach censorship "event" is actually a complex locus in which multiple issues and interests are represented'.

[97] Gigliola Fragnito, 'La censura libraria tra Congregazione dell'Indice, Congregazione dell'Inquisizione e Maestro del Sacro Palazzo (1571–1596)', in Ugo Rozzo (ed.), *La censura libraria nell'Europa del secolo XVI: convegno internazionale di studi Cividale del Friuli, 9–10 novembre 1995* (Udine: Forum, 1997), 163–75.

The context is that the *Conseil* were in the process of slowly abrogating the ecclesiastical *Compagnie*'s power to do this, and causing friction by rebalancing the relationship between the two bodies in their own favour. They were beginning to authorize publications directly and to favour economic considerations over religious concerns—in the name of 'secure commercement'. At the same time, however, they were also seeking to exercise their direct jurisdiction over religious affairs, and to find occasions to regulate the *Compagnie* itself.[98]

The *Registres du Conseil* make no mention of the remonstration the *Compagnie* had decided to make. However, when the matter is picked up again by the *Compagnie des Pasteurs* on 23 April 1602, the record clearly states that it was indeed made to *Messieurs* (on the *Conseil*) some time after 19 February. The *Compagnie* is on this occasion advised that pastors Perrot and Pinault will go before *Messieurs* on the *Conseil* the following Monday to remonstrate with them concerning the shamefulness of the book, and the impudence and lawlessness of the publishers in printing this work without permission ('pour leur remontrer l'indignité du livre, l'audace et contravention des libraires à imprimer ceste oeuvre mesmes sans congé').

Again, the emphasis is on the book and on the audacity and transgressiveness of the people who have produced and distributed it in this city, threatening the authorities' control of public order. The author is not an agent in the process in the way that he was in Rome in 1580–1. 'Libraires' in the plural is the first indication that more than one audacious publisher has been printing the work. *Messieurs* will be asked to punish this reversal of all good order ('tout bon ordre') and to give order that the *imprimerie* of the city should not be profaned in this way. They will also be asked to ensure that regular inspections by a three-man commission of officials, which had been instituted in 1560, are re-established.[99]

This time the remonstration is entered in the *Registres du Conseil* for 26 April 1602. Perrot and Pinault are recorded as appearing before *Messieurs* to prohibit Matthieu Berjon from printing the *Essais* of Montaigne, 'which have also been printed by seigneur Candolle' ('qui ont...esté aussi Imprimez p[ar] le sr de Candole')—which may be a belated acknowledgement of the previous remonstration. The record therefore associates the enterprises of Candolle and Berjon in printing the *Essais*. An officer is charged with seizing all the copies then going through 'the press of Berjon, [Pierre de la] Rovière and others' ('sur la presse d[udit?] berjon, Rouvier et dautres'). Does the use of 'presse' in the singular tell us that this was a group enterprise on the part of several *libraires*, but printed on one press? Or are they all printing it separately on their own presses? In addition, the three-man commission is charged with inspecting all the 'impressions' or 'livres' to check that they have been permitted and reported ('permises [et rapportées]'). So, those caught printing the *Essais* were to be subjected to a general inspection.[100]

---

[98] Jostock, *La censure négociée*, 45, 147–51.

[99] For this and the previous paragraph, see Cahier and Campagnolo (eds.), *Registres de la compagnie des pasteurs de Genève: tome VIII, 1600–1603*, 141–2 (23 April 1602); Jostock, *La censure négociée*, 40.

[100] For this and the previous paragraph see Geneva, Archives d'État de Genève (AEG), Conseil ordinaire—Petit Conseil—Conseil des XXV, Registres du Conseil, vol. 97, fol. 59r (26 April 1602) (<https://ge.ch/arvaegconsult/>, accessed 5 September 2011). The record appears to read 'sur la presse

However many presses were involved, the circumstances suggest that informal associations of *libraires* and printers—with Candolle as the entrepreneur—were producing the *Essais* in clandestine fashion in 1602. Such an arrangement, with a publisher or financier behind the scenes employing various printers and booksellers, was normal in Geneva.[101] The stimulus for this enterprise was commercial: the arrival in Geneva of copies of the successive octavos (1598, 1600, and 1602) published by L'Angelier, which were themselves in part a response to the *contrefaçons* already published in Lyon (1593) and Geneva (1595), and which rendered the republication of a heavily expurgated text such as Lyon [Geneva] 1595 commercially unviable.

It is very difficult to track such associations, as the *libraires* could act variously as publishers, booksellers, and printers and were all related to one another through various business and family connections. They were also, as we shall see in what follows, associated with Genevan pastors who might unofficially approve, or even propose, certain publications—Candolle knew both Goulart and Perrot, senior members of the *Compagnie* who were privately handling copies of L'Angelier's full-text *Essais* by the turn of the seventeenth century. There is also later evidence of associations between Candolle and the *libraires* named by the *Compagnie* in connection with the *Essais*, and a clue concerning the identity of at least one of the unnamed others who might have been involved.

The latter involves the choice of 'Leiden: Jehan Doreau' as the false imprint for both Genevan editions of 1602 (see Illus. 2.2.1 and 2.2.2). Philippe Desan has pointed out that another work by Philippe de Marnix, also published at Geneva in 1602, carried the same imprint on its title page. Goulart juxtaposes a passage from this work and a passage from the *Essais* in his *Histoires admirables*.[102]

The idea of using this false imprint probably originated with the Marnix edition (because the edition by Paets with which it was entering in *concurrence* was published in Leiden), and was then transferred to the Montaigne edition that was being printed around the same time. So it is likely that whoever was involved in publishing the Genevan Marnix was also involved in the Genevan Montaigne. Another *libraire*, Jacob Chouet, was held responsible and fined for publishing the Marnix edition by the *Conseil* on 12 May 1602.[103]

Had Chouet been Candolle's partner in publishing Leiden A [Geneva] 1602? They had certainly been partners in the past, and Chouet had been involved before Candolle in running Eustache Vignon's enterprise after his death. In 1598,

---

d[...] berjon, Rouuier et dautres'. The editor of the registers of the *Compagnie* interprets this as 'l'officine de Berjon et de Rovière [Pierre de la Rovière]'. See Cahier and Campagnolo (eds.), *Registres de la compagnie des pasteurs de Genève: tome VIII, 1600–1603*, 142n.96. It appears that the *Essais* were being printed in several printshops, but that Berjon was held principally responsible by the *Compagnie* and the *Conseil*.

[101] Jean François Gilmont, *Le livre réformé au XVIe siècle* (Paris: Bibliothèque nationale de France, 2005), 57–8.

[102] Philippe de Marnix, *Tableau des differens de la religion* (Leiden: Jean Doreau, 1602); Goulart, *Thresor d'histoires admirables et memorables de nostre temps*, 1614–20, vol. 1, sigs. P7v–8r.

[103] Jostock, *La censure négociée*, 394. The title given in the registers of the *Conseil* for 12 May 1602 is 'Miroir des différends de la religion' but the similarity of the title, and the date, make it almost certain that this refers to the 1602 *Tableau*. Chouet was fined ten florins.

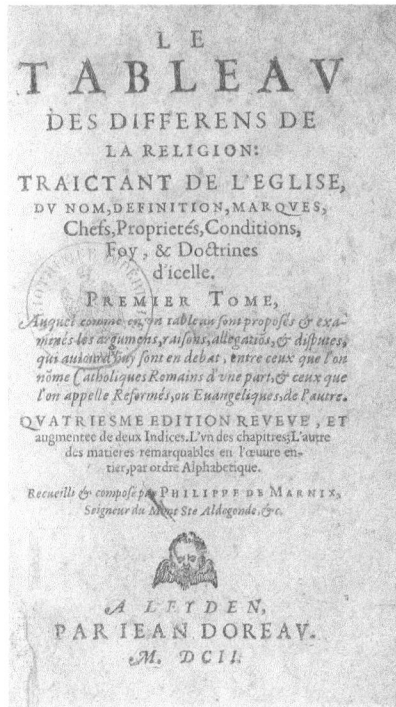

Illus. 2.2.1. Philippe de Marnix, *Le tableau des differens de la religion* (Leiden: Jean Doreau, 1602), Bibliothèque nationale de France, pressmark D2-9214 (1), title page. Reproduced by permission of the Bibliothèque nationale de France, Paris.

the *maison* run by Candolle joined with Chouet to publish an edition of *Corpus juris civilis a Dio. Gothofredo J. C. recognitum*, printed by Guillaume de Laimarie.[104]

Candolle was already a publisher and bookseller in 1602, but it is difficult to be sure at what point prior to 1619 he owned and began to run presses. We shall see that both de la Rivière and Berjon printed books for him in the early 1600s. Originally from Provence, he was first and foremost a draper, inheriting the trade from his uncle Bernadin. He became involved in the print trade when in 1591 he married Anne Vignon, the eldest daughter of an established Genevan printer, Eustache Vignon (d. 1588). For ten years he ran the Vignon family firm ('Héritiers d'Eustache Vignon') with a brother-in-law, during which time he was accredited in print as the editor of authors including Tacitus and Belleforest. This period gave him the opportunity to become a very substantial and well-networked

---

[104] USTC 451613/GLN15–16 3972. This was probably the work that Candolle then sought a licence to publish in August of 1601, after he left the Vignon family firm. See the entry for Pyramus de Candolle in RIECH.

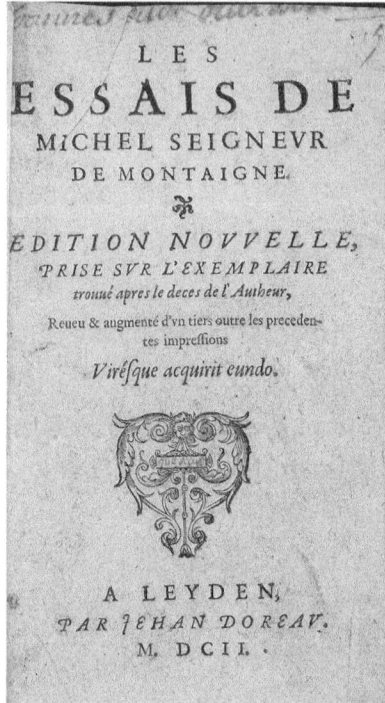

LES
ESSAIS DE
MICHEL SEIGNEVR
DE MONTAIGNE.

EDITION NOVVELLE,
PRISE SVR L'EXEMPLAIRE
trouué apres le deces de l'Autheur,

Reueu & augmenté d'vn tiers outre les preceden-
tes impressions

Viréſque acquirit eundo.

A LEYDEN,
PAR JEHAN DOREAV.
M. DCII.

Illus. 2.2.2. Montaigne, *Essais* (Leiden: Jehan Doreau, 1602), Bodleian Library, pressmark Vet.B2 f.37, title page. Reproduced by permission of The Bodleian Libraries, the University of Oxford.

figure in the Genevan and international book trade, a *marchand libraire* in his own right.[105]

In early 1597 Candolle went before the *Compagnie* to request permission—on behalf of the héritiers de Vignon—to print a mathematical work by Adrianus Romanus against Scaliger. In fact, he had already gone direct to the Recteur of the Academy and received permission—subsequently deciding, perhaps, that he also needed the *Compagnie's* endorsement. When he was refused by the *Compagnie*, who strongly supported Scaliger, Candolle went behind their backs to the *Conseil*, who reversed the decision, with the condition that the invectives against Scaliger were removed. The *Compagnie* were forced to back down and the edition duly appeared with a false place of publication (Würzburg).

However, the very next month, the *Compagnie* signed a contract with Candolle and the héritiers de Vignon (they insisted it was issued in both names) to sell him a vast stock of 1588 Genevan bibles and psalters. Correspondence the following

[105] Liliane Mottu-Weber, Anne-Marie Piuz, and Bernard Lescaze (eds.), *Vivre à Genève autour de 1600*, 2 vols. (Geneva: Slatkine, 2002–6), vol. 2, 33–5; Perret, *Les Imprimeries d'Yverdon*, 27–51, 376–9; Paul Chaix, Gustave Moeckli, and Alain Dufour, *Les livres imprimés à Genève de 1550 à 1600* (Geneva: Droz, 1966), 141–3.

month with Calvinist pastors in southwest France reveals their motive: they believed Candolle was the ideal merchant to distribute Genevan bibles in France at a good price.[106]

In 1601, the Vignon family inheritance was divided between the three surviving children. Jean Vignon inherited the publishing house and became the sole director. As we shall in section 2.2.6, it was this brother-in-law, Jean, who attended the *Conseil* and paid a fine for Candolle in 1602. There is documentary evidence that Candolle published or sought to publish other books, besides the *Essais*, in 1601–3, including three for which he was condemned by the *Compagnie*.[107]

None, however, bore his name or the name of an enterprise he owned until 1606, when a few editions, often under the false imprint of 'Coligny', began to advertise their origins in the 'Societas caldoriana', 'Societe Chaldorienne', or the 'Imprimerie Caldorienne'. This was Candolle's own, branded publishing enterprise. He was still, however, using other printers. One of these, as early as 1606, was Pierre de la Rovière. Another was Mathieu Berjon, who printed at least three works for Candolle's Société in the 1610s, before Candolle established his own press at Yverdon ('Ebroduni').[108]

The evidence therefore suggests that even by 1602 Candolle was an international merchant with agents and contacts in several countries, and with good connections both on the *Conseil* (he was a member of the larger *Conseil* from 1595) and the *Compagnie*. He is likely to have taken the *Essais* on in 1602 because he knew L'Angelier's octavos of the full, posthumous text were selling well in France and he

---

[106] For this and the previous paragraph, see Gabriella Cahier and M. Grand-Jean (eds.), *Registres de la compagnie des pasteurs de Genève tome VII: 1595–1599* (Geneva: Droz, 1984), 55–9, 62, 269–71.

[107] See the entries for Pyramus de Candolle and Jean Vignon in RIECH; Cahier and Campagnolo (eds.), *Registres de la compagnie des pasteurs de Genève: tome VIII, 1600–1603*, 257 and n.371.

[108] Other printers who printed for him included, (unsurprisingly) Jean Vignon, Paul Marceau, and Pierre Aubert. The following list of publications (I have not seen copies) is derived from the Consortium of European Research Libraries' 'Heritage of the Printed Book' database (<http://www.cerl.org/resources/hpb/main>) and 'Thesaurus' database (<http://www.cerl.org/resources/cerl_thesaurus/main>): *Epistolae graecanicae mutuae antiquorum rhetorum, oratorum philosophorum, medicorum, theologorum, regum, ac imperatorum aliorumque praestantissimorum virorum* (Aureliae Allobrogum [Geneva]: Sumpt. Caldorianae Societatis, 1606); *Erasmi Roterodami Adagiorum chiliades juxta locos communes digestae* (Aureliae Allobrogum [Geneva]: sumptibus Caldorianae societatis, 1606); *Homeri quæ extant omnia* (Aureliæ Allobrogum [Geneva]: sumptibus Caldorianæ Societatis, 1606); *Hoi tēs hēroikēs poiēseōs palaioi poiētai pantes. Poetae Graeci veteres carminis heroici scriptores, qui extant, omnes*, ed. J. Lectius (Aureliae Allobrogum [Geneva]: excudebat Petrus de la Roviere: sumptibus Caldorianae societatis, 1606); *Controversiae memorabilis inter Paulum V. Pontificem Max. & Venetos* (In villa Sanuincentiana [Geneva]: Apud Paulum Marcellum, sumptibus Caldorianae Societatis, 1607); *Corpus Iuris Civilis: In quinque partes distinctum* (Lugduni [Geneva]: Vignon: Societas Caldoriana, 1607); Claude Fauchet, *Les antiquitez et histoires gauloises et françoises* (Geneva: Par Paul Marceau pour la Societé Caldorienne, 1611); *Lexicon iuridicum juris Romani* (Coloniae Allobrogum [Geneva]: excudebat Matthaeus Berjon: sumptibus Caldorianae Societatis, 1612); *Adagiorum Des. Erasmi Roterodami Chiliades quatuor, cum sesquicenturia* (Coloniae Allobrogum [Geneva]: Excudebat Petrus Aubertus: Caldorianae societatis, 1612); Jean Bedé de La Gormandière, *Les droicts de l'Eglise catholique, & de ses prebstres, dediés au serenissime Roy de la Grand Bretagne* (Geneva: par Matth. Berjon: pour la societé Chaldorienne, 1613); Claude Duret, *Thresor de l'histoire des langues de cest univers*, ed. Pyramus de Candolle (Cologny [Geneva]: Societe Caldoriene: Berjon, 1613); *Codicis Justiniani* (Lugduni [Geneva]: Johannem Vignon, Caldorianae Societatis, n.d.).

knew he could sell his own stock of copies in France, Germany, and England, thereby raising cash for his purchases of wool.

When he moved his enterprise (now the 'Société helvétiale caldoresque') from Geneva to Yverdon in 1617, the main attraction for the *Conseil* in Yverdon was the wool trade and cloth manufacture. But Candolle explained in negotiations how the two trades were interrelated. He would use the monies gained from selling the products of his presses in France, Germany (especially Frankfurt), and England to buy wool for importing and manufacture (so that no cash needed to be transported across Europe). In 1617, he certainly had a stock of printed books in two warehouses in Geneva.[109]

2.2.6 WHO ALLOWED THE *ESSAIS* TO BE PRINTED AT GENEVA IN 1602?

Did the seizure ordered at the end of April 1602 by the *Conseil* go ahead, and, if so, was it successful? Or did the copies on the presses of these associated printers and publishers in fact constitute what is now thought of as the second surviving Genevan edition of 1602, Leiden B? It is difficult to be certain. What is clear is that a copy of L'Angelier's new octavo edition, first published in early 1602, reached Geneva soon after publication, but after the publication of Leiden A [Geneva] 1602. The publisher of Leiden B [Geneva] 1602 noted that it contained two new tables or indices: one listing the subjects in the book and one giving references to passages on the life of the author. These tables were perhaps included by L'Angelier in response to the tables that had appeared in Lyon 1593 (actually published in Lyon) and Lyon [Geneva] 1595, though they were more thorough (especially in indexing references to Montaigne's life) and covered the full text of Gournay's posthumous edition.[110]

So a reset of Leiden A [Geneva] 1602 was published (Leiden B [Geneva] 1602), with the addition of these two indices from L'Angelier's edition, again destined for the French and other international markets accessible via Lyon and Frankfurt. The work of changing the page numbers was hastily done, as in some cases the Leiden B [Geneva] 1602 version of the index of subjects refers incorrectly to the page numbers as they were in Paris 1602.[111]

In the meantime (*c.*1598–*c.*1603), Le Febvre was shifting unsold copies of Lyon [Geneva] 1595 with inserts of prefatory materials copied from L'Angelier's publications. He was clearly stimulated to do this by the arrival in Geneva of these new octavo editions from Paris, which he saw both as an end to the commercial viability of the shorter, corrected text and as an opportunity to sell his remaining stock. A couple of years later the *concurrence* between these Genevan *libraires* and

---

[109] Perret, *Les Imprimeries d'Yverdon*, 27–48 (27–8).

[110] Sayce and Maskell, 41–4; Balsamo and Simonin, *Abel L'Angelier & Françoise de Louvain (1574–1620)*, 323–4. Some copies of Paris 1602 carry the old *privilège* of 15 October 1594 and not the new *privilège* of 1 April 1602, indicating that they were printed and published early in the year.

[111] Sayce and Maskell, 48.

L'Angelier takes a new turn in the other direction: L'Angelier appears to have reissued seized copies of Leiden A [Geneva] 1602 with his own title page, alongside his own new edition of that year. The story ended in 1609, with the reissue of some remaining copies of Leiden A [Geneva] 1602 with the new and false Genevan imprint of 'Jean Can' (who was not a printer at Geneva), and an edition (once again Leiden, Jean Doreau) reset from Leiden B [Geneva] 1602.[112]

When it is reported to the *Compagnie* on 11 June 1602 that 'they have just completed printing the *Essais* of Montaigne in this town' ('on acheve d'imprimer en ceste ville les *Essais* de Montaigne'), the inference it seems safest to make is that the edition which the group of *libraires* associated with Candolle had begun to send to press at the end of April, had either not in the event been seized by the officers of the *Conseil*, or had been carried through successfully on some presses despite the officers' attempts. It is likely, that is, to correspond to what is now labelled Leiden B [Geneva] 1602.[113]

The language used in the record indicates an escalation of the public scandal caused—from the *Compagnie*'s point of view—by the clandestine printing of this work. The *Essais* are now described as a profane and cynical book that forms men in atheism ('livre prophane et cinique formant les hommes à l'atheisme'). In mid-1602, then, the *franchise* of Montaigne's—or rather of the *book*'s worth—was, as a matter of public record, not allowed by one of the main bodies representing the Genevan church, despite what Florio and Daniel say in the paratexts to London 1603. Once again the pastors resolve to go before *Messieurs* on the *Conseil* to implore them to prevent this scandal from being further disseminated by means of this town ('pour les prier d'empescher que ce scandale ne soit davantage semé par le moyen de ceste ville'). Once again, there is no record of this remonstration in the registers of the *Conseil*.[114]

However, it appears that the three-man commission did finally—as charged on 26 April—inspect the printshops of Candolle, Berjon, de la Rovière, and the others in early July. The results of these inspections follow one another in the records of the *Conseil*'s session on the morning of 5 July 1602.[115]

The findings are that Berjon has printed the *Calendrier historial* without permission, and that Candolle has printed 'le Cantique des cantiques mis en rithme par une femme' without permission, using the name of a publisher of Thonon. Both are summonsed before the *Conseil* for the following day. In the absence of Candolle, his brother-in-law Jean Vignon, now running the Vignon *maison*, stands in. Berjon confesses that he was given the copy of the *Calendrier* for publication by a minister, Osée André, and is censured but not, it appears, fined. Jean Vignon is fined 25 florins for Candolle's 'Cantique', and he also reveals that a minister—this time an

---

[112] Balsamo and Simonin, *Abel L'Angelier & Françoise de Louvain (1574–1620)* 336; Sayce and Maskell, 49, 53, 60.

[113] This conclusion is supported by Jostock, *La censure négociée*, 259.

[114] Cahier and Campagnolo (eds.), *Registres de la compagnie des pasteurs de Genève: tome VIII, 1600–1603*, 151.

[115] Geneva, Archives d'État de Genève (AEG), Conseil ordinaire—Petit Conseil—Conseil des XXV, Registres du Conseil, vol. 97, fol. 93v (5 July 1602) (<https://ge.ch/arvaegconsult/>, accessed 5 September 2011).

important and long-standing member of the *Compagnie*, Charles Perrot—had been behind the publication in question.[116]

We know this because the following day Perrot is called before the *Conseil*. The entry in the margin is 'Libraires':

> The reputable minister Charles Perrot was called in for having had printed without leave the Song of Songs, put into French verse by a woman; As also the Essays of Montaigne, which he corrected, and this without the leave of the Seigneurie ('Spectable Charles Perrot ministre a esté appelé ceans pour avoir fait imprimer sans congé le Cantique des Cantiques mis en rithme francois par une femme; Comme aussi les Essais de montaigne qu'il a chasties et ce sans conge de la Seigneurie').[117]

The syntax of this record indicates that Perrot was called for having effectively published ('pour avoir fait imprimer') both the 'Cantique des Cantiques' and the *Essais*, and for having corrected the latter without the permission of the *Conseil*. Some commentators on the Genevan Montaigne assume this record to be referring to a separate, now lost edition of the *Essais*, produced independently by Berjon and censored by Perrot, for no copies of a clearly censored edition of the *Essais*, other than Lyon [Geneva] 1595, have yet been found.[118]

There is another possible interpretation of this evidence, however. If it is true that no corrections have yet been detected in Leiden A [Geneva] 1602 or Leiden B [Geneva] 1602, it is also true that a full collation has not to my knowledge been undertaken. Given that it was Candolle who printed the 'Cantique', and that the information about Perrot's involvement in this must have come from his brother-in-law Vignon the previous day, it is more likely to have been Vignon who revealed at the same time that Perrot had previously authorized Candolle's edition of the *Essais*.

It is therefore probable that the edition unofficially authorized and supposedly *chastié* by Perrot is indeed Leiden A [Geneva] 1602. The claim that Perrot both allowed and corrected the edition is a defence against the *Compagnie*'s original accusation that Leiden A [Geneva] 1602 was an edition prepared without official correction.[119] Either the correction was undertaken with so light a touch as to be invisible, or Vignon exaggerated the nature of Perrot's intervention in an attempt to legitimize his associate's publication, or Candolle simply printed the uncorrected text regardless.

There is a more important general point. In both the cases that came before the *Conseil* on 5 July 1602 the defence offered by the *libraires* in question (Berjon and

---

[116] Geneva, Archives d'État de Genève (AEG), Conseil ordinaire—Petit Conseil—Conseil des XXV, Registres du Conseil, vol. 97, fol. 94v (6 July 1602) (<https://ge.ch/arvaegconsult/>, accessed 5 September 2011).

[117] Geneva, Archives d'État de Genève (AEG), Conseil ordinaire—Petit Conseil—Conseil des XXV, Registres du Conseil, vol. 97, fols. 95v–96r (7 July 1602) (<https://ge.ch/arvaegconsult/>, accessed 5 September 2011).

[118] Giacone, 'Gli *Essais* di Montaigne e la censura calvinista', 680–1, though Giacone speculates that the lost Perrot edition resurfaced in a line of editions, starting in 1608, that cut I 21 ('Le profit de l'un est dommage de l'autre'). To my knowledge, no such cut was made in these editions.

[119] Though we cannot rule out a coincidence: that both Candolle and Berjon reported in the same session that Perrot had unofficially allowed and promoted the printing of a work with each of them.

Candolle) was that a minister had unofficially approved, even initiated, the publication in question. So here is clear evidence of a situation in which individual pastors are exercising private liberties of judgement on their own authority, in collusion with *libraires*, without the knowledge of the *Compagnie*, and in some cases without any reference to the *Conseil*. There are other instances of this in the records involving some of our protagonists—as when the pastor Gabriel Cusin took it upon himself to publish a treatise of Félix Huguet's with Matthieu Berjon at Geneva, enlisting Goulart and Antoine de La Faye as unofficial censors. Cusin gained permission from the *Conseil*, but did not consult the *Compagnie*.[120]

Within or around the official institutional process of regulation, conducted amidst political tensions between the *Conseil* and the *Compagnie*, more informal relations between *libraires* and pastors were instrumental in shaping not only what was published at Geneva, but also the circulation of books in the round. It is in this context that two of the most senior pastors on the *Compagnie*, Simon Goulart and Charles Perrot, prove in rather different circumstances to have been the prime movers behind Lyons [Geneva] 1595, published by François le Febvre, and Leiden [Geneva] 1602 (A and B), published in the first instance by Pyramus de Candolle.

From the perspective of the current study, these editions can be considered as part of the *œuvre* of these Genevan pastors, and—because readers saw through the thin disguise offered by title pages stating 'Lyon' or 'Leiden'—more broadly of Geneva as a city, rather than just as part of the story of the dissemination and reception of the *Essais*. Florio, Scaliger, and Lipsius variously attributed these editions—or at least Lyon [Geneva] 1595—to 'the Genevans'.

Perrot and Goulart were closely associated throughout their careers, and both were instrumental on a number of different levels in the transmission and correction of texts at Geneva. The main difference was that Goulart was a polyhistor, a major editor and producer of texts for a Francophone audience across Europe. As d'Aubigné put it in an *éloge*, he 'filled Europe with books'.[121]

It is crucial to understand that although both acted as censors, Goulart in particular saw himself as enfranchising the decent, Christian, private reader-writer—not excluding ordinary Catholics—across northern Europe with a circumscribed liberty to read and understand devotional and secular literature for themselves in cheap, readily available copies. In many of his editions he provided notes and summaries that made this intent explicit.

Perrot was not engaged in this enterprise of vulgarization, but he was involved for several decades in both regulating the circulation of books and liaising with *libraires* at Geneva. Both men were regularly charged by the *Conseil* with examining and correcting works on behalf of the city authorities, and both were on the liberal wing of the *Compagnie*, concerned where possible to use correction as a way of facilitating rather than prohibiting access to literature.

In the records of an interrogation that took place in February 1570, for example, there is a glimpse of Perrot acting in a private capacity to supervise the reading of

[120] Jostock, *La censure négociée*, 231–4.   [121] Jones, *Simon Goulart, 1543–1628*, 455.

his brother-in-law, a wayward pastor's son called Lucas Cop. Perrot personally corrected Cop's copy of Catullus, which contained extra illicit materials in manuscript, by erasing certain French verses that had been written therein before handing the copy back. He was also assigned more public duties of regulation and correction. In May 1578, Eustache Vignon presented a copy of Goulart's famous *Memoires de l'estat de France* to the *Seigneurie* in order to obtain a licence for publication. The *Seigneurie* consigned it for examination to Perrot, who declared a few days later that the book could be published with a few corrections. His liberal stance was, however, rejected by the *Conseil*, who prohibited publication.[122]

There is no direct evidence of Perrot's motives in having 'had printed' the *Essais*. But there are some very interesting circumstances, relating to the same period, which may offer a partial explanation. He was the son of a *conseiller* of the *Parlement* of Paris and his correspondence shows that he was in touch with Parisian *parlementaires* around the turn of the century. There were long-standing relations between the Perrots and the Pithous, and Charles was in regular correspondence with Jean Pithou (in Basel, then Lausanne) throughout the 1590s and early 1600s.[123]

This is very likely to be the explanation for his role in the dissemination of the unexpurgated *Essais* in Geneva. As we saw in 2.1, this was the moment when the parliamentary network was actively promoting and circulating the book, together with praise of the author.

In a letter to Pithou of 20 March 1601, Perrot opens by telling him that the opportunity to write arose because he met 'sre de Candole' after dinner—which suggests that Candolle might have conveyed correspondence between them regularly.[124] In *c.*1602–3 he wrote to de Thou in Paris, informing him that he possessed the copy of de Thou's *Iobus* that had been personally censored by Bèze and that he was sending it to him.[125] In September 1607, Perrot's son was in Paris conversing with Pierre de L'Estoile. L'Estoile gathered from the son's discourse that Charles was passionately in favour of the reunion and reformation of the church, but that he was forced to dissimulate his views in Geneva. These views were expressed in a manuscript treatise ('De extremis in Ecclesia vitandis'), which Charles's son wanted to obtain for publication in Paris.[126]

Just over a year later, Charles Perrot's heterodoxy became public knowledge when the *Conseil* seized his manuscripts after his death, and condemned the

[122] Jostock, *La censure négociée*, 183–7, 170.

[123] Jacob Elisée Cellérier, *Notice biographique sur Charles Perrot pasteur genevois au seizième siècle* (extracted from 'Mémoires de la Société d'Histoire et d'Archéologie de Genève'; Geneva: Imprimerie Ramboz et Schuchardt, 1856).

[124] Dorez, *Catalogue de la collection Dupuy*, vol. 2, 299–300 (re: BnF MS Dupuy 700, fols. 161–200, though Dorez identifies the recipient as Nicolas Pithou); Roger Zuber, 'Tombeau pour des Pithou: Frontières confessionnelles et unité religieuse (1590-1600)', in Verdun L. Saulnier (ed.), *Mélanges sur la littérature de la Renaissance à la mémoire de V.-L. Saulnier* (Geneva: Droz, 1984), 331–42, 332, and n.11, 336; BnF, MS Dupuy 700, fol. 178r.

[125] Ingrid A. R. De Smet, 'La Poésie sur le fumier. La figure de Job à l'époque des Guerres de religion', in Lestringant (ed.), *Jacques-Auguste de Thou (1553–1617)*, 89–106, 93. The letter is in BnF, MS Dupuy 806, fol. 107 and the copy is BnF pressmark Rés. P. Yc. 1127.

[126] Cellérier, *Notice biographique sur Charles Perrot*, 35–6.

De extremis and other works. This was a major scandal that found a place in chronicles of the city, for L'Estoile's information proved correct: Perrot had retained his freedom of conscience in private manuscripts—as far as stating that the Genevan church should never have separated from Rome.[127]

Though Goulart had his troubles with the *Compagnie* and the *Conseil*, neither he nor his reputation suffered an equivalent scandal. Moreover, he was eventually to gain recognition as a public intellectual figure on the European scene (which Perrot did not) with his own entry in Bayle's *Dictionnaire critique et historique*. In particular, for decades he played a crucial role in the transmission or retransmission of texts and information via Geneva to a French and international Francophone public of reader-writers. As he did not wish to exclude a lay Catholic audience this often meant concealing both his own name and vocation (as Calvinist minister) and the place of publication of the works he produced—as in the case of the *Memoires de l'estat de France* mentioned above.[128]

He was above all a compiler, editor, commentator, translator, and corrector who took liberties in republishing, recontextualizing, and rewriting texts that had already been produced by authors and publishers in France. He carried out this activity in the context of his lifelong vocation as a preacher who wished to explain and make texts accessible to a lay audience who could, within decent Christian limits, read and write, and judge, for themselves.

Perhaps more than any other pastor on the *Compagnie*, Goulart had influence and contacts in the Genevan publishing trade. One telling incident can illustrate this. In January 1606, at the request of de Thou, Isaac Casaubon wrote to Goulart to ask him to prevent publication at Geneva of a French translation of de Thou's *Historiae* and in general to assist in enforcing the royal privilege protecting the work.

De Thou had been warned by someone that 'mon Seigneur de Candale' was printing or was wanting to print a French version of the first edition—another indication that Pyramus de Candolle was an important entrepreneur in the transnational book trade before he established his own public brand as a publisher. A month later, Goulart replied that he had not heard Candolle mention such an intention, even though he had talked to him at length a month previously about various affairs.

However, another individual, prompted perhaps by French *libraires*, had brought him a copy of de Thou's first edition and asked him to run over it with a view to suggesting someone who could translate it. He replied that this could only be done with the author's approval. He promises Casaubon he will do all he can to prevent any such publication, and to implore Candolle, 'who has five or six volumes on the go', not to risk displeasing such a grand and illustrious personage (as de Thou).[129]

[127] Jostock, *La censure négociée*, 267–73.   [128] Jones, *Simon Goulart, 1543–1628*, 476.
[129] For this and the previous two paragraphs, see Thou, *Historiarum sui temporis libri CXXXVIII*, vol. 7, pt. I, 20/BnF, MS Dupuy 409, fols. 64–5; Jones, *Simon Goulart, 1543–1628*, 412–13. The volumes Goulart mentions were presumably those which began to appear from 1606 under Candolle's own imprint.

This helps flesh out our sense of the agency of Genevan pastors within networks of scholars and of French and Genevan *libraires*. Goulart was not only publicly but more privately regulating and facilitating the business of the Genevan book trade—in this case by conspicuously showing due respect for the rights of an illustrious French author. De Thou clearly knew that any major text produced in France which was in danger of being reproduced or translated at Geneva was likely to go through Goulart or someone he knew. No doubt copies from France were regularly brought to him with a view to the publication of new Genevan editions or translations—as indeed happened in the case of de Thou's first edition.

Furthermore, if Goulart was in the habit of having discussions with Candolle about various affairs at the end of 1605, it is not difficult to imagine a meeting such as the March 1601 after-dinner encounter between Candolle and Goulart's close associate Perrot giving rise to the 1602 edition of the *Essais*.

Goulart's correspondence is full of evidence of his role and of his relations with *libraires*. In a letter to Scaliger, later in 1606, Goulart reveals that it is the Genevan *libraire* François le Febvre who will be transporting Scaliger's gift of a copy of his Eusebius from Amsterdam to Geneva in a shipment of books he is expecting. The intermediary was his son, also named Simon Goulart, resident in Amsterdam. As we heard above, Goulart the elder and Le Febvre had worked together on Lyon [Geneva] 1595.[130]

2.2.7 GOULART AND THE *ESSAIS*

We shall focus in more detail on Goulart's work at this point because of his profile—discussed in 2.2.6—as one of the most prolific reader-writers of the age. He transmitted what he read and rewrote in the vernacular to a lay Francophone audience across Europe, via the handpress, in an attempt to guide or control their encounters with literature.[131]

He was also the Genevan figure whose encounters with the *Essais* we can most easily trace in detail. When collated with Lyon 1593, Lyon [Geneva] 1595 reveals the way he read and rewrote the *Essais* in a corrective context. The extracts he later took (mostly) from the full, 1595 text—included in the *Thresor* and the *Meditations historiques*—reveal the way he read and rewrote the *Essais* in the context of private reading loosely structured by the commonplace method.

There are some connections and overlaps between the two readings. In some cases, though using the full text, Goulart once again corrects it. In transferring one passage from *Essais* III 12 to the *Thresor* he adapts the opening so that his own reader can understand it in context. But at the same time he removes a reference to the 'barbaric' mortuary rituals of the Neorites, reversing the meaning of one phrase in the process.[132]

[130] Jones, *Simon Goulart, 1543–1628*, 419, 434.
[131] Huchard, *D'encre et de sang*, 91–3, 576–7.
[132] Goulart, *Thresor d'histoires admirables et memorables de nostre temps*, 1614–20, vol. 1, sig. 2F8r/ NP1095.

Likewise, in Lyon [Geneva] 1595, there are signs that the corrector is paying attention to the way the *histoires* are being judged. Consider what he does with the text of Lyon 1593 when he arrives at a Senecan-style list of examples of people who go to their deaths without fear, and with wit or resolution:

> Another asked the executioner not to touch his throat: he was ticklish and did not want to burst out laughing! ~~When the confessor promised another man that he would sup that day at table with Our Lord, he said, 'You go instead: I'm on a fast'.~~ Yet another asked for a drink; when the executioner drank of it first, he declined to drink after him—for fear of the pox.... A similar story told of a man in Denmark, who was condemned to be beheaded: they offered him similar terms [reprieve if he married a woman], but he refused the young woman they brought because she had sagging jowls and a pointed nose. ~~In Toulouse when a man-servant was accused of heresy, the only justification he would give for his belief was to refer to that of his master, a young undergraduate who was in gaol with him: he preferred to die rather than part ways with his master's opinions, whatever they were.~~ <u>Thus do courage and the striving for a resolute resistance against anything that might occur in extreme situations, even if favourable, take over the spirit of man, once it has broken ranks</u>. In our histories, we read about the citizens of Arras....[133]

Two of the examples are cut, on religious grounds—in one case because of the sheer irreverence of the condemned man, in the other because of Montaigne's irreverence in recounting the death of a protestant martyr. But the corrector also finds that Montaigne has not properly commented on the psychological significance of these examples (especially the last one in the corrected text), so he adds a summary of what they tell us about the spirit of man in extreme situations.

In other cases one can see how the same passage is noted first for censorship then for extraction. When Goulart the corrector, defending the public morality of Geneva, read the opening of III 9 in his copy of Lyon 1593, this was his reaction:

> Perhaps there is no more manifest vanity than writing so vainly about it. That which the Godhead has made so godly manifest should be meditated upon by men of intelligence anxiously and continuously. Anyone can see that I have set out upon a road

---

[133] In this and future extracts from Lyon [Geneva] 1595, sentences that are struck through are those present in Lyon 1593 but cut by Goulart in Lyon [Geneva] 1595; sentences with underlining are those added by Goulart. See Lyon 1593, first part, sig. C4r-v/Lyon [Geneva] 1595, sig. b8r-v: 'Un autre disoit au bourreau, qu'il ne le touchast pas à la gorge, de peur de le faire tressaillir de rire, tant il estoit chatoüilleux: ~~l'autre respondit à son confesseur, qui luy promettoit ce jour là avec nostre Seigneur, allez vous y en vous, car de ma part, je jeusne.~~ Un autre ayant demandé à boire, et le bourreau ayant beu le premier, dit ne vouloir boire apres luy, de peur de prendre la verolle.... Et on conte de mesmes, qu'en [Dan]nemarc, un homme condamné à avoir la teste tranchée, estant sur l'eschaffaut, comme on luy presenta un[e] pareille condition, la refusa, par ce que la fille, qu'on luy offrit, avoit les joües avallées, et le nez trop pointu. ~~Un valet à Thoulouse accusé d'heresie, pour toute raison de sa creance, rapportoit à celle de son maistre, jeune escholier prisonnier avec luy, et ayma mieux mourir, que se départir de ses op[in]ions, quelles qu'elles fussent.~~ <u>Ainsi gaignent sur l'esprit de l'homme le courage s'estant une fois desbandé, et les efforts d'un anticipation resolue contre tout autre extremité quoy qu'autrement avantageuse.</u> En nos histoires, nous lisons de ceux de la ville d'Arras...'. In the sentence added by Goulart (underlined) it seems clear that the subjects of 'gaignent sur' are 'le courage' and 'les efforts', but it is not so clear whether the subject of 's'estant une fois desbandé' is 'l'esprit' or 'le courage', and what the exact meaning is in either case. I have translated it with 'l'esprit' as the subject, so that the metaphor is of a force that disbands or breaks rank, to be taken over by 'le courage' and 'les efforts etc.'.

along which I shall travel without toil and without ceasing as long as the world has ink and paper. ~~I cannot give an account of my life by my actions: Fortune has placed them too low for that; so I do so by my thoughts. Thus did a nobleman I once knew reveal his life only by the workings of his bowels: at home he paraded before you a series of seven or eight days' chamber-pots. He thought about them, talked about them: for him any other topic stank. Here (a little more decorously) you have the droppings of an old mind, sometimes hard, sometimes squittery, but always ill-digested.~~ And when shall I ever have done describing some commotion and revolution of my thoughts, no matter what subject they happen upon, when Diomedes wrote six thousand books on the sole subject of philology?[134]

But only five years later he was to reprint exactly this censored passage as a noteworthy extract from the *Essais*. The work in which it appeared—the *Thresor d'histoires admirables et memorables de nostre temps*, as it was entitled from 1614—was analogous in many ways to the 'thresor' he had already published under Montaigne's name. It consisted of 'historical' extracts from many authors, supplemented by anecdotal memoirs from the author's own experience, and a certain, limited amount of commentary.

The first edition of the *Thresor* (1600–1) offered more or less exactly the passage above (cut by Goulart from Lyon [Geneva] 1595) as an extract under the commonplace heading 'Fantastiques', along with many other extracts under various other headings, including some clearly taken from a post-1588 text (which precludes use of Lyon 1593 or Lyon [Geneva] 1595).[135] The only other passage contained under this heading comes from a chapter that Goulart cut altogether from Lyon [Geneva] 1595: III 5, 'Sur des vers de Virgile'.[136] The juxtaposition is in this case provocative

[134] Lyon 1593, second part, sigs. l6v–7r/Lyon [Geneva] 1595, sig. 2l11v: 'Il n'en est à l'avanture aucune plus expresse, que d'en escrire si vainement: ce que la divinité nous en a si divinement exprimé, devroit estre soigneusement et continuellement medité par les gens d'entendement. Qui ne voit que j'ay pris une route, par laquelle, sans cesse et sans travail, j'iray autant qu'il y aura d'ancre et de papier au monde? ~~Je ne puis tenir registre de ma vie, par mes actions, fortune les met trop bas: je le tien sic par mes fantasies. Si ai-je veu un Gentilhomme, qui ne communiquoit sa vie, que par les operations de son ventre: vous voyez chez luy en montre, un ordre de bassins de sept ou huict jours: c'estoit son estude, ses discours: tout autre propos, luy puoit. Ce sont icy, un peu plus civilement, des excremens d'un vieil esprit, dur tantost, tantost lasche, et tousjours indigeste.~~ Et quand seray-je à bout de representer une continuelle agitation et mutation de mes pensées, en quelque matiere qu'elles tombent, puis que Diomedes remplit six mille livres, du seul sujet de la grammaire?'

[135] I have been citing the 1614–20 edition of Goulart's *Histoires*. The first edition of the first book of this four-book work appeared in three parts (in three volumes with discontinuous signatures) over 1600–1: Simon Goulart, *Histoires admirables et memorables de nostre temps*, 3 vols. (Paris: J. Houzé, 1600–1) [USTC 74130—first part, 1600, only], where the relevant quotation appears in vol. 3, at sig. c12r [Gallica page 36r/screen 675]. I have verified that all the passages extracted from the *Essais* by Goulart for book I of the *Histoires*, as listed in G. Banderier, 'Montaigne dans le *Thresor des Histoires Admirables* de Simon Goulart', *Bulletin de la Société des Amis de Montaigne*, 7th series, 41–2 (1995), 52–8, 55–7, first appeared in the 1600–1 edition, though they sometimes appear under different headings. There is one exception. I could not locate the extract from *Essais* I 3 that appears in Goulart, *Thresor d'histoires admirables et memorables de nostre temps*, 1614–20, vol. 1, sig. V7r, in the 1600–1 edition. Many of these passages include text that was only added after Paris 1588, which is the copy text for Lyon 1593.

[136] Goulart, *Histoires admirables et memorables de nostre temps* [1600–1], sig. C11v–12r [Gallica pages 35v–36r/screens 674–5]. Compare Goulart, *Thresor d'histoires admirables et memorables de nostre temps*, 1614–20, vol. 1, sigs. P6v–7r, for the same text of the chapter 'Fantastiques'.

and unmoralized. The III 5 passage concerns people who hide to eat, while the III 9 passage concerns someone who shows people the waste product of his eating!

Like most of Goulart's publications, including the corrected *Essais*, the *Histoires admirables* were aimed at the market in France. In the dedication (12 May 1600) from 'Simon Goulart Senlisien' (as his name appeared on the title page) to his brother Jean, a court official still living in Senlis (France), the background to the collection is explained. During 'our recent miseries' (the civil wars in France and Henri IV's betrayal of the protestant cause in reconverting to Roman Catholicism) Goulart had been marking thousands of 'notable particularities' in books relating to the previous one hundred and fifty years of history. He has now begun to collect them into volumes.[137]

In the address to the 'Lecteur debonnaire', the larger framework within which he offers his collection, and within which he expects the 'admirable' and 'memorable' extracts to be read and re-used, becomes clearer. They are admirable because they are beyond his comprehension, to the extent that he sees miracles amongst them. They are memorable for good and peaceful souls looking for contentment, instruction, and consolation. He invites his readers to go beyond his example in collecting even better extracts for posterity, as it can only serve to reveal God's judgements and acts of grace. He hopes in the new century that God will inspire people in diverse places carefully to record in diaries and annals all those things worthy to be preserved for the education of our successors. He offers the extracts simply as they are, ready to be converted by the reader through 'lecture simple' into revivifying substance. The aim of this and the volumes to follow will be: 'fear God, keep his commandments: there is man in the round'.[138]

So Goulart imagines a whole contemporary community of reader-writers doing what he is doing in these volumes, and what he had been doing in one way or another throughout his publishing career: collecting and recording moral-historical and natural-historical 'pieces and extracts of man' (as we heard Samuel Daniel call them at the beginning of 1.5) while also keeping their own memoirs of contemporary history and personal experiences.

But to what end? In the April 1604 dedication of the second volume, he tells his brother that he leaves 'to you and to any kind reader the free meditation of the fruit that one can and must take' from his collection, having added little of his own. In what follows, however, it becomes clear that he expects this principally to be a meditation on God's justice and grace, even if other shorter and more pathetic lessons are also available.[139]

And in some chapters Goulart adds much along these lines. The collection of recent histories concerning 'Melancholiques' is prefaced by a long commentary on melancholic afflictions that emphasizes how the following miscellaneous mixture ('diversité entremeslee') is designed to bring the reader back to reverence before almighty, just, and merciful God ('la reverence de Dieu tout puissant, juste et

[137] Goulart, *Thresor d'histoires admirables et memorables de nostre temps*, 1614–20, vol. 1, sig. *2r.
[138] Goulart, *Thresor d'histoires admirables et memorables de nostre temps*, 1614–20, vol. 1, sig. *3r–v.
[139] Goulart, *Thresor d'histoires admirables et memorables de nostre temps*, 1614–20, vol. 2, sig. 2M7r. This text also appears in the Houzé 1610 edition of volume 2.

misericordieux'). During the chapter, we see Goulart enact this by including an extract from his own memoirs concerning two men he had seen die of rabies (as we would now identify it), twenty years previously, after being bitten by the same dog. This gives rise to a brief meditation on Psalm 91 and the fact that even such horrible deaths are part of God's grace.[140]

Goulart's great theme throughout his *œuvre* was the operation of divine Providence, and he adds mini-sermons on this topic to the *Thresor*, including a peroration against Epicurean philosophy at the end of volume 1.[141]

In the *Thresor*, then, Goulart takes and translates extracts from vernacular and professional scholarly writings, including some unpublished manuscript writings, groups them together under particular commonplace headings, and adds into the mix extracts from his own 'diaries and annals'. Many of the sources are of course histories, but many are miscellanies like his own that re-present extracts from histories in a particular light.

With respect to his uses of the *Essais*, this has the effect of putting Montaigne in the company of professional and amateur naturalists collecting and rewriting examples of human nature from their reading, and adding their own *expériences* on the same topics. Frequently cited and translated authors incude Camerarius, Ambrose Paré, Andreas Hondorff (*Promptuarium exemplorum*), and Theodor Zwinger (*Theatrum humanae vitae*)—all managers of and commentators on a common but growing stock of commonplaces and related personal experiences.[142]

It is clear that Goulart is using very up-to-date miscellaneous literature alongside a few classic works from the earlier era of humanism. His corrected version of Montaigne's 'De la force de l'imagination' had made some cuts for the sake of moral decency but left many of the chapter's anecdotes and comments intact, especially towards the end.[143] His own chapter on 'Imagination' in the *Thresor* starts with extracts from Pasquier's *Recherches* (book 6, first published 1596), and a passage translated from Vives's *De anima et vita libri tres*. These set the intellectual framework of the chapter.

There then follow three personal *histoires* from Montaigne's 'De la force de l'imagination', though they constitute a single, continous passage in the original text. One variant tells us that in this case Goulart *was* drawing on the 1588, not the 1595 text—indeed, the whole passage could have come from Lyon [Geneva] 1595, as it was left untouched there. This is followed by extracts from a recent Latin commentary (1595) on monsters, including three that involve the commentator, Martin Weinrich, himself extracting passages from Vives, Paré, and an unnamed theologian. Goulart then adds an *histoire* of his own that would not have been out of

---

[140] Goulart, *Thresor d'histoires admirables et memorables de nostre temps*, 1614–20, vol. 1, sigs. X2v, Y6r–v.

[141] Huchard, 'Histoire et providence dans l'oeuvre de Simon Goulart', *passim*; Goulart, *Thresor d'histoires admirables et memorables de nostre temps*, 1614–20, vol. 1, sigs. 2K7r, 2M5r–v.

[142] See Goulart, *Thresor d'histoires admirables et memorables de nostre temps*, 1614–20, vol. 1, sigs. C4r–5r, where Camerarius, Paré, and Montaigne are cited end-to-end.

[143] Lyon 1593, first part, sigs. F1r–4v/Lyon [Geneva] 1595, sigs. d4v–7r.

place in Montaigne's 'De la force de l'imagination', and ends with an extract from *Essais* III 11, a chapter that was cut in its entirety from Lyons [Geneva] 1595.[144]

There are chapters in both the *Thresor* and the *Meditations historiques* that demonstrate the terms on which Montaigne is brought into the conversation between Goulart and Camerarius. In a nutshell, Camerarius provides the framework within which Montaigne's *histoires* should ultimately be understood, though this does not mean that the Gascon's judgement is not respected. When Goulart reviewed Montaigne's principal chapter on custom (I 22) for Lyon [Geneva] 1595, he retained most of the text, bar passages referring to sexually indecent practices and one passage about 'our present quarrel'.[145] He also, at some point, noted a passage near the beginning of this chapter concerning a man and a child without hands who had become equally dextrous with other parts of their bodies. In Montaigne, these *histoires* exemplify the force of custom, even over that of nature.

But Goulart places them in a chapter of the *Thresor* entitled 'Recompenses de nature' and opens it with a long passage from Camerarius, also about a man born with no arms. The passage is very similar to Montaigne's, except that the German scholar begins by declaring the 'providence and solicitude that the Creator of all things has given nature' to be marvellous—it is, in other words, not custom, but Providence working though nature that allows such people to adapt. The rest of the chapter includes a passage from Paré, a further long passage from Camerarius, and another extract from Goulart's own memoirs.

In fact, if we switch to Goulart's version of the *Meditations historiques*, we can see how closely these two projects of his are related and how strong a steer Goulart is taking from Camerarius. The two extracts used in the *Thresor* are taken from a chapter in the *Meditations* entitled 'De la merveilleuse recompense de Nature' (vol. 1, book 2, chap. 17). There is another chapter on the same theme in the third volume of Camerarius (vol. 3, book 5, chap. 2). Here we find that it was in fact Camerarius who had selected the passage from Paré used by Goulart in the *Thresor*. And Goulart in turn inserts into Camerarius's text (in square brackets, to distinguish them) the same passage from *Essais* I 22, together with another two passages from the corresponding chapter in the *Thresor* and a new extract from Du Bartas' *Seconde Semaine*, which Goulart had edited and annotated earlier in his career.[146]

Nevertheless, it remains the case that, in the interests of providing *diverse lecture*, Goulart puts Montaigne's 'free' judgement of well-known topics and *histoires* in

---

[144] Goulart, *Thresor d'histoires admirables et memorables de nostre temps*, 1614–20, vol. 1, sigs. Q8v–R3r; Martinus Weinrich, *De ortu monstrorum commentarius* ([Leipzig]: Osthusius, 1595), sigs. V7v–8r [USTC 630865/VD16 W 1556]. The extract from I 20 at *Thesor*, vol. 1, sig. R1v includes use of the pre-1595 variant 'Ces jours passez' (NP107*a*).

[145] Several references to sexually indecent practices are cut from Lyon 1593, first part, sig. F6r–v— compare Lyon [Geneva] 1595, sig. d9r. See also Lyon 1593, second part, sig. G3r ('du bien qu'on prend. Et Dieu le sçache ... elle à quartier. Il advient de la leur, comme')/Lyon [Geneva] 1595, sig. e1v ('du bien qu'on prend. Il advient comme').

[146] For this and the previous paragraph see Goulart, *Thresor d'histoires admirables et memorables de nostre temps*, 1614–20, vol. 1, sigs. 2E7v–F1v; Camerarius, *Les meditations historiques*, 1610, vol. 1, sigs. Z1v–3r; vol. 3, 2V4v–X4r.

conversation with that of the pious scholar Camerarius. This is, as we noted throughout Volume 1, exactly the kind of conversation in which the *Essais* and their author tended to engage in this period.

One chapter in Camerarius offers observations on the laws of the inhabitants of Marseille. The first he considers is the custom made famous by the classical historian Valerius Maximus: state-regulated, public self-killing by hemlock. Camerarius gives other examples of laws favouring self-killers but then condemns all such 'ingenious and specious pagan inventions [as] repugnant to Christian faith and piety'.

He then quotes Pierre Quiqueran's judgement of Valerius Maximus's account of the custom, from his Latin praise of Provence (*De laudibus provinciae libri tres*). Camerarius finds Quiqueran to be too ambivalent in what he says, seeming in some respects to support the custom, even though he begins by doubting its utility. He insists that however you dress up this custom of the ancient inhabitants of Marseille, the law of God remains, in relation as much to yourself as to your neighbour: 'Thou shalt not kill' ('NON OCCIDES' in capitals in the Latin text). Goulart embellishes the Latin text in his French translation, adding that this remains—and shall remain—the firm, inviolable, immutable, and irrevocable law as long as the children of Adam inhabit the earth.[147]

However, Goulart interrupts Camerarius's text at this point to introduce an interpolation of his own: he knows that in the passage in question Valerius Maximus goes on to link this custom with an incident he witnessed visiting the isle of Cea with Sextus Pompeius. He also remembers that Montaigne translated the whole passage towards the end of his chapter II 3, and commented briefly upon it—thus entering into conversation with other commentators on the passage such as Camerarius and Quiqueran.[148]

When Goulart had reviewed the end of Montaigne's chapter in Lyon 1593 for the purposes of correction, he had left it virtually untouched. Montaigne typically begins his risqué chapter by submitting his fantastical and doubtful ruminations to the 'cathedrant', the professor of theology, whom he equates with the sacrosanct divine will that rules us in all things. This said, he does not make the point of the chapter the statement of this will, as Camerarius does. He goes on instead to juxtapose examples of self-killing, and motives for self-killing, in pro et contra fashion.

In Lyon [Geneva] 1595, Goulart keeps as much of the text as he can, removing one tricky biblical story (Nicanor) and another sexually explicit one (a woman enjoying herself with soldiers), while even adding helpful phrases here and there. He has no problem with the passage on Pauline self-dissolution.[149] But he is sensitive to the pagan connotations of Montaigne's use of 'fortune'. On one occasion

---

[147] For this and the previous paragraph see Camerarius, *Les meditations historiques*, 1610, vol. 2, sig. 2A4v–2B1r; Philippus Camerarius, *Operæ horarum subcisiuarum siue meditationes historicæ… Centuria et editio correctior, atque auctior, altera* (Frankfurt: Typis Ioannis Saurii: impensis P. Kopffii, 1606), sig. Z3r–v.

[148] Camerarius, *Les meditations historiques*, 1610, vol. 2, sig. 2B2r–v.

[149] For this and the previous paragraph see Lyon 1593, sigs. Y3r, Y3v, Y4v/Lyon [Geneva] 1595, sigs. n9v–10r, n5r, n8v–9r; M. A. Screech, *Montaigne and melancholy: the wisdom of the 'Essays'* (London: Duckworth, 1983), 43–4.

he changes it to 'la misere humaine'. On another he has Flavius Josephus saved not by fortune, but by 'la providence divine'—Goulart's characteristic preoccupation once again showing through. In the passage under consideration, at the end of the chapter, the incident happens during Sextus Pompeius's visit 'd'aventure', not 'de fortune'.[150]

The most telling touch comes at the very end, however, when Montaigne finally adds a judgement on the memorable *histoires* that he has assembled, and Goulart chooses to qualify it: 'Of all incitements, unbearable pain and a worse death seem to me the most pardonable, <u>if it were possible to make excuses</u>' ('La douleur, et une pire mort, me semblent les plus excusables incitations, <u>si excuse s'y pourront pre-tendre</u>')[151]—for the sacrosanct divine will, and scholars such as Camerarius, of course insist that no incitation is excusable.

When Goulart came to transpose the same passage to his edition of Camerarius, he did not use the text of Lyon [Geneva] 1595. But he nevertheless made remark-ably similar corrections. He left out 'il advint de fortune' altogether. And at the end of the interpolation he wrote as follows:

> The lord of Montaigne has represented this history and a very large number of others, positing extreme pain and the cruel ordeal of death as amongst the most exusable incitations. But the Holy philosophy is completely of the opposite view. ('Le sieur de Montagnes a représenté ceste histoire et tresgrand nombre d'autres, mettant la douleur extreme et le cruel supplice de mort entre les plus excusables incitations. Mais la Saincte philosophie est totalement de contraire avis.')[152]

We can compare the situation here to the one addressed in 1.5.7, when Lancre disapprovingly watched a Montaigne-type perspective insinuate itself into the learned discourse of Martin Delrio. Here, the *persona* of the author is invoked. Goulart introduces Montaigne's opinion into dialogue with the scholar Camerarius's, even though it is in his view totally against the 'avis' of the Holy Philosophy.

As he does so, it becomes clear that Goulart is not just interested in pillaging the *Essais* as a rich treasure of extracted passages. He gives considerable weight to the *sentence* of the 'Sieur de Montaigne' as someone who both 'represents' histories *and* judges them. It may appear to be one throwaway remark at the end of a chapter full of *histoires*, but Goulart highlighted the fleetingly expressed opinion when he read the text on two different occasions, for two different purposes.

In the *Thresor*, as we have already seen, the reader is left freer to make what he or she will of the extracts from the *Essais*. Goulart's long chapter on vehement passions ('Passions vehementes de dueil, de joye, de jalousie, de peur, de tristesse, &c.') includes no less than six extracts from Montaigne's work, including at least one from the pre-1595 text.[153] Most of the vehement passions are illustrated in

---

[150] Lyon 1593, sigs. Y1r, Y2v, Y4v/Lyon [Geneva] 1595, sigs. n6v, n8r, n9v.

[151] Lyon 1593, sig. Y5v/Lyon [Geneva] 1595, sig. n10r.

[152] Camerarius, *Les meditations historiques*, 1610, vol. 2, sig. 2Br–v.

[153] Banderier, 'Montaigne dans le *Thresor des Histoires Admirables* de Simon Goulart', 56. Banderier states that Goulart always uses the full, 1595 text (57) but the passage extracted from I 18 at Goulart, *Thresor d'histoires admirables et memorables de nostre temps*, 1614–20, vol. 1, sig. 2C5v, uses the pre-1595 variant 'guerriers' (NP 77e).

this chapter from modern *histoires*, which makes it very much like a cruder version of many of the chapters in the *Essais*.

The chapter is anchored at the end by a local and personal experience taken from Goulart's own *mémoires*—again, much as a chapter in the *Essais* might be. Goulart recounts the *histoire* of an honourable woman of his acquaintance who believed her husband to have been killed in the St Bartholomew Day's Massacre, and who was so shocked when he returned unharmed that a pregnancy eleven years later was still affected by it. Like Montaigne, Goulart does not name the family and reserves some of the details out of respect. He himself had just managed to escape the massacre when in France in 1572.[154]

Most of the examples in this chapter result in death, and many in individuals going willingly to their deaths, often in the midst of military conflict. Goulart intervenes a couple of times in the chapter to re-emphasize the Christian canon against self-murder and to insert references to the teachings of the 'true philosophy' and the Holy Spirit. Some passages and authors are given particular weight. Goulart appends a sermon on vanity and God's judgement on the powerful—partly based on the printed marginal annotations in the edition he was using—to a passage from Guicciardini about the Venetians' fearful retreat from their *terra firma*.[155]

He also translates a fascinating story from Laevinus Lemnius (*De habitu et constitutione corporis*) about a condemned man whose overnight physical transformation, out of fear, was so dramatic that he was pardoned. He then selectively translates and adapts Lemnius's own commentary on this *histoire*, which ends with another sermon on human vanity and fragility.[156] There follow further, shorter examples, from other sources, of fear sending people white, and so forth.

None of the examples from Montaigne are given quite the weight of the two *histoires* from Guicciardini and Lemnius. But Goulart does take, without comment, two of his examples of voluntary death from the Montaignean chapter on suicide used in his edition of Camerarius (*Essais* II 3), and follows them up with two examples of genital self-mutilation from *Essais* II 29, both of which had been cut from Lyon [Geneva] 1595.[157] He also recognizes two unsourced Montaignean examples from I 2—about a man dropping dead of grief upon seeing his son dead on the battlefield, and a Pope dropping dead of joy—as borrowings from Paolo Giovio, whom he also cites independently elsewhere.[158]

Furthermore, a lengthy extract from the passage opening Montaigne's own chapter on fear on the battlefield and 'panic terrors' (I 17) plays an important role

[154] Goulart, *Thresor d'histoires admirables et memorables de nostre temps*, 1614–20, vol. 1, sig. 2D1r–v; Huchard, *D'encre et de sang*, 94–5.

[155] Goulart, *Thresor d'histoires admirables et memorables de nostre temps*, 1614–20, vol. 1, sigs. 2B5r, 2B6r–7r, 2C4r–v.

[156] Goulart, *Thresor d'histoires admirables et memorables de nostre temps*, 1614–20, vol. 1, sigs. 2C3v–5r; Levinus Lemnius, *De habitu et constitutione corporis* (Jena: Tobias Steinman, 1587), sig. N6r–v [USTC 670771/VD16 L 1104]. The first edition of this work appeared at Antwerp in 1561 (USTC 405018).

[157] Goulart, *Thresor d'histoires admirables et memorables de nostre temps*, 1614–20, vol. 1, sig. 2B8v–9r; Lyon 1593, sig. 2Z3r–v/Lyon [Geneva] 1595, sig. 2d10v.

[158] Goulart, *Thresor d'histoires admirables et memorables de nostre temps*, vol. 1, sigs. 2B3v–4r, 2B8v (not identified by Villey as taken from Giovio).

in the chapter. Goulart leaves in Montaigne's personal introduction, followed by three examples of the extremities to which fear can lead in military conflicts. But he then adds a series of passages of his own on the same theme from Paolo Giovio, Pontanus, Commines, Jacob Horst, Ascanius Centorius, and a history of the siege of Vienna, including several on 'panic terrors' caused by rumours of Turkish military attacks that chime with the end of Montaigne's chapter. In this case the Montaignean act of invention and judgement sets the agenda for Goulart's own development. Here, one can see exactly how a chapter of Montaigne's might be broken down by another reader-writer and developed with different examples.[159]

The most striking and important example of this, however, occurs in volume 3 of the *Thresor*, which contains by far the lengthiest extract from Montaigne, and from book III of the *Essais* in particular. Modern commentators often emphasize the existential exercises in self-portraiture from book III, such as the opening to III 2 famously analysed by Erich Auerbach in *Mimesis*.[160] But we noted earlier that the indices to the memorable matter in both Lyon 1593 and Lyon [Geneva] 1595 do not refer the reader consistently to the passages making up Montaigne's own personal *histoire*.

They do, however, direct him or her consistently and frequently to all the other *histoires* Montaigne recounts and judges, including, for example, his excoriating discourse on the avarice and cruelty of the Spanish in the New World. This is the discourse, culminating in the passage cited in both indices (concerning the absorption of the pillaged goods by the sea), to which Goulart gives greatest prominence in his *Thresor*.[161]

The reason is not difficult to see. Reflection upon providence was at the heart of Goulart's conception of history and historiographical practice—it was also what he sought to encourage in his Francophone audience, as they read and rewrote his works. If it was neither possible nor legitimate to divine the light of God's judgements in the chaos of the religious wars of the present, then consolation could be found by seeking it in the narrative of the past.[162]

Goulart sought such moments of illumination in all the authors he read, and found a particularly striking one in Montaigne. The Gascon of course more commonly uses the language of fortune, which Goulart frequently corrected in Lyon [Geneva] 1595. But this does not mean there is no talk of divine providence in the *Essais*. When Montaigne does talk of it, he normally describes it as permitting rather than directly causing things to happen.[163]

---

[159] Goulart, *Thresor d'histoires admirables et memorables de nostre temps*, 1614–20, vol. 1, sigs. 2C5v–8r. The extract from Horst comes from a very recent publication—*De aureo dente maxillari pueri silesii*, Leipzig 1595 (USTC 664779/VD16 H 5006).

[160] See 2.7.1.

[161] The passage is multiply indexed in Lyon [Geneva] 1595, though the page references are sometimes wrong. It appears as 'Cruauté des Espaignols', 'Deploration des Conquestes des Indes, faictes contre les Espaignols', and 'Espagnols, leur grand avarice. leur cruauté contre le Roy du Peru etc.'.

[162] Huchard, *D'encre et de sang*, 104; Huchard, 'Histoire et providence dans l'oeuvre de Simon Goulart', 237–8.

[163] Alain Legros, 'Montaigne between fortune and providence', in John D. Lyons and Kathleen Wine (eds.), *Chance, literature, and culture in early modern France* (Farnham: Ashgate, 2009), 17–30.

The most significant instance of this is what he says about the fate of the pillaged treasures that the Spanish attempted to bring back from the New World. After describing at length the cruelty inflicted on the Kings of Peru and Mexico, all in the avaricious pursuit of gold, Montaigne unambiguously states that God 'deservedly allowed [*a meritoirement permis*] that their vast plunder should be either engulfed by the sea as they were shipping it or else by that internecine strife in which they all devoured each other; and most of them were buried on the scene, in no wise profiting from their conquest'.[164]

When Goulart reviewed this long discourse in Lyon 1593, he left it virtually untouched for Lyon [Geneva] 1595.[165] In the third volume of his *Thesor*, he used the fuller, 1595 text of the discourse as the basis for a whole chapter instructing posterity on cruel avarice ('Avarice cruelle, et ses exploits furieux: memorables, pour l'instruction de la posterité'). On this one occasion he gave his source a full introduction:

> I will begin the narrative of the present chapter of our collection with the noteworthy talk and discourse [*le notable propos et discours*] of the seigneur de Montaigne: then I will continue and conclude it with diverse histories we have that provide irreproachable testimonies. Here will be the very picture of cruel avarice and its furious exploits, which will hardly find its like in all the histories of preceding centuries.[166]

Goulart then begins with Montaigne's 'Our world has just discovered another one' ('Nostre monde vient d'en trouver un autre'), again editing the text very lightly.[167] There is only one noteworthy change, but it occurs in the crucial, concluding passage. In Goulart's *Thresor*, God does not permit that the pillaged treasures are 'absorbed' ('se soient absorbez') by the sea in transport, but 'engulfed' ('ayent esté engloutis').[168] Providence is made a touch more proactive than it characteristically is in Montaigne.

Goulart then completes his chapter by complementing Montaigne's use of López de Gómara with further passages from Las Casas and Benzoni, both of whom had been published at Geneva in French. These juxtapositions make perfect sense, given Montaigne's proximity to these writers on the topic of the cruelty and avarice of the Spanish in the New World. Indeed, Montaigne had himself already drawn (in 'Des cannibales') on the Genevan edition and translation of Benzoni by another pastor, Urbain Chauveton, who had added his own anti-Spanish discourses to book 1.[169]

---

[164] III 6, NP958/BVH Paris 1595, bk. III, p. 89/S1034.

[165] Lyon 1593, second part, sigs. i1v–5v/Lyon [Geneva] 1595, sigs. 2k2v–6v. In the whole passage Goulart makes only one significant change. In the parenthesis at the very beginning he substitutes 'tant de nos devantiers' for 'les daemons, les sybilles'.

[166] Goulart, *Thresor d'histoires admirables et memorables de nostre temps*, 1614–20, vol. 3, sig. C6v.

[167] III 6, NP952/ BVH Paris 1595, bk. III, p. 85/S1029.

[168] Goulart, *Thresor d'histoires admirables et memorables de nostre temps*, 1614–20, vol. 3, sig. D1v.

[169] NP209–10, 1424; Frank Lestringant, *Le Brésil de Montaigne: le Nouveau Monde des 'Essais' (1580–1592)* (Paris: Chandeigne, 2005), 191–3; USTC 49933/GLN15–16 2948; USTC 45440/ GLN15–16 720. While Las Casas's work appeared at Geneva only in 1582, various editions of Chauveton's French and Latin translations of Benzoni appeared with Eustache Vignon between 1578 and 1586, followed by a further Latin edition in 1600 (GLN15–16).

As he moves from one selection or author to another, Goulart ties things together with his own commentary, switching between direct quotation and summary, breaking off from his 'representation' of Las Casas's narrative by saying that he was so horrified by the rest that he could not go any further.[170] He concludes with a sermon which restates Montaigne's description of the operations of divine providence in much stronger terms: the sea, as the scourge of God, carried out prompt justice on the majority of the pillagers, while the others perished miserably in various places. Cruel avarice will come to a bad end.[171]

It is once again clear here that Goulart, when he uses the *Essais*, is not merely borrowing *histoires* from another miscellany. Even though he can probably see how closely III 6 follows its source, and even though Montaigne is not a firsthand witness like Las Casas and Benzoni, he builds his own chapter upon 'the noteworthy talk and discourse of the seigneur de Montaigne'. The *persona* of the author as speaker or writer of these discourses is clearly acknowledged. He may not describe the particular qualities of this authorial *persona*, but he does represent his *propos* and *discours* openly and faithfully. Indeed, it is arguable that Goulart no more distorts Montaigne's text and context here than a modern critic such as Auerbach does in the case of the opening to III 2.

For when it came to providence—as to other theological topics such as miracles, prayers, the comprehensibility of God—Montaigne was not that far from a Calvinist preacher such as Goulart.[172] Indeed, when Montaigne was talking about providence, what divided him from Goulart was not what he said, but the irreverent, secular style of his discourse as a layman discussing theological issues.

When Goulart read I 31 ('Qu'il faut sobrement se mesler de juger des ordannances divines') in Lyon 1593, he did not change a single word of Montaigne's reasoning against 'that crowd of everyday interpreters and comptrollers-in-ordinary [*interpretes et controlleurs ordinaires*] of God's purposes who claim to discover the causes of everything that occurs and to read the unknowable purposes of God'. He might even have delivered much of it himself from his pulpit in Geneva.

But there is one passage Goulart could not have delivered from the pulpit and which he does cut: Montaigne imagines someone finding providence in the death of heretics (including a Pope) in a latrine, and then goes to the relevant chapter ('In latrinis mortui aut occisi'/'Dead or killed in latrines') of a well-known miscellany, Textor's *Officina*, to find examples of others, including an early Christian martyr, who met the same fate in the same place. Surely God could not have been saying the same thing in the case of all these latrine deaths?[173]

The largely non-censorious use of the *Essais* in the *Thesor* and the *Meditations historiques*—which corresponds to the moment when Goulart's associate Perrot

---

[170] Goulart, *Thresor d'histoires admirables et memorables de nostre temps*, 1614–20, vol. 3, sig. D5v.

[171] Goulart, *Thresor d'histoires admirables et memorables de nostre temps*, 1614–20, vol. 3, sigs. D1v–5v.

[172] Nakam, *Les 'Essais' de Montaigne, miroir et procès de leur temps*, 107–10.

[173] For this and the previous paragraph, see Lyon 1593, first part, sigs. O3r–4r/Lyon [Geneva] 1595, sigs. h12v–i1v; NP1430n.7; *Officina Ioan. Ravisii Textoris Nivernensis* (Venice: apud Marcantonio Zaltieri & Michele Zanetti, 1584), sig. P4v [USTC 859158].

allowed an uncensored text to be published at Geneva—alerts us to the fact that Lyon [Geneva] 1595 should not be taken to stand in the round for the encounter between the Calvinist reader-writer and the *Essais*.

When charged, or self-charged, as a member of the *Compagnie des Pasteurs*, with censoring the text for publication in a Genevan printshop, Goulart is defending the public morality of his city. When privately reading and extracting the *Essais* alongside many other contemporary works of scholarship and commentary, he for the most part uses a full and uncensored text and 'notes' for communication to his own audience in France, passages and authorial *sentences* that in another context he had cut. Everything depends on the particular nexus of reading and rewriting, which in turn depends upon the nature of the social networks and institutions that facilitate or regulate the 'transpassage' of foreign texts.

2.2.8 THE *ESSAIS* IN THE NORTHEASTERN ITALIAN CITY-STATES

Take the evidence of the early transmission of the *Essais* in Italy, in the decades after Montaigne entered the city of Rome with a copy in 1580. As we saw in 1.3.2–7, an aristocratic culture of extramural learning, collecting, and *conversazione* had taken root across the peninsula by the late sixteenth century. Beyond the universities—and the corresponding offices of university teachers—courts, academies, and other private gatherings provided alternative institutional settings and identities for independent investigation of nature, including human nature, as well as for informal education.

In these contexts reading and writing gave rise to, and interacted with, observing and conversing. The figure of the noble patron—who could be a clergyman or a man of letters—seeking self-knowledge in solitude or in civil conversation with others, and displaying their virtuous activity 'live' or in print, was a normal one in elite social interaction in late Renaissance Italy. We saw in 1.4.5 that Montaigne gained recognition in person as a virtuoso in Italian locations other than Rome; the author of the *Essais* would eventually do the same via the circulation of his book.[174]

The city-states involved in the 'transpassage' of Montaigne's work were Ferrara and Padua-Venice, which uncoincidentally represented the two most important centres for the circulation of French culture in the Italian peninsula. They were centres Montaigne himself visited as a stranger in 1580–1, though the traces of his book's arrival in each city date to a later period. As a French nobleman

[174] The best overall study of this Italian culture remains Paula Findlen, *Possessing nature: museums, collecting, and scientific culture in early modern Italy* (Berkeley: University of California Press, 1994). For this situation in Venice and Padua see Maurizio Sangalli, *Università, accademie, gesuiti: cultura e religione a Padova tra Cinque e Seicento* (Trieste: LINT, 2001), X–XI. For priests as independent investigators in philosophical learning, see Peter Dear, 'The Church and the new philosophy', in Stephen Pumfrey, Maurice Slawinski, and Paolo L. Rossi (eds.), *Science, culture and popular belief in Renaissance Europe* (Manchester: Manchester University Press, 1991), 119–39, 136.

accompanying a high-ranking French dignitary, Montaigne had gained immediate access to the Duke of Ferrara's cabinet. At Venice, he had found it very odd that Venetian gentlemen who conversed more than once with the French ambassador were held under suspicion. He was eventually to compare the *liberté* accorded strangers at Venice unfavourably with the opportunities open to them at Rome.[175]

We saw in 2.2.6 that the early fortunes of the *Essais* in France and Geneva are connected. The fortunes of the *Essais* in France and Italy are also connected, if in a different way. As in France, the evidence suggests that Montaigne's work only became a touchstone in intellectual conversation in northeastern Italy towards the end of the 1610s and during the 1620s. Beyond this shared chronology of reception, there are other parallels with the case of Geneva, as well as divergences. From one point of view it seems clear that Montaigne and his collaborators initially lost jurisdiction over the public record of his *fantasies* in the interconnected city-states of northeastern Italy, as at Geneva.

We heard in 2.2.2 that Lyon [Geneva] 1595 was published in the period between the publication of the poorly distributed Paris 1588 quarto and the successfully distributed Parisian octavos. In the same interim, another bowdlerization was published, in Italian, at Ferrara (1590). This, however, was not the result of clerical censorship or of links between *libraires* and priests. It derived from the close political and diplomatic links between the courts of France and Ferrara, and was re-written and re-ordered in Italian to represent a volume of moral, political, and military *discorsi* suitable for a ducal library such as the Duke of Ferrara's or the Duke of Urbino's. In this volume, Montaigne discourses more like his *politique* friends, showing a different set of qualities, in a less self-conscious fashion, and offering the kinds of ethical, political, and military commentary that would serve Naselli's patrons.[176]

It was itself subjected to a local censorial review in Ferrara in 1600, when a number of *errori* were identified and listed (including two relating to Montaigne's discussion of imagination) for the Congregation of the Index in Rome. As in the case of the objections to the 1580 edition in Rome in 1581, these were not in the event acted upon (by means of the publication of an expurgated edition).

It was, in fact, an inquisitor in Bergamo, in the Venetian Republic, who first brought Naselli–Montaigne's attribution of miracles to the force of the imagination to the attention of a Cardinal of the Index. But Cardinal Valier, who independently ascertained the presence of further errors, sent the book to Ferrara for censorial review with other works of Este literature. In the wake of the 1598 devolution of the duchy to the Papacy, a point was being made about the need to take control of and expurgate Este court literature—using the local inquisitorial officers in Ferrara itself. The important point for our purposes is

[175] R75/F925; R68/F920; R126–7/F961–2. See 1.7.5. 'R' is henceforward the abbreviation for Michel de Montaigne, *Journal de voyage*, ed. François Rigolot (Paris: Presses Universitaires de France, 1992); 'F' is henceforward the abbreviation for Michel de Montaigne, *The Complete Works: Essays, Travel Journal, Letters*, trans. D. M. Frame (Stanford: Stanford University Press, 1957).
[176] Ruggero Campagnoli, 'Girolamo Naselli primo traduttore italiano di Montaigne (1590)', *Studi francesi*, 47–8 (1972), 214–31. Campagnoli's discussion informs much of what follows.

that Naselli's *Discorsi* were indeed identified as a product of the Este court, along with works by Ariosto and Alunno.[177]

In the context of this study, Naselli's *Discorsi* does not merely document an early, rather disappointing stage in the Italian reception of Montaigne. It points to the accessing and redisposing of practical philosophical goods in a particular, Franco-Italian relational and political nexus. As a minor functionary in the conduct of the house of Este's relations with its principal international protector, the house of France, Naselli offers to his patron Don Cesare d'Este 'grand matters, of war, and governments...worthy of all honours' ('cose grandi, di guerra, e di gouerni... degni d'ogni honore').[178]

Naselli appropriately finds many of these *cose grandi* in the work of an illustrious French gentleman of the kind with whom he must regularly have conversed in his diplomatic capacity: a 'Cavaliere dell'ordine del Re Christianissimo; Gentil'huomo ordinario della sua Camera'—namely, Montaigne, a gentleman of the privy chamber of the French King who took so many of his historical examples from the French campaigns in the Italian peninsula. But Naselli also adds another discourse—the long *questione* advertised on the title page.[179]

In this deliberative discourse, very different in kind from anything a modern reader would associate with the *Essais*, and apparently composed soon after the winter 1576–7 Estates General of Blois, the author argues methodically and resolutely against those at the assembly who in a public *ragionamento* demonstrated the employment of foreigners in a republic to be universally undesirable, and who nearly succeeded in having this position passed into law.[180]

There had indeed been a chorus of legal voices in France in the 1570s, and at the Estates in particular, attempting to bar foreigners from the offices open to 'natural' citizens. The deputies of the Third Estate in 1576–7 were exercised by Catherine de' Medici's entourage of Florentines. While she—in their eyes—profligately distributed offices and titles to these foreigners, the King retained the privilege of granting them letters of naturalization. But their attempts to restrict this privilege with new legislation were unsuccessful, and the King retained his powers untrammelled.[181]

The *discorso* published by Naselli first runs through five *ragioni* (two added by the author) as to why foreigners such as these Florentines should not be given offices in governing the republic. It then goes back to first principles and uses historical examples to build up the counter-argument, finding solutions to objections along the way and above all reiterating the shared history and interdependence of

---

[177] Jean-Louis Quantin, 'Les censures de Montaigne à l'Index romain: précisions et corrections', *Montaigne Studies*, 26 (2014), 145–62, 150–62; Armogathe and Carraud, 'Les *Essais* de Montaigne dans les archives du Saint-Office', 89–90.

[178] Ferrara 1590, sig. † 2v.

[179] The authorship of this discourse, and its status as a text that was either composed in Italian or translated from another language, is uncertain.

[180] Ferrara 1590, sigs. R8r–v, T4v.

[181] Peter Sahlins, *Unnaturally French: foreign citizens in the Old Regime and after* (Ithaca: Cornell University Press, 2004), 31–2, 69–70; Georges Picot, *Histoire des États généraux, considérés au point de vue de leur influence sur le gouvernement de la France de 1355 à 1614*, 4 vols. (Paris: Hachette, 1872), vol. 2, 538–9.

the French crown and government and the governing families of the Italian states, as indeed of other European empires and states. In writing this rigorous piece of humanist dialectic, the author genuflects throughout to the *patron* of practical philosophical discourse: Aristotle. The margins constantly refer us to the *Ethica* and, above all, the *Politica*.[182]

So, whether or not he authored or translated them, Naselli finds and disposes useful philosophical goods that redound to the glory of the house of Este, and—as *discorsi*—imitate the patron-author of practical philosophy: Aristotle. They are perfectly at home in the Duke of Urbino's *scansia* 37, overwatched by the image of Aristotle on the wall of his library at Casteldurante (see 1.3.10).

At various points, the author of the *Questione* stipulates that the stranger he would see taking office in the republic is one who is 'judicious, prudent, and apt' ('giuditioso prudente, ed idoneo'), 'a stranger and a good, virtuous, and prudent man' ('un forastiero huomo da bene prudente e virtuoso'). The principle governing Naselli's adaptive translation of the *Essais* is to bring a French *cavaliere* who shows these very qualities into the service of the Ferraran state. He is, again, turned into a prudent *politique* who is fit to give political counsel in the *società civile* of Ferrara and other Italian states.[183]

Furthermore, like Goulart's *Essais*, Naselli's *Discorsi* can be understood as a work of the editor (and—in this case—translator) by placing it in the context of other texts he produced and adapted on a similar pattern. Naselli published three editions of predominantly political discourses based on French texts, with two different Ferraran publishers. His trade in his diplomatic capacity was, after all, information on *cose di Francia*. In each case he customized his translations by adding extraneous *discorsi* that placed the main source texts in dialogue with other voices on contemporary political and military topics. The three editions comprised a single enterprise on the part of Naselli and the Ferraran publishers to translate the whole range of French political discourse—Catholic (Lucinge), *politique* (Montaigne), and Huguenot (La Noue)—for Ferraran and Italian readers wanting to hear the judicious and prudent *ragioni* of virtuous French counsellors.[184]

In the case of Geneva, the arrival of copies of L'Angelier's octavos (1598, 1600, 1602) both rendered Lyon [Geneva] 1595 obsolete and stimulated clandestine production of a full-text edition on the part of Genevan *libraires* led by Pyramus de Candolle. After a short delay, in other words, Montaigne was 'allowed', if in clandestine fashion, at Geneva. Priests such as Goulart himself, and Perrot, were instrumental in this process.

Something similar might be said to have happened in northeastern Italy—this time in the context of informal networks of learned leisure and sociability. These networks linked members of the church, courts, *accademie*, universities, and the publishing profession, and welcomed noble strangers on a highly selective basis. They produced *conversazione civile* and *amicizia*, both in face-to-face social life and

[182] Ferrara 1590, sigs. R8r–V5v.   [183] Ferrara 1590, sigs. V3r, V5v.
[184] Jean Balsamo, 'Naselli, Girolamo (? - v. 1609)', *Dictionnaire*, 809–10.

in manuscript and print, for purposes such as the divulgation of knowledge and the education of the young nobility in practical philosophy.

And, once again, the turn-of-the-century octavos are crucial. We have already seen that a copy of Paris 1602 found its way into the library of the Duke of Urbino (1.3.10). The only other extant copy of the early French editions of the *Essais* currently known to have been collected and owned in Italy in this period is the copy of Paris 1598 that originally formed part of the collection of the *natio germanica iurista* at the University of Padua (now in the Biblioteca Universitaria in Padua).[185] The arrival of such copies in northeastern Italy would eventually lead to the full enfranchisement of Montaigne in a new Italian translation published at Venice, undertaken by a friar (Venice 1633–4).

It may seem unsurprising that this should happen in *la Serenissima*, with its reputation for intellectual and press freedom. But recent historiogaphy has contested the traditional picture of the Venetian state as one that progressively liberated itself, in the name of secular autonomy, from clerical power and censorship, until it definitively broke free in the Interdict controversy of 1606–7.[186]

The new picture situates the Interdict as a temporary disruption to a long-standing process of censorship and control involving both collaboration and tension between the church and state authorities—not unlike the process at Geneva. The Venetian state was as concerned to control the public exercise of liberty of judgement in political and religious matters as the church was; control of the texts produced, read, and written was an important part of this. Both wished to have the power to censor and control lay morality and religion, and both appointed clerics and theologians to important positions of influence in this respect.[187] At the same time, as at Geneva, it was eminently possible for individual publishers, with the connivance of patrons, to evade regulation or serious punishment.

Before the Interdict, an agreement over the publication of the 1596 Clementine Index at Venice—the Concordat—had been reached. And negotiations with the Holy See had resulted in a process whereby prepublication censorship included officials of church (a Roman-appointed inquisitor) and state (a secretary of the Senate and the *Riformatori dello studio di Padova*) working together—with the latter, secular arm still strongly linked to Catholic interests seeking to control the book

---

[185] Anon., *Catalogus librorum altero se correctior comptiorque qui Patavii in Bibliotheca I. N. G. J. inveniuntur sub felicissimo regimine… Caroli Nicolai a' Marpurg Nobilis Lyburni Fluminensis* (Padua: Ex Typographia Pasquati, 1691), 51; Anna Bettoni, 'Livres français de la bibliothèque *germanica* de Padoue à la fin de la Renaissance', *La Lecture littéraire: revue du Centre de recherche sur la lecture littéraire de l'Université de Reims*, no. 7 ('Lire à la Renaissance', ed. Jean Balsamo) (2002), 15–41. I am very grateful to Anna Bettoni for providing me with a copy of this article and other information relating to the copy in question (Biblioteca Universitaria di Padova, pressmark 11.b.131). The *Catalogus* records that the copy in the library in 1691 was an octavo (octavos were designated with the letter 'M'), which makes it very likely that it corresponds to the copy of Paris 1598 still in the collection, even though it has no ex-libris.

[186] See de Vivo, *Information and communication in Venice*, but the new emphasis was already there to a certain extent in Paul F. Grendler, *The Roman Inquisition and the Venetian press* (Princeton: Princeton University Press, 1977), xxii–xxiii.

[187] Mario Infelise, 'Masters of books: ecclesiastic and state censorship in Venice during the Counter-Reformation', paper given at 'Oxford Seminars on the History of the Book', All Souls College, University of Oxford, 28 February 2012.

trade. Even during the Interdict, the Venetian government did not favour removing the Roman inquisitor and taking command of the entire censorship process. After the Interdict, it acquiesced in the Roman prohibition of James I of England's 1609 *Apologia*, and left Sarpi's and Contarini's histories of the Interdict unpublished. As at Geneva, Venetian publishers and booksellers worked with their suppliers to get certain books past customs—by substituting title pages, smuggling, and disguising of wares.[188]

The Servite friar Fulgenzio Micanzio reveals in a letter of 24 February 1617 that he had attempted, and failed, to get a licence to print an Italian translation of Bacon's *Essays* at Venice, due to 'the evil Custome we are fallen into, never to print any thing that is good'. Rather than give censors or 'insolent beasts' the opportunity to 'loppe them', he suggests the translation be printed in London and a good number of copies sent back to Venice via the English ambassador.[189]

This was a fitting 'transpassage', for the nobleman William Cavendish had brought a copy of the *Essayes* (1612 edition) with him from England to Venice, then translated them with the help of an Italian assistant as an exercise, and presented them to Micanzio. But Micanzio must have intervened to warn the composers or correctors of the translation that 'the surly and envious friar' who hindered their printing in Venice objected to certain passages. As printed in three London editions of 1617–18, and one Florentine edition of 1618–19, the translation removed all anti-Catholic remarks and two entire essays ('Of Religion' and 'Of Superstition').[190]

The documents relating to this episode reveal that the friar Micanzio, like the secular priests Goulart and Perrot in Geneva, played a major role in mediating the circulation, translation, and publication of philosophical texts. It was the eagerness of 'some gentlemen' to have an Italian text of the *Essayes* that motivated his initiative, and he later predicted that it 'will be received with great applause chiefly of this Nobility' (in Venice). In the meantime, Micanzio had personally read 'peeces' of Bacon's *Advancement of Learning* to 'Virtuosi' in Venice, who had importuned him to translate it (which he did not).[191]

Micanzio's role in the circulation of Bacon's works fits a wider pattern that we have already begun to observe in other late-sixteenth and early-seventeenth-century contexts. The clergy (regular and secular) in both France and Italy were

---

[188] De Vivo, *Information and communication in Venice*, 201, 214, 250–6; Maclean, *Scholarship, commerce, religion*, 151–3.

[189] Noel Malcolm, *De Dominis, 1560–1624: Venetian, Anglican, ecumenist, and relapsed heretic* (London: Strickland & Scott Academic Publications, 1984), 50 (citing BL Add. MS 11309, fols. 5v–6r). Micanzio's correspondence with Cavendish survives only in an English translation undertaken by the latter's tutor Thomas Hobbes. He and Sarpi collaborated closely, so it is possible that the latter had some involvement in this correspondence. See Filippo de Vivo, 'Paolo Sarpi and the uses of information', in Joad Raymond (ed.), *News networks in seventeenth-century Britain and Europe* (London: Routledge, 2006), 35–49, 37.

[190] Malcolm, *De Dominis, 1560–1624*, 48–51; V. Gabrieli, 'Bacone, la Riforma e Roma nella versione hobbesiana d'un carteggio di Fulgenzio Micanzio', *English Miscellany*, 8 (1957), 195–250, 209. Malcolm's reconstruction of the history of this translation remains the one that most convincingly acccounts for all the available documentary evidence.

[191] Malcolm, *De Dominis, 1560–1624*, 50.

participating prominently in the teaching and dissemination of practical philosophy to elite students and readers, and in its application in the practical
contexts of civil life. This is acknowledged even in England, where Shakespeare
shows an ordained Italian friar making physiognomical 'observations' that put
an 'experimental seal' on his reading in books, and that enable him in practice
to read the innocence of a traduced woman in her face.[192]

In Italy, the foundations of the university discipline lay in exegesis of Aristotle's
Nicomachean Ethics and *Politics*, but beyond the universities other classical and
modern authors, including those who wrote in the vernacular, were becoming
increasingly important. Micanzio, in another letter to Cavendish, describes Bacon's
Essays as 'a new and most neat way of instructing in morals and politics with a most
excellent delightfulness even to the most coy wits'.[193]

In the later 1610s and 1620s, the context of the dissemination of the *Essais* in
northeastern Italy likewise proves to be extramural teaching of morals and politics
to the young nobility and patriciate. As we shall see in more detail in 2.2.9, some
time *c.*1617–23, in Venice, Fra Paolo Sarpi (of the Servite order) commissioned a
new translation of a chapter not in Naselli (I 27, 'De l'amitié') from the same
Servite friar and theologian (Micanzio) as a contribution to a famous Venetian
amicizia between two noblemen. It is very likely to be Sarpi's connections with the
French republic of letters that brought our author to his attention.

A friar of the Jesuate order, Girolomo Canini, then translated a copy of a later
edition of the full text as a work teaching self-knowledge. This full, unexpurgated
Italian text (lacking only II 12) was printed at Venice in 1629 (though not necessarily distributed), then published and distributed in 1633–4 (with II 12 in a
separate volume)—with the potential to render Naselli's edition obsolete. At the
same moment, the linchpin of Franco-Italian intellectual relations, Gabriel Naudé,
paired Montaigne in a publication at Venice with the French priest Charron as the
new Seneca and Plutarch of practical philosophy. In 1644, another secular clergyman, a professor of moral philosophy at Padua and a member of the Accademia dei
Ricovrati, Flavio Querenghi, published a set of 'miscellaneous' vernacular *Discorsi*
that were acknowledged to have imitated the *Essais*, mostly in the form of Naselli's
Discorsi.[194]

However, as these dates and Querenghi's dependence on Naselli already reveal,
there is an important difference between the transmission of the *Essais* in Geneva
and in northeastern Italy. Despite the tensions between Geneva and Lyon and
other centres of French print culture, French books flowed in both directions.
Venice was the main conduit for the arrival of French books in Italy, but it appears
that French copies of the *Essais* were still very rare in the peninsula as late as 1620.
The international market for French books—or, indeed, for transalpine books in
general—did not extend fully into the peninsula.

[192] Shakespeare, *Much Ado About Nothing*, 4.1.163–8.
[193] Gabrieli, 'Bacone, la Riforma e Roma nella versione hobbesiana d'un carteggio di Fulgenzio
Micanzio', 206.
[194] These statements will all be documented in the detailed treatment that follows in 2.2.9–12.

Although it was certainly possible for individual collectors to obtain imports from north of the Alps via strangers and Venetian booksellers, the learned book trade in Italy was all but a closed market by 1600. Foreign publishers did not directly market or sell their wares there. Direct import controls were less significant than a general suspicion—fostered by the post-Tridentine Church—of heterodox thinking spreading from transalpine countries. The Italian Roman Catholic world created its own version of divine and humane learning and only selected imports were incorporated in unadapted forms.[195]

There is no evidence that Naselli, like Goulart and Florio, might have been conscious of readers who would compare his text with the French. In other words, Naselli's reduced version of the pre-1588 text held the Italian market for Montaigne's work for a much longer period than Lyon [Geneva] 1595 could possibly hold the Francophone market. Numerous copies of his 1590 translation survive in Italian libraries, including the Biblioteca Estense at Modena.[196]

And there is documentation of these copies having been acquired and owned in the period itself. For example, between the publication of the Clementine Index in 1596, and 1602, lists were taken for the Vatican of the books found in the libraries and private collections of thirty-one religious orders across Italy, in an effort to gain control of the these orders' libraries and studies. Copies of the *Discorsi* were found in the collections of three monks in the Veneto (Candiana 1 copy, Padua 2 copies), along with others located in Emilia Romagna (one copy Monteveglio) and Milan (one copy). But there were no copies of the French *Essais*.[197]

Indeed, besides the copy Naselli must have had (probably of Bordeaux 1582 or Paris 1587) and the copy of Bordeaux 1580 sent to Pinelli, we have yet to find evidence that any copies of the early editions of the *Essais* to 1588 were possessed by collectors in Italy. The contrast with Florio's remark about the plethora of diverse copies and editions to which he had access could hardly be greater. This supposition is supported by the fact that only one copy of any of these early editions (1580–8) is currently known to be held in Italian public libraries. And relatively few copies of the editions from 1593 to 1630 survive today in Italian collections. The earliest edition held by the Vatican dates to 1611. Nevertheless, the copies of Paris 1598 and Paris 1602, which have verified early owners in Padua and Casteldurante, can still combine with the survival of other early octavos in Italian libraries to suggest that these small format French editions did slowly begin to enter Italian collections between the later 1590s and the 1620s.[198]

[195] For this and the previous paragraph see Maclean, *Scholarship, commerce, religion*, 198, 208–9, 223–4.
[196] USTC/EDIT 16 (19 copies); ICCU ('Istituto Centrale per il Catalogo Unico') Opac SBN ('Servizio Bibliotecario Nazionale'), <http://www.sbn.it/opacsbn/opac/iccu/free.jsp>. Until we have better data, such statements can only be provisional.
[197] See the online database entitled 'Le biblioteche degli ordini regolari in Italia alla fine del secolo XVI', <http://ebusiness.taiprora.it/bib/index.asp>, BIB50580 (erroneously dated 1540), BIB26031.
[198] The main sources for early copies of the *Essais* extant in Italian collections are Sayce and Maskell, supplemented by Balsamo and Simonin, *Abel L'Angelier & Françoise de Louvain (1574–1620)*, USTC, and the ICCU Opac SBN online catalogue. None of these sources are comprehensive, and survival in historic Italian collections cannot be considered a reliable guide to ownership of copies at the time. The earliest editions currently known to be represented in Italian libraries are Paris 1587 (one copy on

2.2.9 PAOLO SARPI: THE VENETIAN SOCRATES

Some of the information we have about the nexuses of transmission of the *Essais* in northeastern Italy between the late 1610s and the early 1630s comes from sources first composed in manuscript at the time, but not printed until the 1640s. Here we shall focus on the evidence relating to a moment in the late 1620s/early 1630s when clerics called upon the French text to assist in the fashioning of *virtù civile* and models of the philosophico-religious life for the noble elite of the Veneto.

The idea for Fulgenzio Micanzio's life of Fra Paolo Sarpi originated in the period immediately following Sarpi's death (*c.*1623–6). A text was circulating in manuscript in the early 1630s and a different text finally appeared in print in 1646 (Leiden).[199] As in the case of de Thou's *De vita sua*, it is crucial to understand the apologetic context of this piece of life-writing, which offered an unconventional hagiography of a friar all but martyred by the Roman Catholic Church.

Micanzio was adumbrating a saintly philosophical *persona* for Sarpi to shore up the authority of his writings, to defend him against the printed calumnies to which he had been subject from the moment he had begun to serve as *consultore* for the Venetian senate in the period of the Interdict. In other words, Micanzio's *imago* of Sarpi's philosophical *persona* is shaped by the religious politics they shared and their identity as Catholic friars who, as officials of the Venetian state, defended Venice's ecclesiastical privileges against the publications and polemics of the court of Rome, and especially the relatively new order of the Society of Jesus.

The philosophical *persona* consists of the offices Sarpi performed for his friends, for the Venetian Republic, and for God; the heroic virtues he exercised in performing those offices; and, above all, a perfect blend of the contemplative and civic or active lives ('mista singolarmente d'attiva e contemplativa').[200] Here was a friar whose cell was visited by the civic elite of Venice, and who left his monastery to serve the Venetian state. His status as an all-round wise man, not just a *teologo*, implicitly contrasted with the theological *persona* of the Roman Catholic militant formed by Jesuit pedagogy—at least according to a certain anti-Roman stereotype.

For the larger backdrop is the manner in which the Jesuits—and, in reaction to their educational initiatives, other religious orders and secular priests—were participating or attempting to participate in the teaching and exegesis of philosophy, alongside theology, in order to shape the education of the elite in the confessionalized

USTC in the Biblioteca Universitaria, Bologna), and Lyon 1593 (two copies on USTC in Milan and Modena, and one further copy in the Biblioteca Federico Patetta del Dipartimento di Scienze Giuridiche dell'Università degli Studi di Torino). The edition with the most surviving copies in Italian collections is Paris 1598 (four copies, including the copy in Padua not listed on ICCU Opac SBN but confirmed on USTC).

[199] Fulgenzio Micanzio, *Vita del padre Paolo, dell'ordine de' Servi; e theologo della serenissima republ. di Venetia* (Leiden: Joris Abrahamsz van der Marsce, 1646). I cite the following edition in what follows: Paolo Sarpi, *Istoria del Concilio Tridentino seguita dalla 'Vita del padre Paolo' di Fulgenzio Micanzio*, ed. Corrado Vivanti, 2 vols. (Turin: Giulio Einaudi, 1974).

[200] Sarpi, *Istoria del Concilio Tridentino seguita dalla 'Vita del padre Paolo'*, vol. 2, 1359.

Europe of the late Renaissance.[201] We have already had reason to note the roles played by Canon Pierre Charron, Bishop Camus, Father Garasse S. J., and Pastors Simon Goulart and Charles Perrot in shaping private reading of the *Essais* and of other secular authors in France and Geneva. Bishop Camus offered the *Essais* in print to the French nobleman Achante, around the same time that Sarpi offered them to the Venetian nobleman Trevisan (see 2.7.3).

What kind of autonomy could be granted by a Christian society to idle, secular philosophical pursuits, and to the secular philosophical *personae* of the lay and clerical elite who wished to pursue them? Beyond hermits, and ascetic monks, how should ordained monks, friars, canons, and educated lay people balance the active and contemplative, the philosophical and religious lives? What rules of behaviour should be applied to their 'conversation', through spiritual discipline, pedagogy, and censorship?

These questions had been current since at least the twelfth century and were answered in different ways across the continent in the late sixteenth century. They were addressed in the *Essais*, in Montaigne's debate with the friar Fabri and others at Rome in 1581, and in many of the early scenes of transmission of the *Essais*—especially where such scenes also involve Charron's *De la sagesse* as a designated companion text.[202]

Sarpi is an important figure for the wider argument of this study, besides his role in the transmission of the *Essais*. For Micanzio's biography provides a post-Erasmian, late Renaissance model of the enfranchisement of the learned reader-writer as civic scholar-saint. His virtues as a wise and learned man, especially his prodigious feats of memory and judgement, arise from his mastery of books and writings, and, through them, of all forms and applications of knowledge and communication, from pragmatic written *consulte* and censorship of the press to civil, Socratic conversation and religio-moral self-scrutiny.[203]

In this respect, Micanzio's work is closer to the relatively new genre of biographies of learned men such as Peiresc and Pinelli than to traditional hagiography.[204] Like those texts, it idealizes forms of learned sociability and private education that in some respects are complementary to the school of Montaigne, especially insofar as they incorporate *conversazione* with the nobility.

Sarpi's earliest education is provided privately by a priest, Ambrosio Morelli, who tutors him in rhetoric, memory, and judgement alongside children of the nobility such as Andrea Moresini. He is soon in demand amongst the *letterati* of

---

[201] Paul F. Grendler, *Renaissance education between religion and politics* (Farnham: Ashgate, 2006), VI, 1–21. On Venice see Maurizio Sangalli, *Cultura, politica e religione nella Repubblica di Venezia tra Cinque e Seicento: Gesuiti e Somaschi a Venezia* (Venice: Istituto veneto di scienze, lettere ed arti, 1999), and on Padua, Sangalli, *Università, accademie, gesuiti*.

[202] Virginia Krause, *Idle pursuits: literature and oisiveté in the French Renaissance* (Newark and London: University of Delaware Press and Associated University Presses, 2003); Ian Hunter, 'The university philosopher in early modern Germany', in Condren, Gaukroger, and Hunter (eds.), *The philosopher in early modern Europe*, 35–65, 43–50.

[203] See de Vivo, 'Paolo Sarpi and the uses of information'.

[204] See Peter N. Miller, *Peiresc's Europe: learning and virtue in the seventeenth century* (New Haven: Yale University Press, 2000).

the court of Mantova, answering all comers on all learned topics for the prince. He has mastered all the liberal arts and the professional disciplines by the age of twenty-two, and combined them with all the Christian and moral virtues. He has read and retained knowledge of books and of persons with equal mastery.[205]

On the one hand, when not carrying out his sacred offices, he spent his time in books, writing out various thoughts on natural, metaphysical, and mathematical topics ('pensieri naturali, metafisici e matematici'). On the other hand, he frequented his usual virtuous conversations ('virtuose conversazioni') at the *ridotto* of the same Andrea Moresini, where gathered all who professed letters—not only noble senators of the *Serenissima*, noteworthy for kindness, religion, learning, and civil prudence ('bontà, religione, dottrina e prudenza civile'), but all kinds of *virtuosi*, both lay and clerical. Sarpi's *ridotto* in Padua was the house of Vicenzo Pinelli—'l'academia di tutte le virtù'.[206]

This is a first glimpse of what may be a distinctive feature of literary and philosophical culture in the Veneto: friars, canons, scholars, and patricians mixing together in civil conversation. But Sarpi balanced his active with his contemplative pursuits. Like Montaigne, but for a shorter period and for the explicit purpose of self-correction, he withdrew to study himself by means of reading, as well as writing in the manner of Plutarch. On the basis of his consultation of Sarpi's archive of notes, Micanzio states that around the turn of the sixteenth and seventeenth centuries the Servite friar, like Socrates, brought philosophy down from heaven to earth, and concentrated for six years on the study of moral philosophy.[207]

Micanzio has reviewed Sarpi's markings throughout his copies of Aristotle and Plato, as well as his 'librizzoli'—that is, notebooks the friar carried about with him, full of *sentenze* and other writings. He has seen only three more elaborated pieces of writing, in the manner of the 'opuscoli' of Plutarch, including a 'medicine for the soul' ('medicina dell'animo') and a portrait of his own defects, and their proposed cure, which showed he had scrutinized the innermost recesses of his own heart and seen and censured all vices in himself.

For the next twenty years, after this period of self-correction, mediated by reading and writing, those that lived in intimacy with him could not detect even a single defect. Like the true possessors of wisdom ('i veri possessori della sapienza') he had clearly cured himself, made himself truly good. And, unlike Montaigne, he had not used only secular literature. He had also read through both the New and the Old Testament, and his Breviary (especially the Psalms), with such profound attention that he marked almost every line for meditation—a great prince sought his copy of the Greek New Testament for this reason.

This period of self-study was to end with the call he received to serve Venice in the Interdict controversy, which turned the friar's thoughts to the author of the

---

[205] Sarpi, *Istoria del Concilio Tridentino seguita dalla 'Vita del padre Paolo'*, vol. 2, 1276–7, 1281–2, 1284–5, 1301.
[206] Sarpi, *Istoria del Concilio Tridentino seguita dalla 'Vita del padre Paolo'*, vol. 2, 1305–6, 1308.
[207] This passage exists in a variant in the manuscript of the *Vita* conserved in the Biblioteca Querini-Stampalia in Venice. See Sarpi, *Istoria del Concilio Tridentino seguita dalla 'Vita del padre Paolo'*, vol. 2, 1322n.3.

biography, Micanzio. Sarpi had privately taught Micanzio, not with ordinary lessons, but using the Socratic method, setting reading then seeking the truth with him in open discourse. He had in this way perfected many gentlemen and clerics in the moral, mathematical, and natural disciplines, never expounding an author such as Aristotle or Aquinas *ex professo*, but instead preparing his students sincerely to seek the truth. He now needed Micanzio alongside him as a faithful companion, and as someone who could collect from books the authorities in civil and canon law he needed to back up his positions in the controversy. And just as Sarpi had mastered, in reading and writing, the whole record of learning, he now mastered the whole archive of the Venetian state, to which he was granted unrestricted access, and to which were added—written out by a professional writer salaried by the senate—his own *consulte*.[208]

The section of the biography which includes the mention of Montaigne concerns Sarpi's mastery of that type of prudence which Micanzio labels 'of conversation' ('di conversare'), and which he rates even above that of Socrates. Sarpi welcomed into his *conversazione* not only the grandest Venetian senators but also the younger nobility, those admitted into office as *savii d'ordini* to learn from their superiors.[209] Sarpi was their archive, their library, their historical chronicle ('archivio, libraria, historia'). Micanzio goes on in an extended digression to tell first of the relationship between Sarpi and one of these young noblemen, Marco Trevisan, then of the famous history of Trevisan's friendship with Nicolò Barbarigo. Sarpi contributes to the building of this friendship by having Micanzio translate *Essais* I 27 ('De l'amitié') into Italian.[210]

Micanzio's narration of the social nexus of this manuscript translation offers another complex early modern example of a participant-observer's description of a text's context. We have been encountering such descriptions throughout this study, and approaching them with two points in mind. The first point is that literary artefacts in this period are not just conveyances of 'text' and 'thought'; they act as traces of the agency relations that are established or reaffirmed by their making, use, and transmission.[211]

In this case, Montaigne's chapter is translated for the idea of friendship it offers, but the making and circulation of the translation at the same time directly indexes the involvement of one pair of 'friends', the friars Sarpi and Micanzio, in the construction of a work of civic virtue—the friendship between another pair of friends, the noblemen Trevisan and Barbarigo.

The second point, already implicit in the first, is that these descriptions of context have their own agenda, their own history. This history is particularly vexed in the case of Micanzio's narrative of Sarpi's involvement in the Trevisan–Barbarigo friendship. In two letters to Galileo of 23 August and 15 September 1635, Micanzio told the story of the manuscript *Vita*, and of the digression about Trevisan in particular.

---

[208] For this and the previous two paragraphs see Sarpi, *Istoria del Concilio Tridentino seguita dalla 'Vita del padre Paolo'*, vol. 2, 1323–4, 1329, 1331–2, 1375–6.

[209] Grendler, *Renaissance education between religion and politics*, XI, 41.

[210] Sarpi, *Istoria del Concilio Tridentino seguita dalla 'Vita del padre Paolo'*, vol. 2, 1392–6.

[211] See the 'General Preface' to Volumes 1 and 2.

He claimed in conventional fashion that the biography had come from his pen without any art, as pure and simple testimony to the truth, but that someone had copied and begun to circulate it before he had had a chance to perfect it. But he then goes on to say that a madman ('un pazzo') had constrained him to include the 'discorsetto' on the famous friendship, which now (in 1635) makes him—rather than, as should be the case, its true author—look mad.

Micanzio reminds Galileo that these heroic friends had caused a lot of paper to be blotted. It would have been more accurate to say that Trevisan—almost certainly the *pazzo* he is referring to—had caused it, for he used writings in print and manuscript throughout his life for self-apologetic and polemical purposes. The semi-official chronicler of the friendship, the Benedictine monk Luigi Manzini, reveals in his *Lettera* of 1629 that Trevisan himself, with 'very wise resolution' ('sagaccisima risolutione') was behind the publication of the legal and literary documents describing the friendship.

This is hardly surprising given that the main beneficiary of the whole episode and its surrounding publicity was Trevisan. He was—briefly—re-enfranchised as a Venetian nobleman by the financial support of Barbarigo and, later, the political support of the doge Nicolò Contarini. But by 1635 it would have seemed perfectly justifiable to characterize Trevisan as a *pazzo*, given that he had foolishly denounced the powerful senator Domenico Molino to the Venetian inquisitors of state in October 1631, and suffered exile as a consequence of Molino's inevitable counter-accusations.[212]

According to his own account, once again distributed in print and manuscript copies, Trevisan accused Molino of transgressing the proper limits of equality and civil modesty ('della egualità e modestia civile'), and of having his dependents elevate him to a quasi-tyrannical position of supremacy with concepts and attributes that were simply too odious and scandalous. His proof? In his submission to the Inquisitors, Trevisan cited the highly inappropriate way Molino had been addressed by the likes of Lorenzo Pignoria and Francesco Pona in the prefaces and dedications to books printed *c.*1628–9, the moment when he himself was being exalted by his own dependents in various writings as the paragon of heroic friendship with Barbarigo. He also recalled that Molino had abused his position as censor (when one of the *riformatori allo Studio di Padova*) by taking sole responsibility for granting the imprimatur to books dedicated to him, when he should have gained the others' signatures.[213]

Clearly, the fashioning of a reputation for noble virtue in and through the making of printed books was very important for these patricians, whether of minor rank like Trevisan or major rank like Molino.

In the *discorsetto* itself, then, Micanzio tells how, under Sarpi's tutelage, Trevisan gave himself to moral philosophy and all other kinds of learning, visiting his master

[212] For this and the previous two paragraphs, see Enrico De Mas, *L'attesa del secolo aureo (1603–1625): saggi di storia delle idee del secolo XVII* (Florence: Olschki, 1982), 260–2 (the Galileo letters), 265–6; Gaetano Cozzi, *Venezia barocca: conflitti di uomini e idee nella crisi del Seicento veneziano* (Venice: Il Cardo, 1995), 332–4, 380–1.

[213] Cozzi, *Venezia barocca*, 385–6.

for informal, conversational tuition almost every day. Their *conversazione* passed into such a degree of *amicizia*, says Micanzio, that they could speak with complete *libertà* to one another, with Sarpi particularly valuing Trevisan's *veracità*. Trevisan tells him, for example, that others call Sarpi *patrone* of his passions, but that he, by contrast, sees intemperance in the fact that Sarpi is always in his cell reading and writing. Trevisan is also exquisitely informed of all the affairs and manners of Venice and reports them to Sarpi.[214]

Then Sarpi hears that Trevisan has in turn entered into a great friendship with another nobleman of Venice, Barbarigo (a friendship which Micanzio remarks has already exhausted all writers' pens), Micanzio describes the nexus of the translation as follows:

> He [Sarpi] was also willing to contribute something to so rare a work [*opera cosi rara*]. It was not fit that so excellent a construction of civil virtue [*fabrica così eccelsa di virtù civile*] should be raised at Venice, without this architect putting his hand to it. And hearing Signor Marco recount the various accidents that had passed between them, and their desire for a total transmutation and transfusion not only of external things but of themselves [*desiderio d'una totale transmutatione, e d'una transfusione, non solo delle cose esterne mà di sè stessi*], according to that precept *amicorum omnia communia* ['friends hold all things in common'], which is in everyone's mouth, but perhaps never practised in any other example, certainly not to the degree it later was in the case of these two lords; and having delivered some excellent teachings concerning friendship, he did command Master Fulgentio to translate out of French into Italian that essay of Michael of Montaigne of friendship. Which once done, I cannot relate how pleasing it was to both these gentlemen, finding in their own hearts and affections not only those conditions of friendship which that great person [*quel grand'huomo*] had expressed with so rare examples as an Idea of perfect friendship [*un'idea d'una perfetta amicitia*], but also to find thereby how far they had exceeded his description.[215]

Sarpi is here a Socratic figure offering a private tutorial to a young nobleman in the practical philosophy of friendship, specifically with a view to shaping the form to be taken by the relationship between him and another nobleman. When Erasmus had begun the *Adagia* with the precept 'friends hold all things in common' ('amicorum communia omnia') he had pointed out that although it was frequently on mens' lips, actual sharing of life and property was extremely rare.[216] One of its most influential ancient occurrences was in Aristotle's highly influential discussion of the relationship between friendship and justice (*Nicomachean Ethics*, 1159b).

The rationale of the Trevisan–Barbarigo friendship is to exceed all other historical examples of great friendships in actually putting this proverb into practice, in relation both to their souls and to their property, and to provide a model for political

[214] Sarpi, *Istoria del Concilio Tridentino seguita dalla 'Vita del padre Paolo'*, vol. 2, 1392–3.
[215] Sarpi, *Istoria del Concilio Tridentino seguita dalla 'Vita del padre Paolo'*, vol. 2, 1393–4.
[216] Desiderius Erasmus, *Collected works of Erasmus Volume 31: Adages Ii1 to Iv100*, eds Margaret Mann and Roger Aubrey Baskerville Mynors (Toronto: University of Toronto Press, 1982), 29–30; Kathy Eden, *Friends hold all things in common: tradition, intellectual property, and the 'Adages' of Erasmus* (New Haven: Yale University Press, 2001).

community in so doing. At the point in its development when Sarpi instructs Trevisan, the two would-be perfect friends *desire* a total transmutation and trans-fusion of external things and of themselves according to that precept—that is to say, it is not yet achieved.

The role of the translated Montaigne chapter is to offer a vernacular, sub-Aristotelian idea of perfect friendship, of total transmutation and transfusion, along with a description of an actual, rare example (the friendship of Montaigne and La Boétie) that Trevisan and Barbarigo can both appropriate and exceed. The author of the translation is not its writer, but the *patron* of all virtues (Sarpi) who commissions it from his friend and disciple Micanzio. It is a unique gift in manuscript for two individuals.

We cannot consult Micanzio's translation, as it is not extant. But we can consult an Italian translation of the chapter on friendship undertaken in these years by a friar of a different order, Girolamo Canini of the Jesuates. Canini was Padua-Venice's answer to Geneva's Simon Goulart—if less prolific, and less well-known in posterity. The translation was commissioned and published (in 1633, after an aborted attempt in 1629) by Venice's answer to L'Angelier, Edward Blount, and Pyramus de Candolle: the *libraio-editore* Marco Ginammi. When we read the chapter in Canini's Italian, and in the light of the summary he included for the benefit of the reader, we can indeed hear how it could have given rise, as part of a Sarpian tutorial on friendship, to features of the friendship as it was subsequently celebrated.

Canini's prefatory and marginal summaries divide Montaigne's chapter into eight sections and clarify the argument from his point of view. Montaigne is describing 'amicitia perfetta' of the kind he enjoyed with La Boétie, whose treatise *De la servitude volontaire* was—in Canini's slightly misleading words—his treatise on friendship ('un suo Trattato dell'amicitia'). Montaigne distinguishes it from other kinds of loving friendship between fathers and sons, brothers, husbands and wives, and from physical love, including Greek 'amore Academico'.

Read within the particular nexus provided by the Trevisan–Barbarigo friendship the chapter has much of relevance to offer. The only philosopher named as offering authoritative definitions of *amicizia perfetta* is—perhaps surprisingly—Aristotle (Cicero is quoted but not named). Canini's section 3 on the esteem in which friendship is held by nature and lawmakers ('Amicitia stimata dalla Natura, da' legislatori') opens by stating that there is nothing to which nature more clearly conducts us than to society ('alla Società'): 'And Aristotle says that good legislators have taken greater care of friendship than of justice' ('E dice Aristotele, chi li buoni legislatori, hanno havuto piu cura dell'amicitia, che della giustizia'—referring to *Nicomachean Ethics*, 1159b).[217]

This is one of many direct citations from Aristotle's text that Montaigne inserts into the *Essais* (after 1588) as a way of entering the conversation on moral philosophy

---

[217] For this and the previous paragraph, see Michel de Montaigne, *Saggi..., ouero Discorsi, naturali, politici, e morali*, trans. Girolamo Canini (Venice: Marco Ginammi, 1633), sig. I2r–v (henceforward abbreviated as 'Venice 1633'; available in a low resolution digital facsimile on Gallica).

to which the Greek's work had given rise in the 1570s and 1580s at Henri III's *Académie du Palais* and in the Ramist controversy.[218]

Later in the chapter Aristotle is name-checked twice on the same page. And it is this page, in the first half of Canini's section 7 on the extraordinary and perfect friendship ('amicitia... straordinaria, e perfetta') of the two Frenchmen, which could most clearly be read as giving rise to the central feature of the Trevisan–Barbarigo friendship, the feature which took it beyond the perfection of Montaigne-La Boétie.

Canini's section 7 begins with Montaigne's description of the universal union ('mescolanza universale') he achieved with La Boétie and of the writings to which it immediately gave rise (in this case a neo-Latin satire). The friendship grew quickly because it was formed on no other Idea, but itself ('alcuna altra Idea, che se medesima'). Each friend's will lost itself in the other's: 'holding back nothing for ourselves, that was our own, that was either his or mine' ('non ci riservando niente, che ci fusse proprio, nè che fusse overo suo, o mio').[219] It is this passage and what follows that Sarpi must principally have had in mind, for the realization of this communality of wills and property was the hallmark of the Trevisan–Barbarigo friendship.

The following, Ciceronian example of Tiberius Gracchus and Caius Blosius is used to consolidate this sense of the perfect communality of wills, before we hear, in Canini's Italian, that the principle uniting their souls was *carità*—the very principle usually invoked in the case of Trevisan–Barbarigo. As Barbarigo might have said when conferring all his worldly goods on Trevisan: 'for my part, I would certainly have more willingly trusted in him, than in myself' ('io mi sarei certamente più volentieri fidato in lui, per conto mio, che di me stesso').

The Italian Montaigne then reinforces the distinction between common friendships or 'amicitie communi' (described with the Aristotelian apophthegm: 'O my friends, there is no friend!') and this noble exchange ('questo commertio nobile'). In this latter perfect union, again, there is complete 'confusione' of wills, with no awareness of services done, gratitude, obligation, and so forth: 'everything actually being in common between them, wills, thoughts, judgements, goods, wives, children, honour, and life... one soul in two bodies, according to Aristotle's very apt definition' ('[e]ssendo tutto in effetto comune fra essi le volontà, i pensieri, i giuditii, i beni, le mogli, i figliuoli, l'honore, la vita... un'anima in due corpi, secondo la propissima definitione di Aristotele').

Here, then, is the ancient adage mentioned by Micanzio (*amicorum omnia communia*), translated from Montaigne's original French into Italian, in the midst of a passage about the transfusion or confusion of wills between perfect friends. In this case the Aristotelian saying is most probably from Diogenes Laertius. There follows

---

[218] François Rigolot, 'Montaigne et Aristote: La conversion à l'*Ethique à Nicomaque*', in Ullrich Langer (ed.), *Au-delà de la Poétique: Aristote et la littérature de la Renaissance = Beyond the Poetics: Aristotle and early modern literature* (Geneva: Droz, 2002), 43–63, 53–7, 62–3; François Rigolot, 'Quand Montaigne emprunte à l'Ethique à Nicomaque: étude des "allongeails" sur l'Exemplaire de Bordeaux', *Montaigne Studies*, 14 (2002), 19–35, 29.

[219] Venice 1633, sig. I4v.

the example of the 'testamento' of the Corinthian Eudamidas, who bequeathed to two of his friends the honour of caring for his mother and daughter.[220]

Sarpi, in other words, uses his friend Micanzio to provide a text—as he had used him to provide legal and historical precedents during the Interdict controversy—which is intended directly to realize the friends' specific desire 'for a total transmutation and transfusion not only of external things but of themselves, according to that precept *amicorum omnia communia*'.

The outcome of Sarpi's Socratic intervention—as narrated by Micanzio—is not, then, just an Italian version of a chapter by Montaigne on the generally relevant topic of friendship (as Cozzi, Benzoni, and others have maintained). It is, first, the re-education and re-enfranchisement of a young Venetian nobleman (Trevisan) who had fallen into moral and financial disrepute; and, second, a civic Venetian 'work' of friendship—based on the specific principle of commonality of property—between Trevisan and Barbarigo, which itself is a contribution to the *conversazione civile* of post-Interdict Venice. There were other texts in circulation in manuscript and print about Trevisan's and Barbarigo's friendship from the mid-1620s and this digression in Micanzio's biography takes its place amongst them.[221]

For Micanzio goes on briefly to tell the story of how all things became common between the two friends before and after Sarpi's death: how Barbarigo invited the quasi-destitute Trevisan to live in and be master of his own house, including his wife and children; the *carità* evident in the way Trevisan instantly divested himself of the vices which had brought his fortunes low; the legal instruments ('procura, e testamenti') they set up within their lifetimes formally to make all their property common to one another. Though many initially doubted its duration, Micanzio states it to be 'at this day one of the glories of our city and our century', the Apotheosis of the heroic virtues ('per le virtù heroiche fù trovata l'Apotheosi'), a new way of virtue ('una strada nuova di virtù'), and its protagonists 'the Numina presiding over all friendships' ('Numi tutelari dell'amicitie').[222]

It is these remarks that above all enable us to group Micanzio's digression with texts that were published in Venice between 1625 and 1629, produced both by lay writers and by clergy, and instigated in many cases by Trevisan himself. A good proportion of these were published by the *libraio-editore* who proves to be a major protagonist in this story: Marco Ginammi. There are two in particular that help us further to explore descriptions of the kind of nexus within which the *Essais* were transmitted and translated in Padua-Venice. The first involves another translation dedicated to the friendship of Trevisan and Barbarigo; the second offers a scene that is both complementary to Micanzio's description of Sarpi's informal tutorial on friendship and indicative of the context of Canini's Montaigne.

---

[220] For this and the previous two paragraphs, see Venice 1633, sig. I5r–v; Rigolot, 'Quand Montaigne emprunte à l'Ethique à Nicomaque', 29–30; Ullrich Langer, *Perfect friendship: studies in literature and moral philosophy from Boccaccio to Corneille* (Geneva: Droz, 1994), 15–20.

[221] Cozzi, *Venezia barocca*, 327–409.

[222] Sarpi, *Istoria del Concilio Tridentino seguita dalla 'Vita del padre Paolo'*, vol. 2, 1394–6.

In 1626, Marco Ginammi published a parallel Spanish and Italian text of Bartolomè de Las Casas's history of the destruction of the West Indies. He commissioned the translation from Giacomo Castellani, an anti-Spanish polemicist, who under the pseudonym of Francesco Bersabita dedicated the work 'To Friendship' ('All'Amicitia')—to, that is, Trevisan and Barbarigo.

The translator of Las Casas for Ginammi and the translator of Montaigne for Sarpi have one important thing in common, with respect to their association with the famous friends. Both were named in the 'Procura, e Testamenti' of Trevisan and Barbarigo, which were printed in several of the publications devoted to the friendship in the late 1620s: Micanzio was a beneficiary of Trevisan's will, dated 16 March 1626, in which he was described as 'my... most loyal Friend,... most faithful servant of the... Republic' ('mio... lealissimo Amico,... fedelissimo servitore della... Republica'); Castellani was a witness to the requests of Barbarigo and Trevisan, presented at the Ducal Chancellory on 17 November 1627, that their wills—founded as they were on the immutable laws of nature and of the true and perfect friendship—be published immediately, as though the two friends were already dead.[223]

So why dedicate a narrative of destruction of the West Indies to Venetian *amicizia*, to Trevisan and Barbarigo? Castellani's narrative of the friendship and its heroic significance is similar to Micanzio's, if more detailed. Once again it is asserted that only three or four pairs of true friends have emerged across the centuries, and that they are the most perfect. The rationale of the dedication is only offered towards the end, and it reveals some affinity with the political philosophy of Ludovico Zuccolo. In Las Casas's history we see only dissension, persecution, ruin, massacres, violence, and death. Only *amicizia*—origin of peace, reconciler of souls, becalmer of minds, and so forth—could repair so much harm, restore harmony between the natives and the strangers, as well as between the natives themselves. Castellani concludes by hoping she will also continue to bring perfect tranquillity to Venice herself.[224]

The context is once again the application of practical philosophy to contemporary politics and morality via an Aristotelian principle: the relationship between friendship and justice as the basis of political community.

The previous year (1625) Ginammi had published a collection of dialogues on miscellaneous topics in practical philosophy by the court intellectual and writer Ludovico Zuccolo. Just as Micanzio represented Sarpi teaching Trevisan the doctrine of friendship in *conversazione* in his own cell, calling on various texts including Montaigne, so Zuccolo (in the dialogue 'Il Molino, overo Della amicitia scambievole fra' Cittadini') represented the noble senator Domenico Molino doing the same for Trevisan in a Venetian *ridotto*, calling on Roman historians and—above all—Aristotle.

---

[223] Giacomo Scaglia, *Breve racconto dell'amicitia, mostruosa nella perfettione, trà N. Barbarigo & M. Trivisano, gloriosi figliuoli della nobiltà Venetiana* (Venice: Francesco Baba, 1627), sigs. ✠✠1r, 4r; ✠✠✠2r; Cozzi, *Venezia barocca*, 341.

[224] Bartolomè de Las Casas, *Istoria o breuissima relatione della distruttione dell'Indie Occidentali*, trans. Giacomo Castellani (Venice: M. Ginammi, 1626), sig. ✠6r.

There is no mention of Barbarigo, but Trevisan is clearly singled out because of his involvement in the developing friendship, and the idea is once again to contribute to the shaping of the outcome. Zuccolo's text is more of a *saggio* on civil discipline with a page of dialogue appended at the end than it is a dialogue in the conventional sense. It culminates in Molino's summary of the ways in which a city-state can govern itself so as to give rise to that 'reciprocal friendship' ('amicitia scambievole') between citizens, which Aristotle (*Nicomachean Ethics*, 1154b) says holds states together, to the extent that lawgivers care more for it than for justice— the same precept singled out by Montaigne.[225]

There follows, again in Latin, a quote from the *Politics* 5.11 (1314a), in which Aristotle describes how the tyrant seeks to do the opposite, to create distrust amongst the people, and to make war on the good precisely because they are faithful to one another and do not accuse one another. Trevisan, 'gentilissimo, ed eruditissimo spirito', then responds by raising various *dubbii*, which are satisfyingly resolved by his senior Molino.[226]

More than Micanzio's, Zuccolo's scene is redolent of an informal *discorso* on friendship, complete with *dubbii*, translated to the civil situation of a *ridotto* for noblemen, clerics, and scholars. Its most significant feature is its informal, vernacular, non-scholastic Aristotelianism: a noble patron goes direct to the text of Aristotle in a civil setting to offer teachings on friendship that are immediately relevant to Venetian society and to the young Venetian nobility. In Canini's hands, Montaigne does something similar.

2.2.10 GIROLAMO CANINI'S *SAGGI*

This, then, is the kind of nexus in which circumstantial evidence suggests we can place the Venetian *Saggi di Michel Sig. di Montagna*. In its own self-image, Venice was run by an aristocracy of virtuous sages or *Savii* at various levels from Trevisan's to Molino's.[227] The moral and cultural formation of these *Savii*, and the public display of their exemplary virtue and learning, was the main cultural business of the republic and its various educational institutions, from the *Studio* at Padua to the *ridotto* represented by Zuccolo. Few strangers were assimilated to this elite. One exception was the French nobleman and intellectual Scipion de Gramont, admitted to the Accademia dei Ricovrati in April 1638.[228]

Montaigne is admitted to Venetian academic culture via his book. He is naturalized as a *Savio*, a sage and noble academician equivalent to the likes of Molino. He becomes an informal, noble teacher of practical philosophy of the kind found in

---

[225] For this and the previous paragraph, see Lodovico Zuccolo, *Dialoghi... ne' quali con varietà di eruditione si scoprono nuovi, e vaghi pensieri filosofici, morali, e politici* (Venice: Marco Ginammi, 1625), sigs. L7v–M5r.

[226] Zuccolo, *Dialoghi*, sigs. M3v–5r.

[227] Grendler, *Renaissance education between religion and politics*, XI, 39–41.

[228] Antonio Gamba and Lucia Rossetti (eds.), *Giornale della gloriosissima accademia ricovrata A: Verbali delle adunanze accademiche dal 1599 al 1694* (Vicenza: LINT; Padua: Accademia galileiana di scienze lettere ed arti in Padova, 1999), 171.

an environment of learned sociability such as an *accademia*, where clerics, nobility, and scholars came together for *conversazione*. Publishers such as Ginammi catered for the printed book market that derived from participation in—or aspiration to participate in—such environments.[229]

Indeed, the Jesuate Canini had been catering for this market through other publishers for some years. His order had not traditionally been associated with learning, or even with the priesthood. As lay brothers, their vows committed them to ignorance, penitence, and poverty, and they were bound to obey ordained clergy. When Montaigne visited the Jesuates at Verona, Vicenza, and Ferrara in November 1580, he noted their commercial activity producing and selling scented and medicinal waters, and the severity of their discipline. But in 1606 Paul V opened the order up to the priesthood, and consequently to studies in humanities, philosophy, and theology.[230]

Only a few years later in Venice in 1612, the Jesuate Canini, who according to the Frenchman Le Secq was a theologian versed in many languages, began his career as a prolific translator, editor, commentator, and manipulator of texts, before becoming prior of the Jesuate monastery at Padua by the late 1620s.[231]

Many of Canini's works were compiled as methodical and practical guides to civil prudence and spirituality for the Venetian nobility and clergy. In 1619 Giovanni Battista Ciotti published *Del bel parlar senatorio di Cornelio Frangipane, … abbellito, distinto, dichiarato in alcune parti principali, e ridotto in metodo, et alla pratica, e dedicato alla gioventù della nobiltà veneta, da D. Girolamo Canini*. As adapted and organized by Canini, this treatise is a practical manual on political speech-making. The *Trattato della corte del Signor di Refuge… Illustrato di annotationi dall'istesso autore, e di diversi metodi dal Canini* (Venice, 1621) provided diagrammatic charts of the forms and laws of courtly behaviour.

In the prefatory discourse to the *Aforismi politici cavati dall'Historia d'Italia' di M. Francesco Guicciardini* (Venice, 1625), entitled 'How usefully to read Histories' ('Del modo di leggere utilmente le Historie'), Canini recommends a progressive approach to reading, suggesting three steps: the first is to read the History; the second is to reduce the observations thereupon made to universal precepts; the third is to apply the latter to our particular actions ('il primo della lettura dell'Historia, il secondo dell'osservationi ridottevi à precetti universali, ed il terzo dell'applicatione di questi alle nostre particolari attioni').[232]

His religious manuals were no less methodical and practical. More explicitly spiritual was the *Somma, overo pratica del foro interiore, e penitentiale, del M. R. P. Fr. Alfonso di Vega da Madrid della Sacra Religione… Nella quale si risolvono innumerabili casi di conscientia appartenenti a tutte le materie teologiche, canoniche, e civili,*

---

[229] So in the Venetian context Ginammi's *Saggi* might be compared to, for example, Giovanni Francesco Loredano (ed.), *Discorsi academici de' signori incogniti, havuti in Venetia* (Venice: Giacomo Sarzina, 1635), which offers 'noble' treatments of an equally wide range of subjects from the apparently trivial to the serious.

[230] Legros, 'Jésuites ou Jésuates?', 138–42.   [231] 'Canini, Girolamo', *DBI*.

[232] Girolamo Canini, *Aforismi politici cavati dall'Historia d'Italia* (Venice: Antonio Pinelli, 1625), sig. A5r.

conforme alla dottrina de' Santi padri, dottori della Chiesa, ed autori più gravi, sì antichi, come moderni, the first part of which advertised itself as 'most useful not only to confessors, and penitents, but also to canons, theologians, preachers, and all sorts of spiritual persons' ('utilissima non solo a confessori, e penitenti, ma ancora a canonisti, teologi, legisti, predicatori, ed ad ogni sorte de persone spirituali').[233]

The culmination of this trend in the publication of practical guides to prudent and spiritually conscientious action in the public and private spheres came with the last two works published in Canini's lifetime. The first was the 1629 edition (unknown until recently) of the *Saggi di Michel Sig. di Montagna*, printed by Marco Ginammi in Venice, but probably not distributed at that point. This edition, like the better-known and better-distributed one that followed (with a significantly different title page) in 1633, included all the *Essais* except II 12, and identified 'Saggi' on its title page with 'most curious natural, political and moral discourses' ('curiosissimi *discorsi* naturali, politici, e morali'; my italics).[234]

The 1629 title page also presented it as a work of philosophy that teaches self-knowledge by means of the representation of a particular *persona* and his way of life. The author, by representing 'to the life' a complete and true image of himself, and of all his life, teaches others with efficaciousness truly to know themselves ('con rappresentar al vivo una compita, e verace imagine di se stesso, e di tutta la sua vita; insegna efficacemente ad altri il vero conoscimento di se medesimo'). Both the translation and the summaries opening each chapter are firmly attributed to D. Girolamo Canini of Anghiari. The summaries work together with the marginal notes—which are translated from a French edition dating to 1608 or later—to turn each chapter into many short 'discorsi' with their own titles, making the text more easily assimilable, as a methodical set of arguments, to the discursive culture associated with the Venetian *accademie* and *ridotti*.[235]

The *Saggi* are as much a work of correction as of translation. Canini had worked as a corrector for at least one publisher and, without using expurgation, he intervened like Goulart in many of the texts he published, in order to provide paratextual forms of direction on how they should be read.[236]

As translated, summarized, and divided by the Jesuate, and as separated from II 12 by Ginammi, the *Saggi* are a much more affirmative text than the self-consuming artefact described by much postmodern Montaigne criticism, particularly when it comes to chapters on the nature of philosophy, belief, virtue, and education. This is nowhere clearer than in the case of I 56, which comes across in Canini's summary as a strong piece of moral censorship: how the prayer to 'Our Father' should be used; the 'error' of praying to God on the wrong occasions; on praying

[233] Published at Venice 'apresso i Giunti', 1621.

[234] Philippe Desan, 'Une édition italienne inconnue des *Essais* (Venise, 1629)', *Montaigne Studies*, 15 (2003), 169–75.

[235] Desan, 'Une édition italienne inconnue des *Essais* (Venise, 1629)'; Paul Van Heck, 'The *Essais* in Italian: the Translation of Girolamo Canini', *Montaigne Studies*, 23 (2011), 39–53, 43–4.

[236] Cesare Rinaldi, *Lettere* (Venice: Tomaso Baglioni, 1617), sig. A3v.

without true repentance; use of the Bible in the vernacular denounced; the abuse of vulgarization and the mishandling of the mysteries of our religion; the abuse of the name of God, and so on.[237]

In general, in Canini's hands, the chapters unfold not as exercises in Pyrrhonism, but as the freely made judgements of a nobleman concerning what we, or a good Christian, should or should not think and do with respect to various moral, natural, and military topics. For example, the final section of III 1, on Epaminondas, is read by Canini as a discourse on what one must and must not do in the name of public utility.[238]

This is not to say, again, that he significantly mistranslates or censors the text. But his summaries are often ingenious in tying together the various sections of each chapter with the syntax of a continuous and positive argument on a particular topic—as we saw in 2.2.9 in the case of I 27.[239] The sections comprise articulated series of *ragioni, cagioni, essempii, precetti, esperienze, racconti, problemi, questioni, detti,* and *dubbii* of the kind that were debated in informal settings of learning in Venice and Padua, and that can, equally, stand on their own. The most common alternative to the affirmative summary of a section is the summary in terms of a *problema* or 'problem if…' or 'whether…', and so forth.[240] Canini summarizes II 33 (which is II 32 in his edition) as a discourse on the *problema* of whether the sensual appetite, in particular of love, is more powerful than the spiritual appetite, such as ambition.[241]

As another example of a positive moral argument, take Montaigne's chapter on solitude in Canini's summary (Illus. 2.2.3).[242] As we heard in 2.2.9 and shall hear in relation to Querenghi in 2.2.11, the question of the solitary or contemplative life versus the active philosophical life was a key topic in civil conversation. Canini gives the chapter on this topic a clear dialectical structure that builds a definition of true solitude ('vera solitudine') and its proper ends, and of the right conduct of the solitary man ('l'uomo solitario').

---

[237] See Venice 1633, sig. Q4r. For further examples of affirmative summaries of sections and chapters, see Venice 1633, sigs. A7r (I 4, sect. 3), B7r (I 11), B8v (I 12; Montaigne is admitting this and that into his model of the constant sage or *huomo savio*), C7v (I 19; on the value of philosophy as a preparation for death), E2v (I 21; a rifutation with proofs), F1v and F3v (I 23, section 5; on which side in doubtful matters a man should put himself), G2v (I 25; prescriptions on the institution of young nobility), Q7v (I 57), R1r (II 1, sections 4 and 5), Y7v (II 15; on the difference between true and vain glory), 2D1v (II 28 [II 27 in Canini], section 3; on how man should conduct himself in his old age).

[238] Venice 1633, sig. 2I1r (III 1, section 8).

[239] For examples, see Venice 1633, sigs. A8r (I 5), B1r (I 6), C3r (I 15), E2v–3r (I 22—continuous argument about *costume* and *novità nociva*), F5v (I 24, sections 1–4), I7v–8r (I 29), K7v (I 31, section 2—what a Christian must believe in relation to events that either favour or thwart their own cause), sig. L4r (I 36), sig. O4r (I 45 becomes a defence of the Duc de Guise with *ragioni* and *essempii*), T5r (II 8, sections 1–10), X4v (II 11), Z5r–v (II 16), 2B4v (II 19 [II 18 in Canini]), 2D6v (II 31 [II 30 in Canini], sections 2–7 all treat the topic of anger), sig. 2G2v (II 37 [II 36 in Canini], broken down into 17 sections of a discourse against medicine).

[240] So, for example, I 13 contains a very short discourse, almost a *sentenza*, 'Dell'utilità, affabilità, reggente delle cerimonie' (sigs. C1v and C2r); I 47 becomes a whole series of *problemi* (sig. O7r, sections 1–6, 'se si debba proseguire la vittoria sopra i nemici rotti', etc.); II 31 ([II 30 in Canini], sig. 2D6v), section 7, 'un detto d'Aristotile'.

[241] Venice 1633, sig. 2E4v.   [242] Venice 1633, sig. L7r.

Della Solitudine.   Cap.   XXXVIII.

1 *Perche ſi fugge la ſolitudine.*
2 *Fine della ſolitudine ricercato con non buono mezzo.*
3 *Vera ſolitudine,e come ſi goda.*
4 *Impedimenti,che ce ne diſtogliono,e come da sbrigarſene.*
5 *Compleſſioni a propoſito per la ſolitudine*
6 *Come l'huomo ſolitario ſi debba portare nelle commodità eſterne,e ne gli accidenti*
      della fortuna.
7 *Occupatione da eleggerſi nella ſolitudine.*
8 *Solitudine per diuotione,quale.*
9 *Studio delle lettere nella ſolitudine,qual debba eſſere.*
10 *Fine di gloria,e di riputatione nella ſolitudine riprobato.*

1   Aſciamo da banda quella lunga comparatione della vita ſolita-
      ria all'Attiua . e quanto a quel bel detto,col quale ſi copre l'am
      bitione,e l'auaritia,che noi non ſiamo già nati per il noſtro par
      ticolare , ma per il publico; rapportiamocene arditamente a
coloro,che ſono in ballo;e che eſſi ſi battino la conſcienza,ſe al contrario
gli ſtati,i carichi , e quel trauaglioſo maneggio del Mondo non ſi ricer-
                                                              chi

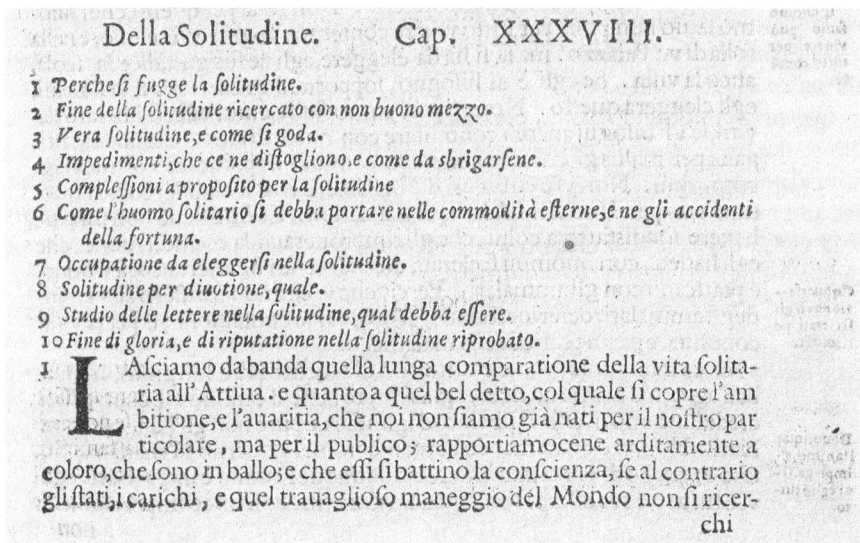

Illus. 2.2.3. Montaigne, *Saggi*, trans. G. Canini (Venice: M.Ginammi, 1633), Bodleian Library, pressmark Vet. F2 d.18 (1), p. 173 detail. Reproduced by permission of The Bodleian Libraries, the University of Oxford.

He divides it up as follows:

1. why we flee solitude;
2. how we seek the end of solitude by a means that is not good;
3. true solitude and how it can be enjoyed;
4. impediments that distract us from it, and how to free ourselves of them;
5. temperaments suited for solitude;
6. how the solitary man should carry himself in relation to external goods, and chance accidents;
7. the occupations we should choose in solitude;
8. devotional solitude, and what it is;
9. what the study of letters in solitude should be;
10. reproval of glory and reputation as the ends of solitude.

At the very centre of Canini's version of the chapter is the short paragraph, section 5, which contrasts (to quote the marginal notes) retired souls ('animi a proposito della ritiratezza e solitudine') with active souls ('animi attivi ed occupati'), while the creation of section 8 clearly distinguishes the devotional solitude of ascetic monks, which is highly praised, from the kind of 'true solitude' Montaigne is advocating for the layman and perhaps the secular clergy.[243]

---

[243] Venice 1633, sigs. M1v–2v, for this and the previous paragraph.

In some cases, Canini has to strain to find a useful and positive argument. The first couple of pages of I 3 are divided into four sections: first, the *cagione* or cause why our affections are transported beyond us—an *errore* in our imaginations; second, the *ragione* why this is an *errore*—because we do not attend to ourselves or focus on present things (backed up by Plato and Epicurus on the self-knowledge of the *savio*); third, that it is not an *errore* particularly in the Prince to transport himself ('nel Prencipe il tra[s]portarsi') with the thought of their reputation after death; fourth, because in this way he can be truly praised, not to say beatified (with an Aristotelian precept from *Nicomachean Ethics* 1.10 strategically opening section 4). Montaigne, of course, does not tie the argument together in this way, and it is clear that Canini is straining a little to find a useful and affirmative *discorso* about the *Principe* in these pages.[244]

On the whole, however, Canini's efforts compare well with the efforts of modern editors who use summaries and paragraph breaks to guide the reader through Montaigne's mazes. The seventeen subdivisions of II 37 (II 36 in Canini) admirably break down the various components of Montaigne's chapter against the art of medicine. II 3 is justifiably structured as a *pro et contra* discourse, separating 'la parte affirmativa' for suicide, from 'la parte negativa' against suicide, with the second and third sections each beginning with a *dubbio*—appropriately, given that the chapter starts by identifying both philosophy itself and Montaigne's own *paroleggiare* with *un dubitare*.[245]

Canini nowhere intervenes in this open but relatively orthodox discussion of suicide in the way that Goulart does, allowing himself only to emphasize in the summary of section 1 that the author doubts the affirmations of the pro-suicide faction in line with the determination of Divine Providence ('sotto la determinazione della Divina Providenza').[246]

The description of the book as an institution in self-knowledge, transferred to the publisher's address to the reader in the 1633 edition, along with a general reference to the 'various places' in which the author defends his own style, is reconfirmed by Canini's other interventions,[247] for these 'places' are highlighted in his summaries. In general terms, section breaks and marginal notes are regularly used to focus our minds on the nature of *saggezza* or *saviezza*, of *l'uomo savio* or *saggio*, and to emphasize the passages which contribute to the author's efficacious self-portrait. Passages of authorial commentary are usually partitioned as distinct *discorsi*.

By contrast with Lyon 1593 and Lyon [Geneva] 1595, those which concern the author himself and his motives for writing are always indicated. The final section of II 6, for example, links directly to the promise on the 1629 title page by offering an authorial discourse on knowing and speaking of oneself. The section ends by telling us that because Socrates had been the only one to take a real bite at his God's precept 'know thyself', only he was judged worthy of the name of *Savio*.[248]

---

[244] Venice 1633, sigs. A4r–5r.   [245] Venice 1633, sigs. 2G2v, R6v.
[246] On the orthodoxy of the discussion, see Screech, *Montaigne and melancholy*, 43–5.
[247] Venice 1633, sig. a6r–v.
[248] See Venice 1633, sigs. B3v (I 9, sections 1–3), B6r (I 10, section 5), C1r (I 13, section 3), L4r (I 36, section 1), M3v (I 39, section 3), M6r (I 40/14, section 7), P6v (I 50, section 1), Q2r (I 54,

But the summaries make a broader contribution to the shaping of a book which both represents an author to the life and teaches self-knowledge to others. In Canini's affirmative summary it is much easier to see how a chapter such as I 26—in which Montaigne recognizes an *errore* of his own, and a corresponding *disordine* in the consciences of Catholics in the French religious troubles—can be seen to offer a self-image that aims to teach others truly to know themselves.[249]

Canini sometimes uses the chapter summaries approvingly to describe the exemplary qualities of the author's discourse, as when Montaigne 'modestly' calls his essays 'Chimere' in I 8, or 'sensibly' discourses on the importance or otherwise of a good death in I 18, or prepares for death with vigilance and marvellous preparation in I 19 ('con vigilanza, e preparatione maravigliosa'), or reveals the 'freedom' of his writing and speech ('il suo parlare, e scriver libero') at the beginning of III 1, not to mention his *veracità, segretezza, fedeltà, modestia,* and *integrità di costumi*.[250]

But other passages of authorial commentary singled out for attention as distinct *discorsi* are not reflexive in kind, and again remind one of the topics and style of discourse in the *accademie*. In the last few pages of II 2, Canini individuates an authorial *discorso* on the 'old and pleasant question, as to whether the soul of the sage would surrender itself to the force of wine' ('vecchia, e piacevole questione, se l'animo del saggio fusse per arrendersi alla forza del vino'), a *discorso* which goes on to consider the nature of *l'uomo savio* and *saviezza* in the round. Elsewhere he singles out an *avvertimento* or a *giudizio* of the author.[251]

In book III, of course, Montaigne makes it more difficult for Canini to render his text as readily assimilable teachings in self-knowledge. One section of III 9—described by Canini as the author's apology for his digressions, his style, his order (i.e. lack of it) in writing the book—declares the author's intention that his subject matter ('la materia') should stand out on its own. It is the undiligent reader who loses the subject, not the author. There is always a word or two in a corner on the topic. The subject matter itself can show well enough ('Ella mostra assai') where changes occur, where the beginnings are and the ends, and where it picks up again, without links and stitches ('di legature, e di costure') for the service of the weak-eared, and without self-glossing ('senza glosare me stesso'). After using frequent divisions of chapters in his first two books, Montaigne started making longer chapters that require commitment from the reader.[252]

In Canini's edition, however, it is not the *materia* itself but the translator who provides the *legature* and the glosses for the service of the weak-eared. He plays the

section 3), Q3r (I 55, section 2), Q4r (I 56, section 1—the author's 'protest' about his writings, section 7), S7r (II 6, section 8), Y5v (II 15 [II 14 in Canini], section 4), 2D1v (II 28 [II 27 in Canini], section 2, where one phrase of Montaigne's is highlighted as 'essempio di se stesso'), 2I1r (III 1, section 3).

[249] See Venice 1633, sig. H8v (I 26).

[250] Venice 1633, sigs. B3r (I 8, section 2), C6 (I 18, section 4), C7v (I 19, section 6), 2I1r (III 1, sections 1 and 5).

[251] Venice 1633, sig. R6r–v. See also: section 3 of I 1 for another 'Discorso dell'Autore' not about himself (sig. A1r); section 2 of II 25 ([II 24 in Canini], sig. 2C4r); section 2 of II 30 ([II 29 in Canini], sig. 2D5v, 'Discorso sopra i mostri'); section 5 of II 31 ([II 30 in Canini], sig. 2D6v—an 'avvertimento' of the author); section 7 of II 33 ([II 32 in Canini], sig. 2E4v—a *giudizio* on the history of Spurina, with *avvertimenti*); section 5 of II 35 ([II 34 in Canini], sig. 2F4r).

[252] Venice 1633, sigs. 2R3r, 2T8v–V1r.

role of the diligent reader-writer who marks the beginnings and ends, emphasizes the words in a corner that are germane to the topic, and provides breaks in the longer chapters. He facilitates and directs the Venetian public's engagement with the text as lessons in self-knowledge based on the author's own example. He does this a lot of the time simply by beginning new sections with key statements or key changes of topic, or by plucking key statements out for the summary.

Canini's summary of the final section of III 4 promises a neo-Platonic philosophical lesson on 'diversione': 'why we hold fast so little to things, and why we do not consider them by themselves, in their essence, but instead consider the images that mask things [*la maschera delle imagini*], circumstantial and superficial appearances, as is the case in many examples'. This is based on just one sentence in the middle of a text crammed with examples ('Noi non riguardiamo guari i soggetti all'ingrosso, e soli; le circostanze, e l'immagini minute, e superficiali ... ci percuotono'), but it serves to give the reader some orientation for the whole final section.[253]

Canini shows no prudishness whatsoever. His edition is—largely—unabashed to tell the truth. Where Montaigne hides a chapter on sex under the title 'On some lines of Virgil', his translator tells the reader from the off that this is a treatise on 'the genital and marital act' ('l'attione genitale, e maritale') and directs him or her to the main *discorso* (section 13) on the core topic ('Attione del generare').

Amongst the total of nineteen sections making up the chapter, Canini further individuates *discorsi* on: the love to look for in a good marriage ('buon maritaggio'), and on how the author conducted himself (section 4); on disloyalty in a marriage, and whence it proceeds in men and women (section 5); on the bad education of our daughters, and the amorous books they read (section 6); on the severity men show to women, with respect to their honour and chastity (section 8); on jealousy, whence is born that severity (section 9); on being a cuckold voluntarily and involuntarily; on the strictness with which women are kept in Italy, and on the liberty that they should be given (section 15); on how the author conducted himself, with respect to promises and fidelity (section 17).[254]

Likewise, Canini lets the reader of III 11 know immediately that Montaigne will discuss the 'extraordinary genital operation' of lame people as an example of the way in which the human mind can find all sorts of contradictory *ragioni* for any phenomenon. His summary of this chapter is particularly helpful—the topic is indeed 'the capacity and excessive liberty of our Discourse in building itself vain and false foundations' and the arguments against judicial execution of witches are emphasized. A counter-example—a chapter summary that obscures the 'scandalous' topic at its heart—is III 6. Canini's summary, unlike Goulart's edition and miscellany, hides Montaigne's excoriating critique of Spanish cruelty in the New World. This is particularly interesting, given that Ginammi was the publisher of Las Casas.[255]

---

[253] Venice 1633, sigs. 2L2v, 2L5r.   [254] Venice 1633, sigs. 2L6v–7r.
[255] Venice 1633, sigs. 2X5v, 2O7r.

Mention of the *autore* and his judgements unsurprisingly becomes more and more prominent in Canini's analyses of book III chapters. Chapter III 8 gives the author's judgement of the utility of the exercise of *conferenza*, and his condemnations of various abuses of the exercise. The reader is pointed to one of the most important justifications of the author's manner of composition of the *Saggi*—he is following his 'Nature' in his writing—in III 12.[256] Chapters III 10 and III 13 dovetail together as chapters that use the author's own example to show us how we should use our self-knowledge to govern ourselves. 'De mesnager sa volonté' becomes 'On how to govern well one's will' ('Del ben governar la sua Volontà') and the summary emphasizes how, in his mayoralty ('Governo di Mere') of Bordeaux, the author put the precepts of moderation into action. Sections 3–11 of III 13 become a continuous set of *discorsi* on the author's experience and government of himself.[257]

Most modern criticism and editorial work on the *Essais* amounts to university teachers' directions for reading Montaigne's difficult text. The interest of Canini's edition, as of Micanzio's anecdote about Sarpi, lies in what it reveals of the way an early modern friar would have directed a reader's attention and glossed Montaigne's practical philosophical arguments. Canini is likely to have done this in close consultation with the publisher, Marco Ginammi. For, once again, as in the case of Naselli's *Discorsi* and Lyon [Geneva] 1595, we need to place a work that is often treated in isolation—as an instance of the reception of the *Essais*—in relation to other publications by the translator and editor.

In the second of the last two works published in Canini's lifetime, the Jesuate offers another edition of a French nobleman's work. With this we move from an ex-mayor (Montaigne) teaching self-knowledge, to a cardinal (d'Ossat) teaching civil prudence. Once again, there is evidence that his goals for the volume were in tune with the publisher's. Just as Canini and Ginammi combined to offer the patrician or would-be patrician reader the philosophical *persona* of a noble French seigneur, represented *al vivo*, who teaches the true way to self-knowledge, so Canini and Sarzina combine in the *Lettere a principi di negotii politici, e di complimento* to offer, *al vivo,* the *persona* of a noble French cardinal who teaches the true way to civil prudence.

Once again Canini exercises the functions of a corrector or editor. This time the letters are reorganized as a sequence and cut ('ridotti sotto l'ordine di un corso continuato'), with the addition by Canini of practical lessons in prudence and other virtues for those conducting similar affairs ('qualche tiro di Prudenza, e di altre virtù, e qualità quivi adoperate...per porgere occasione ad altri esperti in sì fatti maneggi di penetrarvi più a dentro').[258]

In his address to the reader, Sarzina promises:

> You will learn with incredible pleasure and marvellous profit, the true way to handle and to conduct, to the desired end, the most important affairs, even those in desperate

[256] Venice 1633, sigs. 2Q1r, 2Y2v.   [257] Venice 1633, sigs. 2V3v, 2Z6v.

[258] Arnaud D'Ossat, *Lettere a principi di negotii politici, e di complimento, del sig. cardinal d'Ossat. Diuise in tre libri. Tradotte dal francese, messe insieme, & arricchite di alcuni discorsi*, trans. Girolamo Canini (Venice: Giacomo Sarzina, 1629), sig. *a*3r.

straits, and also how properly to discourse of them on any occasion. In the third book 'Of Compliment' you will conceive the image of the entire and truthful disposition, there represented to the life, of that most sincere Prelate. And by that means you will learn the true way to write in this kind with the appropriate decorum, and more with the pure integrity of soul, than with superfluous and vain ceremonies, and with the ambitious industry of the pen.[259]

This promise is in tune with the content of the discourse that Canini adds, 'Del modo di maneggiare un simigliante negotio', which offers a philosophical and practical analysis of d'Ossat's conduct of the negotiations by letter. Canini seeks to emphasize the spiritual context of d'Ossat's negotiating skills by recording how the cardinal always referred the beginnings, progress, and outcomes of his actions to the divine cause of all things ('il cominciamento, il progresso, ed il fine delle sue attioni al supremo Motore di tutte le cose'). He is aiming here at a practical but spiritually conscientious form of politics to counter the worldly politics of those he calls in his vernacular edition of Tacitus the Machiavellians and Atheists ('i Machiavelli, gli Ateisti') and others from the 'caverne d'Acheronte'.[260]

As a Jesuate committed to the Venetian Catholic Reformation, Canini is responding in his late publications to the same religious and cultural need that, on M. A. Screech's reading, had prompted Montaigne at some point in the evolution of the *Essais*: the need for a Roman Catholic spirituality not expressed in the 'subtle' language of academics and clerics, but in the form of a practical guide to lay conduct, both political and personal.[261]

Canini also provides our link to the only figure in this period identified in print as an 'Italian Montaigne'. Flavio Querenghi is of interest here as a reader of Naselli's *Discorsi morali, politici, et militari* who wrote his own *Discorsi morali politici et naturali*. Even though much of Montaigne's most characteristically personal material is removed from Naselli's edition, Querenghi is still able to relate to and imitate the *persona* of the author, whom he refers to as 'a good Frenchman' ('un buon Francese')—demonstrating the point to be made (in 2.7.11) that the original author can remain an agent even in nexuses that involve a reductive translation. In the last years of his life, Canini became the prior of the Jesuate monastery at Padua and it is from there that he dedicated the third book of the *Lettere a principi* to Querenghi as a noble canon of the cathedral, and university reader in moral philosophy ('Monsig. Flavio Querenghi Canonico, e Publico Lettore delle morali in Padova').[262]

---

[259] D'Ossat, *Lettere a principi*, sig. *a*4r ('Apprenderete con incredibil gusto, e maraviglioso profitto, il vero modo di ben trattare, e di condurre al desiderato fine importantissimi affari, ed anco come disperati, ed insieme di regolatamente discorrerne in ogni occorrenza. Nelle Terze di Compliment Voi raffigurete l'imagine dell'intero, e verace affetto, quivi rappresentato al vivo, di quel sincerissimo Prelato; ed in tal maniera v'imparerete la vera maniera di scrivere in questo Genere con la dovuta convenevolezza, e più con la schietta integrità dell'animo, che con le soverchie, e vane cerimonie, e con l'ambiosa industria della penna.')

[260] D'Ossat, *Lettere a principi*, sigs. 2F1, 2F6; Cornelius Tacitus, *Opere...Annali, Historie, Costumi de' Germani, e Vita di Agricola; illustrate con notabilissimi aforismi del Signor D. B. A. Varienti; trasportati dalla lingua Castigliana nella Toscana*, ed. G. Canini (Venice: Appresso i Giunti, 1628), sig. c2v. The first edition of this work appeared in 1618.

[261] Marc Fumaroli, 'A spirituality for gentleman', *Times Literary Supplement*, 6 January 1984.

[262] D'Ossat, *Lettere a principi*, sig. 3a2r.

Perhaps he chose this book for Querenghi not only because Flavio's uncle and guardian Antonio knew d'Ossat, but because because he saw the canon as another 'sincerissimo Prelato' who, like d'Ossat, showed 'la schietta integrità dell'animo'. At any rate, he offers him the book in the hope that it will find a place in the 'Cabinet of the ever chaste and learned Inhabitants [the Muses] of his pleasant and delightful Museum [*suo ameno, e delitioso Museo*]'.[263]

This may refer to the joint collection of his and his uncle Antonio's books that Flavio later (in 1639–41) donated to the Dominican friary of S. Agostino. Along with Naselli's *Discorsi* and around 260 other books, two copies of Canini's work indeed found a place in the small selection—including 'fathers of wisdom' ('padri della sapienza')—that Flavio retained for his personal use when he donated the bulk of the collection. Amongst these patristic and secular *padri*, Aristotle and Aquinas, and their traditions of commentary, were predominant.[264]

Canini goes on in the same passage to portray the secular canon Querenghi as an exemplar of the balance between the contemplative and the active philosophical lives—a sort of secular hermit who teaches practical philosophy. The picture he offers is not unrelated to Micanzio's of Sarpi, though Querenghi's milieu was more sympathetic to the Jesuits and Rome. On the one hand Canini observes—or imagines?—him living a serene and tranquil life of 'conferenza' with the Muses, enjoying a state of meditative pleasure, beyond idleness and beyond the mutual confusion that can arise in civil conversation. So Canini sees him now seated in contemplation, now walking in the field, where even in mid-winter the grasses and herbs flower as he passes:[265]

Now I follow you towards the Sacro Tempio Maggiore, to see you participate amongst the first in divine offices: and now towards the public university of this celebrated Italian Athens, to hear you with pliant mind, a new Aesculapius of spirits, with no less learning than eloquence, intent only on remedies, and focused on the well-being of the audience;...and in this way to put before other people the true example, from which one can learn by a quicker route, more efficiently, and learn not only through school but rather principally through life, the most profitable philosophy.[266]

Canini here attributes Querenghi with the philosophical *persona* of a physician of spirits, a new Aesculapius, intent on the practical healing, through learning and

[263] D'Ossat, *Lettere a principi*, sig. 3a2v.

[264] *DBI*, 'Canini, Girolamo'; Emilia Veronese Ceseracciu, 'La biblioteca di Flavio Querenghi, professore di filosofia morale (1624-1647) nello Studio di Padova', *Quaderni per la storia dell'università di Padova*, 9–10 (1976-7), 185–213, 192, 202; Flavio Querenghi, *Discorsi morali politici et naturali* (Padua: Giulio Crivellari, 1644), sig. S2v; Uberto Motta, *Antonio Querenghi (1546–1633): un letterato padovano nella Roma del tardo Rinascimento* (Milan: Vita e pensiero, 1997), 213–15.

[265] D'Ossat, *Lettere a principi*, sigs. 3a2v–3r.

[266] D'Ossat, *Lettere a principi*, sig. 3a3r–v ('Hora il [V.S. Reverendissima] seguo verso il Sacro Tempio Maggiore, per vedervelo assistere fra i primi a' Divini Offitii: e hora verso la publica Academia di questa celebre Italica Atene, per sentirvi con seguace ingegno da lui novello Esculapio de gli animi, con non minor dottrina, che eloquenza, al sol rimedio intenta, ed al ben de gli Uditori tutta rivolta;...ed in tal guisa metter davanti a gli altri il vero essemplare, donde si apprenda per strada più breve, e più spedita, e vi s'impari non solamente per la scuola, ma ancora principalmente per la vita la più profittevole Filosofia').

eloquence, of his auditors in the university.[267] He celebrates him—as Ginammi does Montaigne on the title page of the 1629 *Saggi*—as someone who teaches philosophy by displaying himself in life, to the life, as a true example to others, as he goes first to participate in divine offices, then to the university to lecture.

The clear implication is that he fulfils his duties as a reader in moral philosophy in the *persona* of a coadjutor-canon (from 1607) of the cathedral. Flavio was coadjutor to his uncle Antonio, a *canonico penitenziere*, who, unlike Flavio, obtained dispensation not to fulfil the obligation of residence in the chapter. The lucrative canonry of Padua cathedral was one of the most illustrious such ecclesiastical offices in the Italian peninsula, and was associated with men of letters; Petrarch was a previous incumbent.[268]

From this living philosophical exemplar, whose decrees on the art of living are reduced to practice in the candour and innocence of his own *costumi* ('già ridotti egregiamente da esso a' Precetti, e...alla pratica nel candore, e nell'innocenza esquisita de' suoi costumi'), they can learn the most profitable philosophy by a shorter and quicker route. The offices from which Querenghi's philosophical *persona* fundamentally derives are those of a *canonico* of the cathedral chapter, first, and university lecturer, second—in Canini's description, his participation in divine offices is significantly prior to his fulfilment of the duties of his secular office. And it is his speech and conduct in person that is paramount, not his manuscript writings, and certainly not his printed books.

Canini's dedicatory portrait is in tune with other *elogia* of Querenghi published and circulated, mostly in Padua, during his lifetime. They all celebrate him as someone living a serene life, amongst his studies, teaching others by example—a secularized version, again, of monastic seclusion. Another canon of the same cathedral city, Giacomo Tomasini, associated Querenghi with Petrarch in his treatment of the latter's period of solitude in Parma ('De solitudine Parmensis'). He recalls Querenghi's own stay at the court of Parma, but describes him as a cultivator and lover of solitude ('solitudinis amator et cultor'), and goes on to evoke his tranquil and happy life in his house near the church of San Antonio di Vienna in Padua, whence, again, he teaches the art of living.[269]

Canini's celebration of the dual offices of Querenghi as canon and professor of ethics in this context is of some historical significance. One consequence of the perceived need for reforming measures in *cinquecento* Venice and Padua was the increasing role played by the Venetian state in the administration of the University

---

[267] On the *persona* of the philosopher as physician of body and soul, see Sorana Corneanu, *Regimens of the mind: Boyle, Locke, and the early modern 'cultura animi' tradition* (Chicago: University of Chicago Press, 2011).

[268] Veronese Ceseracciu, 'La biblioteca di Flavio Querenghi', 187–8; Motta, *Antonio Querenghi (1546–1633)*, 111–12; Francesco Scipione Dondi Dall'Orologio, *Serie cronologico-istorica dei Canonici di Padova* (Padua: Stamperia del Seminario, 1805). I assume Flavio acted as a secular canon who administered the sacrament of penance on Antonio's behalf in the cathedral, but have found no direct evidence of this.

[269] Luciano Stecca, *Tradizione e innovazione: studi sulla cultura francese e italiana tra Cinque e Seicento* (Padua: CLEUP, 1996), 78; Giacomo Filippo Tomasini, *Petrarcha Redivivus* (Padua: Paolo Frambotto, 1635), sigs. Q3v–4r.

of Padua and, consequently, in the formation of the ruling and bureaucratic elite. In 1560 the task of nominating teaching staff at the university was taken from the joint body of masters and scholars and passed to the *Riformatori dello Studio* and the *Senato* itself.[270]

One response of the body of conservative patricians who perceived a particularly acute moral crisis in the late sixteenth century was to encourage the role of Jesuits as educators of the young nobility in the traditional values of private and public morality—even if, in 1591, they were expelled and their college at Padua closed.[271] Another, via the *Riformatori*, was to elect to the chair of Aristotelian ethics at Padua in 1594, for the first time since its inauguration in 1407, a priest: Giovanni Belloni. From then until the eighteenth century the chair was held by ecclesiastics of various kinds. The second to be elected was Flavio Querenghi in 1624.[272]

Besides church and university, however, there was a third setting in which Querenghi taught his audience by presenting himself as a living philosophical exemplar of the contemplative life. In so doing, he was following the example provided by his predecessor Belloni, who had also been a *Ricovrato*—a member and *Principe* of the Accademia dei Ricovrati—in Padua.[273] Querenghi was participating in a philosophical and educational culture that crossed the boundaries between church, *studio*, and *accademia*, and between ecclesiastical, university, and noble patrician identities.

2.2.11 THE ENFRANCHISEMENT OF FLAVIO QUERENGHI?

On 21 May 1633, at Padua, Monsignor conte Flavio Querenghi, canon and public reader of moral philosophy ('canonico et publico lettor della Morale'), opened the first public meeting of the Accademia dei Ricovrati since 1619 with a learned discourse 'on the life of solitude and repose' ('della vita solitaria e reposta'). We know this because the secretary made a record of Querenghi's noble *attione* in the register of the Accademia's proceedings. The secretary's principal role in making this record was to describe the performances of the speakers in such a way as to reveal their noble qualities:

> In which [discourse]...he [Querenghi] represented in his speech almost as if in a noble portrait his solitary life, free from public affairs, dedicated only to his studies, that was applauded by the most illustrious and excellent governors [*rettori*], with the

[270] Sandro de Bernardin, 'I Riformatori dello Studio: indirizzi di politica culturale nell'università di Padova', in Gianfranco Folena (ed.), *Storia della cultura veneta* (Vicenza: Neri Pozza, 1976–86), vol. 4.1, 61–91, 61; A. Poppi, 'Il problema della filosofia morale nella scuola padovana del rinascimento: Platonismo e Aristotelismo nella definizione del metodo dell'etica', *Platon et Aristote à la Renaissance: XVIe Colloque international de Tours* (Paris: J. Vrin, 1976), 104–46,107.

[271] De Bernardin, 'I Riformatori dello Studio', 73–4.

[272] Poppi, 'Il problema della filosofia morale', 106–7, 137–8.

[273] Gamba and Rossetti (eds.), *Giornale della gloriosissima accademia ricovrata A*, 86–7.

most illustrious and reverend monsignor bishop, and all the flower of the city there gathered to hear him.[274]

This was a grand civic event that brought together the ecclesiastical, intellectual, and aristocratic establishment of Padua and Venice. The occasion of the reopening of the Accademia was the triumphant return to Padua of the brother of its Venetian founder (Federico Cornaro), Marcantonio Cornaro, who, after suffering disgrace mid-career, had secured the bishopric in 1632, in succession to his brother (who held it 1629–32). In 1599 Federico Cornaro had been a young abbot, and the academy he founded was an offshoot of the episcopal curia of the diocese of Padua. The diocese became in these decades a quasi-feudal possession of the San Polo Cornaro family (Federico's and Marcantonio's branch), as they out-manoeuvred their dynastic rivals, the San Maurizio Cornaro family, and consolidated their connections in Rome.[275]

Amongst other functions, the academy's role—as on this occasion in 1633— was both to see off and to welcome powerful Venetian patricians. Along with the Venetian governors (*podestà, capitano,* etc.) of the city, and the scholars and students of the university, many noble priests and Venetian aristocrats were present. This was above all a union of the nobility of the ruled (Padua) and ruling (Venice) cities, under the aegis of a dynasty of worldly Venetian clerics.

When the academy had reopened with a private sitting on 16 April, the secretary had described it as having, during the absence of Marcantonio Cornaro, remained like a barren widow in solitude and withdrawal ('rimasta vedova nella solitudine e ritiratezza incolta').[276] The topic of Querenghi's public discourse—solitude—was, in this context, highly appropriate. The only version extant is the one printed 11 years later in Querenghi's collected *Discorsi.* The text we have opens by telling the 'Signori Eminentissimi' and 'Celebratissimi Academici' of the ecclesiastical, secular, and literary republic that, having hung up his arms in the temple and retired to a hidden life in the country, he never believed he would have to show himself on the public scene again.[277]

Querenghi goes on to say he will demolish 'la Politica' in order to use the stones to lay the foundation of 'un'Heremo' (a hermitage), though he promises also to rebuild the former in the public schools.[278] His spoken argument in this public forum is thus in favour of solitude and silence. This apparently paradoxical aspect of his performance is in tune, however, with the Impresa and motto of

---

[274] Gamba and Rossetti (eds.), *Giornale della gloriosissima accademia ricovrata A,* 158.

[275] Achille Olivieri, 'I Ricovrati e le trasformazioni dell'idea di prudenza: "l'antro e le parole"', in Ezio Riondato (ed.), *Dall'Accademia dei Ricovrati all'Accademia Galileiana: atti del Convegno storico per il IV centenario della fondazione (1599–1999): Padova, 11–12 aprile 2000* (Padua: Accademia Galileiana di scienze, lettere ed arti, 2001), 361–74; Giuseppe Gullino, 'I Corner e l'Accademia', in Ezio Riondato (ed.), *Dall'Accademia dei Ricovrati all'Accademia Galileiana: atti del Convegno storico per il IV centenario della fondazione (1599–1999): Padova, 11–12 aprile 2000* (Padua: Accademia Galileiana di scienze, lettere ed arti, 2001), 59–73; Niccolo Antonio Giustiniani, *Serie cronologica dei Vescovi di Padova* (Padua: Stamperia del Seminario, 1786), clxiv–clxv.

[276] Gamba and Rossetti (eds.), *Giornale della gloriosissima accademia ricovrata A,* 156.

[277] Querenghi, *Discorsi morali politici et naturali,* sig. V3v.

[278] Querenghi, *Discorsi morali politici et naturali,* sig. V4v.

the academy, to which Querenghi alludes: a cave with two entrances, open to both the active and the contemplative lives, 'a refuge for souls, open in two directions' ('bipatens animis asylum').[279]

For this was a place where a range of elite patricians from indigenous secular clerics such as Cornaro to studious foreign noblemen such as Scipion de Grammont could come together to form and to project a single range of philosophical *personae* and forms of life that to varying degrees were both active and contemplative, both worldly and spiritual. So, although Querenghi alludes to the monastic life of true, ascetic contemplation throughout his discourse, and although he made arrangements to be buried in a Certosa (Vigodarzere), he is ultimately a secular canon offering a secularized (though still religious) version of the contemplative or monastic life, one that opens equally onto civil life, and that is suitable as such for an audience of the noble, governing classes of church and state in Padua-Venice.[280]

In forming and projecting his philosophical *persona* on this occasion, Querenghi was in dialogue, via their books, with classical and contemporary figures. Aristotle is in the background throughout as the philosopher of the active life. Querenghi begins by contradicting the famous dictum from the *Politics* about man as a sociable animal with the statement from the opening to *The History of Animals* that man is both sociable and solitary. This is the cue for his argument that man lives—as in the Ricovrati's cave—in the midst of the two lives, Solitary and Civil ('in mezzo delle due vite, Solitaria, e Civile'), with a greater inclination towards the more ancient and natural existence (the solitary life)—like God, Christ, and Adam. He took up the same theme in another discourse on the life of the villa.[281]

Seneca also has a key role to play, as we shall see later in this section. But two of the contemporary figures invoked by Querenghi deserve particular mention, even though neither is directly named. The first is 'one of my own family' ('un mio di casa')—his powerful uncle, and principal social and intellectual *patron*, Antonio Querenghi. The second is 'a good Frenchman' ('un buon francese'), Michiel di Montagna (as he was named in Naselli's edition). Flavio's argument is that art—or civilization, as we might now call it—creates false civil needs and separates man from his natural solitude, as Adam was separated from the Garden of Eden. He takes the Edenic theme from a neo-Latin poem ('De ruris laudibus') published (1616, 1618) in the printed *carmina* by his uncle Antonio, an ex-*Ricovrato* whose death would be commemorated in the academy only a few months later. In the poem Adam's marriage leads directly to the beginnings of fallen civil life, and to the vices of the city.[282]

---

[279] Derived from the cave described in the thirteenth book of Homer's *Odyssey* (13.96ff.) and from a phrase in Boethius's *Consolation of philosophy* (3.m10.6). See J. L. Heilbron, *Galileo* (Oxford: Oxford University Press, 2010), 96, and Giovanni Belloni, *Discorso intorno all'Antro delle Ninfe Naiadi di Homero. Impresa de gli Academici Ricovrati di Padoua* (Padua: Francesco Bolzetta, 1601).

[280] Veronese Ceseracciu, 'La biblioteca di Flavio Querenghi', 193.

[281] Querenghi, *Discorsi morali politici et naturali*, sigs. V4v–X2r, O4v–P4r.

[282] Querenghi, *Discorsi morali politici et naturali*, sig. X2r–v; Antonio Querenghi, *Hexametri carminis libri sex. Rhapsodiae variorum carminum libri V* (Rome: Apud Bartholomæum Zannettum, 1618), sigs. D8v–9r. A first, incomplete and inadequate edition of Querenghi's *carmina* appeared at

It is particularly clear that Querenghi is simultaneously secularizing the monastic life and sanctifying the philosophical life when he distinguishes true solitude from the barbaric solitude of individuals such as Timon of Athens. It is a characteristic of the former that, like the Greek philosopher Archytas of Tarentum, the individual can compare his studies with those of his friends and show them the fruits of his contemplation. Querenghi then equates, as examples, the fact that two of the founders of Christian monachism—Saint Paul the Hermit and Saint Anthony (who died in Padua)—visited together (in St Jerome's account), and the fact that the founders of Greek philosophy—Thales and the other six wise men of Greece—gathered together for conversation (in Plutarch's account).[283]

When Querenghi comes to explain how it is that only man of all God's creatures appears not to have been provided by Nature with protection against the elements, he inserts, without acknowledgement, a long passage from Naselli's translation of Montaigne's I 35 ('De l'usage de se vestir'). The passage argues that we have in fact covered the traces of Nature's original provision—still evident in the way of life of the inhabitants of the recently discovered New World—with our own artifices.[284]

Luciano Stecca identifies a further borrowing from Montaigne shortly after this in Querenghi's speech, this time from the French text of 'De la solitude' (I 38), which Naselli did not translate.[285] But it is important to realize that at this point Querenghi is in fact drawing directly on yet another important classical source for the solitary philosophical life—Seneca's *Moral letters to Lucilius* 1.6–8—and that this is the context for his resort to 'a certain Frenchman' ('un certo francese': Montaigne).

Seneca's epistles to Lucilius aim to teach the young man how to withdraw into himself to live the free philosophical life by enjoying what is really his—his nature, his time, his friends, and so on—without physically separating himself from human society. Letter 1.6 centres on the precept that friends hold all things in common, and on Seneca's desire to teach Lucilius what he has learned, not just by sharing studies (books with marked-up passages) and by lecturing him, but by summoning the young man to watch his teacher actually living by his own rules (as we heard Canini watching Querenghi). Letter 1.7 is still more important for

Cologne in 1616. See Motta, *Antonio Querenghi (1546–1633)*, 331–2n.265. The second, 1618 edition was dedicated to Francesco Maria II della Rovere, Duke of Urbino.

[283] Querenghi, *Discorsi morali politici et naturali*, sig. X3r–v.

[284] Querenghi, *Discorsi morali politici et naturali*, sig. X4r–v; Stecca, *Tradizione e innovazione*, 106–9, which considers the borrowing in detail. The original passage is to be found in Ferrara 1590, sigs. F8v–G1r.

[285] Stecca, *Tradizione e innovazione*, 135. Stecca states elsewhere (98–9n.71, 138) that Querenghi drew directly on the French text, in addition to Naselli's translation. But the evidence is not conclusive, and many of the examples he gives could result from the independent use of common sources by Montaigne and Querenghi (as in the case above). There is one example (see Stecca 111) that does show Querenghi's awareness in general terms of the content of one passage in the French text of a chapter (I 24) that was not translated by Naselli. But the inventory of Querenghi's personal collection contains no evidence that he owned any French vernacular books—all are in Latin or Italian. He owned copies of Naselli's and Canini's translations of the *Essais*, and of an Italian translation of Honoré d'Urfé's *Epîtres morales*. See Veronese Ceseracciu, 'La biblioteca di Flavio Querenghi', 206–7, 210.

someone arguing in favour of solitude. Seneca warns Lucilius of the dangers of spending time with the crowd, especially at the games: 'Retreat into yourself' ('recede in te ipsum'; *Moral letters* 1.7.8). Letter 1.8 is the text in which Seneca reveals that he is communing not only with himself but with future generations, via the writings he is leaving, and that this is more valuable than his activity in court or in the senate.

Querenghi remarks that while in *Moral letters* 1.6 Seneca says that no good thing is pleasant to possess without friends to share it, he immediately retracts this view in the following letter, *Moral letters* 1.7. There Seneca says that one need not fear that one has wasted one's efforts if one cannot share things one has learned—it was for oneself that one learned them. Purity and tranquillity of soul ('la quiete dell'animo') are best conserved in solitude. To back this up, Querenghi very selectively quotes Aristotle saying that the solitary man is a God, and associates that dictum with the motives of those who close themselves in hermitages and monasteries. Then he extensively paraphrases 'quel Savio' ('that wise man') Seneca from *Moral letters* 1.7–8, on the dangers of crowds and on the utility of staying at home to write instead for posterity. Of *quiete* itself he does not speak, because who does not know that solitude is the haven from all cares?

As it happens, there is someone who appears not to know this—a nobleman whose book Querenghi had been using as a vade mecum for many years, a nobleman with whom he was used to interacting in conversation:

> A certain Frenchman claimed not to have found in solitude that tranquillity he was hoping for, and to have acted like the horse which, escaped from the hands of his master, torments himself on his own a hundred times more than working for others. Excuse me! [*Perdonimi*] He is still resting in a field, while by escaping he freed himself from the command of his master, and from the laboursome vocation of arms [*fuggendo si sottrasse dall'imperio del suo Signore, e dal faticoso mestiere dell'armi*].
>
> But it is also true that in the midst of leisure our spirit gives birth to fantastical chimerae—such as, indeed, these Discorsi of mine [*chimere fantastiche; come appunto sono questi miei Discorsi*]. These will be happy births, that do not burden the mind, but refresh it: where initially our brain, caught up in the affairs of men, is always full of objects that inflame and sadden it; where those first images of leisure [*quei primi simulacri dell'otio*] do nothing but serenely exercise our soul.[286]

Querenghi's explicit engagment with Naselli's version of *Essais* I 8 ('De l'Oysiveté') in this context is very telling. He reads the work of 'a certain Frenchman'—some members of the audience would have known who Querenghi was referring to— with a strong image of the classical *Savio* Seneca in the background. Specifically, he places Seneca's *Moral letters* 1.6–8 in dialogue with Michiel di Montagna's 'Dell'otio' as two related accounts of the kind of philosophical retreat into solitude that he is enacting and describing for his audience, and of the kind of writing that is ultimately the outcome. Montaigne's chapter does not draw directly on the *Moral letters*, but it is very clear throughout his text—even in Naselli's bowlderization—that he is drawing on Seneca's advice to Lucilius: we should

---

[286] Querenghi, *Discorsi morali politici et naturali*, sig.Y2v–3r; Ferrara 1590, sig. B1r.

retreat into ourselves as far as we can, rather than be corrupted by the vices of the mob.[287]

Still more striking is Querenghi's recognition of Montaigne's unconventional departure in relation to the classical tradition represented by Seneca, and the nature of his retort or correction as he reads and rewrites the passage from 'Dell'otio'. Montaigne had hoped that to leave his mind at leisure to entertain itself, to stay and settle itself in itself, would be to find the rational, serene tranquillity in retirement promised by Seneca. But his mind proved inconstant, more inclined to run away with itself, less subject to control. It turned out that all he could do was record its erratic movements in writing with a view to making it ashamed of itself.

We can almost feel Querenghi's reaction to this in the margin of his copy: 'oh come on!' He sides viscerally with the classical *patron* Seneca, and brings Montaigne back into line with the classical norm. For Querenghi, Montaigne's errant horse— the mind of the individual retired from civil life—is still in *riposo*, and he has still freed himself from the *imperio* of his *Signore*, and from slavery to his vocation. He is still free, in classic Senecan style, from domination by others, and at leisure.

Nevertheless, Querenghi directly identifies his own *Discorsi* with Montaigne's 'chimere fantastiche', specifying that they have a more assuredly therapeutic role, both for himself and for others. They are serene exercises, not the frettings of a bolted horse. Of course, the fact that he uses the phrase 'questi miei Discorsi' reveals that he has edited the text of his speech after the event for the purposes of collecting it with all his other occasional discourses in a book called *Discorsi*, a book that consciously imitates, but also 'improves' or corrects the Italian *Discorsi* of Naselli–Montaigne. Though only a proportion of Querenghi's discourses originate in speeches given on special occasions, they all address the same kind of mixed 'academic' audience in Padua and Venice (including strangers visiting those cities) from the point of view of the same philosophical—and professional—*persona*. Most originate in short manuscripts of practical philosophical advice offered to specific ecclesiastical and aristocratic patrons.

We have looked in detail at the context of Querenghi's use of Montaigne at the Accademia dei Ricovrati in 1633 because it changes our perspective both on the book in which his speech was eventually to appear and on the comparison we are implicitly making between the *Discorsi* and the *Essais*. Querenghi's book is, like the discourse on solitude it contains, a noble *attione* performed before a civic audience of churchmen, university scholars, and aristocrats. It indexes the social performance of philosophical solitude before a public of 'friends', as well as the enfranchisement of a 'natural' and noble proponent of the new, practical philosophy. The portrait of Querenghi entered in the manuscript register of the academy inscribes his noble title and offices and the quasi-monkish *persona* that goes with it.

Though the concepts of nature it utilizes are very different from Montaigne's, in these respects it is directly comparable with the *Essais*. Indeed, it helps to bring out the story of the *Essais* themselves as that of a 'noble book'—a portrait of noble

---

[287] Green, *Montaigne and the life of freedom*, chapter 2.

attioni on the part of a self-consciously retired aristocrat, performed before an audience that likewise included the secular nobility, clerics, and scholars.[288] Both books, furthermore, come with ready-made reception histories—even if, as we shall see in the rest of this section, the contrast between the two mens' publishing strategies is ultimately the most revealing point.

Peter N. Miller has found in Querenghi's *Discorsi* the 'philosophical foundation of [the] view of the scholar as a member of a civil society'. They incarnate, that is, the ideal of learned sociability espoused by figures from Guazzo to Peiresc. The model is that of a community of friends drawn together by a shared desire for philosophical self-perfection. Querenghi's particular evocation of this life 'illuminates the relationship between *constantia*, conversation, and its lived practice in a circle of provincial friends, aristocrats and scholars'.[289]

This is true, but it is also true that much of Querenghi's lived practice, in both social and intellectual terms, is dictated by his patrons and the relationships between them, and by the duties of his offices as a *canonico*-philosopher, coadjutor to his uncle, client to that same uncle and other patrons. The constraining conditions of the author's enfranchisement are more visible in the *Discorsi* than in the *Essais*. Querenghi's discourse on solitude, for example, appears to be a kind of command performance; its *dessein*, in Montaigne's terms ('Au lecteur'), is both for the *service* of others and for the *gloire* of the speaker.

Silvia de Renzi has shown how the professional physician Giulio Mancini, in exactly the same period (1600–30), used scribal publishing to build the networks that sustained his career: 'even in the "age of print", scribal practices—lending, copying, assembling manuscripts—worked to create and sustain the diverse relations—among peers and between junior and senior colleagues—which constituted a physician's professional network'. Manuscript *consilia* were lubricants for social and intellectual relations. They could go to a variety of patrons, who would 'mention' and re-circulate them in influential circles, or they could be collected by just one patron: the Pope himself (in the later stages of Mancini's career).[290]

Querenghi's career as a 'civilized priest', whose social distinctiveness rested both on a form of quasi-monastic seclusion and on his participation in civil philosophical conversation, was built in similar ways.[291] The circulation of his written discourses, and the written record of others' responses to them, created and sustained the networks which shaped his philosophical *persona* as a *canonico*-professor—only very late in life did he put all this on the printed record.

But Flavio was in a more dependent position than Mancini. In the period between *c.*1606 and *c.*1620, Flavio's manuscript *consilia* on topics in practical and natural philosophy were understood not as personally authored texts circulated by

---

[288] As we shall see in section 2.2.12, this is exactly how Ginammi presented it to the dedicatee of the 1633 *Saggi*.

[289] Miller, *Peiresc's Europe*, 64–5, 73, 68.

[290] Silvia De Renzi, 'A career in manuscripts: genres and purposes of a physician's writing in Rome, 1600–1630', *Italian Studies*, 66, no. 2 (2011), 234–48, 248.

[291] For Federico Borromeo's fashioning of the model of the 'civilised priest' in this period, see Wietse de Boer, *The conquest of the soul: confessions, discipline, and public order in counter-Reformation Milan* (Leiden: Brill, 2000), 141–54.

his initiative in private, but as scribal publications of the court of Parma at the court of Urbino, and as those of a family client of the important intellectual patron Antonio Querenghi (Flavio's uncle). In other words, he was effectively ordered by one patron to compose and send fruits of his private reading and writing to another patron. His reputation, furthermore, is subsidiary to that of his uncle, and his activities and offices are largely dictated by his uncle's connections.[292]

Flavio documents this himself in his *Discorsi*, and his printed documentation broadly corresponds to the archival records and manuscript copies extant in Florence and the Vatican.[293] He describes how his patron Ranuccio Farnese, Duke of Parma—derived from his uncle Antonio, who served the Duke—ordered him to 'publish' them at the court of Urbino as fruits of the *disciplina* of Ranuccio's court. He duly sent various *scritti* to the Duke over the years, as manuscript separates. But when, a long time after, he visited the Duke's *studio* at Casteldurante he found these disparate writings were kept there in the form of bound *libri* (books), and that they had a title: 'Discorsi Morali, e Naturali'. The latter ('Naturali') were 'scholastic' discourses, while the former ('Morali') were more informal and persuasive. The reported title corresponds exactly to that contained in an extant manuscript volume in the Urbino collection at the Vatican Library. Far from feeling encouraged by this experience to publish them also in print, Querenghi decided it was much more prudent not to.[294]

Querenghi elsewhere tells Padre Giovanni Battista d'Este, who in 1629 had ceased to be Alfonso III (of Modena) in order to cultivate solitude as a Capuchin friar, that the choice in his later years to concentrate on the *morali* at the expense of the early *naturali* had not been entirely his.[295] In an authoritative neo-Latin poem, printed both in the *Discorsi* and in Antonio's collected *carmina*, his uncle Antonio had dictated that Flavio cease writing abstruse discourses on natural-philosophical topics and come down to earth, like Socrates, to discourse of moral philosophy. The occasion—some time between *c.*1611 and *c.*1618—had been Flavio's composition of a natural-philosophical discourse, sent in manuscript to

---

[292] See, for example, how Davila's praise of Flavio is subsidiary to his praise of Antonio Querenghi in Angelo Calogierà (ed.), *Nuova raccolta d'opuscoli scientifici, e filologici: Tomo duodecimo* (Venice: Simone Occhi, 1764), 345.

[293] Querenghi's letters (1607–31) from Padua to the Duke of Urbino, including many that accompany manuscript *discorsi*, can be found in Florence, Archivio di Stato di Firenze (henceforward abbreviated as 'ASF'), Fondo Ducato di Urbino (henceforward abbreviated as 'Urbino'), classe I, divisione G, filza 219, fols. 745r–73r. He had already written once to the Duke from the court of Parma, on 7 November 1606 (ASF, Urbino, cl. I, div. G, fil. 248, fol. 843r). Minutes of some of the letters sent back from the Duke to Querenghi can be found in ASF, Urbino, cl. I, div. G, fil. 304, fol. 579r–v and fil. 306, fols. 214–15, 441, while more can be found in print at the front of the *Discorsi*, sigs. a4r–b4r. The manuscript *discorsi* themselves can be found in Vatican City, Biblioteca Apostolica Vaticana (henceforward abbreviated as 'BAV'), Urb. Lat. MS 860, fols. 408–44 and MS 861, fols. 1–56. The latter manuscript begins with a three-part neo-Latin work on philosophical style, also by Querenghi, entitled 'Problemata'.

[294] Querenghi, *Discorsi morali politici et naturali*, sig. a1r–v; BAV, Urb. Lat. MS 861, fol. 31r.

[295] Querenghi, *Discorsi morali politici et naturali*, sig. 2M4r–v; *DBI*, 'Alfonso III d'Este, duca di Modena'.

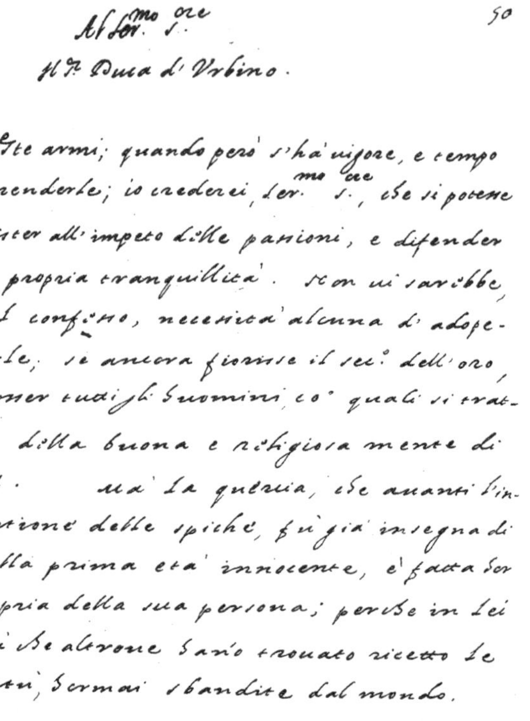

Al Ser.mo Sig.re
Il Sig. Duca d'Urbino.
50

Con queste armi; quando però s'hà vigore, e tempo
di prenderle; io crederei, Ser.mo Sig.re, che si potesse
resister all'impeto delle passioni, e difender
la propria tranquillità. Non vi sarebbe,
io 'l confesso, necessità alcuna d'adope-
rarle, se ancora fiorisse il sec.o dell'oro,
ò fosser tutti gli huomini, co' quali si trat-
ta, della buona e religiosa mente di
V. A. Ma la quercia, che avanti l'in-
ventione delle spiche, fù già insegna di
quella prima età innocente, è fatta hor
propria della sua persona; perche in lei
più che altrove havrò trovato ricetto le
virtù, hormai sbandite dal mondo.

Illus. 2.2.4. Biblioteca Apostolica Vaticana, Urb. Lat. MS 861, fol. 50r (manuscript *discorsi* sent by Flavio Querenghi to the Duke of Urbino). Reproduced by permission of the Biblioteca Apostolica Vaticana, Vatican City.

the Duke of Urbino, on the question of whether and how the air of the middle region comes to be cold.[296]

It is likely that, in advising concentration on moral philosophy, Antonio Querenghi was already positioning his nephew for the chair in that discipline at Padua. Flavio would eventually obtain this office in 1624, through the patronage of the founder of the Ricovrati, Federico Cornaro, who sued to the future doge Giovanni, his father.[297]

In order to come down to earth to discourse of moral philosophy, and to assume a more natural and independent voice in his speech and writing so as to offer his friends 'a natural portrait of myself' ('un mio ritratto del naturale'), Querenghi had resort to Naselli's Montaigne.[298] He had already produced some moral-philosophical compositions, but he now more boldly wrote to the Duke promising him 'arms' with which one could resist the onslaught of the 'passions' and defend 'one's own tranquillity' (Illus. 2.2.4). The accompanying discourse was entitled 'The way to

[296] Querenghi, *Discorsi morali politici et naturali*, sigs. 2H2r–K3r; Querenghi, *Hexametri carminis libri sex. Rhapsodiae variorum carminum libri V*, sig. G8r–v.

[297] Laura Megna, 'Federico Cornaro e l'Accademia padovana dei Ricovrati', *Studi Veneziani*, 43 (2002), 331–48, 344–5.

[298] Querenghi, *Discorsi morali politici et naturali*, sig. a2r.

convert our displeasures into delights' ('Modo di convertire i nostri dispiaceri in diletti'; Illus. 2.2.5).[299]

So, this apparently more personal and natural discourse was, like the others, a made-to-order manuscript text published in a bound volume at the court of Urbino by order of Flavio's uncle's major patron, the Duke of Parma.

However, c.1620, Querenghi repackaged the discourse with a new title ('The alchemy of the soul's passions') and had it printed anonymously in Padua and Vicenza, re-dedicated to the Venetian patrician Domenico Molino. This is likely to have been part of a campaign to consolidate his connections amongst the Venetian governing elite, with a view to gaining office at the *Studio*. Though it appears Cornaro was directly instrumental in his appointment to the chair, other patrons were also important, such as the *procuratore* of San Marco, Francesco Morosini. And Molino's support will also have been significant. The Querenghi family papers include several letters from the senator to Flavio, including one of 1626 in which he records how Enrico Davila had informed him of the applause with which his at once learned and most gracious lectures ('le sue dotti, et leggi-adrissimi lettioni') were received by the numerous scholars and other auditors who heard them.[300]

The discourse itself opens the 1644 volume and begins with a preface (identical to the one that featured in the manuscript sent to the Duke of Urbino) that reworks or 'corrects' Naselli's 'Ai Lettori', and other passages, in the same way that the passage discussed above reworks 'Dell'Otio'. For although Querenghi borrows Montaigne's language and tone, he also pointedly promises a taste, a *saggio*, of a more useful self-portrait than Montaigne does his readers: 'Reader, I propose to you a new Alchemy, not of metals, but of the passions of the soul: let your heart try it out [*il tuo cuore ne faccia il saggio*], and see if it takes the hammer.' It will be a discourse delivered in good faith, expressed in simple, natural language, while the prescriptions he offers will be nude, without ornament, born in him spontane-ously, rather than extracted from books (Illus. 2.2.5).[301] He goes on in the passages that follow directly to address the reader with the voice of Nature herself, which counsels retreat into philosophical solitude.

Copies of the anonymous *Alchimia*, and of another anonymous discourse Querenghi had printed around the same time (*Ragionamento dello Studio di Padova*),

[299] BAV, Urb. Lat. MS 861, fols. 50r, 51r.

[300] Querenghi, *Discorsi morali politici et naturali*, sig. 2Y2v (Francesco Morosini); Reggio Emilia, Archivio di Stato, Archivi Privati, Archivio Turri, busta n.161, fasciculo n.1 ('Querenghi'), no num-bering, Domenico Molino at Venice to Flavio Querenghi at Padua, 27 February 1626.

[301] Querenghi, *Discorsi morali politici et naturali*, sig. [A1]r: 'Il mio dire è schietto, e naturale, perche non iscrivo per pompa d'ingegno, mà per tuo, e mio beneficio…Sarà questo discorso di buona fede, ed anderò notando in semplici parole quelle considerationi, ch'm'han servito tal volta per medicina. Attendi alla sola intelligenza di queste ricette, le quali troverai altrettanto utili e vere, quanto nude d'ornamenti. Non aspettar, ch'io t'alleghi Aristotile, e Platone: perche non le hò cavate da' libri; ma son nate in me spontaneamente, senza seme di dottrina.' Cf. Ferrara 1590, sigs. †3v–†4r: 'Questo è un libro di buona fede Lettore…io non mi son proposto altro fine, che domestico e privato…Io l'ho dedicato alla particolare commodità de' miei parenti, ed amici…Io voglio esservi scorto nella mia semplice maniera, naturale, ed ordinaria, senza studio, ed artificio…molto volontieri mi ci sarei dipinto tutto intiero e nudo.'

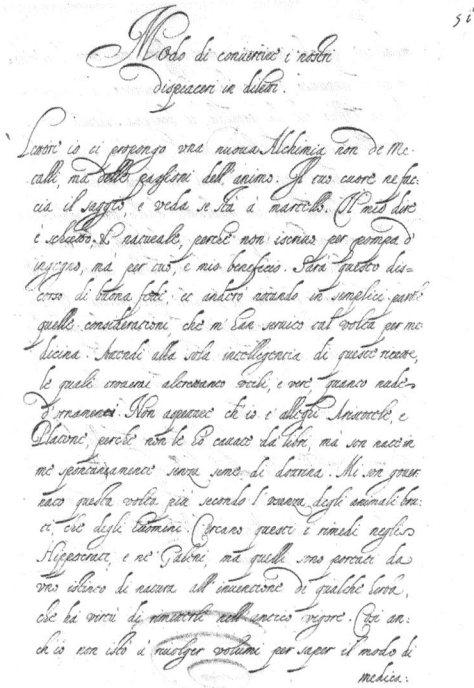

Illus. 2.2.5. Biblioteca Apostolica Vaticana AV, Urb. Lat. MS 861, fol. 51r (manuscript *discorsi* sent by Flavio Querenghi to the Duke of Urbino). Reproduced by permission of the Biblioteca Apostolica Vaticana, Vatican City.

both dedicated to Molino, are extremely rare.[302] As Querenghi printed nothing else until late in his life (*c.*1640), it seems fair to assume that *c.*1620 he used local printers as an alternative to having scribal copies made—just as Montaigne pretends to do in the *Essais*. We do know that he distributed the resulting copies widely to patrons and friends, and solicited replies.

The publication of the *Alchimia* to family and friends was clearly meant to mark an important moment in his career, a moment at which—prompted by his *patron* and uncle Antonio Querenghi—he assumes the *persona* of a moral philosopher who abandons abstruse science and worldly affairs and speaks from nature in his solitude, just a few years before he becomes an official moral philosopher. One copy found its way into the library of the Duke of Urbino, and another into that of Gabriel Naudé in Paris. The latter copy was immeasurably dignified by being packeted up with copies of other, much more substantial treatises of medico-moral

---

[302] Flavio Querenghi, *Alchimia delle passioni dell'animo* ([Padua and Vicenza]: [n.p.], [1620]); Flavio Querenghi, *Ragionamento dello Studio di Padova nella partenza dell'illustrissimo sig. podesta Ottauiano Bon* (Padua: G.B.Martini, [*c.*1622–3]). According to the online catalogue of the ICCU (Opac SBN) at the time of going to press (June 2016) three copies of the *Alchimia* and two of the *Ragionamento* are extant in Italian libraries.

wisdom, probably also from the Veneto region: Cardano's *De consolatione* and Matteo Franceschi's translation of Simplicius's commentary on Epictetus. It was Epictetus, and his disciple Arrian, that Antonio Querenghi declared his nephew to be imitating in the *Alchimia*.[303]

The best testimony we have of the significance of the circulation of the *Alchimia* is printed at the back of the *Discorsi* in the form of a ready-made reception history in its own chapter entitled: 'Judgements of various people on the Alchimia, printed anonymously in Padua and Vicenza'. The offices of these recipients and respondents are carefully specified: Signor Alessandro Guarini, Counsellor and Secretary to the Duke of Mantova, as well as son to the author of the *Pastor Fido*; Signor Enrico Davila ('H.D'), Governor for the Republic of Venice (in Cattaro); Padre Paolo Bombini, Counsellor of the Duke of Mantova, and so on.[304]

As elsewhere in Querenghi's volume, the circulation of copies of his discourses indexes the social relations with courts, corporate entities, and individual patrons that shaped his career and his *persona*. The recipients' letters all testify in one way or another to the practical effects that they understand this treatise of moral alchemy was meant to have—the conversion of *dispiaceri* into *diletti* and the consolidation of Querenghi's *persona* as a *canonico*-philosopher, a physician of spirits or minds.

Davila had been born near Padua, but had fought in the later civil wars in France, before returning to his native city and going on to serve as Venetian Governor of Cattaro from 1618.[305] In his letter to Querenghi, he reports that the *Alchimia* arrived just as he had tasted the perfidy of a friend, giving him occasion to 'put this Philosophy into practice, and to put Philosophy to work' ('metter questa Filosofia in atto pratico, e ridur la Filosofia alla operatione'). He goes on to declare this practical philosophy to be the true philosophy, which follows the nature of things, including man, and provides useful and natural remedies for everyday infirmities, not abstractions and cavils in the manner of the 'Academici' and the 'Stoici'.

In Davila's mind Querenghi is promoting 'human and natural ways of doing philosophy' ('modi di filosofare humani, e naturali'), which centre on the provision of medico-moral remedies that need to be gently and soothingly introduced, with eloquence—which Querenghi would continue to do both in his private *consilia*

---

[303] University of Rome, 'La Sapienza', Biblioteca Alessandrina, pressmark XIV.c.7 (9); Estelle Bœuf, *La bibliothèque parisienne de Gabriel Naudé en 1630: les lectures d'un libertin érudit* (Geneva: Droz, 2007), 355; Querenghi, *Discorsi morali politici et naturali*, sig. 2Y1r. Bœuf was not able to identify Querenghi as the author of the *Alchimia* listed in Naudé's inventory. The three works are grouped by a bracket in the margin and appear in a section of the inventory headed 'Livres qui sont empaquetez' (Littré defines a 'paquet' in this sense as a bookbinder's term denoting 'plusieurs volumes tournés tous du même sens et cousus, préparés pour être endossés et liés ensemble à l'entour, mais séparés l'un de l'autre par de petites planches qui en font sortir le dos'). The *paquet* in question is not extant so it is not possible to be certain which editions of the works Naudé possessed. USTC lists two sixteenth-century editions of Franceschi's translation, published in Venice in 1582 and 1583, and two editions of Cardano's work, published in Venice in 1542 and Nürnberg in 1544.

[304] Querenghi, *Discorsi morali politici et naturali*, sigs. 2X1r–Y1r.

[305] 'Enrico Caterino Davila', *DBI*.

and in the university lectures that, a few years later, Davila would commend to Domenico Molino.[306]

To achieve this human and natural-philosophical mode, according to Davila (in his letter of 1620), Querenghi has perfectly imitated the style of Montaigne. If he wishes to persist in this he could compile a set of discourses not entitled 'Conatus', as in Montaigne's case, but 'Profectus'. Davila goes on to say that he knew Montaigne (while in France during the civil wars) and that he found him to be but superficially 'stained' with letters ('tinto di lettere, ma non profonde'). His style of writing was natural, as he was more of a soldier than a *letterato*. Querenghi by contrast supplements nature with art, and thus exceeds Montaigne. Davila's letter is complemented over the page by another written from Venice on 30 July 1621 by a Flemish gentleman of the court of Cardinal Barberini, Signor Guglielmo Sohier.[307]

Sohier appears in the acts of the *natio Germanica artistarum* in early 1619 ('dominus Guilelmus Sohir Belga') as an intermediary in a dispute involving his co-Fleming, the illustrious anatomist Adriaan van den Spieghel, who was an active member of that nation, and a regular donator of books to their library. Sohier was named in Spieghel's will of 9 March 1625 as a resident of San Francesco Grande at Padua, and put down still firmer roots in the city the following year by marrying Isabella Zorzi. He was clearly considered a font of bibliographical information. On 19 June 1627, Lorenzo Pignoria recommended Sohier—who was back in Padua after an interval—to Domenico Molino as a very learned gentleman who could let him have the title of an unidentified 'Libro di Messina'.[308]

Though Sohier's is the only letter which does not directly mention the *Alchimia*, it does foresee that posterity, considering the conformity of Querenghi's and Montaigne's minds, shall one day say 'O how Montaigne Querenghises, how Querenghi Montaignises' ('O Montagnes Querengheggia, ò Querengo Montagneggia'). The occasion of Sohier's missive is a belated reply to a letter of Querenghi's in which he had offered Sohier the news that he had recovered his copy of Monsignor di Montaigne's book (in Naselli's translation)—a cause for celebration on Sohier's part.

Sohier's excuse for not replying earlier was illness—of which van den Spieghel would doubtless have informed Querenghi. He cannot quite say he is over it, so instead he can say, with Seneca (in fact Serenus, addressing Seneca), at the

[306] Querenghi, *Discorsi morali politici et naturali*, sig. 2X1v (for this and the previous paragraph); Flavio Querenghi, *Institutionum moralium epitome. De sapientiae & eloquentiae divortio. De consiliario. De honore. De numero virtutum moralium. Introductio in philosophiam moralem Aristotelis* (Paris: Apud Viduam Mathurini Dupuis, 1643). A previous edition of this collection, without the last four treatises listed, had appeared in Leiden in 1639: Flavio Querenghi, *Institutionum moralium epitome; alter, de genere dicendi philosophorum, seu, de sapientiae et eloquentiae divortio* (Leiden: ex officina J. Maire, 1639).

[307] Querenghi, *Discorsi morali politici et naturali*, sigs. 2X1v, 2X2v–3r.

[308] Lucia Rossetti (ed.), *Acta nationis Germanicae artistarum, 1616–1636* (Padua: Editrice Antenore, 1967), 75; Francesca Zen Benetti, 'Nuove ricerche sull'anatomico fiammingo Adriaan van den Spieghel (1578-1625)', *Quaderni per la storia dell'università di Padova*, 5 (1972), 45–71, 51 and n.4, 71; Venice, Bibliotheca Nazionale Marciana, MS It. XI. 20–6789, fol. 39r (Lorenzo Pignoria to Domenico Molino, 19 June 1627). My thanks to Mary Laven for checking the last item.

beginning of the *On tranquillity of mind* (1.2): 'my state of mind, though not the worst possible, is a particularly discontented and fretful one: I am neither ill nor well'. Serenus is telling Seneca, as Sohier is telling Querenghi, that his soul is not as free from perturbations as his philosophical master's. The Senecan quotation is highly appropriate: once again Querenghi is positioned as a physician of minds, here on the model of Seneca. The juxtaposition of Seneca and the other author (Montaigne) who Querenghi is using as a vade mecum—so much so that he was particularly anxious to get his copy back—corresponds to the pairing Querenghi would himself use a few years later when reopening the Ricovrati.

Sohier also promises to use every diligence to find a copy of Montaigne in French, so that Querenghi can more perfectly 'taste' that author, and advance his knowledge of that language ('userò ogni diligenza di trovarglielo in Francese; accioche possa perfettamente gustar quell'Autore, ed avanzarsi nell'intelligenza di quella lingua'). This gives us a precious glimpse of the role of transalpine scholars such as Sohier in sourcing foreign language texts for Paduan and Venetian patrons such as Querenghi, and tying them to potential language tuition. It also tells us that in Venice in July 1621 copies of the French *Essais* were rare enough to require a special effort on his part.[309]

This tallies with the evidence offered by the record of acquisitions made by the library of the *natio Germanica artistarum* to which Sohier's close associate Spieghel belonged. Acquisitions of books in the French vernacular between 1590 and 1621 were extremely rare, with a small spurt in the period 1618–21 and only one major author represented (Du Bartas).[310]

The case of Querenghi, particularly as seen through the optic of Canini's description and of the speech he gave to reopen the Ricovrati in 1633, has helped establish one of this study's fundamental points concerning the culture of practical philosophy in this period: the teaching of philosophical doctrines cannot be separated from the social performance of philosophical *personae*, through particular offices such as that of *canonico, accademico,* and *lettore,* in particular spaces such as the cathedral, the academy, and the *studio*.

Querenghi performed philosophical solitude for his audience of ecclesiastical and civic nobility, and of students and parishioners, in all these public spaces, drawing on ancient precedents such as Seneca and Epictetus and modern precedents such as the good Frenchman, Montaigne. He did it both in person and in writing, for the circulation of manuscript and printed writings, and the written or printed record of the 'reception' to which they give rise, were understood to index this live social performance and the reaction of the audience to it.

---

[309] Querenghi, *Discorsi morali politici et naturali*, sigs. 2X2v–3r, for this and the previous two paragraphs. Querenghi's personal library contained no French texts and there is no evidence that he took up Sohier's offer of tuition in the language.

[310] Antonio Favaro (ed.), *Atti della Nazione Germanica Artista nello Studio di Padova*, 2 vols. (Venice: R. Deputazione Veneta di Storia Patria, 1911), vol. 2, 8 (1591 'Epistolas gallice'), 185 (1601, two books), 216 (1604, 'Libro gallico quodam'), 233, 234 (1605, Latin–French dictionary), 266 (1607, Du Bartas in French), 343 (1612, two books), 398 (1615, two books); Rossetti (ed.), *Acta nationis Germanicae artistarum, 1616–1636*, 51 (1618), 53 (1618), 62 (1618, French commentary on Hippocrates?), 71–2 (1619, 5 books), 125 (1621, 'Les pseaumes penitentiaux').

However, in the particular social conditions of the late Renaissance world of Italy and France, heavily determined by hierarchical relations between patrons and clients, and by the obligations of particular offices, this performance could be described not as an enfranchisement of the mind but as social and intellectual enslavement—to classical *patrons* such as Aristotle and Aquinas, and to social and intellectual *patrons* such as Antonio Querenghi and Domenico Molino.

On the one hand, the 'precedent' of Flavio Querenghi, applied retrospectively, helps us see the *Essais* in similar terms as the record of a practical philosophical performance, consisting of noble *attioni*, before an audience of 'patrons', of family and friends, past and present. On the other hand, it helps us see how the *Essais* attempt to delineate a freer, less conventional—because less official, less professional, less society-bound—kind of philosophical career.

In other words, Querenghi's is an 'ordinary' case of enfranchisement by means of letters and philosophical retreat that helps us see how extraordinary Montaigne's was, in the terms of his own day. Montaigne, furthermore, does not use the technology of the printed book as an afterthought to a life of social transactions with patrons, carried out via scribal culture, collected and bound together by a Duke in an aristocratic library. From the start he collects himself in one constantly evolving printed book, describes himself as his own *patron*, carrying out offices without names, and seeks to find new friends via the circulation of that book nationally and internationally.

2.2.12 MODERN RE-INVENTERS OF ETHICS

The most important new friend Montaigne found in Italy was not Querenghi but the self-styled publisher-bookseller (*libraio-editore*) Marco Ginammi. We heard in 2.2.8 that he commissioned the Jesuate friar Canini to translate and correct the French *Essais*. So Venice 1633 can be described as an index of Ginammi's work in employing Canini's 'studious care' to help him achieve the 'safe transpassage' of the *Essais* to Venice.

It is important to understand that in doing this, just as his publishing house was re-launching itself (after plague struck) in 1633, Ginammi was making a statement. In 1629 he had himself received a dedication as a 'Bibliopola insigne' ('distinguished bookseller'). He saw himself as reviving the virtues and values of great cinquecento houses such as that of the Giolliti and the Manuzii—at a moment when the Venetian publishing industry was in serious decline. Just as they had employed clerical intellectuals such as Erasmus and Dolce to correct their works, so he employed the cleric Canini. Just as they claimed to work not for commercial profit, but to win recognition for moral and intellectual virtue, so did he.[311]

He first tried to publish an edition of the *Essais* in Italian in the same year (1629), but as only one copy—still in publisher's binding—has so far been found,

---

[311] Maria C. Napoli, *L'impresa del libro nell'Italia del Seicento: La bottega di Marco Ginammi* (Naples: Guida Editori, 1990), 29, 32, 79–84.

it is reasonable to assume that the onset and outbreak of plague between 1628 and 1631 prevented full distribution. Indeed, the 1633 edition may amount to a reissue of retained stock of 1629, with a new title page. As we noted in 2.2.8, the title page of that aborted edition advertised it as a truthful self-portrait that effectively teaches true self-knowledge to others. It also attributed the translation and summaries to Canini.[312]

The 1633 title page displaces the name of the translator (Canini died in 1631), and describes the *Saggi* or *Discorsi* as having been transported from the French to the Italian language by the work of Ginammi and offered to the dedicatee, the nobleman-philosopher David Spinelli (Illus. 2.2.6). In the dedication to Spinelli, whose philosophical dialogues he published in the same year, Ginammi described the book as the portrait of the *attioni* of the Signor di Montagna, whom he clearly saw as a French equivalent to a noble academician of Venice such as his dedicatee, illustrious both for *scienza* and *nobiltà*.[313]

It is perfectly possible, then, to describe the *Saggi*, and the *Apologia* of the following year (1634), as the work of Ginammi, part of an *œuvre* he produced to an identifiable cultural programme, focused more on *lettere* and less on religion than was the norm, between the 1620s and the early 1650s. This and the well-known fact that he defied the Roman Index (in publishing, for example, Machiavelli) does not mean, however, that he was some kind of champion of anti-clerical, secular thought. Not only did he commission a Jesuate to translate Montaigne, he worked closely with the religious orders, especially the Minorites, to publish editions and commentaries as part of the Scotist revival. Compared to a literary publisher of the previous era, such as Gabriele Giolito, his whole list had a moral, edificatory slant to it, in tune with the reforming zeal of the times in the Veneto.[314]

By means of paratexts, including personal dedications and lists of titles (on sale in his *Libraria*) ordered by format size, he maintained a continuous relationship with his principal readerships of university and ecclesiastical scholars, and of *letterati*. The latter comprised the broader cultural elite of the city in their *personae* as free literates (from university and monastic scholars, through to patricians and the cultivated *borghesia*). So the folio books heading the list at the back of Venice 1633 were dominated by scholarly Scotist literature in Latin, including the works of a Dominican friar from the Polish province of Poznan ('F. Petri Posnaniensis'), and of the Franciscan friar Filippo Fabbri, who had denounced Cremonini but who himself had some problems with the Inquisition in relation to his own work. The *Saggi* appeared beneath these, amidst a group of elegantly produced quartos offering *discorsi*, *considerationi*, and *dialoghi* to the *letterati*.[315]

---

[312] Desan, 'Une édition italienne inconnue des *Essais* (Venise, 1629)'. The registers of the printers' company at Venice record no activity in 1628–9 (Napoli, *L'impresa del libro*, 26).

[313] Venice 1633, sig. a2r.

[314] Michel de Montaigne, *Apologia di Raimondo di Sebonda*, trans. Anon. (Venice: Marco Ginammi, 1634); Napoli, *L'impresa del libro*, 44–5, 55, 57–68.

[315] Napoli, *L'impresa del libro*, 53–4, 66–8; Venice 1633, sig. 3C7r–v; Thomas F. Mayer, *The Roman Inquisition: a papal bureaucracy and its laws in the age of Galileo* (Philadelphia: University of Pennsylvania Press, 2013), 148.

SAGGI
DI MICHEL
SIG. DI MONTAGNA,
Ouero

DISCORSI, NATVRALI, POLITICI, E MORALI,

Trasportati dalla lingua Francese nell' Italiana,

Per opera di MARCO GINAMMI.

Al Clariss. Sig. Sig. Osseruandiss.

IL SIG. DAVID SPINELLI.

INVENETIA, MDCXXXIII.

Presso Marco Ginammi.

Con Licenza de' Superiori, e Priuilegio.

Illus. 2.2.6. Montaigne, *Saggi*, trans. G. Canini (Venice: M. Ginammi, 1633), Bodleian Library, pressmark Vet. F2 d.18 (1), title page. Reproduced by permission of The Bodleian Libraries, the University of Oxford.

Ginammi most obviously cultivated this latter readership, and the 'academic' circles they frequented, with his contributions to political, ethical, and historical literature. Two examples evident in the Venice 1633 list are the literature of the Trevisan–Barbarigo *amicizia*, in the late 1620s, and of the pro-French, anti-Spanish consensus (e.g. the works of Las Casas on the Spanish destruction of the new world), through from the 1620s to the 1640s.[316]

Indeed, one of Ginammi's specialisms was the faithful 'transportation' of modern, foreign language works into Italian. Though he used several different translators, he commissioned translations that were always of the same style (close and literal), often with the original text on the facing page. As in the case of Canini's Montaigne, Ginammi first published an edition of Las Casas (the *Istoria*) which attributed the work to the translator Giacomo Castellani, then two years later issued another text by Las Casas (*Il supplice schiavo Indiano*), translated 'per opera di Marco Ginammi'.[317]

Ginammi's prefatory address to the reader in the *Saggi* reinforces his *persona* as one who is in the book trade for reputation rather than for profit. He reminds his customers that they know him as the one who, for their benefit, defied the Index to offer the works of Machiavelli and Aretino under pseudonyms ('Niecollucci' and 'Partenio')—works duly listed at the back of the volume. He has now gone on to spare no expense in securing them a faithful translation of the *Essais*, which more than any other volume he has produced makes clear his own motives. He invites them to speculate how much it might have cost him to secure the services of the virtuous D. Girolamo Canini in translating such a copious volume, to employ such expensive printers, and to use such high-quality paper. He has outdone himself to offer them these natural, historical, political, and moral discourses—'a perfect philosophy'. He whets their appetite for the follow-up volume the following year, the 'Apologia di Raimondo di Sabundia', as learned as it is curious ('altretanto dotta quanto curiosa').[318]

Ginammi clearly thought that this luxury quarto volume would capture a whole readership of *letterati*, whom he imagined were in the market for such learned and curious works in the vernacular. He does not give us the numbers but we do know that the retail price of the *Saggi* was a staggering 118 soldi, where many of his other publications sold for between 16 and 40 soldi. The presence of copies in a later inventory (the source of the retail price) that included stock inherited from Ginammi, and the fact that he never published another edition of Montaigne, probably indicates that it was a commercial failure.[319]

[316] Angela Nuovo, 'L'Editoria veneziana del XVII secolo e il problema americano: La pubblicazione delle opere di Bartolomè de Las Casas (Venezia, Marco Ginammi, 1626-43)', in Angela Caracciolo Aricò (ed.), *L'impatto della scoperta dell'America nella cultura veneziana* (Rome: Bulzoni, 1990), 175–86, 177–85; Napoli, *L'impresa del libro*, 68–79.
[317] *DBI*, 'Marco Ginammi'; Napoli, *L'impresa del libro*, 40–1.
[318] Venice 1633, sig. a6r ('Lettore'). See the entry on Ginammi in *DBI*.
[319] Napoli, *L'impresa del libro*, 11, 50, 71. Napoli's source is a post-mortem inventory (Archivio di Stato di Venezia, Giudici di Petizione, inventari, b. 381/46, n. 85), dating to 1678, of the goods of Francesco Brogiolli, who very probably inherited the Ginammi house and its stock. Another French author, Nicolas Caussin, was more of a commercial success for Ginammi than Montaigne.

Why invest so much in this particular work at this moment? The appearance of Ginammi's edition in 1633–4 can be related to an international bibliographical trend that had the effect in Padua-Venice of making the full *Essais* seem a desired 'rarity'. The market increasingly defined that quality in intellectual, not material terms, in relation to recent authors who were reinventing particular disciplines.[320] We have seen Sarpi (2.2.9) and Sohier (2.2.11) testify to this effect in the period before the appearance of Ginammi's edition.

Originating in distinctively Franco-Italian cultural exchanges, and associated with the presence of Francophone intellectuals and Francophile book collectors in Padua-Venice and Rome, this early seventeenth-century trend gives new legitimacy and credibility to the French *Essais* in Italy, which had until then circulated mainly in the form of Naselli's *Discorsi*. The primary promoter of the full French *Essais* in Italy was the French scholar, editor, and bibliographer Gabriel Naudé.

Naudé spent 1626–7 in Padua, where he probably met Flavio Querenghi, and where he certainly followed the *lezioni* of Cesare Cremonini, before spending eleven years in Rome serving Cardinal Francesco dei conti Guidi di Bagno. He even had clear connections with Urbino. He knew Paduan scholar Giovanni Colle, who had served as Francesco Maria's physician from 1600 to at least 1615. He became a member of Urbino's academies, discovered (according to a printer's preface) a Cardano manuscript in Urbino and published his Montaigne-influenced *De syntagma de studio liberali* there in 1632. In that treatise he paired, for the Italians, two of 'our compatriots', Charron and Montaigne, as the scourges of pedantic learning.[321]

This was not the first time Naudé had named Montaigne in print. By 1625, Naudé's intellectual-bibliographical works were standardizing and diffusing a tip to collect Montaigne in French that must have been circulating in the Franco-Italian republic of letters for a number of years (at least since the 1610s).[322] Of course, we do not know exactly when the last Duke of Urbino acquired his French copy of the *Essais*, but the example of Padre Raffaele Aversa's request in 1626 that missing early works of Galileo's be supplied to the library provides a foundation for saying that a copy of the 1602 edition might have been obtained in the 1610s or later, at the request of a specific intellectual.[323]

At any rate, in the *Advis* of 1627, Naudé famously described how the book collector should assemble the new generation of commentators and philosophers around the traditional authorities and their older commentators. With obvious

[320] Warren Boutcher, 'Collecting manuscripts and printed books in the late Renaissance: Naudé and the last Duke of Urbino's library', *Italian Studies*, 66, no. 2 (2011), 206–20, 212.

[321] Jack Alden Clarke, *Gabriel Naudé, 1600–1653* (Hamden, Conn.: Archon Books, 1970), 13–16, 33–5, 48–9; Anna Lisa Schino, 'Incontri italiani di Gabriel Naudé', *Rivista di Storia della Filosofia*, 44 (1989), 3–36, 9, 30; Paul Oskar Kristeller, *Studies in Renaissance thought and letters III* (Rome: Edizioni di Storia e di Letteratura, 1993), 613–43 ('Between the Italian Renaissance and the French Enlightenment: Gabriel Naudé as an editor'), 617–18; Millet 224.

[322] In his *Apologie* of 1625 Naudé groups Montaigne with Seneca, Charron, and Vives as authors who have excelled in the formation of a free judgement, and calls him the French Seneca (Millet 205).

[323] Enrico Gamba and Vico Montebelli, *Le scienze a Urbino nel tardo Rinascimento* (Urbino: QuattroVenti, 1988), 101–2.

exceptions (Erasmus, Vives, Bacon) this new generation was predominantly a combination of French and Italian writers and intellectuals. Thus 'Clavius, Maurolic et Viette' were to be gathered 'auprès d'Euclide et Archimède'; 'Commines, Guicciardin, Sleidan, auprès de Tite-Live et Corneille Tacite'; 'l'Arioste, Tasso, du Bertas, auprès Homère et Virgile'; 'Montagne, Charon, Vérulam, auprès de Sénèque et Plutarque'.[324] In the inventory he made of his Parisian library, just before he left for Italy to serve the cardinal in Rome, these last three modern authors were indeed grouped together—in the same sub-collection of packeted books that contained his copy of Querenghi's *Alchimia*.[325]

In the very same year and city that Ginammi publishes his successful edition of the *Saggi*, Naudé publishes a *Bibliographia politica* (Venice, 1633) that qualifies and contextualizes the recommendation in specific terms. As we shall see, the nature of the recommendation explains the form taken by Ginammi's edition. It occurs in a treatise that describes an extra-curricular disciplinary trend away from slavish dependence on formal, especially scholastic Aristotelian ethical commentary. The move—within the context of continuing respect for non-scholastic Aristotelianism—is towards freer, because more inventive and systematic, reorganizations of the discipline of moral philosophy, including ethics and politics.[326] The principal classical precedents for the post-Aristotelian incorporation of practical new 'discoveries' and examples in moral discourse are Seneca and Plutarch, who together and respectively provide models of passionate abundance and order or methodical re-arrangement.[327]

While far from his books and other aids in Cervia, Naudé has been asked, as a librarian with knowledge of many books and writers, for a list of useful writers on politics by the learned priest and theologian Jacques Gaffarel. The context is the conduct of Franco-Venetian diplomatic relations. Gaffarel has been chosen by the French ambassador to Venice (Gaspard Coignet de La Thuillerie) to converse with him on important affairs, especially in his hours of leisure.

Naudé begins with a conventional outline of the reasons why the study of politics should begin with ethics and oeconomy, the other two parts of moral philosophy as traditionally conceived. Many of the ancient philosophers became known to posterity for the rule of their manners and the medicine of their most

---

[324] Millet 216.

[325] Bœuf, *La bibliothèque parisienne*, 355. Naudé collected his books in subject clusters and in this section of the 'livres qui sont empaquetez' (though it is not clear exactly how the books are packeted) we find several modern works of moral and political philosophy, including Palingenius's *Zodiacus vitae*, La Mothe Le Vayer's *Dialogues*, the 'Essais de Montaigne', the 'Oeuvres morales et politique[s]' of Francis Bacon, Epictetus, the 'Sagesse de Charon', Cardano's *De sapientia* and *De consolatione*—then Querenghi's *Alchimia* bound with Simplicius and Cardano (*De consolatione*, again). Some of these authors (Epictetus, Montaigne, Charron, Simplicius) were again grouped together in the section on moral philosophy in Naudé's *Bibliographia politica*. See Gabriel Naudé, *Bibliografia politica*, ed. Domenico Bosco (Rome: Bulzoni, 1997), 277.

[326] Jill Kraye, 'Conceptions of moral philosophy', in Daniel Garber and Michael Ayers (eds.), *The Cambridge history of seventeenth-century philosophy: Volume II* (Cambridge: Cambridge University Press, 1998), 1279–316, 1282.

[327] Schino, 'Incontri italiani di Gabriel Naudé', 16; Naudé, *Bibliografia politica*, ed. Bosco, 104–5/Gabriel Naudé, *Bibliographia politica* (Venice: Apud Franciscum Baba, 1633), sig. A8r. I add references to the 1633 edition because Bosco uses the 1642 edition for his text.

excellent souls—especially Socrates, who was the first to pass from the obscure study of nature to the contemplation of manners, and to found a *schola* thereon. Though many Greek sages followed and continued his teachings, and gained reputations for their moral qualities, none of them—with the sole exception of Aristotle—left anything written with order and method on this *disciplina*. What Aristotle did leave can be supplemented with Theophrastus, Seneca ('full of emotion and heat in all his books'), Plutarch ('calmer and better composed'), and others including Epictetus—and, of course, Biblical wisdom literature such as Proverbs and Ecclesiastes.[328]

Naudé then moves on to the moderns, dividing them between those who 'invent' the subject directly and those who comment—avoiding the corruptions of the scholastic method—upon Aristotle. It is not surprising to find the former category dominated by French and Italian teachers who wrote in both Latin and the vernacular as prelates, professors of moral philosophy or humane letters, lawyers, and office-holders: Odoardo Gualandi (Bishop then Archbishop of Cesena), Francesco Piccolomini (university professor), Alessandro Piccolomini (lecturer in moral philosophy at Padua, 1539, then an archbishop), Guillaume Du Vair (lawyer, *conseiller*, later bishop), Nicolas Coëffeteau (Dominican, lecturer in philosophy, preacher, ambassador, bishop), Pierre Charron (doctor of law and theological canon), Elie Pitard (*conseiller* and *aumônier*), Léonard Marandé (*greffier* in the *Cour des aides*, then *aumônier*, priest and anti-Jansenist theologian), and Tomasso Campanella (Dominican, philosopher, astrologer).[329]

Naudé's recommendation of Montaigne comes, then, in his treatment of a subsection of the group of modern authors he assembles for Gafferel who have reinvented a methodical ethics, as opposed to just commenting on ancient authors. This subsection consists of those clerical figures of various kinds who have offered their treatments not in Latin, but in the Italian and French vernaculars. He compares Alessandro Piccolomini, the author of an elegant 'institution' in Italian, with two very illustrious French prelates who had treated the same matter with similar elegance in French (Du Vair and Coëffeteau).

Almost in a parenthesis he then inserts his judgement that, in this company, Montaigne in his *Essais* ('in suis Tentamentis') is to be commended for *copia* of *sententiae*, for striking home more often in the manner of Seneca ('ad modum Senecae'), but found wanting in orderliness and elegance ('sic minus ordine et nitore praevalet'). In the same respect he judges the theological canon Charron wiser than Socrates, because he is the first modern to reduce wisdom to art, with an admirable method, with learning and judgement ('Socrate sapientior...quod sapientiae ipsius praecepta primus quod sciam admirabili prorsus methodo, doctrina, iuditio, in artem reduxerit'). Charron's book gives us Aristotle, Seneca, and Plutarch, but with something more divine ('ac divinius etiam aliquid') than any of the ancient or more recent authors. The subsection on those who have used the

[328] Naudé, *Bibliografia politica*, ed. Bosco, 98–105/Naudé, *Bibliographia politica*, 1633, sigs. A3r–7v [Gallica page 5/screen 6–page14/screen 15].

[329] Naudé, *Bibliografia politica*, ed. Bosco, 106–7/Naudé, *Bibliographia politica*, 1633, sig. A8r–v [Gallica page 15/screen 16–page 16/screen 17].

riches of the vernaculars to treat of moral philosophy ends with Pitard and Marandé. Four of the six discourses in Marandé's *Jugement des actions humaines* of 1624 had, in the manner of Charron, built material from the *Essais* into a more methodical philosophical framework.[330]

Naudé's passage describes the bibliographical and intellectual ideas that shape the nexuses of 'transpassage' of the French *Essais* to northeastern Italy through from the 1610s to the 1630s. The first of two important points concerns the primary discipline to which the *Essais* are understood to be contributing and the associated type of philosophical *persona* their author is understood to be fashioning. In modern histories of seventeenth-century philosophy, Charron and Montaigne are primarily grouped as sceptics in chapters on developments in epistemology, against the background of the *persona* of Pyrrho and the written tradition of Sextus Empiricus.[331]

Naudé, however, groups them with authors who are reinventing ethics—as one part of the tripartite discipline of moral philosophy (*ethica, oeconomica, politica*)— in the vernacular, against the background of the *personae* of philosophers in the post-Socratic tradition who 'became known to posterity for the rule of their manners and the medicine of their most excellent souls', and of the written traditions of Aristotle, Seneca, and Plutarch. We have seen on several occasions that to read and rewrite Montaigne in the Veneto at this moment was to do so in the company of texts such as Aristotle's *Nicomachean ethics* and Seneca's *Moral letters*.

The second important point concerns the nature of the practical philosophical culture in which Montaigne, via the fortunes of his work in northeastern Italy, participates. It centres on the *persona* of the priest-philosopher who both teaches and embodies a reinvented, more methodical, and applied form of moral philosophy, who interacts in civic life with the secular noble elite, and with scholars and bibliographers, offering physic for the soul.

We have encountered three different instances of this participation in one and the same year (1633): the performance of solitude by the *canonico*-philosopher and acknowledged imitator of Montaigne, Querenghi, at the reopening of the Accademia dei Ricovrati; Naudé's printed recommendation of the *Essais* to Gaffarel, a priest and philosopher involved at that moment in diplomacy, and possibly in the Accademia degli Incogniti; and the successful republication (after an aborted first attempt in 1629, just as the plague hit) of a close translation of the full French *Essais*, with methodical divisions and summaries, by a Jesuate friar.[332] But there are

[330] Naudé, *Bibliografia politica*, ed. Bosco, 106–7/Naudé, *Bibliographia politica*, 1633, sig. A8r–v [Gallica page 15/screen 16–page 16/screen 17]; Millet 224–5; Alan Boase, *The fortunes of Montaigne: a history of the 'Essays' in France, 1580–1669* (London: Methuen & Co., 1935), 195–203 (on Marandé), henceforward abbreviated as 'Boase'.

[331] So Montaigne and Charron are barely mentioned in Kraye, 'Conceptions of moral philosophy', but are central to Charles Larmore, 'Scepticism', in Daniel Garber and Michael Ayers (eds.), *The Cambridge history of seventeenth-century philosophy: Volume II* (Cambridge: Cambridge University Press, 1998), 1145–92.

[332] Gaffarel is not listed as a member of any academy on the British Library's online 'Database of Italian Academies' (<http://www.bl.uk/catalogues/ItalianAcademies/>), but Naudé ends the *Bibliographia* by saying that Gaffarel is in the 'most famous academy in the world'. See Naudé, *Bibliografia politica*, ed. Bosco, 188–9/Naudé, *Bibliographia politica*, 1633, sig. E9v [Gallica page 114/

also the instances of Sarpi's recommendation (less easy to date with any precision) of a new translation from the French *Essais* to his independent young noble Venetian friend Trevisan, and the French-speaking Flemish scholar Sohier's recommendation of a French copy to *canonico* Querengi in 1621.

Beyond these, and Naudé's other printed recommendations, we have encountered various nexuses of transmission of the *Essais* in northeastern Italy that are related to various degrees to the same trend: the presence of a copy of the Paris 1598 *Essais* in the library of the *natio Germanica iurista* at Padua; Davila's epistolary response (1620) to his receipt of a gift copy of Querenghi's *Alchimia*, which he describes as an imitation of his one-time French acquaintance's work; the presence, in an inventory of Naudé's Parisian library *c.*1630, of a French *Essais* in a cluster of packeted books on ethics and politics including Querenghi's *Alchimia*, Charron, and Bacon, amongst others; the presence, in an inventory of *c.*1631, of the 1602 French *Essais* in *scansia* 37 ('Oethica Oeconomonia et Politica') of the Duke of Urbino's library, formed from the late 1610s for the monks of the local order of the Minims ('Preti Chierici Minori Regolari del Crocefisso di Casteldurante'), alongside the 1590 bowdlerized Italian translation (see 1.3.10); Querenghi's formation, at the moment (1639–41) when he donated the majority of his books to the Dominican monastery at S. Agostino in Padua, of a personal, selective collection of 'most serious authors and fathers of wisdom' that included both Naselli's and Canini's translations of Montaigne, together with his own works.[333]

It might be argued that the legitimacy earned by the *Essais* during the 1620s as part of an international, Franco-Italian trend in moral philosophy, is double-edged. Though considered exemplary in the Senecan abundance and efficaciousness of their *sententiae* they are understood to be 'lacking' in *ordo* and *nitor*, as Davila already indicates in his letter to Querenghi upon receipt of the *Alchimia* in 1620. They need the accompaniment of a more elegant, more orderly exposition of the clerical kind offered by Pierre Charron's *De la sagesse*, the methodical 'companion'

screen 115]. There is one piece of evidence that this was likely to have been the Incogniti: Loredano (ed.), *Discorsi academici de' signori incogniti, havuti in Venetia* is dedicated to La Thuillerie, who Gaffarel was advising.

[333] For Querenghi's personal collection see Veronese Ceseracciu, 'La biblioteca di Flavio Querenghi', 198–213. Querenghi's personal library contained about 260 titles, with the largest proportion falling in the discipline of moral philosophy, including many of the authors and works mentioned by Naudé in his *Bibliographia*: editions and translations of, and commentaries upon Aristotle's *Nicomachean Ethics* and *Politics* (e.g. nos. 11, 14, 39, 50, 58, 76, 110 Muret on the *Ethics*, 173, 223); several editions of Seneca and Plutarch (nos. 4, 13, 30, 42, 53); editions of other ancients mentioned by Naudé including Epictetus and his commentators (no. 56); editions of moderns who either re-invented ethics in Latin or the vernacular (no. 29 Francesco Piccolomini; nos. 60, 72 Flavio Querenghi *Discorsi*; no. 94 Du Vair's *De la constance* in Italian; nos. 96 and 247 Lipsius *De Constantia*; no. 101 Flavio Querenghi *Alchimia*; no. 103 Flavio Querenghi *Introductio*; nos. 163 and 255 Bacon *Saggi morali*; 169 Montaigne *Saggi morali*; no. 210 Montaigne *Discorsi* trans. Naselli), or politics (nos. 33, 45, 177, 214; no. 246 Lipsius *Politica*; no. 237 Lipsius *Monita politica*); editions of miscellanous other works (nos. 73 d'Ossat's letters, 206 Canini's translation of de Refuge on the court). Ceseracciu does not identify the Italian translation of Du Vair (trans. Giovanni Paolo Tonsis, published by the Zanni in Cremona in 1619). For *scansie* 37–9 (moral philosophy) of the Duke of Urbino's library see 2.7.4. Bosco's edition of the *Bibliographia politica* has a convenient index (277–84) of all the authors mentioned, distributed under the subject and topic headings he uses.

to Montaigne for those beyond the reach of Roman Catholic regulation (Charron's work was placed on the Index in 1605). In this scheme, a new, more autonomous, more practical, and contemporary ethics is seen to find its foundations in abundant Seneca's and orderly Plutarch's departures from Aristotle and Plato, and in turn from abundant Montaigne's and orderly Charron's departures from Seneca and Plutarch.[334]

In the preface to the orderly, elegant exposition of the *Essais* published in two volumes by Marco Ginammi in 1633–4, the publisher justifies the work with a different evaluation of the very features used by some critics to condemn it. The description of the book as teachings in self-knowledge is transferred from the 1629 title page to Ginammi's address to the reader and expanded. Montaigne's *discorsi* offer all that 'a perfect philosophy' ('una perfetta Filosofia') makes desirable for us. Lancre, we may recall, had complained that Montaigne's thoughts were regulated neither by authoritative books nor by particular subjects, but simply followed the author's own 'conceptions'.[335]

Ginammi markets the book positively, using similar descriptive terms borrowed from 'various places' ('diversi luoghi') in which the author apologizes for his own text. For him it is valuable as a book of noble singularity, as a 'rare' commodity that all noble libraries had to have. From such a noble philosopher, who wrote capriciously, obliging his pen only to his *ingenium*, not to custom ('ha scritto di cappriccio obligando la penna al genio, non all'uso'), we have to accept the odd tasteless expression.[336] He doubtless knew, when financing such an expensive publication, that even prestigious collectors such as the Duke of Urbino had been investing in French copies.

However, it is important to realize that Ginammi was selling not just Montaigne's *Essais* in Italian, but what Ian Maclean has called an 'acte médiateur'. For in the learned book trade, as in intellectual life, mediation—whether by translation, commentary, or correction—on the part of professional interpreters (theologians, jurists, medics, humanists) and on the part of publisher-booksellers, was the order of the day.[337] It is this very order of things—the agency assumed by and attributed to professional interpreters and major publishers in nexuses of learning, and the relative patiency of the particular well-born reader-writer—that motivates Montaigne's intervention as an amateur in learned conversation.

It is all the more interesting, then, that Ginammi's *Saggi* are a perfect vernacular example of Maclean's *acte médiateur*: they self-consciously mediate the unmediated, uncensored Montaigne, for the Venetian edition is the work of—it is authored

[334] Millet 236; Lorenzo Bianchi, *Rinascimento e libertinismo: studi su Gabriel Naudé* (Naples: Bibliopolis, 1996), 143–8.

[335] Millet 201.

[336] Venice 1633, sig. a6r–v; Montaigne, *Apologia di Raimondo di Sebonda*, sig. a2r: 'questa Apologia di Raimondo di Sebonda…riputata singolare nel suo genere'. See also the dedication to David Spinelli in Venice 1633, sig. a2.

[337] Ian Maclean, 'L'Économie du livre érudit: le cas Wechel (1572-1627)', in Pierre Aquilon, Henri-Jean Martin, and François Dupuigrenet Desroussilles (eds.), *Le livre dans l'Europe de la Renaissance: actes du XXVIIIe Colloque international d'études humanistes de Tours* ([Paris]: Promodis, Éditions du cercle de la librairie, 1988), 230–9, 236.

by—the professional interpreter Canini and the publisher-bookseller Ginammi. It both realizes the terms in which the rarity of the *Essais* had been advertised to collectors by scholar-advisers in the Franco-Italian republic of letters and compensates for their principal perceived defect. The translator has adorned the text with most useful and necessary summaries of each chapter ('Sommarii ad ogni Capitolo come utilissimi, e necessarii'). From Ginammi's *bottega* one could now buy in two volumes the full, abundant *Essais* in Italian with *ordo* and *nitor*, with some of the *arte* that Davila had said Montaigne lacked.

Here, then, is another example of the way in which the documents of Montaigne's early heritage can be seen as the deposits of complex agency relations between participants positioned in particular nexuses as: noble reader-writers (Montaigne himself; Ginammi's readership of Paduan-Venetian patricians; Trevisan; Querenghi in his non-professional, 'academic' identity); professional interpreters (Naselli, Sarpi, Querenghi as professor of moral philosophy, Canini) and scholarly bibliographical advisers (Sohier, Naudé); privileged social and intellectual *patrons* (Cesare d'Este, Domenico Molino, David Spinelli, the Duke of Urbino, Antonio Querenghi); publisher-booksellers (Mamarello, Ginammi); classical fathers of wisdom (Aristotle as author of the *Nicomachean Ethics* and *Politics*, Seneca, Plutarch); and recent authors inventing the same topics (Lucinge and La Noue, Charron and Bacon).[338]

As an intellectual historian, one cannot simply recover 'a reading' of an author such as Montaigne without taking account of such nexuses of relations. In the next chapter we shall consider those surrounding another translation into a European vernacular that was much more successful than Ginammi's and Canini's, and that was likewise marketed as a rare commodity suitable for noble household libraries. First published in 1603, Florio's Montaigne would still be considered 'vendible' in 1657; it shaped the English reader-writer's use of the *Essais* throughout the first half of the seventeenth century.[339]

[338] The double inclusion of Flavio Querenghi in this list is meant to emphasize that these are positions in a particular nexus rather than fixed identities across all nexuses.
[339] Though there is more research to be done on the role of French copies of the *Essais* in seventeenth-century England. See John O'Brien, 'Montaigne, Sir Ralph Bankes and other English readers of the *Essais*', *Renaissance Studies*, 28 (2014), 377–91.

2.3

Learning Mingled with Nobility in Shakespeare's England

The arrival of Montaigne's *Essais* in early modern England is often identified with the introduction of sceptical free-thinking, whether of the safe and humane or the libertine and radical variety. Montaigne had had a sceptical crisis in writing the book (so Villey and his followers said), so when the book arrived in London its readers must have caught the same epistemological virus directly. We are told in one recent study, for example, that 'sceptical crises... were sweeping through the intelligentsia of London in 1608 in the wake of Florio's Montaigne'.[1]

There is no doubt that the translation stimulated much reflection on, for example, the topic of custom and its tyrannies.[2] This was due in no small part to the author, Samuel Daniel, of London 1603's most important paratext, which was retained for both the 1613 and 1632 editions. But as we heard in 1.4.1, Daniel saw the book as a preservative against the debilitating effects of a pre-existing crisis of learning rather than the cause of such a crisis. He described Montaigne as an intellectual knight-adventurer making bold sallies out to enfranchise the reader from the 'presse of writings' and from the tyrant custom.

If the influence of the text on sceptical currents of thought has commanded much attention, the agency relations typically indexed by the book itself have not. It is important to give proper prominence to the fact that the book and its author were involved by the translator in private household, quasi-diplomatic relations with three pairs of noblewomen (in the dedications to the three books of 1603), and with Queen Anna herself (1613).

In the 1613 edition, a book produced by a 'Gentleman of the French Kings Chamber' is taken by two gentlemen of the English Queen's privy chamber, Florio

[1] Rob Carson, 'Hearing voices in *Coriolanus* and early modern skepticism', in Graham Bradshaw, T. G. Bishop, and Peter Holbrook (eds.), *The Shakespearean international yearbook 6: special section, Shakespeare and Montaigne revisited* (Farnham: Ashgate, 2006), 140–69, 159. For a critique of this assumption, see William M. Hamlin, 'The Shakespeare-Montaigne-Sextus Nexus: A Case Study in Early Modern Reading', in Bradshaw, Bishop, and Holbrook (eds.), *The Shakespearean international yearbook 6*, 21–36.

[2] William M. Hamlin, 'Florio's Montaigne and the tyranny of "Custome": appropriation, ideology, and early English readership of the *Essayes*', *Renaissance Quarterly*, 63 (2010), 491–544. A revised version of this article has been incorporated as chapter 3 of William M. Hamlin, *Montaigne's English journey: reading the 'Essays' in Shakespeare's day* (Oxford: Oxford University Press, 2013). I am indebted to Hamlin's study—the most important we have of Florio's Montaigne and its readership—throughout this chapter, and the first half of 2.4.

and Daniel, and dedicated to her.[3] Montaigne had of course never been to England; his introduction into noble household society in Florio's paratexts is metaphorical. But there were clear, recent precedents for French authors on diplomatic missions whose books had been welcomed into English noble households, including the royal court, in tandem with their actual persons. Philippe Duplessis-Mornay came to the English court in 1577–8 to seek help for the Huguenots and befriended Philip Sidney; works of his were later translated by both Sidney and his sister the Countess of Pembroke.[4]

The parallel and the contrast with the French poet Du Bartas are still more instructive. Du Bartas visited the Scottish court in 1587 as an emissary promoting the possibility of a marriage between James VI and Catherine de Bourbon (after landing in England and acting briefly as a representative of Navarre there). He was personally welcomed by James, who became involved in translating his works (and vice versa). The literary and personal encounters between the monarch and the poet shaped the fortunes of the *Semaines*' reception in both England and Scotland. Joshua Sylvester's became the standard translation from 1605, and sealed the reputation of the Gascon poet as an English court author directly associated with the dedicatee, the King.[5]

Montaigne, by contrast, was metaphorically introduced as a foreign dignitary who befriended noblewomen in their households and courts; he became not the king's but their and (in Florio's 1613 edition) the Queen's author—as is most apparent when Daniel presents a play based partly on the *Essayes* to 'her Maiestie and her Ladies', in Oxford in August 1605 (see 2.3.8). Indeed, Florio's *Essayes* seeks the same kind of readership, and reading, as Sidney's *Arcadia*; like that work it is presented to an audience of ladies—led by one in particular (the Countess of Bedford)—whose 'pleasure and leasure' will not be misplaced or mis-employed in perusing it. He genders his translation female in the first dedication, before retreating to use of the neuter pronoun ('it').[6]

The English text's rhetorical, schematic style is Arcadian and Euphuistic, preparing it for admiring readers and imitators of the balanced phrases and amplificatory devices that originated in the vogue for Guevara and Spanish romance.[7] Daniel's

---

[3] Michel de Montaigne, *Essayes* (London: Melch. Bradwood for Edward Blount and William Barret, 1613), title page and sigs. A2r–4r.

[4] Mary Sidney Herbert, *The collected works Vol. 1: Poems, translations, and correspondence*, eds Margaret P. Hannay, Noel J. Kinnamon, and Michael G. Brennan (Oxford: Clarendon, 1998), 208–10.

[5] Peter Auger, 'The *Semaines*' dissemination in England and Scotland until 1641', *Renaissance Studies*, 26 (2011), 625–40, 634–5; Peter Auger, 'British responses to Du Bartas' *Semaines*, 1584–1641', unpublished doctoral dissertation (University of Oxford, 2012), part I, chap. 1.i.

[6] SCETI London 1603, p. R3r; Heidi Brayman Hackel, *Reading material in early modern England: print, gender, and literacy* (Cambridge: Cambridge University Press, 2005), 150–4. In the case of the *Arcadia* it is clear from the relatively high proportion of female ownership that it did circulate widely amongst the female audience to whom it was addressed (p. 159). Hamlin's studies of the extant copies of Florio's work have not yet explicitly addressed the extent of the female readership. For the gendering of Florio's work, see Georgianna Ziegler, 'En-gendering the subject: Florio's feminization of Montaigne's "Moy-mesmes"', *Montaigne Studies*, 8 (1996), 125–43.

[7] Frances A. Yates, *John Florio: the life of an Italian in Shakespeare's England* (Cambridge: Cambridge University Press, 1934), 225–34; Barry Taylor, 'Learning style from the Spaniards in sixteenth-century

idiom in his 1603 dedicatory poem to the English *Essayes*, shared by Florio in his prose dedications, is likewise rooted in the elite literary culture of Elizabethan humanistic romance. It is one indication that the relations mentioned in the third paragaph of this chapter centred not only on the construction and deconstruction of theories of knowledge, but on the private schooling and self-schooling of the gentry and nobility, and on aristocratic scenes of learned leisure—as would also be the case in Padua-Venice between the late 1610s and the early 1630s.[8]

Indeed, as we shall see in 2.3.4–5, Florio's translation originated in the chapter on the institution of young noblemen. The testing and implementing of various solutions for the training and cultivating of gentle selves, both male and female, via reading and writing and other entertainments and exercises, was the foundation of non-university practical philosophy in this period, while scenes of instruction were at the heart of post-Reformation English culture from page to stage. The problems surrounding the fashioning of gentlemen and gentlewomen in virtue—whether conceived in more classical or in more Calvinist terms—provided a central thread in the elite literary and dramatic culture of late Elizabethan England from Lyly's romances and plays of the late 1570s and 1580s to the works of Sidney, Spenser, and Shakespeare in the 1590s.[9]

So the performance of Florio's translation indexes household relations in which noblewomen and queens are educated to play enhanced roles in the patriarchal, courtly world of diplomacy, learning, and entertainment, especially where these involve use of the vernaculars. The precedent for this in 1590s England, aside from Queen Elizabeth's role in her own court, was the agency of the Countess of Pembroke in what Samuel Daniel calls his 'best Schoole' at Wilton, which (in literary terms) most famously produced the compositions and translations of the nobleman, Sir Philip Sidney.[10]

The process with which we are concerned throughout this chapter might be described, then, as the institutionalization, within the elite household, of the free or noble literate's reading, its actualization in conversation and action, and its

---

England', in S. K. Barker and Brenda Hosington (eds.), *Renaissance cultural crossroads: translation, print and culture in Britain, 1473–1640* (Leiden: Brill, 2013), 63–78.

[8] See 2.2.8–12.

[9] Corneanu, *Regimens of the mind*, 6–7; Kathryn M. Moncrief and Kathryn Read McPherson (eds.), *Performing pedagogy in early modern England: gender, instruction and performance* (Farnham: Ashgate, 2011); Jeffrey Andrew Dolven, *Scenes of instruction in Renaissance romance* (Chicago: University of Chicago Press, 2007). Corneanu joins the 'recent challenge to the "epistemological paradigm" in historical understanding, according to which early modern philosophy was primarily confronted with the epistemological question of the justification of knowledge, following the historical event of the challenge of scepticism'. In her view, this fails to appreciate that for early moderns themselves 'the pursuit of philosophical inquiry was organised by the idea of leading an exemplary life', a matter of 'practical regimens and formative disciplines for shaping the individuals engaged in the philosophical or scientific life'. I concur, but would add that these regimens were often specifically designed for the gentle and noble class, and were mediated in important ways by specific uses of reading and writing.

[10] Samuel Daniel, *A panegyrike congratulatory delivered to the Kings most excellent maiestie at Burleigh Harrington in Rutlandshire.… Also certaine epistles. With a defence of ryme, heeretofore written, and now published by the author* (London: Valentine Simmes for Edward Blount, 1603), sig. E8v [ESTC S107347].

commercialization and theatricalization in print and on the stage.[11] With respect to the relationship between reading and writing, we shall see that reading or 'lecture' is understood as an informal verbal or conversational extension of a particular read-aloud text, or of pre-digested texts, which may then itself be written down— whether by a noble reader-writer or by one of their servants or gentleman friends. The noble household school—its learned servants and tutors, its forms of education and leisure, its outcomes in the literary and behavioural productions of its masters and mistresses—was conceived in opposition to more standard pedagogical relations between a schoolmaster in a classroom and a pupil rote-learning Latin grammar.

The hunt was on for alternative, more suitable cultures of extra-curricular instruction and counsel, rooted in the real-life experience of the gentry and nobility and in the production of literature that would appeal to them. The English Montaigne was introduced in this context as a custodian of gentlemanly, experience-based, non-pedantic uses of books, learning, and knowledge. These centrally included the exercise of noble liberty of judgement and of satirical wit at the expense of tyrannical customs and fashions. But it was never quite clear that these uses were in safe hands, that the experience could be exemplary, or that the outcomes would be virtuous. Even Florio was unsure about his author, comparing his text to the perilous labyrinths which romantic heroes were required to traverse.

2.3.1 THE PARATEXTS TO FLORIO'S MONTAIGNE

The three editions (1603, 1613, 1632) of Florio's *Essayes* were vital in shaping the seventeenth-century English reception of Montaigne, turning his work into a resource—like Sidney's *Arcadia*—for the non-institutional, active reader-writer, studying vernacular texts in private, alone or with the facilitation of learned servants.[12] So, it is important to take account of two important facts—already touched upon in 1.4.1—that are revealed in the paratexts to the first edition of 1603, together with a third that is but half-revealed.

The first is that Montaigne was perceived to have deliberately hidden the traces of his formation and activities as a reader-writer of 'authors'. Florio understood the French work to provide the encrypted key to the educative formation of a contemporary orator and statesman comparable with Quintilian's imagined orator, with Crassus and Antonius in Cicero's *On the orator*, and, by implication, with contemporary Elizabethan patrons such as Sir Edward Wotton, the originator of the translation.

---

[11] For a compatible approach to a similar topic undertaken within the framework of American comparative literary studies, see the chapter on 'Institutional authority' in Hassan Melehy, *The poetics of literary transfer in early modern France and England* (Farnham: Ashgate, 2010), which begins with *Essais* I 25, and argues that Montaigne's book 'extends reading and writing beyond the institutions that have conventionally restricted them; hence it moves away from a strict delineation of masculinity and femininity [in relation to the educative context of the aristocratic household]' (146).

[12] The case is made with ample evidence in Hamlin, *Montaigne's English journey*. On readers as writers in the case of Sidney's *Arcadia*, see Brayman Hackel, *Reading material*, 156–95.

The encryption lies in Montaigne's manner and matter of speech, the particular kind of oratorical eloquence he brings, which, despite doubts, Florio ultimately (on Sir Edward Wotton's say) endorses. What makes Montaigne very different from Cicero's orators is the fact that he can speak in an extravagant and satirical manner, and on topics such as women and sex, which makes it harder for him to win friends. He is a wit. As we heard in 1.4.1, he can seem 'capriccious,…opiniative…paradoxicall…sometimes extravagant, often od-crocheted, and ever selfe-conceited to write of himselfe out of himselfe'.[13]

In the epistle 'To the curteous Reader' Florio alludes directly to the introduction to the second book of Cicero's dialogue, where Cicero reminds his brother that, when they were boys, sophists sought to divert them from their father's prescribed course of learning by disseminating the belief that Crassus in his early education had just dabbled with learning (*doctrina*), and that Antonius had had no instruction (*eruditio*) at all. The two famous orators colluded with this misinformation because, for political reasons, one (Crassus) wished to be seen to be looking down, as a Roman, on foreign Greek learning, while the other (Antonius) thought that his speeches would be more acceptable to Romans if they believed he had never studied at all. Yet the two brothers could call witnesses from their own family, where they were being taught Crassus's favourite subjects by teachers he had befriended, that he could speak Greek perfectly, and that he could propound upon any topic by way of inquiry, handle any matter. Likewise, they knew Antonius was always in conversation with learned men on his travels, and in his speech showed that there were no studies of which he was ignorant.[14]

So the classical orators dissimulated their learning for public relations reasons, and refused in conversation to reveal the art and method behind their philosophical formations. Florio finds that his orator Montaigne does exactly the same in writing:

> [I]n this specially finde I fault with my maister, that as Crassus and Antonius in Tullie, the one seemed to contemne, the other not to know the Greeks, whereas the one so spake Greeke as he seemed to know no other tongue: the other in his travells to Athens and Rhodes had long conversed with the learned Græcians: So he [Montaigne], writing of himselfe, and the worst rather than the best, disclaimeth all memorie, authorities, or borrowing of the ancient or moderne; whereas in course of his discourse he seemes acquainted not onely with all, but no other but authours; and could out of question like Cyrus or Cæsar call any of his armie by his name and condition.[15]

As a *noble d'épée*, like Cyrus or Caesar, Montaigne appropriately commands a copious arsenal of textual authorities, but does not want to admit to having studied them. It is not difficult to agree that he did indeed dissimulate in this respect in the *Essais*, as we shall see in 2.3.4 (in the case of I 25). Yet, as Florio goes on to say on the same page: 'Essayes are but mens school-themes pieced together; you might as wel say, several texts. Al is in the choise and handling'. And as Montaigne himself

---

[13] SCETI London 1603, p. R2v.
[14] SCETI London 1603, p. A5v; Cicero, *On the orator*, 2.1.
[15] SCETI London 1603, p. A5v.

says, his text represents '[w]hat I discourse according to my selfe, not what I believe according unto God, with a laycall [i.e. laical] fashion, and not a clericall manner; yet ever most religious; As children propose their essayes, instructable, not instructing.'[16]

So, Montaigne has been schooled in the learning that turns study of authors and conversation with learned men into speech or compositions, in this case 'writing of himselfe'. The *Essayes* are a continuation of this schooling in adulthood. They are a nobleman's virtuoso performance of reading and writing—'mens school-themes'. The performance is a rhetorical one: we observe how he chooses his matter and disposes or judges—handles—it in a self-consciously 'laycall', not 'clericall' fashion.

But such observation is difficult because, like Crassus and Antonius, he wants to cover his traces. He gives no citations and speaks in an extravagantly digressive way, leaving Florio and his assistants with the task of translating, of bringing forth the learning encrypted in the author's speech (as Cicero does with Crassus and Antonius in *On the orator*). This requires a heroic effort; the translators or inter-preters are like the heroes of a chivalric romance. One assistant was to Florio 'in this inextricable laberinth like Ariadnes threed... in these darke-uncouth wayes, a cleare relucent light'—the Italian's only help in dissolving the knots in the text. The other drew all the citations that Montaigne refused to name like 'bugge-beares' out of 'their dennes'.[17]

The second fact is that noble reader-writers of the early modern period, unlike the free literates of Petrucci's late medieval period, do not do all the manual labour of actually reading and digesting, annotating and explicating texts for themselves. The Italian's work is the outcome of his reading and translating of the *Essais* with and for noble pupils as a tutor in elite family service—a profession he inherited from his father Michael Angelo Florio.[18] It is they who are reading the *Essais* in private, but with his and other servants' facilitation.

The translation is the product of these relations. Indeed, Florio describes the translation metaphorically as a female foreign language tutor whom he has taught English and helped into service with the Countess of Bedford and others; she in turn is described as commanding him (Florio, her servant) to complete it, and as supervising and encouraging him in the work, and supplying him with the above-mentioned assistants.[19] Her role in so doing is, again, implicitly modelled in the second dedication on that of the Countess of Pembroke in the household school at Wilton, where she commanded various people, including her brother, to write.[20]

Florio, then, translated the *Essais* as someone in service, charged with facilitating his female superiors' private household formation in learning and virtue. This for-mation was gendered, for it was in turn geared to the protection and preservation

[16] I 56, NP341–2/BVH Paris 1595, p. 205/SCETI London 1603, p. 175.
[17] SCETI London 1603, p. A3r.
[18] Yates, *John Florio*, 7–8. Here I am following on from the preliminary discussion in 1.4.1.
[19] SCETI London 1603, pp. A2r–3r.
[20] Sidney Herbert, *The collected works Vol. 1*, 12–14.

of the reputations of noble male relatives, and the education of noble male children in a civilized household—as the Countess of Pembroke preserved the literary legacy of her brother (Philip Sidney), even after death, and educated her son, William Herbert, the future Earl of Pembroke.

This is most apparent in the dedication to the second book of London 1603, when Florio uses passages in Plutarch's *Lives* to compare his patronesses Lady Penelope Rich and Lady Elizabeth Manners, Countess of Rutland (née Sidney), to two Cornelias of ancient Rome. As quasi-Roman wives and mothers, Florio's patronesses' qualities of learning and virtue serve them to take joy in their own nobly born young scholars (i.e. their sons), to invite learned and virtuous strangers—even 'forraine Princes'—into their households, to drive them (partly through their mastery of languages) to admiration, and to bring their husbands an invaluable dowry of 'Nobilitie, Learning, Language, Musicke...an uncurious gravitie, and all-accomplish't vertue'.[21] This is the formation, as we shall see in 2.3.7, that would be satirized so ruthlessly by Ben Jonson in the figure of Lady Would-Be.

But the reason the dedicatees are paired is of course that they were the 'friend' (i.e. publicly acknowledged mistress) and daughter of the most learned and literarily productive nobleman-soldier of the Elizabethan age, Sir Philip Sidney. This is the occasion for Florio to acknowledge that even though he praises Montaigne as 'the greatest wit without example' in 'Essayes', of which he was the first author (as Homer was the first author of epic verse), Sidney's achievement in the 'perfect-unperfect' *Arcadia* remains the incomparable archetype of noble literary achievement. There then follows his much-discussed defence of the 1590 *Countess of Pembrokes Arcadia* over the 1593 hybrid version.[22]

How could Florio's second-hand work, a translation, even come near to Sidney's original invention? Well, that 'Worthie' (Sidney) himself divinely translated part of Duplessis-Mornay and Du Bartas from French, so though we (Florio and his patronesses) 'more meanely do in meaner workes...where our Protonotaries doe holde the chaire, let us poore Secondaries not be thrust out of doores'. In passing, Florio nods to the fact that he has actually seen the Sidney translation of Du Bartas, and to the potential agency of the two Sidney-related women in seeing it into print: 'which good Ladies, be so good to all, as all this age may see, and after-ages honor'.[23]

The whole point of this, of course, is to establish the Countess of Rutland's *Essayes*, the Lady Rich's *Essayes*, and so on, as worthy secondaries to the acknowledged protonotaries, the *Arcadia* (though not in the Countess of Pembroke's hybrid version) and Sidney's own translations from the French, now in the custody of the female protectors of his legacy. Even though performed at one remove,

---

[21] SCETI London 1603, pp. R2r–v.

[22] Yates, *John Florio*, 199–204; Helen Moore, 'Sir Philip Sidney and the *Arcadias*', in Mike Pincombe and Cathy Shrank (eds.), *The Oxford handbook of Tudor literature, 1485–1603* (Oxford: Oxford University Press, 2009), 637–51.

[23] SCETI London 1603, p. R3r; H. R. Woudhuysen, *Sir Philip Sidney and the circulation of manuscripts, 1558–1640* (Oxford: Clarendon Press, 1996), 235–6.

insofar as they are translations done for the mistress and daughter (not the sister) of the archetypal noble English patron-author, they are still literary compositions in the school of Sidney, performed in household schools modelled on his—perhaps displacing his, as the Countess of Bedford is implicitly displacing the Countess of Pembroke. One tutor of the Countess of Bedford's brother, James Cleland, would read Florio's praise of Montaigne's text and appropriate it without acknowledgement as his own praise of Sidney's *Arcadia*, thereby confirming the association between the two texts.[24]

The problem is that Florio's author, his 'prototype', on occasion speaks like a 'Satyrizing censor' on the subject of women. Florio even compares him in this respect to that 'dog-Satyrist' of ancient Rome, Juvenal, who 'causelesse barks, bites, and is bitter, even to deprave that untaintable Cornelia [mother of the Gracchi]' in *Satire* 6. Much of the text of the dedications to books 2 and 3 becomes a dialogue—it is a characteristic, as we shall see, of the English Montaigne that he gives rise to dialogue—between the translator and his satirizing censor on the subject of women's nobility and learning.[25] It is likely this is based on discussions that took place while Florio was reading the French *Essais* with his noblewomen pupils.

So Florio engages his author in relation to a particular passage in III 3 on a topical subject that was very close to his heart: the institution of young noblewomen in learning, including the question of their part in books and in dispersing their knowledge of books abroad. On the one hand, Montaigne suggests that the learned and learned advisers possess the ears of ladies with scholarly books so as better to govern them; if they stick to their own natural 'riches' they will over-rule school learning. On the other hand, he prescribes a conventionally limited curriculum for them, while using Juvenal *Satire* 6, mid-discourse, to declare them 'learned...in copulation':

> The learned stumble willingly on this blocke: making continuall muster and open show of their skill, and dispersing their bookes abroad: And have in these dayes so filled the closets, and possessed the eares of Ladyes, that if they retaine not their substance, at least they have their countenance: using in all sorts of discourse and subject how base or popular soever, a newe, an affected and learned fashion of speaking and writing.
>
> Hoc sermone pavent, hoc iram, gaudia, curas,
>
> Hoc cuncta effundunt animi secreta, quid ultra?
>
> Concumbunt docte.
>
> They in this language feare, in this they fashion
>
> Their joyes, their cares, their rage, their inward passion;
>
> What more? they learned are in copulation. (Iuven. sat. 6. 189)
>
> And alledge *Plato* and Saint *Thomas* for things, which the first man they meete would decide as well, and stand for as good a witnesse. Such learning as could not enter into their minde, hath staid on their tongues. If the well-borne will give any credit unto me, they shall be pleased to make their own and naturall riches to prevaile and be of

---

[24] James Cleland, *Hērō-paideia, or, The institution of a young noble man* (Oxford: Joseph Barnes, 1607), sig. T4v.

[25] SCETI London 1603, p. 2R2v.

worth:...When I see them [women] medling with Rhetoricke, with Law, and with Logicke, and such like trash, so vaine and unprofitable for their use, I enter into feare that those who advise them to such things, doe it that they may have more law to governe them under that pretence. For what other excuse can I devise for them? It is sufficient, that without us, they may frame, or roule the grace of their eyes, unto cheerefulnesse, unto severity, and unto mildnesse: and season a 'No' with frowardnesse, with doubt and with favour; and require not an interpreter in discourses made for their service. With this learning they command without controule, and over-rule both Regents and Schooles. Yet if it offend them to yeeld us any preheminence, and would for curiosity sake have part in bookes also: Poesie is a study fit for their purpose, being a wanton, ammusing, subtill, disguised, and pratling Arte; all in delight, all in shew, like to them-selves. They may also select divers commodities out of History. In Morall Philosophy they may take the discourses which enable them to judge of our humours, to censure our conditions, and to avoid our guiles and treacheries; to temper the rashnesse of their owne desires, to husband their liberty: lengthen the delights of life, gently to beare the inconstancy of a servant, the peevishnesse or rudenesse of a husband, the importunity of yeares, the unwelcomnesse of wrinkles, and such like minde-troubling accidents. Loe here the most and greatest share of learning I would assigne them.[26]

Learned books are everywhere in ladies' closets and in their ears—this is the 'presse of writings' Daniel complains about in the dedicatory poem. But they do not know how to use this learning, which gives rise to an affected fashion of speaking and writing, as they fall into superficial citation of authorities such as Plato and Aquinas.

Montaigne's caricature of the superficially learned woman would shortly walk onto the English stage as Jonson's Lady Would-Be (see 2.3.7). The Frenchman reacts to this trend by assigning women a share in humane learning—the arts of poetry and love, moral philosophy and history—that is analogous (at least in terms of the humanistic disciplines mentioned) to the share he assigns himself in II 10. He just differentiates (from the perspective of the conventional gender politics of the time) the uses to which this share is put by men and women. Women should only read books for the kinds of knowledge they actually need, and which they already naturally have: knowledge of the art of love, of the constancy needed to live a long life in the household, and so on.

Florio replies directly to his satirizing censor in the third dedication, perhaps punning as he does so on the name of one of the dedicatees of the second book (Lady Penelope Rich):

Nor do I well brooke...even this Satyrizing censor my prototype [Montaigne], that he after him in this your part affordes you small share of Rhetorique, Logique, Law; whose tongue to him is Rhetorique, reason Logique, and commandement Law. Your other perfections ô let him not draw downe to imperfection. If you by them may rule Regents; more may you do it, if you have more perfections. In Poesie, in Historie, yea in Philosophy if you have good allowance, why should you have any limites?...What

[26] III 3, NP862–4/BVH Paris 1595, bk. III, pp. 24–5/SCETI London 1603, pp. 494–5. 'Iuven. sat. 6. 189' appears as a marginal note (not in parenthesis) in London 1603.

neede you to enquire but what you neede? You are rich and may require such ornaments as fitte your state.... Woulde not your noble Husbandes, even in house-affaires, dislike to speake to you, or you to them, by a trouchman? How then would you like it in strange matters to talke with a Stranger by an interpreter? How can you knowe his sufficiencie? How dare you trust his faithfulnesse? Tenne to one he knowes not, or shoulde not knowe what he speakes-of: or more, or lesse, or worse hee expresseth, one or both. And why should men, more then you, talke with the dead, the truest, and take counsell of Bookes, the best Counsellours?[27]

Florio picks up Montaigne's acknowledgement that women should not need an interpreter in discourses produced for their service to push back—if only a little—the limits his author places on female learning. The ability to read books in foreign languages directly indexes the ability to converse with important strangers and to assess their 'sufficiencie' and 'faithfulnesse'—in exactly the way Florio assesses that of Montaigne in the course of the dedications. Noblewomen certainly played roles as intermediaries and information brokers, and served in informal diplomatic capacities in Elizabethan England—if in a secondary, gendered fashion. A prominent example from the early part of the reign is Lady Mary Sidney's role in Elizabeth's marriage negotiations with the Spanish ambassador Alvaro de Quadra—a role which required spoken Italian.[28]

Florio had in mind here a pragmatic role for noblewomen in the entertainment of diplomatically important figures such as Du Bartas and Duplessis-Mornay in noble households. He and unspecified noble ladies—perhaps including Lord Treasurer Buckhurst's daughter Lady Mary Neville—were involved in entertaining the Venetian representative Scaramelli at Buckhurst's Horsley residence in September 1603.[29] But there remain limits to what Florio himself is advocating, and it is ultimately more the Juvenilian tone than the content of Montaigne's prescriptions that he contests.

The relevant Plutarchan sources on the two Cornelias make Florio's point about the institution of noblewomen still clearer. Cornelia, a widow and the daughter of Metellus Scipio, married Pompey. She 'was properly learned, could play well on the harpe, was skilfull in musicke and geometrie, and tooke great pleasure also in philosophie, and not vainely without some profit'. In terms of her conversation, she was 'very modest and sober of behavior, without brawling and foolish curiositie'; her father 'was a noble man, both in bloud, and life'. Her role in Pompey's life is companion to his son, custodian of his reputation, and mourner of his death.[30]

Cornelia, daughter of Scipio Africanus, widow of Tiberius Sempronius Gracchus, is described in North's English translation, as a 'noble Ladie' who 'loved

[27] SCETI London 1603, p. 2R2v.
[28] James Daybell, 'Gender, politics and diplomacy: women, news and intelligence networks in Elizabethan England', in Robyn Adams and Rosanna Cox (eds.), *Diplomacy and early modern culture* (Basingstoke: Palgrave Macmillan, 2011), 101–19; Natalie Mears, 'Politics in the Elizabethan privy chamber: Lady Mary Sidney and Kat Ashley', in James Daybell (ed.), *Women and politics in early modern England, 1450–1700* (Farnham: Ashgate, 2004), 67–82, 70.
[29] The National Archives, Public Record Office, SP 99/2 fols. 157–8, 183, 184.
[30] Plutarch, *The lives of the noble Grecians and Romanes*, trans. Thomas North (London: Thomas Vautroullier and John Wight, 1579), sig. 3L5v.

ever to welcome straungers'. She kept a 'very good house, and therefore had alwayes great repaire unto her, of GRÆCIANS and learned men: besides, there was no king nor Prince, but both received giftes from her, and sent her againe'. Those who frequented her would hear her report the deeds and manner of her father's life, and wonder to hear her tell, without grief and with quasi-masculine virtue, of the acts and deaths of her sons—'to be noblie borne, and vertuouslie brought up, doth make men temperatly to disgest sorow'.[31]

For this Cornelia was known first and foremost as mother of the Gracchi (her sons Tiberius and Gaius). After the death of her husband, she had taken upon herself the rule of her house and children, 'led such a chast life, was so good to her children, and of so noble a minde', that everyone thought Tiberius a wise man for having left her behind him. She refused to remarry and dedicated herself to the education of Tiberius and Gaius. They were 'so carefully brought up, that they being become more civill, and better conditioned, then any other ROMANES in their time: every man judged, that education prevailed more in them, then nature'—both 'happely borne to be valiant, to be temperate, to be liberall, to be learned, and to be nobly minded'.[32]

Florio's dedications, then, are all about the arrival and use of strange books, languages, and servants in noble households focused on the institution of young noblewomen and of young noblemen. The French stranger Montaigne is brought into an Italianate literary environment already populated by authors such as Tasso and Ariosto, with classical authors such as Cicero and Plutarch in the background. What is striking about Florio's paratexts is just how often he steals—or, rather, borrows (as citations are given)—from Montaigne's and his Italian authors' texts in the course of his own conversations with his aristocratic dedicatees. These authors provide material for scenes of dialogue with and involving such noble patrons. As we shall see, in England in the early years of the seventeenth century, Montaigne is very much an author to steal from—much of the time without acknowledgement—if one is composing such dialogues, whether in pedagogical or theatrical contexts.

The home-educated Lord of Montaigne is appropriate for the environment described in the dedications because learning is a noble family affair. In the case of Lady Mary Neville, for example:

> I knowe not, if native inclination, proceeding from a Father, in wisedome none greater; a Mother, in goodnesse none better; or informing instruction, applied by his prudent direction, used by her kind discretion, received by your [Lady Mary's] quicke ingenuitie, or confirming example of both them above all example, and your noble husband excellently qualified, exquisitely languaged, and your as learned as well graced brothers; or all these in concourse have made-uppe such accomplishment, as againe I knowe not, if you, or wee all, owe more to them for you.[33]

---

[31] Plutarch, *The lives of the noble Grecians and Romanes*, sig. 4F3r.
[32] Plutarch, *The lives of the noble Grecians and Romanes*, sig. 4D6r.
[33] SCETI London 1603, p. 2R2v.

The Sackvilles and Nevilles are shining examples of the noble family transmission of learning in households that, unlike public educational institutions, see father and mother, brother and sister, instructing and being instructed in the same spaces. Florio is promoting the idea that unofficial household institutions of this kind involved women more in the transmission of learning.

This is of course true relative to public and charitable institutions. But the dedications are also, from Florio's indignant point of view, about the household hierarchy that downgrades female learning. For, from another perspective, it might be said that Florio was himself stuck lower down this hierarchy, reading Italian and French books with young noblewomen. The young John Harrington was Latin-literate; his sister the Countess was not. Florio nevertheless uses his dedications to argue for greater recognition of her and the other ladies' learned skills and virtues. His work both testifies to and attempts to consolidate the potential overlap in household nexuses between the otherwise distinct cultures of male and female learning.

As we shall see in more detail in 2.3.4, the chapter which originated the fully Englished *Essayes* (I 25) offered both a direct household method for Latin-learning, and an alternative, vernacular route to philosophical virtue. Montaigne's work self-consciously straddles vernacular and Latin-literate learning, not least by including so many citations in Latin, some translated or paraphrased in the accompanying text, some not. This does mean that to read and translate it one needs Latin. Florio draws attention to his own exclusion from the Latin-literate world in his epistle 'To the curteous reader', referring to '*Quintilians* Orator; a learned man I warrant him, for I understand him never a word'.[34]

But the Countess was able to provide him with Latin-literate assistants. He did not undertake the work alone, but as part of a group of tutors and advisers who were all serving the same noble households in different capacities. One, Samuel Daniel, Florio's brother-in-law, was in a similar position to himself. Although there is no evidence Daniel had a direct role in the execution of the translation, he composed the most important paratext, he served as tutor to a young noblewoman in this milieu who read the *Essayes* (Lady Anne Clifford), and he wrote works in 1603–5 that drew heavily on Florio's text.

Indeed, it is important to see Florio and Daniel as closely associated reader-writers of Montaigne's text with and for noble patrons. Florio translated Montaigne and taught specific Italian authors, and Daniel wrote literary and dramatic works that borrowed from Montaigne and the same Italian authors, in the same milieu, and for some of the same patrons, in the same early years of the seventeenth century. Ben Jonson wrote words for the Globe stage that alluded to this fact in 1606.[35]

The two assistants actually provided by the Countess were Florio's superiors, and were more closely associated with the male, Latin-literate sphere of the household's patriarchal intellectual world. 'Maister' Theodore Diodati was directly involved as a tutor in the education of the son and heir of the Harrington-Russell household,

---

[34] SCETI London 1603, p. A5r.
[35] These points will all be developed and referenced in the sections that follow.

the young John Harrington: 'like Aristotle to Alexander, he...in all good learning,...doeth with all industrious attention, instruct, direct, adorne that noble, hopefull, and much promising spirit of your beloved brother and house-heire Maister John Harrington'.[36]

His other assistant, 'Maister Doctor' Matthew Gwinne, described by Florio as his La Boétie, as an orator and a poet, a philosopher and a medic, was a Gresham Professor of Physic and a senior medical adviser to the nobility, as well as a neo-Latin dramatist.[37] It was he who assumed the Italianate identity of 'Il Candido' in paratexts and who undertook to source—and probably to translate—all Montaigne's citations of Latin prose and all quoted poetry in foreign languages. No one but he, says Florio, could have 'quoted so divers Authors, and noted so severall places'.[38] Gwinne read the French text in order to re-invent—to quote and note—the *loci* used by Montaigne.

So, although after publication of the translation Florio went on to become reader in Italian to Queen Anna, and both he and Daniel grooms of her privy chamber, Diodati and especially Gwinne had much more distinguished careers as university intellectuals who also saw court and private household service. When Florio talks of his noble patronesses receiving learned and virtuous strangers into their households he must have had Diodati in mind as the latest in a line of intellectual visitors to Scottish and English households and courts that included Du Bartas and Duplessis-Mornay.

The son, like Florio, of an Italian protestant exile, Diodati was born in Geneva in 1573, and was the father of the more famous Charles Diodati, friend of Milton. He is very likely to be the source of Florio's information about Genevan editions of the *Essais*. He matriculated in medicine at Leiden University on 3 August 1594, where he remained until 1598, when he accepted the invitation to become John Harrington's tutor in England. By 1609 he was tutor and physician to the royal children.[39]

Gwinne had accompanied Fulke Greville on his travels in 1587–8, having been released from St John's College, Oxford, at Francis Walsingham's request. He had also accompanied Sir Henry Unton on his ambassadorship to France in 1596, and was to become a successful court physician under James I, as well as holder of various public offices and lectureships as a physician.[40] Gwinne delivered two lectures in Michaelmas term 1598 and Hilary term 1599, on the occasion of his being elected foundation Professor of Physic at Gresham College in London.[41]

Where Florio's dedications place the *Essais* in the courtly and familial world of household learning, these lectures place them in the international world of neo-Latin scholarship. The second lecture begins on the theme of the passing of this

---

[36] SCETI London 1603, p. A3r.   [37] See the following paragraphs for references.

[38] SCETI London 1603, p. A3r.

[39] William Birkin, 'Diodati, Theodore (1573–1651)', *ODNB*.

[40] Warren Boutcher, 'Gwinne, Matthew (Londres 1558–1627)', *Dictionnaire*; Iain Wright, 'Gwinne, Matthew (1558–1627)', *ODNB*.

[41] These were first printed as *Orationes duæ* (London, 1605). The date of the lectures is established in John Ward, *The lives of the professors of Gresham College* (London: John Moore for the Author and W. Innys et al., 1740), pp. 261–2.

brief life ('de vita brevi transigenda'), citing St Paul, Hippocrates, Seneca, and Plato. Moving from these to the 'neoterical' authors, Gwinne offers first a quotation from Marc-Antoine Muret's *Annotationes in Seneca*, and then Montaigne (French verses) 'most cleverly from the inventions, expositions, and inquiries' ('de inventionibus, interpretationibus, inquisitionibus scitissimè *Sieur de Montaigne*').[42] The verses are amongst those he was not able to quote and note, as they were by Montaigne's obscure friend La Boétie.

This extremely significant early English reference to the most clever Seigneur de Montaigne's work is another indication (alongside, in the English context, the acquisition of a copy of Paris 1598 for the Bodleian library by 1605) that the *Essais* had 'crossed over' into the world of neo-Latin scholarship. It offers three Latin clues—*inventiones, interpretationes, inquisitiones*—which indicate that Gwinne understood the *Essais* to be an extremely elegant work of miscellaneous *commentatio*. This understanding is compatible with Florio's statements in his epistle to the reader that Montaigne's worth 'then being so eminent, his wit so excelent, his inventions so rare, his elocutions so ravishing', his patrons' 'pleasure and leasure' will not 'be mis-placed or mis-employed in perusing him'; that there are in the French work 'so pleasing passages, so judicious discourses, so delightsome varieties, so perswasive conclusions, such learning of all sortes, and above all, so elegant a French stile' that he must be recognized as the 'greatest wit without example'.[43] With this statement, Florio backs Gournay's estimation—in her preface of 1595— of Montaigne's status as a patron-author.

Still more important than the careers of the team behind the translation is the third, half-revealed fact we can glean from the dedications. We saw in 2.2.9 that the naturalization of Montaigne as a citizen of Padua-Venice began with Sarpi's commissioning of a translation of one chapter (I 27) whose theme, *amicizia*, proved to be indicative of his role there. Florio began his work with one unnamed chapter, which a combination of textual and circumstantial evidence proves beyond reasonable doubt to be 'De l'institution des enfans' (I 25).

This chapter starts with Montaigne dissimulating his learning, in the manner of Crassus and Antonius, but does then go on to reveal both how he was educated in Latin and how he would advise a Countess to have her own young noble son edu-cated in the philosophical pursuit of freedom and virtue. Florio was commissioned to undertake the translation, in the first instance, by 'Noble and vertuous Sir Edward Wotton', most likely in relation to the education of his eldest son Pickering Wotton, who was born in 1587. He completed the chapter in the Countess's house

---

[42] Matthew Gwinne, *Orationes duæ* (London: Richard Field, 1605), sigs. C6v–7r. The two lines of French verse ('Toursjours l'eau va dans l'eau, et tousjours est ce/ Mesme ruisseau, et tousjours eau diverse') are extracted from a longer citation of Montaigne's (from La Boétie) to be found towards the beginning of III 13, 'De l'experience' (NP1115). In the same printed lecture the marginal annotations record allusions to I 19 (sig. D2r) and II 7 (sig. E1v). It is tempting to suggest that the prominence of Montaigne in the second lecture and his absence from the first may indicate that Gwinne started reading the *Essais* at Christmas 1598–9, which may be when he first started sourcing and translating Montaigne's citations for Florio. It could also be, however, that, in contrast with the first lecture, the moral theme chosen for the second lecture made the *Essais* an appropriate source.

[43] SCETI London 1603, p. R3r. On the Bodleian copy of Paris 1598, see 2.7.4 and 2.7.8.

and presented it to her for reading; she commanded him to finish the rest.[44] We shall consider it in detail in 2.3.4. First we must consider the broader literary and cultural tradition of institutions of the gentry and nobility.

2.3.2 THE INSTITUTION OF THE ENGLISH NOBILITY

The circumstances described in 2.3.1 on the basis of Florio's paratexts prove to be broadly indicative of the pedagogical and social context of the *Essais'* introduction into England between the 1590s and the early 1700s: the institution of the gentry and the nobility in philosophical learning in households, courts, and other spaces beyond formal classrooms—including private tutorials at college and the spaces of educative travel on the continent—and related scenes of learned leisure and self-instruction in adulthood. In this context, reading and writing is often carried out on behalf of noble patrons by servants, and is normally understood to index 'conversation' and other forms of social and political action. This is not to say, of course, that Montaigne's work was only received by gentle and noble readers.[45] Rather, it was received as suitable for the unofficial education and study of such readers.

In its ideal form, this institution amounted to a *cultura animi* (or *cultus animi*), a culture of the soul or mind for the noble or gentle subject, alongside a culture of the body and an education in the practical-philosophical judgement needed for elite life, supported by appropriate books and servants.[46] It aimed to fashion noblemen and noblewomen in learning and virtue, in distinctively gendered ways.[47] Much of the literature from Elyot and Ascham through Cleland and Milton to Locke deals with the institutions of noblemen and gentlemen, but noblewomen and gentlewomen are present in these treatises, and receive instruction separately in works such as Vives's *De institutione foeminae Christianae*, translated by Hyrde and printed in multiple editions.[48]

Gentlewomens' institutions in virtues such as chastity and patience are largely conceived in ways that complement the formation and needs of their male relatives (as we saw in relation to Florio's dedications in 2.3.1). The noble pupils were required to be as much masters and mistresses of reading and writing, and of the

---

[44] See Warren Boutcher, 'The origins of Florio's Montaigne: "Of the Institution and Education of Children, to Madame Lucy Russell, Countess of Bedford"', *Montaigne Studies*, 24 (2012), 7–32, 7, 18. This article is complementary to the current chapter and presents detailed textual and circumstantial evidence to support the statement that Florio began with I 25.

[45] See Hamlin, *Montaigne's English journey*, for an overview of the range of readers.

[46] Hugo Friedrich, *Montaigne*, ed. Philippe Desan, trans. Dawn Eng (Berkeley: University of California Press, 1991), 11, 377–8.

[47] For early modern England, see Brayman Hackel, *Reading material*, 196–213; Pamela Selwyn and David Selwyn, ' "The profession of a gentleman": books for the gentry and the nobility (*c.*1560 to 1640)', in Elizabeth Leedham-Green and Teresa Webber (eds.), *The Cambridge history of libraries in Britain and Ireland: Volume I to 1650* (Cambridge: Cambridge University Press, 2006), 489–515 (specifically as it relates to the collecting of books in private household libraries).

[48] For the editions of these translations see the online catalogue of early modern English translations: Centre for the Study of the Renaissance, University of Warwick, 'Renaissance Cultural Crossroads', <http://www.hrionline.ac.uk/rcc>.

servants who offered learned skills, as they were of valour and chastity—with the important proviso that the rationale of reading and writing was to index gendered versions of noble conversation and virtue, not to be an end in itself. This style of education was conducted as a matter of relations between family members, between fathers and sons, mothers and daughters, between tutors and counsellors and their masters and mistresses. It was mediated by books and by examples and sentences extracted from books, and it drove a market in printed and manuscript literature— including the romances of Lyly, Spenser, and Sidney—for those who aspired to the culture and values of the gentry and nobility.

The market in printed literature mentioned in the last paragraph was very much the province of the publisher of Florio's Montaigne, Edward Blount, the Abel L'Angelier of late Tudor, early Stuart London. Blount had been apprenticed for seven years to the publisher of Sidney and Spenser, William Ponsonby, the first stationer comprehensively to exploit the developing market for contemporary ver- nacular literature. Blount, though, was an unusually secular and cosmopolitan bookseller; throughout his career he focused on European histories and travel books, dictionaries of Italian, Spanish, and Latin, and translations from French, Italian, Spanish, Dutch, Greek, classical Latin, and neo-Latin. He also revived Lyly's works late in his career.[49]

The noble household scene of cosmopolitan literary culture apparent in Florio's dedications is designed, from Blount's point of view, to appeal to the market he was simultaneously serving and shaping—hence the lengthy treatment of the issues surrounding the publication of Sidney's *Arcadia*, and Sidney's various trans- lations. In this market, there was no boundary between Englished versions of for- eign authors, and what we now consider to be English literature; Blount's edition of Florio's Montaigne was closely related, for example, to his edition of Samuel Daniel's poetry and prose, published in the same year (see 2.3.6).

Future research will need to assess whether the manner in which Florio's trans- lation shapes use of the *Essais* in England holds for use of French copies.[50] The earliest dateable reference of any kind to ownership of a specific French copy of the *Essais* in England occurs in February 1596. It places the copy in the context of a multilingual teaching library geared to the needs of noble patrons. The copy is listed amongst one M. Le Douz's books, inventoried as he left the Harrington- Russell household on instructions from the Earl of Essex to substitute Dr Hawkyns at Venice (which, in the event, he did not do).

Le Douz's list, which is complementary to a separate list of Le Douz's papers and manuscripts, points to a noble household institution such as that we shall hear described methodically by James Cleland in 2.3.7. It co-opts the professional

---

[49] Gary Taylor, 'Blount, Edward (*bap.* 1562, *d.* in or before 1632)', *ODNB*. See also Leah Scragg, 'Edward Blount and the History of Lylian Criticism', *The Review of English Studies*, 46, no. 181 (1995), 1–10.

[50] Some of the contexts involving English readers of French copies (Bankes, Locke), discussed in O'Brien, 'Montaigne, Sir Ralph Bankes', are compatible with the perspective outlined on the basis of Florio's Montaigne in this chapter. Bankes does not reference Florio's Montaigne, but he reads the text as an account of the self-fashioning of a free-talking gentleman such as himself.

humanist core of Latin language-teaching (including Castellio's *Dialogi*, Freigius's *Paedagogus*, Junius's *Nomenclator*) but extends itself across an eclectic, multi-vernacular range of languages and studies. It complements Latin books with Italian, Spanish, and French books. The book list contains the scriptures, canonical classics (Terence, Plautus, Sallust, Caesar), Tasso, and the *Cortegiano*—all in several languages. In secular literature, the emphasis is on poetry, history, and moral philosophy. A copy of the 1588 *Essais* is complemented by a copy of Lipsius's *De constantia*.[51]

As we heard in 2.3.1, Florio did some of his translation of Montaigne in the very same household, and it is likewise closely tied to his reading lessons in French with his noblewomen pupils. This is clearest when he describes how the translation will 'serve you two to repeate in true English what you reade in fine French' and when he tackles the thorny pedagogical problem of how to read with his ladies a text which finds only three good women, all of whom committed suicide for love of their husbands.[52]

Florio appears to have had no Latin but he likewise used Montaigne in the context of an informal curriculum of recent Italian, French, and perhaps Spanish books that, like learned servants, mediate 'intelligence' and learning to noble patrons such as Sir Thomas Egerton. Such servants play the role given to Italians in general in a sonnet added to a copy of Florio's dictionary: they bear 'inteligence with moste' and best invent or best invented choose, and in writing show, what Greece or Rome, ages or places knew ('Philosophie of nature, manners, witt'); that is, they mediate both the intelligence they glean from networks, and the philosophical knowledge they find in classical texts. The words are Matthew Gwinne's, and apply to an Italian–English dictionary, but they give us a strong clue as to the value in this context of a book such as Montaigne's, for we can infer that it is likewise judged by Gwinne to have best invented or selected, and in writing shown— with Florio's direct assistance—what Greece and Rome knew, for the purposes of noble patrons.[53]

Florio and Le Douz were not alone as foreign tutors who used the French *Essais* to read with the nobility. In 1626, Sieur Jonatan de Sainct Sernin published his *Essais et observations sur les Essais du seigneur de Montaigne* with Edward Allde. In his dedicatory letter, he draws on I 8 to claim them as his own 'imaginations', produced while in exile in London, confined indoors during the plague. But this small volume is clearly a product of Sainct Sernin's French language lessons with the English nobility, and comprises two of his own essays followed by commentary on the first six of Montaigne's—once again, reading Montaigne directly gives rise to writing. There is an epistle to the nobility of Great Britain ('tres-genereuse, tres-magnanime, et tres-invincible noblesse de la Grande Bretagne') in which all

---

[51] Lambeth Palace Library, Bacon MS 655, fols. 185r–6r; Warren Boutcher, 'Michel de Montaigne et Anthony Bacon: la familia et la fonction des lettres', *Montaigne Studies*, 13 (2001), 241–76, 272.

[52] SCETI London 1603, p. A2r; pp. R2r–v. The reference is to *Essayes*, II 35, 'Of three good Women'.

[53] Warren Boutcher, 'Vernacular humanism in the sixteenth century', in Jill Kraye (ed.), *The Cambridge Companion to Renaissance Humanism* (Cambridge: Cambridge University Press, 1996), 189–202, 189–90.

the 'discours' his wit has engendered in their country as a foreigner is credited to them as strong lovers of the French language ('vos Excellences et Seigneuries, comme fort amateurs de la langue Françoise').[54]

Another English reader-writer of Montaigne in the 1590s, the gentleman-scholar William Cornwallis, clearly indicates in his extensive remarks on an English manuscript translation of the *Essais* in circulation *c.*1600 (though probably not Florio's) that the whole work was understood at the time through the optic provided by the principal chapters on noble education: I 24 and I 25. Montaigne, he says, 'hath made Morrall Philosophy speake couragiously, and in steed of her gowne, given her an Armour; he hath put Pedanticall Schollerisme out of countenance, and made manifest, that learning mingled with Nobilitie, shines most clearly'.[55] 'Pedanticall Schollerisme' clearly refers to I 24, and 'learning mingled with Nobilitie' most probably refers to I 25.

Montaigne is being judged here to have found a new voice for moral philosophy, a noble voice that satirically discountenances the pedant and exemplifies a new kind of social relationship between philosophical wisdom, the learned and learned books, and the nobility. Montaigne does not teach like a professional humanist. He knows how to keep pedagogues' and schoolmasters' learning in their proper (low) place in the noble household, to employ the right kind of scholars and the right kind of learning with gentlemanly discretion. The new voice heralded by Cornwallis was used in 1607 by James Cleland, who dedicated the fourth book of *Hērō-paideia, or, The institution of a young noble man* (Oxford, 1607) to the young John Harrington as 'one of/ Your most faithfull and loving Tutors', and the one for whose instruction, he says, he 'cheifly intended the whole worke'.[56] As we shall see in 2.3.7, much of this text on the education of the nobility speaks (without acknowledgement) with the voice of Florio's Montaigne.

At the other end of our period, there is evidence pointing in the same direction. Milton's 'Of education', dedicated to Samuel Hartlib in 1644, may not borrow directly from Montaigne, but his description of the right path of a virtuous and noble education, so smooth, so green, so full of goodly prospect, shares much with I 25.[57] Hartlib himself, who took education in a more egalitarian, less aristocratic direction, was to publish an extract from Florio's version of Montaigne's account of

---

[54] ESTC S3784. There are only two known copies of this in Britain, both in the British Library. The first (pressmark 1472.aa.11) is bound in with seventeenth century catechisms, dialogues, and pastoral letters. It declares 'A Londres de l'imprimerie d'Edward Allde 1626' on the title page, and bears a dedication to 'Monsieur Edoward Osburne'. The other copy (pressmark 820.a.17) appears to have a defective title page, with no mention of a printer, and is dedicated to 'Monsieur Jean Chasteau'. My citations are from the former copy: Jonatan de Sainct Sernin, *Essais et observations sur les Essais du Seigneur de Montagne* (London: Edward Allde, 1626), sigs. A3r–v, A6r, A7v.

[55] William Cornwallis, *Essayes* (London: Edmund Mattes, 1600–1), sig. H4v. The passage occurs within the long essay 'Of Censuring' and is the culmination of an essay-within-an-essay on books. I am grateful to William Hamlin for sharing the early fruits of his research on Cornwallis's references to Montaigne, which suggests that Cornwallis is quoting directly from an English translation but that the translation is not Florio's. See Hamlin, *Montaigne's English journey*, 242–3.

[56] Cleland, *Hērō-paideia*, sig. Q2v.

[57] John Milton, *Of education. To Master Samuel Hartlib* (London: printed for Thomas Underhill and/for Thomas Johnson, 1644), sig. A2r [ESTC R10430].

his own education in that same chapter in 1654 as part of his plans for an 'advancement of learning in these nations'.[58]

We shall see in 2.4.1 that the bookseller William London in 1657 gave much prominence to Florio's Montaigne in a catalogue of vendible books for the private institution of the northern gentry in philosophical learning. Section 2.5.7 will demonstrate how Pierre Coste's early work on Montaigne, before he published his epoch-making London edition of 1724, centred on the relations between John Locke's educational philosophy and his reading of Montaigne, especially *Essais* I 25.

There is much evidence, then, to indicate that in early modern England many reader-writers related to the text primarily via the concept of a non-scholastic, noble 'institution' in philosophy and virtue conducted in the mode of aristocratic learned leisure. They inferred such an institution and mode from the book and they used the book in the course of their own learned leisure, their ongoing self-institutions, or in designing institutions, exercises, and entertainments for others.

Again, this does not mean that only gentry and nobility read the text at leisure in their households. But it does mean that it was received as a book by a noble gentleman who himself, as William London put it, knew how to use books—in the sense of personalize, customize, and domesticate them for the purposes not of a scholar but of one such as himself, studying for pleasure and profit in his leisure time.[59] The author had had the kind of informal education in Latin and modern languages, history, moral philosophy, and law that English writers from Elyot on had advocated, and he had put it to virtuoso or overly extravagant and paradoxical use—depending on one's point of view.[60]

More particularly, early English users—including, as we have seen, Florio—inferred that this strangely unmethodical institution in the art of living for the freeborn was based in extremely wide-ranging but relatively undisciplined private reading and writing. Ben Jonson makes this clear in a collection that is cognate in genre (as a miscellany of observations) with the *Essais* themselves. For he describes *Timber* as discoveries 'made upon men and matter: as they have flow'd out of his daily Readings; or had their refluxe to his peculiar Notion of the Times'.[61]

---

[58] Samuel Hartlib, *The true and readie way to learne the Latine tongue* (London: R. and W. Leybourn, 1654), title page and sigs. H1r–2v [ESTC R19399]. The extract could be taken from SCETI London 1603, pp. 84–5 ('The Athenians (as *Plato* averreth)... containe: So exact was my discipline'), or from the equivalent texts in the later editions of Florio's translation (1613 and 1632).

[59] See the discussion of William London in 2.4.1.

[60] R. C. Stephens, 'John Locke and the education of the gentleman', *The University of Leeds Institute of Education: Researches and Studies*, 14 (1956), 67–75, 68.

[61] Ben Jonson, *Workes*, 3 vols. (London: Richard Bishop [and Robert Young] for Andrew Crooke [vol. 1]; John Beale, John Dawson, Bernard Alsop and Thomas Fawcet for Richard Meighen [Thomas Walkley and Robert Allot] [vols. 2–3], 1640–1), vol. 3, sig. M1r [ESTC S112456; ESTC S111824; ESTC S428]. The printing history of the so-called second folio of Jonson's *Workes* is extremely complex, with extant volumes often including the various parts, with separate title pages, in different orders. I am here referring to a volume whose pagination and signatures are continuous and start with *Horace his art of poetrie*, but which includes separate title pages for *The English grammar* (1640), and for *Timber: or, Discoveries* (1641). See Joseph Loewenstein, *Ben Jonson and possessive authorship* (Cambridge: Cambridge University Press, 2002), 211–14.

Contemporaries might well have described the *Essayes* in the same way: a record of Montaigne's observations on men and matter, as they emerged from the application of daily readings to the author's private, individual ('peculiar') conception of the times.

If Jonson's collection has any sort of organizing principle, it is that of an institution in reading and writing well—which is to say, virtuously. It includes a self-contained piece of advice requested by an unspecified 'Lordship... touching the education of your sonnes', in which Jonson warns against an education in the family and prefers public schooling. He describes the dangers of bringing sons up amongst 'ill servants' and of only conversing 'with singulars': 'I like no private breeding.'[62]

At one point he includes a series of notes on 'the difference of wits' or *ingeniorum discrimina*. This is a pedagogical topic treated by Quintilian in relation to the ability of the teacher of the orator to see the beginnings of—and to nurture—different natures and styles.[63] Jonson then shows his skill in discriminating between such natures and styles—what he calls 'compositions'—on the basis of their writing.

Once again, the context of a significant mention of Montaigne and the *Essais* is the pedagogy and method of reading and writing:

> *Some* that turne over all bookes, and are equally searching in all papers, that write out of what they presently find or meet, without choice; by which meanes it happens, that what they have discredited, and impugned in one worke, they have before, or after extolled the same in another. Such are all the *Essayists*, even their Master *Mountaigne*. These in all they write, confesse still what bookes they have read last; and therein their owne folly, so much, that they bring it to the *Stake* raw, and undigested: not that the place did need it neither, but that they thought themselves furnished, and would vent it.[64]

Montaigne is the master of a school of wits who turn over books and search in papers in random fashion for matter to invent in speech and writing. He has initiated a vogue that inheres in a recognizable lay *persona*—here sketched as a caricature. Jonson is contrasting the virtues of those who read and write with 'Art' with those free literates—the English school of Montaigne—who write with what they presently find or meet, without choice. He thereby inverts Florio's defence of Montaigne: all is in the choice and handling, yes, but the essayists do not show any. Jonson's criticism corresponds closely to the antagonistic point of view entertained by Florio in his paratexts, but ultimately put to one side; namely, that Montaigne's is a discourse which extravagantly and randomly veers from discrediting and impugning to extolling.

---

[62] Jonson, *Workes*, vol. 3, sigs. P3v–4r. The source for this passage is Quintilian, *Institutes of oratory*, 1.2, esp. 1–20.

[63] Jonson, *Workes*, vol. 3, sigs. N3v–4r; Quintilian, *Institutes of oratory*, 2.8.1.

[64] Jonson, *Workes*, vol. 3, sig. N4r. Jonson may still have Montaigne in mind when he continues on the same page to talk of 'some, [who] by a cunning protestation against all reading, and false venditation of their own *naturals*, thinke to divert the *sagacity* of their Readers from themselves, and coole the sent of their own *fox-like* thefts'.

If, then, free-thinking or free-talking is the outcome of the *Essais*' arrival in England, it is undertaken, received, and judged in many nexuses as gentle or noble free-thinking that is shaped by particular kinds of learned leisure—assisted study, reading and writing and conference (in the general sense of 'conversation')—that are liable to veer extravagantly into random quotations and the experience of pleasurable licence. For some, as we have just seen, it could be seen to nurture an over-free style of study, of reading and writing, of speech—sometimes wittily satirical speech—that lacked a frame of art and gave all over to chance and nature.

This was especially dangerous—from a conservative, Jonsonian point of view—for women. As it began in the household, women were in the vicinity in a way they were not in formal classrooms, whether as pupils or educators, and could be considered as either a corrupting influence, or as subject to corrupting influences. Ideally, this freer form of study would be safely embedded in the performative, instructive relations that aim to institute gentle and noble subjects in a virtuous life. These are relations such as those in the Bedford-Harrington or Sackville-Neville houses, between noble fathers and children, brothers and sisters, husbands and wives, relations visibly or invisibly mediated by learned servants and advisers, and by the prototypes and precedents of philosophical wisdom so abundantly present in the *Essayes*. Florio memorialized these relations in his dedications; authors of romances fictionalized them in verse and prose; playwrights dramatized them on the stage.

2.3.3 'LECTURE AND ADVISE'

At the beginning of the 1590s Shakespeare wrote a comedy centred on the institution of young gentlewomen. The main play begins with Lucentio instituting '[a] course of learning and ingenious studies'; 'Vertue and that part of Philosophie/ Will I applie, that treats of happinesse/ By vertue specially to be atchiev'd'; his servant recommends less Aristotle, more Ovid, and a practical approach to logic and rhetoric.[65] But they are on Italian travels and this course of learning quickly dissolves into the pursuit of the experience of love. The rest of the play alternates between stage images of two very different institutions provided for Baptista's daughters. While one (Bianca) is provided with a lute and a set of perfumed books, and tutors in music and literature who are suitors in disguise, one of whom gives her 'lectures' (readings) in the art of love, the other (Katherina) breaks the lute over the music tutor's head, then finds herself in a household 'taming-school' run by a much harsher master.

At the end of the decade Shakespeare returns to the theme in a tragedy. Early in *Hamlet*, a young noblewoman and a young nobleman are given lessons in self-knowledge by the male relatives who govern their education. One is ready to

---

[65] William Shakespeare, *Comedies, histories, and tragedies*, eds Henry Condell and John Heminge (London: Isaac Jaggard and Edward Blount, 1623), sig. 3v (SCETI p. 210) [*The Taming of the Shrew* 1.1.18–20].

travel, while the other must stay at home protecting her chastity. In the first part of the scene, Ophelia is lectured on 'the ste[e]p and thorny way to heaven' by her brother, though she turns the tables by warning him against playing the 'reckles libertine' and following 'the primrose path of dalience'. Laertes's fraternal 'good lesson' is exclusively concerned with the 'wisdom' required to conserve his sister's 'chast treasure'. Ophelia must not listen to Hamlet's songs with 'too credent eare'.[66]

Her father Polonius then takes up the lesson in the second half of the scene by telling her bluntly that '[y]ou doe not understand yourselfe so cleerly/ As it behooves my daughter, and your honor'. He goes on to instruct her in the war-like strategy needed by a young girl who is properly anxious to conserve her 'maiden presence'.[67]

Laertes is about to return from Elsinore to Paris after a flying visit for the new king's coronation. As tradition demanded on such occasions in cultivated Renaissance households, his father Polonius, in the same scene, provides him with a quick institution in moral philosophy:

> And these fewe precepts in thy memory
> Looke thou character, give thy thoughts no tongue,
> Nor any unproportion'd thought his act,
> Be thou familier, but by no meanes vulgar,
> Those friends thou hast, and their adoption tried,
> Grapple them unto thy soule with hoopes of steele,
> …
> Give every man thy eare, but fewe thy voice,
> Take each mans censure, but reserve thy judgement,
> …
> Neither a borrower nor a lender b[e],
> For love oft looses both it selfe, and friend,
> And borrowing dulleth [the] edge of husbandry;
> This above all, to thine owne self be true
> And it must followe as the night the day
> Thou canst not then be false to any man[68]

As such instructions go, these are somewhat constrictive. They betray an anxiety about the directions Laertes might take once out of sight, the liberties he might take as heir with the family's reputation and other resources. In the moral

---

[66] William Shakespeare, *The tragicall historie of Hamlet… Newly imprinted and enlarged to almost as much againe as it was, according to the true and perfect coppie* (London: James Roberts, 1604), sig. C3v [*Hamlet* 1.3.49–50, 45, 30–1].

[67] Shakespeare, *The tragicall historie of Hamlet*, sig. C4v [*Hamlet* 1.3.96–7, 121].

[68] Shakespeare, *The tragicall historie of Hamlet*, sig. C4r [*Hamlet* 1.3.58–80]. In the 1603 (the so-called bad) quarto of the play the (rather different) text of these precepts was printed with inverted commas: William Shakespeare, *The tragicall historie of Hamlet Prince of Denmarke* (London: [Valentine Simmes] for N[icholas] L[ing] and John Trundell, 1603), sig. C2r–v. The period offers many historical and literary examples of such sets of precepts, most usually offered by fathers to sons as they are about to leave for study or travel. See William Shakespeare, *Hamlet*, ed. Harold Jenkins (London: Methuen, 1982), 440–3, and Horace Howard Furness (ed.), *A new variorum edition of Shakespeare: Hamlet*, 2 vols. (15th edn., Philadelphia and London: J. B. Lippincott, 1918), vol. 1, 65–70.

literature available to a father of the time it was certainly possible to find more liberal institutions. Montaigne was criticized at Rome for advising in I 25 that, in Florio's words, '[h]e [the young nobleman] shal laugh, jest, dally, and debauch himselfe with his Prince. And in his debauching, I would have him out-go al his fellowes in vigor and constancie'.[69] In other respects, however, surrogate father Montaigne and fictional father Polonius are recognizably drawing on the same set of commonplaces in instituting civil and courtly behaviour in their young noblemen.[70]

Will this culture bring forth seeds of virtue, though? Pierre de Montaigne's 'exquisite toyle' did not overcome his son Michel's natural 'idle drowzinesse'.[71] Might Laertes succumb to idleness and vice? Polonius's anxiety finds more direct expression three scenes later, when he briefs a family servant on how to get intelligence about Laertes' behaviour in Paris. Reynaldo is to seek out Danes who know Laertes—perhaps the 'wrong' kind of friends—and drop some leading remarks about his 'youth and libertie' (gaming, drinking, fencing, etc.) as a bait to catch a 'carpe of truth'. The idea is that the Danes are then likely to confirm what they know of Laertes' vices with concrete information of his visits to brothels and the like: 'with windlesses and with assaies of bias,/ By indirections find directions out'.[72]

The joke here—if joke is the word when it comes to the rather sinister character of Polonius—derives from the paradox of the two briefs. One is a set of directions on how to be true to yourself, the other a set of directions on how to be false in order to find out if somebody else is being true to themselves.

As the father in a noble household, Polonius is anxious to direct his offsprings' conduct, and as minister of state he is anxious to give direction to the king's handling of affairs. For the first he needs intelligence about his own son's character, for the second intelligence about the king's son-in-law's ostentatious melancholy and political intentions—he will go on to use exactly the same kind of tactics to catch a carp of truth about the state of Hamlet's soul. In using various instruments and servants to glean both, he is a principal focus for the culture of moral and political 'lecture and advise'—the phrase is Polonius's own—with which the play deals and which by the 1590s was an established feature of elite life in England.[73]

In 1.3 the 'lecture' is entirely oral, but elsewhere in the play the role of books and writings in mediating this culture is visualized on stage, especially when it

---

[69] I 25, NP173/BVH Paris 1595, pp. 94–5/SCETI London 1603, p. 80. Montaigne defended himself against the Roman censors' criticism of the 1580 version of the passage on debauchery. See R119/F955–6 ('item: qu'il falloit nourrir un enfant à tout faire') and Malcolm Smith, *Montaigne and the Roman censors* (Geneva: Droz, 1981), 87–97.

[70] Compare, for example, I 25, NP159–60/BVH Paris 1595, p. 85/SCETI London 1603, p. 72: 'In this schoole of commerce, and society among men, I have often noted this vice, that in lieu of taking acquaintance of others, we only indevor to make our selves known to them...Silence and modestie are qualities very convenient to civill conversation. It is also necessary, that a yong man be rather taught to be discreetly-sparing, and close-handed, then prodigally-wastefull and lavish in his expences, and moderate in husbanding his wealth when he shall come to possesse it.'

[71] I 25, NP181/BVH Paris 1595, p. 100/SCETI London 1603, p. 85.

[72] Shakespeare, *The tragicall historie of Hamlet*, sig. E1r–v [*Hamlet* 2.1.1–68].

[73] Shakespeare, *The tragicall historie of Hamlet*, sig. E1v [*Hamlet* 2.1.67].

comes to the institution of the young nobleman at the centre of events. Both Ophelia and Hamlet read books on stage. Ophelia promises to lock her brother's lesson in her memory, but Hamlet, just back from the reformed university of Wittenberg, writes his own father's lesson down on tables he extracts from his pocket. The prince wields a sword and fights a duel, but he also writes a speech for a play and directs the actors thereof; he has even learned to write 'fair' so that he can forge a royal commission when necessity demands. At other times he has his friend Horatio on hand to advise him orally. Most strikingly of all, he punctuates the action with satirical railings against women and mankind and meandering confessions of his own folly and vanity. The latter take the form of digressive moral essays redolent of Montaigne's printed meditations—as, for example, when he reflects upon the way in which an actor portraying grief can seem more genuinely overcome by that emotion than he can, as the son of a murdered father.[74]

Are these confessional 'essays' diverting him from action rather than directing him to action? And what has happened to his institution in godly learning?

Much of the work done on the Elizabethan and Jacobean culture of 'lecture and advise' in the 1990s concentrated on the intellectual and social history of scholarly services for the nobility and governing classes in the areas of education, politics, military strategy, and natural science.[75] The foundations of this culture lay in the Tudor demand for an education appropriate to the needs of the gentry and nobility of a reformed nation. The result both combined and opposed a formally instituted arts education with an intensification of informal, 'household'—or 'grand tour'—style tertiary education.[76] Key pedagogical works such

---

[74] Compare Shakespeare, *The tragicall historie of Hamlet*, sig. F4v [*Hamlet* 2.2.492–501], with SCETI London 1603, pp. 503–4: 'An Orator (saith Rhetorick) in the play of his pleading, shall be mooved at the sound of his owne voyce, and by his fayned agitations; and suffer himselfe to be cozoned by the passion he representeth: imprinting a lively and essentiall sorrow, by the jugling he acteth, ... *Quintilian* reporteth, to have seene Comediants [*sic*] so farre ingaged in a sorrowfull part, that they wept after being come to their lodgings: and of himselfe, that having undertaken to moove a certaine passion in another, he had found himselfe surprised, not onely with shedding of teares, but with a palenesse of countenance, and behaviour of a man truly dejected with griefe.'

[75] See Lisa Jardine and Anthony Grafton, ' "Studied for Action": How Gabriel Harvey Read His Livy', *Past and Present*, 129 (1990), 30–78; Lisa Jardine, 'Mastering the Uncouth: Gabriel Harvey, Edmund Spenser and the English experience in Ireland', in J. Henry and S. Hutton (eds.), *New perspectives on Renaissance thought: essays in honour of Charles Schmitt* (London: Duckworth, 1990), 68–82; Lisa Jardine and William Sherman, 'Pragmatic readers: knowledge transactions and scholarly services in late Elizabethan England', *Religion, culture and society in early modern Britain: essays in honour of Patrick Collinson* (Cambridge: Cambridge University Press, 1993), 102–24; Paul E. J. Hammer, 'The uses of scholarship: The secretariat of Robert Devereux, second Earl of Essex, c.1585–1601', *English Historical Review*, 104 (1994), 26–51; Paul E. J. Hammer, 'The Earl of Essex, Fulke Greville, and the employment of scholars', *Studies in Philology*, 91 (1994), 167–80; William H. Sherman, *John Dee: the politics of reading and writing in the English Renaissance* (Amherst: University of Massachusetts Press, 1995); Paul E. J. Hammer, 'Essex and Europe: evidence from confidential instructions by the Earl of Essex, 1595–6', *English Historical Review*, 111 (1996), 357–81; Lisa Jardine and Alan Stewart, *Hostage to fortune: the troubled life of Francis Bacon* (London: Gollancz, 1998); Paul E. J. Hammer, *The polarisation of Elizabethan politics: the political career of Robert Devereux, 2nd Earl of Essex, 1585–1597* (Cambridge: Cambridge University Press, 1999), 298–315.

[76] See Warren Boutcher, 'Pilgrimage to Parnassus: local intellectual traditions, humanist education and the cultural geography of sixteenth-century England', in Yun Lee Too and Niall Livingstone

as Laurence Humphrey's *Optimates* and Roger Ascham's *Scholemaster* ('specially purposed for the private bringing up of youth in gentlemen and noblemens houses') were focused on methods and tutors appropriate to the noble family setting, which Humphrey said should be set up like a *liberalis officina* ('free study workshop').[77]

By the 1560s, when Philip Sidney was at school, the acquisition of a humanistic education in the arts was firmly and widely integrated into elite family strategies and elite household culture. A standard task for a philosophical adviser such as Montaigne in France or—much later—Locke in England, was advice on special approaches to education of the young.[78] The manner of acquisition and use of the programmatic, methodical arts education on offer in schools and colleges had become a means of social differentiation and an instrument of family strategy. The elite young, even when they went away to school or university, were being educated as part of the gentle or noble household, by 'governors' or tutors who were allies and *famuli*, and who tailor-made the education on offer according to the needs and the imagined future of that household.

This, of course, was even more literally true of gentlewomen and noblewomen, whom we have seen were educated within—and as ornaments for—the elite household.[79] For young elite men, the imagined future would include continued employment of scholars and readers. As they undertook travels accompanied by scholarly friends, their early 'institution' blended into a continued relationship to learning and the services provided by the learned in adulthood. The other side of the coin was that men from relatively inferior backgrounds were more likely to follow the formal curriculum. Learning to profess, to teach, and to serve, and learning to judge, to know, and to govern, were quite different things—or so it was repeatedly insisted by those who had an interest in promoting learning to the gentry and nobility, or in basing their gentility and nobility on learning. At the same time, masters and servants were brought into close and intimate contact by the experience of education.[80]

The consequence of this was that the socially and culturally reproductive relationship between the gentle or noble dynast and his successfully cultivated male and female heir(s) increasingly came to the fore—as in Florio's dedications and in Shakespeare's plays of the 1590s. It provided an institutional—social, financial,

---

(eds.), *Pedagogy and power: rhetorics of classical learning* (Cambridge: Cambridge University Press, 1998), 110–47.

[77] Roger Ascham, *The scholemaster or plaine and perfite way of teachyng children, to understand, write, and speake, the Latin tong* (London: John Day, 1570), title page; Humphrey, *Optimates*, III, sigs. r6v–7r.

[78] On Locke, see 2.5.7.

[79] Edith Snook, *Women, reading, and the cultural politics of early modern England* (Farnham: Ashgate, 2005), 10–11.

[80] For England, see V. Morgan, 'Approaches to the history of the English universities in the sixteenth and seventeenth centuries', in G. Klingenstein, H. Lutz, and G. Stourzh (eds.), *Bildung, Politik und Gesellschaft: Studien zur Geschichte des europäischen Bildungswesens vom 16. bis zum 20. Jahrhundert* (Vienna: Verlag für Geschichte und Politik, 1978), 138–64, 145–8; and for a similar trend in Austria, see K. J. MacHardy, 'Cultural capital, family strategies and noble identity in early modern Habsburg Austria', *Past and Present*, 163 (1999), 36–75.

ethical, ideological—foundation for learning, to rival that between the official university teacher and the arts student.

As applied in service, humane learning increasingly sought to realize its raison d'être in authentic noble agency; that is, in the learned conversation and virtuous deeds of a noble philosophical life in the Tudor present that would match those of the Gracchi—mother and sons—and similar figures in the ancient Roman past. The figures of the wise dynast (accompanied by his dynastic adviser) and the successfully educated son or daughter became the ultimate guarantors of humane learning's value and purpose—not classical philology, not antiquity, not the canonical author, and not the literary values of the individual humanist (though all, of course, continued to have a vital role in the process). It was through elite agency that the learned literary 'conference' or 'readings' of gentle and noble persons and their learned friends and servants were to be realized as autonomous actions and words performed in the sphere of politics, war, and business (in the case of men) or virtuous household behaviour (in the case of women).[81]

With the advent of the printed templates of humanist pedagogy and the formalization of school and university arts education came a new definition of the noble male 'individual' that incorporated a model of nobly free literacy. This was the *persona* whose compellingly *in*formal, free-ranging, occasion-specific mode of appropriation of classical wisdom—through experience—aimed to define itself against and above the systems, types, and routines of institutionalized arts pedagogy. This was attractive even to the aspiring mercantile family or to the elite scholar who was in practice dependent on a profession or on selling or bartering his skills.[82]

If one was an elite parent, one would attempt to buy and control this process of self-definition for one's male offspring by acquiring the right experts and the right extra-curricular books. At the same time, as I indicated in 2.3.2, this trend in elite education was intimately related to the top end of the commercial market for continental and translated books, which was in turn related to the selection of sources for the dramatization of elite life and values on stage, in new or more avant-garde genres such as pastoral tragicomedy.

From *c.*1580 Elizabethan literature began to test the humanist institutions on offer. There is a close relationship between Ascham's *Scholemaster* and the most successful elite romance of the 1570s and 1580s, Lyly's *Euphues, the anatomy of wit*. After the narrator recounts the idleness and vice into which Euphues fell by ignoring his education and seeking experience, the prodigal son repents and in the second half sounds like Ascham as he offers an institution based on the pseudo-Plutarchan 'Of the education of free-born children' *(De liberis educandis)*, and moral epistles redolent of school exercises. However, Lyly's second novel about the same character

---

[81] See especially Jardine and Grafton, '"Studied for Action"', and 1.1.6 in this study.

[82] See the brilliant short piece by Margaret Ferguson, '1549: A new intellectual élite', in Denis Hollier (ed.), *A new history of French literature* (Cambridge, Massachusetts: Harvard University Press, 1989), 194–8.

moves further away from Ascham's culture of learning towards the opening of an elite market in 'reading for pleasure' for free literates.[83]

The argument here is that there was one imported and translated continental book which, along with others by authors such as Castiglione, Machiavelli, Lipsius, Tasso, and Guarini, crystallized both this trend in the household institution of the nobility and the doubts and anxieties surrounding it. It did so all the way through from the 1590s, when copies began to arrive in numbers from France and when a major English translation was commenced, until the early eighteenth century, when the post-Restoration translation of Charles Cotton, together with Pierre Coste's monumental London edition of the French text, reconfirmed its place in elite English letters. The book was the *Essais* of Montaigne; the foundational chapter was that on noble education (I 25)—though, as we shall see, another form of more apparently licentious schooling was gleaned from other chapters such as III 5.

Above all, it is Montaigne who makes the gentle and noble consumer (including the female consumer) the agent of literate knowledge use, who subordinates pedantic learning to the leisurely scenes and practical purposes of a noble philosophical life. He forces the distinction between, on the one hand, the practical motives and routine methods of school-based Latin humanist pedagogy and, on the other hand, the utilization of all occasions and texts—including vernacular texts—in the service of the well-born consumer's moral needs in his or her daily experience. His deliberately unscholarly work consumes a vast battery of texts, apparently without regard for origin, context, or language. The state of being he portrays in print assumes—because it contrasts in every way with—the fixed norms and forms of humanist textbooks.[84]

At the same time, the printed *persona* of Montaigne somehow sits at the crossroads of early modern English elite identity and has something to say to all-comers. He stands between the worlds of vernacular court literature and of neo-Latin scholarship, bridging both markets and addressing both lay and specialist readers. He seems at once a noble lord, a bourgeois citizen, and a humanistically trained gentleman-lawyer; he is at once 'retired' on a country estate and experienced in court business and politics. He is at once in (unpaid) service to higher masters and an employer of scholars in his own household. He defines himself and his values as virile, but addresses himself in writing, at leisure, to female patrons. He is at once an advocate for the preservation of elite society's norms and mores, and a cuckoo in the nest of morally safe social and dynastic reproduction, a dog-toothed, witty satirist in the cynical or Juvenilian mould.

---

[83] Fred Schurink, 'The intimacy of manuscript and the pleasure of print: Literary culture from *The Schoolmaster* to *Euphues*', in Michael Pincombe and Cathy Shrank (eds.), *The Oxford handbook of Tudor literature, 1485–1603* (Oxford: Oxford University Press, 2009), 671–86.

[84] See Elizabeth L. Eisenstein, *The printing press as an agent of change: communications and cultural transformations in early modern Europe: Volumes I and II* (Cambridge: Cambridge University Press, 1979), 230–1—still two of the best pages ever written on Montaigne. See 2.7.11 for further discussion of these pages.

As was briefly indicated at the beginning of this section, the topic of I 25—early education—was the foundation of a broader culture that mingled learning with nobility. This highly pragmatic, Tudor variety of humanism formed social and cultural continuities between (in the case of servants) early tutorial work or (in the case of gentleman friends) wise conference with noble children, and both the scenes of learned leisure and the more directed advice on politics, conduct, intelligence, law and strategy that would serve the same aristocrats as adults. As the fictional case of Polonius makes clear, tutorial supervision of offspring and the collection of political intelligence were part of the same culture. Historians have identified a

> specific category of employee in a noble household...the scholar, retained to 'read' with his employer and his employer's associates....Such readers read, either alone or in company, on their employers' rather than on their own behalf, for purposes and with methods that varied dramatically from occasion to occasion.[85]

The higher-ranking figure, the special gentleman 'friend' or follower, whom the aristocrat did not strictly 'employ' as a servant or secretary, but who nevertheless fulfilled a related higher function, would not only 'brief' but also 'counsel' and direct his aristocratic friend, conduct his business, and orchestrate the work of lower-ranking scholar-readers and intelligencers on his behalf.[86] Examples of this more noble, non-professional kind of figure in England would be Robert Sidney and Anthony Bacon, and—in France—Michel de Montaigne and Pierre de Brach.

In his last extant letter (2 September 1590), written to Henri IV, Montaigne is anxious to specify his independence from royal liberality and paid service.[87] His avoidance of paid public employment and preference for the provision of private services and counsel (as occasion demands) is also emphasized at various points in the *Essais*. In general terms, there is an important continuity between the role Montaigne sketches for the non-professional *gouverneur* of the young nobleman in I 25, his own role in advising the Comtesse on the *gouverneur*'s office, and the 'office sans nom' he imagines for himself in advising the King on his *meurs*—not by scholastic-style readings—in III 13.[88]

---

[85] Jardine and Grafton, '"Studied for Action"', 34.

[86] For the distinction between secretarial servants who were recognized as being paid or 'entertained' by noble masters and special gentlemen friends who were never paid a salary but received recompense by means of favours and gifts, see Hammer, 'Uses of scholarship', 29, 35, 44–5, and (less explicitly) *The polarisation of Elizabethan Politics*, 285–315. Within each category, of course, there were still considerable gradations in rank, and the distinction between the two categories could be blurred in specific cases. The range went on the one hand from the unambiguously servile messenger and tutor in modern languages to the scholar-diplomat who aspired to be less a paid employee than a worthy 'friend'. Within the other category, the range went from the lower-ranking gentleman friend and scholar (e.g. Anthony Bacon) who was occasionally in danger of looking like a dependent, to the minor nobleman with a considerable estate and learned servants of his own (Robert Sidney, Fulke Greville).

[87] Montaigne, *Œuvres complètes*, 1400 (letter to Henri IV): '[j]e n'ai jamais recu bien quelconque de la liberalite des Rois non plus que demandé ny merité et nay receu nul payement des pas que j'ay employes a leur service'.

[88] I 25, NP155/BVH Paris 1595, p. 82/S168 ('la charge du gouverneur'); III 13, NP1125/BVH Paris 1595, bk. III, p. 203/S1223 ('office sans nom'). See 1.4.2.

Although Montaigne plays down the role of mothers in the actual delivery of young noblemens' education, his chapter (I 25) and his book acknowledge the agency and influence of powerfully literate noblewomen in his milieu—a fact, as we saw in 2.3.1 and 1.4.1, that is strongly highlighted by Florio's edition. In English studies, the scholarship's initial focus on the history of goal-oriented, professional, and contestatory readings has tended until recently to elide the role of women in this culture of leisurely but applied learning.[89]

In 1.1.6, the Bishop of Carlisle's sermon at the funeral of Lady Anne Clifford pointed us to the importance in elite contexts of the household 'oeconomy' of learning—the administering and application of divine and humane learning in the spaces and rooms of the household, and in contexts shaped by familial relations that involved women. Servants, books, and spaces were shared by women in the household in ways they could not be in schoolrooms and universities; they could be responsible—if under their husbands' or sons' authority—for gathering and mediating medical remedies or legal advice, and for determining and eliciting the access of scholars to the household, their employment in the household.

This has been demonstrated, using a variety of documentation, in the case of particular English noblewomen such as the Countess of Pembroke, Lady Elizabeth Russell, Lady Frances Stanley, and Lady Anne Clifford. Margaret P. Hannay's pioneering work on the learning and agency of the Countess of Pembroke is well known. Brought up in the household academy of her father, Sir Anthony Cooke, Lady Elizabeth Russell went on not only to make a translation of John Ponet that contributed to theological debate under the new monarch, but also to wield political influence via her support for pedagogues and preachers who were moving through the households of landed gentry. The evidence in the case of Lady Frances Stanley is scantier and consists of a catalogue of her books and some of the books themselves. These documents testify to the circulation of books within a network of family members and associates, more than to the acquisition of learning or any 'active' reading.[90]

The case of Lady Anne Clifford is different again.[91] Scholarship has examined the evidence behind the statements in Rainbowe's sermon (to which we limited

---

[89] Brayman Hackel, *Reading material*, 196. Among the many studies available in this field, see Micheline White (ed.), *English women, religion, and textual production, 1500–1625* (Farnham: Ashgate, 2011); Snook, *Women, reading, and the cultural politics of early modern England*; Moncrief and McPherson (eds.), *Performing pedagogy in early modern England: gender, instruction and performance*.

[90] Margaret P. Hannay, *Philip's Phoenix: Mary Sidney, Countess of Pembroke* (Oxford: Oxford University Press, 1990); Chris Laoutaris, 'The Radical Pedagogies of Lady Elizabeth Russell', in Moncrief and McPherson (eds.), *Performing pedagogy in early modern England: gender, instruction and performance*, 65–83; Brayman Hackel, *Reading material*, 240–54.

[91] There is an extensive literature on Lady Anne Clifford. For a good brief guide, see James Daybell, 'Clifford, Anne', in Garrett A. Sullivan and Alan Stewart (eds.), *The encyclopedia of English Renaissance literature* (Chichester: Wiley-Blackwell, 2012), vol. 1, 196–200. For some of the most important recent studies, see Karen Hearn and Lynn Hulse (eds.), *Lady Anne Clifford: culture, patronage and gender in 17th-century Britain* (Leeds: Yorkshire Archaeological Society, 2009).

our discussion in 1.1.6) and revealed her to be an excellent example of the house-hold service model of reading and writing with which we are concerned. Lady Anne used scholarly facilitators and readers in the domestic sphere in the way that noblemen used them in the political and diplomatic spheres.[92] Within her diaries, we find her employing a theological scholar, Mr Ran, to read the Bible with her during a period when her attempts to secure her inheritance against her husband's and the king's wishes are putting her under almost intolerable strain. Her husband intervenes to return Ran to his own studies. The prohibition may signify an acknowledgement that Lady Anne's reading and writing, facilitiated by learned servants, was a key part of her pursuit of land and position.[93]

Lady Anne's supervision and conduct of reading and writing in books is one part of a broader household practice of record-keeping that is as much administrative as intellectual, as much about finances as about the self. This practice testifies to her agency as a woman of property responsible for the past and future generations of her noble stock, and for her household family, servants, and neighbours. She did not of course do all her own writing, but she was the authorial agent—as we heard Rainbowe insist in 1.1.6. She directed and attested what her servants actually wrote—as Florio represents Lucy directing what he wrote—and supervised a complex process of transference of written records from ephemeral notes to more monumental registers, such as her 'Great Books'.

As Adam Smyth says, 'the world of written scraps, collected, passed on, revised, rationalized—this *was* Clifford's character'.[94] Whether 'retreating from an unsympathetic marriage, managing her own sizeable household, or making a claim to her inheritance', Lady Anne turned to books, and to the servants, gentlemen friends, and ministers who could help her use them. She used 'the inscription, accumulation, and deployment of texts in legal, managerial, and political activities as well as in her scholarly pursuits, devotional exercises and personal reflections'.[95]

As we shall see in 2.3.7, Lady Anne, who owned and had read to her both Florio's *Essayes* and Sidney's *Arcadia*, who performed in masques at Queen Anna's court, is the best-documented female example we have of the culture and outcomes of the noble household institution that mediates Montaigne's arrival in England.

---

[92] A. B. Kunin, 'From the desk of Anne Clifford', *English Literary History,* 71 (2004), 587–608.

[93] Julie Crawford, 'Lady Anne Clifford and the Uses of Christian Warfare', in White (ed.), *English women, religion, and textual production, 1500–1625,* 101–23, 107–11, 123.

[94] For this and the previous paragraph see Adam Smyth, *Autobiography in early modern England* (Cambridge: Cambridge University Press, 2010), 72–93 (79, 93). See also Nancy E. Wright, 'Accounting for a life: the household accounts of Lady Anne Clifford', in Ronald Bedford, Lloyd Davis, and Philippa Kelly (eds.), *Early modern autobiography: theories, genres, practices* (Ann Arbor: University of Michigan Press, 2006), 234–51, 248–9.

[95] Brayman Hackel, *Reading material,* p. 240; Eve Rachele Sanders, *Gender and literacy on stage in early modern England* (Cambridge: Cambridge University Press, 1998), p. 187.

2.3.4 FLORIO'S 'INSTITUTION AND EDUCATION OF CHILDREN'

Polonius appears to have purchased the best moral precepts available for character-ing the memory of a son about to travel. Had he been a real English noble father of the 1590s, where might he have found them? I have shown elsewhere that Florio's translation originated in a manuscript English version of Montaigne's *institution* (I 25), re-addressed to the Countess of Bedford, in relation to the education of her future son (which she did not in the event have), and her brother John Harrington.[96]

In what follows, I shall consider this manuscript chapter (insofar as we can assume it was broadly continuous with the printed version) not as a work by Montaigne transmitted via an English translation, but as a work commissioned by an English patron and performed by Florio in a nexus of service relations. The resulting text took its place in an English tradition—informed by continental sources—of courtly educational writing that stretched from Sir Thomas Elyot's *Governour* to Locke's *Some thoughts*.[97]

One example of this tradition of writing that is closely related to Florio's manu-script chapter and redolent of Polonius's precepts for a noble traveller is another translation (1592), probably by the gentleman-scholar John Stradling, dedicated to the Countess of Bedford's husband, entitled *A Direction for Trauailers. Taken out of Justus Lipsius, and enlarged for the behoofe of the right honourable Lord, the young Earl of Bedford, being now ready to travell.*[98]

In this text, the translator-author reads Lipsius's letter with and for the Earl in the way that I am arguing Florio reads I 25 with and for his wife and his mother-in-law—though Florio goes on to read the larger text for an extended group of noble and gentle patrons, including the broader readership of the printed book. From the start, Stradling regularly intervenes in the original text to direct its mes-sage in accord with the young Earl's needs. He inserts lengthy amplifications of and digressions from Lipsius's text, returning sporadically to a more or less faithful translation of the Latin.

Indeed, Stradling gradually gets more courageous in leaving the text and address-ing the Earl directly. At one point he demonstrates the ennobling value of famili-arity with learned men by textually enacting a three-way conversation with a learned foreign scholar (Lipsius), a scholar whom Bedford might actually meet on his travels. The implication is that the translator-author is not himself a profession-ally learned man, but a potential 'friend' who will accompany the Earl and guide and encourage him in his dealings with such learned men.[99]

---

[96] Boutcher, 'The origins of Florio's Montaigne'.

[97] Stephens, 'John Locke and the education of the gentleman'.

[98] USTC 512170/ESTC S101412 (and attributed to Stradling in the 'Renaissance cultural cross-roads' database). On Stradling and the attribution see *ODNB* and Boutcher, ' "Learning Mingled with Nobilitie" ', 342n.10.

[99] For a more detailed discussion, see Boutcher, ' "Learning Mingled with Nobilitie" ', 342–5.

Stradling's text is just one indication that Russell and a number of other young noblemen and noblewomen (including the Earls of Southampton and Rutland), all associated to a greater or lesser degree with the cult of Sir Philip Sidney and the career of the young Earl of Essex, were the focus in the 1590s of the cultural expectations of a large number of both poorer, base-born and higher-ranking gentlemen scholars. These expectations concerned noble employment of scholars and of scholarly advice, and of the wisdom and advice of select 'friends'.[100]

Young noble offspring were to be surrounded from an early age both in their households and in their travels with the right kinds of friends, tutors, and advisers. By this means they would pick up the habit of seeking and acting upon the right kind of advice, thereby learning to avoid the intemperate, expensive behaviour feared by Polonius and, more generally, disreputable associations with the 'wrong' religious and political causes. Specific occasions connected with the emergence of this new crop of young nobility—from married noblewomens' pregnancies to actual births and, later, early education and travel—were crucial opportunities for individuals to seek places in particular households as scholarly employees and gentlemen friends by proffering advice establishing the desirability of investment in learning and the learned. Servants and gentlemen might also be placed in these circumstances in particular households or travelling retinues by other patrons hoping through them to cement alliances or glean intelligence.[101]

Furthermore, the production of related advisory literature could represent an opportunity for politically prominent figures—from Sir Henry Sidney through King James I to Sir Henry Slingsby—to define themselves, their values, and their dynasties in coterie circles or in the public eye by publishing institutions as manuscript or printed letters to their sons, protégés, and younger brothers.[102]

With this tradition of institutional writings in mind, we can listen anew to the chapter presented by John Florio in *c.*1598–9 to Lucy Russell, the Countess of Bedford, and hear it as an English work addressed to an English patroness, in exactly the way that Stradling addressed the *Direction* to her husband, the Earl. The opening section of the printed version re-delineates Montaigne's noble, non-scholarly *persona* as that of someone who has 'seene but the superficies of true learning', and who is 'not sufficiently taught to instruct others'.[103]

But the manuscript version of this chapter most probably began with the first address to 'Madam'—who, in the English nexus, we should understand to be Lucy Russell and/or her mother:

---

[100] See the various studies by Hammer listed in the 'Bibliography', and Mervyn Evans James, *Society, politics and culture: studies in early modern England* (Cambridge: Cambridge University Press, 1986), 416–65.

[101] Hammer, *Polarisation of Elizabethan politics*, 299.

[102] Alan Stewart, *Philip Sidney: a double life* (London: Chatto & Windus, 2000), 47–8; Jason Scott-Warren, *Sir John Harington and the book as gift* (Oxford: Oxford University Press, 2001), 4–10, 17–18 (on the motives behind the private then public printing of James' advice to his four year-old son, entitled *Basilikon dōron*). On Sir Henry Slingsby, see 2.4.2–3.

[103] I 25, NP150–1/BVH Paris 1595, pp. 79–80/SCETI London 1603, pp. 67–8.

Some having read my precedent Chapter, tolde me not long since in mine owne house, I should somewhat more have extended my selfe in the discourse concerning the institution of children. Now (Madam) if there were any sufficiencie in me, touching that subject, I could not better imploy the same, then to bestowe it as a present upon that little lad, which ere long threatneth to make a happie issue from out your honorable wombe: for (Madame) you are too generous to beginne with other then a man childe.... [M]oreover the ancient and rightfull possession, which you from time to time have ever had, and still have over my service, urgeth mee with more then ordinarie respectes, to wish all honour, well-fare and advantage to whatsoever may in any sorte concerne you and yours.[104]

The question—'the nurture and institution of young children'—is shortly after this passage defined as the 'greatest difficulty' in 'all humane knowledge'. We are asked to consider 'what doubts and feares, doe daily waite on ... parents and tutors'. The problem is that natural dispositions are easily changed and soon disguised, 'men headlong embracing this custome or fashion, following that humor or opinion, admitting this or that passion, allowing of that or this law'. Then, just over the page from the first address to Madam, Florio addresses the Countess directly, with words (here underlined) that have no equivalent in the French text (Illus. 2.3.1):

Madam, Learning joyned with true knowledge [*la science*] is an especiall and gracefull ornament, and an implement of wonderfull use and consequence, namely in persons raised to that degree of fortune, wherin you are. <u>And in good truth, learning hath not her owne true forme, nor can she make shew of her beauteous lineaments, if she fall into the hands of base and vile persons. For, as famous Torquato Tasso sayeth; Philosophie being a rich and noble Queene, and knowing her owne worth, graciously smileth upon, and lovingly embraceth Princes and noble men, if they become sutors to her, admitting them as her minions, and gently affoording them all the favours she can; whereas upon the contrarie, if shee be wooed, and sued unto by clownes, mechanicall fellowes, and such base kinde of people, she holds hir selfe disparaged and disgraced, as holding no proportion with them. And therfore see we by experience, that if a true Gentleman or nobleman followe hir with any attention and wooe her with importunity, hee shall learne and knowe more of hir, and proove a better scholler in one yeere, then an ungentle, or base fellow shall in seaven, though he pursue hir never so attentively.</u> She is much more ready and fierce to lend hir furtherance and direction in the conduct of a war, to attempt honorable actions, to command a people, to treate a peace with a prince or forraine nation, then she is to form an argument in Logick, to devise a Sillogisme, to canvase a case at the barre, or to prescribe a receit of pills.[105]

---

[104] I 25, NP153/BVH Paris 1595, p. 81/SCETI London 1603, pp. 68–9. Florio is using Paris 1588 as well as Paris 1595 in translating this passage—one of the reasons it is likely to have been the beginning of the manuscript version. For the textual evidence, see Boutcher, 'The origins of Florio's Montaigne', p. 11 and the 'Appendix' to that article. We do not know for sure whether the Countess of Bedford was pregnant when she received this dedication from Florio.

[105] I 25, NP154/BVH Paris 1595, p. 82/SCETI London 1603, p. 69. As can be seen in Illus. 2.3.1, the 1603 edition places inverted commas down the right-hand margin alongside this passage from the line containing 'For, as famous...' to the line containing 'receit of pills'. This is not to indicate that the lines are an interpolation, for inverted commas appear elsewhere in the 1603 edition merely to highlight a passage of particular interest or of noteworthy sententiousness. The 1595 text of the equivalent passage in the French reads as follows: 'Madame c'est un grand ornement que la science, et un util de merveilleux service, notamment aux personnes eslevees en tel degré de fortune, comme vous estes. A la verité elle n'a

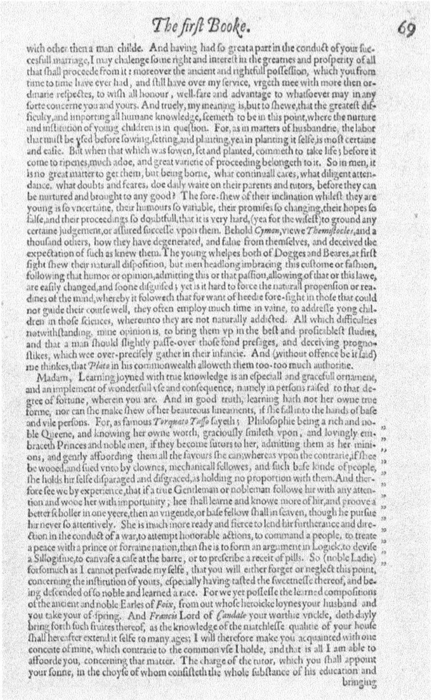

Illus. 2.3.1. Montaigne, *Essayes*, trans. Florio, London 1603, Bodleian Library, pressmark Douce M. 731, p. 69. Reproduced by permission of The Bodleian Libraries, the University of Oxford.

Once again, we hear how our French author is brought into a conversation in which a learned servant is constantly quoting Italian authors such as Tasso to his patroness and using the language of courtly romance. To learn philosophy is now to court philosophy, which means that gentlemen and noblemen who have the manners of a courtier will be able to woo her much more effectively and quickly than base persons.

I have shown in detail elsewhere that this whole passage, including the interpolation (underlined) is closely related to Florio's rhetoric in the dedications to the three books, especially the first to Lucy, Countess of Bedford, and Lady Anne Harrington (Illus. 2.3.2).[106] It also alludes back to his invocation of Learning as a Mistress in his epistle to the courteous reader.[107]

---

point son vray usage en mains viles et basses. Elle est bien plus fiere, de prester ses moyens à conduire une guerre, à commander un peuple, à pratiquer l'amitié d'un prince, ou d'une nation estrangere, qu'à dresser un argument dialectique, ou à plaider un appel, ou ordonner une masse de pillules.'

[106] SCETI London 1603, p. A2r. See Warren Boutcher, 'Florio's Montaigne: Translation and pragmatic humanism in the sixteenth century', unpublished doctoral dissertation (University of Cambridge, 1991), 161–6, 178–9, 212–16, 222–5, 228, 251–78, and 'The origins of Florio's Montaigne'.

[107] SCETI London 1603, p. A5r: 'Yea but Learning cannot be too common, and the commoner the better. Why but who is not jealous, his Mistresse should be so prostitute? Yea but this Mistresse is like ayre, fire, water...'.

TO THE RIGHT HO-
norable my best-best Benefactors, and most-
most honored Ladies,

Lucie Countesse of Bedford;

and hir best-most loved-loving Mother,

Ladie Anne Harrington.

Trange it may seeme to some, whose seeming is mis-seem-ing, in one worthlesse patronage to joyne two so severall all-worthy Ladies. But to any in the right, it would be judged wrong, to disjoyne them in ought, who never were neerer in kinde, then ever in kindnesse. None dearer (dea-rest Ladies) I have seene, and all may say, to your Honora-ble husbands then you, to you then your Honorable huf-bands; and then to other, then eyther is to th'other. So as were I to name but the one, I should surely intend the other : but intending this Dedication to two, I could not but name both. To my last Birth, which I held masculine, (as are all mens conceipts that are their owne, though but by their col-lecting, and this was to *Montaigne* like *Bacchus,* closed in, or loosed from his great *Iupiters* thigh) I the indulgent father invited two right Honorable Godfathers, with the ONE of your Noble Lady-shippes to witnesse. So to this defective edition (since all translations are reputed femals, delivered at second hand ; and I in this serve but as *Vulcan,* to hatchet this *Minerva* from that *Iupiters* bigge braine) I yet at least a fondling foster-father, having transported it from *France* to *England*; put it in English clothes; taught it to talke our tongue (though many-times with a jerke of the French *Iargon*) would set it forth to the best service I might ; and to better I might not, then You that deserve the best. Yet hath it this above your other ser-vants; it may not onely serve you two, to repeate in true English what you reade in fine French, but many thousands more, to tell them in their owne, what they would be taught in an other language. How nobly it is descended; let the father in the ninth Chapter of his third booke by letters testimoniall of the Romane Se-nate and Citty beare record : How rightly it is his, and his beloved, let him by his discourse in the eight'th of his second, written to the Lady of *Estissac* (as if it were to you concerning your sweete heire, most motherly-affected Lady *Harring-ton*) and by his acknowledgement in this first to all Readers give evidence, first that it is *de bonne foy,* then more than that, *c'est moy* : How worthily qualified, embellished, furnished it is, let his faire-spoken, and fine-witted Daughter by alli-ance passe her verdict, which thee neede not recant. Heere-hence to offer it into your service, let me for him but do and say, as he did for his other selfe, his peerlesse paire *Steven de Boetie,* in the 28. of this first, and thinke hee speakes to you my praise-

A 2

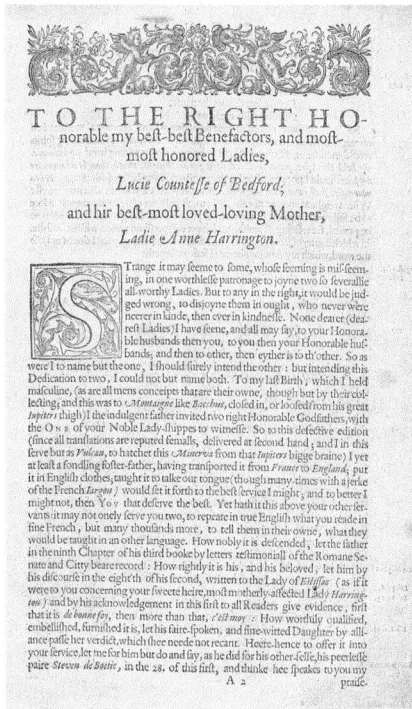

Illus. 2.3.2. Montaigne, *Essayes*, trans. Florio, London 1603, Bodleian Library, pressmark Douce M. 731, sig. A2r. Reproduced by permission of The Bodleian Libraries, the University of Oxford.

Florio clearly inserts this passage here because of the prominence given in the text (directly afterwards) to the 'noble Ladie' (the Comtesse) as a descendant of 'so noble and learned a race' as the Foix. The Foix are equivalent to families such as the Sidney-Pembrokes and the Bedford-Harringtons in England. The Countess's male ancestors were all learned, her uncle Francis Lord of Candale daily wrote learned compositions, and she herself has agency in the appointment and briefing of the tutor for her son.[108] So, although the principal noble products of the house are virtuous young noblemen and learned compositions by noble male relatives, her own learning and her position in the house do give her some agency in the process of production; again, there is some overlap between the female and male oeconomies of learning.

As we heard in 2.3.1, the same is true in the Countess of Bedford's household: her mother most likely had agency, or at least 'discretion', in appointing and instructing Diodati as tutor to the young John Harrington; she is able to appoint him as an assistant to Florio, along with Gresham professor Gwinne.[109]

---

[108] I 25, NP154–5/BVH Paris 1595, p. 82/SCETI London 1603, p. 69.

[109] BL, Lansdowne MS 108, fol. 158r (an undated letter from Lady Anne Harrington to Adam Newton, tutor and eventually secretary to Prince Henry, concerning her son's studies and tutors).

Pragmatically, then, Florio was seeking to consolidate his position as a tutor in the Harrington-Russell household and to consolidate that sense of female agency in male learning, from which he—as a tutor to noblewomen—secondarily derives his own. All of this is conveyed by the metaphorical representation of Philosophy as a queen who receives gentle male suitors at her house and court.

The overall argument Florio makes with this interpolation is Cornwallis's (see 2.3.2): that learning mingled with nobility shines most clearly. Learning does not have its true uses in the hands of poor grammar school boys and university arts students, for whom it is just a matter of ready discourse for logic, law, and medicine, but in the hands of promising young noblemen such as Lucy's brother, John Harrington, who are likely to be involved in war, honourable actions, command, and diplomacy. Philosophy and learned men are ennobling; nobles hold proportion with philosophy and her teachers. Gentlemen and noblemen are the proper end-users of learning, not logicians, lawyers, and physicians. This is so primarily because of the functions it falls to them, rather than to people of lower rank, to perform, and because, of course, they can pay for it.

Florio's elaborate insistence via Tasso that *la science*—'learning joyned with true knowledge'—is 'an implement of wonderfull use and consequence' when directed to the nobility's aims is a sales pitch for the elite scholarly services that I have been describing. The terms of the pitch could be reversed, in a situation where it is the scholar who must be persuaded of the value of employment with the nobility, or with the gentlemen friends of the nobility, as when Lionel Sharpe writes to John Coke at Trinity College, Cambridge, to persuade him to work for Sir Fulke Greville: 'You will live by means of letters with a man who is noble in the eyes of all courtiers, in the eyes of the earl of Essex especially, and a man who is in good favor with the queen' ('Vives in literis cum homine nobili apud omnes aulicos, apud Comitem Essexium imprimis et apud principem gratioso').[110]

Either way, the ideal package puts together learning, the practical knowledge on how to apply learning, and the leisure and higher purposes of noble males as mediated by their female relatives and their special gentlemen friends, and as served by scholarly retainers. The young nobleman is the English Renaissance incarnation of Petrucci's 'free literate', surrounded by servants who facilitate his 'independent' reading, writing, and speaking. Going private is quicker than going to school. With the personalized attention of individual tutors and advisers, a 'true Gentleman or nobleman' can learn in one year what a master of arts can in seven, and he is less enslaved to the directions of a textbook.

2.3.5 THE CHARGE OF THE TUTOR

Is this not precisely what Montaigne is telling us with the example of his own early institution as paid for by his father? Towards the end of I 25 he declares: 'I will tell you how they ["Greeke and Latine tongues"] may be gotten better cheape, and

---

[110] Hammer, 'The Earl of Essex, Fulke Greville, and the employment of scholars', 178, 180.

much sooner then is ordinarily used...I was above six yeares olde...I had gotten as pure a Latine tongue as my maister could speake'. Montaigne's father—himself a wealthy but uneducated merchant-bourgeois and soldier—had purchased 'a most exquisite and readie way of teaching': a household institution in pure Latin. Before he could speak, Montaigne's wet-nurse was substituted by a Latin-speaking German humanist who, aided by two assistants, had the child continually in his arms.[111]

Montaigne's father eventually yielded to common opinion and sent him to college, though he continued to demand (in Florio's words) 'the best and most sufficient Masters' and to institute 'particular rules' for his son, against the 'usuall customes of Colleges'. Soon, the formal arts curriculum began to corrupt Montaigne's Latin. But the carefully chosen *precepteur de chambre* indulged Montaigne's tendency to duck the 'prescript lessons' and allowed him to read the humanist classics—Virgil, Terence, Plautus—alongside vernacular 'Italian comedies'. Indeed, as he tells us at the beginning of the other essay on education (I 24), these comedies provided him with derisory images of humanist pedants against which to measure his personal tutors.[112]

However, in his own personalized prescriptions for a noble institution, Montaigne makes it clear that it is not a perfect knowledge of Latin that he wants to preserve from the example of his own education, but, via whatever languages and examples are needed, the special, free-ranging, vernacular informality of approach to the regular curriculum.

If, with the period's own eye, we view the entrance to the translated *Essayes* via I 25, we find ourselves ushered by Florio and the tutors who assisted him into an informal, semi-independent culture of leisurely philosophical learning. It derived from a father's 'institution' and was shared privately with friends and betters such as Montaigne's great friend La Boétie and his patroness Diane de Foix. Wittingly or not, for different readers and producers at different moments, I 25 and the *Essayes* as a whole could be seen—like much indigenous Elizabethan literature, from Lyly's first novel about *Euphues* to Sidney's revised *Arcadia*—to dramatize both confidence in and uncertainty about the contribution made by the privatized and pragmatized study of rhetorical style and philosophical learning to elite family strategies for dynastic and social reproduction.

How strong an institutional foundation did the relationship between the lord of Montaigne and his heir appear to provide? Could this rambling, unstructured, free-talking text really be the outcome of an exemplary and utilizable education in philosophy and noble virtue?

The chapter on noble education does seem, from one angle, to record a failure on the part of the Lord of Montaigne. Montaigne's father buys the best Italian advice on direct methods of Latin teaching, then changes his mind and sends him for formal training, then is disappointed in his son, who does not go on to have a

[111] I 25, NP180/BVH Paris 1595, p. 99/SCETI London 1603, p. 84.
[112] I 25, NP181–3/BVH Paris 1595, p. 100/SCETI London 1603, pp. 85–6; I 24, NP138/BVH Paris 1595, p. 71/SCETI London 1603, p. 60.

brilliant and learned career in the national establishment. One can read into it specific tensions surrounding the indeterminacy of the character (or 'humour') and action (or other outcome) that might be produced by ever-shifting educational and political ideas, as well as the general social anxiety as to whether the fruits would correspond to the intentions of parents and to religiously and politically acceptable norms. As we have seen, there are related doubts voiced in the paratexts to Florio's work about the extent to which the outcome of Montaigne's own institution might be seen as 'humorous' or 'troubled'.

At the same time, one can read Montaigne in that chapter—and in general—as a very positive model of an autonomous and learned member of the noble elite who traverses the routine pathways of humanist Latin pedagogy with informally added value and sophistication, and who travels to Rome without losing his moral integrity. He powerfully holds his moral and intellectual balance and retains an authoritative presence in the midst of shifting ideas and factions, whilst preserving the traditions of his father, the friendship of the members of his *familia*, and conformity to the religious and political establishment of France.

Indeed, from Florio's perspective, it is not difficult to see how the whole of I 25 and its companion chapter I 24 might have translated as an extended endorsement of the institutional origins of the culture of leisurely household learning and pragmatic humanism, practical scholarly services, and gentlemanly, scholarly counsel for the elite, within which Florio and his assistants sought to make their living. From this point of view, I 25 is a chapter which re-appropriates philosophy from the school and the textbook and gives it back to the development of the gentle and noble self in the company of a tutor both in the household and, in the case of the male self, on his travels.

As, insists Montaigne, a well-born child must above all else be free, and understand the difference between 'bondage and freedome, subjection and libertie', let us among 'the liberall Sciences' begin with 'that which makes us free'.[113] Travel at home through books, and abroad in person through different nations, is the principal means to this end. In this kind of life, or 'Prentiship', any action or object can serve in the place of a book as occasion for an exercise of speaking or judging. An 'idle tale or any discourse else, spoken either in jest or earnest, at the table or in companie, are even as new subjects for us to worke upon'—which is why 'visiting of forraine countries, and observing of strange fashions, are verie necessary', so as to 'be able to make certaine relation of the humours and fashions of those countries they have seene, that they may the better know how to correct and prepare their wits by those of others'.[114]

Florio—through Montaigne—recommends to the Harrington-Russells and other gentle and noble houses a 'schoole of commerce, and societie among men' which conflates 'acquaintance with men ... by the memorie of books' with actual

[113] I 25, NP165/BVH Paris 1595, p. 89/SCETI London 1603, pp. 75–6.
[114] I 25, NP158/BVH Paris 1595, pp. 84–5/SCETI London 1603, pp. 71–2.

commerce in the world.[115] A method for the household learning of Latin is offered, but knowledge of the tongues of 'my neighbours with whom I have most commerce' is also strongly recommended, along with travel abroad from 'infancie', familiar acquaintance with 'the customes, with the meanes,...the state,...the dependances and alliances of all Princes', and—as we shall see later in this section in more detail—the use of 'some learned man' who will furnish the principal tutor and adviser in manuscript with 'such munition', such 'notable discourses' as are appropriate to 'his best use'.[116]

Despite their mockery of pedants and grammarians, I 25 and the chapter which preceded it in print (I 24, 'Of Pedantisme') steadily maintain the idea that the true, classical philosopher is 'great in knowledge' acquired in contemplative leisure, yes, but 'greater in action'.

Think of the 'Syracusan Geometrician' who was taken from his 'bookish contemplation' to apply his learning in the construction of 'terror-moving engines' for the 'defence of his countrie'; the philosopher Thales, who was able to start up a 'traffike, which within one yeare brought him such riches, as the skilfullest in the trade of thriving, could hardly in all their life devise how to get the like'; Lucullus, the Roman general 'whom learning made and framed so great a Captaine without experience'—who, that is, read up history on the way to war with Mithridates and instantaneously became a great general; the Spartan, whose 'minde [is] in an uncessant practise of well-doing'; the modern scholar Adrianus Turnebus, 'sundry times of purpose' urged by Montaigne 'to speak of matters furthest from his study' and who was able to judge of such matters as 'hee seemed never to have professed or studied other facultie then warre, and matters of state'.[117]

These, indeed, are the examples Montaigne uses to make the argument that there is nothing wrong with philosophy per se, but only with our route to it, our institution, the kind of approach to learning and the kind of scholars in which we have invested our money and our belief—'[t]hey knowe the Theorike of all things, but *you* muste seeke who shall put it in practise' (my italics). Learning without the 'skill to manage the same' is a 'dangerous Sworde'—a highly appropriate metaphor when you are addressing the nobility.[118] So it is that when Montaigne comes to offer the Countess his conceit about education 'contrarie to the common use' he puts the emphasis on the 'charge of the tutor...in the choyse of whom consisteth the whole substance of his education'.[119]

At the heart of I 25, and of the work as a whole, when viewed from Florio's perspective, is the question of how humane learning and experts in humane learning

[115] I 25, NP159/BVH Paris 1595, p. 85/SCETI London 1603, p. 72; I 25, NP162/BVH Paris 1595, p. 96 [87]/ SCETI London 1603, p. 74.

[116] I 25, NP180/BVH Paris 1595, p. 98/SCETI London 1603, p. 84; I 25, NP158/BVH Paris 1595, p. 84/SCETI London 1603, p. 72; I 25, NP162/BVH Paris 1595, p. 96 [87]/ SCETI London 1603, p. 74; I 25, NP166/BVH Paris 1595, p. 90/SCETI London 1603, p. 76.

[117] I 24, NP140/BVH Paris 1595, pp. 72–3/SCETI London 1603, p. 61; I 24, NP142/BVH Paris 1595, p. 74/SCETI London 1603, p. 63; I 24, NP144/BVH Paris 1595, p. 75/SCETI London 1603, p. 64.

[118] I 24, NP144–5/BVH Paris 1595, pp. 75–6/SCETI London 1603, pp. 63–4.

[119] I 25, NP155/BVH Paris 1595, p. 82/SCETI London 1603, p. 69.

such as Diodati—recently brought in at considerable expense from Geneva—should be used in the culture of a well-born person such as the young Harrington. Montaigne's father took advice from learned men around him on the best way to fashion a son with the grandeur of mind and knowledge of the ancient Romans and Greeks. He was told that the key lay in finding a fast, early route to mastery of their languages: Latin and Greek. So he hired a very expensive German humanist and medical doctor who would only speak Latin to his son, and who would be aided by two less learned men. But when his original advisers were no longer around him, Pierre lost faith in his household scheme and sent Michel off for a formal collegiate education in the arts.

Montaigne's own 'conceite' is to put amateur, non-expert gentlemen such as himself in charge in a way that he implies his father did not. The crucial point is that he adjusts the relations between expert readers, books, and gentle laypersons such that it is a tutor with the qualities (if not the attested social status) of a gentleman who judges what use is to be made of books and of professional processors of books in an everyday school of philosophical inquiry without walls—with, of course, another noble gentleman (himself) in the background to advise on the role of the tutor. Instead of putting a learned expert in charge of two less expert assistants, as his father did, he puts a less expert tutor with gentlemanly judgement in charge of two 'readers' who do no more than provide material. So the experts' reading serves the tutor's purposes, which are the exercise of judgement and virtue, not the display of 'reading'—that is, learning and expertise.

The French words used by Montaigne to describe the role of this figure are 'gouverneur', 'conducteur', and 'guide'.[120] The passage in which he is first described, which falls just after the passage into which Florio interpolates the saying of Tasso, is tellingly amplified in the English version:

> The charge of the tutor, which you [the Countess] shall appoint your sonne, in the choyse of whom consisteth the whole substance of his **education and bringing-up**; on which are many branches depending, which (forasmuch as I can adde nothing of any moment to it) I will not touch at-all.... To a **gentleman borne of noble parentage, and heire of a house**, that aymeth at true learning, and in it would be disciplined, not so much for gaine or commoditie to himselfe (because so abject an end is farre unworthie the grace and favour of the Muses, and besides, hath a regarde or dependencie of others) nor for externall **shew and ornament**, but to adorne and enrich his inward minde, desiring rather to shape and institute an able and sufficient man, than a <u>bare</u> learned man. My desire is therefore, that <u>the parents or overseers of such a gentleman</u> bee very **circumspect, and carefull** in chusing his director, whom <u>I would rather commend</u> for having a **well composed and temperate braine**, then a full stuft head, yet both will doe well. And I would rather prefer **wisdome, judgement, civill customes,**

and modest behaviour, then <u>bare and meere literall</u> learning; and that in his charge he hold a new course.[121]

In the English version it is more clearly implied that he is not a professional *homme de lettres*, but someone with the qualities of a gentleman: 'wisedome, judgement, civill customes, and modest behaviour, [rather] then bare and meere literall learning' ('plus les mœurs et l'entendement que la science'). It is a sign of 'a noble, and effect of an undanted spirit' ('l'effet d'une haute ame et bien forte') in this 'director' to be able to guide the first steps in learning of a child, and not by the book. Only such a man will be able to facilitate the enfranchisement of his well-born pupil's mind:

> our minde doth move at others pleasure, as tied and forced to serve the fantasies of others, being brought under by authoritie, and forced to stoope to the lure of their bare lesson; we have beene so subjected to harpe upon one string…our vigor and libertie is cleane extinct.

There follows the example of a professor at Pisa who was not only enthralled to Aristotle, but consequently to the Inquisition at Rome.[122]

The tutor, then, is not a professional provider of 'theorike', but a wise guide to the skill of managing learning in conversational practice. Furthermore, the relationship between the tutor and his charge becomes the paramount social relationship in the household—not even the parents can interfere with it.[123] For it is the tutor who will direct the student's learning, not the textbook—he must have a perfect grasp of the pace and strengths of his charge's mind and adapt his lesson accordingly and gently. How could there be a standard, printed *institutio*, 'one selfe-same lesson, and like maner of education, to direct many spirits of diverse formes and different humours'? This would, again, be to stoop like a tamed hawk to 'the lure' of a 'bare lesson'.[124]

If the pupil embraces the opinions of Xenophon or Plato, 'they shall be no longer theirs, but his'. He needs not to learn precepts and their provenance, but how to apply them. The book is only there to enable you to move on to something else, to the direct disposition of knowledge—in our terms, it indexes conversation

---

[121] I 25, NP155/BVH Paris 1595, p. 82/SCETI London 1603, pp. 69–70. Bold type indicates amplifications of the original, and underlining added phrases—though the distinction is a subjective one. Florio takes at least one reading ('les lettres et la discipline') from an earlier edition here (NP155*a*). The French text reads as follows: 'La charge du gouverneur, que vous luy donrez, du chois duquel depend tout l'effect de son institution, elle a plusieurs autres grandes parties, mais je n'y touche point, pour n'y sçavoir rien apporter qui vaille …. A un enfant de maison, qui recherche les lettres [80–8: les lettres et la discipline], non pour le gaing (car une fin si abjecte, est indigne de la grace et faveur des Muses, et puis elle regarde et depend d'autruy) ny tant pour les commoditez externes, que pour les sienes propres, et pour s'en enrichir et parer au dedans, ayant plustost envie d'en reussir habil'homme, qu'homme sçavant, je voudrois aussi qu'on fust soigneux de luy choisir un conducteur, qui eust plustost la teste bien faicte, que bien pleine: et qu'on y requist tous les deux, mais plus les mœurs et l'entendement que la science: et qu'il se conduisist en sa charge d'une nouvelle maniere.'
[122] I 25, NP156/BVH Paris 1595, p. 83/SCETI London 1603, p. 70.
[123] I 25, NP159/BVH Paris 1595, p. 85/SCETI London 1603, p. 72.
[124] I 25, NP154–5/BVH Paris 1595, p. 82/SCETI London 1603, pp. 69–70.

and action, not the learning of grammar and other feats of memory.[125] And in a great book such as Livy's or Plutarch's there are a thousand institutions or pointers of 'ways to walke in', which it takes a skilful reader to see.[126] Beyond this, the 'Schollers choise-booke' is 'this worldes-frame' itself.[127]

As to the practicalities of the noble pupil's intellectual exercise, Montaigne envisages a team of paid scholarly readers working under the tutor and directing him in his daily, changing conference with books and learning. We heard above that the situation described had become an institution in English noble house-holds by the 1590s. Once he has been taught 'what is fit to make him better and wiser' he can move on to more traditional disciplines such as rhetoric and logic. 'Talk' and 'book' are to be alternated:

> His lecture [*leçon*] shalle be sometimes by way of talk [*devis*], and sometimes by booke: his tutor may now and then supplie-him with the same Authour, as an ende and motive of his institution: sometimes giving him the pith and substance of-it readie chewed. And if of-him-selfe he be not so throughly acquainted with bookes, that he may readily find so manie notable discourses as are in them to effect his purpose, it shall not be amisse, that some learned man being appointed to keepe him company, who at any time of neede, may furnish him with such munition, as he shall stand in neede-of; that he may afterwarde distribute and dispence them to his best use.[128]

Here, again, is the household service model of learning. Instead of the standard textbook lessons in rhetoric and logic, the pupil's father employs a non-professional man of gentle temperament to supervise exercises appropriate to the specific changing needs of his particular son's education, and this 'gouverneur' in turn employs scholarly facilitators who will furnish materials for his purposes. The 'lecture' (Florio's translation of 'leçon') or verbal instance of instruction is always based on reading.[129]

---

[125] I 25, NP159/BVH Paris 1595, p. 85/SCETI London 1603, p. 72.

[126] I 25, NP162/BVH Paris 1595, p. 96 [87]/SCETI London 1603, p. 74.

[127] I 25, NP164/BVH Paris 1595, p. 97 [88]/SCETI London 1603, p. 75.

[128] I 25, NP166/BVH Paris 1595, p. 90/SCETI London 1603, p. 76: 'Sa leçon se fera tantost par devis, tantost par livre: tantost son gouverneur luy fournira de l'autheur mesme propre à cette fin de son institution: tantost il luy en donnera la moelle, et la substance toute maschee. Et si de soy mesme il n'est assez familier des livres, pour y trouver tant de beaux discours qui y sont, pour l'effect de son dessein, on luy pourra joindre quelque homme de lettres, qui à chaque besoing fournisse les munitions qu'il faudra, pour les distribuer et dispenser à son nourrisson.' For a direct comparison (in a context relating to the 'continuing' education of an older nobleman) see the letter to Greville on his studies: 'You tell me that you are going to Cambridge, and that the ends of your going are to get a scholar to your liking to live with you, and two or three others to remain in the University and gather for you; and you require my opinion what instruction you shall give these gatherers.... He that shall out of his own reading gather for the use of another, must (as I think) do it by Epitome or Abridgment, or under Heads and Commonplaces. Epitomes also may be of two sorts; of any one art or part of knowledge out of many books, or of one book by itself etc.' There is the same emphasis as in Montaigne on the inadequacy of a 'mere scholar'. See Francis Bacon, *The letters and life*, ed. James Spedding, 7 vols. (London: Longman, Green, Longman, and Roberts, 1861–74), vol. 2, 21–2, 25.

[129] See OED, 'lecture *n.*', senses 3 ('The action of reading aloud. Also, that which is so read, a lection or lesson. *arch.*'), 5a ('The instruction given by a teacher to a pupil or class at a particular time; a lesson. *Obs*'), 5†b ('*fig.* A "lesson", an instructive counsel or example. *Obs.*').

Sometimes, as in the case of Stradling with the Earl of Bedford and the Lipsius letter, the tutor will supply just one author as the 'ende and motive of his institution', so that a direct reading of the text gives rise to the discussion. On other occasions, the direct reading of the text will have been undertaken beforehand (by the assistants) and the tutor will present a digested version of the substance verbally.

This passage provides us with a key to the early English reception of the *Essais* in informal tutorial contexts: they offered a rich compendium of 'lectures', or readings-aloud with discussion, of the kind that corresponded to the practice of Florio and other tutors in noble households. These 'lectures' also provided a rich resource for the staging of free-form elite conversation in the public theatres.

The situation described in this passage, then, uncannily matches the situation in the Harrington-Russell and other noble households where Montaigne's own work was being read in leisurely tutorials and digested in English, by a team of lower-ranking readers and higher-ranking tutors including Florio, Diodati, and Gwinne, as the 'ende and motive' of the institutions of young noblemen and noblewomen.[130] This kind of household 'institution'—not just for young children but also for young adults and beyond—proves to be the typical context of the translation of Montaigne's text to England.

2.3.6 FLORIO AND DANIEL ON STATELY VIRTUE

To put it another way, the 'one chapter' (I 25) turns out to be not just the origin of the printed translation, but its raison d'être. And at the centre of that chapter is Florio's amply expanded version of Montaigne's description of the 'aim' of all philosophy: noble virtue:

> [Philosophie] aymeth at <u>nothing but</u> vertue: <u>it is vertue shee seekes after</u>; which as the schoole saieth, is not [i.e. which is not, *pace* the school] pitcht on the top of an high, steepie, or inaccessible hil; <u>for</u> they that have come unto hir, affirme, that cleane-contrarie, shee keeps hir stand, <u>and holds hir mansion</u>, in a faire, flourishing, and pleasant plaine, whence <u>as from an high watch Tower</u>, she survaieth all things, **to be subject unto hir**, to whome any man may <u>with great facility</u> come; if he but knowe the way <u>or entrance to hir pallace</u>: for, the pathes <u>that leade unto hir</u>, are certaine fresh, and shadie <u>greene</u> allies, sweete and flowerie wayes, whose ascent is even, easie, <u>and nothing wearisome</u>, like unto that of **heavens**-vaultes. Forsomuch as they have not frequented this vertue, <u>who gloriously, as in a throne of Majesty sittes</u> **soveraigne, goodly,** triumphant, **lovelie,** equally delicious, and couragious, <u>protesting her-selfe to be</u> a professed and

---

[130] I do not have space here to raise in a satisfactory way the issues of gender and rank within the community of scholars and readers attending on the members of these noble households. The principal tutor to the male heirs (a position later held by Adam Newton, in John Harrington's case) clearly ranked highest, but, as letters written by one tutor (Jacques Petit) from the Harrington household show, there were a large number of other tutors jostling for lower positions as modern language tutors to the young noblewomen of the house. The key point is that Florio's oft-noted concerns with 'female' secondarity in the dedications to the translation ultimately relate to this social context. See Boutcher, 'Florio's Montaigne', 214–16.

irreconciliable enemie to al sharpenesse, austerity, feare and compulsion; having nature for hir guide, fortune and voluptuousnesse for her companions; they according to their weakenesse have imaginarily fained hir, to have a foolish, sadde, <u>grimme</u>, quarelous, spitefull, threatning and disdainfull visage, <u>with an horride and unpleasant looke</u>; and have placed her, upon a <u>craggy, sharpe, and</u> unfrequented rocke, amidst **desart cliffes, and uncouth crags**, as a skarre crowe, <u>or Bugge-beare</u>, to affright the <u>common</u> people with. Now the tutour, which ought to know, that hee should rather seeke to fill <u>the minde, and store</u> the will of his disciple, as much or rather more, with <u>love and</u> affection, then with <u>awe, and</u> reverence unto vertue, **may** <u>shewe and</u> tell him, that Poets followe common humours, <u>making him plainly to perceive</u>, and <u>as it were</u> palpablie to feele, that the Gods have rather placed <u>labour and</u> sweat at the entrances, which leade to Venus chambers then <u>at the dores, that direct</u> to Pallas cabinets.

And when he shall <u>perceive his scholler</u> to have a sensible feeling of himselfe, presenting *Bradamant*, or *Angelica* before him, as a Mistresse to enjoy, <u>embelished</u> with a natural, active, generous <u>and unspotted</u> beautie, not <u>uglie or</u> Giant-like, but **blithe and livelie**, in respect of a <u>wanton</u>, softe, affected, and artificiall-<u>flaring</u> beautie; the one **attired** like unto a yoong man, coyfed with a bright-shining helmet, the other <u>disguised and</u> drest about the head like unto an <u>impudent</u> **harlot**, with embroyderies, <u>frizelings, and carcanets</u> of pearles: he will <u>no doubt</u> deeme his owne love **to be a man and no woman,** if in his choice he differ from that effeminate shepheard of <u>Phrigia</u>. In this new kinde of lesson, he **shall declare** unto him, that the prize, <u>the glory</u>, and height of true vertue, consisteth in the facility, profit and pleasure of his exercises: so far from difficultie, <u>and encombrances</u>, that children as well as men, the simple as soone as the wise, may come unto hir. <u>Discretion and</u> temperance, not force <u>or way-wardness</u> are the instruments <u>to bring him unto hir</u>...If so it happen, that his Disciple proove of so different a condition, that he rather love to give-eare to an <u>idle</u> fable, then unto the report of some **noble** voiage, or other <u>notable and</u> wise discourse, when he shal heare-it; that at the sound of a drumme <u>or clang of a Trumpet</u>, which are wont to <u>rowze and</u> arme the youthly heate of his companions, turneth to another that calleth him to <u>see a play</u>, tumbling, jugling tricks, <u>or other idel loose-time sports</u>; and who for pleasures-sake doth not deeme it more delightsome to returne all sweaty and **weary** from a victorious combate, <u>from wrestling or riding of a horse</u>, than from a Tennis-court, or dancing schoole, with the prize <u>or honor</u> of such exercises; The best remedy I know for such a one, is, to put him **prentise to some base occupation**, in some good towne or other, yea were he the sonne of a Duke; according to *Platoes* rule, who saieth, *that children must be placed, not according to their fathers conditions, but the faculties of their mind.*[131]

[131] I 25, NP167–9/BVH Paris 1595, pp. 91–2[76]/ SCETI London 1603, pp. 77–8. Underlinings indicate material added by the translator; bold type indicates modified sense; italics represent italics in the original text. The French text reads as follows: '[La philosophie] a pour son but, la vertu: qui n'est pas, comme dit l'eschole, plantée à la teste d'un mont coupé, rabotteux et inaccessible. Ceux qui l'ont approchée, la tiennent au rebours, logée dans une belle plaine fertile et fleurissante: d'où elle void bien souz soy toutes choses; mais si peut on y arriver, qui en sçait l'addresse, par des routtes ombrageuses, gazonnées, et doux-fleurantes; plaisamment, et d'une pante facile et polie, comme est celle des voutes celestes. Pour n'avoir hanté cette vertu supreme, belle, triumphante, amoureuse, delicieuse pareillement et courageuse, ennemie professe et irreconciliable d'aigreur, de desplaisir, de crainte, et de contrainte, ayant pour guide nature, fortune et volupté pour compagnes: ils sont allez selon leur foiblesse, faindre cette sotte image, triste, querelleuse, despite, menaceuse, mineuse, et la placer sur un rocher à l'escart, emmy des ronces: fantosme à estonner les gens. Mon gouverneur qui cognoist devoir remplir la volonté de son disciple, autant ou plus d'affection, que de reverence envers la vertu, luy sçaura dire,

This is a vision of the path through learning and experience to virtue for elite Elizabethan readers of courtly, pastoral romances from Lyly to Sidney, from Ariosto to Tasso. In Florio's English version, this passage links with his Tasso-inspired interpolation on Queen Philosophy, re-invoked here by the amplification in the first line: '[Philosophie] aymeth at <u>nothing but</u> vertue: <u>it is vertue *shee* seekes after</u>' (my italics). Just as to learn philosophy was to court Queen Philosophy, so now to seek virtue is to court Queen Virtue in a pastoral scene of sweet and flowery ways that meander to the palace of an enthroned sovereign. There is no labour and sweat in this pleasant plain, just love and affection.

Florio's slanted interpretations and amplifications are so numerous in this passage as to amount to a running gloss for the Countess and her noble ilk—a 'lecture' on Montaigne's text. Remember, also, that Florio was a tutor in Italian who taught French as well: the use of two heroines from Ariosto's *Orlando Furioso* for the choice between vice and virtue could hardly be more appropriate.

In his reading, Florio consistently unfolds Montaigne's text to explicate the 'aim' of philosophy as a distinctively noble, because stately, majestic and glorious, even heavenly virtue: 'logee' yields a 'mansion'; 'd'où elle void' becomes a picture of 'vertue' surveying all things from 'an high watch Tower'; 'souz soy' gives her 'subjects'; 'l'addresse', a pallace entrance; 'voutes celestes' becomes 'heavens-vaultes'. These precedents herald the textually unjustifiable introduction of Queen Virtue's state ('who gloriously, as in a throne of Majesty sittes') and prepare for the gentle expurgation of some of her Venerean aspects ('goodly' for 'belle', 'lovelie' for 'amoureuse').

Queen Virtue's scholastic counterpart, according to the logic of the translator, must become a vicious counterpart, a tyrant cowing the 'common' people. These readings are all continuous with emphases introduced in the English version later in the passage ('the prize, <u>the glory</u>'; '<u>idle</u> fable... **noble** voiage'; '**base occupation**'). Florio retains Montaigne's ironically severe judgement that if the pupil proves to be of the wrong 'condition' (which, as a well-born heir, he should not be)—that is, not naturally inclined to virtue—then he should be disenfranchised and sent to serve as an apprentice in a base occupation. He adds the popular theatre to Montaigne's list of 'idel loose-time sports' to be contrasted with the report of some noble voyage, or other notable and wise discourse.

que les poëtes suivent les humeurs communes: et luy faire toucher au doigt, que les dieux ont mis plutost la sueur aux advenues des cabinetz de Venus que de Pallas. Et quand il commencera de se sentir, luy presentant Bradamant ou Angelique, pour maistresse à jouir: et d'une beauté naïve, active, genereuse, non hommasse, mais virile, au prix d'une beauté molle, affettée, delicate, artificielle; l'une travestie en garçon, coiffée d'un morrion luisant: l'autre vestue en garce, coiffée d'un attifet emperlé: il jugera masle son amour mesme, s'il choisit tout diversement à cet effeminé pasteur de Phrygie. Il luy fera cette nouvelle leçon, que le prix et hauteur de la vraye vertu, est en la facilité, utilité et plaisir de son exercice: si esloigné de difficulté, que les enfans y peuvent comme les hommes, les simples comme les subtilz. Le reglement c'est son util, non pas la force.... Si ce disciple se rencontre de si diverse condition, qu'il aime mieux ouyr une fable, que la narration d'un beau voyage, ou un sage propos, quand il l'entendra: Qui au son du tabourin, qui arme la jeune ardeur de ses compagnons, se destourne à un autre, qui l'appelle au jeu des batteleurs: Qui par souhait ne trouve plus plaisant et plus doux, revenir poudreux et victorieux d'un combat, que de la paulme ou du bal, avec le prix de cet exercice: je n'y trouve autre remede, sinon qu'on le mette patissier dans quelque bonne ville: fust il fils d'un Duc: suivant le precepte de Platon, qu'il faut colloquer les enfans, non selon les facultez de leur pere, mais selon les facultez de leur ame.'

In his preliminary poem to London 1603, Samuel Daniel represents Florio's work as one of the best books to have introduced, in a situation of confusion and uncertainty, the 'likeliest images frailtie can finde', and to have made sallies out upon the tyrant custom. The English Montaigne's challenge in I 25 to the customary scholastic image of 'vertue' is one of these images. We can infer this from its presence in another poem of Daniel's that was addressed, like Florio's chapter in its manuscript version, to the Countess of Bedford. The poem appeared in a volume that had very close connections with London 1603, beyond the fact that Daniel had poems in both. Like Florio's volume it was issued as a folio (though a much slimmer one) by Edward Blount, printed by Valentine Simmes in 1603—a rare departure from Daniel's normal practice of publishing his works with Simon Waterson.[132]

The showpiece poem had been written to be presented to the new King James at the Harringtons' house at Burley-on-the-Hill in Rutlandshire—one of the houses in which Florio might have performed his translation under the supervision of the dedicatees of book 1 (Lady Anne Harrington and her daughter the Countess of Bedford). According to one contemporary account, King James, on his progress south to take the throne of England, arrived there on 23 April 1603, having just visited another household associated in Florio's dedications with the translation, that of the Earl and Countess of Rutland.[133]

Daniel's poem to King James at one point describes it as the greatest glory 'to give/ The institution with the happy birth/ Unto a King, and teach him how to live' (alluding to the *Basilikon dōron* addressed to Prince Henry, translated by Florio into Italian in 1603), and the poem's didactic tone makes it readable as his own gift to James of an institution in how to live and to rule.[134] The message of the poem is that James shall not change the frame of the Tudor state but continue the work, begun by Henry VII, of the restoration of England to its native ancient modesty, and of the English to themselves, from out of tyranny and foreign sins (under Richard III). He will help the English to continue to unlearn false arts and recover their plainness, while resisting all the stratagems of art.

The first important point for this argument is that Daniel's slim folio volume already makes use of Florio's translation in several places, including in the final

---

[132] Daniel, *A panegyrike* [ESTC S107347]. I used the British Library copy, pressmark C.102.K.17(2), which contains an inserted manuscript letter to Edward Seymour, the Earl of Hertford. The textual history of the various editions and issues of this collection is complex. The folio edition I am citing has a variant issue with no text of the 'defence of ryme', with a title page which does not mention that the 'Panegyrike' was delivered to the King at 'Burleigh Harrington in Rutlandshire', and with various other differences [ESTC S107436]. A smaller octavo edition was also issued by Blount in the same year, not printed by Simmes [ESTC S109270]. The British Library holds an undated folio holograph of the 'Panegyrike' with fewer stanzas than the printed version (BL, MS Royal 18. A. LXII).

[133] M. T., *The true narration of the entertainment of his Royall Majestie, from the time of his departure from Edenbrough; till his receiving at London* (London: Thomas Creede for Thomas Millington, 1603), sigs. E2v–E3r. He returned to the Harrington household on the 25 April (sig. E4r).

[134] Daniel, *A panegyrike*, sig. A3v; Curtis Perry, *The making of Jacobean culture: James I and the renegotiation of Elizabethan literary practice* (Cambridge: Cambridge University Press, 1997), 25–6.

prose treatise, the 'Defence of Ryme'. As the same publisher issued both volumes during 1603, this makes it very likely that Daniel had access to Florio's manuscript. 'Defence' parallels the 'Panegyrike' in arguing for the preservation of the customary state of England at a time of potential upheaval (as a foreign king and queen, and two new courts, travel south). In the case of the prose treatise, the argument is in response to a proposal to bring classical quantitative metres into English verse, which is treated as a viper-like innovation that would overthrow the whole state of rhyme in the kingdom.[135]

In 1602, the neo-Latin poet Thomas Campion had dedicated a treatise to Lord Buckhurst proposing a new 'art' of English verse to be regulated by the rules of classical metrics. In the style of an English Montaigne, Daniel receives this new art, this 'strange shape of opinion and discourse', with the caution it deserves: 'I thanke God that I am none of these great Schollers, if thus their hie knowledges does but give them more eyes to looke out into uncertaintie and confusion'. He faces down this expert in the new classical learning on behalf of his own patron, the Earl of Pembroke, in whose mother's household 'school' he had resided and learned to rhyme at Wilton.[136]

Daniel's *Defence* is so redolent of Florio's Montaigne in its theme and mode of argument that it almost constitutes an extra chapter for that work. It also helps us understand what Daniel means when he says in his dedicatory poem (to Florio's translation) that Montaigne's essays constitute sallies out upon the tyrant custom. In the *Defence*, Daniel makes a sally out upon a new and tyrannical custom (quantitative metrics), a custom which derives from a broader custom of servile, unexamined imitation of the Greeks and Romans.

Daniel had learned to judge better than Campion of such matters in the noble household school of Wilton. He correspondingly identifies Campion's proposal as a *false* sally out—in the name of tyrannical rules of rhetorical art based on the prosody of Greece and Rome—upon a seemingly 'barbarous' custom (rhyme), that turns out to be a perfectly natural and rational custom for the English and for many other nations. In the course of doing this he quotes the experience with which Montaigne opens I 30: the Greek King Pyrrhus's discovery that the Romans were self-evidently not as barbarous as he had been led to believe.[137] None of this means that Daniel does not recognize—as Montaigne recognizes—that long-standing customs can turn out to be 'ill customs' needing examination and reform.

In the same volume, Daniel's discussion of the endless verbal contentions in the science of law, from the opening of *Essayes* III 13, informs his praise of the learning and virtues of a noble lawyer, Sir Thomas Egerton, Lord Keeper of the Great Seal (who also received the dedication to Gwinne's *Orationes*).[138] The poem to Egerton

[135] J. I. M. Stewart, 'Montaigne's *Essays* and *A Defence of Ryme*', *The Review of English Studies*, o.s. 9 (1933), 311–12.

[136] Daniel, *A panegyrike*, sigs. G3r, H3r–v.

[137] Daniel, *A panegyrike*, sigs. G6v–H1r; SCETI London 1603, p. 100.

[138] See Daniel, *A panegyrike*, sigs. C2r (the last stanza), C3r (the top two stanzas), and compare with SCETI London 1603, pp. 634–5. The borrowing is most apparent in the relationship between Daniel's description of law as 'a Science, that by nature breeds/ Contention…: For altercation controversie feeds' and Florio's description of 'a Science that of her owne nature engendreth altercation and

is one of several poetic epistles to diverse members of the nobility, three of whom are noblewomen from the same milieu as those who feature in Florio's volume. They include Lady Margaret (née Russell), Countess of Cumberland, and her daughter Lady Anne Clifford, whom Daniel was tutoring during this period, and who is later represented on canvas and in writing with a copy of Florio's Montaigne (see 2.3.7).[139]

But the most important connection for the current argument is with Daniel's poem to Lady Lucy, Countess of Bedford,[140] for it is clearly connected with Florio's dedication of the manuscript of I 25 and of book 1 of the printed *Essayes* to the same patroness. Daniel's poem offers a picture of the Countess as the 'learned Lady' whose studies are the only way to glory, to a place on high, in state, in residence with virtue.

The poem opens with a description of this stately virtue that is complementary to the one addressed by Florio to the Countess in I 25. Though virtue is the same in the humble shadows of obscurity as when she is sat 'in Court, clad with authoritie' yet, 'Madame' (says Daniel to the Countess, echoing Florio's address), her ability is confined unless 'she [h]ath mounted in open sight/ An eminent, and spacious dwelling got'—a dwelling such as Florio's mansion or palace of virtue. In such an eminent dwelling, '[w]ith such a goodly and respected face / Doth vertue looke, that's set to looke from hie,/ And such a faire advantage by her place/ Hath state and greatnesse to doe worthily.' It then transpires that the dwelling is the house of the Countess herself, who has let virtue in—'a house so sweete/ So good, so faire; so faire, so good a guest,/ Who now remaines as blessed in her seate,/ As you are with her residencie blesst'.

So the Countess is identified with Virtue, and her house with Virtue's mansion. If the first half of the poem is related to Florio's 'vertue' and its addressee, the second half is closely related to the first half of Daniel's poem in London 1603, 'concerning *his translation of* Montaigne'. The message to the Countess in the *Panegyrike* volume is that 'all the good we have rests <u>in the mind,</u>/ <u>By whose proportions</u> onely we redeeme/ <u>Our</u> thoughts from out <u>confusion</u>, and do finde/ The measure of our selves, and of our powres' (my underlining). This is exactly what Daniel shows himself doing, in Montaigne-like manner, in the *Defence*, when he redeems thinking on prosody from out of confusion.

Later in the poem to the Countess he addresses the role of books, which he says cannot on their own make the mind capable of this. The mind must already be apt to be set aright. Yet do books 'rectifie it [the mind] in that kinde,/ And touch it so, as that it turnes that way/ Where judgement lies'. And though 'we cannot finde/

division'. In Florio, this immediately follows an anecdote about 'Ferdinando, King of Spaine', who sent 'certaine Colonies into the Indies' without any lawyers, which is used by Daniel in the following stanza. Over the page, Florio has: '*Difficultatem facit doctrina: Learning breeds difficulty.* Wee found many doubts in *Ulpian*, we finde more in *Bartolus* and *Baldus*'. This informs the inclusion of the same Latin tag as a marginal note to Daniel's next stanza, which concerns the 'Bartolists', whose 'learning.../...opened wider passages of doubt'.

[139] Daniel, *A panegyrike*, sigs. E1r, E5r.
[140] Daniel, *A panegyrike*, sigs. E3v–4r, for all the quotations that follow. I have emended 'shath' [*sic*] to '[h]ath'.

The certaine place of truth, yet doe they [books] stay,/ And intertaine us neere about the same./And give the <u>Soule the best delights</u> that may/Encheere it most'.[141]

This is exactly what Daniel says Florio's book can do in his preliminary poem on the translation, whose originary chapter had been shown to the Countess and whose entire first book was at the same moment being dedicated to the Countess and her mother. Florio's work provides an experience, in its own genre, similar to the experience of being led in a Sidneian prose romance through confusion, then entertained near about the place of truth, cheered with best delights. In Daniel's mind, Montaigne's book plays the role in the institution of young noblemen and noblewomen in the Countess's household that Plutarch's book was to play in the household of Montaigne's noble young scholar. Daniel and Florio, in preparing the material for 'lecture' by talk and by book, play the roles of the tutor and learned servant described by Montaigne in I 25.

To recall, once again, the chivalric terms of Daniel's dedicatory poem to Florio's Montaigne: when we are overcharged with the mass of books that stuff the world, that figure man's 'manifold incertaintie', and the appetite of our skill as readers is confounded, when we are oppressed on all sides with the 'presse of writings', 'the strange shapes of opinions and discourse' shadowed in paper leaves and with '[c]ustome, the mightie tyrant of the earth' seemingly subjecting us from our tender births, it is Prince Montaigne who we need as a companion, who will make sallies out upon the tyrant, who will adventure his own estate to <u>'give the best proportions to the minde / Of our confusion'</u> and find 'the likeliest images frailtie can finde', wherein the 'skill-desiring <u>soule</u>/ Takes her delight, <u>the best of all delight</u>', and 'where her motions evenest come to rowle/ About this doubtfull center of the right'.

Montaigne is, in short, the gentleman adviser who will put one's 'lectures' from books on the best footing, who will best conduct one's commerce with books and one's employment of the learned and learned arts, and who will best guide one to the stately mansion of virtue, for wherever one may go 'the franchise of his worth is allow'd'. The richest library can be but poor without him, and those who profess letters and have him not will be beaten more soundly by their fate than the pedant without a copy of Homer was beaten by Alcibiades.[142]

Reading between Daniel's lines, the promise is that this book is one of a choice few—including Sidney's *Arcadia*—that, through 'lectures', could provide intellectual and ethical substance to a whole noble household-service culture focused on the provision of learning relevant to the lives and purposes of the gentle and the noble, both female and male. It was a culture which desperately needed, as its justification, the image of the self-possessed noble consumer of knowledge—whether a noble lawyer such as Thomas Egerton or a noblewoman such as Lucy Russell—who, aided by books such as Montaigne's, and tutors or 'directors' such as Daniel, would not lose their way amidst so many 'directions', especially after 1601.

[141] Daniel, *A panegyrike*, sig. E4r–v. The underlined phrases are those which can be compared directly with similar phrases in Daniel's dedicatory poem to Florio's *Essayes* (see the next paragraph, where the equivalent phrases are again underlined).
[142] SCETI London 1603, pp. [para]1r–v.

Florio's translation was commissioned and begun some time in the years before 1599, years of great expectancy for followers of the Earl of Essex and Essexian culture. But it was completed during the years of Essex's downfall and execution (1599–1601), years of imprisonment, disgrace, and debt for followers such as Rutland and Bedford—hence their position firmly in the background in Florio's dedications. In this context, Florio's brief invocation of the fathers of Lady Elizabeth Grey ('daughter to the right Honorable Earle of Shrewsburie') and of Lady Mary Neville (Lord Buckhurst, 'this ages *Cato*, our *Englands Hospitalis*') in the third dedication looks like a piece of court diplomacy. Gilbert Talbot, Earl of Shrewsbury, a privy councillor, had been a commissioner at the first trial of the Earl of Essex. Buckhurst had also sat in judgement on some of the Essexians, and probably colluded in the non-payment of Rutland's large fine.[143] Even Daniel's patron, Mountjoy, had been closely associated with Essex until a very late stage, only backing out in 1600.[144]

The work on English pragmatic humanism of the 1590s has, as I mentioned earlier, made much of the case of Henry Cuffe.[145] Cuffe was a university man who became a scholar-reader in the employ of the Essexian nobility. The advice he gave—subsequently disowned by the nobles in question—was judged to have been one of the causes of the treasonous actions in which many of the young noblemen mentioned above (including the Earls of Bedford and Rutland) participated to one degree or another in 1601. In the process, a firm and very questionable distinction was drawn between Cuffe, 'a base fellow by birth, but a great scholler, and indeed a notable Traytor by the booke' and some of the nobles and gentlemen he misled, who were judged less guilty and praised for confessing freely and liberally when they realized the error of their ways. Here, the rhetoric—used by Florio—which excludes the 'base' from proportion with 'true' learning is used to blame the base scholar for 'false' or treasonous applications of book-learning. Cuffe was executed.[146]

In other words, the post-Sidneian, Essexian household institution of nobles, gentlemen friends, and scholar-readers, and the relationship between learning, the learned, and action, collapsed in the disarray and disgrace of a failed rebellion in 1601–2, just as the translation was nearing completion. The arrival south of King James and Queen Anna, just after Florio's translation went to press (the dedications

---

[143] Bedford was fined £10,000 and imprisoned (but soon released). Rutland was fined £30,000 and also imprisoned. See G. E. Cockayne, *The complete peerage*, ed. Vicary Gibbs et al., 13 vols. (London: St Catherine's Press, 1910–40), vol. 2, 78; vol. 11, 260; Michael Hicks, 'Talbot, Gilbert, seventh earl of Shrewsbury (1552–1616)', *ODNB*; Rivkah Zim, 'Sackville, Thomas, first Baron Buckhurst and first earl of Dorset (*c*.1536–1608)', *ODNB*; SCETI London 1603, pp. 2R2v–R3r.

[144] Alexandra Gajda, *The Earl of Essex and late Elizabethan political culture* (Oxford: Oxford University Press, 2012), 38.

[145] I am particularly indebted in what follows to Alan Stewart's unpublished paper 'Henry Cuffe, the "Hollowe Penman": Authorship, Attribution and Blame in the Essex Circle'. I am grateful to Prof. Stewart for providing me with a copy of his paper.

[146] Alan Stewart, '"Hollowe Penman"', citing [Francis Bacon], *A declaration of the practises & treasons attempted and committed by Robert late Earle of Essex and his complices, against her Maiestie and her kingdoms* (London: Robert Barker 1601), sig. D2v. See also Gajda, *The Earl of Essex*, 45, 56–7, 225.

contain references to Queen Elizabeth, still alive) but just before the publication of Daniel's volume, did provide new hope for this group of noble families. Southampton was released from prison and restored to court; the Harringtons were awarded the governorship of the Princess Elizabeth; and the Countess of Bedford and Florio gained positions at Queen Anna's court, as did some of the other ladies he names.[147]

Samuel Daniel, meanwhile, was recommended to Queen Anna by the Countess, wrote a masque for performance at the queen's court in January 1604, then became licenser of her company, the Children of the Queen's Revels. Through Daniel's masque, which saw two of Florio's goddesses (the Countess of Bedford and Lady Rich) appear as the goddesses Diana and Venus, the queen and her ladies were able to play the kind of intermediary role in international diplomacy envisaged by Florio's dedications. The queen, for political reasons, was insistent on inviting the learned Spanish ambassador to the masque, rather than the French.[148]

Nevertheless, some of the generation of young nobles from the milieu described in Florio's dedications lost direction in politics, and some even lost their way (from their Protestant fathers' point of view) in religion, finishing their lives as Roman Catholics in the closet or in exile.[149]

There remained, to return to Daniel's dedicatory poem to the *Essayes*, a problem with Montaigne's text, a problem acknowledged in Florio's paratexts—a problem we also saw (in 2.2.10) acknowledged in Venice, and solved in a particular way there by the translator and corrector Canini. Montaigne's 'genius'—Daniel implies—needs deciphering. His excellency is wrapped up in 'Hierogliphicques, Ciphers, Caracters', in strange speech. His directions for reading his work and following his advice are very indirect, they are hidden away inside the text. He does not present his 'lectures' methodically enough, in an *institutio* that can be easily followed. As Daniel says, when approached in its French edifice, the house of his learning is 'in a troubled frame confus'dly set'. It is difficult to see from the outside why we should wish to enter, or what we shall find inside.

But, says Daniel, using the metaphor of a house once again, 'as a guest in gratefulnesse/ For the great good' to be found within, we should enter anyway. Besides, when we now approach him in English, we find he has been placed 'in the best lodging of our speech' and given the proper frame of dedications and

---

[147] See, in *ODNB*, Park Honan, 'Wriothesley, Henry, third earl of Southampton (1573–1624)'; Jan Broadway, 'Harington, John, first Baron Harington of Exton (1539/40–1613)'; Helen Payne, 'Russell Lucy, countess of Bedford (*bap.* 1581, *d.* 1627)'.

[148] John Pitcher, 'Daniel, Samuel (1562/3–1619)', *ODNB*; Berta Cano-Echevarría and Mark Hutchings, 'The Spanish ambassador and Samuel Daniel's *Vision of the Twelve Goddesses*: A new document [with text]', *English Literary Renaissance*, 42 (2012), 223–57.

[149] See, for example, 'Wotton, Edward, first Baron Wotton (1548–1628)', *ODNB*, and Cockayne, *The complete peerage*, vol. 12, pt. 2, 867. Wotton's eldest son, Pickering (for whose education he may have commissioned the translation of *Essais* I 25), died a Catholic in Valladolid in 1605, and Wotton himself confessed to being a Catholic recusant later in life. One of the families honoured in Florio's dedication to the third book of his translation is the Sackville family. The son of Thomas Sackville, Lord Buckhurst (also called Thomas), travelled widely in Europe then returned to Padua in 1615 as a Catholic exile. See Jonathan Woolfson, *Padua and the Tudors: English students in Italy, 1485–1603* (Toronto: University of Toronto Press, 1998), 267–8.

recommendations, including Daniel's own poem. He has, in short, become a noble household institution, if a rather paradoxical one.[150]

In the 1632 edition, Daniel's poem, self-consciously standing at the gate of Montaigne's house, is complemented by another poem 'To the Beholder of this Title'. On the facing leaf is an engraving of a gate, with a title-bearing shield above, through which one can see Daniel's troubled frame confusedly set—a crowded jumble of buildings, columns, and arches. The 'title' of the book, hung above the gate, is both the noble title of the author ('Lo: Michael de Montaigne, Knight of the noble Order of Saint Michael, and one of the gentlemen in ordinary of the French Kings chamber') and the title ('Essayes') to which the name is annexed (Illus. 2.3.3).[151]

The 1632 edition, then, more clearly makes a virtue of the digressive, learned abundance of the English Montaigne. The book is offered to casual viewers of the frontispiece, in the bookseller's shop, as an intriguingly confusing palace of invention, an aristocratic house whose rooms, galleries, and closets are filled with rarities, with learned emblems and pictures, to entertain the visitor with a variety of pleasures and profits in a kind of school of wit.

Originally, the producers of the frontispiece had thought to provide a full '*Model or Epitomie*'—a 'frame'—of all these rooms, so that every reader casting thereupon a glancing eye would be informed, at the first aspect, of the rarities within. But when they walked through the palace for the purpose of compiling such an epitome, they found such a variety, scattered here and there, that the epitome itself would have run to a whole volume—beyond a 'briefe *expression*'. For a 'diligent unfolder' can bring concealed fruits to light from every angle and leaf, where 'the rash *Beholders* eye' perceives no shows or promises of such choice things. They therefore show only the gate, previously barred by a French guard, but now open to anyone with an English key (the English language), who would pass at pleasure every way within.

2.3.7 FROM PRIVATE READING TO PUBLIC STAGE

The 1632 frontispiece suggests that, in England, to read and diligently unfold Montaigne's text is to enter an aristocratic palace of invention, a scene of learned leisure and instruction, a noble household school of wit. The producers of this edition decided that this school should not be reduced to a methodical epitome of the kind offered in so many printed miscellanies.

Related conclusions can be drawn from various pieces of evidence relating to the years immediately after the publication of the English Montaigne in 1603, including five to which I shall give particular emphasis in this section and 2.3.8: James Cleland's *Institution* (1607); the left-hand panel of Lady Anne Clifford's 'Great

---

[150] SCETI London 1603, p. [para]1v.
[151] Michel de Montaigne, *The essayes or morall, politike and millitarie discourses*, trans. John Florio (London: M. Flesher for R. Royston, 1632), verso of title page and sig. A1r.

Illus. 2.3.3. Montaigne, *Essayes*, trans. Florio, London 1632, Bodleian Library, pressmark Buxton 34, frontispiece engraving. Reproduced by permission of The Bodleian Libraries, the University of Oxford.

Picture' (depicting her at the age of fifteen in 1605) and her diaries for 1616–17; Robert Tofte's *The blazon of jealousie* (1615) and Marston's use of Montaigne in *The Dutch courtezan* (*c.*1604); the sub-plot to Ben Jonson's *Volpone* (performed early 1606, printed 1606); the relationship between Samuel Daniel's court play *The Queenes Arcadia* (performed 1605, printed 1606) and Shakespeare's *The Tempest* (1610–11).

What Cleland does with the English *Essayes* in 1607 is comparable to what Charron does with the French *Essais* in 1601. Like Charron, Cleland nowhere mentions Montaigne by name. But he takes, unacknowledged, many passages from Montaigne's chapters on the bringing up of children and incorporates them into a methodical institution not of a generic wise man (as Charron does) but of a young Protestant nobleman, at one point explicitly identified with John Harrington, the brother of the Countess of Bedford. He displaces the 'troubled frame' described by Daniel with a new frame. He gives '[t]o the noble reader' an account of how he has discharged his office of the 'Tutorship of young Nobles', speaking through his book as 'an unpartial Counceller, and a faithful Admonisher' to his noble pupils in his absence.[152]

Cleland's treatise is ordered into six books addressed to different participants in the educational process: the first is addressed to a noble father and 'patterne' (Lord Hay), and shows the duty of parents towards their children; the second is addressed to the tutors of the royal princes (Adam Newton and Thomas Murray) and advises tutors in general of their duty; the third is addressed directly to a young nobleman (George, Earl of Enzie) and shows a young nobleman's duty towards God; the fourth, addressed directly to the Countess of Bedford's brother, John Harrington, shows a young nobleman's duty towards his parents and tutor; the fifth, addressed to 'two most vertuous, and wel-learned young gentlemen' (Francis Stewart and John Stewart) shows a young nobleman's duty in civil conversation; the sixth, addressed to the young Earl of Essex and Ewe, points out a young nobleman's way in travelling.

From the perspective of the history of educational literature, the significance of Cleland's treatise is that it participates in a recent tradition of printed treatises that institutionalize—for the English gentry—the private acculturation of the free, noble literate. Study and recreation become one and the same in a household 'Schoole-chamber' that Cleland would have painted—following Florio's Montaigne—with images of the three graces 'as they were above *Speusippus* Schoole, that they [the noble pupils] may see their pleasure joined with profit'.[153] The books and methods of professional humanists and philosophers are adapted to the private spaces and relations of a nobleman's everyday life, at home, at court, on

---

[152] Cleland, *Hērō-paideia*, sigs. Q2v, ¶3r. I have shown elsewhere that Cleland borrows extensively (without acknowledgement) from Florio's translations of Montaigne's three chapters on the bringing up of children (I 24, 'Of Pedantisme'; I 25; and II 8, 'Of the affection of fathers to their Children') and from at least two others that precede the educational chapters in book I (I 20, 'Of the force of imagination'; I 22, 'Of Custome, and how a received Law should not easily be changed'), as well as less extensively from other chapters. See Boutcher, 'The origins of Florio's Montaigne', 24–6, including the footnotes.

[153] Cleland, *Hērō-paideia*, sig. I3v. SCETI London 1603, p. 80.

his travels. Even his free reading and writing, the way he judges books for himself, without a tutor or counsellor present, is a prescribed part of this institution.

Cleland adopts from I 25 neither Pierre's method for learning Latin through colloquial speech nor Montaigne's plan for an early education in philosophical conversation as substitutes for the traditional study of grammar and logic. But he alludes to both and speaks with Florio's words in the course of laying out a programme that incorporates a scholarly and professional training in Latin, Greek, liberal arts, and the law, alongside private reading, civil conversation at court (in Prince Henry's academy, instead of Oxford or Cambridge), and travel.

The programme is delivered entirely as a matter of household and court relations between parents, tutors, inferior servants, noble companions, and the prince. Its foundations in the learning of Latin, with the assistance of both French and English, closely link speaking (correct pronunciation), hearing, reading (aloud), writing (copying), and translating (double translation). Cleland alludes pejoratively to Pierre Eyquem's method of having his son brought up to hear and speak only Latin (described in I 25), though he co-opts it as the best way of acquiring French.[154]

When the tutor teaches the young nobleman more advanced grammar, he uses the humanists' classical Latin canon, 'revolves' their commentaries for the most appropriate annotations and marginal notes, and introduces his pupil to the practice of grammatical correction upon his own writing.[155] It is when Cleland describes how the 'study of Humanity' rests upon the teaching of '*Histories*', especially Livy and Plutarch, and how it should be studied for 'the Anatomy of Philosophy and the study of Judgement', not for 'the phrase, and Grammatical construction', that he draws more extensively on Florio's Montaigne.[156]

Later, in the book addressed directly to John Harrington (the brother of the recipient of *Essayes* I 25 in manuscript) he prescribes '[w]hat bookes you [i.e. Harrington] should read privatly by your selfe', and how they should be read and judged. The emphasis is once again on 'historie', which includes everything from the Old and New Testaments, and classical Greek and Roman chronicles to 'the historie, or rather Poeme of *Sr Philip Sydneyes Arcadia*', praised—as we have already noted—with the very terms Florio uses to praise the *Essayes*.[157]

Again, it is when he moves on in the same book to '[h]ow yee [Harrington] should make good use of your reading, and judge of books' that he borrows verbatim from Florio's Montaigne. This time Cleland rewrites a passage in Florio in which the Frenchman advises on how to read according to the *persona* of the author: 'And to this purpose am I wont, in reading of histories (which is the subject of most men) to consider who are the writers: If they be such as professe nothing but bare learning, the chiefe thing I learne in them, is their stile and language'.[158]

At the end of the same chapter, still addressing Harrington, Cleland specifies that this private reading by himself, the goal of which is to exercise his judgement,

---

[154] Cleland, *Hērō-paideia*, sigs. K1v–3v.   [155] Cleland, *Hērō-paideia*, sigs. K4r–L1v.
[156] Cleland, *Hērō-paideia*, sig. L2r–v; SCETI London 1603, p. 74.
[157] Cleland, *Hērō-paideia*, sigs. T1v–4v.
[158] Cleland, *Hērō-paideia*, sig. V2r–v; SCETI London 1603, p. 26.

should always be accompanied by writing. He should make short annotations in the margins of his book; then, when he has finished the book, he should copy them out into another book in one of two ways. If the author of the work he has been reading is 'methodicall' he should copy them out into a book of commonplaces. If the author's work is a 'Rapsodie, without anie coherences of the parts thereof', he tells him, you should copy out 'your observation in your reading'.[159]

Cleland goes on to give examples of books of both types, which he says almost every man is now personally compiling. We can infer from this list that Cleland considered the *Essayes* to be the result of a reader having re-copied his notes and observations from books and other sources not into a methodical commonplace book, but into a miscellaneously ordered compilation (*variae lectiones*). The result is a 'store house of al humane learning' comparable to the more miscellaneous collections he names, such as the *Noctes atticae* of Aulus Gellius, the *Dies geniales* of Alexander ab Alexandro, and the *Adversaria* of Adrianus Turnebus.[160]

But we can be more specific than this. In Cleland, Montaigne is not a patron-author. He is neither a cited and named authority nor a 'patterne' of the outcome of a noble institution, comparable to Cyrus in the *Cyropaedia*, King James in the *Basilikon dōron*, or Sidney in the *Arcadia*. Rather, his observations from his reading are a source for the discourse in which Cleland deals throughout: the educative and recreational conversation between noble fathers, learned tutors, and young noblemen. To adapt Florio, they are noblemens'—and noblewomens'—school themes, comparable in their wit, invention, and elocution to the *Arcadia* itself. In the masculine sphere of the educational household they do not have the status that Florio tries to give them in his 1603 dedications. Nevertheless, it was the introduction of Montaigne into the Harrington-Russell household via Florio's manuscript chapter I 25 that shaped Cleland's use of the *Essayes* in this manner.

Florio's Montaigne is a noble reader-writer whose voice and ethos is perfect for the conversation described in the last paragraph. This is most apparent in Cleland's preface 'To the noble reader'. There, he cuts and pastes, as his own, without acknowledgement, Florio's versions of Montaigne's descriptions of his *persona* as a reader-writer and discourser from II 17, I 56, II 18, I 25, II 10, and III 2.

So, we are told, in Montaigne's words, that Cleland does not think his advices perfect, and that as many times as he looks them over, he is vexed at them, just as Ovid says he is ashamed when he rereads his own writing. Cleland proposes them like those scholars in schools who publish doubtful and sophistical questions to be disputed, not to be resolved. He does not intend to puff up his pages with inflated trifles (this via a citation from Persius's *Satires* selected by Montaigne). He is too meanly instructed to teach others ('I am not sufficiently taught to teach others', in Florio). He hides the names of famous authors (such as Seneca and Plutarch) in using their reasons and comparisons, to bridle the temerity of those who would

---

[159] Cleland, *Hērō-paideia*, sig. V4v.
[160] Cleland, *Hērō-paideia*, sig. V4v; Blair, *Too much to know*, 126–31.

censure him. He is happy if men of understanding think he might have been able to make use and benefit of learning, if he had been endowed with any.[161]

The 'Preface describing who are Nobles, and the nature of Nobilitie' likewise draws extensively and widely from all corners of the *Essayes*. Most significantly, it adopts Florio's version in III 13 of the 'warning-lesson given to all men' by Apollo, 'God of wisedome, knowledge, and light', on the 'frontispiece of his temple', as (in Cleland's words) 'the plaine and full exposition of the title or subject of this Institution; that you would learne to KNOW YOUR SELVES'.[162]

Cleland clearly believes, then, that the voice of the English Montaigne is the voice an impartial counsellor and faithful admonisher needs to use to talk about learning to the nobility, to show them how to use learning.

At around the same moment, in the years immediately following the publication of Florio's first edition, stage plays began to draw on the *Essayes* in ways that are related to their role in furnishing topical matter, ethos, and discourse for the private institution and conference of the noble elite. Take the example of the topic of unruly fathers. Approximately half of Cleland's chapter 10 of the first book ('Of the Fathers allowance for his Sonnes maintenance') is taken verbatim or paraphrased from Florio's 'Of the affection of fathers to their Children'.[163]

The borrowed matter deals with the problem of fathers who spend liberally on their son's early education but then hoard resources and power later in life and fail to follow testamentary customs. In this case the tyranny lies in a new custom brought in to suit overweening fathers. Villey thought Francis Bacon drew on this chapter of Montaigne's when he added 'Of Parents and Children' to the 1612 edition of his own *Essays*.[164]

At exactly this moment, in 1608, a play was published on the same topic of unruly fathers (*King Lear*).[165] As Leo Salingar has convincingly argued, Montaigne's chapter II 8 furnished the playwright with much material for the first two acts, as the two fathers, Lear and Gloucester, spin out of control in their relations with their principal heirs. The play even contains a letter-essay on tyrannical fathers as a crucial element in its plot. And Salingar goes on to show how Shakespeare uses Montaigne to supply the King, Lear, with themes, terms, and telling illustrations throughout the rest of the play. It is ultimately the King, we might say, who is borrowing counsel, themes, and language from Montaigne. As Salingar puts it, 'Montaigne has furnished Lear with the "matter" for his exposure of contradictions at the basis of social life.'[166]

---

[161] Cleland, *Hērō-paideia*, sigs. ¶3v–4v. Compare SCETI London 1603, p. 370, p. 172, p. 384, p. 68, p. 236, p. 484.

[162] Cleland, *Hērō-paideia*, sig. A1r. Compare SCETI London 1603, pp. 639–40.

[163] Cleland, *Hērō-paideia*, sigs. F1r–4r. A1r. Compare SCETI London 1603, pp. 224–31.

[164] Pierre Villey, *Montaigne et François Bacon* (Paris: Revue de la Renaissance, 1913), 30–7.

[165] William Shakespeare, *True chronicle history of the life and death of King Lear and his three daughters* (London: Nathaniel Butter, 1608).

[166] Leo Salingar, 'King Lear, Montaigne and Harsnett', *Anglo-American Studies*, (Salamanca) 3, no. 2 (November 1983), 145–74, 163–4, 166. Douglas Trevor, 'Love, anger and cruelty in "De l'affection des peres aux enfans" and *King Lear*', *Montaigne Studies*, 24 (2012), 51–66, reconfirms Salingar's conclusions: 'if we focus our attention on the familial dynamics of Lear's family in particular, the

However, Salingar interestingly goes on to argue that 'Montaigne had too much influence on *King Lear*' in this respect. The passages of Montaignean thought 'are like Essays in miniature, speculative and sententious... [but] they are felt as marginal commentaries rather than essential to the action'.[167] Cleland, remember, recommends the copying out of such marginal commentaries as part of the nobleman's preparation for civil conversation—the kind of preparation exemplified by the *Essayes*.

The suggestion that arises here, as it does in Florio's dedications, is that Montaigne in England could be associated by some with that form of 'marginal' or miscellaneous commentary which is informal, digressive, and personal—even satirical and 'humorous' in the early modern senses of disorderly, fanciful, capricious, whimsical, odd, fantastic. The forms of elite conversation to which the *Essayes* contributed are refracted, critiqued, even mocked when Florio's words are incorporated into drama, especially popular drama. Not only in *King Lear*, but also in *Hamlet* and in *The Tempest* (act 2, scene 1) we see this form of marginal, digressive commentary dramatized. Hamlet's spoken essays are as marginal to the action as Lear's. And we shall see later in this section that in the figure of Gonzalo we can picture Montaigne as a 'lord of weak remembrance' who prates amply and unnecessarily, a lord who against his own intentions stimulates others to rebellious thoughts. He is a caricature equivalent in some respects to Lady Would-Be in Jonson's *Volpone*—though a gentler one.

If Cleland does not actually put Florio's Montaigne on his reading list for the young nobleman, there is evidence in one case that the book *was* on the reading list in these years for a young noblewoman we have already encountered, and who was tutored by Samuel Daniel: Lady Anne Clifford.

'It vexeth me', says Florio's Montaigne in III 5, 'that my Essayes serve Ladies in lieu of common ware and stuffe for their hall: this Chapter will preferre me to their cabinet'.[168] He is thinking of his book as a household object, one that he wants to see lodged in the most private rooms, where the ladies do their most private reading and writing. And there is striking visual evidence that Florio's Montaigne *did* gain access to this English noblewoman's cabinet in a tryptych she commissioned in 1646. The triptych is especially striking for literary historians; it includes representations of fifty-three volumes, all but one with titles legibly inscribed.[169]

---

unmistakable traces of a careful consideration of Montaigne's work, specifically "Of the affection of fathers to their children", seem impossible to deny' (65).

[167] Salingar, 'King Lear, Montaigne and Harsnett', 168.

[168] III 5, NP889/BVH Paris 1595, bk. III, p. 42/SCETI London 1603, p. 508.

[169] Attributed to Jan van Belcamp, *The Great Picture*, 1646, Abbot Hall Art Gallery, Kendal, AH2310/81. See Giles Waterfield, *Art treasures of England: the regional collections* (London: Merrell Holberton, 1998), 106–7. For the most authoritative recent discussion of this painting by an art historian, see Karen Hearn, 'Lady Anne Clifford's Great Triptych', in Hearn and Hulse (eds.), *Lady Anne Clifford: culture, patronage and gender in 17th-century Britain*, 1–24. There is no completely accurate transcription of the titles as they appear on the spines. See George C. Williamson, *Lady Anne Clifford, Countess of Dorset, Pembroke & Montgomery, 1590–1676: her life, letters and work* (Kendal: Titus Wilson, 1922), 498–500, for an approximate transcription (with two titles missing), and Richard T. Spence, *Lady Anne Clifford, Countess of Pembroke, Dorset and Montgomery (1590–1676)* (Stroud, Gloucestershire: Sutton, 1997), 190–1, for a list of the books displayed. For authoritative recent

Illus. 2.3.4. Attributed to Jan van Belcamp, *The Great Picture*, 1646. Reproduced by courtesy of Abbot Hall Art Gallery, Lakeland Arts Trust, Kendal, Cumbria.

The painting provides a visual analogue—in the case of a noblewoman—to Cleland's guide to the begetting, education, and introduction to civil conversation of a nobleman. For its three panels show—within the broader context of an ongoing noble family history—the conception, institution, and continuing self-education of Lady Anne through to maturity. All the objects depicted—including the books, and including the copy of Florio's Montaigne—serve as material indexes of this process of formation.

The left-hand panel depicts Lady Anne Clifford at the age of fifteen in 1605, the year in which her father died and in which she should have inherited her estates (Illus. 2.3.4).[170] It draws on the same symbolism as the scene with the lute and the set of books in Shakespeare's *The Taming of the Shrew*. Her left hand rests on a book of music, above a lute propped against the table. On the wall above her head are portraits of her tutor, the poet Samuel Daniel, directly above a copy of Sidney's *Arcadia*, and her governess, Anne Taylor, who presides over copies of Sylvester's Du Bartas and other works directly beneath.

Lying horizontally to the right of the poet's portrait, above imposing folios of biblical and patristic works, are the verse works of Daniel ('tutor to this young lady'). The inscription corresponds to that on the monument Lady Anne erected to Daniel in a Somerset church ('Tutor to the Lady Anne of Clifford in her youth').[171] On the shelf below, again lying horizontally, is the prose chronicle of England by Daniel (once more, 'Tutor to ye young Lady'), and, directly beneath, 'Lo: Michael de Montaigne his Essaies'. As we have seen, all the editions of Florio's translation include an important dedicatory poem by Daniel in the preliminary matter, guiding the reader on how to receive and use the book.[172]

Books and portraits figure within the other two panels as well. The central panel shows Lady Anne's mother (Margaret Russell, daughter of Francis Russell, 2nd Earl of Bedford) and father, and her two brothers. An inscription specifies that the imaginary assembly dates to June 1589, by which time the Countess was already pregnant with Lady Anne, who is therefore present *in utero*. Portraits of her mother's four sisters, her Russell aunts, hang on the walls. Her mother holds the Psalms, while above her head rest the Bible, Seneca, and a manuscript of alchemical extractions.

The right-hand panel mirrors the left and shows Lady Anne as she was 'to the life' in 1646. Portraits of her two deceased husbands hang on the walls. The books on these shelves are less neatly arranged than on the left. They include a higher proportion of religious and devotional works, though there are still many secular

---

discussions of Lady Anne's books, see Brayman Hackel, *Reading material*, 222–40; Heidi Brayman Hackel, 'Turning to her "Best Companion[s]": Lady Anne Clifford as reader, annotator and book collector', in Hearn and Hulse (eds.), *Lady Anne Clifford: culture, patronage and gender in 17th-century Britain*, 99–108.

[170] George Clifford settled his estates upon his younger brother.

[171] Williamson, *Lady Anne Clifford*, 63.

[172] The title page of 1603 offers 'Essayes...of Lo: Michaell de Montaigne' (Illus. 1.4.1) where 1613 has 'Essayes...By Michael Lord of Montaigne'. See SCETI London 1603, p. A1r, p. [para]1r; Montaigne, *Essayes*, 1613, sigs. A1r, A3r–4r. Transcriptions are mine.

works, including (on the lower shelf) Plutarch in French, and Greville's works. Lady Anne's hand rests on the Bible and on Pierre Charron's 'Booke of Wisedome translated out of French into English'. Montaigne has been displaced by the author who systematized his work as an institution in practical philosophy to be used in parallel with the Bible.

The painting offers a retrospective image, but records relating to 1616–17, soon after Lady Anne's marriage, complement the picture it offers. She married Richard Sackville, Earl of Dorset, son of the Elizabethan patron best known as Lord Buckhurst. She was still based in the north, but passed much of her early married life in various Sackville houses, from what she calls Great and Lesser Dorset house, to Horsley, to her main retreat: Knole in Kent.

On the 31st October 1616 she was in the north waiting for word as to whether she could join her husband in London. She records that she spent the month 'working and Reading', and that one 'Mr Dumbell' read a great part of an unspecified history of the Netherlands to her. Ten days later she is still at her work and hears her servants Rivers and Marsh read 'Montaignes Essays which book they have read almost this fortnight'. The following month she leaves for London and the court. By 8 January she is at Knole. The following day she is sorting things in her closet, where she has George Sandys's book on the government of the Turks read to her, 'my Lord [her husband] sitting the most part of the day reading in his closet'. After another trip to court she is back at Knole, and in January of 1617 records that 'Rivers used to read to me in Montaigne Essays and Moll Neville in the Faery Queene'. In the summer of the same year she records hearing Moll Neville reading Sidney's *Arcadia* to her.[173]

We heard in 2.3.1 and 1.4.1 that Florio and his assistants consciously reproduce Montaigne's work within and for a network of noble houses and learned families, families imbued with the literary culture of Elizabethan romance centered on texts such as Sidney's *Arcadia*. Two of these are closely related to Lady Anne Clifford's 'house': the Sackvilles and the Russells. Her diary reveals her relations with members of some of the other families invoked by Florio—the Bedford-Russells, the Talbot-Greys, the Riches, the Sidneys, the Manners, the Nevilles.[174]

Florio's third dedication addresses the daughter of Lord Buckhurst, Lady Mary Neville, and declares that no small part of the translation was 'done under your Fathers roofe, under your regiment'—another cameo of relations between father, young noblewoman, and learned servant.[175] We cannot be sure whether the 'roof' in question was that of Knole or of some other Sackville house such as Horsley. Florio was certainly helping a number of noblewomen, including one named Mary, entertain the Venetian representative at Horsley in 1603.[176] We cannot be absolutely sure that the Moll or Mary Neville reading Sidney and

[173] Katherine O. Acheson (ed.), *The diary of Anne Clifford, 1616–1619: a critical edition* (New York: Garland, 1995), 59, 65, 69, 90.

[174] See the following notes to Acheson (ed.), *The diary of Anne Clifford*: 39², 39⁹, 40¹, 40⁶, 40¹², 42³, 46², 62², 65¹, 89¹, 90³, 102⁶⁻⁷.

[175] SCETI London 1603, p. 2R3r.

[176] PRO SP 99/2 fols. 157–8, 183, 184; Boutcher, 'Florio's Montaigne', 237–9.

Spenser to Lady Anne a few years later was Florio's dedicatee's daughter, but it is very probable.[177]

Either way, the important point is the close fit between the scene of composition in the paratexts to the first edition (London 1603) and the place of the same book in Lady Anne Clifford's diary and in the 'Great Picture'. London 1603's preliminary matter frames the *Essayes* for consumption in an aristocratic household scene of learned leisure 'hung' with portraits of patrons and their learned helpers—just as Lady Anne Clifford's famous triptych does. Montaigne is introduced into England as a learned noble friend to specific families, a friend who performs a service, an 'unnamed office' for those families. He reads and writes in private *with* and *for* them; his service in so doing is then commodified in print for a wider audience by Edward Blount. Florio summarizes the point in the second dedication: 'Why wrote he [Montaigne] then? for him and his. But why doe I translate him? For your Ladiships and yours.'[178]

Furthermore, it seems that Lady Anne Clifford is having Florio's Montaigne read to her in a leisurely context that is very different—freer from direct, patriarchal supervision—from her reading with the minister Ran (see 2.3.3). An important distinction between her and some other educated ladies is her revelation that her father would not have her tutored in languages—one justification for the polemic dominating Florio's dedications.[179]

We cannot ultimately know exactly how Rivers read the *Essayes* with Lady Anne—whether he just read the text aloud, or whether he paused to gloss it for her or discuss it with her in the form of 'lectures' of the kind described in *Essayes* I 25. And we may well ask how likely it is that he read III 5—the risqué chapter that Montaigne hoped would get him into ladies cabinets—to her. For, although we have so far placed much emphasis on the kind of schooling described in I 25, III 5 relates the *Essayes* to a European—especially Italianate—elite tradition, associated above all with Aretino, of private schooling in sex and courtship, including for gentlewomen.[180]

In III 5, Montaigne describes how his daughter, who he says was being brought up by her mother, was one day reading a French book aloud to him, with her private governess present—another example of a scene of noble 'lecture'. The governess interrupted her to make her skip over an obscene word, which of course imprinted it in her mind all the more efficaciously. Montaigne does not intervene because he does not meddle with female government. But he does go on to claim, in Florio's amplified English, that girls naturally school themselves in the games of love: 'it is a cunning bred in their vaines and will never out of the flesh … which these skill infusing Schoole-mistresses nature, youth, health and opportunitie, are ever buzzing in their eares, ever whispering in their minds'.[181]

---

[177] Acheson (ed.), *The diary of Anne Clifford*, 137 (note for 40).

[178] SCETI London 1603, p. R2v.

[179] Barbara Kiefer Lewalski, *Writing women in Jacobean England* (Cambridge, Mass.: Harvard University Press, 1993), 137.

[180] James Grantham Turner, *Schooling sex: libertine literature and erotic education in Italy, France, and England, 1534–1685* (Oxford: Oxford University Press, 2003).

[181] III 5, NP898–9/ BVH Paris 1595, bk. III, pp. 48–9/SCETI London 1603, p. 514.

Just a year before the scene recorded in Lady Anne's diary, Robert Tofte, a poet and learned gentleman companion to the gentry and nobility, published a translation of the Italian Benedetto Varchi's lecture at the Accademia degli Infiammati of Padua on the poetry of jealousy. We saw in 2.2.10 and 2.2.11 that Italian 'academic' culture shaped the context in which Montaigne was received in Padua-Venice, just as the analogous noble household culture of 'lecture and advise' (see 2.3.3)—we are now seeing—had welcomed him in England. Tofte describes the Italian academies as the 'private Exercises' of 'the better sort of learned Gentlemen', who also present 'before the Ladies and Gentlewomen' excellent comedies, 'with such like delightfull Exercises'.[182]

Tofte extends these exercises himself in the 'speciall Notes' he adds to the text. The interesting point for us is that in the course of this marginal commentary he helps ladies and gentlewomen respond to Varchi as he might have done in a live 'lecture'. The notes engage the ladies in conversation using passages from and references to Florio's Montaigne, III 5, which is itself a series of 'lectures' on sex and marriage based in readings of poetry. In other words, Tofte glosses Varchi for his female readers by glossing Montaigne with and for them. The tone of his interventions in response to what Montaigne has to say about women is remarkably similar to that adopted by Florio in his second dedication to his noble patronesses, discussed at the beginning of this chapter. Tofte is, like Florio, bringing the French author Montaigne into a scene of reading centred mainly on Italian authors.

In one case Varchi takes a particularly ardent Petrarchan sonnet as a pretext to warn women about the differences in the temperaments of men. Some men, says Varchi, take any occasion to get angry, some are 'jocond and blithsome, and not troubled at all'. Tofte, in turn, takes this opportunity to refer his gentlewomen friends in a marginal note to III 5 (though he gets the reference wrong).

'I see no reason', says Tofte, 'why the better sort [of men] should take this false playing of their Wives [i.e. adultery] so much at the heart as they doe; especially when it is their Destinie, and not Desert, to be so used.' Montaigne, 'that brave French Barron', says Tofte, is of the same mind, for he gives examples of worthies such as Lucullus, Caesar, Anthony, and Cato, who were all cuckolds but 'made no stirre about it'. Read the third chapter (in fact the fifth) of the third book of the *Essayes*, says Tofte, and he will 'satisfie you at large in this poynt.'[183] A few pages on he states that he considers what Montaigne has to say about the vulnerability of the female sex to the fury of jealousy to be too frank to quote, so he simply refers his readers once again to this chapter.[184]

Towards the end of his lecture Varchi argues that, 'with Wisedome, Discretion, and Patience' we may 'easily drive away and expel the force and rage' of jealousy. But Tofte feels this passage needs to be corrected, and he once again uses Florio's

[182] Benedetto Varchi, *The blazon of jealousie ... with speciall notes upon the same*, trans. Robert Tofte (London: T[homas] S[nodham] for John Busbie, 1615), sig. C1r [USTC S119026].
[183] Varchi, *The blazon of jealousie*, sig. F3r. Tofte makes further use of the same passage in III 5 over the page (sig. F3v).
[184] Varchi, *The blazon of jealousie*, sig. G1v.

Montaigne III 5 to do this.[185] Even as he does so, he glosses and qualifies Montaigne's words in the course of his own 'lecture', finding them to be too bold. Trying to cure jealousy in the female sex, writes Montaigne, were but time and labour lost: 'Their Essence, as he [Montaigne] affirmeth, (for I [Robert Tofte] will not in any way subscribe to such an Hereticall opinion as this is, and therefore I allege authoritie, Certissima omnium regula) being so much infected wth JEALOUSIE, ... that there is no hope to cure them'.

After a further passage from III 5, in which Montaigne claims that even when women do free themselves of jealousy, it is only to transfer it to their husbands, Tofte once again intervenes:

> But 'holla' pardon mee (fayre Ladies and Gentlewomen) to whose lot it shall fall by chance to read this Note. Had it not beene but that I should have left this part Defective, and a meere Heteroclite, I would not have proceeded so farre as I did [i.e. in quoting Montaigne]: and now for amends, (yet not to flatter you at all,) speake Mounsieur *Montagnie* in French what he list, yet could I, and can allege as much, if not more, against our owne Male-kinde, the Italian and others, and (I am sorry so to say) some here in our owne Countrey of England ... who are and have beene as violent, and virulent in this Bedlam-like Humour, as any Woman Virago whatsover.[186]

This is once again very redolent of Florio's 'lectures': the dialogues Florio conducts with Montaigne on behalf of and in the presence of his gentlewomen readers in the dedications to his translation. Tofte brings Florio's translation in to gloss and to correct Varchi's over-idealistic notion of the curability of jealousy, but then he himself glosses and corrects his own alleged authority (Montaigne) for the benefit of his gentlewomen readers.

The nature of Tofte's commentary, and its proximity to Florio's dedicatory discourses, gives us a real insight into the nature of the 'lectures' to which the *Essais* gave rise in early modern England. They were read and glossed as a bold, frank, and—on some topics—satirical text that could challengingly enter conversations with other texts on any topic, but that itself provoked its own readers and auditors to gloss, to challenge, to amplify. Tutors such as Tofte and Florio intervened in the text as they read it with their noble pupils.

These readings and glossings of Montaigne in private household or courtly, 'academic' nexuses of learning and learned entertainment—nexuses in which gentlewomen and noblewomen can be prominent—are related to uses of the same work in stage plays of the same years. Again, this is not to say that plays simply reflect such nexuses. In what follows in the rest of this section I shall consider some of the borrowings in Marston, before showing how Jonson's *Volpone*, for the King's Men (1605–6), directly caricatures aristocratic readers of Florio. In 2.3.8 we shall move on to the relationship between Daniel's use of Montaigne in *The Queenes Arcadia* and Shakespeare's in one scene of *The Tempest*. The re-use in a related scenario in another King's Men play (*The Tempest*) of a passage from Florio previously used in

---

[185] Varchi, *The blazon of jealousie*, sigs. K1v–2r.
[186] Varchi, *The blazon of jealousie*, sig. K1v, for this and the previous paragraph.

a play closely associated with the Queen's Revels (Daniel's *The Queenes Arcadia*) testifies to Shakespeare's competitive engagement, in a more popular context, with a particular elite entertainment already staged at court, and associated with a rival theatre company.[187]

In one Italianate play (*The fawn*) presented at the Blackfriars by the Children of the Queen's Revels in 1604–5, Marston puts in the mouth of Duke Ercole, disguised as a fawn, exactly the same examples of Roman worthies turning a blind eye to adultery as were pulled by Tofte out of III 5 in his commentary. In another Marston play put on by the same company at the Blackfriars in 1603–4, the playwright turns lines from the same chapter into a dialogue between the libertine gentleman Freevil and his friend Malheureux—including one passage which is already an exchange between two people in the original text.[188]

But the principal trend apparent in Marston's use of Florio in these years is the way he uses *Essayes* III 5 to shape the bold speech or 'lectures' of articulate and uninhibited gentlewomen such as Crispinella, Dulcimel, and Sophonisba—stage representations (already caricatures?) of the gentlewomen behind Florio's dedicatory manifesto for the relaxing of limits on women's access to and use of learning.[189] Marston's *The Dutch courtezan*, played by the Queen's Revels c.1604, makes extensive use of III 5, and lighter use of other chapters.[190]

Consider one instance from *The Dutch courtezan* that offers parallels with Tofte's scenario of reading and commentary. Act 3, scene 1 is a private scene of 'lecture' between the two gentle daughters of Sir Hubert Subboys and their nurse Putifer. As the scene opens the nurse asks Beatrice to read her once more the sonnet that Beatrice's suitor Master Freevill has sent her concerning the kiss she gave him. Later in the scene, the nurse says to the sisters, 'I now will read a lecture to you both, how you shall behave your selves to your husbands the first monneth of your nuptial'.

But in fact the scene is dominated by an entirely different 'lecture', given by the bold, free-thinking, but virtuous second sister, Crispinella. Crispinella speaks directly with the first-person, satirical voice of Florio's Montaigne, III 5:

> lets neere be ashamed to speake what we be not ashamd to thinke…we pronounce boldly Robbery, Murder, treason, which deedes must needes be far more lothsome then an act which is so naturall, just and necessary, as that of procreation…as in the

[187] On the role of such competitive engagement in the shaping of Shakespeare's plays, see Janet Clare, *Shakespeare's stage traffic: imitation, borrowing and competition in Renaissance theatre* (Cambridge: Cambridge University Press, 2014).

[188] Peter Mack, 'Marston and Webster's use of Florio's Montaigne', *Montaigne Studies*, 24 (2012), 67–82, 73, 68. There is a large literature on Marston and Montaigne, both in articles and in editions of the former's works. For the most recent authoritative treatment of the topic (especially Marston's use of Montaigne on the tyranny and artificiality of custom), and survey of the literature (in the notes), see Hamlin, *Montaigne's English journey*, 95–109, 276–80.

[189] Mack, 'Marston and Webster's use of Florio's Montaigne', 73; Charles Cathcart, *Marston, rivalry, rapprochement, and Jonson* (Farnham: Ashgate, 2008), 65.

[190] Mack, 'Marston and Webster's use of Florio's Montaigne', 66–72. Mack shows that III 5 is used in 'several different ways: for the confused and infatuated puritan Maleureux, for the wily prostitute Francishina, but also for the witty conversation of the lively but virtuous Crispinella'.

fashion of time, those books that are cald in, are most in sale and request, so in nature those actions that are most prohibited, are most desired.[191]

Notice here how the scenes of conversational reading or 'lecture' line up. Montaigne's chapter centres on readings of two pieces of verse: one about married love, one about adulterous love. In Tofte's translation, Varchi reads sonnets and other poems in relation to problems of love and jealousy. In directing his ladies and gentlewomen in how to approach Varchi, Tofte in turn brings new readings, including a reading from Montaigne III 5 about ancient worthies who turned a blind eye to adultery. Others brought in from Montaigne have to be glossed or corrected for his audience of gentlewomen. In *The Dutch courtezan*, as printed for reading by a public, we are told that the argument of the fable is 'the difference betwixt the love of a Curtezan, and a wife' (in the preliminary matter).[192]

Finally, in a scene of private 'conference' within the play, two gentlewomen sisters and their nurse—in an Italianate setting—comment upon a love sonnet and digress daringly onto the topic of the realpolitik and the language of love, using Montaigne III 5. A number of readers and commentators, including a playwright, bring various texts to bear on problems of love and jealousy, and the English Montaigne is prominent amongst them.

The argument should now be clear. Thanks largely to Florio and Daniel, Montaigne was introduced in Jacobean England as a participant in such scenes of private 'institutional' reading and leisurely 'conference': 'lectures' or 'readings-aloud' that were sometimes based on direct consideration of particular, cited texts, and sometimes based on uncited, pre-digested texts. He was used by scholars, tutors, and advisers to furnish the real aristocracy—and by playwrights to furnish the onstage aristocracy—with matter for topical philosophical discussion. But the latter scenes did not simply reflect the former. We shall turn in a moment to Jonson's parody of this trend (the stage figure of Lady Would-Be in *Volpone*).

The general point is not just that lords and ladies politic would-be and their servants and friends naturally draw upon Montaigne's text in such nexuses of reading and conference. Montaigne's text is a kind of master-text of 'lectures' for the gentry and nobility; it *shows* how one can comment and digress freely upon themes and topics thrown up by experience and by other texts in a manner that is suitable for the well-born, private reader-writer, not the professional scholar. It is itself a highly informal—indeed, potentially licentious—institution in the process of private reading, commentary, and conference. This process was at the core of the household education and learned leisure of the gentry and nobility at the turn of the sixteenth and seventeenth centuries—hence the selection of I 25 for translation in manuscript.

The idea in Florio that Montaigne was translated for 'your Ladiships' at court—ladyships conversant in Italian and other continental literature thanks to tutors of

---

[191] For this and the previous paragraph, see John Marston, *The Dutch Courtezan. As it was playd in the Blacke-Friars, by the Children of her Maiesties Revels* (London: T. P. for John Hodgets, 1605), sig. D3v. SCETI London 1603, pp. 508–9. The first phrase comes from the page before (SCETI London 1603, p. 507).

[192] Marston, *The Dutch Courtezan*, sig. A2r.

Florio and Daniel's ilk—shapes the first mention of the name 'Montaigne' on the English stage in early 1606. This mention is also likely to be, in part, a response to Marston's prolific use of Montaigne the year before in *The Dutch courtezan* and *The fawn*—Queen's Revels' plays.

In act 3, scene 4 of Ben Jonson's *Volpone*, Lady Would-Be responds to Volpone's desperate attempt to stem her torrent of words with the declaration of an ancient poet that the highest female grace is silence. She takes him to mean Italian poets and says she has two or three about her, starting with Guarini. She remarks that all 'our *English writers*', at least those happy in Italian, will 'deigne to steale out of this *Author* [Guarini], mainely; / Almost as much, as from *Montagnié*: /He has so moderne, and facile a veine,/ Fitting the time, and catching the *Court*-ear'. There follows further comment on other Italian authors, including 'for a desperate wit…*Aretine*', whose '*pictures* are a little obscene'. She then moves on to a practical-philosophical discourse on how we can cure ourselves by diverting our passions—which may owe something to Florio's 'Of diversion'.[193]

It is worth digressing briefly to note that Lady Would-Be and Crispinella have female descendants in the printed and dramatic literature of the Jacobean era. The free-talking female aficionado of new fashions and newfangled continental literature, centrally including Italian texts and the *Essayes*, becomes a recognizable stage stereotype. One such descendant appears in a play acted before King James by his company of the revels some time before 1620. In the second scene, the Duchess Dorigene is putting down a country gentleman suitor. She says that his country virtues may perhaps serve 'for a Doctors daughter,/ Though shee have read Orlando Furioso'. But for the Duchess, who has looked higher into poetry and who 'has talkt with Montaigne and with Machivel,/ And can make use of them; note him in this/Place shallow, here profound: and be th'only Starre/ Whereto all Wits advance their Jacobs Staffe', what would his three hundred pounds a year do for her?[194] Here, again, is the stage stereotype of the learned court noblewoman who has not only read Montaigne, she has *talked* with him, made use of him, annotated and judged his text.

The much-quoted pamphlet *Haec-Vir*, a reply to *Hic-Mulier* of the same year (1620), resembles a printed playbook and takes the form of a theatrical dialogue between a mannishly dressed Lady and an effeminately dressed Knight.[195] The mannish woman (Hic Mulier) is accused by Haec Vir of following foolish fashions similar to those indulged by Lady Would-Be—wearing 'jealous yellow jaundis'd bands' instead of 'innocent white Ruffes'.[196]

Like Crispinella, Hic Mulier at one point offers a 'lecture' that draws without acknowledgement (in the printed marginalia, which do acknowledge other

---

[193] Ben Jonson, *Volpone or the foxe* (London: T. Thorpe, 1607), sig. G2r–v.

[194] Anon., *A pleasant comedie, called the two merry milke-maids. Or, the best words weare the garland. As it was acted before the King, with generall approbation, by the Companie of the Revels* (London: Bernard Alsop for Lawrence Chapman, 1620), sig. B3r–v [ESTC S107366].

[195] Anon., *Hæc-Vir: or, the womanish-man: Being an answere to a late booke intituled Hic-Mulier. Exprest in a briefe dialogue betweene Hæc-Vir the womanish-man, and Hic-Mulier the man-woman* (London: [John Trundle], [1620]) [ESTC S106169].

[196] Anon., *Hæc-Vir*, sig. B4v.

borrowings) on Florio's Montaigne. This time the theme is that '*Custome* is an Idiot' and the sequence of borrowing is from I 49, 'Of ancient customes', a chapter that begins with a critique of those who allow themselves to be blinded and deceived by the authority of present custom. Hic Mulier uses the material to make an impassioned speech on the liberty of the freeborn woman and the tyranny of custom.[197]

To return to the origins of this stage stereotype, *Volpone* 3.4, let us begin by placing Lady Would-Be's remark about Montaigne in two overlapping contexts. The first is the satirical treatment throughout the scene and the play of Sir Politic and Lady Would-Be as representatives of a new breed of fashionable noble intellectuals who are patrons of continental literature, of the learned servants who facilitate their access to it, and of court or private theatre plays which, again, borrow from that literature for source material. The second is the fact that a play acted by the King's Men is making an allusion—via Lady Would-Be—to the culture of a rival company (for which Jonson also wrote), the Queen's Revels. This company was associated with pastoral tragicomedies that drew on recent continental literature made fashionable at court by the likes of Florio and Daniel.

Sir Politic and Lady Would-be are caricatures of the noble English audience for Montaigne and for the books, knowledge, and services promised by the new learning and by learned servants such as Florio and Daniel: gentle students who would eschew the '*craggy pathes of study*' and '*come to the flowrie plaines of honour, and reputation*'.[198] They carry or allude to books and name authors throughout the play. The overarching irony is that none of this helps Lady Would-Be be a virtuous woman in the sense of chaste, silent, and obedient, or Sir Politic a politic man of the kind Polonius's precepts would fashion. She ends up behaving like a courtesan in pursuit of Volpone's riches; he babbles about a plot to sell Venice to the Turks and is made a fool of.[199]

Sir Politic, who loves '[t]o note, and to observe', quickly agrees to offer Peregrine instruction for his behaviour and bearing, but is astonished he came forth to Venice without 'rules, for travayle [travel]' such as those prepared for the Earl of Rutland

---

[197] Anon., *Hæc-Vir*, sig. B2r–v; Susan Gushee O'Malley, *Custome is an idiot: Jacobean pamphlet literature on women* (Urbana: University of Illinois Press, 2004), 255–7, 302. O'Malley argues that the author might have counted on the fact that readers of the pamphlet would have known of the obscene material surrounding Hic Mulier's borrowed material in Florio's text, in order to undercut her impassioned plea. But she acknowledges that the pamphlet also allows for a reading sympathetic to her defence of the freeborn woman's liberty (256). For an expansion of the argument, see Susan Gushee O'Malley, 'Was Anonymous a jokester?': The anonymous pamphlet *Haec-Vir: Or The Womanish-Man*', in Janet Wright Starner and Barbara Howard Traister (eds.), *Anonymity in early modern England: 'what's in a name?'* (Farnham: Ashgate, 2011), 129–40. The materials assembled in this chapter suggest that borrowings from Florio were rarely mindful of the original context, and that the author of the pamphlet was unlikely to have expected his readers to bring such knowledge.

[198] Jonson, *Volpone or the foxe*, sig. E2r (in 2.2); italics in original. For a compatible study centred more on early Jacobean information-gathering see Mark Netzloff, 'Jonson's *Volpone* and the Information Economy of Anglo-Venetian Travel and Intelligence', in John Watkins and Kathryn Reyerson (eds.), *Mediterranean identities in the premodern era: entrepôts, islands, empires* (Farnham: Ashgate, 2014), 73–91.

[199] Michael J. Redmond, *Shakespeare, politics, and Italy: intertextuality on the Jacobean stage* (Farnham: Ashgate, 2009), 46–59.

by Stradling, or given by Polonius onstage to Laertes. Peregrine admits to only having some 'common ones' from a 'vulgar *Grammar,* / Which hee, that cri'd *Italian* to mee, taught mee'—a direct allusion to Florio and his *Second frutes* (1591). Aping the kind of advice offered in Florio's manuscript version of I 25 for the Countess, Sir Politic regrets that 'our hopefull *gentry*' are entrusted to pedants. Noting that Peregrine seems to be a gentleman of 'ingenuous'—that is, noble—race, he reveals that he has been 'consulted with,/ In this high kinde, touching some great mens sonnes,/ Persons of bloud, and honor'.[200]

In a later scene he takes up these instructions for the traveller, which he reveals he has 'set downe' in writing, along with other 'projects' he has in various notes and papers. He cannot find his note on how he could sell the state to the Turk, but he pulls out his '*Diary*/ Wherein I note my actions of the day', which prove to be entirely mundane and trivial. In the comic denouement of the sub-plot, Peregrine fools him into believing warrants have been signed to search his study for papers. Sir Politic pathetically reveals that he has 'but *notes,*/ Drawne out of *Play-bookes*' and 'some *Essayes*'.[201]

He is a stage caricature of the noble reader-writer in the school of Montaigne, one of those who in Jonson's words (in *Timber,* quoted in 2.3.2) 'turne over all bookes, and are equally searching in all papers, that write out of what they presently find or meet, without choice'.

In 3.4, Lady Would-Be enters complaining that her 'band' (a fashionable ruff) does not reveal enough of her neck.[202] It is a scene of satire against the loquacious, would-be learned woman who slavishly follows modish new customs in dress, discourse, and literature. As one editor of the play says, Jonson's lady is a would-be Countess of Bedford, a caricature of the learned court woman described in Florio's dedications in response to Montaigne's image of women adopting 'a newe, an affected and learned fashion of speaking and writing'.[203]

Lady Would-Be harangues her women servants about the way they have dressed her, before haranguing Volpone with her knowledge of physic and the liberal arts: 'I would have / A *Lady*, indeed, t'have all, *Letters*, and *Artes*,/ Be able to discourse, to write, to paynt'. As we heard above, when Volpone mentions poetry she moves on to Italian poets including Guarini and Cieco di Hadria. She is carrying two or three of them and produces a copy of Guarini's *Il pastor fido* from 'about mee'. Her Italian reading list corresponds closely to that in the preface to the first edition of Florio's Italian–English dictionary, which also alludes to dialogues by Aretino.[204]

But in the remarks already quoted concerning writers who thieve from Guarini and Montaigne, Jonson is using her to take aim at two reader-writers of the *Essayes* who were both associated with the new genre of tragicomedy and the Children of

---

[200] Jonson, *Volpone or the foxe,* sig. D3v.
[201] Jonson, *Volpone or the foxe,* sigs. I1r–v, I3r (4.1), M2r (5.4).
[202] Jonson, *Volpone or the foxe,* sigs. G1r–3r. All following quotations are from these leaves of the 1607 edition.
[203] Ben Jonson, *Volpone,* ed. Philip Brockbank (London: E. Benn, 1968), 76.
[204] John Florio, *A worlde of wordes, or, Most copious and exact dictionarie in Italian and English* (London: Arnold Hatfield for Edward Blount, 1598), sigs. a5v–b2r [USTC 513650/ESTC S102357].

the Queen's Revels at the time: John Marston, and Florio's associate Samuel Daniel. As Lucy Munro argues, Jonson is glancing at 'the Queen's Revels in general, and their use of modish literary works favoured by Queen Anna'. Munro points to the queen's fondness for Guarini and other Italian writers, and to the fact that London 1603 was dedicated to a group of women who then became prominent at her court, while London 1613, as we heard at the beginning of this chapter, was dedicated to the queen herself.[205]

Daniel promoted the translation of both these authors into English—in the process promoting his own association with them. His instrumentality in the translation of *Il Pastor Fido* into English is advertised in his preliminary sonnet to the anonymous printed translation of 1602, issued by his publisher Simon Waterson.[206]

So in 1602–3, Daniel heralded, in print, the enfranchisement as English denizens of both Guarini and Montaigne. Marston's *The malcontent*, the first play advertised as a 'tragicomedy', borrowed heavily from Guarini's play and we have already seen that he used Florio's Montaigne in *The Dutch courtezan* and *The fawn*. But the more direct reference, first noted by Jason Lawrence, is to Daniel's *The Queenes Arcadia* (1605). This pastoral tragicomedy drew on 'Cieco di Hadria' (Luigi Groto).[207] It is a play, furthermore, which stole almost as much from Guarini as from Montaigne and which, with its modern and facile vein, unquestionably caught the court-ear in the summer of 1605, a few months before *Volpone* was first put on.

2.3.8 MONTAIGNE'S ARCADIA IN DANIEL AND SHAKESPEARE

The occasion for *The Queenes Arcadia* was King James's and Queen Anna's progress with their courts to Oxford for the annual Act of the university in 1605. An extraordinary array of court nobility accompanied them—many with established reputations for learning and patronage of learning, including some, such as Southampton, Rutland, and the Countess of Bedford, who were patrons of Florio and/or Daniel. A large number were incorporated masters of arts during the progress. The main events were rhetorical exercises held in a special auditorium constructed in the university church. The King was an active participant in these, one of which featured Matthew Gwinne. A sequence of plays was put on in the Serlian theatre (designed by the Comptroller Simon Basil) in the hall at Christ Church, Oxford. Three academic neo-Latin works played across three

---

[205] Lucy Munro, *Children of the Queen's Revels: a Jacobean theatre repertory* (Cambridge: Cambridge University Press, 2005), 105.

[206] Battista Guarini, *Il pastor fido, or, The faithfull shepheard. Translated out of Italian into English* (London: [Thomas Creede] for Simon Waterson, 1602), verso of title page [ESTC S103502].

[207] Jason Lawrence, *'Who the devil taught thee so much Italian?': Italian language learning and literary imitation in early modern England* (Manchester: Manchester University Press, 2005), 99–101, 143–51.

evenings, representing the generic range of drama from satire, through tragedy to comedy—the last written by Gwinne (*Vertumnus, sive annus recurrens*).

The following morning, Samuel Daniel's pastoral tragicomedy, at that point entitled 'Arcadia Reformed' ('Arcadia restaurata' in Isaac Wake's Latin), was played in English in the same theatre for the court of Queen Anna, which included Prince Henry. Throughout the ceremonies and entertainments there was a clear distinction between the academic events put on in Latin for the court of the 'rex platonicus' James and the vernacular translations and entertainments needed for the court of Queen Anna—a reflection at the highest social level of the distinction Florio noted at work in the aristocratic household he served.[208]

Nevertheless, Daniel's entertainment was taken very seriously by the scholar and diplomat Isaac Wake, who included a long eulogy of the play and description of its action and themes in his Latin account of the 1605 progress, which otherwise concentrated on the scholarly disputations and orations put on for James.[209]

This in itself is significant for the argument earlier in this chapter concerning the role of learned noblewomen in the patriarchal world of the aristocratic household: Daniel clearly succeeded in providing, for the queen's court, a learned drama in the vernacular that made a social and intellectual impact on the larger occasion of James's 1605 progress to Oxford. Indeed, it is recorded as having been more successful than the academic Latin dramas that preceded it, and it was published the following year as *The Queenes Arcadia*.[210]

The intellectual impact of the vernacular play depended in part on a book that at least some ladies of the court were reading, and that had been translated at the request of one of them (the Countess of Bedford)—his brother-in-law Florio's *Essayes*. The humour of Lady Would-Be's reference to Guarini and Montaigne hangs on the fact that a fashionable court lady in early 1606 would know when a writer was stealing from fashionable continental books she had read with her learned servants. For the 1605 entertainments, Daniel takes works by those very authors and fashions a court play whose overarching plot concerns the efforts of two ancient Arcadians, Melibæus and Ergastus, to restore Arcadia to its natural state, uncorrupted by the 'arts' and the associated new customs that have been brought in by various outsiders.[211]

[208] For this and the previous paragraph, see John Nichols, *The progresses, processions and magnificent festivities of King James the First, his royal consort, family and court*, 4 vols. (London: J. B. Nichols, printer to the Society of Antiquaries, 1828), vol. 1, 530–59; Anthony Nixon, *Oxfords triumph* (London: Edward Allde for John Hodgets, 1605) [ESTC S120953]; Isaac Wake, *Rex Platonicus: sive, de potentissimi Principis Iacobi Britanniarum Regis, ad illustrissimam Academiam Oxoniensem, adventu, Aug. 27. Anno. 1605* (Oxford: Joseph Barnes, 1607), sig. R3v [ESTC S119457]; John Orrell, *The human stage: English theatre design, 1567–1640* (Cambridge: Cambridge University Press, 1988), 119–20. I am using the first edition of Wake's text. A second edition appeared in 1607; see ESTC S119454.

[209] Wake, *Rex Platonicus*, sigs. R3v–4v.

[210] Munro, *Children of the Queen's Revels*, 103 (citing a letter of John Chamberlain to Ralph Winwood); Samuel Daniel, *The Queenes Arcadia. A pastorall trago-comedie presented to her Majestie and her Ladies, by the Universitie of Oxford in Christs Church, in August last, 1605* (London: G. Eld for Simon Waterson, 1606) [ESTC S121848].

[211] He also draws on Tasso's *Aminta* and Luigi Groto's *Il pentimento amoroso*. See Lawrence, 'Who the devil taught thee so much Italian?', 97–102.

The plot is similar, then, to the plot Daniel used for England's history in seeking to persuade James in the 1603 'Panegyrike' to continue the restoration of England to its native English modesty by reforming corrupt customs where necessary, rather than by overthrowing the whole frame of the state with foreign innovations.

The interesting question for us concerns the relationship between the way in which Florio's brother-in-law reads—or indicates his patrons might read—Montaigne in the preliminary poem to London 1603, and the way he reads the same text for the purpose of writing a court entertainment to present to the ladies and gallants of Queen Anna's court in 1605. We heard at the beginning of this chapter (2.3) that, for Daniel, Montaigne's essays are sallies out upon the tyrant custom, which has left us in a state of uncertainty and confusion. In 2.3.6 we saw him, in the 1603 *Defence*, make a sally out upon a new (to English) custom—quantitative metrics—that was in danger of further enslaving us to imitation of the Greeks and Romans.

Daniel's 1605 play represents further dramatic sallies out upon the same tyrant. It ends with Melibæus exiling the intrusive agents of uncertainty and confusion, those whose example would otherwise make 'us slaves unto/ (That universall Tyran of the earth/ Custome) who takes from us our priviledge/ To be our selves .../ And…inchaynes our judgements, and discourse/ Unto the present <u>usances</u>' (my underlining). Thus enchained, we find we have no other touch of truth than 'the nations of the times/ And place wherein we live' and being 'our selves Corrupted, and abastardized thus/Thinke all lookes ill, that doth not looke like us'. Let us then, Melibæus concludes, recollect our selves, be again Arcadians in manners and habit, and solemnize a happy day of 'restauration'.[212]

It is a replay for the queen's court of Daniel's solemnization, in the 1603 'Panegyike', of the new union of Britain, in which, through James, men will reckon how 'this State/ Became restor'd, and was made fortunate' (by the first Tudor king, Henry VII).[213]

In the final speech of the play, as he restores Arcadia and Arcadian selves, the 'ancient' Melibæus draws on a chapter in Florio that includes a description of an Arcadia of sorts—the community of the newly discovered Amerindian peoples in I 30, which Europeans deem barbarous and bastardize with their artificial tastes because it does 'not looke like us' (in Melibæus's words). Daniel even glances at the French. Florio had written that 'we have no other ayme of truth and reason, than the example and *Idea* of the opinions and customes of the countrie we live in', where the French has 'opinions et <u>usances</u>' (my underlining). Further down in the very same passage, as we shall see later in this section, Montaigne replies to classical, pastoral visions of the golden age, including Aristotle's account of the Carthaginians' discovery of a 'great fertill Iland' beyond the straits of Gibraltar, with a report on the customs of the real Arcadia just discovered in the new world—a report used verbatim by Gonzalo in *The Tempest*.[214] But this is not the only Arcadia Daniel found in the *Essayes*.

---

[212] Daniel, *The Queenes Arcadia*, sig. L1v.   [213] Daniel, *A panegyrike*, sig. B3r.
[214] I 30, NP211–12/BVH Paris 1595, p. 120/SCETI London 1603, pp. 101–2. Kenji Go, in 'Montaigne's "Cannibals" and *The Tempest* Revisited', *Studies in Philology*, 109 (2012), 455–73,

The overall genre and composition of Daniel's play, including the main plot with its various lovers, rely on Guarinian and other Italian precedents, along with verbal material translated directly from Tasso's *Aminta* and Groto's *Il Pentimento Amoroso*. However, the overarching plot and further verbal material is derived directly from an existing translation of Montaigne, *Essais* II 37—Florio's 'Of the resemblance betweene children and fathers'.[215]

As we heard in 1.4.2, Montaigne in that chapter tells the story of a 'benefice' that is 'situated at the feete of our Mountaines, named *Lahontan*'. This 'petty state' had 'from all antiquitie' continued in so happy a condition that no 'pety-fogging Lawyer' had ever been called for. They avoided 'commerce' with the outside world until one of them, 'puffed up with a noble ambition', sent his son to be educated as a 'petty-fogging Clarke' in another town. He began to disdaine the 'ancient customes' of his co-villagers and never ceased 'to sow sedition and breede sutes amongest his neighbours'; indeed, he did not leave 'till he had confounded and marrd all'.

After this 'corruption or intrusion of law', worse mischief followed by means of a 'quagge-salver, or Empirike Physition' that married one of their daughters and settled amongst them. This 'gallant' taught them the 'names of agews, rheums and impostumes' and began to introduce 'strange compositions and potions' and to 'trafficke' their health. They began to perceive that the 'evening Sereine...bred the head-ach' and that the autumn winds were 'more unwholesome and dangerous, then those of the Spring-time'. Since his potions came first into use, they find themselves 'molested and distempered'; they 'plainely feele and sensibly perceive a generall weaknesse and declination in their antient vigor'.[216]

This is the point the English found themselves at, in 1603, as the new King and Queen arrived south to renew the work of restoration of the native English modesty—at least in Daniel's imagination. It is also the point at which Daniel's 1605 play for Queen Anna starts, with Melibæus and Ergastus expressing exactly these perceptions in Arcadia, described at the end of the play in terms redolent of those used by Florio of Lahontan: 'Montaynous Arcadia, shut up here/ Within these Rockes, these unfrequented Cliftes... [where the shepherds] have continued still the same and one/ In all successions from antiquitie'.[217]

Back in the first scene, Ergastus follows Florio almost word-for-word in declaring that 'the Syrene offends us more/ (Or we made thinke so) than they did before,/ The windes of Autumne, now are said to bring/ More noysomnesse, then those do of the Spring'. These changes of perception cause the two ancient Arcadians to set out to discover exactly what Montaigne, in Daniel's poetic account, set out to

469–72, argues that the description of the Carthaginians' discovery of this fertile island in Florio's Montaigne influenced Shakespeare's conception of the uninhabited island in *The Tempest*.

[215] Munro, *Children of the Queen's Revels*, 102–3; Lawrence, '*Who the devil taught thee so much Italian?*', 97–102. In identifying *Essayes* II 37 as a source for Daniel's play, Lawrence cites Lyle H. Butrick, '*The Queenes Arcadia* by Samuel Daniel, edited, with introduction and notes' (unpublished PhD thesis, SUNY: Buffalo, 1968), p. 149. I have not been able to see this thesis, and have independently compared the play with Florio's translation of the chapter.

[216] SCETI London 1603, pp. 445–6, for this and the previous paragraph.

[217] Daniel, *The Queenes Arcadia*, sig. I4v.

discover: '[w]hence the contagion of these customes rise/ That have infected thus our honest plaines'. They do so in order to 'restore/ Our late cleane woods, to what they were before'.[218] What Daniel adds to the Lahontan scenario, from his Italian sources, is the change that drives the main plot: the 'distemperature' of love amongst the young nymphs in Arcadia.

Melibæus and Ergastus quickly discover that the sources of the corruption of love in Arcadia are Colax and Techne. The latter's name means 'art'—in this case not the art of 'honest huswiferie', but the tricks of courtship, cosmetics, and fashion that change the apparel of the Arcadians.[219] By the end she has also acquired a friend, Pistophœnax ('a disguiser of Religion' in 'The names of the Actors'), whose role it is to introduce 'hote dispute' about religious rites amongst them.[220]

Colax is partly derived from the son of the over-ambitious father in Lahontan, for he is described as the son of '[a] man though low in fortune, yet in minde/ High set, a man still practising/ T'advance his forward sonne beyond the traine/ Of our *Arcadian* breed'. Together, these bringers of pernicious customs and arts are discovered to have battered at 'all the maine pillors of our state,/ Our Rites; our Customes, Nature, Honestie./ . . . / Reckning us barbarous, but if thus their skill/ Doth civilize let us be barbarous still'.[221] There is thus a distinction between the custom-nature of the Arcadians, and the custom-art of those who corrupt Arcadia by 'civilising' it.

In the middle act, we encounter for the first time two characters derived directly from Montaigne's Lahontan: Alcon, 'a Quacksalver' (the 'quagge-salver', in Florio), and Lincus, a 'Petyfogger' (the 'petty-fogging Clarke', in Florio, who would never cease sowing sedition and breeding suits until he had confounded all). When Alcon describes the 'abstruse and mysticall' art he will use to confound his Arcadian patients he uses some of the very words Florio's Montaigne uses in satirical vein to rip 'up the mysteries of Phisicke' for Madame Duras in II 37.[222]

The really interesting point, however, is that Daniel draws on exactly the passage in Florio that Shakespeare will pick up in *The Tempest*. Alcon and Lincus's dialogue uses *Essayes* I 30 in cynical vein when they describe their amazement at having discovered a community that lacks their own customs—a fact they regret. In trying to introduce legal disputes, Lincus finds that he has nothing to work with as the Arcadians are contented with the way things are and cannot be drawn to contestation. He has no legal base for actions of the kind he can use elsewhere:

---

[218] Daniel, *The Queenes Arcadia*, sigs. B1r–2r. Ergastus also reports that the 'milke wherewith we cur'd all maladies,/ Hath either lost the nature or we ours' (sig. B1v). The source for this is in the same chapter of Florio's, and may even have suggested the whole idea of an Arcadian play on its themes: 'As the Arcadians (saith *Plinie*) cure all malladies with Cowes milke'; SCETI London 1603, p. 439.

[219] Daniel, *The Queenes Arcadia*, sigs. C2r, C1r.

[220] Daniel, *The Queenes Arcadia*, sig. K1v. This character is one of the casualties of the cuts Daniel made for the text of the play published in his 1607 volume of *Certain small works*. See Munro, *Children of the Queen's Revels*, 103 and n.33.

[221] Daniel, *The Queenes Arcadia*, sigs. C1v, K2r.

[222] Compare Daniel, *The Queenes Arcadia*, sig. E4v with SCETI London 1603, p. 441. Daniel picked up the name Alcon from a Latin quotation from Ausonius that Montaigne inserts just above the story about Lahontan: SCETI London 1603, p. 445.

> No tenures, but a constumarie [*sic*] hold
> Of what they have from their progenitors
> <u>Common</u>, with out individuitie;
> No purchasings, <u>no contracts</u>, no comerse,
> No <u>politicque commands, no services</u>,
> No <u>generall Assemblies but to feast</u>
> And to delight themselves with fresh pastimes;
> How can I hope that ever I shall thrive?
> Alc[on]:
> Ist possible that a societie
> Can with so little noyse, and sweat subsist?
> Lin[cus]:
> It seemes it may, before men have transform'd
> Their state of nature in so many shapes
> Of their owne managements, and are cast out
> Into confusion by their knowledges.[223]

Lincus here voices the concept of confusing shapes of knowledge used by Daniel in his poem to Florio concerning the translation of Montaigne; there it is specified that the less choice books bring the strange shapes of knowledge that cause this confusion.

In the play, Daniel then goes on to develop Alcon's sense of amazement:

> For this poore corner of Arcadia here,
> This little angle of the world you see,
> Which hath shut out of doore, all th'earth beside
> And are barrd up with mountaines, and with rocks;
> Hath had no intertrading with thereste
> Of men, nor yet will have, but here alone,
> Quite out of fortunes way, and underneath
> Ambition, or desire, that waies them not,
> They live as if still in <u>the golden age</u>,
> When as the world was in his pupillage.[224]

In I 30 Florio's Montaigne had described, in less cynical and more celebratory vein, the discovery of a society yet commanded by the 'lawes of nature... but little bastardized by ours'. It exceeded all 'the pictures wherewith licentious Poesie hath proudly imbellished <u>the golden age</u>', and all the philosophical fictions generated by philosophers such as Plato:

> It is a nation, would I answer Plato, that hath no kinde of traffike, no knowledge of Letters, no intelligence of numbers, no name of magistrate, nor of <u>politike superioritie; no use of service</u>, of riches or of povertie; <u>no contracts</u>, no successions, no partitions, no occupation but idle; no respect of kindred, but <u>common</u>, no apparell but naturall, no manuring of lands, no use of wine, corne, or mettle. The very words that import lying, falshood, treason, dissimulations, covetousnes, envie, detraction, and pardon, were never heard of amongst them.

[223] Daniel, *The Queenes Arcadia*, sig. E3r (my underlinings).
[224] Daniel, *The Queenes Arcadia*, sig. E3v (my underlining).

Like the Arcadians, the new worlders are 'encompassed...with huge and steepie mountaines'; when their prophets come down from these mountains 'there is a great feast prepared, and a solemne assembly of manie towneshipes together'.[225]

Montaigne goes on to describe how the Portuguese seduce the cannibals away from their old fashions of relatively virtuous cruelty to new and more barbarous customs of punishment brought from Europe. So Lahontan combines with the society of the cannibals in both the ancient Arcadians' and the invaders' conception of Arcadia (in Daniel's play). It represents a state of natural knowledge and customs, which the invaders aim to corrupt with their arts, and which the ancient Arcadians, Ergastus and Melibæus, aim to restore by the play's end.

For a brief moment at the beginning of the seventeenth century, Daniel was in the avant-garde of vernacular court drama and literature. He introduced both the masque and the pastoral tragicomedy, based on recent continental sources, and was associated as licenser with the Children of the Queen's Revels. After 1607, the King's Men began to take these forms and sources, and the court and private theatre audiences that came with them, in related but distinct directions.[226]

On 1 November 1611, just over six years after the Oxford entertainments for James and Anna, the King's Men played a different style of Italianate, pastoral tragicomedy—labelled 'romance' in modern criticism—before the King at court in Whitehall. *The Tempest* 2.1 famously draws on the passage just quoted from Florio's 'Of the Caniballes', used by Daniel in *The Queenes Arcadia*, for Gonzalo's pastoral vision of a Utopia with 'no kind of traffic' or arts. It is interesting that two of the elements apparently added by Shakespeare—'[no] [b]orne, bound of Land' and 'Women...innocent and pure'—take his commonwealth further in the direction of a Daniel-like pastoral Arcadia.[227]

Kenji Go has convincingly argued in a recent article that the second part of Gonzalo's speech ('All things in common Nature...To feed my innocent people') is derived from another longer passage in 'Of the Caniballes', two pages on, in which the English Montaigne elaborates on the reasons why we should not describe the customs of their community—close as they are to nature and to natural virtues—as barbarous. The third and concluding part, in which Gonzalo declares that he would with perfection govern to excel the golden age, is likewise drawn from the passages immediately preceding and following the 'no kinde of traffike' passage, in which the English Montaigne declares that the 'perfection' of the New World nations does exceed Plato's and all antiquity's fictions of the golden age.[228]

The key point here is that the Montaigne Shakespeare uses for source material is not just Florio's Montaigne, it is Daniel's dramatized, Arcadian Montaigne. For it is important to recognize Daniel's role, alongside Florio, in introducing Montaigne

---

[225] SCETI London 1603, pp. 102–3 (my underlinings, to indicate where Daniel is drawing verbatim on Florio).

[226] Munro, *Children of the Queen's Revels*, 104–6, 133; Robert Henke, *Pastoral transformations: Italian tragicomedy and Shakespeare's late plays* (Newark: University of Delaware Press; London: Associated University Presses, 1997), 48, 60–5.

[227] Shakespeare, *Comedies, histories, and tragedies*, sig. A4r (SCETI p. 7).

[228] Go, 'Montaigne's "Cannibals" and *The Tempest* revisited', 458–63.

to elite English patrons as a gentle knight using his learning and judgement to enfranchise us from tyrannical custom, and in using the *Essayes* as a source text for a pastoral court drama, associated with the Queen's Revels, that imagines an Arcadia and exposes newfangled customs derived from human art.

Daniel reads Montaigne for Arcadia and for the critique of tyrannical custom-arts that threaten it. This reading shapes the environment in which Shakespeare, for the King's Men, borrowed from the same source for gentle Gonzalo's vision a few years later. Shakespeare alighted on the two passages in Montaigne's long report on the cannibals' society that present it most readily as an Arcadia. Much of the content in between is not assimilable to such a presentation.

As Munro says, it may be that any text derived from a source is a 'reading' of that source, but the question is, who is reading? In analysing the Queen's Revels' and the Kings Mens' rival developments of tragicomedy, we need to consider a range of readers from dramatists and audiences to shareholders and patrons. These playing companies shared various sources, from Virgil and Ovid to Guarini and Montaigne, sources that they self-consciously used in tragicomedies, in related but distinct ways, even as the same sources were being read and used in private 'lectures' by elite patrons of the theatre, real-life Would-Be's.[229]

The Queen's man Daniel's use of a text (Montaigne's *Essayes*) associated with Sidney's *Arcadia* by Florio, and read by the pair's noble patrons as part of their learned leisure, in order to imagine, for a private court audience, an Arcadia in danger of corruption by new, artificial customs, informs King's man Shakespeare's reading of the same author in writing his own play about art and nature, about enfranchisement and enslavement. I shall argue that Shakespeare's scenario engages critically with Daniel's play and with elite uses of Montaignean themes—if not as mockingly as Jonson's.

The Tempest was not composed for a specific court occasion, as Daniel's drama was, and most likely played at the Blackfriars and the Globe, as well as at Whitehall.[230] But it does experiment throughout—in the context of a play destined to be performed on the popular stage—with learned forms of entertainment and leisure that draw on classical and continental sources to entertain and educate a court audience. Many of these scenes are staged or controlled on stage by Prospero's bookish art and its instrument, Ariel. As might befit a King's Men play, an aristocratic dramaturge and scholar with the power both to enfranchise and to enslave is at the centre of events, with little trace of Queens or court women.

Will Prospero use his books and his learned arts gently to contain his own vengeance, his power to submit others, and to restore virtuous, authoritative rule in Milan and Naples? In his dramatic exploration of this question, Shakespeare returns to the theme we saw him (in 2.3.3) exploring earlier in his career in *The Taming of the Shrew* and *Hamlet*: the institution of gentle youth and the learned leisure of adults in noble households and courts.

---

[229] Munro, *Children of the Queen's Revels*, 97–8, 104–6, 133.
[230] William Shakespeare, *The Tempest*, ed. Stephen Orgel (Oxford: Oxford University Press, 1987), 1–4.

Consider *The Tempest* 1.2 and 2.1 as a pair of scenes of learned leisure or 'lecture' that aim to rouse a prince and his father (the King) from grief to acts of noble virtue using school themes from classical and continental literary sources. One begins as a scene of domestic schooling for a young gentlewoman, the other as a courtly exercise for a king and his court, centred on an 'idle discourse' furnished from his reading by a knight-counsellor. For an elite Jacobean audience of *The Tempest* many things are in play at once: dynastic politics, the representation and manipulation of disturbed noble emotions, the uses of learned arts and the transmission of knowledge, and the operation of authority over domestic household and distant spaces (the island).[231]

The central point for us, though, is the play's concern with the dialectic between enfranchisement and enslavement and its relationship to the definition of truly gentle uses of books and learned arts, which centres on the interactions between Prospero and Gonzalo, and between Prospero and his servants.

There is also a more particular point. The scenario (in 2.1) that has Gonzalo choose and handle the school theme from Florio's Montaigne dramatizes—even satirizes—the elite household process that mediated the arrival of the *Essais* in late Renaissance English culture. As we have seen, Montaigne describes this process in the first chapter translated by Florio: the 'institution' of the nobility, especially on their travels, in the free judgement of customs and manners via private exercises and entertainments self-consciously based on half-hidden classical and continental sources. It is interesting and noteworthy in this respect that I 25 ends with the English Montaigne firmly endorsing the participation of gentlemen and even princes as actors and audiences in the 'honest exercises of recreation' offered by the 'Players' and their theatrical companies. Such plays are extensions of their other exercises, based in 'lectures'.[232]

Act 1, scene 2 quickly becomes a scene of schoolmasterly instruction in which Prospero sits his daughter down to inform her of her own history. We slowly gather what has happened in Milan, then on the island. In both cases the story centres on the different outcomes of the institutions of pairs of siblings. Prospero reveals that while he was rapt in secret studies of the liberal arts, bettering his mind in over-close retirement and neglecting worldly ends, his perfidious brother was awakening his evil nature by learning the Machiavellian arts of courtship and stateship.

His parental trust in his brother bred only falsehood: 'Good wombes have borne bad sonnes'. His brother subjected both Prospero and Milan to most ignoble stooping. Banished to sea, he and his daughter were saved only by the charity of a noble Neapolitan, Gonzalo, who furnished him with rich stuffs and necessaries: 'of his gentlenesse/ Knowing I lov'd my bookes, he furnishd me/ From mine owne Library, with volumes, that/ I prize above my Dukedome'. This sets Gonzalo up as

[231] On the play's dynastic politics, see D. Scott Kastan, '"The Duke of Milan/ And his brave son": Dynastic politics in *The Tempest*', in V. Mason Vaughan and A. T. Vaughan (eds.), *Critical essays on Shakespeare's 'The Tempest'* (New York: G.K. Hall, 1998), 91–103.
[232] SCETI London 1603, pp. 86–7.

a custodian of gentle uses of books and learning, a tutor of gentility and honesty, in the play.[233]

Prospero then tells Miranda how 'I, thy Schoolemaster' have 'made thee more profit' than can other princes that have more time for vainer hours, 'and Tutors not so carefull'. But this was no ordinary 'institution'. Later in the same scene the audience learns that Prospero also took Caliban into his household cell, where he and Miranda together taught him language and the knowledge that came with it. But, according to Miranda, he turned out to be of 'vild [vile] race', not capable of good-natured learning. After attempting to rape Miranda, Caliban was confined in slavery. In the final part of the scene it becomes clear what Prospero has educated Miranda for: to recognize the gallantry and nobility of Ferdinand, and to appear as desirable to him as Venus did to Aeneas.

Prospero's family strategy—the restoration of his dynasty's authority via Miranda—assimilates a Virgilian school theme to its own purposes, as, under his direct sway, the heir of Naples falls for Miranda, the heiress of Milan, in the manner of Aeneas' vision of Venus: 'Most sure the Goddesse . . . '. Ferdinand's spirits are diverted away from grief at his father's apparent loss in the shipwreck ('hee's something stain'd/ With greefe') to admiration for the goddess he now wants to make his queen, just as Aeneas is diverted from his woes by the goddess-like maid who crosses his path (*Aeneid* 1.305–34).[234] This is part of a pattern of recollections of and allusions to the *Aeneid* throughout the play. In the final part of the scene, Prospero arranges a trial of virtue for the prince, a 'lesson' in hard living less directly related to a textual source.

As the following scene (2.1) begins, Alonso, King of Naples, silent and grief-stricken at the apparent loss of his son Ferdinand, is behaving in anything but the manner of Aeneas shipwrecked on the shore of Carthage. It is a sophisticated scene of tragicomedy in Shakespeare's new vein—far more sophisticated than Daniel's pioneering efforts, including as it does both satirical and pastoral notes. For the players, if not for the audience, there is the tragedy of Ferdinand's supposed death and the potential tragedy of Sebastian's and Antonio's double assassination attempt. The latter is foreseen by Prospero's art and averted by Ariel, who awakens Gonzalo and the rest of the court at the crucial moment towards the end of the scene.

The sophistication of Shakespeare's scene relative to prior efforts at pastoral tragicomedy, such as Daniel's, partly derives from the fact that it includes a cynical onstage audience, Sebastian and Antonio, who constantly interrupt and satrically undermine the court counsellors' attempts to entertain the King with their learned wit. Indeed, the scene is built around a counterpoint between the way the gentle and honest lord Gonzalo seeks to counsel King Alonso, and the way the politic lord Antonio, himself a usurper, seeks to counsel the would-be usurper Sebastian, the king's brother. This is not to say the former is in any sense idealized. Gonzalo

[233] Shakespeare, *Comedies, histories, and tragedies*, sig. A2r (SCETI p. 3) [*The Tempest* 1.2.119, 165–68].

[234] Shakespeare, *Comedies, histories, and tragedies*, sigs. A2r (SCETI p. 3), A3r (SCETI p. 5) [*The Tempest* 1.2. 172–4, 358–9, 422, 415–16].

is literally shown to be sleeping while '*Open-ey'd Conspiracie*'—words from Ariel's song in his ear—seizes the moment.[235]

Remember that in Montaigne's nobleman's school of commerce in the world, all occasions, especially when visiting foreign countries, can serve as new subjects to work on in the search for philosophy's truths. This, of course, is not a conventional journey—it is a shipwreck. How will the members of the court make this unexpected occasion on their travels to and from north Africa speak truths to the King, and how wisely will he respond? What themes will they use?

The counsellors Adrian and Gonzalo try gently to persuade the King wisely to weigh their sorrow with their comfort. They seek to divert him from his grief with witty entertainments that suggest how miraculously the court has been preserved, in fresh garments, how likely it is his son is alive, and how worthily his daughter has been invested as the new Queen of Tunis. But they are nowhere near as successful or authoritative as Prospero has been in the analogous case of the King's son in the previous scene. Other members of the onstage audience for this learned exercise, Sebastian and Antonio, snipe constantly at the counsellors' performance of wit, read their themes in cynical vein, and make the occasion speak more bitter truths to the King about the state of his dynasty. They can do this because the King is largely unresponsive, repeatedly commanding Gonzalo and Adrian to 'spare' him their erudite banter.[236]

It is Adrian who turns it into a pastoral exercise by re-envisioning the apparently uninhabitable island as one of 'subtle, tender, and delicate temperance', where the air breathes most sweetly. Under heavy cynical fire ('*Temperance* was a delicate wench') Gonzalo picks up the theme ('How lush and lusty the grasse lookes') and incorporates a retrospective celebration of the marriage of Claribel.[237]

As Sebastian and Adrian appear to play along he introduces the theme of 'Widdow *Dido*', the virtuous Queen of Carthage/Tunis in medieval tradition. But the Cynics immediately re-read Dido in Virgilian vein as the fallen whore of 'Widdower *Æneas*'. As the King finally speaks only to regret the marriage of his daughter and the loss of his son, his brother Sebastian seizes the opportunity to rub the sore of his double loss. Trying to save the day, Gonzalo reprises the pastoral theme by suggesting that Alonso entertain the thought of himself as 'King' of 'this Isle'. How would he govern this invitingly temperate isle?[238]

This is precisely the question Daniel thought that King James and Queen Anna could be entertained with in court settings in 1603–5. The answer he hoped they would give is that they would govern the isle of Britain *as* Arcadia—they would restore Arcadia from the grasp of tyrannical custom, they would with such perfection govern to excel the golden age. Within Shakespeare's play, to answer the question on his king's behalf, Gonzalo entertains Alonso with an imaginary Arcadian

[235] Shakespeare, *Comedies, histories, and tragedies*, sig. A4v (SCETI p. 8) [*The Tempest* 2.1.299].

[236] Shakespeare, *Comedies, histories, and tragedies*, sig. A3v (SCETI p. 6) [*The Tempest* 2.1.1–26].

[237] Shakespeare, *Comedies, histories, and tragedies*, sig. A3v (SCETI p. 6) [*The Tempest* 2.1.43–5, 53].

[238] Shakespeare, *Comedies, histories, and tragedies*, sig. A4r (SCETI p. 7) [*The Tempest* 2.1.74–8, 141–3].

commonwealth based on the chapter from Florio that had already been used by Daniel a few years previously, along with another chapter, for an Arcadian entertainment at the court of James's queen.[239]

The scenario is of course very different, and the difference might tend to support Sebastian's and Antonio's view of Gonzalo's imaginary commonwealth as naïve and self-contradictory (no sovereignty, yet Gonzalo would be king). The audience already knows that the history of the isle (like that of Britain) is not that of an Arcadia. It has no indigenous inhabitants apart from the corrupted Caliban. It already has a powerful lord and sovereign who has brought letters and use of service, enslaving Caliban.

It is interesting in this respect that Gonzalo nevertheless persists in his *naïveté*, his predisposition—in Montaigne-like vein—to see the island and its inhabitants as a potential Arcadian lesson for the Europeans. When Prospero's enslaved spirits later come on to stage the Virgilian episode of the harpies' banquet, he takes them (though of 'monstrous shape') for the people of the island, and immediately imagines what he will report back in Naples, in the way Montaigne's servant reports on the cannibals in I 30. Would they believe him if he told them the islanders' 'manners are more gentle, kinde, then of/ Our humaine generation you shall finde/ Many, nay almost any'? In an aside Prospero endorses what the '[h]onest lord' has said, given that some of the Europeans present (i.e. Alonso, Sebastian, and Antonio) are worse than devils.[240]

In I 30, Montaigne uses a report of the real experience of the New World to *reply* to Plato's poetic Golden Age commonwealth ('T'Excell the Golden Age').[241] In *The Tempest* 2.1, Gonzalo reapplies Montaigne's reply as a Utopian *challenge* to Alonso, to wake him up to his fortune and to make him resolve what actions he will take in the immediate future. But without any wise response or direction from Gonzalo's master, who continues to dwell unhealthily on the loss of his dynasty's future, this application gains no force or authority. The lack of royal response to the ancient counsellor's 'lecture' from Florio's Montaigne opens opportunities for the two politic, cynical lords to 'comment' upon it in sniping and satirical fashion.

In their eyes, Gonzalo is just a 'Lord of weake remembrance' prating 'amply, and unnecessarily', an 'ancient morsell', a rambling intellectual knight—'Sir Prudence'. He is, for them, a caricature of the counsellor who idly participates in elite 'lectures'

[239] Shakespeare, *Comedies, histories, and tragedies*, sig. A4r (SCETI p. 7) [*The Tempest* 2.1.145–66]: 'Gon. I'th'Commonwealth I would (by contraries)/ Execute all things: For no kinde of Trafficke/ Would I admit: No name of Magistrate:/ Letters should not be knowne: Riches, poverty,/ And use of service, none: Contract, Succession,/ Borne, bound of Land, Tilth, Vineyard none:/ No use of Mettall, Corne, or Wine, or Oyle:/ No occupation, all men idle, all:/ And Women too, but innocent and pure:/ No Soveraignty.... / Gon. All things in common Nature should produce/ Without sweat or endevour: Treason, fellony,/ Sword, Pike, Knife, Gun, or neede of any Engine/ Would I not have: but Nature should bring forth/ Of its owne kinde, all foyzon, all abundance/ To feed my innocent people.... / Gon. I would with such perfection governe Sir:/ T'Excell the Golden Age.' Compare SCETI London 1603, p. 102.
[240] Shakespeare, *Comedies, histories, and tragedies*, sig. B1r (SCETI p. 13) [*The Tempest* 3.3.31–6].
[241] See Margaret Tudeau-Clayton, *Jonson, Shakespeare and early modern Virgil* (Cambridge: Cambridge University Press, 1998), 213–14.

based on classical and continental themes.[242] So when Gonzalo begins his lecture by saying that he 'would (by contraries) Execute all things' he is momentarily, from the perspective of Sebastian's and Antonio's sniping, a stage caricature of the *persona* given to the English Montaigne by Daniel and Florio: that of a knight-adventurer making sallies out upon custom in daring intellectual exercises.

But they are no more than exercises. The real action is elsewhere. Prospero's brother Antonio reapplies Gonzalo's theme of the sovereignty of the isle much more pragmatically to *his* chosen lord's present needs. He makes the occasion speak to Alonso's brother Sebastian, rather than to Alonso himself, in a different and more dangerous way. He imagines not an Arcadia but a crown dropping on Sebastian's head after multiple assassinations.

Unlike Alonso, Sebastian engages with his counsellor's reading of the situation. He appears almost ready to accept the invitation to bypass '[t]wentie consciences' and to contemplate seizing the occasion of Ferdinand's and Claribel's supposed loss to establish sovereignty over both the island and the kingdom at home. Just as he seems persuaded to apply the precedent of Antonio's usurpation in his own case, the art of a greater master (Prospero) intervenes, by means of its instrument Ariel, to achieve what Gonzalo had been attempting earlier in the scene. Ariel awakens Alonso, who immediately resolves to search for his son.[243]

Where Daniel had presented the queen's court with an Arcadian entertainment based partly on Montaigne, Shakespeare insets an Arcadian entertainment by 'Sir Prudence', again based on Montaigne, in a more sophisticated tragicomedy for various audiences at court and in the public and private theatres. Gonzalo, who is like one of Daniel's ancients, is constantly turned into a comedy fool by Sebastian and Antonio, who are like Daniel's corrupted courtiers, as he tries to tell Alonso and his court how he would restore a kind of Arcadian commonwealth to the island—something the offstage audience knows is a pointless intellectual exercise for the elite.

Gonzalo's efforts are shown to be ineffective and naïve, with no purchase on reality; he literally sleeps through the hatching of a conspiratorial plot against his king. His pastoral vision never really gains purchase in the play, with the exception of one approving aside by the lord of the island, and is trumped by that lord's Virgilian, masque-like entertainments. But the counsellor who in Sebastian's and Antonio's eyes prates amply and unnecessarily is nevertheless shown throughout the play to be the custodian of gentle and honest, if insufficiently politic, uses of learning.

It is not, then, Shakespeare's direct, personal reading and reworking of Virgil and Montaigne that is at stake in these scenes and in *The Tempest* as a whole. What *is* at stake is the outcome of the institution of the nobility, and of the kinds of free-ranging, idle lectures and exercises, based on classical and continental sources, with which, as they seek to plot their dynasties' futures, they are advised and entertained—including in court plays such as *The Queenes Arcadia*.

[242] Shakespeare, *Comedies, histories, and tragedies*, sig. A4v (SCETI p. 8) [*The Tempest* 2.1.230, 262, 284].
[243] Shakespeare, *Comedies, histories, and tragedies*, sig. A4v (SCETI p. 8) [*The Tempest* 2.1.276].

Florio and Daniel had introduced Montaigne into England as a master of such lectures and exercises based in reading and writing facilitated and supported by servants. In *The Tempest* 2.1, we see the discussion, circulation, and application of the themes of an idle pastoral lecture lose direction and begin to spin out of control, because the noble master on stage (King Alonso) does not command and protect the process and its outcome. This almost results in regicide, as two other lords turn Gonzalo's Arcadian theme in politic, conspiratorial directions.

What is at stake, in other words, is also at stake in the whole acculturative process whereby serviced reading and writing indexed noble conversation and action. Classical and continental sources were applied humanistically as school themes in the formation of the liberty of judgement of the elite, the resolution of their emotional and political needs, and the constant reformulation of their family strategies in very uncertain moral, political, and dynastic circumstances.

This process at one and the same time comprehended and found a key focus in the circulation, translation, and use of the *Essais* in late Elizabethan and early Jacobean England, both in private readings and in private court entertainments for the elite that are partly based on those readings. In the first half of the next chapter, we shall review evidence that the English Montaigne continued to serve as a touchstone for the practice and value of private 'lectures' in Stuart England, as copies of the book reached members of the gentry across the country.

2.4

Reading Montaigne and Writing Lives in the North of England and the Low Countries

In the final chapter of Volume 1 (1.7) and in the first three chapters of Volume 2 (2.1, 2.2, 2.3) we have followed the *Essais* on their travels to Rome, to Paris, to Geneva, northeastern Italy, and to England. We have seen how, in each location, the book, rather than simply meeting with one or other kind of critical reception, became the focus of relations between various agents seeking to secure its 'commercement' (Samuel Daniel's phrase) on their own terms.

The book's transpassage through Geneva is less 'safe', less secure and open than Florio and Daniel imply, and Ferrara exacts a heavy toll, even if an unfavourable ecclesiastical review does not lead to actual censorship. But it is arguable that the Montaigne of the 1580 *Essais* is enfranchised in Rome, as if born there, while Montaigne the ex-*conseiller* of the 1595 *Essais* is made an honorary friend of the Parisian parliamentary elite in the early 1600s. Likewise, the Signore di Montagna of the 1633–4 *Saggi* becomes a citizen in Venice-Padua, and the Lord Montaigne of the 1603 *Essayes* is accommodated in London.

As well as continuing to explore the networks of agents involved in the book's travels across Europe, we began, in the first chapter of this volume (2.1), especially in the discussion of L'Estoile (2.1.8), to focus on the sixteenth- and seventeenth-century descendants of Petrucci's late-medieval free literate.[1] This is less a social identity than a social situation in which an act of reading and writing, on the part of anyone (male or female), might take place in *relatively* free conditions. It might involve the exercise of private rather than public offices, a setting that is non-institutional or free of direct supervision, an ethos or *persona* that is lay rather than clerical—all three of which pertain in L'Estoile's case.

In Florio's milieu, Montaigne was a *patron* of the noble intellectual friend to high-ranking individuals such as Sir Philip Sidney and Lady Anne Clifford (see 1.4.1). These noble aristocrats were in a position to command the counsels and services of others who, to varying degrees, performed the manual labour of reading and writing (or translating, in Florio's case) on their behalf and facilitated their conversation and other actions. Their capacity to act as free literates derived from their noble status, and its extent depended on gender and other factors (Lady Anne Clifford's religious reading, for example, was supervised).

---

[1] See the 'General Introduction' to both volumes, in Volume 1.

In this and the following chapter (2.5) we shall continue to focus on private reader-writers in different locations, though none will be of such high rank. We shall see that their interactions with Montaigne's work are shaped in each case not only by the circumstances of its safe transpassage to their environment, but also by the histories of their families, especially with respect to education in the liberal arts. They all read the book in the course of writing accounts of their own lives, in books they fashioned in manuscript for their families' posterities.

They relate to the book, that is, as an index of the act of self-accounting. The current chapter brings together two fathers who use the *Essais* in the first half of the seventeenth century to leave what Natalie Zemon Davis describes as an 'ethical bequest' to their sons.[2] Though one reads Florio's English translation and writes from Yorkshire, and the other reads a French copy and writes from The Hague, they share a relationship to the work as a register of a wise nobleman's experience of the religious troubles and conflicts that tormented Europe between the 1560s and the 1640s. Pieter van Veen used blank leaves in the back of his copy to write his memoir, while Sir Henry Slingsby entered his in a separate journal.

2.4.1 WILLIAM LONDON'S CATALOGUE OF VENDIBLE BOOKS

In 1657–8, nine years after the execution of Charles I, the Newcastle bookseller William London addressed a catalogue of 'vendible books' to the gentleman-scholars of the north: 'To the gentry, ministers of the gospel and others of a peculiar choice...the wise, learned and studious in the northern counties of Northumberland, Bppk of Durham, Westmerland and Cumberland.' He neither explicitly mentions nor explicitly excludes gentlewomen, though Lady Anne Clifford, hereditary Sheriffess of Westmorland, must surely be imagined amongst his potential customers.

To judge from London's dedicatory address, his market is an elite public, consisting mainly of gentlemen and secular clergy, who will purchase books for private study and writing and who are to be distinguished from tinkers and vulgar brains. But he also has in mind people without formal education, including artisans and merchants such as himself. His typical customer is not the advanced university scholar, but the 'diligent free-booter' that 'reads, *Conferrs*, and writes' with the 'Auxiliary aid of Books'—the mid-seventeenth-century English incarnation of the free literate with whom we have been concerned throughout this study. London's own introduction to the uses of books itself exemplifies the way that reading in the kinds of publications he markets can lead to informally learned writing, on the part of a merchant who probably had little formal education, certainly not at university.[3]

---

[2] See 2.4.4 for discussion of this concept.

[3] For this and the previous paragraph, see William London, *A Catalogue of the most vendible books in England (1657, 1658, 1660)* (London: Gregg Press in association with Archive Press, 1965), sigs. A3r, D1r; Margaret Schotte, '"Books for the use of the learned and studious": William London's

The catalogued books are mainly in English, including large numbers of translations from the classics and continental literature, but with a smattering of learned volumes in Latin, some of them imported from the continent, and of volumes in foreign vernaculars, together with multilingual dictionaries and foreign language manuals. It is a relatively broad and open catalogue, as London himself claims in the dedication (where he denounces catalogues that leave out 'Heterodox Books'), including both Catholic literature and works by Thomas Hobbes.

London speaks for his customer when, citing the sayings of an unnamed 'noble mind', he declares: '[t]he freedom of my soul hath a Charter to uphold it....I can traffick for Knowledge, in the midst of fiery combustions and perturbations, and no Cannon can reach me; I can sit in a contemplative Cabin, and no Martial Alarme can disturbe me'. Here, the traffic in knowledge conducted by the soul-as-merchant via books-as-commodities is one that—unlike other trades—is unaffected by the wars. London hints elsewhere, however, that the 'Tempestuous winds' of the 'civil War' have depressed the market for learning, and he hopes that 'the generous education of very many hopefull branches, from good families' will kick-start it again.[4]

This may explain why, in a catalogue that does emphasize recent publications, London keeps stating that books in England are embarrassingly under-used, and why a book last published in 1632 (Florio's *Essayes*) is listed in a catalogue of 1657. It could be that booksellers and publishers still had a glut of unsold stock in their stores following the disruptions to the trade during the conflict. 'Vendible' was a concept also used by publishers in the scholarly Latin trade ('vendibiles') to distinguish stock that they were confident of selling from those 'minus vendibiles' that they might have to write off—that is to say, London is assuring the reader of his catalogue that the older books listed are not remainders and leftovers that nobody wants, but marketable and desirable items.[5]

London's theme in his dedication is that 'Nobility of Blood, *Gentlemen*, is but the fruits and effects of Learning, and the culture of the mind', that 'Learning and *Knowledg* [sic] is the Essence, and true being of a Gentleman.' Where learning meets with a 'Generous and Brave mind', all must needs acknowledge and bow to him with respect'. Indeed, while 'Tinkers and vulgar Brains' drown their wits in a country alehouse, a truly 'Noble and brave deportment...is only to be accomplished by *Study, Reading*, and converse with Discreet and Wise men'. There is already a clue in this dedication that William London considers one vendible book

Catalogue of Most Vendible Books', *Book History*, 11 (2008), 33–57. I quote the text of 1658 from this facsimile edition. The 1658 edition (ESTC R202769) is a reissue of the 1657 edition (ESTC R3792) with a new title page and a supplement up to mid-1658 (it is likely that copies of the 1657 edition, with its original title page, were also sold with the supplement). London did issue another supplement in 1660 (ESTC R202769). It is not entirely clear whether London was listing books actually available via his shop or an 'ideal stock' of the best or 'choice' books of learning printed in England. But at least one study builds a good case that he stocked most of the books. See Schotte, ' "Books for the use of the learned and studious" '. The main objection to this argument is that the 1660 supplement was presented simply as a catalogue of new books printed between 1 June 1658 and the Easter term 1660.

⁴ For this and the previous paragraph see London, *A Catalogue*, sigs. E1v–2r, B1v; Schotte, ' "Books for the use of the learned and studious" ', 46–8.

⁵ Maclean, *Scholarship, commerce, religion*, 176, 216.

in particular to be an exemplary outcome of the meeting between learning and a generous and brave mind. The aim of the catalogue is to let all know which books 'are daily *prest* for their service', for though there is 'a complaint that the world seems opprest with Books, yet do we daily want them'.[6]

London is alluding here to Samuel Daniel's prefatory poem to Florio's Montaigne:

> But yet although we labor with this store
> And with the presse of writings seeme opprest,
> And have too many bookes, yet want we more,
> Feeling great dearth and scarsenesse of the best.[7]

This allusion, on the part of a bookseller, provides further confirmation of the importance of Daniel's paratextual poem, published with all three editions of Florio's translation (1603, 1613, 1632). Daniel goes on in the same poem to identify the *Essayes* as the answer to such oppression, as one of the select books that should be daily pressed into service, along with elite servants such as himself to read and interpret or translate them. London is using paratextual advertising copy from Florio's Montaigne in his own paratextual advertisement for books in general.

This is not an isolated reference to Florio's work. In the epistle to the reader, London apologizes for including a section of 'Romances, Playes and Poems', saying he will neither take pains to promote their study, nor hinder their sale. He then asks us to hear 'a Learned Author' speak about romances and adapts a passage from Florio's version of II 10, 'Of Bookes', in which Montaigne describes how they never had credit 'so much as to allure my youth to delight in them'. 'The wonder in this is the greater,' says London, 'that he was a French man'—an allusion to the fact that French works had cornered the market for romance in the 1650s. Here the nobleman Montaigne clearly features as a foreign model for the gentle public London is trying to reach, a model of a scholar-gentleman who 'reads, *Conferrs*, and writes'.[8]

To promote sale of his books London then adds 'An introduction to the use of books in a short essay upon the value and benefits of *Learning and Knowledge*'. The principal inspirations for this are Francis Bacon's *Advancement of learning* and *Essays*, but he also quotes various English and translated guides to use of the 'stock of choice Books' that he is keen to clear and that he deems appropriate for a scholar-gentleman who is aiming to 'discourse in company, or frequent wiser society', to undertake 'publique Service', or to seek 'private retirement'. They include Burton's *Anatomy of melancholy* and Stanley's *History of philosophy*. Another is once again the English Montaigne, which appears in the catalogue itself in the section on 'History with other pieces of humane learning intermixed'.[9]

The author cited is always referred to in the marginal note as '*Lord* Montaigne' (my italics). When making the point that learning does not necessarily lead to

---

[6] London, *A Catalogue*, sigs. A3v–4v, B2r.
[7] SCETI London 1603, p. [para]1r.   [8] SCETI London 1603, p. 237.
[9] London, *A Catalogue*, sigs. I3r, X4r ('Ld Mountaigne. Essaies translated from the French folio').

wisdom and sound knowledge, London calls extensively on Florio's description of 'letter-strucken' pedants and the value of a true education in knowledge in I 24.[10]

London uses Florio's Montaigne to delineate the free literate to whom he would sell his stock. In recommending diversity of study and extensive reading to his customers, and freedom from exact attention to any particular science, he calls on *Essayes* II 10:

> For what I see not at first view, I shall less see (saies Ld Montague [*sic*]) if I opinionate
> to it. . . . Therefore in reading Books, One said, He had a skipping wit, for if one Book
> (saies he) seems tedious, I take another, and so I am not weary with doing nothing.

The soul's freedom to traffic in knowledge is here explicitly tied to an unregulated practice of reading of the kind described in and enacted by the *Essayes*. Much that London says elsewhere, though not directly based on Florio, is compatible with the English *Essayes*: 'To converse with our selves in our studies, and private retirements, is better company and society, than I see by most now adaies frequented'.[11]

Towards the end of his lengthy introduction, London cites various classical figures who greatly estimated books, including Solomon and Zeno. He then moves on to more recent worthies, including Robert Burton and King James. He ends with Montaigne, quoting once again from II 10: '*I generally enquire after Books* (saies One that knew how to use them.)' Montaigne is declaring a preference for precisely the kind of books that London is offering in his catalogue: books that use sciences rather than books that institute them (the latter are books for school study, which London puts in a separate, short list).[12] He is the *patron* of the private, gentle (whether by birth or aspiration) reader-writer to whom London would sell his vendible stock.

2.4.2 FLORIO'S MONTAIGNE AND SIR HENRY SLINGSBY'S 'COMMENTARIES'

The prominence given to Florio's Montaigne in London's catalogue of vendible books for daily service is in tune with evidence that has recently emerged of a whole body of seventeenth-century reader-annotators across the country—not just the northern counties—who read intensively in their copies of Florio. Like

---

[10] London, *A Catalogue*, sig. D1r–v; SCETI London 1603, p. 63 (re: 'letter strucken men'), p. 66 (re: Antipater and the Athenians).

[11] London, *A Catalogue*, sig. F3v; SCETI London 1603, pp. 236–7 ('Should I earnestly plod upon them, I should loose both time and my selfe, for I have a skipping wit. What I see not at the first view, I shall lesse see it if I opinionate my selfe upon it. . . . If one booke seeme tedious unto me I take another, which I follow not with any earnestnesse, except it be at such houres as I am idle, or that I am wearie with doing nothing.'); p. 52 ('a wise man ought inwardly to retire his minde from the common prease, and holde the same libertie and power to judge freelie of all things').

[12] SCETI London 1603, p. 239 (where the phrase is: 'I generally enquire after bookes that use sciences, and not after such as institute them'). See London, *A Catalogue*, sig. G1v for another reference to SCETI London 1603, pp. 431–2. There are other pages in London's catalogue on which 'Ld Montague. Essa.' or suchlike appears as a printed marginal note (sigs. E1v, F1v, G1r), but in these cases I was not able to identify particular source passages in Florio's text.

Sidney's *Arcadia*, Florio's *Essayes* left an archive of traces of 'the reader as writer' in seventeenth-century England.[13]

William Hamlin's remarkable research into the extant copies of the three early modern editions has revealed the public of free literates (in England) for whom Montaigne was writing, for the owners and users of these copies left an extraordinary archive of writing—often personal writing—in the margins. Hamlin has also argued that the nature of the text they were reading—itself authored by a 'diligent free-booter' who 'reads, *confers*, and writes'—facilitated these kinds of personal written interventions.[14]

The annotators, we might say from the perspective of this study, were enfranchised as reader-writers by 'one who knew how to use' books. They were continuing and amplifying the free and frank dialogue that Montaigne had initiated with his own authors and his own lived experience; they were rewriting and redirecting extracts from his text in the way he had done extracts from his authors' works. By richly elaborating and interacting with Florio's own reading and rewriting of Montaigne's French text, each hybrid print and manuscript copy, each new reader-writer, became a distinct 'English Montaigne'.

But how, exactly? And in what contexts? In 2.3 we encountered a whole variety of tutors and servants who read Montaigne with and for the gentry and nobility or used him to find a voice to address them, and of playwrights who used him to stage their dialogue. We encountered stage caricatures (in Jonson's *Volpone*) of would-be politic reader-writers of both genders who kept a diary of daily actions or flaunted their studies in conversation. But we invoked only one or two instances of actual gentlemen (Cornwallis) or gentlewomen (Clifford) who themselves 'talked' with him. With the exception of one or two known figures such as Sir William Drake, Hamlin rarely has enough evidence to identify and to retrieve the biographical circumstances of his early annotators and extractors.[15]

So let us focus in what follows on one gentleman reader-writer who can be identified, even though his copy is not to my knowledge extant. A contemporary of Drake's, he was part of the northern county elite addressed by London (though from a county—Yorkshire—London did not name). Like Drake, he used Florio's Montaigne in the period of what have recently been re-described as Britain's wars of reformation or religion.[16]

Sir Henry Slingsby is exactly the kind of customer William London had in mind, though he was executed as a Royalist conspirator only a year after London's catalogue

---

[13] Brayman Hackel, *Reading material*, 156–95 (195).

[14] Hamlin, *Montaigne's English journey*, 169–71.

[15] On Drake, see Kevin Sharpe, *Reading revolutions: the politics of reading in early modern England* (New Haven: Yale University Press, 2000); Hamlin, *Montaigne's English journey*, 148–57.

[16] Where once most attention was given to 'the English civil war' or 'the English Revolution', the new focus on a multi-kingdom approach to British history has placed this war in the broader history of conflicts driven by religious politics across the three kingdoms of England and Wales, Scotland, and Ireland (sometimes also described as the 'war(s) of the three kingdoms', which are in turn to a greater or lesser degree seen as part of the continental European wars described as the 'Thirty Years' War'). See Charles W. A. Prior, *A confusion of tongues: Britain's wars of Reformation, 1625–1642* (Oxford: Oxford University Press, 2012); Charles W. A. Prior and Glenn Burgess (eds.), *England's wars of religion, revisited* (Farnham: Ashgate, 2011).

first appeared (1658). He might well have declared, in London's words, that '[t]he freedom of my soul hath a Charter to uphold it.... I can traffick for Knowledge, in the midst of fiery combustions and perturbations, and no Cannon can reach me; I can sit in a contemplative Cabin, and no Martial Alarme can disturbe me.'

In the legacy he wrote to his sons in the Tower of London in 1658 (listed in William London's 1660 supplement), as he faced execution, he exhorted them to:

> Prefer *restraint* of the *Body* before that of the *Mind*: there can be no true freedom, so long as the Soul is liable to thraldom.

> I have been known to *sundry Holds*; Yet I found my infranchised mind, when I was most estranged from enjoyment of *Liberty*, to be the freest injoyer of it self.[17]

One of the places in which his enfranchised mind had been the freest enjoyer of itself was in a manuscript journal he had kept in previous decades, especially at moments of enforced 'solitarinesse' and 'leasure', when he could set down and 'revew' his 'perigrination' in his 'close retirement'.[18]

One such moment had been twelve years earlier, after the fall of Newark in May 1646 and the effective defeat of the Royalist cause, when Slingsby had been deprived of his physical liberty, constrained to hide in his own house. His motive was to avoid being apprehended and forced to take the Negative Oath and National Covenant, which would have required him to renounce his good faith (both his religion and his allegiance to the King).[19]

---

[17] Henry Slingsby, *A father's legacy.... Instructions to his sonnes. Written a little before his death* (London: J. Grismond, 1658), included in and cited from Henry Slingsby, *The diary... A reprint of Sir Henry Slingsby's trial, his rare tract 'A father's legacy.' Written in the Tower immediately before his death, and extracts from family correspondence and papers, with notices, and a genealogical memoir*, ed. Daniel Parsons (London: Longman, Rees, Orme, Brown, Green, and Longman, 1836), 226.

[18] Slingsby, *Diary*, 118/Nottingham University Library, Department of Manuscripts and Special Collections (hereafter abbreviated to 'NUL'), MS Ga 12714, fol. 46r. For convenience, as well as references to the extant manuscript in Nottingham, I give references to the printed edition, based on an eighteenth-century manuscript copy of what the editor calls the Scriven manuscript (which he says is lost). They are almost certainly the same manuscript, as Sir Savile Slingsby records that 'half a sheet was wanting on both sides' (p. 61) at one point in the Scriven manuscript. This corresponds exactly to fol. 25, the bottom half of which has been cut out, in the Nottingham manuscript. In the case of direct quotations, transcriptions are from this manuscript. It is a folio book, with all-round margins ruled in pencil, containing a fair, lightly corrected copy in ink, in the same hand throughout. It is likely to have been written out from drafts, not in one but in several goes (as there are changes in the ink and in the writing), as and when Slingsby had moments of leisure. Apart from the very beginning ('1638', erased) there are no prominent date or day headings, only occasional mentions of the date at the beginning of paragraphs and a small marginal note at the beginning of each year. It therefore has more the aspect of a continuous memoir than a diary. The text of the nineteenth-century edition, though based on an eighteenth-century copy, is close to the manuscript original, with some light editing (either on the part of the eighteenth-century copyist or the nineteenth-century editor). So, at this point in the printed edition (117–18), 'The end of ye first part' and the beginning of the '2 part' is indicated, but the Nottingham manuscript (fol. 46r) has no such indications or divisions, other than the beginning of a new paragraph (not indented). Also, a correction that appears in the margin of the manuscript (fol. 46r: 'Here is a mistake it was the 7th of May when my Commission was dated 1642') is silently incorporated into the printed text (p. 119). At the very end of the manuscript the memoir is written in the wrong order on the leaves (fol. 71v continues straight on to fol. 72v, which then continues back on to fol. 72r, then on to 73r), and this is silently corrected in the printed edition.

[19] Edward Vallance, *Revolutionary England and the national covenant: state oaths, Protestantism, and the political nation, 1553–1682* (Woodbridge: Boydell Press, 2005), 125.

But he had been free to register the thoughts in this written journal, which claimed 'a Libertie for tender Consciences' from those who imposed the 'new religion', who had but recently claimed the same from the Royalists. In doing this, he of course drew inspiration from biblical texts. But he also drew on his reading in classical histories of the kind given great prominence in London's catalogue. He summoned precedents, from Tacitus's *Germania* 14 and Suetonius's 'Life of Tiberius' 41, for noble ancients who had refused to renounce their allegiance to chiefs when defeated or captured by the enemy.[20]

But in commencing his journal in 1638–9, he had also made great use of a contemporary book that appeared in William London's 'History' section. He had used Florio's Montaigne to shape both his commentary upon and account of wars that he had initially wished to contemplate from a free 'retirement'. How had his education prepared him to do this?

Slingsby was not a university scholar, but he was in the market for learning in the vernacular and Latin. He resided as a fellow-commoner at Queens' College, Cambridge, from January 1618–19 until 1621, without taking a degree. His tutor was the puritan divine, John Preston, one of the most prolific seventeenth-century educators of the gentleman-students and fellow-commoners whose admission to Oxford and Cambridge colleges transformed the universities in this period.

The letters exchanged between the young Henry and his father between 1618 and 1621 once again reveal the extreme solicitude of fathers for the details of the education of their gentle sons in this period. Besides lectures on moral conduct, Sir Henry senior instructs him in detail in the arts of handwriting and letter writing, and sends him books. He was certainly prepared to send his son on a continental tour, if accompanied by the right guide. In the summer of 1621, according to Preston's early biographer and pupil Thomas Ball, Sir Henry must have authorized Preston to play the role described in *A direction for trauailers* (see 2.3.4) and take his son on travels to the continent (the Low Countries). Polonius-like arrangements appear to have been made—tutor and pupil were observed, with intelligence sent back to England on their movements.[21]

But beyond this we do not have detailed instructions concerning the family strategy for the institution of the young Sir Henry. There are some indications in Sir Henry senior's accounts of the books coming into the household, including a copy of Francis Bacon's 'Assaies' in February 1613. According to the same accounts, Henry junior's elder brother William (d. 1617) spent two years in France in 1610–12 accompanied by one Mr Snell.[22]

Sir Henry's 'Articles' to Snell—equivalent to those issued directly by Polonius to Laertes (see 2.3.3)—concerning the institution of the young William on his travels

---

[20] Slingsby, *Diary*, 118–21/NUL, MS Ga 12714, fols. 46v–47r.

[21] For this and the previous paragraph see Slingsby, *Diary*, 302–13, 316–18; Geoffrey Ridsdill Smith, *Without touch of dishonour. The life and death of Sir Henry Slingsby, 1602–1658* (Kineton: Roundwood Press, 1968), 12–21; *ODNB*, 'Slingsby, Sir Henry (1602–1658)', and 'Preston, John, D.D. (1587–1628)'; John Morgan, *Godly Learning* (Cambridge: Cambridge University Press, 1986), 285; Slingsby, *Diary*, 304, 306–8, 310–11, 316.

[22] Slingsby, *Diary*, 269.

do survive. They open with 'the principles of religion', those of the 'reformed Churche'. William should spend time reading the scriptures and 'other books teaching good life and doctrine'. All this should be performed in French, which he should learn in parallel with Latin. The tutor, indeed, is enjoined to address William only in Latin or French from their first landing on the continent. For his French studies, ancient and modern histories and sometimes other kinds of learning are most appropriate, as long as care is taken to improve his Latin at the same time. Even his personal meditations should be in French. There are various other precepts regarding his conduct and conversation, health and diet. Writing is given equal weight with his weapon, dancing, and riding. Indeed, he is instructed to keep a written journal of his travel, together with a note of his expenses, which he must also register in fair copies in two separate books, one of which should contain notes of his correspondence.[23]

William's younger brother Henry would later school his own children, including at least one daughter, in languages. Though he hardly mentions his daughter Barbara in his memorial writings, we know from exercises written into a pre-existing manuscript account-book that she was privately tutored in French when aged ten in 1643.[24]

We shall see later in this section that the younger Henry used similar methods to those used on his elder brother to immerse his own son in Latin—this time on the pattern of Montaigne's account of his early education in I 25. It would also appear that the younger Henry was instituted in the record-keeping habit described in his father's 'Articles', for, as we have already seen, between 1638 and 1648 he compiled in manuscript what has been described since the nineteenth century as a 'Diary'. As edited by Daniel Parsons (1836) from an eighteenth-century copy, this has become an important manuscript source in the historiography of the English civil war.[25]

But historians have not considered the exact nature and sources of this document. Slingsby compiled his book within a very fluid genre of life-writing and account-keeping that does not correspond to what are now described as diaries or autobiographies.[26] This genre comprehended different types of writing in different types of books and manuscripts, from commonplace books to spiritual narratives, from financial accounts to the margins of almanacs.

In England, in the same year (1638) that Slingsby began writing his 'Booke of Remembrance' (as he called it), Elizabeth Isham of Northamptonshire began writing her 'Booke of Rememberance', a spiritual memoir inspired by Augustine's

---

[23] Slingsby, *Diary*, 259–64.

[24] Jerome de Groot, '"Euery one teacheth after thyr owne fantasie": French language instruction', in Moncrief and McPherson (eds.), *Performing pedagogy in early modern England: gender, instruction and performance*, 33–51.

[25] Slingsby, *Diary*, 1–193; Keith Lindley (ed.), *The English Civil War and Revolution: A Sourcebook* (London: Routledge, 1998), 53–7.

[26] See, for the English case, Smyth, *Autobiography*. For the Low Countries and France, see 2.4.4–8, and 2.5 *passim*.

Confessions.[27] In France, there is the directly comparable example of Guy Patin's manuscript precepts of a doctor to a son ('Précepts particuliers d'un médecin à un fils'), compiled in the same period (*c.*1638–48). Patin recommends Montaigne alongside classical authors as one of the *sages* who will boldly and freely tell his son the truth, without fear of tyrants or tyranny.[28]

Slingsby might have chosen a form more like that of a manuscript common-place book, as his contemporary Sir John Gibson of Wilburn, Yorkshire, did. The Royalist Gibson, another potential customer of William London, was imprisoned during the 1650s. He extracted and adapted lines of verse and prose that invoked virtuous precedents for the life of exile, unjust punishment, and suffering that he himself was living.[29] But there was no chronological element to Gibson's book.

Slingsby also extracts and adapts material from other books. Besides the references to Tacitus and Suetonius mentioned above, he includes, for example, vernacularizations and adaptations of a passage in Caesar's *Commentaries* (4. 17–18) describing a bridge over the Rhine as a description of a bridge built by the Scots, and a passage in Tacitus's *Annals* (2. 64–5) as an account of the treacherous manner in which the King was retrieved from the Scots by the English Parliament and imprisoned in 1646–7.[30]

But, relative to Gibson, Slingsby uses a form more like that of a journal. Entries are made at irregular intervals, sometimes months or years apart, and weave together domestic events; memoranda of accidents, sickness (including details of medical treatment), and deaths; records of housekeeping activities; building works and expenses; spiritual and moral meditations; and detailed accounts of military campaigns and political events in the national wars.

Slingsby himself nowhere describes the book as a diary, though a heading at the very beginning of the manuscript has been crossed out in black and rendered largely illegible. Only the phrase 'Or/A Booke of Remembrance' can be (tentatively) deciphered beneath the erasure, while the preceding word may be 'Journall'. At the very end he refers to 'these Commentaries or Booke of Remembrance Beginning in the yeare 1638 and Ending in the yeare 1648'.[31]

With this phrase Slingsby tells us that his book is a cross between classical commentaries on wars and politics by the likes of Caesar and Tacitus, and household books of remembrance of the kind described by Montaigne (see later in this section). He elsewhere compares it to the *liber commentariorum* in which, in the Old Testament (Esther 2.21–3 and 6.1–2), Mordecai's deeds in exposing a conspiracy against the King are written, then read aloud before the same King, who rewards him.[32]

[27] A transcription of the relevant leaf (fol. 2v) in Princeton University Library, Robert H. Taylor Collection RTC 01 no. 62 (Isham's book) is available at <http://web.warwick.ac.uk/english/perdita/Isham/bor_p2r.htm>. See also Elizabeth Clarke's and Erica Longfellow's introduction to the online edition at <http://www2.warwick.ac.uk/fac/arts/ren/projects/isham/texts/>.

[28] Millet 233–4.   [29] Smyth, *Autobiography*, 130–43.

[30] Slingsby, *Diary*, 163–4/NUL, MS Ga 12714, fol. 66v; Slingsby, *Diary*, 182–3/NUL, MS Ga 12714, fol. 72r.

[31] Slingsby, *Diary*, 185/NUL, MS Ga 12714, fol. 73r.

[32] Slingsby, *Diary*, 55/NUL, MS Ga 12714, fol. 22v.

The reference is not accidental. Slingsby was himself a Royalist and his so-called Diary records both his actions and his conscience as a cavalier supporting the King against Scottish rebellion and a parliamentary conspiracy. It is related to the written 'legacy' that he was later to leave his sons in print when awaiting execution—most obviously when he gives his views on soldiering as a commendable way of breeding for a young gentleman, or on the best way for his son to be taught Latin.[33] Unlike the Old Testament precedent, Slingsby's book of record would never be read aloud before the King, and he was rewarded only with a beheading.

William London at one point recommends the study of the Bible above all books. For this 'sacred *Verbum Dei*, will teach us the true-keeping of those Account-Books of our consciences, which one day must be open'd when our Shop-books are burnt'. He is alluding here to the kinds of paper books that so many of his customers kept for written records: on the one hand, commercial or financial records ('Shop-books'); on the other hand, more personal or domestic records ('Account-books of our consciences'). As well as being a household memoir and chronicle history, Slingsby's book could indeed be described as an account-book of his conscience. The interesting point, however, is that London does go on to recommend 'Moral Studies' in, above all, history (with 'other pieces of humane learning intermixed'), alongside bible study.[34] And it is not only the Bible and classical history that teaches Slingsby the true-keeping of this account-book. The other book he uses for this purpose is Florio's Montaigne.

We are told this explicitly nearly a third of the way through the journal. In his account of the spring and summer of 1640, Slingsby weaves together national and domestic events. The King, seeking supplies for his campaign against the Scottish rebels, dissolves Parliament after only three weeks in which they brought their grievances concerning the innovations in religion, the ship money tax, and other matters. Slingsby, as always, is thinking about the future of his house and his family. He is contemplating more building works at Redhouse (his estate), but also the vanity of all such worldly things. He turns to the crucial question of the institution of his eldest son Thomas, heir to his knighthood and estate. He commits him to the charge and tuition of one Mr Cheny, who will be his schoolmaster. He wants him to learn to speak Latin, more by practice than by grammatical rule; already, before he was four years old, Thomas knew the Latin words for various parts of his body. Slingsby is worried, though, that Thomas is not making so much progress this year.[35]

He then records his decision to,

> make triall of this way of teaching my Son Latine without Rule or Grammer: And herein I doe follow the patterne of Michaell de Montaigne who as he himselfe sayth was so taught Latine, that he could at six years old speake more Latine then French. But I want that meanes whiche he had having those about him being a child that

[33] Slingsby, *Diary*, 38/NUL, MS Ga 12714, fol. 15r; Slingsby, *Diary*, 53–4/NUL, MS Ga 12714, fol. 22r–v.
[34] London, *Catalogue*, sigs. F3v, F4r.
[35] Slingsby, *Diary*, 48–53/NUL, MS Ga 12714, fols. 20r–22r.

could speake nothing but Latine Him I doe take to be my Patterne herein of educating my son as I doe likewise his advise in Registring the dayly accidents which happens in my House.[36]

Slingsby finds no difficulty in extracting Montaigne's account of his own early education, from its context in Florio's version of I 25 (where Montaigne says it failed in his case), as a 'pattern' for application to the institution of his own son—though he is aware he does not have the financial means of Montaigne's father. This nexus of use of the text fits with others examined in 2.3, and with William London's promotion of Florio's work to his customers in the 1657–8 catalogue (see 2.4.1).

But, as the last clause in the quotation indicates, Slingsby also uses Florio's work for patterns to shape his own continuing self-instruction in adulthood. We heard earlier in this section that his elder brother, William, had been instituted in record-keeping habits. In the passage that immediately follows on, Henry reveals that he has taken his inspiration for his own book directly from Florio's version of I 34 ('Of a Defect in our policies'). Once again he emphasizes a passage in which Montaigne describes the legacy of his own father:

I doe likewise take his advise in Registring the dayly accidents which happens in my House

He saith his father observed this order in his House he had one man that kept the Booke of Houshold affaires wherein weare registred all expences payments gifts bargains sales. An other man that was his clarke kept a <u>Journall Booke</u> wherin day by day he Registred the memories of the Hystories of his House. A thing pleasant to read when time began to weare out the <u>Remembrance</u> of them. As to sett downe when such a worke began when ended, what way or course was taken what accidents hapned, how long it Continued: Likewise to sett downe all our voyages where and how long we weare from home; our mariages, who died and when: the receaving of good or bad tidings who came who went changing or removing houshold officers taking of new, discharging of old servants and suche like.

Such a Booke had King Assuerus wherein that Treason which Mordecai had discovered to be plotted against the King was sett downe which he caused to be red before him Edixit afferri librum Commentariorum Chronica quæ fuerunt lecta coram eo ['He ordered the book of records, the chronicles, to be brought, and they were read in his presence'].

Hereupon I followed the advise of Michaell de Montaigne to sett downe in this Booke such accidents as befalles me not that I make any studie of it, but rather a recreation at vacant times without observing any stile method or order in my wrighting or rather scribling Et quicquid in buccam venerit effutire ['And to blurt out whatever comes into my mouth'].[37]

---

[36] Slingsby, *Diary*, 54/NUL, MS Ga 12714, fol. 22r–v; SCETI London 1603, p. 84 ('And as for my selfe, I was above six yeares olde, and could understand no more French or Perigordine, then Arabike, and that without arte, without bookes, rules, or gramer, without whipping or whining. I had gotten as pure a Latine tongue as my maister could speake'). The printed edition of Slingsby's book adds 'a frenchman' to this passage after 'Michaell de Montaigne', omits 'being a child' after 'about him', and introduces a full stop as follows 'educating my son. I do likewise'. In the manuscript 'who as himselfe sayth' is a correction above the line.

[37] Slingsby, *Diary*, 54–5/NUL, MS Ga 12714, fol. 22v (my underlining); SCETI London 1603, p. 111. The printed edition has a number of variants in this passage, including 'our servants' for 'old servants', and 'my study for 'any studie', 'any time' for 'any stile'.

Here, then, is the source for the phrase he uses later in the same journal to describe the book in which he is writing: 'book of remembrance'. We shall see in 2.5.5 that Pierre de L'Estoile claimed the same passage as inspiration for the *registre* of the French religious troubles that we have already seen (2.1.8) he was keeping in Paris in the early 1600s.

Slingsby did not keep his register of the British troubles over so long a period, or with such diligence, as either Montaigne or L'Estoile did theirs of the French troubles. And like L'Estoile, but unlike Montaigne, Slingsby did not gather his whole written archive into just one book, for communication via the printing-press. Furthermore, his fate—beheaded on the scaffold for his religious and political conscience—might make him seem a strangely militant figure to compare with the two Frenchmen, who kept their heads down during the French conflicts.

Nevertheless, to triangulate the manuscript books of L'Estoile and Slingsby with the printed book of Montaigne is to understand what all three were doing at different moments in the era of European religious troubles: keeping a book of 'good faith', wherein they could account for themselves and preserve their liberty, their enfranchised minds, in times of universal confusion and sickness.[38] In all three cases the keeping of such a book was associated with or derived from the keeping of other kinds of household account-books. In 2.4.4 we shall see that a Dutchman, Van Veen, did something similar in the second and third decades of the seventeenth century, though he wrote his memoir directly in a copy of the *Essais*.

There is some evidence to suggest that Slingsby had been following Montaigne's advice in I 34 quite closely since starting to keep his register. It starts with an accident that befell not Slingsby, but his wife's sister's son. Only a couple of pages before the passage quoted above he had written of changes in his household staff. He is careful throughout to record all voyages and their duration. This is not to say that he started the journal entirely as a result of encountering Montaigne's 'advice'; Slingsby had just been made a baronet and his reference to the *liber commentariorum* of King Ahasuerus (quoted not from the English but from the Latin Bible), and his references to Tacitus and Caesar, indicate that he considers the keeping of a book of commentaries to be a noble activity, appropriate to his station.

Florio consistently uses the term 'register' throughout his translation, on many occasions to refer to Montaigne's own book. And the important point here is that Slingsby clearly understands the *Essayes* themselves, especially book III, to be a kind of 'register' or 'journal Book', and a breviary for the compilation of such a book. The English Montaigne is a pattern in a much broader sense, along with biblical and classical precedents, for the record he is keeping.

It is a pattern, more particularly, for a distinctively free and open style of reading and writing or account-keeping, one more akin to recreation and not constrained by the specialist techniques and methods of 'study'. There are clear hints of this in the final sentence, where he is surely following Montaigne's general example (as opposed to his particular 'advice' on journal-books) in not observing any style,

---

[38] Nakam, *Montaigne et son temps*, 87, 233.

method, or order in his writing, and in letting 'accidents' determine what he sets down. He is joining the English school of Montaigne we heard Ben Jonson describe so disparagingly in 2.3.2.

The still more telling evidence, however, lies in the fact that the opening quarter of Slingsby's book incorporates extensive material from Florio's book, largely unacknowledged—more than he subsequently takes either from the Bible or from classical histories. Whenever in this opening section Slingsby comes to comment upon the accidents he is registering, whether domestic or political, he is rewriting, as his own, commentary found in Florio—especially in book III. He uses Florio's book as a breviary for the compilation of a free-ranging register.

The majority of the material from the early pages in Slingsby's journal comes from III 12, 'Of Phisiognomy', but in these pages he also draws heavily on the end of III 10 ('How one ought to governe his will'), which concerns Montaigne's approach to public office, with some phrases also taken from III 2 and III 11. He occasionally adds 'as one saith' to acknowledge that the borrowed words are not his own, but he never names his source. The result is that when modern historians quote Slingsby's voice of free conscience from this manuscript document, they are often quoting, without realizing it, Florio's Montaigne.[39]

What was it in the third book that particularly caught Slingsby's eye? In an atmosphere of growing religious tension over the Laudian imposition of ceremonial uniformity, and of troubled individual consciences, spiritual directors were only too keen to suggest books that were appropriate to the times. Slingsby records a conversation with Timothy Thurscross, a prebend of York, in the York Minster library, and notes that the prebend gave him a copy of the recent English translation (from the Italian) of the Spanish reformer Juan de Valdés' *Consideraciones divinas*. The prebend was himself troubled in his conscience and was living a holy way of life much admired by the Yorkshireman. But their conversation centres on the 'late imposed Cerimonies of Bowing and adoreing towards the Alter', which clearly trouble Slingsby himself. Meanwhile, his wife has summonsed a preacher from York to receive both absolution and 'some wholsome Councell for her soule'. Again, Slingsby records his unease about the possibility that the sacrament of confession might be imposed as 'absolutely necessary'.[40]

But another book provided a more amenable voice for his free conscience, at least at this moment in 1638–9. The next entry in Slingsby's book extends the disquiet to the national stage and is based, without acknowledgement, on Florio's version of Montaigne's meditations on thirty years of French religious wars in III 12.[41]

It is not difficult to see why Slingsby, in reading this passage, marked it up to facilitate the writing of the account-book of his conscience as religious wars began in Britain for the first time. Montaigne was a country gentleman writing from the midst of a region, Guyenne, which had been particularly ravaged by the troubles. In

---

[39] See, for example, Peter Newman, *The old service: Royalist regimental colonels and the Civil War, 1642–46* (Manchester: Manchester University Press, 1993), 190–1.

[40] Slingsby, *Diary*, 7–10/NUL, MS Ga 12714, fols. 3v–4v; Juan de Valdés, *The hundred and ten considerations*, trans. Nicholas Ferrar (Oxford: Leonard Lichfield, 1638).

[41] Slingsby, *Diary*, 10–15/NUL, MS Ga 12714, fols. 4v–6r; SCETI London 1603, pp. 620–4.

1638, Slingsby was already seeing upheaval in Yorkshire and the northern counties, the frontier with rebellious Scotland. Indeed, the Slingsbys were as fractured by the wars of the 1640s as the Montaignes and the L'Estoiles were by the wars of the League of the 1580s and (to anticipate the second half of this chapter) the Van Veens were by the wars in the Low Countries of that same decade.

Furthermore, Montaigne had had a similar education to Slingsby. In III 12, the Frenchman drew on classical Latin poets and historians to find a voice to describe the troubles and express his good conscience—exactly the task facing Slingsby. Montaigne, in this and other passages, declared himself against innovations in church and state, and in favour of peace and quiet. He was a Royalist Roman Catholic who sympathized with his neighbours of the Reformed religion, and who as a result was '[t]o the Ghibelin...a Guelf, to the Guelf a Ghibelin'.[42]

Slingsby likewise declared himself disposed to quietness. He was a Royalist who in the early years of the troubles sympathized with Parliament's defence of its traditional liberties and privileges, but not with their campaign against episcopacy, even though the imposition of Laud's ecclesiastical regime had made him uneasy.[43]

The opening to Florio's translation of Montaigne's chapter (III 12) reflects on the way in which peasants, without book-learning, show more constancy and patience in suffering than specialists in Aristotle and Plato. Montaigne then breaks off in a manner typical of a 'journal-book' to reflect on the circumstances of his reflections:

> I was writing this about a time that a boistrous storme of our tumultuous broiles and bloody troubles, did for many months space, with all it's [*sic*] might and horror, hang full over my head. On the one side, I had the enemies at my gates; on the other the *Picoreurs* or free-booters, farre worse foes....Oh monstrous Warre: Others worke without; this inwardly and against hir selfe: And with her owne venome gnaweth and consumes her selfe.[44]

Later in the same meditation, Montaigne states:

> True-perfect liberty, is, for one to be able to do and work all things upon himself. *Potentissimus est qui se habet in potestate.* [Sen. *epist.* 9] *Hee is of most power, that keepes himselfe in his owne power.* In ordinary and peacefull times, a man prepares himselfe for common and moderate accidents: but in this confusion, wherein wee have beene these thirty yeeres, every French man, be it in generall or in particular, doth hourely see himselfe upon the point of his fortunes over-throwe and downefall. By so much more ought each one have his courage stored and his minde fraughted, with more strong and vigorous provisions:...As I reade not much in Histories, these confusions of other states, without regret, that I could not better them present: So doth my curiositie make me somwhat please my selfe, with mine eies to see this notable spectacle of our publike death; her symptomes and formes. And since I could not hinder the same, I am content to be appointed as an assistant unto it, and thereby instruct my selfe. Yet seeke we evidently to know in shadowes, and understand by fabulous representations upon

---

[42] SCETI London 1603, p. 622.
[43] Slingsby, *Diary*, 66–7/NUL, MS Ga 12714, fols. 25v–26r.
[44] SCETI London 1603, p. 620 (my underlining).

Theatres, the shew of the tragicke revolutions in humane fortune....And good Historians avoide calme narrations, as a dead water or mort-mere; <u>to retreeve seditions and finde out warres</u>, whereto they know we call them.[45]

These two passages in particular caught Slingsby's eye as he sat down to write his account of the way he instructed himself when witnessing—as a curious spectator— the beginnings of what is now called the First Bishops' War of 1639:

> The third of Januarie (out of Curiositie to se the <u>spectacle of our publicke death</u>) I went to Bramham moore to se the Training of our light horse, for which servise I my selfe had sent two horses, by Commaundment from the Deputie Leitenants and Sir Jacob Ashley, who is laite [Comd] downe with speciall Commission from the King to traine and exercise them. These are strang strang spectacles to this nation in this age, that have lived thus long peaceably...it is I say a thing most horrible that we should engage our selfe in a war one with an other, and with <u>our owne venome gnaw and consume our selfes</u>.[46]

This is the very beginning of Slingsby's narrative of the wars, and for several pages, whenever he switches from chronicling events to commenting upon events, he is cutting, pasting, and rewriting passages from Florio's version of 'Of Phisiognomy' and other chapters in book III.

The enforced military mobilization in Yorkshire was in response to the Scots, who were become 'most warlike'—'The Cause of there grievance as they pretend is matter of religion'. When Slingsby comments that this can be a 'faire pretext' but that what is more usual is 'to make religion a pretence and cloake for wickednesse', and that ambition and cruelty are quite vigorous enough not to need arming with justice and devotion, he is drawing on Florio's words.[47]

But these words are not necessarily directed at the Scots alone; he goes on to explain their religious grievances in terms that hint at wrongs on both sides. There then follow two pages of rewritten, adapted commentary from Florio, interspersed with phrases of Slingsby's own, starting with a statement that could apply equally to the Scots and the King: 'I like there opinion who would not have violence offered to the quiett repose of a Country, noe not to reforme and cure the same, nor allow of that reformation which is purchased with the Bloud and ruine of the Citizens.'[48]

Slingsby's use of 'Of Phisiognomy' culminates in a passage that clearly shows how he adapts Florio's words to his own situation in early 1639:

> These are times for Hystorians to wright of, who seeke <u>to avoyd all calme narrations as a dead water, to fill there volumes with cruell wars and seditions</u>. I desire not imployment in these times it is for those that will purchase it, at any rate. Undique totis, usque adeo turbatur aquis ['Such revel and tumultuous rout/ In all the country

---

[45] SCETI London 1603, p. 623 (my underlining).
[46] Slingsby, *Diary*, 10–11/NUL, MS Ga 12714, fol. 4v (my underlining). The manuscript very clearly reads 'Bramham moore', where the printed edition has 'Bramton [Bramham]'.
[47] Slingsby, *Diary*, 11–12/NUL, MS Ga 12714, fol. 5r; SCETI London 1603, p. 622.
[48] Slingsby, *Diary*, 13–14/NUL, MS Ga 12714, fol. 5r–v.

round about']. Where to doe evill is Common, to doe nothing is in a manner
Comendable. Yet I hapned to be in some imployment though it were but short.

The first sentence is from a passage in III 12 that Slingsby had already used once.
The first two phrases of the second sentence are his own, followed by a Virgilian
quotation from nearby in the same chapter of Florio's and a phrase from the
beginning of III 9 that was italicized in London 1603.[49] The final sentence is
Slingsby's own, and suggests—in tune with the Montaignean *persona* upon which
he is drawing—that he was not actively seeking employment ('I hapned to
be...'). He goes on to explain in his own words that the employment he did
find was not a proper commission and lasted but a short time—even 'taking the
vew of Armes' was unusual for Slingsby, who declares himself one 'who doe little
affect busines'.[50]

At this point, to justify his ethos as one who did not desire employments,
who little affected business, he turns to Florio's version of III 10, where he saw (if
he was using the 1603 edition) an italicized proverb that was highly germane to his
situation: '*Abstinence from doing, is often as generous as doing: but it is not so apparent*
[emphasis in original].' The whole passage that follows in Slingsby's journal is a
rewritten version of phrases from the final two pages of Florio's III 10, which
praises a lack of ambition in men of meaner fortunes, and justifies, on Montaigne's
part, his low-key tenure of public office (the mayoralty).[51]

The passage in III 10 that caught Slingsby's eye begins with declarations that he
must have felt applied to him during the early stages of the British wars:

> My humours are contrary to turbulent humors; I could pacifie an inconvenience or
> trouble without troubling my selfe, and chastise a disorder without alteration...For
> my part I commend a gliding, an obscure and reposed life.... But my fortune will have
> it so; I am descended of a family that hath lived without noise and tumult, and of long
> continuance particularly ambitious of integrity. Our men are so framed to agitation
> and ostentations that goodnesse, moderation, equity, constancy, and such quiet and
> meane qualities are no more heard of.[52]

The journal then appears to change tack completely, as Slingsby records his dealings with John Goodhand, the Feodary of the West Riding, whom he accuses of
corrupt practices in matters of wardship. But his meditations on the corruption

[49] Slingsby, *Diary*, 14/NUL, MS Ga 12714, fol. 5v (my underlining); SCETI London 1603,
p. 623 ('calme narrations', etc.); p. 622 ('undique totis', etc., with Gwinne's translation of the Virgilian
verses given in square brackets above); p. 566 ('where to do evil', etc., from a passage near the beginning of III 9 on 'the corruption of the times we live in'). On the importance of the italicization of
maxims in Florio's translation, the origins of a general trend to 'maximize' the text of the *Essais* in
England, see Hamlin, *Montaigne's English journey*, 143–4.
[50] Slingsby, *Diary*, 14/NUL, MS Ga 12714, fol. 5v. Slingsby did not receive a proper commission
until December 1642. See Newman, *The old service*, 36.
[51] Slingsby, *Diary*, 14–15/NUL, MS Ga 12714, fol. 6r; SCETI London 1603, pp. 610–11 (source
for 'Abstinence from doing', etc.; 'cannot for Conscience, at least for ambition', etc.; 'more solide and
firme', 'lett us not usurpe those of greatnesse', etc.; 'actions are most Commendable...hands of a
worke man', 'Muntebankes that shew the operation of there skill upon skaffolds', etc.; 'so ambitious
are we of renowne...equitie Constancie and such qualities are little sett by').
[52] SCETI London 1603, p. 610.

of the times continue, and are once again based on passages in Florio's book III. This time it is the beginning of III 2, where Montaigne muses on the satisfactions of the 'testimonies of an unspotted conscience': 'excuse wee here what I often say that I seldome repent my selfe, and that my conscience is contented with it selfe; not of an Angels or a horses conscience, but as of a mans conscience'. Montaigne declares in the same passage that 'I have my owne lawes and tribunall, to judge of me, whither I addresse my self more, then any where els'. As we shall see in 2.4.3, this version of 'liberty of conscience', connected specifically with the writing of memorial records, is the most lasting contribution of Florio's Montaigne to Slingsby's ethical legacy.[53]

This is by no means the end of Slingsby's use of Florio's work. He draws on many other chapters in the pages that follow. In one passage he uses Florio's words from various chapters to discuss husbandry.[54] In another, occasioned by news of a violent lightening strike on a church in Devon, and the memory of an accident that killed a Papist at Blackfriars in the Jacobean era, he co-opts Florio's 'That a man ought soberly to meddle with judging of divine lawes' (I 31) in opposing those who claim to see Divine providence at work in events, especially when their enemies are smitten down. In this latter case it is possible to imagine that Slingsby first annotated the chapter in his copy with his own examples, then turned the annotated passages into an entry in his journal book.[55]

He might have done something similar when reading Montaigne's short meditation in I 28 upon the theme that '[o]ur studies and our desires should sometimes have a feeling of age'. When reflecting upon the vanity of older men's building projects, Slingsby incorporates many of Montaigne's Latin citations into his own version of the contemplation, which he says is 'unseasonable at noe time' (alluding to the title of the chapter, 'All things have their season').[56] A good portion of the

[53] Slingsby, *Diary*, 16–18/NUL, MS Ga 12714, fols. 6r–7r; SCETI London 1603, p. 484 (source for 'the approbation of others in so corrupt an age... God keep every man', etc.; 'That which was accounted vice', etc.; 'that whose deformitie, and incommoditie is palpable', 'to preserve ones self from the Contagion of an age... without reward'). One sentence is put together from the page before, the very beginning of the chapter: SCETI London 1603, p. 483 (source for 'unquietly and staggeringly... Circumstances and Considerations'). One Ciceronian quotation is brought in from III 11: SCETI London 1603, p. 613 (source for 'Sanitatis patrocinium est insanientium turba').

[54] Slingsby, *Diary*, 25–6/NUL, MS Ga 12714, fol. 10r–v; SCETI London 1603, p. 397 (an italicized passage in Florio which is the source for 'we stray from our selfes... I am not ambitious say we... I am not sumptuous, but the citie requires greate charges'); p. 145 (source for 'Laws to Moderate the vaine expences of belly cheare and apparell as one sayth seameth contrary to its end... eate dainties... increase there creditt and price. The best Course weare to begett... It was a good invention of Seleucus... and pernitious [for 'precious' in printed edition] Dainties'); p. 167 (source for 'Attilius Regulus... attended on with seaven servants').

[55] Slingsby, *Diary*, 28–30/NUL, MS Ga 12714, fols. 11v–12r; SCETI London 1603, p. 107 (source for 'to goe about to find out the cause of every accident... since we read that Arius, Leo, and Heliogabalus died upon a privie... It is the part of a Christean to beleeve... interpreters and controwlers of gods secret designes... ground and establish our religion upon the prosperitie of our enterprises... hazard the overthrow of oure faith').

[56] Slingsby, *Diary*, 44–5/NUL, MS Ga 12714, fol. 18r; SCETI London 1603, p. 404 (source for 'Diversos diversa iuvant... as one saith young men should make there preparations... how we might best and with the most ease leave this world... when he should be going to his grave puts Marble out

diary concerns his wife's attempts to 'take physic' for her ailing health, often record-ing how the rules of this or that physician failed to ameliorate her condition. After one such occasion Slingsby meditates on the failings of physicians and incorporates a rewritten passage from III 13.[57]

2.4.3 THE LIBERTY OF A SUBJECT

The foregoing discussion has established that Florio's Montaigne was constantly by Slingsby's side when he was writing his journal for 1639 and the first half of 1640, and that he consciously used it as a 'pattern' both for the education of his eldest son and for his own enterprise in unmethodically recording and moralizing on events for posterity. He understood posterity principally in terms of the futures of his sons and daughter. Book III, in particular, offered a *persona* and a voice, in writing, that allowed Slingsby in the early stages of the British wars of religion to try out a dis-engaged and sceptical ethos, a form of liberty of conscience, even as he moved ever closer to a proper military commission and to action on the battlefield.

What remained, if anything, of his relationship to Florio's Montaigne as he faced execution for treason twenty years later? As was mentioned in 2.4.2, his writ-ten 'legacy to his sonnes', the ground of which was 'Instruction', found its way into print shortly after his death. This discourse is on the one hand related to the kinds of 'institutions' of young gentlemen we were considering in 2.3.2 and 2.3.4, and on the other hand represents a piece of self-justification that faces down the spe-cific accusations put to him at his trial.

The voice adopted by Slingsby in this text owes more to Proverbs than to Montaigne. But we heard earlier that the condition he most wished his sons to enjoy after his death was 'true freedom' of mind and body. He was concerned above all to instruct them, as Polonius had instructed Laertes, in how to remain 'Freeborn Subjects':

> But to return to You, my dear Sons, to whom and for whose benefit these my last direc-tions are addressed; Be it your care in the free enjoyment of a private condition...to mould your Spirits to that temper, as Your discreet carriage may free You from publick censure, Many eyes and many ears require cautious and preventive Thoughts. The only way to be secure is not to be active in the affairs of State.[58]

He goes on to say once again that it is 'the mind that makes the undertaker free' and that he who desires 'too Officiously to engage his Person in others Concerns' opens himself to dangers. Make 'Your Thoughts your own and loyal desires cannot redound to your prejudice', for the 'Liberty of a Subject, as I hold it to

to worke...should our studies and desires [for 'designs' in printed edition] have alwayse a feeling of age...imponit finem sapiens in rebus honestis').

[57] Slingsby, *Diary*, 46–7/NUL, MS Ga 12714, fols. 18v–19r; SCETI London 1603, p. 642 (a passage which begins in italics in Florio and which is the source for 'as it is sayd Plato...effects of what they professe').

[58] Slingsby, *Diary*, 208.

be a brave but rare Interest; so I should account him . . . unworthy the title of so eminent a priviledge, who will not stick to engage that Liberty to the ear of a stranger.'[59]

Slingsby is thinking of his own downfall, caused by the fact that he did not stick to engage his liberty to the ears of strangers—the garrison officers in the prison at Hull whose testimony condemned him. But there is also a residue of the moment in 1638–9 when he turned to Florio to assist him in the attempt, in writing, to preserve his free enjoyment of a private condition, to make his thoughts his own in the midst of the emerging conflict.

The important point here is not so much that Florio's Montaigne was an influence on Slingsby (though it was at one key moment). It is more that Slingsby in his written memorials to his sons was doing something analogous to Montaigne in his book to friends and family, but using a different mixture of religious and secular languages and concepts. The transmission of practical regimens for soul and body, including dispositions embedded in particular confessional allegiances, was a vital cultural process, mediated by written texts and other forms of instruction, within elite families in post-Reformation Europe.

In the rest of this chapter and in 2.5 we shall consider three more instances of this process, in the Low Countries and France, all shaped in part by use of the *Essais*. In his 'Legacy', as in his journal book of remembrance, Slingsby aimed in writing to form and preserve the freeborn mind and conscience, which he considered the essential part of the liberty of a subject, and to transmit it to posterity via the instruction and education of his sons. The next section (2.4.4) will describe this as the making of an ethical bequest, and consider the case of a copy of the *Essais* which found its way to the Low Countries and became a family memorial designed as a gift for a son.

2.4.4 PIETER VAN VEEN'S COPY OF PARIS 1602

The subject of the rest of this chapter[60] is a copy of the 1602 Paris edition of Montaigne's *Essais* owned by a Dutch lawyer and painter called Pieter van Veen.[61] The last chapter (2.3) approached Florio's 'Institution' not as a work by Montaigne that was received by an English reader and translator, but as a work by Florio that originated in an English context. In the first half of this chapter, we saw not how Florio's Montaigne was received by a reader, but how it could give rise to another

[59] Slingsby, *Diary*, 209.
[60] I should like to thank the following for helping me with my research on Van Veen: Marrigje Rikken of the University of Amsterdam, Paul Lang of the Musée d'Art et d'Histoire in Geneva, Anton van der Lem of Leiden University Library, Brigitte Monti of the Musée d'Art et d'Histoire in Geneva, Katherine O'Mahoney, Jan Papy of the Catholic University of Louvain, Paul Smith of the University of Leiden, An Vanderhelst of University College London, Laura Willett of the Centre for Reformation and Renaissance Studies, Toronto.
[61] There is an inscription 'Ex lib: P. van veen'—which to my eye could be in Pieter's hand—on the first preliminary leaf (recto) before the title page. But the identification of the annotator and illustrator rests securely on the 'Memoire' written in the endleaves at the back. See 1.1.14 for some preliminary discussion of the Van Veen copy and its context.

work, originating in another English context—Slingsby's book of remembrance. Similarly, in what follows below, I approach the copy of Paris 1602 not as a work by Montaigne that reached a Dutch reader, but as a work by Van Veen that originated in a Dutch context.

British Library C.28.g.7 was annotated and illustrated by Pieter at some point during the period between 1602, when the edition was published, and 1629, when he died. At the time he was living and working as a lawyer in The Hague, having grown up in Leiden.[62] References in the annotations to the religio-political controversies of the 1610s, including several to the execution of the Advocat of Holland, Johan van Oldenbarnevelt (for whose fate Pieter shows some sympathy), point in particular to the period after 1619.[63]

Van Veen's manuscript interventions in his copy comprise the following: marks including manicules, underlinings, and vertical lines; Greek and Latin citations, including a number on the preliminary leaves before the title page that have yet to be properly transcribed and identified; shorter summative notes and remarks; longer marginalia offering essays—in the style of Montaigne's own—on Pieter's experiences and opinions; 191 thumb-nail sketches in ink, mainly illustrations of concepts and figures delineated in the text (Illus. 2.4.1); a memoir of Pieter's early life from the age of twelve to the age of about twenty-eight (Illus. 2.4.2), written on the endleaves.

My general contention is that these interventions have to be considered together as a coherent 'work' by Pieter; the copy becomes an illustrated miscellany, or personal emblem book, addressed by Pieter, with a memoir included, to his son. Most of the discussion that follows focuses on the memoir, which deals with the siege of Leiden, with Pieter's travels, his relations with his literary mentor Justus Lipsius, his

[62] On the copy and on Pieter van Veen, see N. J. Pabon, 'Iets over Mr. Pieter van Veen en zijn familie', *Oud Holland*, 41 (1923–4), 241–9; Alan Boase, 'Un lecteur hollandais de Montaigne: Pieter van Veen', *Mélanges offerts à M. Abel Lefranc par ses élèves et ses amis* (Paris: Droz, 1936), 408–17; L. Thorpe, 'Pieter van Veen's copy of Montaigne', *Rivista di letterature moderne*, 3, second series (1952), 168–79; Elmer Kolfin and Marrigje Rikken, 'A very personal copy: Pieter van Veen's illustrations to Montaigne's *Essais*', in P. J. Smith and K. A. E. Enenkel (eds.), *Montaigne and the Low Countries (1580–1700)* (Leiden: Brill, 2007), 247–61, and the further references in their footnotes 1, 3, and 15. See also K. van Mander, *Lives of the illustrious Netherlandish and German painters, from the first edition of the Schilder-boeck (1603–1604): preceded by the lineage, circumstances and place of birth, life and works of Karel van Mander, painter and poet and likewise his death and burial, from the second edition of the Schilder-boeck (1616–1618)*, ed. H. Miedema, 6 vols. (Doornspijk: Davaco, 1994–9), vol. 6, 52, 56, 58–9 [abbreviated hereafter as 'Van Mander']; P. C. Molhuysen and P. J. Blok (eds.), *Nieuw Nederlandsch biografisch woordenboek* 10 vols. (Leiden: Sijthoff, 1911–37) [abbreviated hereafter as '*NNBW*'], 'Veen, Mr. Pieter van'; records of his presence at Leiden University in H. J. Witkam, *Immatriculatie en recensie in de Leidse Universiteit van 1575 tot 1581* (Leiden: H. J. Witkam, 1975). The details of Pieter's biography are still uncertain and vary from account to account. Miedema (Van Mander, vol. 6, 58) states that he studied law in Leiden in 1585–9. But if we believe Pieter's own memoir, this is not possible (he was travelling in Italy and France). *NNBW* gives the year of his birth as 1562, and Thorpe as 1561, but if we combine the information in Pabon with the information in his own memoir it appears that Pieter must have been born some time after 5 March and before 30 November 1563: he was sixty-six years old by 30 November 1629; twenty-six by 5 March 1590; twenty-four when he arrived in France some time—at least a couple of months—after the death of his employer's brother the Cardinal de Rambouillet on 23 March 1587. See Pabon, 'Iets over Mr. Pieter van Veen en zijn familie', 244, and Thorpe, 'Pieter van Veen's copy of Montaigne', 169, 175–9.

[63] Thorpe, 'Pieter van Veen's copy of Montaigne', annotations I, VIII, IX, and page 179.

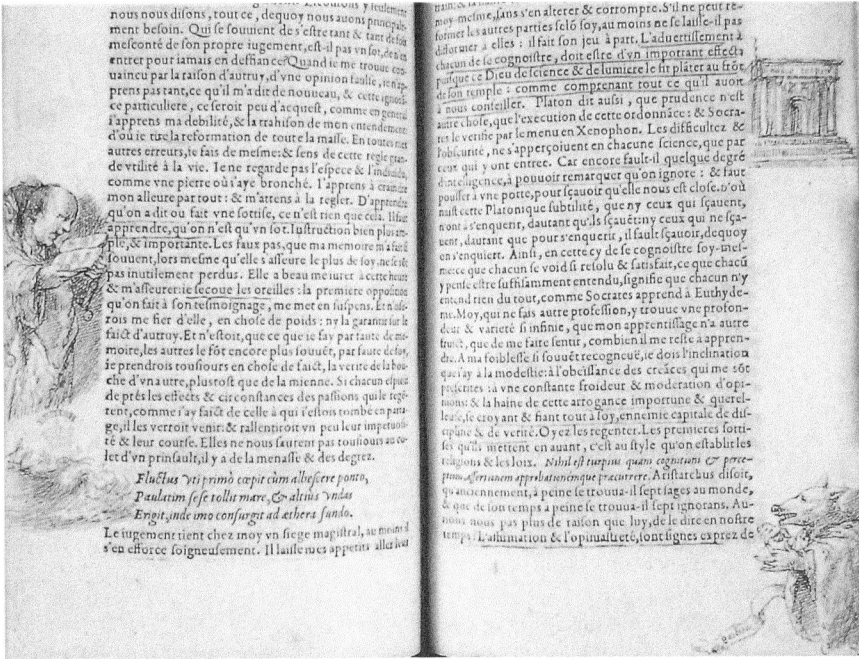

Illus. 2.4.1. Montaigne, *Essais*, 1602, British Library, pressmark C.28.g.7, pp. 1116–17 (Pieter van Veen's copy, with annotations and illustrations). Reproduced by permission of The British Library Board.

father Cornelis, and his elder brothers Gijsbert and Simon. Although, significantly, there is no direct mention of the most famous of his brothers, Otto van Veen, teacher of Rubens, I shall argue that it is ultimately Otto's formation and reputation that explains the distinctive mixture of drawings and annotations to be found in the copy.

The copy has attracted attention from scholars interested in one of two things: the fortunes of the *Essais*, or the art-historical aspects of the illustrations and their relationship to the text. Elmer Kolfin and Marrigje Rikken have added to Paul Smith's unpublished work on the copy. They show how Pieter uses pictorial and emblematic traditions to draw scenes and people from antiquity and history. They describe the book as a 'personal' copy, one not intended for publication.[64]

The present chapter takes their description further by arguing that the book is best understood as an heirloom, a secular equivalent to the Books of Hours passed down within medieval and early modern families. With his book, Pieter is passing on to the next generation a portrait of himself and a recipe for living wisely in troubled times—as we saw Slingsby do (in 2.4.2) via a journal and written 'Legacy' in the following decades in England. Van Veen is making an 'ethical bequest' (Natalie Zemon Davis's phrase) of a very sophisticated kind. The memoir is the

[64] Kolfin and Rikken, 'A very personal copy'.

TABLE.

fir à luy aduenu. 860.861. de sa
pierre.   862.1134 1135
De ses maladies. 1018. d'vne siéne
fieure quarte.   1143
De sa patience à supporter la douleur. 780.781.1137.1138, des pen-

sees à sa mort.
De son officiosité enuers les morts.   1134.
1034. sur sa mort.   1134.
1014.1018. ses prieres au lecteur.
997.999. son action de graces à
Dieu.   1001

Memoir

Estant en france en ma Jeunesse en l'age de 29 ans, et me
trouuant au seruice du S.r de fargis gouuerneur du pais de
Maine en l'an 1589, cest Autteur cy est tombé en mes mains
Duquel en ce temps la j'ay faict, selon ma capacite grand
estat, principalement entendant que le S.r Lipsius, l'esa bien
nommer Thalecim gallicum. Et comme volunteirs la Jeunesse
s'attache à des authoritez (et que Jauois en mon adolescence ouy
a Leyden leduct S.r Lipsius, et le tenu comme de raison) pour un
de plus grand Personages de nostre temps, principalement qu'il m'auoit
aussy pour son Client, escriuant certaines lres a moy, qui ne sont
Imprimés) Je ne m'en pouuois departir de ce liure et relire.
Puis apprès en ma asuellita; ne le prenant plus par aut Escrits
... considerant que ses conceptions

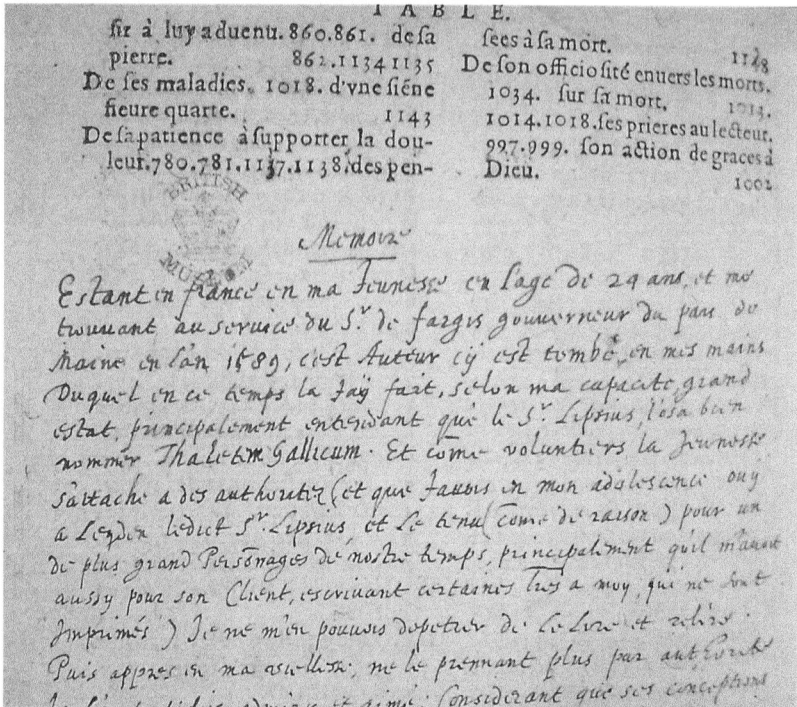

Illus. 2.4.2. Montaigne, *Essais*, 1602, British Library, pressmark C.28.g.7, sig.4K5v (Pieter van Veen's copy, with annotations and illustrations). Reproduced by permission of The British Library Board.

element that will direct us to this conclusion; it fits a pattern of early modern writing about the self in private family contexts.[65]

It is of course significant that Pieter uses the *Essais* in particular for this purpose. In his hands the volume assumes functions analogous to those he understands the original work to have had in its own setting. He portrays *traits de mes conditions et humeurs* for *parens et amis* who might frequent his book in his absence, after his death, just as Montaigne says he does in the preface 'Au lecteur' and as Slingsby does in his book of remembrance.

But the really crucial point is the manner in which Pieter uses the copy to portray his *forme naïve*. He shows his audience, *au vif*, how he has practised the liberal and visual arts through from youth to old age—what we might think of as his

[65] See Natalie Zemon Davis, 'Beyond the market: books as gifts in sixteenth-century France', *Transactions of the Royal Historical Society*, 5th. Ser., 33 (1983), 69–88, 85; Natalie Zemon Davis, 'Fame and secrecy: Leon Modena's life as an early modern autobiography', in M. R. Cohen (ed.), *The autobiography of a seventeenth-century Venetian rabbi: Leon Modena's 'Life of Judah'* (Princeton: Princeton University Press, 1988), 51–70, 51, 57 (re: 'ethical bequest'); Natalie Zemon Davis, 'Boundaries and the Sense of Self in Sixteenth-Century France', in T. C. Heller, M. Sosna, and D. E. Wellbery (eds.), *Reconstructing individualism: autonomy, individuality, and the self in Western thought* (Stanford: Stanford University Press, 1986), 53–63, 332–5, 56–9.

'pre-professional' formation. In so doing he aims to transfer skills and 'self-knowledge' that will be of pragmatic and moral use in times of war and oppression. Montaigne and Slingsby, again, might be said to have done something similar in their own settings—without recourse to drawing.

Support for this hypothesis comes in the form of two further considerations. The first is that Pieter relates to the book and to Montaigne as a one-time disciple of the school of Justus Lipsius. Pieter's acquisition and use of the *Essais* is mediated by his relations with Lipsius and with the pragmatically oriented programme of liberal arts and philosophical studies outlined by his teacher in the 1580s.[66] In particular, it is mediated by publications we began to explore in relation to the *Essais* in 1.6.5: the dialogue published at Leiden in three different language editions by Plantin in 1583–4 with the title *De constantia... in publicis malis*, and the complementary *Epistolarum selectarum centuria prima miscellanea* of 1586.[67]

As we saw in 1.6.3 and 1.6.5, the 1586 letters included Lipsius's public endorsement of Montaigne, and we shall see in 2.4.5 that they also included his praise of Pieter's brother, the young Otto van Veen. The *Politica* followed in 1589, and focused on the complementary political virtue of prudence. Constancy and prudence during the troubles were exactly the virtues Pieter's father had lacked, and the virtues Pieter learned by following the literary studies recommended by Lipsius—including the *Essais*.

The second consideration is that we should understand the volume to have been prepared by Pieter for a specific recipient, his eldest son Cornelis (b.1602), perhaps on a particular occasion such as his departure for the grand tour or his matriculation as a law student.[68] Cornelis van Veen of The Hague is entered in the *Album studiosorum* of Leiden University as a student of law at the age of twenty on 6 June 1622.[69] It is likely that he had studied the arts, and that at some point he travelled southwards in Europe, as so many of his male relatives did in their late teens and early twenties—his grandfather (Cornelis senior), his father Pieter, and his uncles Otto and Gijsbert.

Whether or not the copy relates to a particular event, the general occasion is the transition of Pieter's eldest son from youth to professional maturity via education in the liberal arts and painting, as well as—probably—travel and service. Cornelis would have been about seventeen in 1619 and twenty-seven by the time his father died. The memoir deals with his father's experiences at the same stage of life. As an heirloom, I argue, the book is equivalent to the family portraits

---

[66] For Pieter's marginal drawing of Lipsius, see Kolfin and Rikken, 'A very personal copy', fig. 32.

[67] For the complementarity of the two works, see Jan Papy, 'Le sénéquisme dans la correspondance de Juste Lipse: Du *De Constantia* (1583) à la *Epistolarum Selectarum Centuria Prima Miscellanea* (1586)', paper given at 'Aspects du néo-stoïcisme en Europe aux XVIe et XVIIe siècles', Centre d'Études Supérieures de la Renaissance (Tours), 8–10 October 1998. I am very grateful to Jan Papy for supplying me with a copy of his paper.

[68] Might Pieter even have chosen a copy of the 1602 edition to mark the year of his son's birth? My thanks to Philippe Desan for this suggestion.

[69] W. N. Du Rieu (ed.), *Album Studiosorum Academiæ Lugduno Batavae, 1575–1875*, 2 vols. (The Hague: Martinus Nijhoff, 1875), I, 93. He reappears in the register on 9 August 1638 as a doctor of law, aged thirty-six (I, 298).

and self-portraits that we know for sure were passed down within the Van Veen family.

The principal piece of external evidence for this hypothesis is a hitherto unnoticed connection between the memoir at the back of the copy and one such portrait. Jan Anthonisz van Ravesteyn's 'Portrait of Pieter van Veen with his son Cornelis and his clerk Hendrick Borsman' (Illus. 1.1.11) currently hangs in the Musée d'Art et d'Histoire in Geneva. It was listed as a possession of one of Pieter's descendants in 1694. Bob Haak dates the painting to before 1620 on the basis that Cornelis was born *c.*1595 and looks about 20. In fact he was born in 1602—which would, if we accept Haak's estimate of his age, make it contemporaneous with Cornelis's entrance to Leiden University to study law. The Musée d'Art and d'Histoire dates the painting towards 1620 or 1622; another authoritative catalogue dates it to 1625–9.[70]

Either way, it is clearly from the same general period as the illustrated and annotated Montaigne and, I argue, indicates the figure to whom the volume was principally addressed. Furthermore, the painting shows Pieter doing what he is doing by different means in the illustrated book; namely, showing Cornelis junior the desirability of becoming not just a professionally trained lawyer, but also—in Lipsius's words—'a young man of most cultivated mind and hand' (see 2.4.5), like his uncle and his father before him. To make this connection convincingly, we shall need first to reconsider in detail the history of the Van Veen family and the role of paintings and books in the transmission of the family culture.

On the one hand, it will be important to realize that the Van Veens were known after 1572 as *glippers*. *Glippers* were those native Catholics who—to translate the idiom literally—'slipped' out of Leiden after the city defected to the Revolt in that year. Some actively worked with the Spanish commander and wrote letters urging surrender in the famous sieges that followed in 1572–4. Even though many Catholics stayed to resist the Spanish, and were praised and tolerated for so doing, the *glippers'* actions turned Leiden's Catholic community into second-class citizens and laid them open thereafter to suspicion of pro-Spanish sympathy. This did not mean, however, that the ruling families of Leiden after 1572–4 were enthusiasts for the 'new religion'. They still inclined towards traditionalism in matters of belief. Post-war scholarship has overturned the older view that the northern Low Countries became rapidly and uniformly Protestant during the Revolt.[71]

---

[70] B. Haak, *The golden age: Dutch painters of the seventeenth century*, trans. Elizabeth Willems-Treeman (New York: Harry N. Abrams, 1984), 217–18; P. t-D. Chu, *Im Lichte Hollands: Holländische Malerei des 17. Jahrhunderts aus den Sammlungen des Fürsten von Liechtenstein und aus Schweizer Besitz* (Zurich: VerlagsHausZürich, 1987), 206. I am grateful to M. Paul Lang and Mme Brigitte Monti of the Musée d'Art et d'Histoire in Geneva for supplying me with a copy of the museum's internal dossier on the painting, and with other bibliographical materials.

[71] For a nuanced picture of the religious politics of Leiden and the Low Countries at this time, see C. Kooi, *Liberty and religion: church and state in Leiden's Reformation* (Leiden: Brill, 2000); S. A. Lament, 'The Vroedschap of Leiden 1550–1600: The Impact of Tradition and Change on the Governing Elite of a Dutch City', *Sixteenth Century Journal*, 12, no. 2 (1981), 14–42, 24–7.

With prudence, Catholics and even offspring of *glippers* such as the Van Veens could be re-assimilated in the new United Provinces (post-1581). Only after 1618–19, the execution of Oldenbarnevelt in The Hague, and the outbreak of the Thirty Years War, did militant Calvinism become embedded in the political and legal establishment in the north. This is, significantly, the moment when Pieter annotates and illustrates his Montaigne. It compares directly with the moment when the English Catholic Slingsby read his Florio in 1638–9.[72]

On the other hand, we shall need to understand that the Van Veen family prided itself on its young mens' cultivation in the liberal arts and painting. The most eminent patron of the literary and artistic education of the Van Veen boys, especially Otto and Pieter, was Lipsius. Lipsius became professor of history at Leiden University just before Pieter matriculated as a student of *bonae artes* and *litterae* in 1578. Pieter held him to be one of the 'greatest characters of our times' ('plus grand Personnages de nostre temps'), and describes himself—in specific connection with unpublished letters he received from the great man—as Lipsius's 'client'.[73]

As patron of the young Van Veens' participation in the liberal arts, Lipsius publicly and privately marked the family's talent for combining and alternating literary and artistic study. Within the family, fathers and elder brothers were active in nurturing and fostering this 'natural' talent. They not only set an example but also directly tutored younger members and servants in domestic or office settings. Paintings such as Van Ravesteyn's and books such as the copy of Montaigne were passed down as heirlooms in this context. But let us start with the best-known Van Veen heirloom, which dates to a precise moment in 1584. Otto van Veen's self-portrait with family hangs in the Louvre and shall serve as a way further into the family's history (Illus. 2.4.3).

2.4.5 OTTO VAN VEEN'S 'SELF-PORTRAIT WITH FAMILY'

When Gijsbert van Veen arrived at a lodging in Rome looking for his long-lost brother Pieter, he asked some of his own countrymen if 'some Fleming' ('quelque flamend') was staying there. The host replied that there were some Poles and 'a Frenchman' ('ung francois')—meaning Pieter, who had clearly been able to pass for a Frenchman on his travels. Hearing Gijsbert's group speaking 'flameng' Pieter leaps up from his table and identifies himself as a 'flamend' from Leiden in Holland.[74]

In Rome, then, the Van Veens identified themselves as Flemings, even though they were not inhabitants of the historical province of Flanders, and even though Pieter clearly preferred French as his literary language. Was this because it was safer to be identified as a Fleming, a southern Netherlander, in Rome, or because

---

[72] Kooi, *Liberty and religion*, 35–7; Lament, 'The Vroedschap of Leiden 1550–1600'.
[73] References for these statements will follow in 2.4.5.
[74] Thorpe, 'Pieter van Veen's copy of Montaigne', 177/BL C.28.g.7, sig. 4K7r.

the family really were of 'Flemish'—in whatever sense—origin? Back in Leiden in the 1580s, 'Fleming' tended to designate an ardently Reformed immigrant from the southern Low Countries, though Catholic Flemings such as Lipsius were also resident there.[75] If the Van Veens, and Otto in particular, did at one point claim—via descent from a natural son of one of the Dukes of Brabant—southern noble origins, the claim appears not to have been sustained with any persistence or conviction.[76]

All we know for sure is that by the 1560s, they were firmly settled as a Catholic family in Leiden. The father Cornelis, originally a pensionary of the town before becoming a burgomaster by 1566–7, was married to Gertrude van Neck.[77] When Otto painted his self-portrait with family in 1584 (Illus. 2.4.3), Cornelis and Gertrude had six sons (Jan, Simon, Otto, Pieter, Gijsbert, Timon), four daughters (Elisabeth, Maria, Aldegonda, Agatha), six grandchildren (four of Simon's, two of Elisabeth's), and one daughter-in-law (Anna van Nes, Simon's wife).[78]

The painter—Otto van Veen—was probably born in about 1557. At age fifteen or so he fled the siege of Leiden with his father, who took him to Liège in 1572 or 1573, where he studied with Dominicus Lampsonius. Between 1575 and 1580 he was in Italy, spending much time in Rome. By 1583 he was back in the Low Countries, possibly in the service of the Bishop of Liège, and at the age of about twenty-seven in 1584 he definitively entered service as a painter at the court of Alessandro Farnese of Parma in Brussels.[79] This is the occasion of the self-portrait with family we are considering. It is contemporaneous with a number of inscriptions made by scholarly friends in his *Album Amicorum*, including a *testimonium* of 2 June 1584 by Justus Lipsius.[80]

The detail of this *testimonium* is crucial to the link I am making between the copy of Montaigne and the painting of Van Ravesteyn. Lipsius's inscribed vow of protective friendship describes Otto as 'a young man of the most cultivated mind and hand' ('cultissimae mentis et manus adolescens'). Just two years later Lipsius published a letter dated 31 May 1584 (two days before the date of the inscription

[75] Kooi, *Liberty and religion*, 105. In the sixteenth century Flanders was a province on the North Sea bounded by Zeland and Brabant but could also designate the Low Countries as a whole, especially the Southern Low Countries. Now, Flanders designates the Dutch- or Flemish-speaking part of Belgium, though this does not mean that every Dutch- or Flemish-speaking Belgian wishes to be described as a Fleming. The term, in other words, is fraught with historical and political difficulties. I am very grateful to Dr Anton van der Lem of the University Library of Leiden for clarifying these points.

[76] C. Deri, 'Otto Vaenius ou Van Veen dit "de Brabant"', *Le folklore Brabançon*, 184 (Dec. 1969), 343–6.

[77] *NNBW*, 'Veen, Cornelis Jansz. van'.

[78] The right-hand cartouche includes a numerical key identifying the figures. See E. Michel, *Catalogue raisonné des peintures du moyen-âge, de la renaissance et des temps modernes. Peintures flamandes du XVe et du XVIe siècle* (Paris: Éditions des Musées nationaux, 1953), 265; Pabon, 'Iets over Mr. Pieter van Veen en zijn familie', 245–7.

[79] *NNBW*, 'Veen, Otto van'. Other authorities state Otto to have been born in 1556 or 1558. See Michel, *Catalogue raisonné*, 263, and the entry for Otto in *Biographie nationale*, 44 vols. (Brussels: L'Académie royale des sciences, des lettres et des beaux-arts de Belgique, 1866–1986).

[80] J. van den Gheyn (ed.), '*Album Amicorum' de Otto Venius: reproduction intégrale en facsimilé* (Brussels: Société des Bibliophiles et Iconophiles de Belgique, 1911), no. xx and 121–2. The manuscript *Album* is in the Bibliothèque royale de Belgique, shelfmark II. 874.

in the album) to Otto's tutor Lampsonius. In this printed letter, Lipsius went on the public record to praise the young man in similar terms. He regrets Otto's departure for court service, describing him as an outstanding young man for his character and artistic ability ('insignis moribus et arte adolescens'), a young man who could have been very helpful to him in illustrating many objects from antiquity ('et cuius manus usui mihi esse poterat ad multa Antiquitatis illustranda').[81]

Otto was indeed to be useful to many patrons and audiences in the illustration of objects and narratives from antiquity, as when he published an illustrated version of Tacitus in 1612. His younger brother, Gijsbert, made himself useful in the same way, though less famously. Van Mander's biographies place Otto as one of a number of figures in the Low Countries who sought and acquired reputations for both the liberal and visual arts at this time. But it was not only Lipsius who witnessed to his particular distinction in this respect. In March 1598 Abraham Ortelius credited him in the same *Album amicorum* with having been the first in 'our' world to combine liberal 'letters' with the art of painting. Ortelius's *testimonium* cites a passage in Pliny (35,10) concerning Apelles' teacher Pamphilus, who in the time of Alexander the Great was the first painter with expertise in all the liberal arts.[82]

The reputation of Otto—specifically as endorsed by Lipsius in *testimonia* inscribed in a private manuscript album and in a letter disseminated across Europe— as 'cultissimae mentis et manus adolescens' becomes, I argue, cultural capital for preservation and transmission through the generations (Gournay saw Lipsius's description of Montaigne as *Thales Gallicus* in the same way). The resulting process of familial and cultural reproduction links together Cornelis senior's education of Otto and Pieter in the 1570s with Pieter's education of Cornelis junior in the 1610s and early 1620s, as well as Otto's painting and album of the 1580s with Pieter's portrait (the Van Ravesteyn) and book (the copy of Montaigne) of the 1620s.

And it is not only literary and artistic skills that are transmitted. In the face of increasingly bitter religio-political conflict, there is an implied philosophy of non-partisanship, a philosophy shaped in part by the civic culture of Leiden itself and in part by a Lipsian reading of Montaigne. The troubles in the Low Countries would disperse the Van Veens between north and south. Otto settled in the Imperial Catholic south in court service, as did his brother Gijsbert, while Pieter and Simon returned to live and work in the United Provinces. But this did not mean they were necessarily estranged on religio-political grounds, at least until 1618–19. Otto was still having dealings with Pieter in the 1610s, when he delivered his commission of paintings of the Batavian revolt to The Hague. This was not

---

[81] Justus Lipsius, *Iusti Lipsi epistolarum selectarum, centuria prima* (Antwerp [Leiden]: Plantin, 1586), epist. I. 60, sig. K8v; ILE II, 84 05 31. Lipsius had already marked Otto's return from Rome, his affection for him, and his acquaintance with his father Cornelis in a letter to Lampsonius of 8 October 1583 (not printed in the 1586 volume). See ILE I, 83 10 08 L.

[82] *Album amicorum*, no. XVII and 113: 'Scribit Plinius XXXV, cap. X de Pamphilo pictore celebri, qui fuit sub Appelle et Alexandro Magno, quod hic primus in pictura omnibus litteris eruditus. Ego de te, Veni, idem dico te primum in nostro orbe qui litteras liberaliores cum hac arte iunxisti.' There are further references in the *Album* to Otto's reputation in both poetry or letters and painting. See nos VII, VIII, and 85–6; no. XIII and 97.

Illus. 2.4.3. Otto van Veen, *Otto van Veen peignant, entouré des siens*, ©RMN (Musée du Louvre)/Gérard Blot.

the only time Otto helped glorify the independent Low Countries while simultaneously catering for audiences in the Spanish Low Countries.

Pieter may have abjured his Roman Catholicism, and certainly his allegiance to the Spanish king, after his return to the northern Low Countries in 1591 (see Buytewech's letter in this section). But the terms in which he expresses his sympathy with Montaigne's stance on religion make it clear that his private beliefs resembled the Erastian views of the average Dutch magistrate of the 1580s and 1590s, and suggest that he privately remained 'catholic' with a small 'c'. He is against any public dissidence or controversy on pure grounds of religion. His views are consistent with the support of the authorities in Holland in 1590–1 for the statist stance of Lipsius's *Politica* and their condemnation of the 'troublemaker' Coornheert.[83]

Let us turn, then, to Otto's composition of 1584 with these circumstances in mind (Illus. 2.4.3). The painting is exceptional as a family- and self-portrait in

---

[83] For this and the previous paragraph, see Kolfin and Rikken, 'A very personal copy', 248 and n.6; M. Morford, '*Theatrum hodiernae vitae*: Lipsius, Vaenius, and the rebellion of Civilis', in K. Enenkel et al. (eds.), *Recreating ancient history: episodes from the Greek and Roman past in the arts and literature of the Early Modern Period* (Leiden: Brill, 2001), 57–74; Thorpe, 'Pieter van Veen's copy of Montaigne', 175, and annotations IV, XII; G. Vougt, 'Primacy of individual conscience or primacy of the state? the clash between Dirck Volckertsz. Coornhert and Justus Lipsius', *Sixteenth Century Journal*, 28, no. 4 (1997), 1231–49, 1246–7 and n.106. According to notarial sources used by Pabon, many of Pieter's children were Roman Catholic, while Pieter himself took the Roman Catholic rite on his deathbed (Pabon, 'Iets over Mr. Pieter van Veen en zijn familie', 248).

bringing so many figures together, figures who could not have been brought together in reality in 1584.[84]

The virtual scene depicted by Otto is a response to the troubles that in the previous fifteen years had threatened to divide the family, the citizens of Leiden, and the Low Countries as a whole. It presents a vision of familial and national—'Belgian', north and south—unity and harmony. The composition is organized around the diagonal from bottom left to top right and the relationship between three groupings of figures. We see the ongoing family history of the male Van Veens represented in the transition from left to right, as the younger men study the liberal and visual arts in preparation for travel south into Europe, which will culminate in professional lives as lawyers or artists. The three younger brothers are grouped on the left, near to their mother: one—Timon—with a book; one—Gijsbert—with a design of the ruins at Rome (his actual location in 1584); one—Pieter—less visible in the background. They are in apposition to the group consisting of matured professional brothers and retired civic grandee Cornelis senior on the right, holding what looks like a small devotional volume in his left hand.

In the middle, arranged along the line of the diagonal, is the head and upper torso of Otto at the moment of his departure for court life, aspiringly observed by Gijsbert on the left. This process of institution of artistic purpose and social function from left to right is complemented by a vertical grouping of female relatives and children. The inscription in the cartouche in the bottom left of the painting reveals that Otto intended the work to be a family heirloom transmitted down through his own male heirs or those of his eldest surviving brother, in the event of his having no children.[85]

At the moment of his entry into service after his years of study and travel, Otto bequeaths the eldest surviving male Van Veen a memorial of himself. He shows himself in relation to his own younger selves—his younger brothers, especially Gijsbert—as they step onto the same path to experience and to Rome, the path that leads either to the dignified profession of painting or to the civic offices already occupied by his father and elder brothers.

We shall see that Pieter's memoir—in which Gijsbert is also a pivotal figure— shares the same family narrative of early male formation and culminates at the same point: namely, the moment when Pieter enters permanent professional life (alongside his elder brother Simon in The Hague) at the age of about thirty. Pieter's copy of the *Essais*, I argue, is an analogous artefact in the family's private cultural tradition: a self-portrait designed for the eldest surviving Van Veen.

---

[84] When Pieter met Gijsbert in Rome he was twenty-two years old (*c.*1584–5) and had already spent time studying in Paris. It is possible, but unlikely, that he could still have been in Leiden when Otto did his family portrait. But in 1584–5 Gijsbert, aged twenty-three, had already been in Rome for three or four years. See Thorpe, 'Pieter van Veen's copy of Montaigne', 177/BL C.28.g.7, sig. 4K7r.

[85] Michel, *Catalogue raisonné*, 264–5.

2.4.6 PIETER VAN VEEN'S MEMOIR

Early modern manuscript memoirs were most usually written for younger siblings, children, nephews, or nieces. Felix Platter, for example, wrote an account of his student years for his nephew, starting with his departure from home and ending with the return home to marry. As Felix described them, these were free, even licentious years, so the narrative established 'a family tradition of allowing a young man his breathing space'. In Holland, the Huygens family composed autobiographical writing as a way of passing on information and culture to the next generation. Constantijn Huygens (b. 1595) studied law at the University of Leiden and wrote an autobiography as an example for his children when he was barely thirty, around the age at which Pieter ends his narrative.

Rudolf Dekker concludes that the primary function of early modern 'egodocuments' was the transfer of a family's culture and identity from one generation to the next. And many of the documents—500 in Dekker's sample—were travel journals, accounts of grand tours by young men who travelled abroad after university study to make the transition from youth to adulthood.[86]

Pieter's narrative fits this general pattern: an autobiographical narrative of early study and travel designed to transfer his own and his family's identity and culture from one generation to the next. But unlike Dekker's examples it is written in the back of a printed book and starts out as a judgement of that book. We have to take the particular book, and the particular format of the edition Pieter was using, into account.

The last printed item in the 1602 edition is an index to passages in the text concerning the life of the author.[87] Its heading incorporates the first reference: 'Life of Michel de Montaigne taken from his Essays, beginning with how from the cradle his father sent him to be cared for in one of his poor villages, and how long he was there. 1145' ('Vie de Michel de Montaigne tiree de ses Essais, premierement comme dés le berceau son pere l'enuoya nourrir à vn pauure village des siens et combien de temps il y fut. 1145').

The first group of references tell us where to find passages on Montaigne's 'education' in Rome, his memories of his youth ('Du resouvenir de sa jeunesse'), his 'humeur'; others, on the next page, where to look for accounts of his voyages, his father, and of various accidents that befell him (including 'prise de sa personne'; 'accident infortuné à luy aduenu'—Montaigne's capture, and his fall from his horse, illustrated by Pieter on sig. Z5v).

Many of these topics recur in the manuscript 'Memoire' of Pieter's life that immediately follows the printed 'Vie' of Montaigne (Illus. 2.4.2). And amongst the various dramatic scenes from Pieter's early life—including the family's flight from Leiden, and his recognition of his brother in Rome after years of separation—there are two with direct equivalents in Montaigne's text: Pieter's fall from his horse

---

[86] For this and the previous paragraph see Davis, 'Boundaries', 56–7, 60; R. M. Dekker, *Childhood, memory and autobiography in Holland: from the Golden Age to Romanticism* (Basingstoke: Palgrave Macmillan, 2000), 23, 14–15.

[87] BL C.28.g.7, sigs. 4K4v–5v.

at Le Mans, and his subsequent imprisonment by the Catholic League. Here, we can begin to appreciate how many of Montaigne's reported *expériences* would have been shared by his contemporaries and near contemporaries.

The marginalia and the memoir are complementary to one another. The main text spurs Pieter to recall anecdotes from his own life and experience in marginal notes—exactly the way Hamlin argues it acts, in Florio's translation, on English readers (see 2.4.2). The second half of the last extended marginal annotation is written at a different time from the first half, and at the same time as the 'Memoire' at the back. The ink and handwriting are the same and it refers to the period in Pieter's life at which the memoir begins, the moment when he was in the retinue of the Seigneur de Fargis ('estant a la Suite du S.r de fargis frere du Cardinal de Rambouillet alors decedé').[88]

But it is specifically the paratextual 'Index', I argue, which prompts Pieter to include a sustained piece of life-writing on the endleaves, rather than just a brief judgement of the book of the kind described by Montaigne himself in II 10.[89] In both margins and endleaves, Pieter consciously overwrites Montaigne's life as part of the process of making the book his own—a plausible enterprise given the extent to which their experiences overlapped (they were even at Blois at the same dramatic moment in 1588, described in 2.1.6–7).[90]

Pieter takes the book of an ex-lawyer who, having studied the liberal arts using a special method brought in by his father (Pierre Eyquem), and having impressed professionals (such as Lipsius) with his amateur talents (as described in *Essais* I 25), managed in adult life prudently to survive the troubles. He remakes it as the book of another lawyer (Pieter van Veen) who, having learned the liberal arts and painting using a method espoused by his father, and having been implored by professional painters to make his natural 'talent full of painterliness' his special craft, also managed in adult life prudently to survive the troubles—in a way that we saw Sir Henry Slingsby did not.[91]

The memoir begins *in media res* with the moment in mid-1588 when he entered France in service aged twenty-four, and when—in early 1589—a copy of the *Essais* first fell into his hands, probably in connection with his master's attendance at Blois in the aftermath of Guise's assassination.[92] This is most probably because he

---

[88] Thorpe, 'Pieter van Veen's copy of Montaigne', 174–5/BL C.28.g.7, sig. 4B3r.

[89] II 10, NP439–40/BVH Paris 1588, f. 375v [175v]/S469–70.

[90] Thorpe, 'Pieter van Veen's copy of Montaigne', 178n.54, and 176/BL C.28.g.7, sig. 4K6r, where Pieter directly compares himself with Montaigne, noting that—as a 'simple lawyer'—he is lower in degree than the Frenchman.

[91] Van Mander, vol. 1, 438–9.

[92] Thorpe and Boase both mis-transcribe the date at which Pieter says he was in France as '27', when in fact it reads '24'. Pieter must be saying that he entered France aged twenty-four—that is, in mid-1588, before his twenty-fifth birthday, but that the *Essais* did not fall into his hands until 1589, by which time he must have been twenty-five. His master Philippe d'Angennes, seigneur du Fargis, was called to Blois some time in early 1589, but then returned quickly to Le Mans—where he had left Pieter—upon hearing that the League were trying to take the town. But du Fargis was taken prisoner and Pieter never saw him again (Thorpe, 'Pieter van Veen's copy of Montaigne', 178/BL C.28.g.7, sig. 4K7v).

was bequeathing the book—a different copy, acquired later—to Cornelis at a similar age in the late 1620s, when Pieter was in his sixties facing death.

The memoir and its writer's relationship to Montaigne are conditioned by the fact that Pieter continued to study 'under' Lipsius even after he left the University of Leiden some time around 1582–4 to travel south into Europe for experience. By publishing the *De constantia* with a companion volume of letters, letters that included specific *testimonia* such as the remarks about Otto van Veen and Montaigne, Lipsius allowed ex-students burdened by the troubles to continue to be part of his intellectual *familia*, to live by his recommendations and his philosophy. The letters were—in Jan Papy's words—'an extension, illustration or elaboration of his oeuvre and person'.[93]

Pieter begins by telling the reader—his son Cornelis, I am hypothesizing—that he set much store by the *Essais* because he had heard that his ex-professor, Lipsius, had described its author as the French Thales (Illus. 2.4.2):[94]

In 1589, finding myself in France in my youth, aged 24, and in the service of Seigneur de Fargis, governor of the province of Maine, this author here fell into my hands. At that time I esteemed him—within the limits of my capacity to do so—greatly, principally because I had learned that Sieur Lipsius dared to name him the French Thales. And as youth willingly attaches itself to authorities (I had in my adolescence heard the said Sieur Lipsius lecture, and held him with good reason to be one of the leading lights of our time; more significantly, he had also taken me as a client, writing some letters to me that are not printed) I could not desist from reading and rereading him. Then afterwards in my old age, no longer taking him on authority, I still admired and loved him. I considered that his ideas show his great mind to be little concerned with the authority of the authors he quotes—he examines not their reputations, but what they actually say.... His way of expressing his ideas is gentle and amiable, completely in accord with my nature. He has something to offer in response to the factious spirits of our time, but he prefers to just show us, rather than to enter into debate...just letting it be known what he has chosen for the best, holding on to the ancient beliefs so as not to err for evermore./...And to tell you the truth, in telling us about his nature, and showing it in action in his discourse, he reveals, without vanity, what man is.[95]

93 M. Morford, 'Lipsius' Letters of Recommendation', in T. Van Houdt et al. (eds.), *Self-presentation and social identification: the rhetoric and pragmatics of letter writing in early modern times* (Leuven: Leuven University Press, 2002), 183–98, 197; J. Papy, 'Lipsius's (Neo-)Stoicism: Constancy between Christian Faith and Stoic Virtue', *Grotiana*, 22–3, new series (2001–2), 47–71, 48.
94 Thorpe, 'Pieter van Veen's copy of Montaigne', 175–6/BL C.28.g.7, sigs. 4K5v–6r. I have checked Thorpe's transcription against the original and corrected it where necessary, referring to the three endleaves of the copy after the 'Index' as sigs. 4K6–8. The most important such correction has already been mentioned: Pieter clearly begins 'Estant en france en ma Jeunesse en l'age de 24 ans', not '27 ans' as Thorpe has it.
95 'Estant en france en ma Jeunesse en l'age de 24 ans, et me trouvant au service du Sr. de fargis gouverneur du pais de Maine en L'an 1589, c'est Auteur cy est tombè en mes mains Duquel en ce temps la Jay fait, selon ma capacite, grand estat, principalement entendant que le Sr. Lipsius, l'osa bien nommer Thaletum Gallicum. Et comme volintiers la Jeunesse s'attache a des authoritez, (et que Javois en mon adolescence ouy a Leyden ledict Sr. Lipsius, et Le tenu (comme de raison) pour un de [*sic*] plus grand Personnages de nostre temps, principalement qu'il m'avoit aussy pour son Client, escrivant certaines lettres a moy, que ne sont Imprimés) Je ne m'en pouuois depetrer de Le Lire et relire. Puis appres en ma viellesse, ne le prennant plus par authorite Je L'ay toutefois admire et aimé: Considerant

Though largely neglected in the literature on the fortunes of the *Essais*, this is an invaluable account of the manner and circumstances in which one early read-er-writer joined and then lived in the school of Montaigne. The relationship he describes with the book is closer, more durable, than the one Slingsby describes. It extends over a lifetime. As Pieter describes it, it is not the book, but the 'Auteur' Montaigne, endorsed by Van Veen's own teacher Lipsius as a *vir illustris*, that falls by chance into his hands at a crucial moment in his early life.

His attachment to Lipsius as a university authority, and as a client to a patron, informs his early attachment to the *Essais* as a book that he cannot help but read and reread in private, when not serving his master. But his relationship with the book changes as he grows older. He begins to appreciate that Montaigne himself is unconcerned with the authority of the 'authorities' that he makes speak on his behalf—it is the ideas the Frenchman can express through them in a properly examined fashion that matters, not their reputations.

So Van Veen himself begins to relate to the Lipsius-endorsed author less as an authority and more as someone whose style of thought he admires and loves as one appropriate to his own *naturel*. Also, Montaigne provides a way of responding to the factious spirits of the age ('esprits contentieulx de nostre temps'), a way that involves showing by example, rather than by debating or entering into controversy. In so doing Montaigne turns out to deserve the title Lipsius gave him as a modern 'sage'—much more than those who seek to claim it explicitly in their writings.[96]

Arguably, then, Pieter's membership of the school of Montaigne is subsidiary to his membership of the school of Lipsius. He chooses to begin his short piece of life-writing with two separate references to Lipsius's letters: one to a published letter, and one to several unpublished letters that he personally received. The latter were presumably a prized possession in the family papers and available for consultation in tandem with the memoir. Pieter's remark reveals a one-time expectation—hope, even—that the letters might be published. Lipsius did later publish a 1601 letter to Pieter's brother Otto, commissioning a painting, but Otto, unlike Pieter, was settled in the Spanish Low Countries, to which Lipsius had defected in 1591.[97]

We know from an unpublished letter of Franciscus Bencius (to Lipsius) that Pieter was in possession of a printed copy of Lipsius's first volume of letters in Rome in July 1587, and that he was very actively putting the book to use. Bencius tells Lipsius that he has written to him without answer, but that the 'most modest young man' Pieter van Veen has passed on Lipsius's greetings and shown him a

que ses conceptions monstrent son grand esprit peu preoccupé par authorite des autheurs qu'il fait parler; examinant plus leur Dire, que leur renommè. … La maniere de proposer ses conceptions, est douce et amiable totalement conuenant a mon naturel. Il a de quoy pour respondre aux esprits con-tentieulx de nostre temps: mail il ayme mieulx de le monstrer que de le debatre. . . . donnant seulement a cognoistre ce qu'il a choisy pour le melieur [*sic*], se tenant aulx anciennes Creances pour ne rouler tousiours. / . . . Et pour dire la verité en raccontant son naturel, et L'appliquant a ses discours il monstre, sans vanitè, que c'est de lhomme.'

[96] 'En sorte que si tous qui font plus les sages, qu'ils ne sont; se tiendroient en telle demesche, peult estre, qu'on ne les estimeroit aultant, comme ils se veulent faire valoir par leurs fardez escrits.'

[97] ILE XIV, 01 05 22. This is *ep.* 83 in the 1605 Moretus edition (Antwerp) of *Iusti Lipsi episto-larum selectarum centuria tertia ad belgas*.

printed letter from Lipsius to Bencius in the 1586 edition—a letter Bencius did not actually receive in person. Bencius then immediately mentions his desire for a copy of the *De constantia*, thereby closely associating the two books, before talking of the great things Pieter has told him of Lipsius.[98]

This is an invaluable snapshot of the way in which Pieter uses a printed copy of the letters to act on behalf of his patron and to register his minor place and role in Lipsius's network of like-minded correspondents. In beginning his memoir, Pieter says rather vaguely that he 'heard' or 'learned' that Lipsius had called Montaigne the 'French Thales'. But the Bencius letter makes it certain that he read the reference for himself in his own copy of the very book in which he would also have seen his elder brother named an outstanding young man for character and artistic ability, equipped to illustrate objects from antiquity.

As we heard in 1.6.3, the remark about Montaigne occurs in a passage in a letter to another figure associated with Leiden University, Theodorus Leeuwius, dated to 1583 (published in 1586). It is emphasized with a printed marginal note (Illus. 1.6.4). Pieter almost certainly knew of Leeuwius. He was the first student to register at Leiden University in 1575 and was still there when Lipsius arrived in 1578 and Pieter matriculated in the same year. The letters to Leeuwius anchor the composition and authorial exposition of the purpose of the *De constantia* in Lipsius's early Leiden years, the years in which Pieter followed the master human-ist's lectures. The work was originally written for the 'Belgians'—the spiritual community of the northern and southern Low Countries—but in particular for the community centred on Leiden University, the community that included the Van Veens.[99]

We can catch a glimpse of Pieter's participation in this 'Belgian' literary commu-nity. The unpublished letters he mentions can be dated to the moment of his return from his travels in the early 1590s, the moment with which the memoir ends. Pieter's narrative builds to a dramatic climax. Seized at Le Mans by the French Catholic League, his French master imprisoned, Pieter manages to escape and arrives in Vlissingen in January 1591. He finds his way via The Hague (where he visits his brother Simon) to Leiden, where he visits his parents. But his mother dies a couple of months later, followed by his father in August 1591, after which event Pieter soon returns to The Hague to work with his brother.[100] The moral is perhaps that sons, at the end of their travels, should return home to their parents and to a civic vocation in their country of origin.

---

[98] ILE II, 87 07 12.

[99] On Leiden, Leeuwius, and the *De constantia*, see J. De Landtsheer, 'From Ultima Thule to Finisterra: Surfing on the Wide Web of Justus Lipsius' Correspondence', in K. Enenkel and C. Heesakkers (eds.), *Lipsius in Leiden: studies in the life and works of a great humanist on the occasion of his 450th anniversary* (Voorthuizen: Florivallis, 1997), 47–69, 55 and n.49; N. Mout, ' "Which tyrant curtails my free mind?" Lipsius and the reception of *De constantia*', in Enenkel and Heesakkers (eds.), *Lipsius in Leiden*, 123–40, 124–8; Papy, 'Le sénéquisme'.

[100] Thorpe, 'Pieter van Veen's copy of Montaigne', 178–9/BL C.28.g.7, sigs. 4K7v–8r; *NNBW*, 'Veen, Cornelis Jansz. Van'.

This narrative can be supplemented with circumstances not directly mentioned in the memoir, but which are revealed in the unpublished letters in question. On 15 March 1591, after some bitter public polemics with Coornhert in the previous year, Lipsius left Amsterdam to travel to a health resort in the German Empire. But at Easter in Mainz he privately confessed and reconciled himself to the Roman Catholic Church. The rector of the Mainz college wrote an eyewitness account of this event to Franciscus Bencius in Rome. That summer, he handed in his resignation in a letter to the authorities in Leiden from Spa.[101]

In January 1592 Lipsius writes from Liège that he has heard from a brother of Otto van Veen—perhaps Simon, perhaps Pieter—of the death of their excellent parents. In April 1592, he drafts a letter to Pieter van Veen at Otto's suggestion. Lipsius reveals in a letter of the following month that due to 'the circumstances' he did not send the drafted letter, though he does appear to forward it finally in June.[102]

The circumstances in question are his re-avowal of Roman Catholicism and his 'flight' to Liège, with the intention of moving to a post at the Catholic university of Louvain. Lipsius's reputation is under great threat in the northern Low Countries. Circulation of his letters in the wrong hands could fuel the scandal. From Liège he writes to Pieter, as to other friends and Catholic sympathizers back in the northern Low Countries, because it gives him an opportunity to defend his reputation and reaffirm his affection for the 'Batavians' in the territories he has abandoned.[103]

Lipsius acknowledges that '[doles] in discessu meo'—'my departure pains you'—before going on to affirm that he would have stayed in the north had there only been peace. In the interim, before receipt, Pieter writes to Lipsius to reaffirm both his own and Lipsius's good faith, of which he finds evidence in his patron's writings. In further letters to Pieter, Lipsius accepts these assurances, associates Pieter with his own philosophy of *litterae* and the *bonae artes*, and reaffirms his allegiance to right-minded people in the northern Low Countries and to the 'ancient religion'—the 'anciennes Creances' espoused by Montaigne, according to Pieter's 'Memoire'.[104]

There is no trace of any further correspondence beyond June 1592. After he arrived in Louvain in August 1592 Lipsius had very little correspondence with his friends in the north. But he continued to receive news of Pieter. Gerard Buytewech was the son of Jan Gerritsz. Buytewech, one of the sixteen members of the Leiden magistracy who fled Leiden between 1572 and 1574—the so-called *glippers*. Like Cornelis senior, Jan returned to Leiden; unlike Cornelis senior he took up civic

---

[101] Mout, 'Justus Lipsius at Leiden University', 97–8. For all the details and documents of Lipsius's journey from Leiden to Liège in 1591, see J. De Landtsheer, 'From north to south: some new documents on Lipsius' journey from Leiden to Liège', in D. Sacré and G Tournoy (eds.), *Myricae: Essays on neo-Latin literature in memory of Jozef Ijsewijn* (Leuven: Leuven University Press, 2000), 303–31.

[102] ILE V, 92 01 14, 92 04 21, 92 05 16 V.

[103] Landtsheer, 'From Ultima Thule to Finisterra', 57–60.

[104] ILE V, 92 04 21, 92 06 10, [92 06 16], 92 06 16 V2, 92 06 21 V.

office again, if as a relatively lowly *weesmester*. Jan sent his son to study with Lipsius in Louvain in 1593.

Back in Leiden by 1595, Gerard was one of the few who continued to corre-spond with Lipsius, giving him news of the university and of Catholic friends. So when he reports with some amazement the appointment of Simon van Veen as Advocate General of Holland—an office that would involve him in the prosecu-tion of Roman Catholic, pro-Spanish sympathizers—and of the marriage of Pieter in The Hague, his comment is particularly significant: 'we who up to now have been good Catholic counsellors, ... we serenely abjure the [Spanish] king'.[105]

What is the significance of all this? Pieter's early studies at Lipsius's Leiden, and his subsequent relationship as a client via 'letters' to Lipsius's *persona* as a philo-sophically authoritative *patron* is, I argue, a shaping intellectual and social context both for Pieter's early life, and for the volume that is our subject. Pieter's minor position in the school of Lipsius provided him, on his travels, with a continuing education and a means of social orientation as he gained experience of the world beyond the lecture room.

At the same time, as I stated earlier in this section, his 'Memoire' should be read in the light of the fact that his initial recourse to Montaigne as an 'authority' is mediated by a particular nexus: his relationship as a client to a patron, to his lec-turer Lipsius (a relationship in turn mediated by his elder brother Otto and by his father Cornelis). His cue for seeing himself in Montaigne's text is Lipsius's punning marginal comment—in the 1586 printed *Epistolae*—that the 'Tastes' of Montaigne are to his taste (Illus. 1.6.4).[106] When Pieter empathetically describes the 'naturel' of Montaigne as witnessed by his writings, he is also, I would argue, empathizing with the literarily expressed *naturel* of the authority who first 'tasted' Montaigne for Leiden students—just as he does in the letter he wrote to Lipsius in 1592.

But Pieter does, as we also heard earlier in this section, go on to register a shift in his attitude in old age. Is the implication that, in the event, a more direct rela-tionship with Montaigne taught Pieter the importance of critical independence from all 'authorities'—including those close to home, such as Lipsius and Cornelis senior? How might this relate to the problem of those who 'slipped' from one place and one religious identity to another during the troubles, the problem which hung over the Van Veen family and over Lipsius himself?[107] These are difficult questions

---

[105] For this and the previous paragraph, see Landtsheer, 'From Ultima Thule to Finisterra', 57–8, 60; Lamet, 'The Vroedschap of Leiden 1550–1600', 26; *NNBW*, 'Veen, Simon Cornelisz. Van'; ILE VIII, 95 01 29 B. The translation is mine, but it is tentative. The whole passage reads as follows: 'Lugdunensis ille noster magister Simon van Veen nunc creatus est advocatus fiscalis Hollandiae et c[etera]. Partes nunc eius erunt partes illas serio fovere, in Catholicos, in exercitia eorum inquirere. Et hoc iam iuravit. Non miraris de illo? De fratre debes Petro Vaenio, illis tibi noto, cui praeibit mat-rimonii verba minister Haghensis. Et haec facimus adhuc boni catholici, quippe pro modo secure regem abiuramus advocati. In summa ita Haghae vivimus, ut conscientiae laxandae non opus nobis sit lectione Caietani.'

[106] ILE I, 83 05 25/Lipsius, *Centuria prima*, ep. I 43.

[107] On the problem of Lipsius's migration from location to location, and confession to confession, see A. Gerlo, 'Les études lipsiennes: état de la question', in A. Gerlo (ed.), *Juste Lipse (1547–1606): colloque international tenu en mars, 1987* (Brussels: VUB University Press, 1988), 9–24, 10–13, 22–4.

to which, on the basis of a brief 'Memoire', there can be no definitive answers. But he does, like Montaigne himself, subtly mark his distance from his father and his teachers.

To see this, let us turn now to Pieter's portrait of his own 'naturel'. The moment of this transition is crucial to my argument:

> As for me, if there is a need as one goes to show one's own nature to friends and descendants, there is nothing more agreeable to honest and far from ambitious spirits than to learn of the true nature of their father, their grandfather, or some other predecessor. And as for my nature, I find an infinity of characteristics in this author that almost resemble my own humours.[108]

This is the clearest indication in the 'Memoire' that Pieter is using the copy to re-actualize Montaigne's self-portrait in his own circumstances, with the crucial difference that he shows his true 'naturel', his 'conceptions', as much in his drawings as in his writings. The switch from Montaigne's audience of 'amis et nepveuls' to 'Pere, grand Pere, ou aultre predecesseur' is a strong clue: the memoir indeed portrays 'le vray naturel' of Cornelis junior's father Pieter and his grandfather Cornelis senior. One can feel the paternal 'edge' to the remark that there is nothing more agreeable to honest, unselfish types than to learn of the natural selves of their fathers and grandfathers.

The portrait of Cornelis junior's grandfather follows in the next passage, which deals with the siege of Leiden and its aftermath from 1572 to 1576. Here, the memoir invokes two authority figures whose reputations suffered when they defected or 'slipped away' during the troubles—both implicitly contrasted with Pieter himself. Given the invocation of Lipsius at the beginning, it does not seem unreasonable to suggest that Pieter's moralized narrative is inflected by Lipsius's *De constantia*.

We have already heard, earlier in this section, that the occasion of the unpublished letters mentioned by Pieter was his teacher's notorious defection from Leiden via Liège to Louvain in 1591. Lipsius did this after having twice fled earlier in his career, and after having fictionalized an escape to neutral territory in *De constantia*. The setting of the dialogue probably relates to a real occasion in the 1570s. Lipsius fled the Spanish troops and visited his friend Langius in neutral territory in Liège. There Langius admonishes him for thinking that flight from home is the solution to his troubles and teaches him the philosophy of constancy he needs to survive in times of oppression and civil strife.[109]

Pieter's memoir likewise relates the events that threw his family into turmoil. Leiden itself was one of the first towns in the south of Holland to go over to the

---

[108] Thorpe, 'Pieter van Veen's copy of Montaigne', 176/BL C.28.g.7, sig. 4K6r: '[Q]uant a moy, s'il est besoing qu'en passant on monstre a les amys et nepueuls, son naturel, Il n'y a rien plus aggreable a des honestes et poinct ambitieuls esprits que d'entendre le vray naturel de leur Pere, grand Pere ou aultre predecesseur. Et venant sur mon Naturel, Je trouue un infinite des parties en cest autheur qui quasiment resemblent mon humeur'.

[109] Papy, 'Lipsius's (neo-)Stoicism', 52–6.

revolt. Staunch royal loyalists on the city council were quickly overwhelmed by Orangists led by the town pensionary, Paulus Buys.[110]

As the head of a Catholic family living in an increasingly rebellious town, what was Cornelis senior to do? Pieter is careful to stipulate that his father was not a Spanish loyalist. He tells of Cornelis's horror at the way in which (in 1567) the Duke of Alba had repressed the magistrates in power in Leiden at the time of the first revolt—the iconoclasm of 1566—and relates a story illustrating his solidarity with the municipal authorities at that time. But in 1572 Cornelis nevertheless made a fateful decision, a decision that branded him and his family as *glippers* in the eyes of Calvinists and supporters of the Revolt. He decided they should flee. Simon, a captain in the civic militia, smuggled the three youngest brothers—Timon, Pieter, and Gijsbert—out of the besieged city on a riverboat. He took them to Amsterdam, which had remained Royalist and Catholic, where they stayed with their mother's sister.[111]

A separate escape party consisting of the mother and four daughters followed. Their father, one-time pensionary and then burgomaster of Leiden, fled with Otto (though Pieter does not mention Otto) to the Prince-bishopric of Liège, a part of the Habsburg Low Countries that remained neutral. One contemporary document declares Cornelis of the Spanish party and places him, on 20 October 1572, near Antwerp, 'far away from the malignant and rebellious people'.[112] Eventually, Cornelis himself arrived in Amsterdam, where, Pieter tells us he 'occupied himself teaching his children', waiting for the outcome of the siege.[113]

Spanish troops resumed an earlier siege in May 1574. Leiden's supplies were completely cut off and the city was on its knees, starving, until the famous breakthrough of the relief fleet in October 1574. Leiden was saved from the Spanish. Pieter van Veen's best-known extant painting—in Leiden's Lakenhal—depicts the 'Relief of Leiden' and was donated by him to the city in about 1619. Pieter's glorification of the Beggars' arrival may well have been part of a lifelong attempt to distance himself and his elder brother Simon from his father's actions during the siege, to rehabilitate the Van Veens as loyal citizens of the United Provinces.[114]

After the signing of the treaty between the southern and northern provinces—the 'Pacification of Ghent' of 8 November 1576—Cornelis abruptly returned to Leiden, where he had left all his goods. To the surprise of his son Pieter, he was welcomed back by the town's community. Thenceforward, however, he never again took civic or provincial office, and retired to private citizenship. *De constantia*

---

[110] J. Israel, *The Dutch Republic: its rise, greatness, and fall 1477–1806* (Oxford: Oxford University Press, 1985), 174.

[111] Thorpe, 'Pieter van Veen's copy of Montaigne', 176/BL C.28.g.7, sig. 4K6r.

[112] F. J. P. van den Branden, *Geschiedenis der Antwerpsche Schilderschool*, 3 vols. (Antwerp: Buschmann, 1883), vol. 1, 402 and 403n.1; Israel, *The Dutch Republic*, 150. Branden's source, which I have not been able to check, is Scabinale Protocollen der stad Antwerpen, 1572, sub Asseliers & Martini, vol, I, fols. 531, 499v.

[113] Thorpe, 'Pieter van Veen's copy of Montaigne', 176/BL C.28.g.7, sig. 4K6v: 'il s'amusa la a enseigner ses enfans qui estoient La'.

[114] Israel, *The Dutch Republic*, 181–2. For Pieter van Veen's 'Relief of Leiden', see Kolfin and Rikken, 'A very personal copy'.

implicitly questions Lipsius's own actions by valorizing inner fortitude over physical flight. Pieter questions his father's actions on similar grounds. Cornelis's fear ('timidité') in leaving his home and all his worldly goods to go to neutral country was, says Pieter, the cause of many of the troubles of his house.[115]

The moral is the constancy Cornelis senior lacked, and which Pieter—though 'fort timide' himself at a young age—has learned from studies and experience under the aegis of Lipsius and the French Thales. Pieter is teaching his own male heir the value of staying spiritually and physically 'at home', even if this means living privately as a Catholic in a non-Roman Catholic country. The virtue in question is exemplified by Lipsius's friend Montaigne, who manages—unlike Cornelis senior and Lipsius himself—not to succumb to panic and 'slip' away, even though he ascribes to the 'anciennes Creances' in a region (southwest France) inclining to the Reform.

The memoir ends with a story about Cornelis senior that leaves Cornelis junior—perhaps about to travel himself—with a better image of his grandfather. While a burgomaster at Leiden during the iconoclastic revolt of 1566–7 Cornelis was hurrying to the Town Hall to fulfil his civic duties—something, Pieter implies, he did not do in 1572—when he slipped and broke his leg.[116]

Notwithstanding all the books in the world of the doctors and surgeons, says Pieter, this was never set right—hence Cornelis's disability in Otto's painting. But Cornelis took his fortune in good part, saying that God had justly visited punishment on one of his legs for the pleasure he had frivolously taken in dancing during his youth in France. This leaves the young Cornelis with an image of his grandfather as a good citizen of the United Provinces.

2.4.7 VAN RAVESTEYN'S PORTRAIT OF THE VAN VEENS

The passage immediately following the account of the siege takes us to the moment when Pieter, in his teens, heard Lipsius lecture at the University of Leiden:

> He [Cornelis senior] sent me to study at the new University of Leiden, which my eldest brother, as Captain of the said town, by order of the Prince of Orange, set up with his company in Leiden. Still young, I there heard the Sieur Lipsius, and as I was of a delicate, strongly phlegmatic humour, I undertook (having beforehand an inclination towards painting, music, and other exercises) to practice painting. My father permitted me to do this, one hour after another, saying that in his youth and

---

[115] Thorpe, 'Pieter van Veen's copy of Montaigne', 176/BL C.28.g.7 sig. 4K6v: 'la Pacification de Gand estant publie, Il retourna incontinent a Leyden, ou il fut bien receu du Commun, non obstant qu'il s'avoit retire de Leyden a Liege Pais neutral, ayant este premierement Pensionaire et (apres avoir quitte cest Estat), Bourgemaistre de La dicte ville. Homme Docte et Jurisconsulte, Et ne voulant depuis se mesler de L'Estat, demeura tout sa vie personne privee. Il avoit eu en extreme horreur le *sic* procedures du Ducq d'Alba, Lequel ruina tous ceulx qui avoient este en Magistrat au temps qu'on fit avecq grand ravage changement de L'ancienne relligion En sorte qui'il quita le Pais et tous ses biens, allant en Pais Neutral. Sa timidite fut cause de beaucoup des Inconvenients en sa maison.'

[116] Thorpe, 'Pieter van Veen's copy of Montaigne', 179/BL C.28.g.7, sig. 4K8r.

throughout his life he had seen and considered that it was a good thing for young men to practice some art amongst their studies, so as to be able to make use of it when they are desirous to travel—as he saw I was—especially when resources are not abundant.[117]

Lipsius arrived in Leiden before the end of March 1578 and was appointed on 5 April. Before proceeding, it is crucial to grasp the significance of his arrival and of his rectorships, which began the following year. Simon van Veen's company founded the University of Leiden by order of the Prince of Orange in 1575. The charter provided for an institution that would supply the Low Countries with leaders of church and state. They would be trained in the right knowledge of God and in the liberal arts and sciences before serving the legal administrations of the various states, from Holland and Zeeland to Flanders and Brabant. But until Lipsius arrived, the arts and the philosophical disciplines were neglected. Lipsius brought a vigorous plea for a thorough education in the liberal arts and literature as a necessary tool to every student destined for the law or priesthood. He also brought and developed a specific philosophy of *constantia, sapientia*, and *prudentia*, a philosophy addressed to the circumstances of 'Batavians' who were living through the troubles.

In the five months after Lipsius arrived (April to August 1578) thirty people were matriculated—as many as had enrolled in the whole of the previous year. One of them, on 2 July 1578, at the age of fourteen or fifteen, was Pieter. He appears in the list as 'Petrus Cornelius vander feen Leidensis bonarum artium et literarum studiosus'—an anomalous entry insofar as most were listed as students either of the liberal arts or of *litterae*, but not of both. It was probably the foundation of the university by his brother rather than the arrival of Lipsius that directly prompted Cornelis senior to enrol Pieter as one of the first fifteen or so arts students. The important point is that Pieter's education was wrapped up in a new drive to provide pre-professional students with a propadeutic training in the liberal arts, especially in literature.[118]

But there was an added element, derived from the nature of the Van Veens themselves. The *humeur* of this particular student inclined him to exercises in

---

[117] Thorpe, 'Pieter van Veen's copy of Montaigne', 176–7/BL C.28.g.7, sig. 4K6v: 'Il [Cornelis senior] fit estudier moy dans la Nouvelle universite de Leyden, Laquelle mon frere aisné comme Cappiteine de ladicte ville per ordre du Prince d'Oragne [*sic*], Introduisoit avecq sa compagnie dan Leyden. La estant encore Jeune iouys Le Sr. Lipsius; Et comme J'estois d'une humeur molle fort flegmatique, J'entrepris (ayant auparavant Inclination à la Peinture, musique et autres exercises) de m'exercer a la peinture: Ce que successivis horis mon Pere permettoit disant qu'en sa Jeunesse et par tout sa vie il avoit veu et considere qu'il estoit bon pour des Jeunes hommes d'exercer quelque artifice parmy leurs estudes, pour s'en pouvoir servir quand ils desirent de Voiager, come il voioit que Jen estois desireulx, principalement quand les moyens ne sont pas grands.'

[118] For this and the previous paragraph, see R. J. van den Hoorn, 'On course for quality: Justus Lipsius and Leiden University', in Enenkel and Heesakkers (eds.), *Lipsius in Leiden*, 73–92, 74–7; M. E. H. N. Mout, 'Justus Lipsius at Leiden University 1578–1591', in Gerlo (ed.), *Juste Lipse (1547–1606)*, 85–99, 85, 88–9; Witkam, *Immatriculatie en recensie in de Leidse Universiteit*, 3, at number 76. Pieter was still there in November 1581 (113, at number s298).

painting and, we might assume, drawing—as it had his elder brother Otto, who in the years before the foundation of the university had followed private studies with the poet-painter Lampsonius, a friend of Lipsius, in Liège. Cornelis senior permits Pieter to practice some art amongst his studies, one hour after another. The impression is of his father directing his studies—just as he did in Amsterdam during the siege a few years earlier ('il s'amusa la a enseigner ses enfans qui estoient Là'), and just as Pieter directs Cornelis junior's studies in Van Ravesteyn's portrait, inviting him to practice some art amongst his literary studies.

Why does Pieter specify that his father *permitted* him to study painting? Painting and drawing were not amongst the liberal arts. In sixteenth-century Europe, the apprentices who trained to practise painting as a trade did not normally come from wealthy, educated families and did not simultaneously study the liberal arts in private tutorials and prestigious schools. But Pieter's contemporaries were aware of a custom specific to the Low Countries that bucked this trend. Many well-to-do parents did allow their sons to mix study of painting and drawing with their literary studies, and even to take positions as apprentices with master painters.

This is a very important thread in the biography of Karel van Mander (included in the 1616–18 edition of the *Schilder-boeck*). We are told how Karel, like Pieter, was naturally inclined to painting and drawing, as to poetry and rhyming. Seeing this, his father and uncle thought it wise to apprentice him with Lucas de Heere, a skilful painter and poet. Like Otto and Pieter, Karel travels to Rome, where his artistic skills are in demand from various patrons. We later catch him 'reading and writing in his father's house, and occasionally painting for his own pleasure'— clearly, to anticipate the argument, the theme of Van Ravesteyn's painting. When the troubles of his country force him and his family to flee, his artistic skills provide work that enables them to survive.[119]

In the 'life of Jooris Hoefnaghel, painter and poet of Antwerp' in the *Schilder-boeck*, Van Mander comments directly on this trend:

> I find that a better custom prevails among us Netherlanders than is in use with other peoples—namely that parents, even when empowered by wealth, often get their children to learn one or another art or trade early in their youth; that can be wonderfully useful, especially in times of war and emigration. For we find that cruel fortune, the bane of this world, has less power over a skill than over riches, and that the art which one has learned in one's youth is often the last resort in necessity and a refuge of consolation to avert the shipwreck of oppressive poverty [*en dat de Const, die men in zijn jeught heeft gheleert, dickwils den uytersten plicht-ancker in den noot, en een troostlijcke toevlucht wort, om d'ellendighe schipbreuck van de perssende armoede voor te comen*].

In Hoefnaghel's case, Van Mander tells us, his parents would *not* permit the boy at home or school to do what Mother Nature continually insisted. It takes an intervention from a schoolmaster and from an ambassador of the Duke of Savoy, a

---

[119] For this and the previous paragraph (for the latter see also the passage that follows in the next paragraph), see Van Mander, vol. 1, 10–33, 21.

guest in his father's house, before he is allowed to occupy himself with drawing, while also being taught literature.[120]

The opposite is true of Otto van Veen, in Van Mander's account. The 'life' of Otto in the main text stipulates that he was born in Leiden to a good family, and was drawn by nature towards the art of painting. The appendix adds crucial information about his early formation:

> Until he was 14 years old Octavio van Veen applied himself to learning the art of painting with Isack Claesz. in Leiden and in the between times some hours a day to literature [*'Octavio van Veen' heeft tot zijn 14. Iaren toegheleyt te leeren de Schilder-const, by 'Isack Claesz'. te Leyden, en ondertusschen eenighe uren des daeghs in de Letter-const*]. And after that he was sent by his father to Dominicus Lampsonius, secretary to the Bishop of Liège, a learned poet who also had much understanding of the art of painting....[121]

The outlines of an institution specific to the Van Veen family—and to other families like them in the Low Countries—begin to emerge here, and point us back to the van Ravesteyn and to the Montaigne with a fresh perspective. There are two complementary scenarios: in one, a young man earmarked for a living as a painter is encouraged in between times to study literature (Otto); in the other, a young man destined to use his literary training in legal practice is encouraged in between times to study painting (Pieter, Cornelis junior). Both do so not just for cultivation, but also for pragmatic reasons.

Where might Van Mander have got this information about Otto's early education? He knew very little about the Antwerp group of painters, and probably relied on one or two informers. Given that Pieter wrote commendatory verses for the *Schilder-boeck*, he may also have provided Van Mander with the information included in the appendix about his elder brother. This is the view of Van Mander's modern editor, Miedema.[122] Miedema's supposition can be strengthened by turning to the scene that Pieter commissioned Van Ravesteyn to paint, for the scene elucidates—and is elucidated by—the passages cited above from Pieter's memoir and from the appendix to the *Schilder-boeck*. It also provides us, I will argue, with a description of the nexus of another work: Van Veen's Montaigne.

Art historians have associated Van Ravesteyn's painting with an iconographical tradition of paintings of masters and clerks or secretaries. This is the light in which it was shown at an exhibition in Basel in 1987. The author of the official catalogue pointed to Sebastiano del Piombo's painting of Cardinal Carondolet and his secretary (1510–12), and to Thomas de Keyser's of Constantijn Huygens and his clerk (1627). Chu notes evidence of the presence of a copy of the former in the Low Countries at the right time, and proposes that the figure on the left of the painting should therefore be identified as the clerk.[123]

There is no reason to dispute that del Piombo's model may have influenced the composition of the painting. But it does not explain exactly what is happening in Van Ravesteyn's scene and why. The documents adduced here clearly do. When we

---

[120] Van Mander, vol. 1, 306–9.   [121] Van Mander, vol. 1, 438–9, 463; vol. 6, 54–5.
[122] Van Mander, vol. 6, 52, 56, 58–9.   [123] Chu, *Im Lichte Hollands*, 206.

catch Van Mander 'reading and writing in his father's house, and occasionally painting for his own pleasure' we are surely dealing with a commonplace scene that informs Van Ravesteyn's composition and the Van Veen copy alike.

For this is yet another culturally specific instance of the 'free literate' with whom we have been concerned throughout. The reader-writer is in this case invited to practice some art amongst his studies.

In what is probably a room in Pieter's house—or perhaps his office—in The Hague, Cornelis sits on the left immersed in his literary studies (Illus. 1.1.11 and cover illustration, Volume 2).[124] The books scattered on the table cannot be identified. But given the likely date (*c.*1622, the year of his matriculation as a law student), the setting, and the presence of the clerk, these studies are likely to be of a legal nature.

Pieter enters the room with his clerk Hendrik—who holds Pieter's cane in his left hand and a palette and brushes in his right—with the intention of gently interrupting his son. With a rolled up document in his left hand, Pieter leans forward on the chair to attract his son's attention with his right hand, and to suggest that it is now the hour to switch to some exercises in painting. The easel awaits in the background, alongside the bookcase. Pieter has learned from Cornelis senior— who directed his and his brother's studies as he is now directing his son's—that it is wise to alternate study in literature with exercises in painting or drawing.

We may infer from the passages in the memoir and in Van Mander that the young Cornelis we see in the painting is intending to travel, for both passages emphasize that the visual arts are good fall-backs on a voyage. Since the copy dates from roughly the same period as the Van Ravesteyn, the inclusion at the back of the narrative of Pieter's travels would lend some weight to this speculation. As yet, no other documentary evidence has come to light to support it.

But there is one other piece of documentary evidence which helps to differentiate the painting's theme from the subjects of del Piombo's and de Keyser's works. Van Ravesteyn's portrait appears in a 1694 inventory of eighty-two paintings passed down in the family via Pieter's granddaughter Elisabeth. As a family heirloom it had probably been in the possession of Cornelis until his death. The inventory describes '[a]nother large painting in which Mr Pieter van Veen stands in front of a table on which books are lying, tutoring his clerk Hendrick Borsman and his son Cornelis'.[125] This offers strong confirmation that we are viewing an informal tutorial scene, a scene rooted in a particular feature of contemporary biographical accounts of Dutch painter-poets, and planted in Van Veen family tradition. Like Otto, like Pieter himself, Cornelis junior is to study both painting and letters *successivis horis.*

---

[124] Pabon, 'Iets over Mr. Pieter van Veen en zijn familie', 241.

[125] A. G. J. Mosmans, 'Een belangrijke maltenschap van oude schilderijen', *Oud Holland,* 54 (1937), 214–18, 216: 'Noch een grote schildery waer in dat staet Mr. Pieter van Veen voor een tafel daer boecken opleggen, onderwysende synen clerck Hendrick Borsman ende synen soon Cornelis'. It may be that Pieter tutored his clerks in painting as well (see Pabon, 'Iets over Mr. Pieter van Veen en zijn familie', 242).

Van Mander's prefatory comments to the life of Hoefnaghel are particularly helpful, then, in describing the nexus of this copy prepared by a father with his son in mind. On one level, the book is a concrete reminder to Cornelis junior of the family tradition of alternating literary studies with exercises in painting and drawing—especially with a view to the utility of both in paying one's way as one travels, and in providing for long-term financial survival in very unstable political circumstances. Cornelis junior's uncle Gijsbert van Veen survived in precisely this way, making engravings in Rome and Venice, then settling to live in Brussels as an engraver and painter. He was following closely in the footsteps of Otto. Pieter survived on his travels by working as a secretary. He performed notarial services such as the writing of the acts of the process against the murderers of the Cardinal de Rambouillet.[126]

But it is not just that the arts of painting and literature learned in youth can be pragmatically useful on one's journey south, or in times of war and migration. The volume plainly shows that they provide a 'refuge of consolation' in philosophical terms as well. After reading a printed letter of his teacher on his travels, Pieter acquires a copy of the *Essais* as a young adult in his mid-twenties. Then, over many re-readings, he finds his 'natural' self in the text. Later in life, he acquires a different copy and the work continues to provide consolation. He uses the margins to show his *naturel* to his son and wider posterity in writings and drawings, and uses the endleaves to memorialize his early life and travels during times of war and migration. Pieter's whole life and attitude, as memorialized in the volume, are informed by the Lipsian virtues of constancy and prudence, and by the search for a wisdom beyond religious controversy. Despite his father's mistake, these virtues see him through to moral tranquillity and career success in legal practice in The Hague.

2.4.8 *LES ESSAIS DE PIETER VAN VEEN*

Thus far, I have concentrated heavily on the clues contained in the memoir. But let us conclude with a question that must have occurred to the reader of the second half of this chapter. How might the hypothesis defended above translate into a reading/viewing of the annotations and illustrations in the rest of the copy?

The juxtaposition of the volume and Van Ravesteyn's painting has already, I hope, provided a general answer. In both we see Pieter encouraging Cornelis to be aware of his father's natural inclination—as a young student of the liberal arts—towards painting/drawing, and to follow the pattern of studies pursued by his father and uncle under the tutelage of his grandfather, Cornelis senior. As Cornelis junior studies the text and his father's written interventions in the text, Pieter's hand—by means of the marginal illustrations—moves him gently towards parallel studies in the art of drawing.

For a more particular answer take, very briefly, Pieter's layer of additions to Montaigne's I 8 (Illus. 2.4.4). This example usefully combines several of the

---

[126] Thorpe, 'Pieter van Veen's copy of Montaigne', 178/BL C.28.g.7, sig. 4K7r–v.

elements listed in 2.4.4—underlining, marginal drawing, personal annotation—in what Paul Smith has appositely called a 'lecture emblématisante'. He argues that the combination of drawing, Latin tags, and longer pieces of text—whether Montaigne's or Pieter's own—suggest the *pictura*, *motto*, and *subscriptio* of the emblem tradition.[127] Van Veen turns the copy into a kind of miscellaneous emblem book.

Chapter I 8, 'De l'Oysiveté', is a pivotal chapter in the *Essais* because it contains the first reference in the main text to the circumstances of composition outlined in Montaigne's preface 'Au lecteur'. We saw in 2.2.11 how Flavio Querenghi used Naselli's version of this chapter. Pieter's text derived from Montaigne's first posthumous edition (1595), but it was not drastically different from the text that appeared in the first edition of 1580. There, Montaigne describes how he had recently retired to his estate, thinking to leave his mind—mature and weighty enough to look after itself—in pleasant idleness.

But instead his imagination bolts off like a runaway horse. It turns out, Montaigne says, that if we do not keep our minds occupied with particular subjects, they fashion—in Horace's words—vain apparitions as in the dreams of sick men ('velut ægri somnia, vanæ/ Fingitur species'). When Montaigne read over the chapter between the 1580 and 1588 editions he added another layer consisting of no more than two Latin quotations, four verses from Virgil, and one from Martial.[128]

When Pieter read over the resulting chapter he too added a layer consisting in part of further classical verses. Alongside Montaigne's Horatian quotation he draws a sick man asleep, with an apparition from his dreams above the bed. He underlines Montaigne's comment immediately after the quotation: 'the soul that has no definite aim, gets lost' ('[l]'ame qui n'a point de but estably, elle se perd'). But having visualized Horace's words ('... ægri somnia ...'; my underlining) in a drawing, he also finds they remind him of verses in Persius's satire 3: 'Ægroti veteris meditantes somnia, gigni/ De nihilo nihil [*sic*], In nihilum nil - posse reverti [*sic*]' ('Musing on the dreams of some sick old one, nothing is brought forth from nothing, and nothing can return to nothing'; my underlining).

On the same page as the drawing, Pieter chooses a marginal space alongside the final passage of the chapter, where Montaigne describes how his mind gives birth to orderless fantasies and how he resolves to keep a record of them. Pieter writes out the verses from Persius, and continues in French:

> Which also happens to me quite frequently when I want to put my ideas down sometimes in writing, sometimes in painting. But before I am able put my hand to work half the idea has escaped me, as variations in the style and context cause it to take

---

[127] P. J. Smith, '"Son dire au faict de la langue françoise est admirable": Pieter van Veen, lecteur de Montaigne', paper given at 'La langue de Rabelais et de Montaigne', 'La Sapienza' University, Rome, 13–19 September 2003. I am very grateful to Prof. Smith for supplying me with a copy of his excellent paper.
[128] I 8, NP54–5/BVH Bordeaux 1580, vol. I, pp. 30–2/BVH Paris 1588, ff. 9v–10/S30–1. There were no further additions between 1588 and 1592.

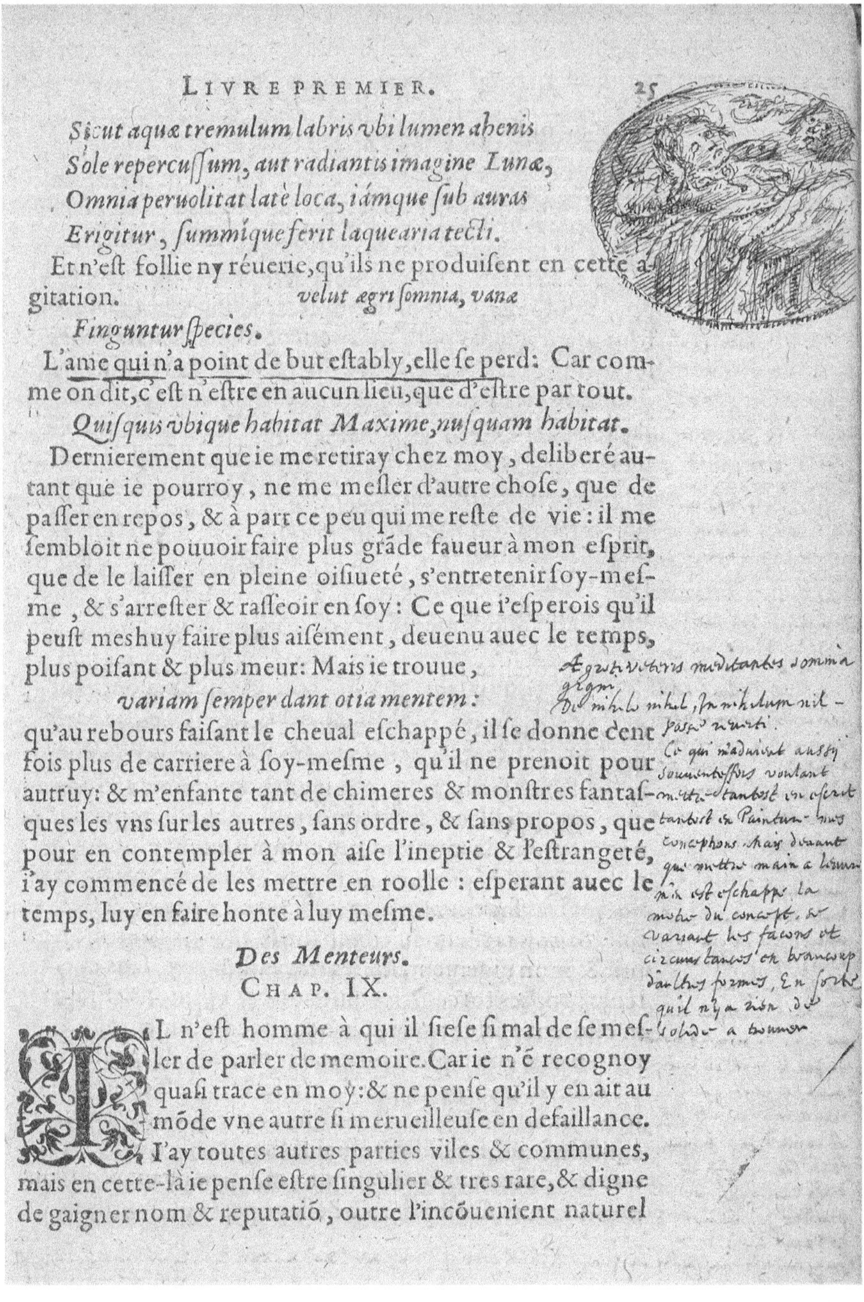

LIVRE PREMIER.

Sicut aquæ tremulum labris vbi lumen ahenis
Sole repercuſſum, aut radiantis imagine Lunæ,
Omnia peruolitat latè loca, iámque ſub auras
Erigitur, ſummíque ferit laqueariatecli.
Et n'eſt follie ny réuerie, qu'ils ne produiſent en cette a-
gitation.   *velut ægri ſomnia, vanæ*

Finguntur ſpecies.

L'ame qui n'a point de but eſtably, elle ſe perd: Car comme on dit, c'eſt n'eſtre en aucun lieu, que d'eſtre par tout.

Quiſquis vbique habitat Maxime, nuſquam habitat.

Dernierement que ie me retiray chez moy, deliberé autant que ie pourroy, ne me meſler d'autre choſe, que de
paſſer en repos, & à part ce peu qui me reſte de vie: il me
ſembloit ne pouuoir faire plus gráde faueur à mon eſprit,
que de le laiſſer en pleine oiſiueté, s'entretenir ſoy-meſme, & s'arreſter & raſſeoir en ſoy: Ce que i'eſperois qu'il
peuſt meshuy faire plus aiſément, deuenu auec le temps,
plus poiſant & plus meur: Mais ie trouue,

variam ſemper dant otia mentem:
qu'au rebours faiſant le cheual eſchappé, il ſe donne cent
fois plus de carriere à ſoy-meſme, qu'il ne prenoit pour
autruy: & m'enfante tant de chimeres & monſtres fantaſ-
ques les vns ſur les autres, ſans ordre, & ſans propos, que
pour en contempler à mon aiſe l'ineptie & l'eſtrangeté,
i'ay commencé de les mettre en roolle: eſperant auec le
temps, luy en faire honte à luy meſme.

Des Menteurs.
CHAP. IX.

IL n'eſt homme à qui il ſieſe ſi mal de ſe meſler de parler de memoire. Car ie n'é recognoy
quaſi trace en moy: & ne penſe qu'il y en ait au
móde vne autre ſi merueilleuſe en defaillance.
I'ay toutes autres parties viles & communes,
mais en cette-là ie penſe eſtre ſingulier & tres rare, & digne
de gaigner nom & reputatió, outre l'incóuenient naturel

Illus. 2.4.4. Montaigne, *Essais*, 1602, British Library, pressmark C.28.g.7, p.25 (Pieter van Veen's copy, with annotations and illustrations). Reproduced by permission of The British Library Board.

many other forms, such that nothing solid [of the original idea] remains to be found.[129]

To us, this is Pieter sounding like Montaigne. To a member of Pieter's family, the effect might have been the reverse: Montaigne ends up sounding like Pieter. Pieter overwrites Montaigne's cue for reading the *Essais* as a 'roolle' or register of his 'conceptions' with a cue for reading *his*—Pieter's—work (the copy with alternating marginal drawings and writings) as a register of his 'conceptions'.

Remember that when in the memoir Pieter comes on to the subject of his own 'naturel', he says that he finds 'an infinity of characteristics in this author that almost resemble my character' ('un infinite des parties en cest autheur [Montaigne] qui quasiment ressemblent mon humeur'). This is in the context of the need 'en passant' to show one's 'naturel' to friends and relatives. A little further on Pieter specifies that his 'soft, very phlegmatic humour ('humeur molle fort flegmatique') inclined him in his youth to exercises in 'la peinture', which his father allowed him to alternate with his literary exercises.

With this and the example of I 8 in mind, we can now see how Cornelis junior might have read and viewed this copy not as a work that sketches the 'conditions et humeurs' of its author Montaigne and that has been annotated and illustrated by Pieter, but, rather, as a work authored by Pieter purposively to show his 'humeurs' and 'conceptions' to his son as they develop naturally in both drawing and writing.

So, what Cornelis junior sees on the page we have been considering is his father revealing his own 'humeur' and expressing his own 'conceptions' by the integrated means of a marked-up text, a pair of recalled classical verses, a self-reflexive comment on the whole elusive process of expressing concepts now visually, now literarily—a comment that links up with the memoir at the back and its description of Pieter's education in the liberal and visual arts.

On this and other pages Cornelis sees a coherent work by his father—*Les Essais de Pieter van Veen*. The desired outcome of this act of knowledge transfer is, of course, similar 'essays' of Cornelis van Veen in parallel literary and visual forms—those, perhaps, he appears to be producing in Van Ravesteyn's painting. And again, in leaving his son this book, Pieter is making the same gesture his painted self makes. He extends his hand to encourage Cornelis to pursue a pattern of studies tried and tested in Van Veen family history—studies that will provide 'a refuge of consolation' throughout his life. Besides practising law in The Hague, Cornelis did indeed become a painter. In 1656 he was the co-founder of 'Pictura', a painter's society.[130]

---

[129] Thorpe, 'Pieter van Veen's copy of Montaigne', 172 (annotation VI)/BL C.28.g.7, sig. B5r: 'Ce qui m'advient aussy souventesfois voulant mettre tantost en escrit tantost en Painture mes conceptions. Mais devant que mettre main a loeuvre m'en est eschappe la moitié du concept, se variant les facons et circonstances en beaucoup d'aultres formes, En sorte qu'il n'y a rien de solide a trouver'. Paul Smith has suggested in his unpublished paper ('"Son dire au faict de la langue francoise est admirable"') that this remark may explain the rather chaotic and disordered style of the drawings.
[130] Pabon, 'Iets over Mr. Pieter van Veen en zijn familie', 243.

Illus. 2.4.5. J. A. van Ravesteyn, *Pieter van Veen, His son Cornelis and His Clerk Hendrick Borsman* (detail), Musée d'art et d'histoire, Geneva. Reproduced by permission of the Musée d'art et d'histoire, Département de la culture et du sport, Ville de Genève.

One could use this hypothesis to explain the thrust of other annotations and illustrations: Pieter's objection to Montaigne's remark in I 56 that you are fully formed at twenty, and his drawing of a young man of that age; a series of illustrations showing young men in the company of fathers and older men instructing them.[131]

But there is one final piece of visual evidence supporting this chapter's hypothesis about the familial nexus of the copy. A comparison of the figure in the Van Ravesteyn painting (Illus. 2.4.5) with figures in the margins of the copy suggest that Pieter may have drawn either portraits of Cornelis junior, or portraits of himself as a young man, into the book (Illus. 2.4.6).

Certainly the same young man appears more than once in the margins, often in the company of books—like Cornelis junior in the painting. The receding hair and narrow mouth, the strong, pointed nose and chin, are the features most obviously shared with Cornelis as portrayed by Van Ravesteyn. One of the marginal illustrations shows a young man sitting at a table with books, and very closely resembles the figure in Van Ravesteyn's painting (Illus. 2.4.7).

In 1.1.7, I briefly discussed the image drawn alongside a passage that refers glowingly to Brutus's night-time annotations in Polybius during a time of

---

[131] BL C.28.g.7, sigs. V8v, 2A7r.

Illus. 2.4.6. Montaigne, *Essais*, 1602, British Library, pressmark C.28.g.7, p. 509 (Pieter van Veen's copy, with annotations and illustrations—detail). Reproduced by permission of The British Library Board.

Illus. 2.4.7. Montaigne, *Essais*, 1602, British Library, pressmark C.28.g.7, p. 543 (Pieter van Veen's copy, with annotations and illustrations—detail). Reproduced by permission of The British Library Board.

universal crisis (Illus. 1.1.9, Illus. 1.1.10). Montaigne concludes: 'To compose our manners and morals is our duty, not to compose books, and to win, not battles and provinces, but order and tranquillity in our conduct. Our greatest and most glorious master-piece is to live fitly [*vivre à propos*].'[132] Can we now see this as an image of Pieter and his son? At the very least, the moral is in harmony with Pieter's use of *this* book, the *Essais*, as placed in context by the memoir at the end.

There is of course no definitive proof of the hypothesis presented here. But to view the copy as a work of art embedded in a family history is to make sense of the object, to make it richer in significance. Not only this: Pieter's work and Slingsby's book of remembrance send us back to the original *Essais* with a fresh sense of their relevance to the experience of private reader-writers across a Europe ravaged with religious troubles.

Montaigne's work grew from a moment of schism and civil war that split his own family, and was addressed to family and friends keen to remember him, in an active sense. The same is true of Van Veen's work, and of Slingsby's. Montaigne, like Van Veen, did not 'slip away' to align himself with militant Catholic authorities, though Slingsby, in the event, did. All three made a book for posterity that showed them—even on their travels—'at home' with themselves and their studies, attempting to survive the religious troubles of the sixteenth and seventeenth centuries. However, we shall see in the next chapter that, from a more scholarly point of view, this could make the *Essais* seem no more than 'the breviary of urbane loafers and ignorant pseudointellectuals'.[133]

---

[132] III 13, NP1158/ BVH Paris 1595, bk. III, p. 225/S1258–9.
[133] See section 2.5.1 for the source of this quotation in the *Huetiana* of 1722.

2.5

Recording the History of Secret Thoughts in Early Modern France[1]

In the last chapter we considered a manuscript journal compiled in England and a copy annotated and illustrated in Holland. Together, they began to place the reading and rewriting of the *Essais* in the context of practices of private record-keeping and life-writing that were current across Europe. The two cases suggested that these practices were especially important in times of religious conflict and war.

This chapter considers two further examples from France: a set of manuscript records including extracts from the *Essais*; and a manuscript journal, likewise with extracts, accompanied this time by the corresponding family copy of Montaigne's text. But, to provide a larger context, we begin with a hostile overview of the first hundred years of the school of Montaigne, produced in the early eighteenth century by a scholar who disapproved of the emergence of a whole public of 'free literates' following the French essayist's example.

2.5.1 URBANE LOAFERS AND IGNORANT PSEUDOINTELLECTUALS

In 1712, Pierre Daniel Huet, scholar and bishop of Avranches, fell gravely ill in the Jesuit house in Paris where he had resided for twenty years. He was about seventy-two years old and every day, since 1681, he had been working on the Hebrew text of the Bible. As soon as he recovered a bit of strength,

> he set himself to write his own life...though not with the order nor the precision of his previous works, because his memory was not the same as it was before. It continued to weaken day by day. Thus, on finding himself no longer capable of compiling a coherent work [*d'un ouvrage suivi*], he contented himself with writing down some unconnected thoughts [*pensées détachées*], a task more appropriate to his current state.[2]

This miscellaneous piece of writing is different from all the others composed and published by Huet. It does not show the operation of a biblical scholar's proper arts

---

[1] 'I took him for the plainest harmless creature/ That breathed upon the earth, a Christian,/ Made him my book wherein my soul recorded/The history of all her secret thoughts.' Shakespeare, *Richard III*, 3.5.

[2] Pierre Daniel Huet, *Huetiana, ou, Pensées diverses de M. Huet* (Paris: J. Estienne, 1722), sig. ã8r–v.

of memory and reason. Detached notions are thrown straight onto paper in a manner that reflects the failure of his memory, for the circumstances—his sickness, his age—mean that he can get away with talking freely, without order and precision.

Since Huet was a noble cleric, an illustrious protagonist in the recent history of the republic of letters, the private memoir was naturally destined for publication. L'Abbé d'Olivet, our source for this information, received the unique copy of the manuscript from Huet with instructions to publish under the title of *Huetiana*. Huet told him he wrote it partly because he feared the appearance of a 'faux' *Huetiana* after his death. He wanted to get the record straight about his private intellectual conversation in case someone else—fraudulently—did it for him. It is an afterthought to a lifetime of rigorous scholarship, designed to act as a memorial of the private man in posterity's eye.[3]

The resulting text, published in 1722, does not by modern criteria resemble a piece of life-writing. It is miscellaneous, comprising 140 chapters on various matters in no particular order. There are some autobiographical elements: an account of his early passion for letters; lives of his sisters and his parents; a few personal anecdotes. But for the most part it tells the story of Huet's escape from his bourgeois origins in Normandy to a life in the republic of letters by making us privy to his remarkably frank talk about authors, books, and intellectual questions.

The sixth chapter, for example, registers how Huet used to talk about Montaigne's book. It had not escaped his attention that the *Essais* were also the work of a sick and dying man putting his 'pensées détachées' on paper without order and precision:

> Montaigne's Essays may truly be called Montaniana, that is, a collection of Montaigne's thoughts without order and without connection [*un Recueil des pensées de Montagne sans ordre et sans liaison*]. This, perhaps, has not a little contributed to rendering him agreeable to our nation, who dislike being subjected to long dissertations [*ennemie de l'assujettissement que demandent les longues dissertations*]; and to the present times, which dislike the serious dedication that coherent treatises written with method require. For the most part it is his free spirit [*esprit libre*], his varied style, and his metaphorical expressions that have procured Montaigne his current popularity, which he has enjoyed for more than a century, and which he still enjoys today; for, truly, it [the *Essais*] is the breviary for urbane loafers and ignorant pseudointellectuals who want to cloak themselves in some knowledge of the world and add some literary hues. You will scarce find a country gentleman [*un Gentilhomme de campagne*], who is keen to distinguish himself from hare-hunters, without a copy of Montaigne on his mantelpiece. But although freedom of thought has its use when confined within proper boundaries, it becomes dangerous when it degenerates into licentiousness [*Mais cette liberté, qui a son utilité, quand elle a ses bornes, devient dangereuse quand elle dégénère en licence*]. Such is the freedom of Montaigne, who seemed to think of himself as above the laws of modesty and shame. When one addresses the public, as all do who class themselves as authors, one must show respect... He thought that his merit placed him above the

---

[3] Elena Rapetti, *Pierre-Daniel Huet: erudizione, filosofia, apologetica* (Milan: Vita e pensiero, 1999), 241 n.34.

rules [*Il a cru que son mérite l'affranchissoit des règles*], that he should set an example rather than follow one.... All his professions of candour and his air of frankness [*Tous ces tours et cet air de franchise qu'il prend*] do not obscure his secret affectation and his pride in boasting of his employments, the number of his servants, and the reputation that he had acquired. Let us collect all of these passages, which he has artfully scattered in his writings, and we will find that he has been his own panegyrist. Scaliger was right in saying, 'What is it to me whether Montaigne loves white wine or claret?' He does indeed abuse his readers' attention by giving them the detail of his own tastes and all his other domestic frivolities [*toutes ses autres fadaises domestiques*].[4]

Like Lancre, Huet is a hostile witness of great acuity.[5] His remarks are equally revelatory of the force of Montaigne's book in seventeenth-century cultural and intellectual life. Once again the primary qualities of the book are identified as those of an ennobled *gentilhomme*: *liberté* and *franchise*. But they are judged to be 'illegal' by this high-ranking citizen of the republic of letters. Montaigne has put himself above the laws of decency, illegitimately erecting himself as an example, a noble patron-author, in the eyes of the public. His book is to the rural gentleman student of humane letters who cannot be bothered to study Seneca in Latin what the breviary is to the average parish priest who cannot be bothered to study the Bible in Latin.[6]

Ultimately, this is not merely a critical response, but a justification for an act of correction. Huet's objections correspond to what Marie de Gournay had described over a century earlier as 'the most general censure with which our book is confronted... that, in an undertaking peculiarly his own, its author depicted himself in it [*d'une entreprise particuliere à luy, son autheur s'y depeint*]'. The problem is 'la particularité' of the post-1582 *Essais*, the fact that they evolve into too private and personal a piece of life-writing on the part of someone whose credentials for publishing a 'memoir' as an exemplary author or *patron* are unclear.

Marie de Gournay replies to this censure with classical and contemporary precedents—precedents not of learned scholars' but of learned soldiers' memoirs. The difference between the fortunes of Caesar's *Commentaries* and Montaigne's *Essais* lies not in the nature of the works or the authors, but in the fame of Caesar's name and the relative obscurity of Montaigne's. Furthermore, contemporary soldiers such as Monluc and La Noue had written 'the register of their actions ('le registre de leurs actions') and offered it to the public, and their memoirs had included private matters such as dreams.[7]

---

[4] Huet, *Huetiana, ou, Pensées diverses de M. Huet*, sigs. A7r–8r. Some of the translation is taken from Krause, *Idle pursuits*, 148.

[5] On Lancre, see the opening section of 1.5, and 1.5.4, 1.5.7.

[6] Literally, a breviary is the summary of the prayers that a priest in orders is obliged to recite, the offices he must say, at set hours of each day. Metaphorically, a breviary is a book which is by one's side, on one's mantlepiece, on one's bedside table, and which habitually informs one's speech and writing. An alternative expression in regular use by the seventeenth century—one applied both to the *Essais* and to his favourite prayer by Pierre de L'Estoile—was 'vade-mecum'.

[7] For this and the previous paragraph, see 'Preface sur Les Essais de Michel Seigneur de Montaigne par sa Fille d'Alliance', NP16/BVH Paris 1595, f. e3.

But from the 1660s, the French republic of letters and the Roman Catholic Church became less and less tolerant of the *particularité* of the fully evolved *Essais* first published in 1595 with an apology by Marie de Gournay. In 1676 the *Essais* were placed on the Roman Catholic Index, more for moral reasons connected with the contemporary critiques of Port-Royal and the Jansenists than for strictly doctrinal reasons.[8]

When Huet writes in 1711 that Montaigne's *liberté* has a certain utility, within bounds, beyond which it degenerates into *licence*, he is implicitly recommending expurgation, not prohibition. He may, indeed, be endorsing the forms in which Montaigne's work had been published in France for nearly forty years. In *L'Esprit des Essais* (Paris: C. de Sercy, 1677), and again in *Pensées de Montaigne propres a former l'esprit et les moeurs* (Paris: Chez Anisson, 1700), the *Essais* were indeed reduced within the bounds of public utility. The *particularités*—the personal digressions, the private memoirs, the *fadaises domestiques*—were removed. The passage Huet recalls Scaliger citing—the passage which most closely resembles a domestic memoir—is just one of the casualties in these editions. In the edition of 1700 the *Essais* become *Montaniana*, a respectable miscellany of sententious and polite literary conversation worthy of public circulation in the republic of letters.[9]

2.5.2 THE *AFFRANCHISSEMENT* OF AMATEUR READER-WRITERS

There is a larger, more important point. The *Essais* are there as a daily book of reference on mantelpieces all over the countryside. They feature in Huet's remarks as *the* index of countless nexuses of informal learning involving those who aspire to noble values and status. These nexuses contribute to a broader social process that had begun in the late medieval period but that had accelerated since the Reformation: the *affranchissement* of a public of private reader-writers consisting largely of lay people and secular clergy pursuing studies in their own time, in their own ways and spaces, for their own purposes ('free literates').

These reader-writers did not necessarily share Huet's inherited passion for rigorous, methodical application to biblical and humane letters. But they did use letters for practical self-accounting, for the assumption in their private reading and writing of the roles of quasi-noble *auteur* and *patron*, roles which might then inform their assumption of public *personae* such as that of the mayor of Bordeaux. In 2.3 and 2.4, we considered some evidence of the role of the *Essais* in the same process in England.[10]

---

[8] Armogathe and Carraud, 'Les *Essais* de Montaigne dans les archives du Saint-Office', 91–4; Quantin, 'Les censures de Montaigne à l'Index romain: précisions et corrections', 147–50 (for information on the censor in 1676, Antoine Gilles).

[9] Sayce and Maskell, 172–6.

[10] English manuscript miscellanies provide evidence of the ways in which '[p]rivate individuals, in thinking of themselves as citizens and using texts to develop their political language, took on public

As a Jesuit-trained scholar of the old republic of letters, Huet judges this process of enfranchisement of amateur reader-writers to be superficial, licentious, vain, and abusive.[11] Furthermore, he associates it—and the *Essais*—with a generic pair of books in which early modern householders from the provinces to the court habitually read and wrote, a pair which denotes the link between their private reading and their miscellaneous, private self-accounting: the breviary (of divine or secular offices) and the written register of daily experiences and readings. These days, Huet is saying, any hare-catcher with a breviary, a pen, and some paper can pretend to be a noble author, can memorialize themselves in writing. They can praise themselves to their posterity as though they were some sort of knightly paragon of piety and learning ('his secret affectation and his pride in boasting of his employments, the number of his servants, and the reputation which he had acquired').

So the copy Huet visualizes on the mantelpiece of the country gentleman is a breviary in the pejorative sense that it symbolically frees him from the obligation to engage with a whole library of learning, to conform quasi-monastically to a rule of study and behaviour, to emulation of scholarly and saintly *patrons*, in the daily reading that informs his conversation. Furthermore, it quickly instructs readers with claims or aspirations to gentle status and values how to assume the distinction of noble *liberté* and *franchise* in writing, how to become exemplary authors themselves, how to erect themselves as *patrons* for an audience.

For the other book implicitly invoked by Huet is a book in which the country gentleman might personally write on a daily basis, assisted by his breviaries and vade mecums: a manuscript book in which he registers domestic and personal matters, in which he distinguishes himself from *preneurs de lièvres*, and acts as his own panegyrist, writing down his *res gestae* in the way that professional writers had chronicled the deeds of truly noble men for centuries. We have already encountered one example of such a book, inspired by the *Essayes*, produced by a country gentleman in England: Sir Henry Slingsby's book of remembrance (see 2.4.2).

Huet points us, then, to the larger relationship between private memory and the written record. In later medieval and early modern pyschology, memory is a power by means of which the soul actively selects and stores images for recall and use. To write, to copy or conserve a written document, is actively to create and store a *mémoire* of something, a *mémoire* that will be sought out and used by someone in the future. The historiography of the use of writing and written documents to keep the memory of public—governmental, corporate, scholastic—institutions is well

---

personae and thus laid claim to the right and obligation to speak, write, and read freely and to participate in the governance of the realm'. See David Colclough, *Freedom of speech in early Stuart England* (Cambridge: Cambridge University Press, 2005), 9.

[11] Roger Chartier, 'The practical impact of writing', in Roger Chartier (ed.), *A History of private life, volume 3: Passions of the Renaissance* (Cambridge, Mass: Belknap Press of Harvard University Press, 1989), 111–59, 124: 'The growing number of those who could read and write and the proliferation of printed matter caused disarray among "clerks"…who had hitherto enjoyed a monopoly of the production and discussion of knowledge.' On Huet and the Republic of Letters, see April Shelford, *Transforming the republic of letters: Pierre-Daniel Huet and European intellectual life, 1650–1720* (Rochester, N.Y.: University of Rochester Press, 2007).

served.[12] The historiography of the use of writing to record the memory of private individuals, families, and networks is relatively new and is advancing in piecemeal fashion in different disciplines.

The scholarly pioneer Armando Petrucci identified the emergence of the figure of the 'free literate' in the twelfth and thirteenth centuries (see the 'General Introduction' to both volumes, in Volume 1), with the production of privately written register-books or *libri-registri* of two principal types: the deluxe register-book, professionally produced for private patrons, and the *zibaldone* or 'hodgepodge' book. The latter type of register-book or *libro-registro* could be written and compiled over long periods by reader-writers within a family, and characteristically accumulated documentary and literary texts in a disorderly and miscellaneous fashion. It was an instrument of the demand for extra-mural, auto-didactic acculturation, a tool for the professional and personal formation of the merchant whose need for writing was connected above all with the conduct of administration both in business and in the household.[13]

Most historians who have followed Petrucci have proceeded by distinguishing a particular type of private memorial writing and analysing it in serial fashion. Madeleine Foisil influentially divided private-sphere writing ('l'écriture du for privé') into 'journals', consisting of *livres de raison* and diaries, and memoirs, which correspond to classical 'commentaries' and were compiled by those who took part in affairs or were eyewitnesses of events. The latter were worthy to be offered to the public in print. The former were concerned with receipts and expenditures, or with other daily transactions, personal and social, and were private forms of writing, of no public utility.[14]

However, the examples of Slingsby in England and L'Estoile in France, encountered in 2.4.2 and 2.1.8, would indicate that this distinction is difficult to maintain in practice. More convincing is Bernard Beugnot's account of the variable 'interferences' between two points of view—that of the documentary *livre de raison* and the reflective *livre de retraite*—in all instances of memorial writing.[15]

Family historians concentrate on the *livres de famille/livres de raison/libri di famiglia* that survive from the thirteenth century on. In the historiography of medieval Italy, Arrigo Castellani first delimited a domain of familial and domestic writings originating in the aptitude of the merchant-bourgeois to write and to inscribe himself in time. Within this privatized tradition of memorial writing, the simple account book could be the germ of more complex works: in one direction historical memoirs, chronicles, and historiography; in the other, moral reflections and intimate journals. The deposition of the memorial notes was normally chronological

[12] The fundamental study is M. T. Clanchy, *From memory to written record, England 1066–1307* (2nd edn., Oxford: Blackwell, 1993).
[13] Armando Petrucci, *Scrivere e leggere nell'Italia medievale* (Milan: Sylvestre Bonnard, 2007), 178–9, 183–9.
[14] M. Foisil, 'L'écriture du for privé', in Roger Chartier (ed.), *De la Renaissance aux Lumières* (Paris: Seuil, 1986), 333–69.
[15] Bernard Beugnot, 'Livre de raison, livre de retraite: interférences des points de vue chez les mémorialistes', in Noemi Hepp and Jacques Hennequin (eds.), *Les valeurs chez les mémorialistes français du XVIIe siècle avant la Fronde* (Paris: Éditions Klincksieck, 1979), 47–64.

(often day-by-day) but could also be thematic (e.g. a section on prescriptions and remedies).[16]

But other historians question how applicable these distinctions are in practice. Klapisch-Zuber and Bérard doubt whether it is useful or practical to consider 'family books' as a distinct genre, or to separate out the writing of such books from other modalities of domestic writing. Though using the label 'livres de famille', they work with a very wide category of 'domestic and memorial writings ('écritures domestiques et mémorielles') or 'memorial family writing' ('écriture familiale de la mémoire'), distinct from 'professional writings' ('écrits professionels') and from authored literary works.[17]

They identify the fundamental trait of these written memoirs of self and others as the fact that they are destined only for 'a family circle...unique, non-communicable to an unknown public, nor transmissible except within the family, *ad usum familiae*'. Their analysis offers three fundamental elements:

> the 'consciousness of the self', and at the same time, the 'representation of the [individual] self' but in relation to the family 'us'; the concept of time, which equally assumes the role of organising the writing and the book; the power of writing, which comprehends at one and the same time a capacity (literacy) and a space of evolution which is historically and socially conditioned.[18]

Furthermore, these documents typically evidence a process of writing and rewriting, as events are transcribed *post factum*, copied from other documents, re-evaluated, in the hope of a good reception within the family, generation, group, or community. They are open works in the sense that the time of writing—which is neither composition after the fact, nor unitary reconstruction, but registration as things happen ('enregistrement contemporain des faits')—remains of necessity discontinuous, irregular, subject to events.[19]

This mode of writing, I argue, fundamentally informs the composition and use of the *Essais* in early modern Europe, in ways that have not been fully recognized. This is partly because social historians and intellectual historians divide up and segregate their sources. The former tend to isolate for analysis the records of family and commercial life. But—especially once we get to the early modern period—there are continuities not just within the ensemble of family registers and journals, but also between those and other kinds of privately compiled or owned books.

From the 1420s and 1430s in Italy the note-keeping method was increasingly identified with humanist education; reading became indistinguishable from writing for subsequent generations of the educated elite across Europe.[20] The more professional forms of this activity required the keeping of highly structured

---

[16] Raul Mordenti, 'Les livres de famille en Italie', *Annales*, 59 (2004), 785–804, 785, 788, 793.

[17] Claude Cazalé Bérard and Christiane Klapisch-Zuber, 'Mémoire de soi et des autres dans les livres de famille italiens', *Annales*, 59 (2004), 805–26, 818, 826, 811, 809.

[18] Cazalé Bérard and Klapisch-Zuber, 'Mémoire de soi', 809, 811.

[19] Cazalé Bérard and Klapisch-Zuber, 'Mémoire de soi', 812–13.

[20] Anthony Grafton, 'Conflict and harmony in the *Collegium Gellianum*', in Leofranc Holford-Strevens and Amiel Vardi (eds.), *The worlds of Aulus Gellius* (Oxford: Oxford University Press, 2004), 282–317.

commonplace books, artificial memory-tools by means of which formal treatises and orations could be systematically compiled for official study and speech-making.

But there were classical precedents—most notably Aulus Gellius—for practices of note-keeping that, like the domestic memorials mentioned above, were 'discontinuous, irregular, subject to events'. In ancient Rome, these types of ephemeral daily notes were compared to merchants' rough daily accounts and distinguished from the *tabula* or *codex*—the *registre*—in which these looser notes and accounts could be re-entered on a monthly or other basis. Early modern scholars and other professionals at leisure could emulate this practice by simply keeping notes in the order they made them, day-by-day, depending on what they were reading or observing. The resulting manuscript and printed collections tended, following Gellius, to claim a greater liberty and to reclaim the subjectivity lost when notes were immediately sorted under pre-existing headings.[21] We have already seen in 2.2.4 how Goulart placed the *Essais* in this tradition at the end of the sixteenth century, and we inferred in 2.3.7 that Cleland did the same in England.

The more arbitrarily compiled miscellanies of readings, together with annotations entered in the margins of books, should also fall, then, into the broad category of private memorial writings we are considering. As William Sherman has pointed out, there was no hard and fast distinction between reading notes made in book margins and other kinds of private written memorials. Reading was closely paired with recording in writing.

Printed books in the early modern period were used to archive memoranda of all kinds, not just commentary on the text. They were used 'to document family histories and financial obligations, to record prayers, poems, and recipes'— described by Heidi Brayman Hackel as 'marks of recording'. The margins, fly-leaves, and blank spaces of Books of Hours were used in late medieval England as places to chronicle personal, familial, and even national events. By the seventeenth century copies of Sidney's *Arcadia* were serving the same purpose.[22] And in a period when religious and worldly concerns were intertwined, should not personalized spiritual exercises and prayers compiled in private writing also fall under the general category of *l'écriture du for privé*?

The problem of what is to be included, and under which generic headings, is less important here than the general trend. The practice of daily note-taking, record-keeping, and account-keeping was widespread amongst the educated elite by the end of the sixteenth century, and was closely associated with reading. It had its roots in the thirteenth century, when we begin to see the documentary traces of

[21] Jean-Marc Chatelain, 'Les recueils d'adversaria aux xvie et xviie siècles', in Henri-Jean Martin and Frédéric Barbier (eds.), *Le livre et l'historien: études offertes en l'honneur du Professeur Henri-Jean Martin* (Geneva: Droz, 1997), 169–86.

[22] For this and the previous paragraph see William H. Sherman, 'Used Books', *Shakespeare Studies*, 28 (2000), 145–8, 146–7; Eamon Duffy, *Marking the hours: English people and their prayers 1240–1570* (New Haven: Yale University Press, 2006), 44–5; Brayman Hackel, *Reading material*, 138, 162–3. For a general study of the relationship between reading and recording in private devotional contexts, see Kate Narveson, *Bible readers and lay writers in early modern England: gender and self-definition in an emergent writing culture* (Farnham: Ashgate, 2012).

a vast accounting enterprise stretching from double-entry book-keeping, communal chronicling, and manorial accounting to the family scrapbook, the personal ledger, and so forth.[23]

During the fifteenth and sixteenth centuries, with the advent and dissemination of humanist note-taking practices, the increasing availability of cheaper paper, the invention of the handpress, the effects of the Reformation, and the further extension of state bureaucracy, more and more heads of household across the social scale from artisans, merchants, and secular priests to magistrates and nobility adopted record-keeping in the conduct of their personal and familial, as in their official and public lives. They began to account for themselves, to write and preserve their own personal archives or 'registers', often in conjunction with their keeping, borrowing, and use of printed books from bibles and breviaries to almanacs and histories.

If one was a prominent scholar like Huet or a nobleman like Monluc, it was more likely that suitably polished, not to say confected, versions of one's personal letters or memoirs would be considered a useful addition to the printed record. But many people who did not fall into these categories were also keeping and 'publishing' (in more limited circles) copies of books, letters, and writings (in so-called 'manuscript miscellanies') for themselves, for their 'particular' use and that of their friends and families, outside the context of any official function in public trade or affairs, in public study or public worship. This was especially true of women. What utility could these possibly have beyond the households and local circles for which they were intended?[24]

This is the trend within which Huet places both the *Essais* and his own *Huetiana*. As we heard in 1.1.4, 1.1.10, and the beginning of 1.3, the *Essais* have many of the characteristics of a privately compiled register of personal notes and memorials distributed under apparently random headings. But Huet associates the unexpurgated *Essais*, and the talk and writing stimulated by the work in provincial households, with the most 'particular' of these personal archival books: those not suitable for public dissemination in print like his own literarily polished *ana*, and the memoirs and letters of high intellectual and political actors.

In such lowly books, written for oneself and for family and close friends, householders might indeed register their *emplois*, the number of their servants, and the reputation they had acquired, along with intimate details of their domestic routine and their 'connoissance du monde'. But Huet sees no value in the *liberté*, the *affranchissement* they evidence. He would keep free literates in their place.

In order to reassess Montaigne's relationship to the trend identified and deplored by Huet, let us consider two such manuscript books and their functions. One—L'Estoile's—has already featured in an earlier chapter (2.1.8). These books draw

---

[23] Mordenti, 'Les livres de famille en Italie', 788; James Alfred Aho, *Confession and bookkeeping: the religious, moral, and rhetorical roots of modern accounting* (New York: State University of New York Press, 2005); Armando Petrucci, *Writers and readers in medieval Italy: studies in the history of written culture*, trans. Charles Radding (New Haven: Yale University Press, 1995).

[24] James S. Amelang, *The flight of Icarus: artisan autobiography in early modern Europe* (Stanford: Stanford University Press, 1998); Richard Beadle and Colin Burrow (eds.), *Manuscript miscellanies, c.1450–1700* (London: British Library, 2011). For women's manuscript writing, see the Warwick University Perdita Project (<http://web.warwick.ac.uk/english/perdita/html/>).

upon the *Essais* at different points during the long seventeenth century between the first publication of Marie de Gournay's remarks and Huet's comments. They are not authored by scholars of the republic of letters, though one of the two is connected with such scholars; they mostly register notes and observations on a daily basis, in the order they occur, subject to events. One is compiled in a centre (Paris), one in a related periphery (Rheims); one by a peripheral participant in the literary circles of the capital's *parlement* (Pierre de L'Estoile), one by a participant in much more limited and local circles of friends and family (Jean Maillefer). But they have much in common with each other, and with Montaigne's project of self-accounting.

Neither L'Estoile's nor Maillefer's project originates purely in reading, whether in the *Essais* or in other books.[25] They are personal projects of self-accounting that are aided in the course of their realization by selected extracts from others' writings. But nevertheless, both, in different ways, privilege the *Essais* as a breviary. The two authors first encounter Montaigne's work in the period just before they start keeping their journals and form a close relationship with it—as Montaigne did with Amyot's Plutarch, published just as he started writing. Montaigne becomes a *patron* for the manuscript writers' own *naturels* as registered in a particular book, in a particular form of memorial writing—as we saw he did for Henry Slingsby and for Pieter van Veen in 2.4. And Montaigne, L'Estoile, Maillefer, Slingsby, and Van Veen all collect their personal daily accounts in just one place—*un registre, un livre de bonne foi*.

Both L'Estoile's and Maillefer's manuscript journals are, furthermore, associated with particular circumstances analogous to Montaigne's own: a 'retreat' from professional or commercial business, melancholy humours, and illness in later life; news and other matters that have to be weighed up; troubled, even shameful emotions that need to be reviewed and regulated. They are associated with particular spaces for reading and writing: a study in a townhouse that is regularly visited by other men of letters (L'Estoile); a cabinet in a country *logis* frequented mainly by close family (Maillefer).

Both works are unmistakeably authored by particular individuals who do indeed memorialize and praise themselves, set themselves up as examples, even if in carefully moderated ways. Although both writers use literary skills and address an audience, neither document is conceived—as Huet's and Montaigne's were—as a literary work destined for the handpress. Neither was published in any form until the eighteenth and nineteenth centuries, and neither has yet been published in a full, critical edition.[26]

L'Estoile's and Maillefer's works have private administrative functions of distinctive kinds. As written records they are kept to be *contrôlés* or reviewed when necessary, for specific reasons. In this respect, both have elements in common—as

---

[25] When I refer to L'Estoile's project, or journal, I am referring principally to his three volumes of 'Tablettes' as a self-contained enterprise, related to but also distinct from his previous *registres-journaux*.

[26] Though a critical edition of L'Estoile's *registres* for the reign of Henri III has been published by Librairie Droz in Geneva.

scholars have claimed the *Essais* do—with a type of archival document mentioned earlier in this section and largely invented by modern historiography: *livres de raison* or *libri-registri*, personal record books.

But it is important to be clear from the outset that the diary of family events is just one 'form' they deploy, if such a form can be said to have existed then. They also incorporate elements that modern historians associate with the ledger, the memoir, the essay, the spiritual exercise, the commonplace book. They are *sui generis* because shaped by a particular person's cultural and administrative needs. They represent the most 'secret' archives kept by the reader-writers in question, those intended primarily for their own and their most intimate family and friends' reference. Over a long *durée*, with *liberté de jugement* and *franchise*, they register in avowed good faith both the religious and the worldly conversation of individual authors embedded in a network of family and friends.

2.5.3 L'ESTOILE AND THE *REGISTRE*

In 2.1.8 we heard how L'Estoile—a near contemporary of Montaigne, a member of the legal bourgeoisie, and a one-time office-holder (royal secretary and *grand audiencier*) in the Parisian *parlement*—used a copy of the *Essais* as his vade mecum in the summer of 1610.[27]

But we did not consider just how familiar various types of *registre* were in his and Montaigne's world. Manuscript registers and paper journals were ubiquitous in the literary lives of humanistically educated *parlementaires* such as Montaigne and L'Estoile, and—as we shall in 2.5.6—of merchants such as Maillefer. Registration was one of the primary applications of writing in the later medieval and early modern period. To register something was to keep a written memoir of something done ('res gestae') for future reference, stored in a book in the way one would store other items in a strongbox.[28]

In Latin, English, and French, the terms *regestum/registrum* and 'register'/'registre' constituted a very wide category of rolls and books in which both originals and copies of letters, acts, minutes, and other documents were kept or collected.[29] There were many different types of *registre*, both more private and more public.

Cotgrave defines the French term in English as '[a] Record, Register, memorial, a book of remembrances, days book; and (more particularly) a book of Entries, Acts, Orders, or Decrets'.[30] Montaigne and L'Estoile would, indeed,

[27] I learned much about L'Estoile from Tom Hamilton, 'Compiling histories of the French Wars of Religion: Pierre de L'Estoile's collection in context (1558–1611)', paper given at 'Transforming information: record keeping in the early modern world', The British Academy, 9–10 April 2014.

[28] Petrucci, *Scrivere e leggere nell'Italia medievale*, 34.

[29] Du Cange cites the following definitions of 'Regestum': 'Liber in quem regerentur commentarii quivis, vel Epistolae Summorum Pontificum'; 'Regestum vocatur liber continens memorias aliorum librorum et epistolas in unum collectas'; 'Registrum, liber qui rerum gestarum memoriam continet'. University of Mannheim, Du Cange, tom. IV, p. 619.

[30] Related entries in Cotgrave's 1611 French–English dictionary (available online at <http://www.pbm.com/~lindahl/cotgrave/>) include 'Livre, ou papier Journal' ('A Journal, Diary, day-book,

have understood a 'registre' most particularly to be a type of record kept by public administrative bodies, and especially by the superior and inferior courts of the French *parlements*.[31] In England they shared the 'common characteristic of being edited collections, books or rolls, which had been compiled from primary sources from separate pieces of parchment'. They could be collections of authentic official records or of transcriptions for internal reference use only.[32]

French parliamentary registers were more likely to be books than rolls and were written by *greffiers* or *notaires*. A *registre* could be both the preliminary redaction of an act made on the day in a notebook and a later transcription made in an official parchment book—a double meaning that is important for understanding the transition in the nature of L'Estoile's *Registres-journaux*. Furthermore, the Paris *parlement* also ordered that *registres secrets* (which could amount to particular leaves) of deliberations that they did not want publicized were kept apart and not copied into the official (that is, public) registers or parchment books. The justification for doing this might be, for example, that the deliberations concerned the internal direction and regulation of the *chambres* of the court.[33] The secret registers of the *Parlement* of Bordeaux were 'an after-the-fact summary record of closed deliberations of the *Grand'Chambre*... [they] often explain the motives, animosities and the alliances of members of the courts'. Members of the court transcribed extracts from these secret registers into their own private manuscript compilations.[34]

We do not know whether Montaigne kept such a compilation, or just knew of them, but we do know that his official life for many years (1557–70) revolved around the reporting of cases from *registres*, and around the registering of decisions in the *Grand'Chambre* of the *Parlement* of Bordeaux. L'Estoile's office as *audiencier*

Register kept of daily occurences'); 'Ephimeris' ('A Journal, or daily Register of things done'); 'Papier jornal' ('A Journal, Diary, or Day-book, a Register kept, or Commentary written, of daily actions or accidents'); 'Controlle, ou Contrerolle' ('A controlement, or contrarolement; the copy of a role (of accounts, & c.) a Parallel of the same quality and content, with the original; also, a controlling, or overseeing; and the Office of a Controler, or overseer; also, a Controler, or overseer'); 'Enregistrer' ('To register, to inroll'); 'L'estat d'une Maison' ('A certain, and setled order of the government, service and expence of a great mans house; also, the List, Catalogue, Register, or Check-roll, containing the names, ranks, and sanctions of all the officers, and servants therein'); 'Greffier' ('A Register, Pregnotary, or principal Clerk to a Court; a Secondary in an Office, or Court; a Clerk of Assize; or of Inrolments'); 'Insinuer' ('To enter; to register; or, to enter into a Register, or Office-book; (or as a French Lawyer describes it) publier, et notifier par Acte par devant le Juge, qui ordonne en estre faict Registre'); 'Inventaire' ('An Inventory; List, Roll; Memorial, Record, Register of many several things'); 'Mettre en ligne de compte' ('To reckon, esteem, account, allow of; to register in the Kalendar of account; to remember, or mention in discourse, as a thing of some importance'); 'Memorial' ('A memorial, record, register; a book of remembrances, a note, mark, or token for remembrance'); 'Roule' ('A rowl, a List, Inventory, Catalogue, Bill, Scrowl, Register, of Names, or of Causes; also, a rowling, folding, turning, rounding; also, mutability, unsteadiness, continual motion').

[31] ARTFL, 'Dictionnaires d'autrefois', 'Registre'.

[32] Clanchy, *From memory to written record*, 61, 103–4.

[33] F. Boutaric (ed.), *Actes du Parlement de Paris. Première série—de l'an 1254 à l'an 1328*, 2 vols. (Paris: Henri Plon, 1863), 'Notice sur les Archives du Parlement de Paris', xii–xviii.

[34] Katherine Almquist, 'Examining the evidence: Montaigne in the *Registres secrets du Parlement de Bordeaux*', *Montaigne Studies*, 16 (2004), 45–74, 47 and *passim*.

(which he left in 1601) gave him responsibility for overseeing a number of registers of the king's incomings and acts, and for having each entry literally 'sealed' in those registers, with the help of a *contrôleur*.[35]

But he also kept, collected, borrowed, and circulated *registres* that had been privately compiled. So, for example, on one occasion he wrote out some extracts from a friend's *registre*:

> On Saturday 23 [January 1610], M. de Bossé lent me a handwritten register of his [*un sien Registre*], bound in parchment, long and narrow [*long et estroit*], like the paper books of apothecaries or those that women keep for their household expenses [*comme sont ces Papiers Dapotiquaires, ou ceux des Femmes pour la Despense de leur Maison*], in which there are several weighty discourses, even theological ones (I have most, including the best ones); many tried-and-tested or unapproved drug recipes, of which I also have many, and all full of drolleries and amusing witticisms [*Drolleries et Rencontres plaisantes*]. From which, for pleasure, I have extracted the following, to add to the masses of others I have...I found in the corner of one leaf of this register the honours of M. de Sully, with the written heading: Noble titles, 1609, July. Maximilian de Béthune, knight, Duke of Sully...[36]

So there was a recognizable kind of paper book, referred to as a 'registre', that might normally be used for an apothecary's or domestic household accounts, but that could also be used for personal records of other kinds, in this case 'graves discours', 'receptes', 'drolleries', and 'rencontres plaisantes'. The key point is that weighty theological discourses could be found copied into paper account-books. It is difficult to say whether L'Estoile's own *registre* could have been described as 'long et estroit'—whether, in other words, it may recognizably have been of this physical type.

L'Estoile appears to say that he already has many of the things Bossé has copied into his *registre*, but he extracts first some 'drolleries' on the topic of marriage. He then finds in the corner of one leaf of the book the titles of M. de Sully, which he does not have, and copies them into his paper book.[37] He often says how much pleasure he took in making such extracts in writing, finding it difficult to take his hand from the paper. In one case (Barclay's *Satyricon*) he writes that he would willingly have transcribed the whole book, so much was the elegant Petronian satire to his taste.[38] And these are just a couple of instances of a whole culture of lending and borrowing, buying and selling of *registres*, and of sharing and copying of *extraits*, that is revealed by L'Estoile's records—including at least three mentions of the sharing of his own 'Registre Journal'.[39]

---

[35] Florence Greffe and José Lothe, *La vie, les livres et les lectures de Pierre de l'Estoile: nouvelles recherches* (Paris: H. Champion, 2004), 95–8.

[36] BnF MS Fr. 10301, fols. 243v, 246v–47r/*Journal Henri IV*, vol. 3, 11–13 (January 1610). On the same day, L'Estoile lends Bossé in return a 'livre de recettes'.

[37] BnF MS Fr.10301 fols. 244r–47r/*Journal Henri IV*, vol. 3, 11–13 (January 1610).

[38] BnF MS Fr. 10301, fol. 132v/*Journal Henri IV*, vol. 2, 639 (August 1609).

[39] In the *Journal Henri IV* see: vol. 2, 45 (October 1601; he takes extracts from the *registres* of the *parlement* with the help of a *greffier* friend); vol. 2, 165–6 (June 1605; he receives an 'extrait' of ten leaves from a Jesuitical tract just arrived from Antwerp, shared by 'un honnête homme et docte'); vol. 2, 214 (BnF MS Fr. 10300, fol. 25r; December 1606; lends his 'Gros Registre Journal in-folio' to M. Despinelle, in return for some 'poésies courtisances' then in circulation); vol. 2, 251–2 (June 1607;

The general point is that L'Estoile is important not just as someone who happened to have read passages he liked in Montaigne. He is an exceptional representative of a whole public of reader-writers in early seventeenth-century France immersed simultaneously and fluidly in both the compilation and circulation of private archival *registres* and in the world of printed books such as Montaigne's *Essais*. He does not study with scholarly rigour. As a free literate, he offers an extreme example of a widespread practice of personal archiving or record-keeping.

2.5.4 L'ESTOILE'S LIFE OF READING AND WRITING

On 2 July 1606, L'Estoile opened a folio book of blank paper and began writing a *registre-journal* (Illus. 2.5.1). In some respects this was nothing new. An obscure *parlementaire*, he is now known to scholars of early modern French history as the memorialist who kept a continuous manuscript journal from 1573 to 1611—from the aftermath of the St Bartholomew Day's massacre to the aftermath of the assassination of Henri IV. L'Estoile's manuscripts were edited by Brunet and printed as a single twelve-volume work, the *Mémoires-Journaux*, between 1875 and 1883, and as a single *Journal* of two kings' reigns by Lefèvre and Martin for Gallimard between 1943 and 1960.[40]

---

the younger M. Dupuy lends a manuscript, other papers, and curious writings, with an inventory of all the books and writings in his *étude*, in return for a loan of one of his own manuscripts, the 'Bigarrures folatres'); vol. 2, 259 (July 1607; Guichard to write further 'belles choses et curieuses' in a large paper book L'Estoile gives him, which already contains the transcription of the old 'Journal' Dupuy lent him); vol. 2, 279 (October 1607; his 'Journal' in-folio of the reign of Henri III is lent to Dupuy, who lends him back in turn 'un registre in-folio' with 'plusieurs notables recueils de ce temps'); vol. 2, 292–3 (BnF MS Fr. 10300, fol. 126r; November 1607; he lends his 'Registre Journal' of the first years of the reign of Henri IV to M. Dupuy, who has shared with him the fruits of his own 'recherches... fort curieuses et secrètes'); vol. 2, 296 (November 1607; M. Dupuy lends him 'un sien gros registre in-folio ... de lieux communs, qu'il a extraits des plus célèbres et meilleurs auteurs, disposés par un bel ordre', and 'un livre d'extraits des Vies de Plutarque'); vol. 2, 415, 421 (January 1609; he lends 'un mien registre, relié en carton, in folio', containing 'ramas curieux' and letters by Scaliger, to M. Justel; then another with 'harangues', etc., a few days later); vol. 2, 447 (BnF MS Fr. 10301, fol. 22v; April 1609; sells a 'registre manuscrit' to M. Lescuyer for an agreed price of 90 livres—but cedes six livres immediately to Lorée, the agent who supplied the coin (twelve 'pistoles'), presumably on Lescuyer's behalf—on condition that Lescuyer supply, at his own expense, a copy of three discourses contained therein; see Illus. 2.5.5); vol. 3, 2–3 (January 1610; a friend sends him on loan an extract of passages from Bellarmine's new book against King James' *Apologia*); vol. 3, 43–54 (March 1610; amuses himself copying 'fadaises' regarding the League from a *registre* of a friend of his, 'M.J.R.'); vol. 3, 91 (May 1610; how 'gens de bien' have contributed to M. Justel's new book from 'leurs vieux registres'). For a detailed study of L'Estoile's exchanges with Pierre Dupuy, see Michel Chopard, 'En marge de la grande érudition, un amateur éclairé, Pierre de L'Estoile', *Histoire et Littérature: Les écrivains et la politique* (Paris: Presses Universitaires de France, 1977), 205–35.

[40] Pierre de L'Estoile, *Mémoires-journaux*, eds. Gustave Brunet et al., 12 vols. (Paris: Librairie des bibliophiles, 1875–96); Pierre de L'Estoile, *Journal pour le règne de Henri III (1574–1589)*, ed. Louis Raymond Lefèvre (Paris: Gallimard, 1943); *Journal Henri V.* Librairie Droz has issued a new critical edition of L'Estoile's journal of the reign of Henri III, but has so far not extended the edition into the reign of Henri IV.

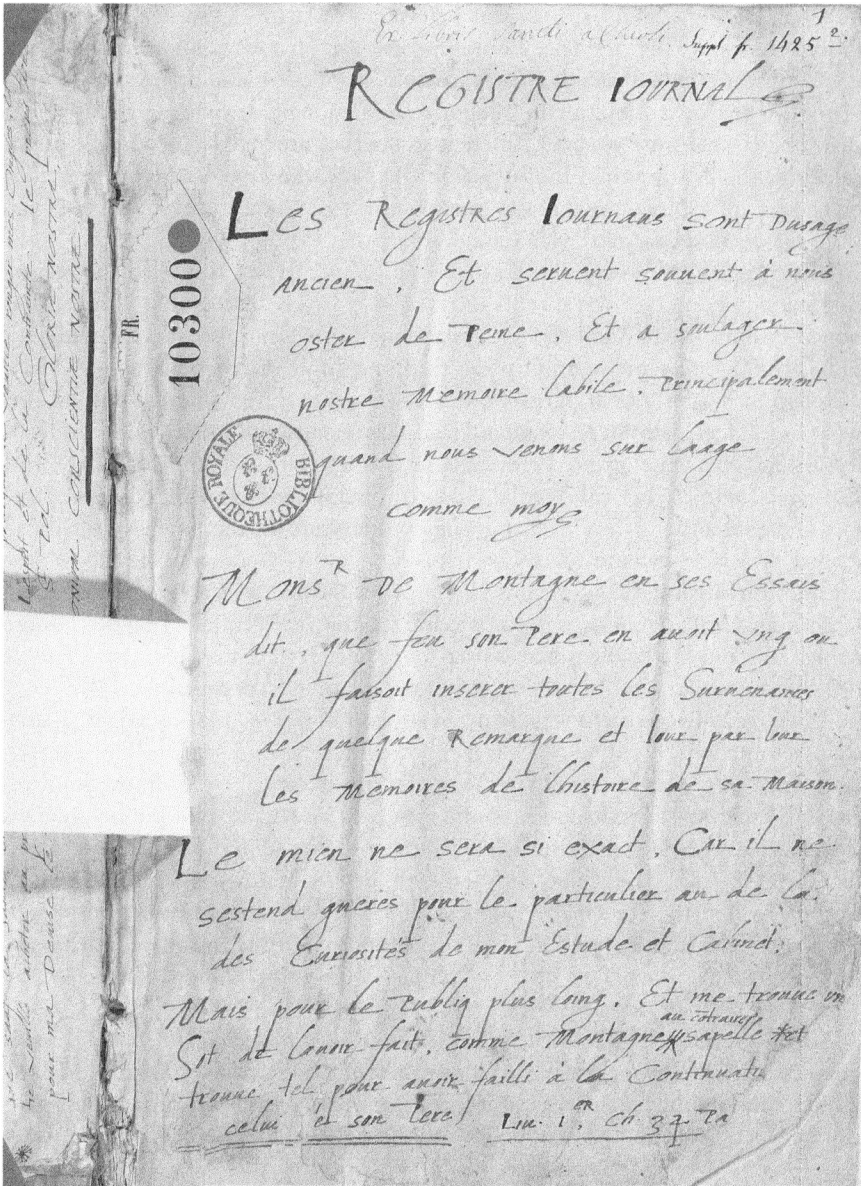

Illus. 2.5.1. Bibliothèque nationale de France, MS Fr. 10300, fol.1r (Pierre de L'Estoile's 'Registre' from July 1606 to January 1609). Reproduced by permission of the Bibliothèque nationale de France, Paris.

When heavily edited by Brunet or Lefèvre and Martin, L'Estoile's writings can indeed appear to be a single, homogeneous text that continuously chronicles the historical events of the day. But the moment one sees and opens the volumes in the Manuscripts room of the Bibliothèque nationale de France, it is apparent that the books themselves tell a different story. They are heterogeneous; the physical form, the handwriting, the layout on the page, the very nature of the record being kept quite obviously mutates from volume to volume and even in some cases from one section of a particular volume to another.[41]

L'Estoile's large folio register of the reign of Henri III was compiled and revised over a long period between *c.*1580 and *c.*1606.[42] It was composed on the basis of notes of public events and of a large collection of copies of miscellaneous materials published in print or manuscript at the time (only a few of which survive). Throughout his entreprise, L'Estoile was writing—or supervising the writing—of what in English historiography would be called 'manuscript miscellanies', and collecting miscellaneous printed materials in conjunction with the compilation of registers. The materials collected and copied predominantly included *libelles*, satires, and contemporary political and religious literature. As they were collected and copied, they were cut-and-pasted, annotated, or commented upon. He was recording and copying out the vituperative literature of the age, with a view to harvesting truthfulness from slander and invective, and shaming the Catholic League.[43] Those copied by hand can be described as user-published texts, in the sense that L'Estoile or his secretaries transcribed them for his and his friends' personal use.

A first, heavily corrected version of the register of the reign of Henri III, a large folio volume with ruled margins, was followed by a second version that incorporates many of the corrections.[44] In the entries themselves, there is almost no material particular to L'Estoile and his family. A Tacitean narrative of public events is interspersed with miscellaneous copied extracts from the published literature collected by L'Estoile. The preliminary leaves to the two manuscripts reveal the ethos of compilation: 'the French liberty of speech' ('la liberté françoise de parler'), which no power on earth can prohibit. This *liberté* finds its principal source in the writings of ancient historians—such as Tacitus—who wrote without flattery of the virtues and vices of princes.[45]

There is a sense in which the ethos of 'freedom of speech' and frank counsel governs L'Estoile's entire project of compilation and composition. We explored the ethical connotations of such historiographical writing in relation to the comparison between de Thou and Montaigne in 2.1.2. Where Tacitus and other classical

---

[41] See McGowan, "'La conversation de ma vie'", for some insights, partly derived from consultation of the manuscripts, that anticipate a few of the points that follow.

[42] BnF MSS Fr. 6678, 6888; Pierre de L'Estoile, *Registre-journal du règne de Henri III: Tome I (1574–1575)*, eds. Madeleine Lazard and Gilbert Schrenck (Geneva: Droz, 1992), 33–5. This register is first mentioned in L'Estoile's own records, as a book he is lending to Despinelle, in December 1606. See *Journal Henri IV*, vol. 2, 214.

[43] See Greffe and Lothe, *La vie, les livres*; Antonia Szabari, *Less rightly said: scandals and readers in sixteenth-century France* (Stanford: Stanford University Press, 2010), 195.

[44] BnF, MSS Fr. 6678, 6888.

[45] L'Estoile, *Registre-journal du règne de Henri III: Tome I (1574–1575)*, 53–4.

historians and satirists most effectively conjure this ethos in relation to the compilation of a 'secret' register of public events and discourses, Montaigne is the author who does the same in relation to the keeping of a 'secret' register of the compiler's own private *fantasies*. Montaigne conjures *liberté* as an ethical quality, a quality whose effects are produced by means of the registering and reviewing of one's private conversation in writing.

By the early 1600s, L'Estoile was also compiling a register for the crucial period from 1589, during which year his house was raided and he was arrested by the League as a *politique*.[46] Nevertheless, in the relevant volume, which covers August 1589 to March 1594, we do find more particular notes: a note of a letter lent to him by M. de Sermoise, *the maître des requêtes*, and where to find it; a note of the price of the butter his wife had bought from Madame de Bellemanière.[47] It is a smaller folio size and presents differently—with a less formal aspect, more scratchily written ('fort griffonné'). This 'Registre Journal' is mentioned as a completed work in a note of 10 November 1607, when L'Estoile lends it to M. Dupuy.[48]

So, the nature of the registers being kept was modulating even as L'Estoile continued, after 1589, to compile and edit the volume dealing with the reign of Henri III, and, later, the volumes dealing with the early reign of Henri IV. But L'Estoile decided to address the issue explicitly for the first time in opening a new set of volumes, in 1606, which consolidated the modulation in a particular way.[49]

When one opens and begins reading these three volumes in their original manuscript form it is immediately apparent that they look more like ledgers, with discrete entries, often rounded off by sums of money spent. The *registre-journal* has become more of a personal administrative document—though an administrative document with moral functions—and the writing of it has become more immediate, more day-to-day. With the first of these three volumes, L'Estoile would begin to write portions of his *registre* in a manner closer to the notes he normally scratched with a stylus as ephemeral aides-mémoires in the 'tablettes' ('tables') he kept in his pocket. Indeed, on one occasion he describes writing an anti-papal 'distique' first in his 'tablettes' then directly into his 'registre'.[50]

At the end of the first volume, in a note scribbled vertically up a page stuck into the back inside cover, L'Estoile says this 'Memorial' he has been keeping full of an infinity of *fadaises*, 'written out freely according to my humour', should after his

---

[46] BnF MS Fr. 10299. A reference to a work by de Thou shows that he was writing up his journal for 1590 in 1604 or later. See *Journal Henri IV*, vol. 1, 82.

[47] *Journal Henri IV*, vol. 1, 35–6, 62.

[48] BnF MS Fr. 10300, fol. 126r/*Journal Henri IV*, vol. 2, 292–3.

[49] Greffe and Lothe, *La vie, les livres*, 150.

[50] On the change in L'Estoile's *registre* from July 1606, see Greffe and Lothe, *La vie, les livres*, 149–50; J. F. Michaud and J. J. F. Poujoulat, *Nouvelle collection des Mémoires pour servir à l'histoire de France depuis le XIIIe siècle jusqu'à la fin du XVIIIe:...Registre-journal de Henri III, publié d'après le manuscrit autographe de L'Estoile*, eds J.J. Champollion-Figeac and A.L. Champollion-Figeac (2nd ser., vol. 1; Paris: L'Éditeur du commentaire analytique du code civil, 1837), i, iv–v, ix–xii. On *tablettes*, see *Journal Henri IV*, vol. 2, 377 (October 1608; 'tablettes' kept in his 'pochette' along with a small format copy of the Psalms); *Journal Henri IV*, vol. 3, 17 (January 1610; the anti-papal 'distique'); Roger Chartier, 'Crossing Borders in Early Modern Europe', *Book History*, 8 (2005), 37–50, 46.

death be burned, as it only served him and his memory, his particular occupations and curiosities ('mes particulieres Occupations, et Curiosités').[51]

The fact that L'Estoile is now consciously keeping a new set of distinct volumes is most apparent at the beginning of the second volume. On one title page he entitles the volume 'Secondes tablettes', with a Latin subtitle that begins by adapting one of the fragments (no. 551) of Varro's *Menippean Satires*: 'So do I fashion a life reading and writing. So do I go in the way of melancholy, and I avoid the pestilential venom of this unappeasable beast, the repulsive vapours, the diverse kinds of phantasms, the fantasies. For me, to live is to think.'[52]

The other title page describes the volume as the second register of his curiosities ('Registre second de mes curiosités'), divided into 'particulieres' corresponding to 'tablettes' for his memory, and 'publiques' (Illus. 2.5.2, 2.5.3).[53] At the end of the second volume, having registered the assassination of Henri IV, he says on the penultimate folio that 'I here finish with the life of my king this second register of my melancholy pastimes and my vain and curious researches, both public and private'. He adds on the final folio that he had intended to finish his 'Ephemerides' with 'this' register (i.e. the second), but the turns and mutations of events, both public (the assassination of Henri IV) and private, had persuaded him to continue into a third. He then entitles this third volume a 'Continuation' of both his public and personal memorial journals ('Continuation de mes Memoires Journaux et Curiosités tant Publiques que Particulieres'), and self-consciously concludes it exactly one year later on 15 May 1611.[54]

These three volumes are therefore considered here and in 2.1.8 and 2.7.7 as a work in their own right—part of a larger set of heterogeneous *registres-journaux*, yes, but also distinct, and distinctly related to the *Essais*.

As has already become apparent, L'Estoile does not use just one but various labels for these three books—'registre-journal', 'journal', 'memoire-journal', 'tablettes', 'magazin', 'ephemerides', 'passetemps', 'recherches'. The record being kept, as well as being constantly reviewed and revised, modulates in form and function in response to events. Indeed, with the assassination of Henri IV, it becomes, once again, more of a chronicle of public events, written in a different style on the page, more redolent of the earlier journal of the reign of Henri III. Nevertheless, the continuing admixture of personal administrative notes is strong enough for one

[51] BnF MS Fr. 10301, fol. 321 (inside back cover)/*Journal Henri IV*, vol. 2, 432. L'Estoile did make similar remarks about the earlier *registres-journaux*, which he nevertheless showed to friends and family.

[52] BnF MS Fr. 10301, fol. 1v: 'Sic legendo et scribendo Vitam Procudo, Sic Melancoliæ Obviam eo. Et huius Implacabilis Bestiæ Virus Pestilens, Tetros Vapores, Diversa Phantasmatum Genera, Et Imaginationes Eludo. Mihi Vivere Cogitare est.' The text neither of this nor of the following title page appears in the printed edition used here—see *Journal Henri IV*, vol. 2, 432. 'Eludo' could also mean 'I mock'. The Varronian fragment 551 normally reads 'legendo autem et scribendum vitam procudito'.

[53] BnF MS Fr. 10301, fol. 2r.

[54] BnF MS Fr. 10301, fols. 339v–40r/*Journal Henri IV*, vol. 3, 82–3; BnF MS Fr. 10302, fols. 1r, 189r/*Journal Henri IV*, vol. 3, 88, 248–9.

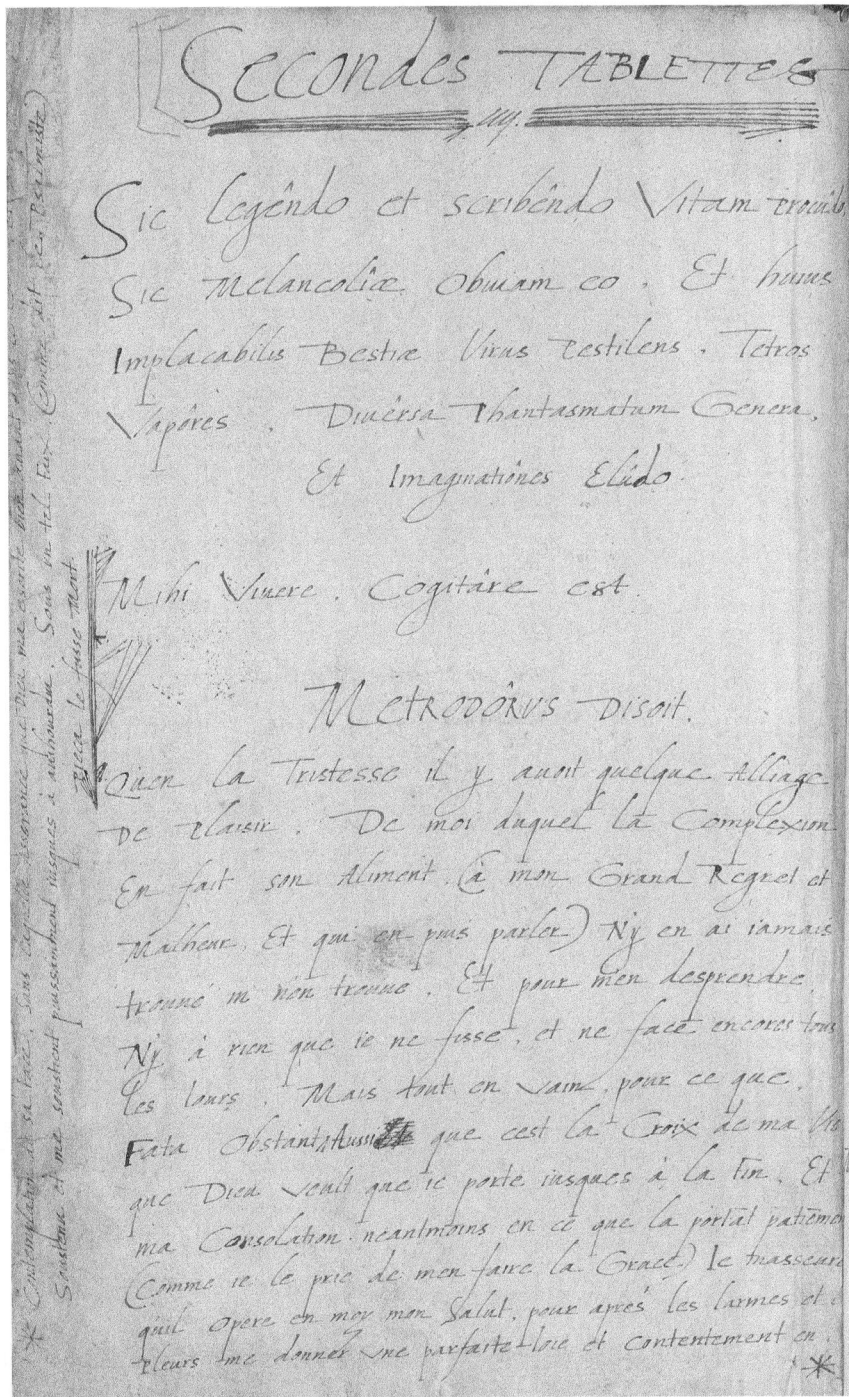

Illus. 2.5.2. Bibliothèque nationale de France, MS Fr. 10301, fol. 1v (Pierre de L'Estoile's 'Registre second de mes curiosités' or 'Secondes tablettes' from February 1609 to May 1610). Reproduced by permission of the Bibliothèque nationale de France, Paris.

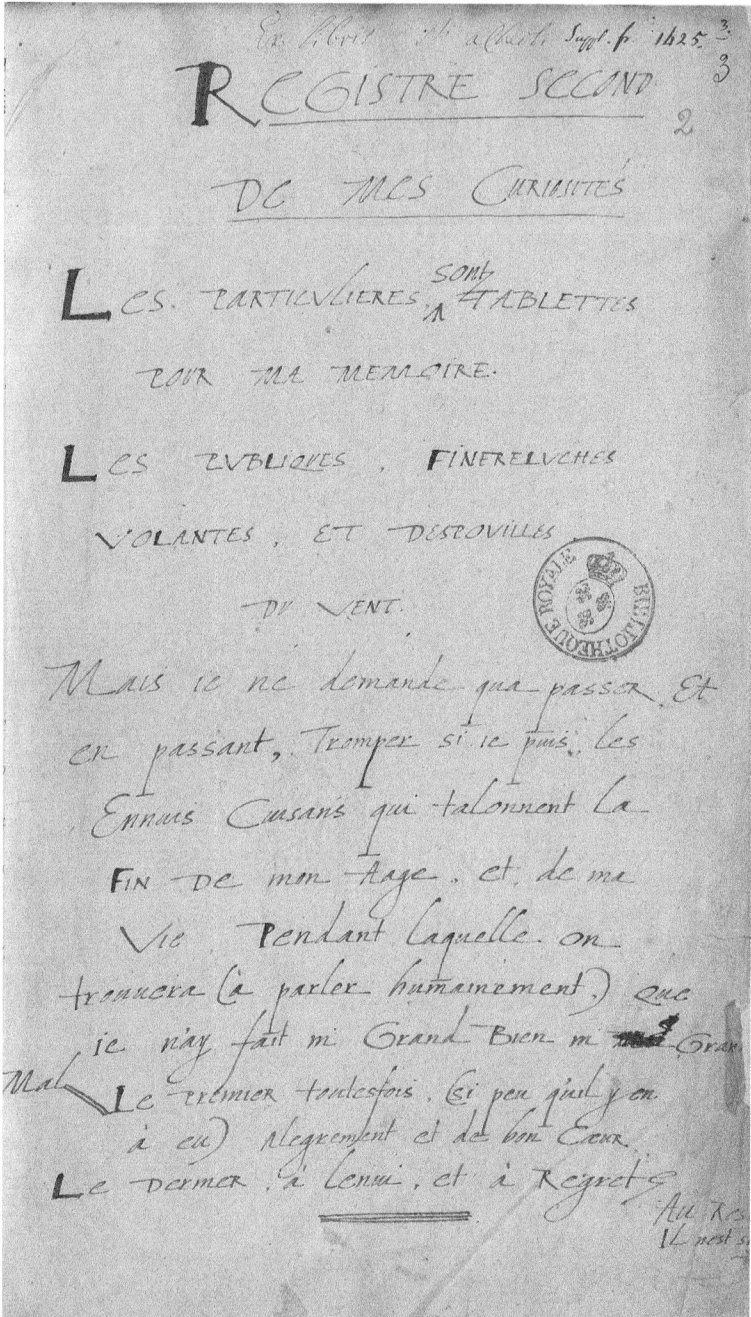

Illus. 2.5.3. Bibliothèque nationale de France, MS Fr. 10301, fol. 2r (Pierre de L'Estoile's 'Registre second de mes curiosités' or 'Secondes tablettes' from February 1609 to May 1610). Reproduced by permission of the Bibliothèque nationale de France, Paris.

early editor to have objected in ink in the margin of the 1610–11 volume that such notes were 'useless' for the writing of history.[55]

For, as I indicated at the beginning of this section, the other thing not apparent in the printed editions—besides the open and evolving nature of the record—is the administrative function of these 'Tablettes'. They are not compiled as a homogeneous and fixed representation of historical events, but as a set of accounts and judgements for review—a *registre et contrôle*. As can be seen in Illustration 2.5.4, L'Estoile is keeping accounts of how many sols he is spending on his *curiosités*, and of other incomings and outgoings such as loans and gifts.

At the top of the page he records the net amount spent (16 sols) on two copies of Tourval's French translation of King James's *Apologia*, which he had picked up at the Palais after the price dropped to a quarter écu a copy (he had already retrieved a one-quarter écu for one of the copies from M. Chouart). He then records spending one sol on a single folio publication. At the bottom, he records how Father Du Breuil loaned him a small folio Cassiodorus, which he judges to be 'fort bon' and which the theologians also rate. But he also reveals that he only accepted it as a way of reminding Du Breuil of the fact that he still had L'Estoile's copy of the *Annales d'Anjou* on loan. Later, he reviews his register and records in the margin that he returned the Father's Cassiodorus on Christmas Eve of the same year.[56]

On one occasion (Illus. 2.5.5) he records netting no less than twelve 'pistoles' (foreign gold coins, worth seven livres each) or eighty-four livres for a *registre*. The purchaser of the *registre* contracted to supply fair copies of some of its contents, and agreed to hand over one of his own manuscripts as a *gage* until he supplied them.[57]

These details reveal the change in the nature of the record L'Estoile was keeping. But what caused it? As one gets older and sicker, one relies more on artificial aids to support one's failing memory. The task of collecting and organizing large amounts of primary materials and notes, in order to write up a polished folio journal of events that had happened years previously, had perhaps got too much for L'Estoile. He needed to manage and record everything on a day-by-day basis, in just one book, which would *be* his memory, both of particular and of public matters, and that would more immediately inscribe materials that passed through his *étude* or that he wrote initially in his *tablettes*. He would keep a more immediate record both of the curiosities of his *étude* and *cabinet* and of family and public events.

By invoking Montaigne in the preliminary leaves to the first two of the three volumes he shows he understands this modulated, personally revealing style of record-keeping to be distinctly related to the precedent of the *Essais*. We shall see

[55] BnF MS Fr. 10301, fol. 330r/*Journal Henri IV*, vol. 3, 75 (May 1610); MS Fr. 10302, fols. 6r, 11r, 14r.

[56] BnF MS Fr. 10301, fol. 149r/*Journal Henri IV*, vol. 2, 523–4 (September 1609). Officially, the gold écu coin was raised in value to 65 sols in 1602, but market rates varied, so one quarter écu might well have been valued exactly 16 sols.

[57] BnF MS Fr. 10301, fol. 22v/*Journal Henri IV*, vol. 2, 447 (April 1609). On the value of the 'pistole' see *Journal Henri IV*, vol. 2, 528.

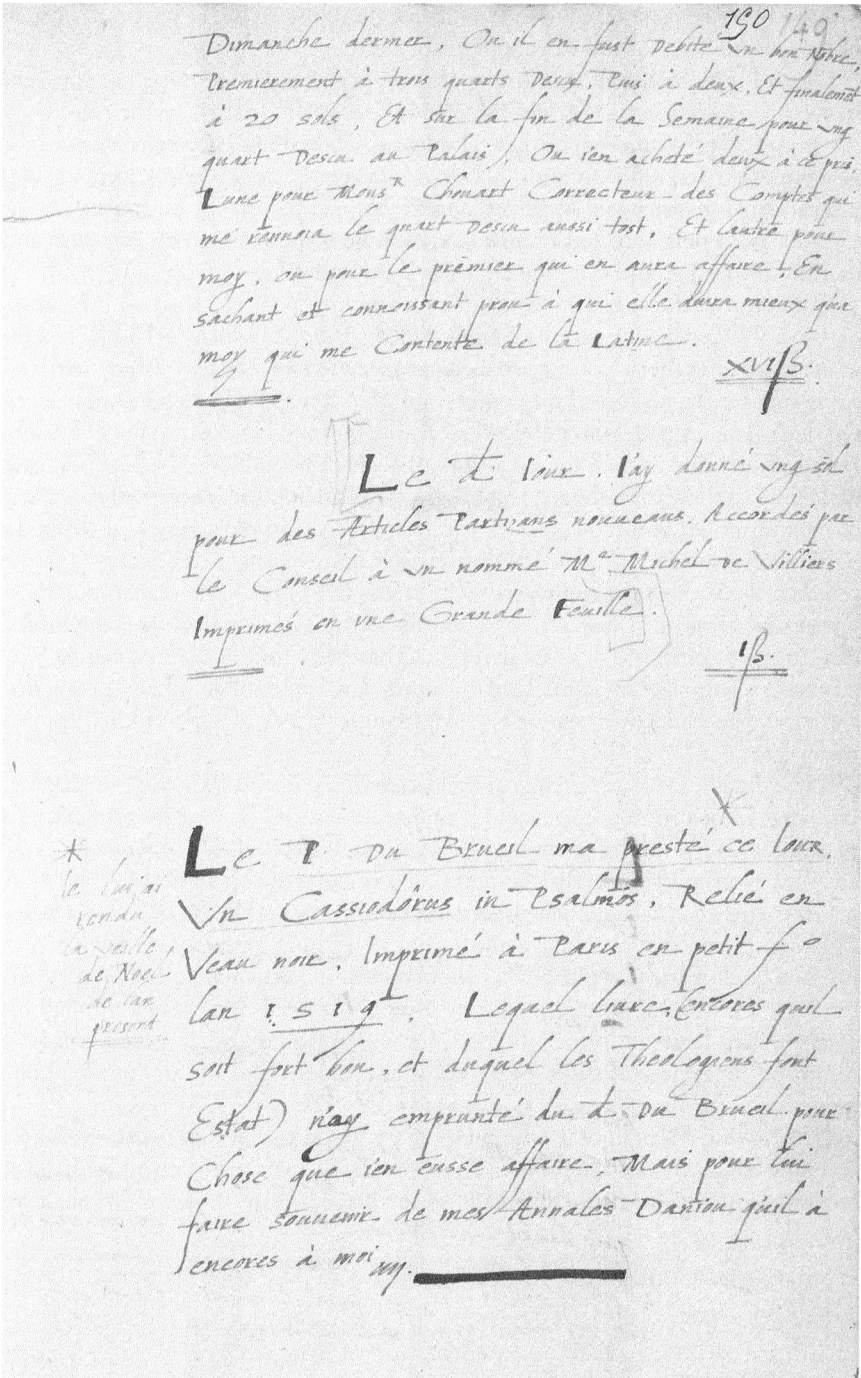

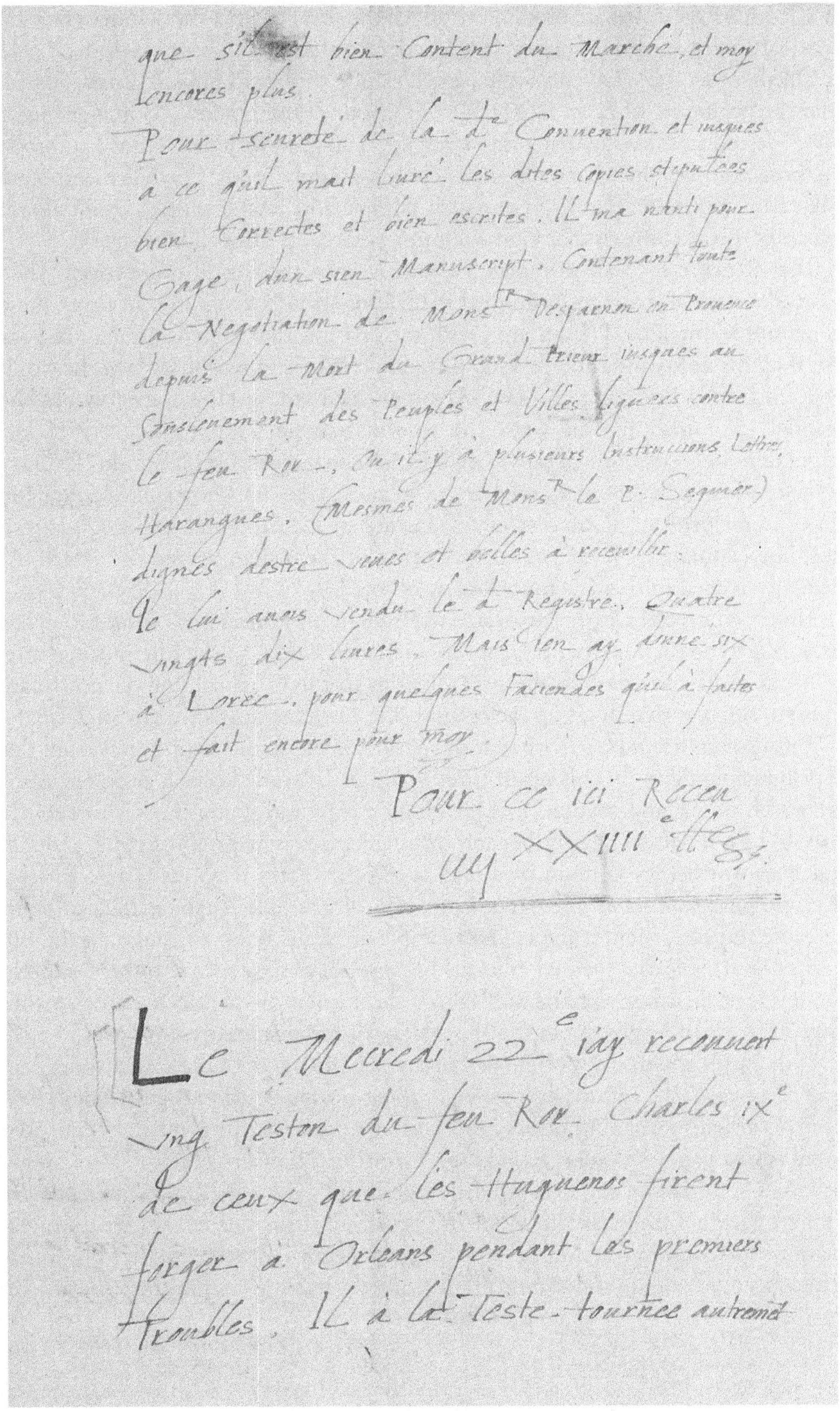

que si est bien Content du marché, et moy
encores plus.
Pour seureté de la d.te Convention et marques
à ce quil mait livré les dites copies stipulées
bien Correctes et bien escrites. Il ma nanti pour
Gage, dun sien Manuscript, Contenant toute
la Negotiation de Mons.r Deyquenem en Prouence
depuis la mort du Grand Prieur iusques au
soubsleuement des Peuples et Villes liguees contre
le feu Roy, ou il y à plusieurs Instructions, lettres,
Harangues, (mesmes de Mons.r le P. Seguier)
dignes destre veues et utiles à recueillir.
Je lui auois vendu le d. Registre, Quatre
vingts dix liures. Mais len ay donné six
à Lacee, pour quelques Faciendes quil à faites
et fait encore pour moy.

                        Pour ce ici Recea
                    uy XXIIII.ée ll.s 5.

_____

Le Mecredi 22.e iay recouuert
ung Teston du feu Roy. Charles ix.e
de ceux que les Huguenots firent
forger à Orleans pendant les premiers
troubles. Il à la Teste tournee autremt

Illus. 2.5.5. Bibliothèque nationale de France, MS Fr. 10301, fol. 22v (Pierre de L'Estoile's 'Registre second de mes curiosités' or 'Secondes tablettes' from February 1609 to May 1610). Reproduced by permission of the Bibliothèque nationale de France, Paris.

in 2.5.5 how the *Essais* are used to introduce the first volume. But Montaigne's text also features in the preliminaries to the second volume.

On the 'Secondes Tablettes' title page L'Estoile applies to himself a passage from near the beginning of *Essais* II 20 ('We can savour nothing pure'). Montaigne interprets Metrodorus's saying that sadness was not unalloyed with pleasure as a comment on those 'complexions' that make melancholy their only 'food'. L'Estoile incorporates a regretful confession that his is one such 'complexion' into a spiritual meditation in which he assures himself that God will bring perfect joy after all his tears.[58]

The 'Registre second' title page continues onto the inside front cover, where L'Estoile uses two passages from near the end of III 9 ('Of vanity'). In using these, he names Montaigne. He declares, with the essayist, that there is no man so good but that, his deeds and thoughts submitted to cross-examination by laws, he would be found worthy of hanging—yes, even men such as himself whom it would be a scandal to punish in this way. The second passage is from the very end of Montaigne's chapter, one of only two in which the Gascon uses L'Estoile's favoured term for man's vain thoughts and speech: 'fadaises'. L'Estoile knows, like Montaigne, that the majority of 'these discourses' are full of inanities and follies ('fadaises'), but, like Montaigne, he can no more get rid of them than get rid of himself. All men are steeped in them as much as any other.[59]

These citations clearly associate Montaigne's project of confession and record-keeping on paper with L'Estoile's own as it comes to the fore in these three volumes. And even though the preliminaries to the third volume do not follow those to the first two in citing the essayist, the contents do, as we saw in 2.1.8.

This is of course not to deny that the nature of the record kept differs from that kept by Montaigne. In this set of three volumes L'Estoile keeps a close record of: (a) which books and manuscripts are coming into and going out of his cabinet; and (b) how much he is spending and earning on books and manuscripts, and how much of worth they contain in moral, intellectual, and religious terms, whether they are pure *fadaises* or not—that is, he critically 'weighs' them as they come in. In some respects, then, it looks like a simple accounts book—though, again, one cannot see this in the printed editions because they simply leave out the sums of money registered by L'Estoile and ignore the format of the block entries on the page in an effort to give them the appearance of more seamless chronicles.

Only in the manuscript originals can one see the traces of the way he goes back over the record, the *registre*, as his own *contrôle*, noting when particular books have been returned, correcting errors, and adding comments in a manner that gives some of his pages a similar look to pages in the Bordeaux copy of Montaigne's *registre*. In one instance, for example, he crosses out a *conte* about the lunatic behaviour of M. du Laurens's wife upon the occasion of his death, and writes in the margin: 'ce Conte verifié Menterie' ('this account proved a lie'; followed by a substitute account, still in the margin). The printed version gives the crossed-out *conte*

---

[58] BnF MS Fr. 10301, fol. 1v; II 20, NP711–12/BVH Paris 1595, p.446/S765.
[59] BnF MS Fr. 10301, fol. 2r, inside front cover; III 9, NP1036/BVH Paris 1595, bk. III, p. 142/ S1120; III 9, NP1047/BVH Paris 1595, bk. III, p. 149/S1132.

2.5.6 Bibliothèque nationale de France, MS Fr. 10301, fol. 96v (Pierre de L'Estoile's 'Registre second de mes curiosités' or 'Secondes tablettes' from February 1609 to May 1610). Reproduced by permission of the Bibliothèque nationale de France, Paris.

and the corrected version as continuous prose, one after the other (Illus. 2.5.6; compare Illus. 1.6.2, 2.5.7).[60]

It is, of course, more than a register of loans and of money spent and received. It doubles up as a book of *diverses leçons* (not a structured commonplace book), for noting particular *sententiae* and transcribing much longer extracts, sometimes twenty to thirty pages at a time, as and when L'Estoile comes across them. This, again, is less apparent in the most current printed edition, where the longer extracts are relegated to notes at the back of the book.

L'Estoile's motives for extracting and copying from the books and manuscripts that pass through his hands vary enormously. On the one hand, he copies about twenty-five folios of material from the second part of Barclay's *Satyricon* for sheer pleasure. On the other hand, he copies four folios of extracts from a scandalous but rare *libelle* (probably, he believes, by a Jesuit), which collectors in Paris, including himself, pruriently wanted to see, to the extent of pushing the price up to seven or eight quarter écus. He made these extracts from a filthy, atheistic tract as a *mémoire* of the holy hypocrites of the age.[61]

This register of individual and family events, of public events, of deaths (including the verified characters of the deceased) also has a frequently advertised set of moral functions. On the one hand, L'Estoile is registering his own *vanité* and *curiosité* in his acquisitions and researches as a bibliophile, and praying to God that he might amend. On the other hand, he is preparing for death, registering his good faith and free conscience.

2.5.5 L'ESTOILE AND DOMESTIC RECORD-KEEPING IN *ESSAIS* I 34

At the beginning of the first volume, then, L'Estoile marks the change in the nature of the record he is keeping by citing the same passage from *Essais* I 34, 'Of a lack in our administrations', that we saw used by Slingsby in 2.4.2. The passage—already cited in 2.1.8—has been used by at least two editors to introduce L'Estoile's *Journal* as a whole.[62] But it makes more sense if we replace it in its proper context, at the beginning of a discrete set of three registers covering 1606–11, described by L'Estoile in the second of the three volumes as 'Tablettes', and if we read it alongside the chapter in the *Essais* to which it refers.

---

[60] BnF MS Fr. 10301, fol. 96v/*Journal Henri IV*, vol. 2, 501 (August 1609). See also BnF MS Fr. 10301, fols. 143v–4r/*Journal Henri IV*, vol. 2, 518–19, for a double page with manuscript additions in all margins, and with correction slips glued in.

[61] BnF MS Fr. 10300 fols. 110v–19r/*Journal Henri IV*, vol. 2, 280–8 (October 1607; extracts from an unnamed 'drôlerie' based on 'le Voiage Denfer', brought to him at his home, but quickly returned); BnF MS Fr. 10301, fols. 107r–32v/*Journal Henri IV*, vol. 2, 509, 616–39 (August 1609; extracts from Barclay's *Satyricon*); BnF MS Fr. 10301, fols. 158r–62v/*Journal Henri IV*, vol. 2, 530, 641–4 (extracts from *Puritanus*).

[62] Michaud and Poujoulat, *Nouvelle collection des Mémoires pour servir à l'histoire de France depuis le XIIIe siècle jusqu'à la fin du XVIIIe:...Registre-journal de Henri III, publié d'après le manuscrit autographe de L'Estoile*, 1; L'Estoile, *Journal pour le règne de Henri III (1574–1589)*, 31.

Before referring to I 34, L'Estoile weaves remarks and *traits* from 'Au lecteur', II 16 and II 17, into his account of his own self-portrait (Illus. 2.5.1, 2.1.8):

> Register-journals are an ancient usage, and often serve to ease our troubles and relieve our failing memory, especially when we reach old age, as I have done. Montaigne, in his Essays, says that his late father had one, where he had inserted all the occurrences of any note, and the memoranda of his house's history day by day. Mine will not be so comprehensive, as it will scarcely extend, with regard to my private individual matters, beyond the curiosities of my study and cabinet; though it will go further with regard to public matters. And I find myself to be a fool for having done it; as Montaigne, to the contrary, calls and finds himself to be this for having failed to continue that of his father (book 1, chap. 34). /*continues on inside front cover* (Illus. 2.1.8)/ In these registers (which I call the storehouse of my curiosities), you will see me (as the lord of Montaigne says in the Essays, speaking of himself) completely naked and as I am, my natural character from day to day [*mon naturel au jour le jour*], my soul free and all mine, accustomed to conduct itself in its own way, neither troublesome nor malign, but too inclined to a vain curiosity and liberty (by which I am marred). Should someone, however, want to remove it from me, that would do wrong to my health and my life, for where I am constrained I am no good at all, being extremely free both by nature and by art. . . . Because, also, he who is not a good man except for show is hardly worth anything. And there I find myself in agreement with the Seigneur de Montaigne, my *vade-mecum*, when he says that, apart from health and life (to which I add the honour and fear of God), there is nothing over which I am willing to chew my nails, nor anything that I am willing to purchase at the cost of a tortured spirit and of constraint. I take therefore as my motto the saying of the Apostle Saint Paul: 'Our glory is the testimony of our conscience' [*Gloria nostra, testimonium conscientiae nostrae*].[63]

In the first sentence of the cited passage, L'Estoile uses Montaigne to define *registres-journaux* as a particular type of register or record, of ancient usage. It is a type of record that can also be referred to as a 'papier journal'. All his manuscript journals and collections indeed belong to this category; we have already seen that

[63] BnF MS Fr. 10301, fol. 1r, inside front cover/*Journal Henri IV*, vol. 2, 193–4 (July 1606): 'Les Registres Journaux sont Dusage Ancien, Et servent souvent à nous oster de Peine, Et a soulager nostre Memoire labile, Principalement quand nous venons sur laage, comme moy. MonsR De Montagne en ses Essais dit, que feu son Pere en avoit ung ou il faisoit inserer toutes les Survenances de quelque Remarque et Jour par Jour les Memoires de lhistoire de sa Maison. Le mien ne sera si exact, Car il ne sestend gueres pour le particulier au de la des Curiosités de mon Estude et Cabinet, Mais pour le Publiq plus loing. Et me trouve un Sot de lavoir fait, comme Montaigne au contraire sappelle et trouve tel pour avoir failli à la Continuati[on de] celui de son Pere Liv. 1er, ch. 34 Pa[]./*continues on inside front cover* (Illus. 2.1.8)/En ces Registres (que j'appelle le Magazin de mes Curiosités,) On my verra, (comme dit le SR De Montagne en ses Essais, parlant de soy) tout nud et tel que [je] suis. Mon Naturel au Jour, [] Ame libre et toute mienne, accoutumé à se Conduire à sa mode, Non toutefois meschante ne maligne, Mais trop portée à une vaine Curiosité et Liberté, (Dont je suis marri), Et laquelle toutefois qui me voudrait retrancher, Ferait tort à ma Santé et à ma Vie, Par ce qu'ou je suis Contraint, je ne vaus rien, Estant extremement libre et par Nature et par Art. ... Car aussi qui n'est Homme De Bien que par la Monstre, ne vault gueres, Et en suis la logé avec le Seingneur [*sic*] de Montagne, (mon Vadé mecum) que sauf la Santé et la Vie, ✳ jajoute l'honneur [de] Dieu Et sa Crainte Il n'est Chose pourquoi je veuille ronger mes Ongles, Et que je veuille acheter au prix du Tourment de Lesprit et de la Contrainte. Je prens donc pour ma Devise le dire de Lapostre S. Pol: GLORIA NOSTRA, TESTIMONIUM CONSCIENTIÆ NOSTRÆ'. For the source passages in the *Essais*, see 'Au lecteur', NP27/Slix; II 17, NP681/BVH Paris 1595, p. 425/S730; II 16 NP660/BVH Paris 1595, p. 412/S708; I 34, NP229–30/BVH Paris 1595, p. 132/S252.

on three separate occasions (in the text of the three-volume set with which we are concerned) he refers both to his large folio journal of the reign of Henri III and his small folio journal of the early years of the reign of Henri IV as a 'Registre Journal'.

But the following sentences also indicate that from now on the record he will be keeping—the volume he is about to start writing, the one that will be more like *Les Essais de Montaigne*—will have a greater admixture of the 'particular', of the personal aide-mémoire, in it. It will become, as well as an ongoing register of public events, a register of the 'curiosités de mon étude et cabinet'. The example of Bossé suggests that this might have been a familiar type of *registre* in L'Estoile's circles. As a general type, it might also encompass examples from other countries—Slingsby's 'book of remembrance' and Maillefer's 'livre secret', to be described in 2.5.6.

The broader significance of L'Estoile's citation of *Essais* I 34 in this context is that it sketches and enacts the privatization and domestication of registers and acts of registration, and hints at their further personalization. The practice of keeping more or less 'secret' registers had migrated to the private sphere of the household in the late medieval period. It was now in the later sixteenth century becoming more personal to heads of household who were more closely involved in reading and writing their own journals, in relation to their own particular curiosities and *naturels*. Montaigne's taking over the writing of his *journal de voyage* from his secretary is an interestingly literal instance of this.

The first version of *Essais* I 34, published in 1580 and left largely untouched in 1588, records Montaigne's father's proposal for the institution of a public registry in each town, where everyone wanting to offer or obtain a given commodity or service could register their particular desires with an officer and be matched off. Montaigne uses this to state a regret that no one thought to match in this way the needs of two destitute scholars with the resources of willing patrons.

But when he came to review this chapter after 1588, he enters a more personal memorandum in the margin of his own book, a memorandum which concerns the history of his own household and the use of more private registers within it (Illus. 2.5.7):

> In his domestic administration my father had this system, which I can praise but not follow: besides the record of household affairs [*outre le registre des negoces du mesnage*] kept by his steward, in which were entered petty accounts, payments, and transactions not requiring the notary's hand, he ordered the servant whom he used as his secretary to keep a journal [*qui luy servoit à escrire, un papier journal*] and insert in it all occurrences of any note, and the memorabilia of his family history day by day [*jour par jour les memoires de l'histoire de sa maison*]. A record very pleasant to look at when time begins to efface the memory of events, and very well suited to get us out of perplexity: When was such and such a thing begun? When completed? What retinues came? How long did they stay? Our trips, our absences; marriages; deaths; the receipt of happy or unhappy news; the change of principal servants; such matters. An ancient custom, which I think it would be good to revive, each man in each man's home. And I think I am a fool to have neglected it.[64]

---

[64] I 34, NP229–30/BVH Paris 1595, p. 132/S252.

ESSAIS DE M. DE MONTA.

qui cela, chacun selon son besoing. Et semble que ce moyen de nous entr'aduertir, apporteroit non legiere commodité au commerce publique : car à tous coups, il y à des conditiõs, qui s'entrecherchent : & pour ne se pouuoir rencontrer, laissent les hommes en extreme necessité. J'entens, au ce vne grãde hôte de nostre siecle, qu'à nostre veüe, deux tref-excellens personnages en sçauoir, sont morts en estat de n'auoir pas leur soul à manger : Lilius Gregorius Giraldus en Italie, & Sebastianus Castalio en Allemagne : & croy qu'il y à mil'hõmes qui les eussent appellez auec tref-aduantageuses conditiõs, s'ils l'eussent sçeu. Le monde n'est pas si generalement corrompu, que ie ne sçache tel homme, qui souhaiteroit de bien grande affection, que les moyens que les siés luy ont mis en main, se peussent employer tant qu'il plaira à la fortune, qu'il en iouïsse, à mettre à l'abry de la necessité, les personnages rares & remarquables en quelque sorte de valeur, que le mal'heur combat quelquefois iusques à l'extremité : & qui les mettroit pour le moins en tel estat, qu'il ne tiendroit qu'à faute de bon discours, s'ils n'estoyent contens.

De l'vsage de se vestir.

CHAP. XXXVI.

OV que ie vueille donner, il me faut forcer quelque barriere de la coustume, tant ell'a soigneusemét bridé toutes nos auenues. Ie deuisoy en cette saison frileuse, si la façon d'aller tout nud de ces nations dernierement trouuées, est vne façon forcée par la chaude temperature de l'air, comme nous disons des Indiens, & des Mores, ou si c'est l'oingle des hõmes. Les gens d'entendement, d'autant que tout ce qui est soubs le ciel, comme dit la saincte parole, est subiect à mesmes loix, ont accoustumé en pareilles considerations à celles icy, où il faut distingüer les loix

Illus. 2.5.7. Philippe Desan, *Reproduction en quadrichromie de l'Exemplaire de Bordeaux des 'Essais' de Montaigne* (Fasano-Chicago: Schena Editore, *Montaigne Studies*, 2002; Classiques Garnier, 2011), fol. 94v/sig. 2A2v. Courtesy of Philippe Desan.

The chapter as a whole gives us an archival genealogy for the *Essais*. It mentions three types of *registre* and implicitly invokes a new sub-type of the third type, the paper journal (as exemplified by the *Essais* themselves, with which L'Estoile associates his own 'Tablettes'). The first is a register of *commerce*, kept by a public officer; the second is a domestic register of business transactions that do not require the hand of a *notaire*, kept by his father's steward ('the record of household affairs kept by his steward, in which were entered petty accounts, payments, and transactions not requiring the notary's hand'); the third is a paper journal in which a secretary inserts 'all occurrences of any note, and the memorabilia of his family history day by day'.

Montaigne here gives us the tip of a whole iceberg of medieval and early modern written records, for it is important to understand—as should be clear by now—that the term 'registre' does not refer to a genre of writings but to a fundamental category of continuous or daily records which are usually kept in one book or roll, that are often transcribed from elsewhere, or copied from one register to another, and which are then reviewed or overseen for various purposes. It can mean anything from a basic list or inventory, whether of goods or of discourses—especially in its private forms, it shifts between these functions easily—to a history of public events. Montaigne refers to a list of classical examples of animal behaviour he compiles within his text as 'ce long registre', with the associated verb 'contreroller' making an appearance in the following sentence with regard to the imagined review of an alternative list of more homegrown examples. He calls Tacitus's histories a *registre public* which pays an unusually large amount of attention to private morals.[65]

We know that Montaigne did use a printed book, Beuther's *Ephemerides*, as a kind of *livre de raison* in which to record signal events in his and his family's life.[66] He claims to have kept, on loose sheets or 'petits brevets descousus', medical notes that he would later consult for a prognosis based on his own experience.[67] He also employed a secretary to keep a journal of events and of his own conversation on his trip to Italy, a journal which he wrote up himself once the secretary had been dismissed. This journal contained, amongst other things, very detailed medical memoranda concerning his condition (renal colic) and the treatments he experimented with.

If we ask why he fails to mention some of these domestic memoranda and says he has neglected his father's practice, the answer lies in the story he tells about this book, the *Essais*, in other passages also largely added in later editions. He is unique in assiduously keeping and publishing (in print) a new sub-type of *registre-journal* over a particularly long period. His journalistic tendencies are channelled into the keeping of a record of his idle mind, a *livre* in which he registers the birth and progress of his *fantasies*. It is this modulation, in a more personal direction, of the *registre-journal* which L'Estoile associates with the *Essais* in the preliminaries to BnF MSS Fr. 10300 and 10301, and which corresponds to the new type of record he will be keeping from now on—a costed record of his vain curiosity and his melancholy—alongside the ongoing record of household events and of memorable public occurrences.

L'Estoile was not alone in noting the affiliations of the *Essais* with a household paper journal of the kind that would not normally be published. We have already

[65] II 12, NP490/BVH Paris 1595, p. 301/S521; III 8, NP986/BVH Paris 1595, bk. III, p. 108/S1065.
[66] Montaigne, *Œuvres complètes*, 1403–12.
[67] III 13, NP1141/BVH Paris 1595, bk. III, p. 213/S1240.

heard Pasquier, Scaliger, and Huet note these affiliations with irritation, especially in book III, where they are most apparent. In the opening lines of III 9 Montaigne declares: 'I cannot give an account of my life [*registre de ma vie*] by my actions: fortune has placed them too low for that; so I do so by my thoughts.' One gentleman registers and talks of the operations and evacuations of his bowels; Montaigne does the same for his *esprit*.[68]

The remark of Scaliger's cited by Huet—'What is it to me whether Montaigne likes white wine or claret?'—is an allusion to the long central section of 'De l'Expe-rience' in which Montaigne discusses 'the detail of his own tastes and all his other domestic trifles'. It is here that Montaigne describes his book as 'un registre des essais de ma vie', a *registre* both of *l'interne santé* and of *la santé corporelle*. 'I have lived long enough now', Montaigne continues, 'to give an account of the regimen [*pour mettre en comte l'usage*] which has got me thus far.'[69] He then takes us into the minutiae of his household routine: how he eats, drinks, and sleeps, how he relates to people of lower class, how he deals with his physical ailments. At the moment of their conclusion, the *Essais* are more like a household journal than they are like polished literary ana of the kind associated with scholars such as Scaliger and Huet.

We shall return to the example of L'Estoile, and the comparison with Montaigne, in 2.7.7. His manuscript journals are interesting in themselves, while also helping us bring out the character of the *Essais* as a *registre*. But although L'Estoile was an amateur, he was not quite the kind of reader-writer envisaged by Huet in the quotation with which we began this chapter. He was a highly educated member of the parliamentary elite, located in Paris—even if he did on one occasion retreat to his house at Gland to pursue his studies and writings.[70] To fully appreciate the force of Huet's remarks we need to find an *honnête paresseux,* an *ignoran studieux,* a *gentilhomme de campagne* from the later seventeenth century, with a Montaigne on his chimney piece, and a *livre de raison* or *livre de retraite* under his pen.

2.5.6 MONTAIGNE ON THE MANTELPIECE IN RHEIMS

On 3 June 1680, Jean Maillefer was sat reading in his logis at Cormontreuil outside Rheims, probably in his cabinet. We can surmise he was sitting because we know the size of the book he was reading. He remarks in his personal journal that it is important to ensure that reading is accompanied and mixed with walking, as the body needs exercise: 'Folio books are read whilst seated, but those in quarto and in octavo can be read whilst walking, and from time to time one can pause to diversify good things and take them in moderation.'[71] It would be very difficult

---

[68] III 9, NP989/BVH Paris 1595, bk. III, p. 110/S1070.

[69] III 13, NP1126–27/BVH Paris 1595, bk. III, pp. 203–4/S1224–6.

[70] *Journal Henri IV,* vol. 2, 203–8.

[71] Jean Maillefer, *Mémoires de J. Maillefer, marchand bourgeois de Reims, 1611–1684, continués par son fils jusqu'en 1716,* ed. Charles Henri Jadart (Paris and Rheims: Alph. Picard and F. Michaud, 1890), 284 (henceforth abbreviated as 'Jadart')/Bibliothèque municipale de Reims (henceforth

to pause and strike a pose with the book he had before him: a copy of the largest folio edition of the *Essais* published before 1700, Paris 1640.[72]

The copy has previously been described as containing 'manuscript annotations by a member of the Maillefer family'.[73] It in fact contains annotations by two members of the family and can be linked with a manuscript held in the Bibliothèque de Reims, two-thirds of which was published by Henri Jadart in the late nineteenth century as the 'Mémoires of Jean Maillefer'.[74] This manuscript contains notes on Maillefer's reading of the *Essais*, not all of which were published by Jadart, and presents itself on its contents page as a book of chapters on different topics by Maillefer (Illus. 2.5.8). In its abridged, published version the notes have been picked up by social historians, though not—to my knowledge—by historians of Montaigne's reception.[75]

But once we return to the manuscript in Rheims, and recombine it with the copy in Bordeaux, we have a major document in the history of the *Essais* in the *grand siècle*. With this document, we can follow the responses of a regional reader-writer as he reacts in private to book III, especially the later chapters, including 'De l'experience'. These were precisely the chapters, first added in 1588, which made learned public intellectuals from Pasquier to Huet nervous about the ultimate value of Montaigne's witty and vivacious work. We quoted Huet's 1712 remark in 2.5.1: 'Scaliger was right in saying "What is it to me whether Montaigne loves white wine or claret?" [alluding to 'De l'Experience'] He does indeed abuse his readers' attention by giving them the detail of his own tastes and all his other domestic impertinences [*fadaises domestiques*].' Maillefer responds in detail to these chapters and gives much detail of his own tastes and other *fadaises*. But we must first consider the context of the copy and the manuscript.

The edition published at Paris in 1640 was 'corrected following the first editions of L'Angelier' but did not have the preface of Marie de Gournay. It omitted the epigraph. It did include, at the beginning, the summary discourse on Montaigne's life, taken from his own writings ('Sommaire discours sur la vie de Michel Seigneur

---

'BmR'), MS 1980, fol. 264r: 'Les livres in folio se lizent assis mais Ceux In quarto et In octavo se peuvent lir en se promenant et faire de temps en temps quelque poze et diversifier les bons et les prendre avecq moderation.' Where I give references to both the printed and the manuscript version of Maillefer's journal, the transcription is from the manuscript; otherwise, it is from the printed version.

[72] According to the measurements given in Sayce and Maskell, 27, 117, 132, 145, though the Paris 1652 folio (Sayce and Maskell no. 30) was equally large. The Maillefer copy is Bibliothèque municipale de Bordeaux, pressmark G. F. 495 rés.

[73] Pierre Botineau and Claude-Gilbert Dubois (eds.), *Montaigne et l'Europe: actes du colloque international de Bordeaux (21–23 mai 1992)* (Mont-de-Marsan: Éditions InterUniversitaires, 1992), plate XIV (between pages 280 and 281).

[74] BmR MS 1980. The link was first made in the first version, in French, of the current chapter: Boutcher, '"Fadaises domestiques": Montaigne marchand bourgeois bordelais lu par un marchand bourgeois rémois'.

[75] Dinah Ribard and Nicolas Schapira, 'À la recherche des écritures protestataires dans la France du XVIIe siècle. Du répertoire à l'action', *Genèses*, 64 (2006/3), 146–62; Stefano Simiz, 'Jean Maillefer, dévot et honnête homme rémois au XVIIe siècle', in F. Gugelot and B. Maës (eds.), *Passion de la découverte, culture de l'échange. Mélanges offerts à Nicole Moine et Claire Prévotat* (Langres: Dominique Guéniot 2006), 223–33.

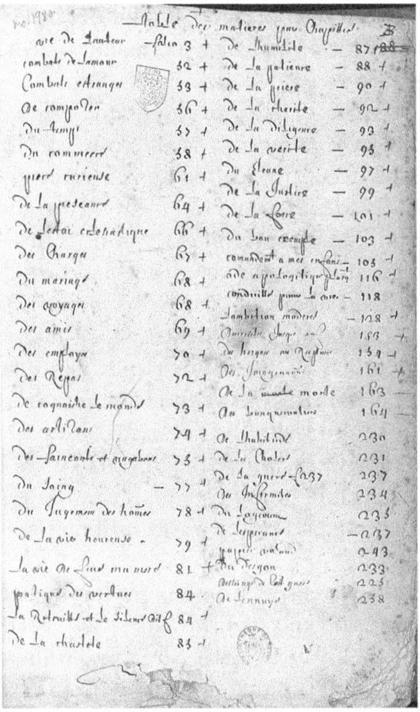

Illus. 2.5.8. 'Mémoires de Jean Maillefer, continués par son fils', Bibliothèque municipale de Reims, MS 1980, index page. Reproduced by permission of the Bibliothèque municipale de Reims.

de Montaigne, extraict de ses propres escrits'), which Maillefer read. The title page has a portrait of a bust of Montaigne facing forward, in an oval border, flanked by two angels, wearing crowns of laurels, carrying palms. The title page of the Maillefer copy corresponds to the state Sayce identifies as Michel Blageart *(b)*. A signature at the top has been written over.[76]

The folio manuscript in Rheims has fewer leaves but it is a similar size. Stefano Simiz has described it as having three distinct parts: a 'History of my life' written up in one go between the 1st and the 20th June 1667, with a short epilogue added after a general re-reading in October 1667; a second part, following straight on, with moral works, consisting of personal and abstract reflections composed over the period of more than a year, using various forms such as the fictive dialogue between father and son, domestic meditations, short essays, and spiritual confessions; and, finally, a journal kept from 1669 to 24 April 1681 by Jean, then continued in less expansive style by his son until 1716.[77] There are also poems Maillefer has composed, transcriptions of letters he has written, transcriptions of speeches he

---

[76] Sayce and Maskell, 128–9; Bibliothèque municipale de Bordeaux, pressmark G. F. 495 rés.
[77] Simiz, 'Jean Maillefer', 224.

has made. In English historical scholarship, it might be called a manuscript miscellany. It is a laboratory in which Maillefer experiments with a wide variety of different forms of *l'écriture du for privé*.

How did Maillefer obtain the copy of the *Essais*? What exactly is its relationship to the manuscript *livre de retraite*? Maillefer's 'Mémoires' offer quite a lot of information about his access to printed books, gazettes (French and Dutch), and journals (*Journal des Savants*), and about the daily and seasonal rhythm of his reading and writing. The most significant point is that he did not, as we are led to believe Montaigne did, exclusively read books that he owned. One dialogue he composed tells us about his daily routine during his years as a merchant in Rheims. After spending the morning stock-taking and making entries in his various *livres de raison* he takes lunch and then reads until two or three o'clock. Then he takes a walk and visits the Capucins or one of the other religious houses in town. He also visits 'the library of Notre-Dame, which opens on Tuesdays and Fridays each week, where the librarian gives me whichever book I please, and I return it faithfully to him.'[78] Maillefer has the same kind of access to this library as Montaigne had to the Vatican library (though Montaigne did not borrow; see 1.7.2).

In a different, journal-style entry he describes a family network of five libraries. These comprised his own and those of: his eldest son, François-Elie, a *conseiller*; Jean Maillefer (junior), who was in trade; Philippe, who was studying theology locally; and Charles, who was running the family business with Jean. Jean senior says that the last of these libraries—Charles's—contained 'my account books and theirs' ('mes livres de raison et les leurs') and is 'entirely necessary for the management of affairs'.[79]

This is a reference to no less than twenty commercial *livres de raison* kept by Jean Maillefer senior and passed on to Charles when he and Jean took over the running of the business. We saw in 2.5.5 how Montaigne's wish that 'each denizen in his own den' ('chacun en sa chacuniere') should refresh the 'ancient custom' ('usage ancien') of keeping registers of small household bills and petty payments ('les negoces du mesnage') and household account-books ('livres de raison') was realized by L'Estoile. Maillefer refreshes the same usage in a manner specific to his circumstances. He exemplifies the notion that the merchant's identity in this period is founded in and through writing.[80]

As a child, he had initially been sent to the college of the Bons Enfants in Rheims and taught Greek and Latin composition by the English Benedictine archbishop, William Gifford. But his father pulled him out and put him into apprenticeship with 'a merchant of drapery and shoes... in order to learn the trade of drapery [*pour gagnier la franchisse de vendre de la draperie*]'.[81]

From that point on, aside from a brief flirtation with a religious vocation, Maillefer acquired his advanced literacy skills not in the context of cultivation, but of commerce. He became a clerk and learned how to keep books and write letters

---

[78] Jadart 115/BmR MS 1980, fol. 70v.   [79] Jardart 229.
[80] Cazalé Bérard and Klapisch-Zuber, 'Mémoire de soi', 812.   [81] Jadart 7.

for merchants. He elsewhere writes 'account books are my talent' ('les livres de raison c'est mon talent') and, in a dialogue clearly intended for the instruction of Charles and Jean junior, he describes in detail the twenty *livres de raison* he has been keeping. They include 'double-entry account books' ('livres par parties doubles') relating to various types of expenditure and income, some to do with household affairs, some to do with business affairs, and various 'grands livres'. They also include cash registers ('livres de caisses') and letter-books.[82]

Of his *livre de caisse* Maillefer says: 'those who go about their affairs alone, must also account for themselves [*se rendre compte à eux mesme*]'.[83] Another of the books fulfils the same function on the level of 'spiritual and temporal morals' ('meurs spirituels et temporelles'). Maillefer calls this the 'third secret book' ('troiziesme livre secret'). The first *livre secret*, which to my knowledge is not extant, concerns 'the pensions of you, my children, and the wages of my servants'. The second concerns 'inheritance funds and the money and estate of my late wife Marie Lefebre'.[84]

These three *livres secrets*, then, are the books of what Montaigne calls the *arrière-boutique*. They are the private household books, those, as the essayist puts it in I 34, beyond the *registre* of household affairs, the *registre* which in Maillefer's case extends to seventeen commercial *livres de raison*. For early modern householders such as L'Estoile and Maillefer, the *Essais* were clearly related to such 'secret' books, those beyond the standard account-books, intended only for friends and family.

The 'troiziesme livre secret' is the manuscript that survives in the Bibliothèque municipale de Reims, the manuscript which contains the notes on reading Montaigne, and which was published in the late nineteenth century in an abridged version as 'Mémoires de Jean Maillefer'. It was originally kept as part of a library of *livres de raison* whose overall function was the keeping of good family accounts— whether financial, historical, moral, or spiritual, whether 'secret' or more public.

After Jean Maillefer senior went into semi-retirement, this library was passed to the sons who took over the running of the business, Charles and Jean junior. In due course, after Jean senior's death, the 'troiziesme livre secret' also passed to one of the two sons who became businessmen, Jean Maillefer junior. This son made further entries after his father's death. There is no space here for a detailed assessment of the extent to which Jean junior's new entries follow the pattern of his father's, mixing personal meditations into a family journal. On the whole, the book reverts to being just a family journal in which are inserted, as Montaigne says in I 34, 'any noteworthy event and the day-to-day history of his household'.[85]

The crucial point, however, is that the 'troiziesme livre secret'—the book which might be described as 'les Essais de Jean Maillefer', the book which contains extensive notes on reading Montaigne—did not originate as an attempt to imitate the *Essais*. It originated in the practice of keeping 'secret' *livres de raison*, household books, beyond ('outre') the more public-facing commercial books—those more like Beugnot's *livres de retraite*. It chronicles events in his life and in the lives of other family members, but it also traces the history of his *meurs*, for the purposes of self-study and self-correction.

---

[82] Jadart 96–9.   [83] Jadart 98–9.   [84] Jadart 97.
[85] BmR MS 1980, fols. 268v–75v.

Maillefer's full description reads as follows:

> In another book which I refer to as the third secret book, curious enough, more curious than necessary, there are remarks that concern myself, my morals both spiritual and temporal, and my family and other incidents that are only too frequent, which is not without use, for God and study help wonderfully well to endure it [life?] and to correct oneself. *Quantas habeo iniquitates* ['How many are my iniquities?'—Job 13. 23], and so on.[86]

Whereas the other books are—to quote Montaigne's words about his 'secret book'—'concerned with some third-hand, extraneous purpose' ('d'une occupation et fin, tierce et estrangere'), this book is 'of one substance with its author' ('consubstantiel à son autheur'). In this book Maillefer accounts for himself 'continuously and... carefully' ('continuellement;...curieusement').[87] Maillefer is indeed not entirely sure of the utility, the necessity of this book—it is perhaps, above all, 'curious'.

The index Maillefer compiled at the beginning of the book presents it as a life-history followed by a number of chapters on moral and oeconomic themes (Illus. 2.5.8). This does bear an interesting resemblance to the format of the 1640 *Essais*, which, as we heard earlier in this section, was prefaced by the brief life of Montaigne. And Maillefer had read Montaigne before. He tells us in 1680 that he first read the *Essais* eighteen or twenty years previously, *c.*1660–2. He tells us that he retained something from that earlier reading, but that it did not make the extraordinary impact on him that it did in 1680.[88]

The evidence indicates that the readings and writings which eventually prompted him, in 1667, to start writing in a single large folio book began in the early to mid-1650s when, as we shall hear him say later, he started to act in his life with more reflection. So, even if the *Essais* did clearly influence the way that Maillefer's book evolved, we must still be clear that Maillefer's work originates primarily in the practice of keeping 'secret' *livres de raison* and in his personal experience—his retreat from business and social conversation due to the onset of deafness and illness, his grief over his second wife's death.

We are therefore tracing not just a reception story, but a parallel between two private household reading and writing projects (Montaigne's and Maillefer's), in two different sets of local and regional circumstances. I argue that the case of Maillefer's 'troizieme livre secret' can join Slingsby's journal (2.4.2) in helping us see the *Essais* themselves as a highly evolved and ennobled form of the household *livre de retraite*, as a work which shares a *mentalité* with private writers in the regions who kept such books, and which was itself intended to be kept and used by private individuals and families as one of their *livres secrets*. This is exactly what happened in the case of the Maillefer family copy of the *Essais*.

---

[86] Jadart 97: 'Un aultre livre que j'intitulle troiziesme livre secret assés et plus curieux que nécessaire, ce sont des remarques pour ce qui me concerne, pour mes meurs tant pour le spirituel que temporelle, que pour ma famille et aultres accidents qui ne sont que trop fréquents, ce quy n'est pas inutil, Dieu et l'estude aydent merveilleusement à la suporter et se coriger. *Quantas habeo iniquitates*, et le reste.'

[87] II 18, NP703–4/BVH Paris 1595, p. 440/S755. Screech leaves out 'Non d'une occupation... comme tous autres livres.'

[88] Jadart 280, 284/BmR MS 1980 fols. 259r, 264r.

As for the other four libraries mentioned by Jean Maillefer, he says that they were, by contrast, 'necessary for the nourishment of the soul'('nécessaires pour la nourriture de l'âme'). He received the copy of Montaigne on loan from one of these: the library of François-Elie Maillefer, his eldest son by his first marriage, who was to become secretary to the King, and therefore acquire (like L'Estoile) noble status, and who died in 1692.

We know this because Jean Maillefer records returning the book to him on 18 June 1680 when he finishes reading it. He also writes: 'I see that my son studies it [the book] and annotates it, and he is right to do so. This book alone is capable of forming one's judgement on the conduct of life' ('Je voy que mon filz le Consilier en fait son estude et le Commente Il a raison Ce livre seul est Capable de former le Jugement sur la Conduitte de la vie'). Maillefer goes on to say, in remarks not transcribed in Jadart, that it is astonishing how many instructions, how many books, how much work it takes to be an *homme de bien* when nature 'has Imprinted it in ourselves' ('nous la Imprimee dans nous mesmes'). The implication is once again that the *Essais* provide a 'natural' short-cut to the formation of the judgement in an environment saturated with books and instructions on how to study to correct oneself.[89]

In June 1680, then, Maillefer senior tells us in his journal that he could already see annotations made by his son in the margins of the family copy. There is indeed a set of annotations fitting this description in the copy extant in Bordeaux. They mostly comprise brief summaries or comments, including references to plays by Molière. There are also annotations that François-Elie made in the copy many years later, in the year of his death, 1692, long after he received it back from his father. In these, much more personal annotations he recalls his father's struggles with illness and describes his own (Illus. 2.5.9).

This means that the *Essais* were read through at least twice by both father and son; by the father in *c.*1660 and again in 1680; by the son some time before June 1680, and again in 1692. The book was consubstantial with their family life. The Maillefer copy of Montaigne as passed between father and son, as commented by father and son, itself becomes a kind of *livre secret*, a book for continuous and special use by family members, for forming their judgement on the conduct of private life.

We can reconstruct the circumstances surrounding Maillefer senior's second reading of the *Essais* in 1680 as follows. Maillefer got to Cormontreuil on 18 May 1680, with his son Philippe and two other individuals, probably servants. He started reading his Montaigne from the beginning at some point before 3 June. At the same time he was reading back over his own writings in the 'troiziesme livre secret', which he had been keeping and composing since 1667. He concludes later that this book of his life would need to be recopied and corrected, but that the result might be a worse copy as he is too infirm and lazy, with too poor a handwriting; besides which, it would divert him too much from his reading.[90] He clearly did not have access to copyists, like L'Estoile.

[89] Jadart 279–80/BmR MS 1980, fols. 258v–59r.
[90] Jadart 284/BmR MS 1980, fol. 264r.

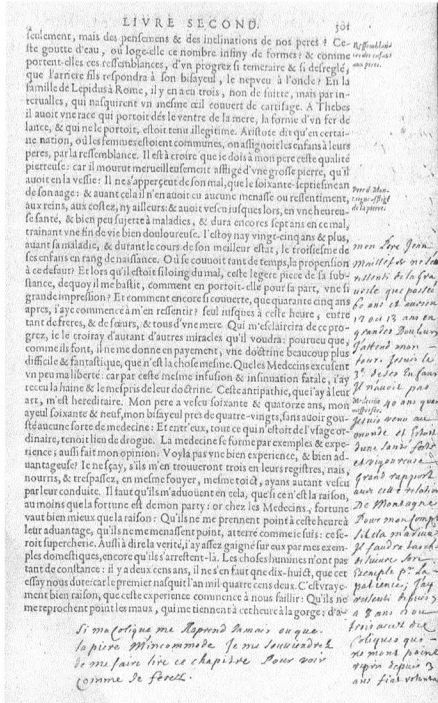

Illus. 2.5.9. Montaigne, *Essais* (Paris: 1640), Bibliothèque municipale de Bordeaux, press-mark G.F. 495 Res, p. 501 (annotated Maillefer family copy). Reproduced by permission of the Bibliothèque municipale de Bordeaux.

On the 1 June he is reading the 'histoire de ma vie' that he wrote thirteen years previously, in 1667. He gets to the point where he is forty-four years old, which corresponds to the year 1655. He sees that in 1667 he had written the following:

> I am now forty-four years old and I can say that all of my actions up to this point have scarcely been preceded by judgement and have been completed almost without reflection [*réflexion*]. But from this day forward, I can say that, with the family which God has given me, he has, in his eternal grace, opened my eyes, as much as I can say, without boasting about it myself, and by his own grace, I weigh [*je peze*] nearly all my actions, if not so strongly my words.[91]

In Maillefer's life-history, then, God is ultimately given the credit for enfranchising him with a liberty of judgement, even if the *Essais* 'alone' prove to be a useful worldly tool in the same process.

---

[91] Jadart 64: 'J'arive à quarante quattre ans et je puis dire que touttes mes actions précédentes ont esté très peue accompagniés de jugement et faittes quasy sans réflexion. Mais du depuis je puis dire que avecq la famille que Dieu ma donné, il m'a par sa grâce ouvert les yeux, d'autant que je puis dire, sans me vanter et par sa mesme grâce: je peze presques touttes mes actions, non pas sy fort les parolles.'

Reading this on the 1 June 1680, he feels he must add a marginal comment:

> At Cormontreuil, on 1st June 1680, where I have been for 15 days, I have not since
> [i.e. since 1667] ceased being at fault in business and civil affairs; but it is our nature,
> my impulsiveness, and the fact that I believed I was doing the right thing. – I am quite
> sickly due to retention and a hernia. I am trying to prepare myself, with the grace of
> God, for death.[92]

In his retreat, Maillefer is glossing his own writing of his own life, layering his
reflections in the course of taking stock of his *meurs*, of his suffering, and of his
preparations for death. On the 3 June, back in his son's copy of Montaigne, he has
read more than fifty folios. He arrives at the opening of I 21, 'One man's profit is
another man's loss' ('Le profit de l'un est dommage de l'autre'), which reads as
follows:

> Demades condemned a fellow Athenian whose trade was to sell funeral requisites on
> the grounds that he wanted too much profit from it and that this profit could only be
> made out of the deaths of a great many people. That judgement seems ill-founded
> since no profit is ever made except at somebody else's loss: by his reckoning you would
> have to condemn earnings of every sort. The merchant can only thrive by tempting
> youth to extravagance....[93]

Maillefer then writes a note in the margin of the copy, the first written trace of his
reading of the *Essais* (Illus. 2.5.10). His handwriting is difficult to decipher but the
gist of the note is clear. Maillefer is comparing Demades the Athenian to a local
tradesman, one Thomas, who also makes a living from funeral requisites, and who
would like there to be deaths every day.

Here I give the French first as it is not coherent or legible enough to convey only
in translation:

[icy] X Du iii Juing 1680 [par? Im?]

Cest le Compte de thomas []neur de nostre paroisse qui voudrait que Ily eut
Chaque jour des mortes [*sic*]

[Here?] 3 June 1680

[It's the reckoning of Thomas [] of our parish, who would like there to be deaths
every day][94]

It is not difficult to see why Maillefer notes this passage. He was a wealthy provincial merchant whose profits had brought him a *logis* in the country to add to his
townhouse on Rue de l'Université in Rheims—the latter a house so splendid that

---

[92] Jadart 64–65: 'A Cormontreuille, ce 1er juin 1680, où je suis depuis 15 jours, Je né pas laissé de
faire encore bien des fautes despuis dans les affaires et conduitte civils; mais c'est nostre nature, ma
promptitude et que j'ay creue bien faire. – Je suis assés incomodé d'une retention et d'une descente de
boyaux. Je tâche de me préparer avecq la grâce de Dieu à la mort.'

[93] I 21, NP110/BVH Paris 1595, p. 53/S121; Bibliothèque municipale de Bordeaux, G. F. 495 rés,
fol. 52.

[94] Even though he saw Montaigne's 'mort', Maillefer wrote 'morte', as he always did in the journal.
The published edition of the journal corrects this spelling.

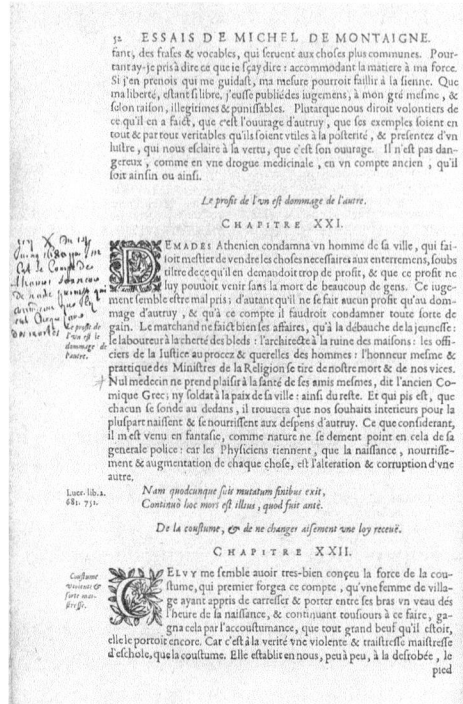

Illus. 2.5.10. Montaigne, *Essais* (Paris: 1640), Bibliothèque municipale de Bordeaux, pressmark G.F. 495 Res, p. 52 (annotated Maillefer family copy). Reproduced by permission of the Bibliothèque municipale de Bordeaux.

it was chosen to host the royal party when they stayed in the town. Book I chapter 21 is one of the least developed of Montaigne's chapters. But Maillefer interestingly does exactly what Montaigne both recommends at various points in the *Essais* and does himself in the margins of the Bordeaux copy. He adduces one of his own experiences, from his own locality. 'Nostre paroisse' is the parish of Saint-Étienne at Rheims, in the life of which Maillefer was deeply involved.[95]

This is the only annotation by Jean Maillefer in the whole volume, although—as we have seen—there are others by his eldest son François-Elie Maillefer. Why is this so? Historians of marginalia who take the sparseness of annotations to indicate a lack of close attention on the part of the reader should take heed at this point; for, after making this one annotation in the margin, Maillefer decided to transcribe extracts from the *Essais* directly into his *livre secret* and comment upon them there. Indeed, the fact that the solitary annotation is dated in the same way as entries in the *livre secret* probably means that he intended to copy it across.

We know from a later entry that Maillefer read on to folio 173, before skipping to folio 595, III 6 ('Des coches'), and reading to the end. He puts this down to 'the

---

[95] Robert Benoit, *Vivre et mourir à Reims au Grand siècle: (1580- 1720)* (2nd edn., Arras: Artois Presses Université, 1999).

impatience of the Frenchman who devours books'.[96] Does this mean that he was impatient to get to those final chapters in particular? They are certainly the chapters with which he most intensively engages. Indeed, there are no extracts from the *Essais* in the *livre secret* until he gets to those chapters. Let us look at the relevant opening (i.e two facing pages) of the 'troiziesme livre secret', dated the 4 June 1680, the day after the first marginal annotation (Illus. 2.5.11).[97]

The first entry on this illustrated opening registers that he is 'invited to the funeral of Madame Lietage's daughter', a neighbour. This is one of more than a hundred such invitations registered in the journal. It explains why, suffering from a terrible hernia, reading back over his own written life, meditating death, he picked out the passage on the tradesman who profits from burials and relates it back to his own parish.

As we go down the left-hand page, there follows a remark about a good soup not needing an elaborate garnish, with a maxim attached: 'often that which is beautiful is not always good' ('souuent Ce quy est beau nest pas toursiours bon'). This is not, it would seem, from Montaigne. There then follow two extracts from III 8 ('De l'art de conférer'). The first extract might also have been made by L'Estoile: Montaigne remarks that there is no greater *fadaise* than to rail at the *fadaises* of the world. Maillefer comments on this by recalling from memory a similar remark in Seneca.

Next is a long extract from III 12 endorsing the notion of a vow of ignorance, to counteract the appetite we have for the study of books:

> I once took pleasure in seeing men somewhere or other, through piety, take a vow of ignorance, as one might of chastity, poverty, and penitence. And that *sic* we need but little learning to live at ease and Socrates teaches us that it lies within us, as well as how to find it there and how to make it help us. All this ability of ours that is beyond the natural is more or less vain and superfluous. It is a lot if it does not burden us more than it serves us.[98]

He then completes the entry for 4 June, the 'essai de Jean Maillefer' for that day. He does so by enacting Montaigne's Socratean wisdom, by suppressing his strong desire to study books:

> Here I closed the book of all things
> moderate and good [*modicum et bonum*][99]

'Modicum et bonum' is the title of one of *Les cent nouvelles nouvelles* by Vigneulles. It is used in the context of culinary morality. In the story a priest asks for 'light' or

[96] Jadart 280/BmR MS 1980, fol. 259r.

[97] Jadart 276–7/BmR MS 1980, fols. 256v–57r. Jadart leaves out four pages of Maillefer's writings at this point (fols. 256v–58r), including several mentions of Montaigne. The quotations that follow in the next few paragraphs are all from the left-hand (fol. 256v) or right-hand (fol. 257r) pages of this opening.

[98] 'Jay pris plaisir de voir en quelque lieu des homes par devotion faire voeu dignorance Comme de Chastete de pauvrete et ~~dey~~ de poenitence et que Il ne nous faut guere de doctrine pour vivre a nostre aise et Socrates nous aprend que elle est en nous et la maniere de ly treuver et de sen aider toutte Ceste nostre sufisance, quy est au dela de la nature est a peue pres vaine et superflue Cest beaucoup sy elle ne nous Charge plus que elle ne nous ~~ser~~ sert'. Compare III 12, NP1084–5/BVH Paris 1595, bk. III, p. 175/S1175–6.

[99] 'icy Jay ferme le livre de touttes choses/modicum et bonum'.

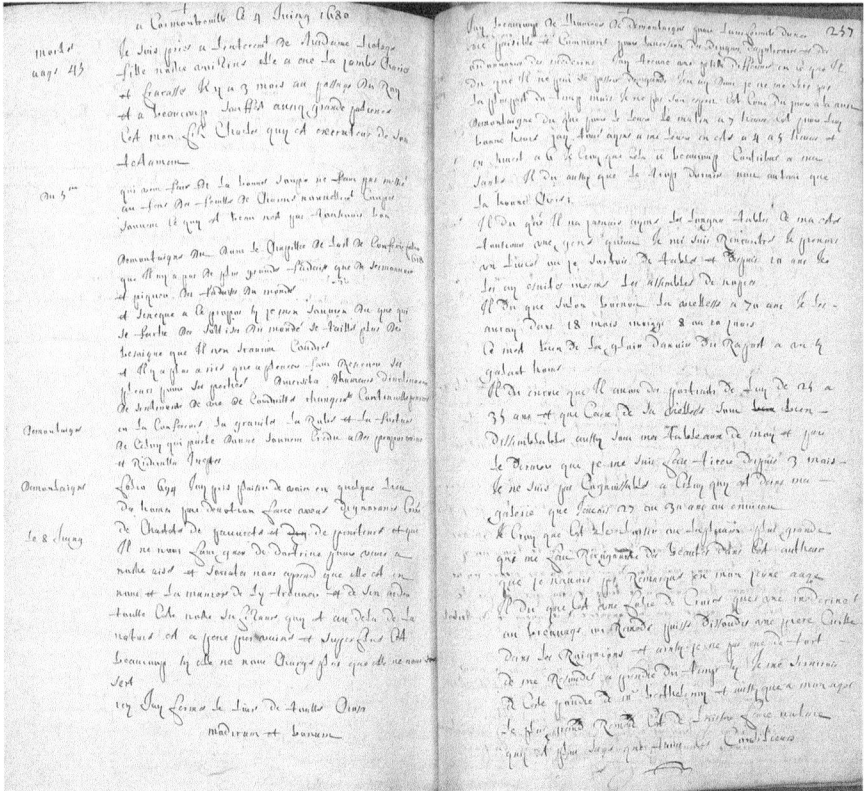

Illus. 2.5.11. 'Mémoires de Jean Maillefer, continués par son fils', Bibliothèque municipale de Reims, MS 1980, fols. 256v–57r. Reproduced by permission of the Bibliothèque municipale de Reims.

'moderate' and good food—nothing heavy and over-rich—to be prepared for a group of gentlemen. (The joke in Vigneulles' tale is that they end up eating a donkey whose name was 'Modicum').[100]

On a page which moralizes about soup, Maillefer is using this Latin phrase to sum up the perfectly judged householder's morality he finds in the final chapters of Montaigne's book, especially, as we shall see in a moment, in 'De l'experience'. Here is a book that even shows one how to be moderate in one's private consumption of books. Again, Montaigne's book and Maillefer's book run together as the paired *livres secrets* in which he can reflect upon his own *meurs* and household conduct.

This is confirmed on the right-hand page, the entry for 10 June 1680, which reveals that he has got to *Essais* III 13, and to Montaigne's long, detailed description of his form of life. It begins:

---

[100] Philippe de Vigneulles, *Les cent nouvelles nouvelles*, eds Robert H. Ivy, Charles H. Livingston, and Françoise H. Livingston (Geneva: Droz, 1972), 68–72 (no. 4).

I share greatly with Montaigne a temperament that inclines towards a peaceful and common life, and against apothecaries' drugs and doctors' regimes. I found a little difference in what he says about being ill at ease without gloves – I have some which I don't use the majority of the time. But I don't have his wit, in that respect we are like day and night.[101]

For the rest of the page Maillefer provides a running commentary on some of the detail of the long section in 'De l'experience' which famously begins: 'I have lived long enough now to give an account of the regimen [*pour mettre en compte l'usage*] which has got me thus far.'[102] Each detail of Montaigne's domestic life prompts Maillefer to give an account of his own usage. Maillefer concludes: 'at my age, the best remedy is to allow nature to run its course, since nature herself is wiser than all other advisers [*les consiliers*]'.[103]

The register of Maillefer's reading of Montaigne does not stop there, even though he has apparently returned the copy to his son. He has clearly taken extracts and notes of passages on separate sheets, which he then copies into his *livre secret* at different points. These reveal that he did go back to read the central portion of the book, which he initially skipped. He tells us, for example, that he wishes 'that this chapter on some lines of Virgil [III 5] was not there; it is too free [*trop libre*]; I only wanted to read some of the marginal notes'.[104]

Maillefer's own marginal note describing the entry for 14 June 1680 summarizes it as 'more of the comparison with Montaigne' ('parallele encore avecq demontaigne'). The entry confirms Huet's analysis of the reasons why every country gentleman has a copy of the *Essais* on his mantelpiece. The comparison this time (between Maillefer and Montaigne) is with respect to the kinds of books the two of them have read, and how they have read them: 'I have after all much in common with Monsieur de Montaigne, who like me could not study with too much application; but I do not have his wit, sure enough' ('apres tout Jay beaucoup de Raport aux humeurs de Monsieur de montaigne qui na peue Come moy estudier par trop dap[lication?] mais Je ne pas son esprit Il sen faut bien'). There follows the passage already quoted, in which he notes his son's annotations and concludes that Montaigne's book alone is capable of forming the judgement.[105]

What conclusions can we draw about the comparison—pursued in writing by Maillefer himself—between these two regional reader-writers? From Huet's point of view they share a lack of application to proper scholarly study. But broader, more generous parallels are possible between the backgrounds and mentalities of these two free literates.

---

[101] 'Jay beaucoup de lhumeur De demontaigne pour luniformite d'une vie paisible et Commune pour laversion des drogues dapoticaire et des ordonnances des médecins J'ay treuve une petite difference en Ce que Il dit que Il ne peut se passer des gands Jen ay Dont je ne me sers pas la pluspart du temps mais Je ne pas son esprit Cest Come du jour a la nuit.' This passage does appear in Jadart (276–7). Compare III 13, NP1131/BVH Paris 1595, bk. III, p. 207/S1230 ('Et me passerois autant mal-aisément de mes gans').

[102] III 13, NP1127/BVH Paris 1595, bk. III, p. 204/S1226.

[103] Jadart 277/BmR MS 1980, fol. 257r.

[104] Jadart 284/BmR MS 1980, fol. 264r.

[105] Jadart 279/BmR MS 1980, fol. 258v.

At the level of family history, one can compare the Eyquems at the beginning of the sixteenth century with the Maillefers in the mid-seventeenth century: a family of merchants, of provincial bourgeois who are beginning to pursue higher forms of literate education, public office, even nobility, and who make a pact with the state, the King, while reserving freedom of judgement and conscience via *l'écriture du for privé*. Maillefer finds in Montaigne's *humeur*, as presented with great wit in an authoritative folio, a precedent for his private identity as a free literate whose own *naturel* guides him in his reading and thought as much as the clerics in the religious houses and libraries in town.

At the level of *mentalité*, it lies in the inclination 'towards a peaceful and common life' ('une vie paisible et commune'). Maillefer was in frequent contact, both in Rheims, and in his own family, with people of religious vocation leading 'exemplary lives' ('vies exemplaires'). His own son-in-law, now known as Saint John-Baptiste de la Salle, is a case in point. Like Montaigne, Maillefer revered such external models, but he established a *patron au dedans*, within himself and within his household, by means of his reading and writing.

Like Montaigne, Maillefer had a positive antipathy to the regimes of the doctors in distant Paris, as to other forms of specialist science other than the official doctrine of the Roman Catholic Church. Maillefer's self-portrait tells us that he also had a profound aversion to the royal decrees which regularly billeted soldiers from other regions and countries in his own house, forcing him to move out—to, more broadly, the incessant civil and international wars that interrupted inter-regional trade. Like Montaigne, he loathed the social obligation to strive for public offices, both those which are bought, and those which are gained by intrigues.

Maillefer's 'troiziesme livre secret' is a private family forum in which he can express these aversions with the same *liberté* and *franchise* claimed in the *Essais*.[106] Montaigne may say that he has abandoned the ancient usage upheld by his father—the keeping of household journals. But the parallel with Maillefer suggests that Montaigne did indeed 'refresh', in a radical and witty way, this usage. At the height of the *grand siècle*, at a moment when public intellectuals were censoring, abridging, and banning the *Essais*, they were being profoundly appreciated as a highly sophisticated and witty version of the kind of book in which a regional merchant might register his domestic *meurs* and form his judgement in the cabinet of his retreat in the country—as, in short, a *livre secret*.

2.5.7 CODA: MONTAIGNE MIGRATES TO ENGLAND

As Alan Boase showed decades ago, the mid-1660s—only a few years after Maillefer first encountered the *Essais*—was a turning point in the fortunes of the *Essais* in France.[107] After that date, increasing numbers of ecclesiastical scholars and

[106] On *franchise* and *liberté* and their Latin cognates, see 2.1.3 and the first footnote there.
[107] Boase, *passim.*

philosophers lined up to expose and condemn Montaigne's *esprit libre* and *air de franchise*. Placed on the Roman Catholic Index in 1676, Montaigne's work was not published in full in France between 1669 and 1725.

Did this affect the reading of a regional merchant in Rheims? He used a copy of the 1640 edition and knew nothing of the prohibition published in Rome. In his study in Cormontreuil he aspired to be the 'country gentleman' imagined with distaste by Huet, the non-scholarly reader-writer who only needed a copy of the *Essais* to acquire some literary hues and form his judgement. But he did declare III 5 too free and could only bring himself to read a few of the summary marginal notes to that chapter.

Huet acknowledged that the *Essais* were still popular in France in the 1710s, despite the lack of new editions. However, as we had cause to note in 2.1.5 and at the beginning of 1.5, the increasingly censorious attitude of members of the French republic of letters during this period, and the placing of the *Essais* on the Index, was noted across the channel.

The response of the producers of Cotton's English translation (Cotton had died in 1687) was to go beyond Samuel Daniel in enfranchising Montaigne as a citizen of England. The 1700 edition, along with the 'Vindication', contained a letter from Cotton's patron Halifax (inserted late in the printing of the work). The letter welcomed the dedication of the previous editions of the translation, and endorsed the idea that Cotton has done the French author more right than his own country, whose impertinent scribblers had damaged his reputation. The nature of the great man was too big to be confined to the exactness of a studied style.[108] The edition greeted the Frenchman as an exile from his own country. It claimed that Montaigne met with a more favourable entertainment in England than in his native France because the latter had become a servile nation.

It sketched, in other words, a far more positive image of Montaigne's education, and of the *Essais*' role in the *affranchisement* of reader-writers, than Huet's remarks in the *Huetiana* would a few years later, and related this to differences in the political and cultural conditions in England and France. The school of Montaigne could flourish in the former where it could not in the latter. The 'Vindication' started by noting the phenomenon that Huet would describe in different terms: even though miscellaneous, without order and connection, 'people of all qualities' made the *Essais* their 'chief study'.[109]

But it went on to characterize the *Essays* as 'the *manuale* of all Gentlemen', due to Montaigne's 'uncommon way of teaching, winning People to the practice of Virtue, as much as other Books fright them away from it, by the dogmatical and imperious way which they assume' (alluding to Montaigne's depiction of virtue in I 25). The *Essays* are also found in the libraries of 'Ladies', who it is wished could 'improve themselves by reading this excellent Book' without having to encounter

---

[108] Michel de Montaigne, *Essays*, trans. Charles Cotton, 3 vols. (London: M. Gillyflower, W. Hensman and R. Wellington, 1700), vol. 1, sigs. [*2]r–[*4]v. I have not found this letter from Halifax in copies of the fourth, 1711 edition.
[109] Montaigne, *Essays*, vol. 1, sig. B1r.

Montaigne's more licentious passages. This is doubtless a reference to III 5, the very chapter Maillefer would have done without.[110]

The main issue in the 'Vindication', which draws on Charles Sorel, is the one implicitly raised by Cornwallis a hundred years before: does learning mingled with nobility in this ostentatiously unmethodical and witty, pleasurable way describe a path to virtuous freedom for the gentry and nobility, or not? His French enemies believe it does not, and draw on Montaigne's own admission in the opening to I 25, where he says that his learning stretches only to an indifferent knowledge of 'practical Morals and History...acquir'd in reading *Seneca* and *Plutarch*'.[111]

The author of the 'Vindication' believes it does, and part of the discourse is aimed at the detractors' image of Montaigne as an over-bold and ignorant country gentleman. It reconfirms Montaigne's culture and status as a nobleman—backed up by the letter from Cotton's noble patron the Marquess of Halifax in the 1700 edition. Half of the 'Life' of Montaigne prefacing the text is lifted and adapted from Cotton's translation of I 25, as when it recounts how Montaigne's father sought 'to Educate his Soul with all Sweetness and Liberty'.[112]

Furthermore, there is evidence that early modern English readers identified with what Montaigne had to say about his noble education. Some time after 1706, Alexander Pope read, in Cotton's translation, one of the passages in I 25 in which Montaigne describes how formal arts education had corrupted his informal household education. Pope placed an 'X' against it and wrote in the margin: 'mutato nomine/ de me/ Fabula narratur' ('with the name changed, he is telling my story').[113] Pope's note again suggests that the *Essays*—and I 25 in particular—could offer a printed template for a personal, 'household' formation, rooted in an unsatisfactory experience of institutionalized humane learning (though in Maillefer's case the unsatisfactoriness lay in its discontinuation).

This is supported also by the case of the collaboration between the gentleman philosopher John Locke, who possessed a copy of Florio's Montaigne (1603) and of the Parisian edition of 1669 (the last—of the full text—until 1725), and the Huguenot refugee Pierre Coste. Locke's journal shows he was reading the *Essais* in 1676–7 and 1684.[114] Though of lower status and wealth than Montaigne, he was praised in his own day in terms similar to those used by Cornwallis of the Gascon nobleman: as someone who brought philosophy out of the schools and 'into the Company of the better and politer Sort' such as nobles and gentlemen. He chose to pursue philosophy as a member of noble and gentle households (that of the first

[110] Montaigne, *Essays*, vol. 1, sigs. B5v–6r.

[111] Montaigne, *Essays*, vol. 1, sigs. P3r, B1v.

[112] Montaigne, *Essays*, vol. 1, sigs. A5r, S7v.

[113] Maynard Mack, *Collected in himself: essays critical, biographical, and bibliographical on Pope and some of his contemporaries* (East Brunswick, London and Toronto: Associated University Presses, 1982), 426.

[114] John Locke, *Some thoughts concerning education*, eds. John W. Yolton and Jean S. Yolton (Oxford: Clarendon, 1989), 13; O'Brien, 'Montaigne, Sir Ralph Bankes', 12–14. On Coste and the broader context of Anglo–French cultural exchange at the time, see Delphine Soulard, 'Anglo-French cultural transmission: the case of John Locke and the Huguenots', *Historical Research*, 85 (2012), 105–32.

Earl of Shaftesbury, in London, then that of Sir Francis Masham at Oates) rather than of a university, and to fulfil philosophical offices 'without names' not dissimilar to those described in 1.4.[115]

As such, one of the capacities in which he acted, and in which Montaigne had acted a century before, was advising the nobility and gentry on the education of their sons. Locke in fact had plenty of early experience tutoring or caring for young gentlemen, whether as an Oxford don, a paediatrician, a private tutor, or a travelling governor on the grand tour. Though generally offered in manuscript letters and separates to patrons who consulted him, Locke did print his advice on the topic as a treatise in England in 1693—a treatise based particularly on letters he had sent from Holland (1684–91) to Edward Clarke about the education of his son.[116]

The question of the literary sources of the treatise is still debated in the scholarly literature.[117] But a contemporary collaborator of Locke, Pierre Coste, thought Montaigne's *Essais*, especially I 25, to be the most important source and analogue. Locke himself mentions Montaigne only once in the treatise, but the context is very telling. He turns to what he says is the most difficult and the most important task in the whole business: the choice of a 'tutor' or 'governour' who is 'fit to Educate and Form the Mind of a Young Gentleman'. You must inquire everywhere for such a man, '[a]nd I remember, *Montaigne* says in one of his Essays, That the Learned *Castalio* was fain to make Trenchers at *Basel* to keep himself from starving, when his Father would have given any Money for such a Tutor for his Son'. Locke is misremembering the detail of a passage in I 34, but the mistake reveals how closely he associates Montaigne with the topics of the choice of the right 'governour' or 'tutor' and of the direct method of Latin-learning—the topics of *Essais* I 25.[118]

Two years after its first publication Locke's treatise was translated by Pierre Coste into French. If Florio, the son of an Italian Protestant exile, shaped reception of Montaigne in England in the seventeenth century by publishing a translation, Coste, a French Huguenot exiled by the 1685 revocation of the Edict of Nantes, shaped his reception in the eighteenth century by publishing a new edition (1724).[119] And just as Florio began his translation with I 25, in household service as an educator of the young nobility, so the entrée to Coste's edition was the same chapter and the same kind of service.

---

[115] Richard Yeo, 'John Locke and polite philosophy', in Condren, Gaukroger, and Hunter (eds.), *The philosopher in early modern Europe*, 254–75, 257–8 (quoting a letter from the third Earl of Shaftesbury), 262.

[116] John Locke, *The educational writings*, ed. James Axtell (Cambridge: Cambridge University Press, 1968), 36–48, 341–96; Locke, *Some thoughts concerning education*, 5–7, 44–7, 68, 79 ('I my self have been consulted of late by so many, who profess themselves at a loss how to breed their Children').

[117] Locke, *Some thoughts concerning education*, 12–13.

[118] Locke, *Some thoughts concerning education*, 149. Sebastien Castellio was the author of a set of Latin dialogues used in teaching Latin.

[119] Locke, *Some thoughts concerning education*, 65; Tilde Sankovitch, '"Un travail vétilleux [...] fort nécessaire": The Coste Edition of 1724', *Montaigne Studies*, 7 (1995), 131–45.

Shortly after publishing his 1695 translation of *Some thoughts*, Coste (via a recommendation from Jean Le Clerc) entered into correspondence with the author, who in turn recommended him for the post of tutor to the young Francis Cudworth Masham, at Locke's patron's house in Oates. He arrived in September 1697, and was there until shortly after Locke died in 1704. Now living in the same household, Coste worked and became familiar with Locke during the period in which the latter was expanding *Some thoughts*, and Coste was both revising his translation of that work and preparing a French translation of Locke's famous *Essay*. He was Locke's preferred translator.[120]

When in 1708 Coste published his revised translation of *Some thoughts*, using the posthumous, expanded edition of 1705, he added numerous notes showing the 'marvellous relationship' between Locke's and Montaigne's thoughts, as there is 'little concerning the education of children that Montaigne has not touched upon in his *Essays*', for the 'matter was close to his heart, he returned to it whatever topic he was on.' Locke, Coste tells us, had read this author, and took account of what he said.[121]

Of the many passages Coste cites and quotes in footnotes, at least seven are from I 25, while five are from the next most important chapter on Locke's topic, II 8. When Locke discusses the best method for learning Latin, and the importance of learning to judge rather than learning to parrot knowledge, Coste aligns him with Montaigne's remarks in I 25.[122]

Coste underlines the centrality of one remark in *Essais* II 8 to Locke's whole ethos of gentle education by capitalizing it. Montaigne is condemning—as Locke does in the passage above on the same page—all violence in the education of tender souls for honour and liberty. Violence is for slaves, not freemen. Montaigne himself was raised without violence; his daughter Léonor has been, too. He would have been even more scrupulous with boys, who are less born to serve and of freer condition: 'I would have loved to make their hearts overflow with openness and frankness' ('J'EUSSE AIMÉ À LEUR GROSSIR LE COEUR D'INGENUITÉ ET DE FRANCHISE').[123]

Coste, himself a tutor to the gentry and nobility, clearly appreciates that shared ideas about the education of the freeborn (male) soul in *franchise* were central to the philosophies of Montaigne and Locke. The question of the extent to which this appreciation informs his edition of the *Essais* is beyond the scope of this study. It is worth noting, though, that his paratexts do highlight Montaigne's quality of 'noble

[120] J. Milton, 'Pierre Coste, John Locke, and the Third Earl of Shaftesbury', in Sarah Hutton, Paul Schuurman, and G. A. J. Rogers (eds.), *Studies on Locke: sources, contemporaries, and legacy: in honour of G.A.J. Rogers* (Dordrecht: Springer, 2008), 195–223; Margaret E. Rumbold, *Traducteur huguenot: Pierre Coste* (New York: P. Lang, 1991), 6–8, 10–13; Locke, *The educational writings*, 88–97.
[121] John Locke, *De l'éducation des enfans ... sur la dernière édition revue, corrigée et augmentée*, trans. Pierre Coste (Amsterdam: H. Schelte, 1708), sigs. **7r–v, A7v.
[122] Locke, *De l'éducation des enfans*, sigs. A7v, C1v, V6r, Z6v (2 passages), 2A8v, 2C7r (all from I 25); D6r, D7r, E3v, L8v, M1r (all from II 8). In subsequent editions Coste added further citations from Montaigne in the footnotes.
[123] Locke, *De l'éducation des enfans*, sig. E3v.

candeur' and its appreciation by no less a critic than the Duke of Buckingham, as well as his role in instructing readers such as his own elite subscribers ('Many of our Chief Nobility and Gentry') in self-study.[124]

Coste's edition and Cotton's translation shaped the place of Montaigne in English letters for a hundred years or more. The former definitively made him a canonical figure, a patron-author, partly by collecting his letters and his critics together with the *Essais* in one edition: Montaigne's literary remains were now an *œuvre*. But in the next chapter we shall see that Pierre Villey's edition and Donald Frame's translation combined to displace them and all other competitors in the mid-twentieth century Anglophone sphere. In this displacement, the person, the mind of Montaigne came to have a life of its own beyond the book.

---

[124] Sankovitch, ' "Un travail vétilleux" ', n.12 (citing the preface to the 1759 edition of Cotton's translation), 136.

2.6

The *Essais* Framed for Modern
Intellectual Life

2.6.1 MONTAIGNE EXPLAINS HIMSELF IN 1946

In 1946, Michel de Montaigne was called before the Committee on Humanism and Society of a major American university.[1] He was required to explain himself in advance of a vote on the inclusion or exclusion of his *Essays* from the university's core course in the humanities. A professor from the Department of Sociology and the School of Education with progressive ideas had a problem with Montaigne. A passive aristocrat sealed in an ivory tower was, he felt, of no use to the teachers of the core course. Indeed, the sceptical *Essays* could only harm a young generation whose task was the reconstruction of a damaged civilization in the immediate aftermath of a war.

Montaigne, in self-defence, starts with a little autobiography. Scepticism, he says, was merely a phase that had taught him to laugh at idealism untested by experience. He agrees with another of the professors present, an ally, that his intellectual career should in fact be seen as developing through three phases: stoic, sceptic, and epicurean. To further rebut the sociology professor's charges, Montaigne's professorial ally adds that the Gascon's experiences of a civil war *were* relevant to a generation whose own world had twice been torn apart by war.

Studied both in a historical context and in a contemporary light the *Essays* could give young men and women an example of those unifying conceptions that 'we are seeking to define in our educational programme'. Montaigne himself then goes on the counter-attack. The 'inner man who must be sought for, awakened, educated and brought to maturity' did not even exist for his opponent, the sociology professor. As for passivity, who could say that Pascal or 'your great countryman, Emerson' were made passive by what they had learned of the French essayist?

We do not know the outcome of the committee's vote. The whole dialogue is of course a fiction, published by the Harvard professor and Shakespearean scholar Theodore Spencer at a moment when the post-war debate about the value and governance of the humanities was gathering steam in America. It is not clear if Montaigne's fictional ally is to be identified with a particular contemporary of Spencer's.

But the person who was to play this professor's role in post-war American culture, who was to chart the development of Montaigne's intellectual career, to make

[1] The source for the first three paragraphs is Theodore Spencer, 'Montaigne in America', *The Atlantic Monthly* 177, no. 3 (1947), 91–7.

him speak to a contemporary American audience of their own experience, to defend Montaigne's value in the context of an educational programme rooted in the great books, was Columbia professor Donald M. Frame. 'Frame's Montaigne' came together over two decades and consisted of a series of related works. He published his first book (his doctoral thesis) on the nineteenth-century reception of Montaigne in 1940; selected translated essays followed for the 'Classics Club' in 1943; the complete translated works in 1957 (with a separate *Complete Essays* in 1958); and the biography with Harcourt, Brace & World in New York, and with Hamish Hamilton in London, in 1965.[2]

Frame was educated at Harvard College (1928–32) and did his graduate work at Columbia University (1934–41). He taught at Columbia from 1938 until his retirement, and saw active duty in the Second World War.[3] He summonsed Montaigne from the past to educate two subsequent generations of American men (and, in his later career, a few American women): those coming of age during the war, and those educated in the late 1950s/early 1960s.

Gore Vidal graduated from high school in 1943 aged seventeen and went straight into active service for two years. In June 1992, as a 66-year-old, he reviewed Michael Screech's new English translation of Montaigne's *Essays* and began to tell the story of another translation that had been part of his life for thirty years. The personally annotated book with maroon binding which Vidal first acquired in the early 1960s and which he had kept—if not at his bedside—always to hand, was a copy of Donald Frame's *Complete Works of Montaigne*. The copy reminded him, amongst other things, of conversations he had had about the classics with the poet Robert Frost in the 1950s. Aware of his reputation as America's finest essayist, Vidal was to opine in interviews later in the 1990s that the essay was the only form of literature that would survive and that Montaigne, not Shakespeare, should therefore be seen as the father of all literature. Vidal's review-essay on Screech's translation took its place in the second edition of his own collected *Essays* in 2001.[4]

In late February of the same year (1992), 48-year-old New York film critic and journalist David Denby attended a seminar on Montaigne as part of Columbia

[2] Donald M. Frame, *Montaigne in France, 1812–1852* (New York: Columbia University Press, 1940); Michel de Montaigne (ed.), *Selected Essays*, trans. Donald M. Frame (New York: W. J. Black for the Classics Club, 1943); Donald M. Frame, *Montaigne's discovery of man: The humanization of a humanist* (New York: Columbia University Press, 1955); Montaigne, *The Complete Works: Essays, Travel Journal, Letters*; Michel de Montaigne, *Complete Essays*, trans. Donald M. Frame (Stanford: Stanford University Press, 1958); Frame, *Montaigne: a biography* (abbreviated as 'Frame'). The biography was reissued in 1984, and a second edition appeared in French in 1994, with a note by Frame and a new 'Bibliographie raisonnée' by François Rigolot (417–35). See Donald M. Frame, *Montaigne: a biography* (San Francisco: North Point Press, 1984); Donald M. Frame, *Montaigne, une vie, une oeuvre, 1533–1592 … Préface et bibliographie générale par François Rigolot*, trans. J.-C.Arnould et al. (Paris: H. Champion, 1994). Frame's own note in the French edition claims that the first, 1965 edition was also reissued in 1980–2, but I have not been able to find any trace of this.
[3] See the preliminary matter to Raymond C. La Charité (ed.), *O un amy!: Essays on Montaigne in honor of Donald M. Frame* (Lexington, Ky: French Forum, 1977).
[4] See the 27 March 1999 *International Herald Tribune* article (Mary Blume, 'Gore Vidal: Taking American history personally') published online at <http://www.nytimes.com/1999/03/27/style/27iht-vidal.t.html?pagewanted=1>; Gore Vidal, *United States: Essays, 1952–1992* (2nd edn.; New York: Broadway Books, 2001).

University's Literature Humanities core course. Denby used a copy of the translation that had been current when he first encountered Montaigne as an undergraduate at Columbia in the early 1960s—Donald Frame's. He went on to publish an intellectual autobiography of his experiences encountering the 'Great Books' on Columbia's core course. At the centre of this autobiography was the chapter on Montaigne's intellectual autobiography about encountering great books.[5]

Studies of Montaigne's nineteenth- and twentieth-century reception emphasize his influence on modern intellectual life. They show him contributing episodes to the intellectual lives of many modern writers and thinkers.[6] This chapter does the reverse. It shows modern intellectuals from the 1860s to the 1970s in central and western Europe and North America influencing the Montaigne readers come to know, or not to know. Generations of these intellectuals called up the real person Montaigne from behind his text and made him explain his value to idealist programmes of humane education.

In Frame's day, these programmes aimed to protect humane values against the reductive forces of 'progressive' modern society. Until the 1970s, the text of the *Essais*, converted into a strange kind of autobiographical *Bildungsroman*, yielded an intellectual career of moral and spiritual development. Thereafter it began to yield the internal workings and mechanisms of writing or discourse itself. Either way, the subject of the text has been claimed as an important historical precedent for the very idea of a 'modern' or 'postmodern' intellectual life based in reading and writing. The subject of the *Essais* has been set up as a prototype, first, of the 'inner man' awakened, educated, and brought to maturity in the conditions of modernity; and second, and more recently, of the fragmented, discourse-bound subject of postmodernity directing us to reflect on the problematic interplay between life and literature.[7]

As we began to see in the second chapter of Volume 1 (1.2), on Pierre Villey and his milieu, Montaigne has been there at hand, a ready-made historical token of whatever version of 'liberty of judgement', or critical agency, the modern text critic wishes to authenticate. This is the weaker version of the current chapter's argument. The stronger is that from an anthropological point of view we have been led to infer the modern critical mind, not the historical *persona* of Montaigne, to be the primary agent behind the text since the end of the nineteenth century.

This means we can read the *Essais* and their modern derivatives as a document of modern intellectual history. Instead of understanding the *Essais*, with Villey, to mark the stages of the evolution of Montaigne's mind (stoic, sceptic, epicurean), we can understand them to mark the stages of evolution of the idealist and post-idealist tradition in philosophical text studies (modern, late modern, postmodern). From the end of the nineteenth to the end of the twentieth centuries, Montaigne's

[5] David Denby, *Great books: my adventures with Homer, Rousseau, Woolf, and other indestructible writers of the Western world* (New York: Simon & Schuster, 1996).

[6] See especially Dudley M. Marchi, *Montaigne among the moderns: receptions of the 'Essais'* (Providence, R.I.: Berghahn Books, 1994).

[7] Richard Regosin, '1595: Montaigne and His Readers', in Denis Hollier (ed.), *A new history of French literature* (Cambridge, Mass.: Harvard University Press, 1989), 248–53, 251.

work *is* the intellectual autobiography of the modern critical mind from proto-modern infancy to postmodern maturity.[8] This is, of course, not to say that the nature, the design of that work as originally composed, has had no agency in the process.

In other words, the *Essays* have not just been another 'Great Book'. They have been used to naturalize a still highly influential way of imagining the part great books have in educated western (usually male) lives. Old-fashioned 'autobiographical' or self-fashioning readings of Montaigne such as Vidal's and Denby's—to which I return in 2.6.5 and 2.6.6—ultimately rely on a distinctively modern biographical picture of Montaigne himself. He is cast in a singular position in his tower-library, communing with books, set-off at a remove from a social context that, perspectively, figures only as a 'viewed' tableau in the background. This modern biographical picture, and its fictive aspects, has already been the subject of a rigorous critique.[9]

Here I want to mount a corresponding critique of the template of Montaigne's self-fashioning modern reader, the template that in the early twenty-first century is perhaps still keeping new readings of the *Essays*—readings more in tune with their early history—out of mainstream literary culture. He (and occasionally she) is also represented communing in solitary fashion with the text, at a remove from any material or social context, fashioning an autonomous inner life against a background of cultural oppression and decline—whether in a literally imagined 'retreat' or in a virtual, set-apart sphere of self, discourse, and textuality.[10]

Exactly, how, in practice did all this come about? A self-reproducing pattern of social relations around Montaigne's book shaped several generations of modern readers' expectations about the kind of intellectual life in which it was meant to play a central part. The relations involved teachers, editors, and translators, as well as institutions and educational programmes—relations analogous to those we have recovered shaping the transmission of the work in early modern Europe. They centred on particular copies of the *Essays*, encountered in specific situations, loaded with inter-personal baggage.

The generational history of the pattern to which I refer extends back from post-war America into interwar and late nineteenth-century Europe. To reveal it I shall

---

[8] I use the terms 'modern', 'late modern', and 'postmodern' not as precise period markers but as descriptions of the critical moments associated here with the intellectual careers of, respectively, Jakob Burckhardt (1818–97), Erich Auerbach (1892–1957), and Stephen Greenblatt (1942–). Sometimes, I use the term 'modern' to comprehend all three terms. Where talking specifically about late modern critics' relationship to the avant-garde literature of the early twentieth century, I also use the term 'modernist'.

[9] Jean Balsamo, 'Biographie, philologie, bibliographie: Montaigne à l'*essai* d'une "nouvelle histoire" littéraire', *EMF: Studies in Early Modern France*, 9 (2004), 10–29, and chapters by other scholars in the same volume, ed. George Hoffmann, on 'The new biographical criticism' (especially Katherine Almquist).

[10] So Marchi's interesting and wide-ranging study of the modern reception of Montaigne uses a heavily idealist notion of intellectual biography and still espouses the notion that engaging with the *Essais* means 'a crucial awakening to intellectual growth'—that is, growth into the inner or textual life as defined by modernism or postmodernism. His study pays no attention at all to the practicalities of the cultural transmission of the text and its perceived meanings, and very little to the specific social contexts of encounters between readers and editions of the *Essais*.

therefore need to add some European intellectual biographies to the American ones briefly sketched above. I shall also need to draw once again on the technical concept from anthropology underlying the present study: the notion that an art object is an index from which relations of agency and patiency are abducted in specific ways. I start with the modern philosophical origins of the relevant concept of an intellectual life. The concept can be traced to German idealism and its heavily individualistic concepts of *Bildung*, of personal and formative culture. The idealist and post-idealist generations of European intellectuals blocked us into reading Montaigne for the operations of the introspective mind.

2.6.2 GERMAN IDEALISM AND THE MODERN MONTAIGNE

A particular critical trend within German academic idealism shaped the range of biographical-critical readings of Montaigne available in the post-war western academy. Two practitioners of the *Geisteswissenshaften* whose combined careers span most of the period from the mid-nineteenth to the mid-twentieth centuries—Jakob Burckhardt (1818–97) and Erich Auerbach (1892–1957)—exemplify the trend in question. Their work steered away from Kantian systems and the grand historical design of Hegelian World History and towards the inner history of western man's *geist*. The evolution and self-discovery of authentically free and thoughtful individuals became the key both to history and to crisis-bound western civilization's future. This had profound implications for the way that intellectual lives have been represented and lived ever since.

The confluence between German and derivative European forms of idealism and the 'evolving' Montaigne provided by Pierre Villey's chronology of composition and Fortunat Strowski's stratified text of the *Essais* issued in a range of biographical-critical approaches defined by the two most influential writers on Montaigne in the post-war period: Hugo Friedrich (1904–78) and Donald Frame (1911–91).[11]

In Friedrich's case, the influence of German academic idealism is of course direct. He cites Burckhardt throughout his study of Montaigne and explicitly compares the two figures. He was educated by the great generation of Germanist and romance philologists that were exiled under Nazism and that included Karl Vossler, Leonardo Olschki, Leo Spitzer, and Auerbach himself (though Friedrich did not study with the latter). Friedrich taught at Freiburg University from 1937 until 1970.

In Frame's case, the influence is indirect. But the general importance of German academic idealism, and of the intellectual migration, in shaping the humanities in

---

[11] On Friedrich, see Erich Köhler (ed.), *Sprachen der Lyrik: Festschrift für Hugo Friedrich zum 70* (Frankfurt: V. Klostermann, 1975) and Fritz Schalk (ed.), *Ideen und Formen; Festschrift für Hugo Friedrich zum 24. XII. 1964* (Frankfurt: V. Klostermann, 1965); on his importance in Montaigne studies, see Hoffmann, *Montaigne's career*, 36 and n.90, and Philippe Desan's introduction to Friedrich, *Montaigne*. On Frame, see La Charité (ed.), *O un amy!*

America from the Second World War onwards, is well documented. One historian has told the story of the post-war American academy's theft of Erich Auerbach's *Mimesis*.[12] Auerbach's work became an American classic for teachers and students of general education and great books courses. As we heard in 2.6.1, Frame was educated at Harvard College (1928–32) and did his graduate work at Columbia University (1934–41). He taught at Columbia from 1938 until his retirement.

Friedrich, of course, did not write a biography, but a philosophical interpretation of Montaigne that drew occasionally on biography, and Frame did not write only a biography, but a critical interpretation and a translation. It is arguable that all criticism necessarily has a biographical aspect.[13] All forms of critical inference relate texts explicitly or implicitly to the lived experience—the inner or outer history, or both—of their producers and readers.

The point here is twofold. First, Montaigne is himself the most compelling practitioner of biographical-critical inference in pre-modern European cultural history. In Plutarchan fashion, he dedicates himself not to history but to biography understood as the *recherche* of signs of the human soul.[14] He is a connoisseur of the physiognomic art of reading souls, and prepares his own textual face accordingly. Second, nineteenth-century German idealism installed a particular modern form of biographical-critical inference at the centre of the humanities. Idealism made the story of the textual and artistic past the story of objectifications of man's philosophical consciousness and self-consciousness—his ideas of man and of himself.[15]

This had profound repercussions for Montaigne criticism.[16] It was only a matter of time before Montaigne's printed self-portrait was claimed as a proto-modern philosophical life. And the *Essais* came to serve the philosophical critic not just as an intimate representation of a historical individual's self-consciousness, but also as a legitimating prototype of the modern philosophical critic's own enterprise. Montaigne himself is pictured participating in the unsystematic collection of an inner history of humanity based in individual experience, in the very principle of individuation.

More particularly, he is refashioned as a humanist thinker in the 'random', self-reflexive, existentialist moulds of the various opponents of the speculative systems of Kant and Hegel. This is most obvious when he is directly compared to unsystematic thinkers such as Burckhardt and Auerbach, essayists who bring biographical and autobiographical anecdote into the practice of philosophical and critical history. The *Essais* become what the practice of cultural history was for both

---

[12] Carl Landauer, 'Auerbach's performance and the american Academy, or how New Haven stole the idea of *Mimesis*', in Seth Lerer (ed.), *Literary history and the challenge of philology: the legacy of Erich Auerbach* (Stanford: Stanford University Press, 1996), 179–94.

[13] George Hoffmann, 'Introduction', *EMF: Studies in Early Modern France*, 9 (2004), 1–9.

[14] Montaigne, *Les Essais*, vol. 1, 13–14,

[15] Fritz K. Ringer, *The decline of the German Mandarins: the German academic community, 1890–1933* (2nd edn.; Hanover: Wesleyan University Press, 1990), 90–102.

[16] See especially Jean Starobinski, *Montaigne in motion*, trans. Arthur Goldhammer (Chicago: University of Chicago Press, 1985), and the essays collected in Harold Bloom (ed.), *Modern critical interpretations: Michel de Montaigne's 'Essays'* (New York: Chelsea House Publishers, 1987).

of these scholars: 'a survival kit for hard times, the repository of what is essentially human and humanly essential about the "old culture of Europe"'.[17]

The intention is not to expose this as a 'misreading' of the *Essais*. The argument of previous chapters in this study has been that the book was designed—in its original context—as a survival kit for hard times. I am extending—into the modern period—the same kind of analysis of the agency relations in which the book has always been involved, since its earliest composition and publication. Clerics and humanists have been participants in its history throughout. Ever since the interventions of the Master of the Sacred Palace from Rome, and Justus Lipsius from the University of Leiden, expert readers have recognized the easy virtuosity of the book's personalized display of humane learning.[18]

This has made it a touchstone for the regulation, authentication, and naturalization of various forms of lay critical agency. 'Montaigne' (the person whose qualities are inferred from the book) has always been vulnerable to those who would make an example of him—whether as a figure to be censured or as a practical prototype of one or other programmatic image of lay intellectual life.

In this chapter, then, the argument is that the *Essais* have, in the long twentieth century, consistently been used to naturalize a particular kind of philosophical-critical agency. They have been interpreted as an index of the receptive and self-reflective agency of the unsystematic critical mind, which is normally gendered male, whether explicitly or implicitly (hence the exclusion of Marie de Gournay from the history of the book). This prototypical mind has a changing history that stretches from Burckhardt to Greenblatt. Its characteristic activity is to seek any cultural source offering intimate access to others' inner histories, and in the process to produce and reflect upon its own inner history before the reader's eyes. At the same time, it aims to bring the combined process to full cultural consciousness so as to preserve or reserve Man's inner history from the degenerate, tyrannical, or chaotic forces of an 'outer' history believed to be in terminal decline. It is not difficult to see how compelling Montaigne's text will be for a critical mind of this kind. The essayist does describe his own contemporary world as degenerate.[19]

In the late modern experience of crisis, of threatened discontinuity with the past, the task of authenticating the traces of free humanity's shared inner history becomes at once more urgent and more difficult, not to say impossible. It relies heavily on the textual—literary and philosophical—heritage. Under such conditions, the Montaigne inferred from the *Essais* is the 'late' humanist reading and writing in his tower, serenely living out the decline of classical western civilization—the happy existentialist surviving without metaphysical supports of any kind, the

---

[17] See Lionel Gossman, 'Cultural history and crisis: Burckhardt's *Civilization of the Renaissance in Italy*', *rediscovering history: Culture, politics, and the pysche* (Stanford: Stanford University Press, 1994), 404–27, 427, for the quotation, which applies to Burckhardt; for similar sentiments expressed by the author of *Mimesis*, see Erich Auerbach, *Literary language and its public in late Latin antiquity and in the middle ages*, trans. Ralph Manheim (New York: Pantheon Books, 1965), 5–7.

[18] See 1.6.3 and 1.7.3.

[19] Consider, for example, his comments on the Spanish imperial corruption of the original, natural world in *Essais* III 6.

knight of non-possession.[20] A template is imposed, a template for an intellectual life lived in a 'late' period of spiritual and cultural decline. The historical precedents for the late modern intellectual life are the declining antiquity lived by Plutarch and Tacitus, the late Renaissance of Montaigne and Shakespeare's Hamlet, and the post-revolutionary, sick Europe of Burckhardt and Nietszche.

2.6.3 BURCKHARDT'S INNER MAN

The historical rediscovery of the lived experience of Renaissance individuals in the nineteenth and twentieth centuries is dominated by the figure of Jakob Burckhardt. Burckhardt 'discovered' the Italian Renaissance in reaction to the first or classical era of German idealist and historical thought that started with Herder (1744–1803) and embraced von Ranke (1795–1886) and Hegel (1770–1831), as well as von Humboldt (1767–1835) and Schleiermacher (1768–1834).[21]

In 'discovering' early Italian Renaissance and *quattrocento* biographical descriptions of individual artists and patrons as 'universal men', Burckhardt was encapsulating, in the crisis conditions of the 1850s, what he saw as the authentic neohumanism of early-nineteenth-century Basel. Renaissance works of art were described as mediating the at once self-conscious and natural Italian genius of individual and free personalities whose life projects from early education to cultivated maturity could be retrieved. In their highest forms—the cultivated lives of Leon Battista Alberti and Federico da Montefeltro—these projects gave rise to the most civilized developments of modern western consciousness.

Equally, in their lowest forms—the lives of Cesare Borgia and Sigismondo Malatesta—they gave rise to the most splendidly wicked and barbaric developments of the same consciousness. Either way, the highly developed individual outgrew the limits of medieval civilization, whether in free and urbane or in excessive and immoral fashion. Indeed, the liberal and noble free-thinker and the monstrous and despotic atheist are somehow two sides of the same coin in Burckhardt's moralized narrative. He writes with a sense of cultural crisis, with a sense that the western European tradition could be coming to an end. Just as the humanist civilization of Basel had entered a crisis in the European revolutions of the first half of the nineteenth century, so Italy—in Burckhardt's worldview—had entered a crisis in the sixteenth century, when the humanists fell via unbridled subjectivity into anxiety and unhappiness.[22]

Burckhardt does not discuss Montaigne in this context in *Civilisation*, though he did name him as a great individual of the late Renaissance in his lectures and notes. Given the nature of the *Essais* as a uniquely detailed self-portrait 'au naturel' of an exceptionally cultivated late Renaissance individual whose early education is

---

[20] Stephen Greenblatt, *Marvelous possessions: the wonder of the New World* (Oxford: Oxford University Press, 1991), 150.

[21] Robert M. Burns and Hugh Rayment-Pickard (eds.), *Philosophies of history: from Enlightenment to postmodernity* (Oxford: Blackwell, 2000), 57–97.

[22] Gossman, 'Cultural history and crisis', 411–12, 418–19, for this and the previous paragraph.

described in detail, it is not difficult to see why it was only a matter of time before someone produced an influential Burckhardtian reading of Montaigne. Hugo Friedrich was eventually to do the honours. Friedrich cites Burckhardt's notes on Montaigne, and explicitly compares the wisdom of the two at several points in his study.[23]

Although Burckhardt treats Montaigne as a precedent for the wisdom of the whole humanistic and philosophical revival from Goethe to Dilthey, Friedrich places him more particularly within a series of post-classical or post-crisis thinkers in different periods: Plutarch (late antiquity), Montaigne (late Renaissance), Burckhardt (late humanist, post-revolution), Friedrich himself (late modern, post-war).

Friedrich, then, sketched Montaigne into the larger Burckhardtian picture of the Renaissance discovery of the individual. In Friedrich's hands, this discovery culminates in Montaigne, who completes—by internalizing—the humanist movement began by Petrarch. The inner idea of man first lived by Montaigne 'signified the return of the former Italian universally educated man (*uomo universale*), now in France'. Montaigne's noble class was thus 'the birthplace of the freest humanity the French and the Europeans had ever enjoyed'. Drawing on the work of a kindred idealist, Pierre Villey, Friedrich installs this return as the source of modern French humanistic idealism: 'Montaigne was the one who made the concept of a liberal, cosmopolitan education a part of the French nation.'[24]

As we saw in 1.2.5, Villey had declared that the pedagogical principles on which western civilization had rested for three centuries derived from Montaigne. Each time secondary education ('enseignement secondaire') revolted against its suppression by practical restraints and relifted itself towards its ideal mission, it called upon the original source of its principles: Montaigne.[25] For Villey, Montaigne's life and works had been the ideal learning outcome.

Frame's less directly Burckhardtian version of the same argument is to demonstrate that Montaigne 'humanized' the early Renaissance humanist by discovering vulgar humanity.[26] Frame places far less emphasis on classical antiquity than Friedrich, but from the point of view of biography it could be argued that he goes on to offer an even more Burckhardtian picture of Montaigne. Friedrich essentially gives us the inner, the phenomenological life, but Frame shows the inner and outer lives developing together. The social life, though, is just a tableau in the background; it is not—Frame insists—the life we infer from the *Essais*.[27]

2.6.4 AFTER BURCKHARDT

There is no definitive work on the *Civilisation of the late Renaissance in Europe* to which we can point. But for a crucial contribution we can turn to the middle

---

[23] Friedrich, *Montaigne*, 68, 180, 249, 302–3, 311.   [24] Friedrich, *Montaigne*, 91–2.
[25] Pierre Villey, *Montaigne devant la postérité* (Paris: Ancienne librairie Furne, Boivin et Compagnie, 1935), 236.
[26] Frame, *Montaigne's discovery of man.*   [27] Frame.

chapters of a book written in exile in Istanbul during the Second World War. It was published in German in Berne in 1946 by the same publisher (A. Francke) who was to issue Friedrich's *Montaigne* three years later, and in English by Princeton University Press in 1953. I refer to *Mimesis: The Representation of Reality in Western Literature*.[28]

Its author, Erich Auerbach, was one of a whole generation of German and Austrian exiles from Nazism who were born around the turn of the nineteenth and twentieth centuries and who shifted our view of Medieval and Renaissance intellectual and cultural history in response to the twentieth-century crisis. It was in *Mimesis*, rather than in the work of other romance philologists such as Ernst Robert Curtius and Leo Spitzer, that Edward Said found the defining work of existentialist-modernist criticism, the one that pointed the way to postmodern and postcolonial perspectives. He found it to be a work whose 'conditions and circumstances of existence' (separation in Istanbul from European culture, from a rich and specialized library) enabled a 'critically important alienation' from the western cultural tradition.[29] As the contingencies of existence, and alienation from official public politics and culture, became the sources of critical agency, Burckhardt's anxieties about western culture were raised to a new pitch. It was, in the academy, Stephen Greenblatt who would most authoritatively orchestrate this raising of the stakes in the postmodern era (see 2.6.10).

The significance of *Mimesis* for this argument lies in its genesis in the interwar crisis of the second major era of German idealist and historical thought that embraced Wilhelm Dilthey (1831–1911), Heinrich Rickert (1863–1936), Georg Simmel (1858–1918), and Ernst Cassirer (1874–1945).[30] In discovering the secularized creatural realism of late Renaissance writers from Rabelais to Montaigne, Auerbach was encapsulating, in the crisis conditions of the 1940s, the new authenticity of the 1920s: existential everydayness.[31] To pass from Burckhardt to Auerbach is to pass, in other words, from one located historicist response to contemporary crisis to another, from one kind of imaginary museum of western cultural artefacts to another. Montaigne has a secure place in both.

For Burckhardt, mid-nineteenth century Basel is a home city that represents a precarious exile from modern culture, a city whose old European civilization is threatened by what he saw as the demi-culture of modernity. For Auerbach, Istanbul is an alien city of exile from which the collapse of western civilization can be viewed in all its late modern finality. Burckhardt's is the aesthetics of the

[28] There is disagreement over whether this should be described as a modern or a late modern work. Carl Landauer convincingly associates it with the legacy of the Renaissance as defined by Burckhardt and with the German ideal of classicizing self-cultivation associated with Goethe and the Weimar classicists (188). Edward Said has a different view (see what follows in the main text).

[29] Edward Said, *The world, the text, and the critic* (Cambridge, Mass.: Harvard University Press, 1983), 8; Herbert Lindenberger, 'On the Reception of *Mimesis*', in Lerer (ed.), *Literary history and the challenge of philology*, 195–213, 207–10.

[30] Burns and Rayment-Pickard (eds.), *Philosophies of history: from Enlightenment to postmodernity*, 155–217.

[31] Hans Ulrich Gumbrecht, '"Pathos of the Earthly Progress": Erich Auerbach's Everydays', in Lerer (ed.), *Literary history and the challenge of philology*, 13–35.

individually cultivated citizen mindful, in times of crisis and anxiety, of the public good and of the preservation of cultural resources for future renaissances of civilization. He salvages the individualizing aesthetic experiences that come with the classicizing art of the Italian Renaissance for the museum that is his most famous book.

Auerbach's book is also an act of salvage, but it is not the western classical tradition and the Renaissance humanist individual that he aims to retrieve for his literary museum. Indeed, classical antiquity and Renaissance humanist individualism more often feature as obstacles to the achievement of authentic representations of human reality. Key representatives of both are noteworthy by their absence. Instead of Cicero, Virgil, and Livy he gives us Petronius, Ammianus, and Gregory of Tours. Instead of Petrarch, Alberti, and Poliziano, he gives us Rabelais, Montaigne, and Shakespeare. The authentic experience of human existence is the basis of Auerbach's aesthetic historicism and these three late Renaissance authors are harbingers of what Auerbach calls modern existential realism.[32]

From the point of view of Auerbach's own figural history, in which later figures retrospectively fulfil the promise of earlier figures, it is surely Montaigne who prefigures Auerbach himself.[33] Auerbach's apparently random method in *Mimesis* draws inspiration from Montaigne's handling of texts and *contes* in the *Essais* (though Auerbach does of course use a broadly chronological scheme and devotes chapters to individual authors). Auerbach infers moments of lived existence from vivid literary fragments, depictions of everyday scenes that draw more on the Bible and saints' lives than on the classics. Again, it is not difficult to see what a compelling precedent Montaigne provides for this kind of critical activity. He too infers 'un tour de l'humaine capacité' from any historical or literary fragment that comes his way.[34]

So Auerbach's true subject, like Montaigne's, is not texts but 'the lives of individuals, both the authors of the texts he examines and the men and women who figure in the texts'.[35] Both, in completely different historical circumstances, enact a form of enfranchisement from purely literary or learned modes of attention to texts. The reading and writing of texts gives rise to something else beyond the purely literary or textual realm.

On the one hand, there are moments of consciousness of individual human growth ('ontogenesis') and collectively shared human reality on the part of authors creating fictions.[36] On the other, there are moments of actual life as lived by biographical prototypes such as St Augustine and St Francis, and as mediated by letters or other autobiographical forms. Auerbach judges all of these as more or less

---

[32] Erich Auerbach, 'Epilegomena zu *Mimesis*', *Romanische Forschungen*, 65 (1953), 1–18, 4.

[33] Hayden White, 'Auerbach's literary history: figural causation and modernist historicism', in Lerer (ed.), *Literary history and the challenge of philology*, 124–39, 125–6; Landauer, 'Auerbach's performance and the American academy, or how New Haven stole the idea of *Mimesis*', 182.

[34] I 20, NP108/BVH Paris 1595, p. 52/S119.

[35] Thomas Hart, 'Literature as language: Auerbach, Spitzer, Jakobson', in Lerer (ed.), *Literary history and the challenge of philology*, 227–39, 235.

[36] Erich Auerbach, *Mimesis: The representation of reality in western literature*, trans. Willard R. Trask (Princeton: Princeton University Press, 1953), 202.

authentic objectifications of human existence considered as a lived phenomenon embedded in time and circumstance. Amongst the most authentic moments in terms of fictions are Dante's Christian figural realism, Rabelais' creatural realism, and the social realism of the French nineteenth-century novel. Each is related to the development of a philosophical groundwork for the consciousness of human reality (a groundwork usually transcended by the related fictional tradition): Christian figuralism, Christian creatural thought, and German *Historismus* itself (the tradition inhabited by Auerbach).

But in terms of real biographical prototypes of authentically and self-consciously lived experience of temporal human reality, it is Montaigne who in Auerbach's scheme first pushes decisively beyond the realist model of the Christian life. He lives the life of the first modern existentialist realist, the life we know from contemporary documents that Auerbach himself attempted to live during the crises of the 1920s and 1930s.[37]

Using Villey's 1930–1 edition of the stratified *Essais*, alongside the 1933 edition of the same scholar's account of the evolving Montaigne, Auerbach brings out the developmental principle behind the text. His whole argument, together with the title of his chapter ('L'humaine condition'), are derived from an analysis of the 1588–92 passage that opens *Essais* III 2. In the modern transmission of the *Essais* great emphasis is placed in general on the so-called b and c additions that ponder and justify Montaigne's project of self-portraiture. The most frequently cited text is Auerbach's text, the opening of 'Du repentir', where Montaigne states that he portrays not being but passing, that each individual man bears the form of 'l'humaine condition'. That word 'condition' is given an anachronistic, existentialist resonance.[38]

In his chapter, Auerbach brings out the terms of Montaigne's interest in others' lives, mediated by the texts he chooses. Montaigne's only specialism was his own random existence (distinguished by Auerbach from humanist 'general culture'). His outer, public life was a mere distraction from this. In fact, Montaigne chose to make 'only so moderate and reluctant a use of his political possibilities'. He emancipated himself from everything that might divert the living man's attention from himself. Montaigne's 'newly acquired freedom was much more exciting, much more of the historical moment [than the rediscovery of classical antiquity], directly connected with the feeling of insecurity'.

The need to orient oneself in the boundless late Renaissance world seemed hard to satisfy and yet urgent. Montaigne had the clearest conception of the problem of man's self-orientation: 'that is, the task of making oneself at home in existence without fixed points of support. In him for the first time, man's life—the random

---

[37] Gumbrecht, ' "Pathos of the Earthly Progress": Erich Auerbach's Everydays'.

[38] See 2.7.1. Tournon argues convincingly that all these readings and citations mistake Montaigne's phrase to mean something like man's existential circumstances, whereas 'condition' is here closer to meaning simply 'social rank'—that is, Montaigne is merely claiming that whatever status one occupies, one still faces a full array of 'philosophical' challenges. See André Tournon, 'Le grammarien, le jurisconsulte et l'humaine condition', *Bulletin de la Société des Amis de Montaigne*, 7th series, 21–2 (1990), 107–18.

personal life as a whole—becomes problematic in the modern sense.' The 'pecu-liar equilibrium of his being' prevents the tragedy inherent in his image of man from unfolding in his work.[39] But Montaigne was the first existentialist, the first phenomenologist of the self, the author of the first work of 'realistic', 'lay introspection'.[40]

Both Friedrich and Frame were of course aware of Auerbach's seminal chapter on the opening of *Essais* III 2, but the point here is not just the direct influence of one chapter of one book. Auerbach's view of Villey's evolving *Essais* through the optic of the III 2 passage was fundamental to the post-war history of interpreta-tions of Montaigne's life and works, especially in the context of American general education (see 2.6.5 and 2.6.6).

But it was the whole developing framework of European idealism, as exempli-fied here in the work of Burckhardt and Auerbach, which shaped the intellectu-al-biographical interpretation of the *Essais* current in the post-war period. The turns taken by the post-Burckhardtian German idealist tradition are especially clear in Friedrich's work, for Friedrich turns Montaigne into a classically educated phenomenologist in the mould of Husserl or the early Heidegger (a colleague of Friedrich's at Freiburg). He adapts Villey's account of the real biographical stages of Montaigne's moral and intellectual growth into an existential movement of thought evident at all levels in the *Essais*: from abasement of man, through description and affirmation of abased man, to self-observation as investigation of the 'human condition'.[41]

Frame, on the other hand, relates Montaigne in the final pages of his biography to modern 'mobilism', the sense of life and existence as process. Evoking Auerbach's key passage, he reveals the whole framework he shares with the generation nur-tured on modernism: 'In portraying not being but passing, Montaigne anticipates not only philosophers like Bergson but novelists like Proust and Joyce'.[42]

Montaigne has, it seems, already investigated to its depths the random human condition discovered in all its horror by modernity, and yet remains serene. By retreating into himself, he has succeeded in not internalizing the subjection to which modern culture and history (this tradition of thinking tends to believe) reduces cultivated selves. The idealist pedagogical framework within which, in common with Friedrich, the whole biography (as well as the translation and the work of criticism) is conceived rises above the surface in these pages. Like Montaigne's actual plan of education (in I 25), his life and works provide 'the training necessary for independent moral living' in the conditions of modernity. In a personal footnote on the last page, Frame identifies Montaigne's central ideas with those expressed in the chapter on noble household schooling, and with the 'commonly held aims' of modern education.[43]

[39] Auerbach, *Mimesis*, 297, 310–11, for this and the previous paragraph.
[40] Auerbach, *Mimesis*, 298, 308, 299, 306, 308.
[41] Friedrich, *Montaigne*, 94–5.   [42] Frame 320.   [43] Frame 322–3.

2.6.5 VIDAL AS READER-WRITER OF
THE *ESSAYS*, 1992

How does all this inform modern reading and writing of the *Essais*? Let us move forwards again to the American afterlife of the European idealist Montaigne; to, first, Gore Vidal's ever-to-hand copy of Donald Frame's *Complete Works*.

Interlocking circles on the binding, Vidal tells us, marked the numerous occasions on which he had set glasses down on top of the book after writing what had since become indecipherable commentaries in the margins. Initially, he had been drawn in by Montaigne's essay against lying. As someone who had spent a lifetime in (political) worlds where the liar is most honoured when known to be lying and getting away with it, he had found the essay consoling. Vidal had never read the copy right through, but he had read here and there and reread favourite essays. Time and again he had found his 'own most brilliant *aperçus*' in Montaigne's text and repossessed them by writing '"How true!"' in the margin. One note of this kind appeared alongside what looked like a tear-stain (that smelt of whisky). Montaigne's remark in III 9 that he is only taken seriously as a famous author in distant places (in his neighbourhood, they find it funny to see him in print) had struck a chord.[44]

By the early 1990s the annotated copy has become for Vidal a symbol of a by-gone era: the 1950s. This was a time when an American poet (Robert Lowell) and an American novelist (Vidal), could still hold in common a small part of the secular classical heritage and share manly knowledge ('so etiolated! so testeronish! so European!') of the old books of Europe. The copy is a material trace, a palimpsest of the intimate thoughts and experiences of his younger selves. His reception of the text is active in the sense that he uses it for self-reflection.

The copy is to Vidal what—in Vidal's own account—Montaigne's books (including the *Essais* once published) were to him; namely, a set of cues to reflect upon himself and his life and to write 'to himself about himself and about what he had been reading which became himself'. Vidal, that is, understands the work to prompt a specific kind of ruminative, self-reflective reading and writing. The external biography of the essayist supplied in précis in his review is no more than a tableau in the background. The true biography is the biography of the developing literary mind.[45]

For the details Vidal relies (as most still do) on Frame's biography, the first biography in English to use the historical record to fill in the gaps in the sketchy self-portrait supplied by the *Essais* themselves. It was Frame who took Pierre Villey's picture of Montaigne's inner evolution and interspersed it with touches of the man of action. The inner life of the mind became a way of preserving integrity and moderation in the midst of an ideological war (the wars of religion) analogous to those which dominated the first half of the twentieth century.

---

[44] Gore Vidal, 'Uncommon sense: the charitable clarity of Montaigne's perceptions', *Times Literary Supplement*, 26 June 1992.
[45] For this and the previous paragraph, see Vidal, 'Uncommon sense'.

In Vidal's précis, we hear of this political background, of Montaigne's family background (his converted Spanish Jewish mother), his humanist education, his legal career (during which he met 'fellow public servant' La Boétie), and then of his greatest 'action', his retirement from public life. Montaigne's description in III 3 of his library retreat is quoted, and accompanied on the same page of the *Times Literary Supplement* by a nineteenth-century engraving of the round tower that housed it. No longer having La Boétie to talk or write to, Montaigne wrote notes to himself on his reading and thinking, notes which eventually became books for the world. He wrote as one still involved in the world both locally and nationally, as a mayor of Bordeaux, courtier and unofficial diplomat who would have been made a counsellor to King Henri IV had he lived longer. The biographical sketch then moves into the area of Montaigne's tastes and predilections (as revealed in the *Essais*), including the fact that 'he was particularly drawn to biographical anecdote'.[46]

And autobiographical anecdote creeps into Vidal's review-essay, as particular strokes of Montaigne's sketch are shaded in with scenes and moments from Vidal's life. The review itself becomes an extension of the commentary that Vidal tells us had developed in the margins of his copy as the aged author reflects ironically on the annotations and their naïveté. We begin to wonder whether Vidal is talking about himself or about Montaigne. Is Vidal not writing to himself about himself, as he writes about the reading through which he 'became himself'? Are we not in fact reading sketches for *The Essays of Michael of Montaigne of Gore Vidal of America*?

As Vidal selects particular details from Montaigne's life and text, he seems ironically to be putting together the elements of a twentieth-century Montaignean *persona* for himself. Quotations from the *Essays* are selected for their relevance to his own literary and political history: '"People say that my period of office passed without trace or mark. Good!"' (Vidal's early political career was similarly undistinguished). He calls Montaigne's words explicitly onto his own side ('I want Montaigne on my side') in the 'great task of reworking my own country's broken-down political system'. The critical agency to which he lays claim via Montaigne is thus in part political, though he states that the Frenchman's 'political interests are aside from the main point, the exploration of self'. He is a man of letters viewing the changes and corruptions of the American cultural and political world from the isolated tower of secular classical culture. The result is an irony-tinged portrait of the reader as artist, holding fast to core Montaignean values in his writing even as society breaks down around him.[47]

2.6.6 DENBY READS FRAME'S MONTAIGNE, 1992

The teacher in the seminar on Montaigne attended by journalist David Denby in late February of the same year (1992) was the Lionel Trilling Professor in the

---

[46] For this and the previous paragraph, see Vidal, 'Uncommon sense'.
[47] For this and the previous paragraph, see Vidal, 'Uncommon sense'.

Humanities, Edward Tayler. The set text was the old Penguin translation of the *Essays*, the one replaced in the following months by Michael Screech's work. In 1961, when Denby first took the course, the set edition of Montaigne's *Essays* had doubtless been the translation by the professor of French, Donald Frame, who had chaired the Humanities A course (as Literature Humanities was originally called) at Columbia from 1950 to 1956.[48] The *Essays* had been on the core curriculum since it emerged in 1937–8 from the General Honors course John Erskine had been teaching for a number of years. In 1992, Denby preferred to use a copy of the old translation by Frame, and the reason for this must be linked to his reasons for enrolling to retake the course he first took as a Columbia undergraduate in 1961.[49]

In the late 1980s Denby had become frustrated with both sides in the 'culture wars' over the role of 'the old books of Europe' on the higher educational curriculum. He was frustrated with the doctrinaire proponents both of safe, traditional humanism and of the principal, politically correct alternatives. The frustration was one part of a wider mid-life crisis of identity, a crisis rooted in a sense that he had become a book-buyer, not a book-reader.[50]

Denby wanted to recover the critical agency that came with being an active book-reader not a passive mass media victim. He invokes the postmodern philosophy of Guy Debord—an antecedent for Jean Baudrillard's work—in describing his agency-less state. Having succumbed to 'the modern state of living-in-the-media', 'the unlived life as spectator', he now 'possessed information without knowledge, opinions without principles, instincts without beliefs'. Though a film critic, he felt that film was part of the problem, that it did not offer the route to critical agency to be found in literature. He therefore resolved to repeat his younger self's run through the 'great books' courses (Literature Humanities and Contemporary Civilization), accompanied by the odd critical classic: 'Erich Auerbach's *Mimesis*, for instance, a half-century-old masterpiece of commentary that could almost serve as a companion to Lit Hum'.[51]

In Denby's account of the class it quickly becomes apparent that despite the change in the assigned translation and the passage of thirty years, he can still access the relevant and modern 'Montaigne' that he had first encountered in the early 1960s. It is not just because he chose to use his old text that we can identify this Montaigne as Frame's updated, adapted, and anglicized version of the figure prepared by Villey, Strowski, and others for educational consumption.[52]

Professor Tayler directs the class in no uncertain terms. He uses the Villey model of an evolving Montaigne in combination with the carefully placed cues in the text itself to shape the class's reading of the work. The breakthrough passage he uses is Auerbach's passage, the opening of III 2. Tayler tells the class that the layers of the essayist's text reveal a passage from an 'early stoicism to a more and more confident

---

[48] See the 'Preface' to La Charité (ed.), *O un amy!*
[49] Denby, *Great books*, 17, 23, 465–6, 269, 271.
[50] Denby, *Great books*, 12, 35–6.   [51] Denby, *Great books*, 15–16.
[52] For Frame's adaptation of Villey, see his 1965 biography, 147–50, 171, 174–5, 179, 193, 302. Frame adapts the existing model by contesting the notion that Montaigne suffered a 'sceptical crisis' around 1576, and by putting more emphasis on his identification with the 'vulgar'.

and joyous epicureanism', thereby playing down—as Frame does—the mid-life sceptical crisis imagined by Villey. Middle age brings 'a greater and greater acceptance of life', an acceptance that Denby personally had lost and wanted to recover.[53]

The class on Montaigne is the occasion for an explicit revelation of the pedagogy informing the whole core course. Tayler had opened it by telling the students that 'your life is at stake, and particularly at this minute'. The class, in other words, is the occasion for an existential challenge issued to the students by the teacher. They are, to say the least, perplexed, and for once the mature student Denby is perplexed too. Then Professor Tayler reads out the opening of Montaigne's 'Of Repentance' (*Essays* III 2), which in his own book Denby quotes in Frame's translation. Tayler accompanies it with what is more or less Auerbach's gloss: the idea that Montaigne is the first to depict modern being in motion, and the contrast with Dante, for whom each person has an essential nature.[54]

For Denby, the clouds part. He observes Huggins—the big football player from California (bated unpleasantly by Tayler earlier in the class)—suddenly leaving his medieval past behind him and 'getting' modern individuality: 'Huggins the football player had begun contributing to the class. Something was stirring in him.... Different selves were coming to the surface, and from these selves would come a Huggins who danced for Dionysus'. In his picture of becoming, then—a picture which amounts to Frame's evolving English *Essays* viewed through the optic of Auerbach and the opening to III 2—Montaigne depicts modern individuality in an active sense (he causes people to *get* it in classrooms).

This is 'the individuality that Columbia couldn't bully—the uniqueness of the "I" that emerged from the multiple selves of each student'. The students' lives were at stake when they read Montaigne, because Montaigne was 'the supreme example of the kind of becoming that Professor Edward Tayler believed in': that of the self-fashioning individual not bullied by institutions and not overwhelmed by the media. 'Montaigne'—the *Essays* in the classroom—both represents and enacts the institutionalized culture of modern American liberal individualism. Significantly (for Denby), the *Essays* made a couple of the religious students, one of Christian and one of Jewish belief, rather nervous.[55]

Denby, however, was relaxed. From his individual point of view he had come more than prepared for such a conclusion. His life was indeed at stake. And Montaigne was the first writer in the core-curriculum readings to whom he felt really close—awkwardly close, when it came to certain passages in which the essayist describes his idiosyncrasies. Montaigne's turns out to be the core book in the core curriculum and the make or break text for Denby's project of writing about the experience of reading 'the books that most engaged me'. Denby, like Vidal, finds himself, as if by chance, everywhere in the text. Montaigne's doubting nature, his lack of specialized knowledge, his defiance of pedants, his sense of his own

---

[53] Denby, *Great books*, 271.   [54] Denby, *Great books*, 269, 274.
[55] Denby, *Great books*, 274–6, for this and the previous paragraph.

judgement as the 'only possible salvation'—all these things made Montaigne the 'patron saint of amateurs' for Denby.[56]

But there was a problem, an existential crisis even. Denby loved Montaigne but feared he would not be able to write about him (thus scuppering his whole project). He would not be able to write about him 'because he is all of a piece... marvelously planted in his own life'. As such, 'to pull him apart would really be murder'. The book is at one and the same time embedded in the making of the lives of the author's and of the reader's minds; identification is total; to pull it apart for the purposes of textual analysis and creative writing would be to take the life both from author and his identical reader. But Denby gets over his angst, as the chapter summary indicates: 'I can't write about Montaigne; I write about Montaigne'. He breaks through into a more serene self-consciousness, one he can write about in essays.[57]

In the 1992 Columbia classroom, the *Essays* are used in ways that are continuous with the European readings of Montaigne discussed in 2.6.2–3 and 1.2—readings with roots up to a century old. They are used as a natural pedagogical paradigm for the ritualistic activation (in Huggins' case) or re-activation (in Denby's case) of the late modern individual's critical agency. Denby steals from Montaigne silently, and the unforced, conversational style of *Great Books* as a whole make the extent of the 'steal' clear.

For, again, *Great Books* is Denby's *Essays*. It is a record, as Denby takes the *Essays* to be, of a 'struggle with difficult and faraway texts, which forced, willy-nilly, the trying on of selves'. At the end of the chapter on this part of the core course Denby declares Montaigne's 'becoming' to be 'an American ideal that I share'. It is by labouring on Montaigne's text, one sentence at a time, that he—'a product of the fifties and early sixties'—recovers his life, himself, the 'form of becoming' he had found at school but lost in contemporary 'media existence'.[58] From his perspective, he recreates his agency as a book-reader and -writer, and the principal intermediary in that recreation has been Montaigne's *Essays*, in Frame's translation.

2.6.7 INDEXING CRITICAL AGENCY

What appears in Denby's account to be an intensely solitary experience of reading and writing as self-fashioning is an institutionalized cultural practice with a history. Both Vidal and Denby abduct the critical agency indexed by Frame's *Essays* as their own and they do so in particular relational nexuses. Vidal is more interested in Montaigne as friend to La Boétie and as public author and man of action because he is reflecting upon his life as a failed or 'retired' politician and as a politically minded artist. He sees himself, and Montaigne, as ironized versions of Burckhardtian Renaissance men living out the decline of civilization. The relations he invokes are those between men of letters and the civic elite in golden age post-war America.

[56] Denby, *Great books*, 271–2, 16.   [57] Denby, *Great books*, 272, 269.
[58] Denby, *Great books*, 455, 276–7.

I refer to the description of Lowell's and Vidal's chat about having Caesar as a house guest, and about Caesar's relations with Cicero.

Denby brings it down to individualized becoming because he is escaping the postmodern 'state of living-in-the-media'. But the process of individualized becoming is also recovered in a specific relational—institutional and pedagogical—nexus: he reads Montaigne in the company of other students guided by a teacher in a classroom who *briefs* him freely to find his unique literary self in Montaigne's model.

The premise of the overall argument of this study is that these are just two of an extraordinary variety of historical instances in which Montaigne's *Essais*, situated as an index of the agency of a liberally educated but naturally evolving reader-writer, in turn serve as a prototype for the creation of further written indexes—essays—of the critical or receptive agency of other reader-writers. In this broad respect, there are continuities between the seventeenth-century English and the late twentieth-century American reception.

But the description of each instance must be carefully handled. We cannot lump all the reader-writers together as 'free literates' who are enfranchised in the same way, with similar positive results. In Alfred Gell's formulaic descriptions of the genres of social events that involve art, there are both primary and secondary agents and patients. There can be complex or 'involuted' situations involving, for example, a patient-as-agent. Such a situation occurs when what we abduct from the index is the artist's passive acceptance of the patron's (recipient's) demands on him. One of Gell's examples is particularly apposite for the present discussion:

> [C]onsider a school situation as follows; the teacher (recipient/patron) enters, and says: 'today, class, I want you all to paint something from your own imaginations, so get busy!...'. The young artists accordingly set to and produce their indexes—under orders. The resulting works of art index the agency of the teacher; but for the teacher giving the class its instructions, none of these exercises in imaginative art would exist. School art is, or at least was, indicative of the lives children lead as 'patients'. School art is produced at the behest of adults, so as to please them, or at least not offend them. Anthropologically speaking, the important feature of school art is what it tells us about the social relations between adults in authority and the children in their charge. On the other hand, the teacher has not, on this occasion, told the children in the class what to represent, so although each child attempts to paint something which will be acceptable to the teacher...each is obliged to exercise agency within the 'patient' role.[59]

In this situation, the artist (the child) is a 'patient' with respect to the index (the painting), because the index mediates the patient relationship he or she has with the recipient (the teacher), who is the primary agent. But for the teacher's order, there would be no painting. On the other hand, the artist is a (secondary) agent with respect to the reference of the painting (the prototype). The difference between this situation and the one in the Columbia classroom is of course that in

[59] Alfred Gell, *Art and agency: an anthropological theory* (Oxford: Clarendon Press, 1998), 54–5.

the latter case the prototypes *are* pre-selected. And the class is instructed to view one in particular of these prototypes as crucial for their essay-writing existence (the *Essays*).

If we substitute 'essay' for Gell's 'painting' we have a simple practical example of a situation in which the primary agency abducted by an observer from a text is not that of the named composer of that text. The background to Montaigne's choice of what in his own time was a unique title ('Les Essais de Michel de Montaigne') is the fact that such situations were normal in early modern literary culture. There was a real danger that readers might—from any text composed by an unknown such as Montaigne—abduct not his and their own personal agency but the agency of classical prototypes and 'teachers' such as Aristotle or Cicero, of contemporary doctors and humanists such as the Roman censor or Lipsius, of aristocratic patrons such as the Marquis de Trans (Montaigne's principal patron) or the Pope.

This is why Montaigne repeatedly insists that a copy of the *Essais* is an index from which we the readers (recipients) can infer the effects produced by the living person (prototype) of the individual responsible for writing them (artist). We can do so in the same way that we might have done had we met the author in person and been able to relate to him directly (see 1.1.4). From this point of view the author-as-prototype is the primary agent and the reader-as-recipient is the patient.

But at the same time, from a different perspective, the reader-as-recipient is also an agent provoked to re-produce his own 'copy' of the *Essais*, a copy that amounts to a new index of his own critical agency directed to new recipients (Vidal's review-essay and Denby's *Great Books*). He (or she) becomes the reader-as-artist. In modern education, four hundred years after Montaigne's time, this process was institutionalized. The essay became the principal outcome of the learning process in the humanities. It became the officially sanctioned index of the *individualized* critical agency that a liberal education aims to bring out.[60]

On the one hand, then, these two copies of Frame's Montaigne, and the further essays to which they give rise, are indicative of long-term historical continuities in the 'reception' of Montaigne. Liberally educated, male and female reader-writers from the late sixteenth to the late twentieth centuries have abducted Montaigne's agency as their own. On the other hand, we should note that they have done so in historically and culturally diverse forms and conditions, and that the agency mediated has been of different types.

Our two readers first encountered the *Essays* in a particular form (a new and 'definitive' English translation by Frame with, later, a new 'life' attached) at a particular moment (late 1950s, early 1960s), though at different points in their respective life-cycles (Vidal is about eighteen years older). The book—the copy of the book—remains a part of their lives. For different reasons, they review its significance at another moment, thirty years later, when a new English translation is about to emerge to challenge the old. Vidal replaces the old with the new on his bedside table, and renews his sense of the making of his own literary life by

---

[60] The 'essay' required by modern programmes of humanistic education is not, of course, directly related to the genre of literary essay associated with Montaigne.

comparing the sharper, more up-to-date translation with the one he is familiar with. Denby holds fast to the old translation, the translation embedded in his formative years as an undergraduate.

2.6.8 THE AMERICAN SCHOOL OF MONTAIGNE

Denby tells us he is a product of the fifties and early sixties, and he rediscovers his moral identity in another product of the fifties and early sixties (Frame's Montaigne). Donald Frame was of precisely that generation of post-war intellectuals described by Denby as 'absorbed in the classics of modernism... and schooled by the disasters of totalitarianism and war'. This generation taught the 'premodernist classics in a modernist way, emphasizing the elements of internal dissonance and conflict, the darker ironies'. So Montaigne became a 'late' humanist living in the period of the 'waning' Renaissance, a humanist who renounced intellectual and spiritual authority, a humanist for whom that renunciation itself became authoritative and transmissible.[61] He provided an authentic origin for the modern literary personality at odds with the times.

Before proceeding, it is important to emphasize once again that Frame's Montaigne is one particular and situated manifestation of a set of related mid-twentieth-century manifestations of the life and works of the essayist. The bibliography to the translated *Works* reveals an interwar and post-war community of western European and Anglo-American readers, editors, and producers of Montaigne's philosophy.[62]

In prime position are the pre-war editions and source studies of Villey. Also listed are writers from the era of modernism who introduced Montaigne to the common reader: Virginia Woolf, André Gide, T. S. Eliot (in the course of introducing Pascal's *Pensées*). All, in different senses, presented him in relation to a contemporary and 'urgent need to communicate the sense of a self at odds with its own time and culture'.[63]

Articles from the liberal American periodicals, including Theodore Spencer's fictional dialogue, join émigré Erich Auerbach's wartime study of the Montaignean 'human condition' and Friedrich's 1949 German study to complete the Anglo-American and western European picture. The contents pages in the *Works* list the essays with their dates of composition as surmised by Villey, so that the reader can distinguish the different layers of Montaigne's mental geology.

In Montaigne's autobiography of the mind as compiled in related ways by Villey, Auerbach, Friedrich, Frame, and others, the intellectual life of the (relatively) optimistic modernist discovers its own geology. At the bottom is a layer resulting from

[61] Denby, *Great books*, 460, 272. See the discussion of Montaigne as part of the 'waning' Renaissance in William James Bouwsma, *The waning of the Renaissance, 1550–1640* (New Haven: Yale University Press, 2000).
[62] Montaigne, *Complete Works*, trans. Donald M. Frame, 'Bibliography'.
[63] Juliet Dusinberre, 'Virginia Woolf and Montaigne', *Textual Practice*, 5 (1991), 219–41, 219.

the clash between the experience of modernity and a *passé* neoclassical or enlightenment faith in the capacity of human rationality to understand and shape the human condition. Frame, for example, identifies a layer upon which Montaigne disdains the vulgar masses who lack literary or philosophical understanding, and obsesses himself with facing the realities of pain and death.

Above this, there is a layer of sceptical 'modern' critique, in which belief in the capacity of classically inspired reason and philosophy is subjected to corruscating doubt (though Frame did not believe this to have been a personal crisis on Montaigne's part, as Villey did). On top is a layer of renewed optimism and affirmation, upon which the weaknesses, contingencies, and uncertainties of the human condition are accepted philosophically and modern fear and trembling are moderated. In Frame's version, Montaigne now identifies himself with the vulgar, accepts pain and death as part of the human condition, and concentrates on preparing for life.[64]

We heard in 2.6.4 how Frame relates Montaigne in the final pages of his biography to modern 'mobilism', the sense of life and existence as process. This is not the whole story. Frame does make good use of the documents which reveal a 'more vigilant mayor and active negotiator than the *Essays* suggest'. 'Than the *Essays* suggest' already tells us, however, that Frame does not imagine the active negotiator he has helped discover in the archives to be the agent behind the text. Rather, the documentation of Montaigne's activities as a lawyer, parliamentarian, and diplomatic intermediary are interpreted as experiences which—reflected upon in tranquillity—contribute to the process of humane reflection upon the human condition that Villey's edition had revealed in the various layers of the text.[65]

Other kinds of document that seem to grate with the Villey–Frame picture of the self-humanizing humanist are scrupulously dealt with. Where literary historians suggest that the letter about La Boétie's death may be not so much a historical document written immediately after the event but a shaped literary artefact, Frame tactfully acknowledges the artistry at work but re-asserts its documentary truthfulness. Where the task of reconciliation is all but hopeless, as in the case of Montaigne's various comments on the genesis of his translation of Sebond, Frame sees the discrepancies as expressions of Montaigne's doubts about a task that was imposed on him by his father.[66]

In the note he wrote in 1988 for the second, French edition (1994), Frame makes a very interesting statement. Were he to have rewritten the biography, he would have made only one change in his point of view. He would have exercised more prudence in accepting the affirmations Montaigne makes about himself in the *Essais*.[67]

[64] Frame 147–61, 289–302.   [65] Frame 318, 62.
[66] Frame 79–80, 346, 105–8, 112–13.
[67] Frame, *Montaigne, une vie, une oeuvre*, 7: 'Si j'avais à le récrire maintenant, je n'y apporterais qu'un changement important: j'accorderais moins de crédit à toutes les affirmations de Montaigne sur son propre compte, sur sa nature, son essence, et montrerais davantage de prudence; mais sans aller, contrairement à la tendance actuelle, jusqu'à penser—ou, si j'en crois mon expérience, feindre de penser—que toute affirmation d'un homme sur ces sujets est *ipso facto* pure fiction et non réalité'. I assume Frame's 'Note sur la seconde édition (la première en français)', which is dated 1988, was composed for the French edition (1994) during the period of its first inception.

For the 1965 biography is indeed fully committed to every word of the *Essays* as a truthful and transparent *registre* of a real, internally consistent self and its development. The *Essais* have to be sincere and authentic in the post-romantic sense because in the context of Frame's educational values it is the reality of the depicted prototype that really matters—as it is for Auerbach.

Furthermore, if we ask exactly what Frame's educational values are, the biography will tell us all we need to know. The pivotal chapter, just over half way through the book, is chapter 11 ('The Writer Finds His Theme [1577–80]'). There, Frame closely follows Villey in finding that the chapters of 1578–80, and the chapter on education in particular, first show Montaigne 'ready to make himself the subject of his book'. For all Montaigne's independence in the 'Apology' (first composed, according to Frame's appendix, in 1573–6), his 'liberation from apprehensive tutelage was still somewhat theoretical'. The experiential test comes in 1578 with the acute pain of renal calculus. Now, in the chapter on education's passage on virtue, he reveals his true philosophy.[68]

In the final pages of Frame's pivotal chapter his own theoretical inspiration becomes apparent:

> Montaigne's awareness of the possibilities of human nature shows most clearly in his faith in education. If the negativism of the 'Apology' is permanent and in earnest, why try to educate? If we can know nothing, what can we learn or teach? Where 'Pedantry' (I: 25) had been mainly destructive, 'The Education of Children' (I: 26) shows what proper training can do. Without Rabelais's vast faith in learning, Montaigne shares his optimism and concern for the training of mind, body, and character. Unlike his reluctant admirer Rousseau much later, he does not believe that infants are angels and that education must be negative; but he anticipates his concern with the child as an entire person and with his active participation in his own education—with learning by doing, and the lessons of things, not only of books. He has many affinities with the modern theories—in their unadulterated form—of John Dewey.[69]

Dewey was Columbia's in-house philosopher of education from 1904 to 1929. In *Montaigne's Discovery of Man*, Frame had described how Montaigne moved the centre of gravity of humanism 'from the scholar to the intelligent man in general'.[70]

Frame's values, in other words, are John Dewey's slanted towards the literary modernist's education of the aesthetic self. The centre of Dewey's pragmatist philosophy of experience was the living human being (as, though, more entirely a social animal than Frame's Montaigne). His version of 'philosophy' was the generalized action of the intelligence, and his pedagogy a practical training that downplayed book-learning.[71]

In intellectual terms, Montaigne provided a historical prototype for what general education Columbia-style ideally should give rise to: the becoming of the intelligent man in general, as witnessed by the writing of the pre- or non-professional literary essay. We have already seen the pedagogy in action in Tayler's classroom.

[68] Frame 184, 190, 192–3.   [69] Frame 198.
[70] Frame, *Montaigne's discovery of man*, 168.
[71] Alan Ryan, *John Dewey and the high tide of American liberalism* (New York: W.W. Norton, 1995).

The outcome is there for all to see in *Great Books*, a kind of extended series of institutionally produced essays for the 'Great Books' course teachers—centrally Tayler—that only secondarily reaches a public audience.

For Tayler is the recipient-as-agent in this scenario. He directs Denby (the artist-as-patient) to become his 'unique' written self by freely interpreting a canonical prototype ('the evolving Montaigne'). Denby is the passive and obedient recipient of an instruction that effectively allows him no freedom of imagination (since both the instruction and the prototype are chosen for him). Denby is *told*, after all, to have an existential crisis at that point on the course, to find that his life was at stake in the reading of Montaigne. He duly obliges in his essays for the teacher.

And there are other participants in this nexus, for, in terms of the performed classroom reading of the *Essays*, is the teacher himself not the patient to a powerful group of absent primary agents, of proactive twentieth-century recipients of the text, from Villey to Auerbach, Friedrich, and Frame? Are they not the ultimate authors of the events, prior even to the author of the *Essais* himself? Their collectively made artefact indexes the getting of modern liberal individuality, and Denby obligingly observes this happening both in others and in himself in the Columbia classroom. Arguably, here, the *Essays* do not enfranchise; they entrap contemporary subjectivity in what Gell calls an enchainment of intention, instrument, and result. Either way, they act as a powerful literary index of schooling—liberally educative schooling.[72]

2.6.9 MONTAIGNE AND THE MODERN CRITICAL AGENT

This institutionalized routine was of course challenged by the radical literary and philosophical pedagogies which took root from the late 1960s. With the challenge, alternative approaches to Montaigne inevitably began to emerge. At the same time, the framework authoritatively summarized by Frame continued to shape the cultural context within which general educated readers such as Vidal and Denby placed the *Essays*.

But Frame's framework also shaped the emergent alternatives, in the sense that poststructuralist critical theory presupposed—as the basis for its own exercises in deconstruction—the 'firm and clear' view of the history of western thought, or liberal humanism, re-drawn by intellectuals between the 1930s and the 1960s. The new pedagogy worked by questioning the 'traditional' notion of 'the integral and self-sufficient subject who exists prior to and outside of any signifying system and the accepted status of language as the authentic representation of truths that lie beyond it in the physical world, in things and in ideas'. What had been a truthful, evolving, self-conscious portrait in the full possession of its author and his lived life became a self-reflexive, self-deconstructing text.[73]

---

[72] Gell, *Art and agency*, 23.
[73] Regosin, '1595: Montaigne and His Readers', 251.

Terence Cave's was one of the first postmodern readings of Montaigne, and it is certainly one of the most enduring.[74] It endures because it is rooted in an intense awareness of a particular moment in the history of critical pedagogy. Cave self-consciously shows us what Montaigne's text looked like at the moment when the commitment and the history I associated above specifically with Frame was convincingly distanced and de-naturalized by particular French and American academic practitioners of literary hermeneutics.

Cave's demonstration also had an intellectual-historical dimension. The assurances, the culture, the twentieth-century intellectual lives that had guaranteed the relationship between study of canonical literature and the safe transmission of humanely lived values were themselves beginning to pass into the historical distance. What appeared to be left was a relationship between literature and an informal kind of literary theory (labelled 'liberal' or 'Enlightenment' humanism by its opponents). This made the substitution of alternative theories possible, some of which claimed their own systematic coherence, some of which cultivated informality.

From an intellectual-historical point of view, it thus became possible for Cave to ask what sixteenth-century 'humanism' amounted to once you took away the guarantees that came with the reputation, the life, and the programmatic pedagogical claims of a humanist like Erasmus. It looked like the sixteenth-century equivalent of an attempt at a systematic theory of literature, an *ars* or 'technology' (a systematic treatise on an art, e.g. grammar).

This consisted of a set of rhetorical strategies for persuasively communicating one's own presence and rational thoughts by means of an artificially 'copious' text. The *Essais* were no longer the transparent document of an actual inner history, but a rhetorically created textual face. The fact that Cave and his contemporaries were still reading and quoting the text in French editions derived from Villey, and in English in Frame's translation, was not considered significant.

Cave's most important contribution to Montaigne studies was his insistence that the 'self-portrait' has no existence independently of the text and a reader's interaction with it. It only exists if the reader faithfully follows Montaigne's own textual instructions for composing it. This is what Denby does obediently in the Columbia classroom. If the reader naturalizes the process of following the instructions he will believe himself to be 'meeting' and 'understanding' a real aesthetic personality of the sixteenth century who is rather like himself (for he composes himself in similar terms as he reads).[75] By denaturalizing this process, Cave was also decentring what had become in the contemporary world an uncritical, institutionalized routine. It had become a museum display of humanist self-reflexive reading (I remember it well from my own undergraduate years in the early 1980s).

In Cave's account, once what used to hold the text together in modern classrooms (and still would in Columbia University in 1992) has been displaced, one is

---

[74] See, especially, the chapter on Montaigne in Terence Cave, *The cornucopian text: problems of writing in the French Renaissance* (Oxford: Clarendon Press, 1979).

[75] Terence Cave, 'Problems of reading in the *Essais*', in I. D. McFarlane and Ian Maclean (eds.), *Montaigne: Essays in memory of Richard Sayce* (Oxford: Clarendon Press, 1982), 133–66.

left with a purely verbal (i.e. textual) Montaignean physiognomy ('disembodied, like the Cheshire cat's grin') designed to engage the complicity of the reader and ensure the survival of the work.[76] The text was somehow no longer a stable possession of the author. At which point, without the 'author', the *Essais* become the archetypally productive, self-deconstructing text. Discourse itself or 'writing' is now the prototype whose primary agency is inferred from the text.

Nevertheless, more than other sixteenth-century texts analysed by Cave, the *Essais* uncannily manifest a self-reflexivity that matches the poststructuralist's own. Once again, showing—as Cave points out—a truly astonishing survival instinct, the *Essais* find a way of indexing the critical agency of their recipient. The text both manifests its own emptiness, turns itself inside out, ironizes itself infinitely, and provides an extraordinarily rich compendium of 'the epistemological and moral arguments available to a secular writer in the later sixteenth century'. They are available, also, to readers across the centuries, who now are held to find not the same human being but 'an indeterminate number of "visages" or physiognomies' that are constituted by readers in the act of reading. The *fortuna* from Pascal to Friedrich is thereby assimilated to this new, poststructuralist description of the way the text acts.[77]

Thus, just as Frame uses Montaigne to anchor the late modern version of humane critical thought in the pre-modern past, so other critical theorists have used him to do the same with their versions of postmodernist theory. Cave uses him to anchor deconstruction there, James Boon post-colonialism, and Jonathan Dollimore cultural materialism.[78] This phenomenon has been the subject matter of the current chapter, which is not to suggest that the modern period has distorted or misread the *Essais* in a way other periods have not.

2.6.10 THE POSTMODERN MONTAIGNE

But let us conclude by asking who the definitive postmodern Montaigne might be, the figure who most evidently follows on from Burckhardt's modern and Auerbach's late modern incarnations? Who has most authoritatively lived and published the Montaignean intellectual life in the later twentieth and early twenty-first centuries? Which reader-writer has most naturally renewed the informal critical essay, packed as it should be with fascinating biographical and autobiographical anecdotes? Who has most plausibly taken up the Montaignean textual *commerce* between the dead and the living?

---

[76] Cave, *The cornucopian text*, 312.   [77] Cave, *The cornucopian text*, 319–20.

[78] James A. Boon, 'Circumscribing Circumcision / Uncircumcision: An Essay Amid the History of Difficult Description', in Stuart B. Schwartz (ed.), *Implicit understandings: observing, reporting, and reflecting on the encounters between Europeans and other peoples in the early modern era* (Cambridge: Cambridge University Press, 1994), 556–85; Jonathan Dollimore, *Radical tragedy: religion, ideology, and power in the drama of Shakespeare and his contemporaries* (Chicago: University of Chicago Press, 1984), 17–18.

The answer is the literary critic who, submitting written testimony to the Appropriations Subcommittee on Interior and Related Agencies (U.S. House of Representatives) on behalf of the National Humanities Alliance, declared, in Montaigne-like style: 'Our strength lies in our multifariousness and our mobility, and it is precisely these qualities that make the humanities so vital. For we do not receive our identity ready-made; instead we are obliged to fashion ourselves.'[79]

Stephen Greenblatt (1942–) is more or less an exact contemporary of David Denby. But *Renaissance Self-Fashioning* (1980) was only too aware that the self-fashioning of the liberally educated modern reader had become an institutionalized ritual of exactly the kind unwittingly reported in *Great Books*. This pedagogical awareness was translated into a critique of the Renaissance artistic legacy, which now threatened to facilitate not the emancipation of the modern subject (à la Burckhardt), but the internalization of subjection. The postmodern 'human condition' is to submit to the narratives of self-fashioning into which power improvisationally writes—'inscribes'—the subject, just as the characters in *Othello* submit to Iago's fashioning narratives. But—and this is the crucial point— Greenblatt nevertheless persisted in believing that late Renaissance Englishmen did cling—just as he does in his own postmodern life—to the lived experience of the self-fashioning human subject, even in the act of suggesting the absorption or corruption or loss of that self.[80]

The key literary touchstone of this act of humane persistence in the face of adverse late Renaissance/postmodern conditions, invoked at telling points throughout Greenblatt's discussion, is Frame's translation of the *Essays*. At one point, for example, Greenblatt discusses the spiritual and material architecture of Thomas More's strategic separation of public *persona* and inner self; that is to say, his inner meditative withdrawal and his chapel, library, and gallery away from the main house. He cites Montaigne's secular substitute for the institutionalized confessional—the *arrière-boutique*—as the authoritative Renaissance model for both, and associates it with the Burckhardtian Renaissance's legacy of 'intense individuality'.

At another point, Greenblatt needs to authenticate Tyndale's printed public experimentation with 'expressions of inwardness that may stand apart from the hated institutional structure' as a precedent for the modern 'critical sense of being set apart from the world and of taking a stance toward it'. The principal Renaissance token of this modern form of critical agency is again invoked: Montaigne's work

---

[79] Greenblatt's written testimony was originally published online at http://www.nhalliance.org/ testimony/2000/00testimony-sgreenblatt.html (accessed 1 July 2002), but has now been taken down. A transcript of the oral testimony is available at <http://www.gpo.gov/fdsys/pkg/CHRG-106hhrg63833/html/CHRG-106hhrg63833.htm>, but this does not include the cited remarks, which come from the additional written testimony. I have not been able to check if the printed volume contains the testimony in question, as it is not available in the United Kingdom: *Department of the Interior and related agencies appropriations for 2001: hearings before a subcommittee of the Committee on Appropriations, House of Representatives, One Hundred Sixth Congress, second session / Subcommittee on the Department of the Interior and Related Agencies* (Washington: U.S. G.P.O., 2000).

[80] See especially the 'Epilogue' to Stephen Greenblatt, *Renaissance self-fashioning: from More to Shakespeare* (Chicago: University of Chicago Press, 1980).

(in Frame's translation). The *Essays* offer a last, late Renaissance flowering of the *'presence'* of existential identity in the written word. The same is found, 'by transference from script back to voice', in the soliloquies of *Hamlet*.[81]

Greenblatt's last two invocations of Montaigne, at the climaxes of the final two chapters on Marlowe and Shakespeare, reveal the ur-source of his sense of the essayist's importance in the imaginary museum of western literature. Marlowe and his heroes know that their life projects are illusions, but they do not withdraw into stoical resignation or contemplative solitude. They embrace the tragic with a strange eagerness. And it is the Montaigne described by romance philologist Erich Auerbach who defines the limits beyond which they push. This Montaigne understands the problem of postmodern selfhood in its full complexity, but nevertheless retains a 'pecular equilibrium' that never tips into tragedy. Greenblatt is quoting from the final pages of Auerbach's essay on the *Essays*, 'L'Humaine condition'.

In the final pages of Greenblatt's last chapter, Montaigne and Shakespeare emerge as complementary figures, figures who share radical perceptions about late Renaissance/postmodern identity. Montaigne is the figure who escapes the narratives of self-fashioning into which power improvisationally inscribes us by inventing 'a brilliant mode of *non-narrative* self-fashioning'. The passage that clinches this is again the passage which Auerbach close-reads in 'L'Humaine condition': the opening of 'Of Repentance'.[82]

Greenblatt's book has often been blamed for closing down the options for a truly critical agency. They appear to include only participation in civilizing violence against the repressed (Spenser), violently nihilistic rebellion (Marlowe), and service to power that achieves liberation only through quasi-erotic submission (Shakespeare). But we have seen that *Renaissance Self-Fashioning* did invoke a guarantor of the possibility of an autonomous self that can regather itself in 'retreat' from the relations of power that dominate external life. Montaigne is still, for Greenblatt, as for his contemporary Denby, the source of the solution to the Hamlet syndrome—the liberally educated postmodern reader's anxiety of agency.

With Montaigne, one can get a life, an inner life, which, unlike one's outer life, is not improvised by power or dominated by the simulacra circulating in the society of the spectacle, and which does not end in tragedy. Such accounts of Montaigne's anticipation of modern and postmodern intellectual life are compelling. But they differ in important ways from the early modern concept of self-accounting that informs the early documentary legacy of the *Essais*. This difference is the subject of the final chapter.

---

[81] Greenblatt, *Renaissance self-fashioning: from More to Shakespeare*, 45–7, 85–7, for this and the previous paragraph.

[82] For this and the previous paragraph, see Greenblatt, *Renaissance self-fashioning: from More to Shakespeare*, 219, 252–3 (citation of 'Of Repentance' in Frame's translation).

2.7

Epilogue

Enfranchising the Reader-Writer in Late Medieval and Early Modern Europe

The 'Prologue' (1.1) to this two-volume study outlined a distinct approach to the literary artefacts that survive from late Renaissance, post-Reformation Europe, and from Montaigne's legacy in particular. We should not limit ourselves to interpreting their textual meanings-in-context. We should use paratexts and other documents to understand how they were made, circulated, and used to do things in social nexuses, to witness to qualities and relations in action. Relevant examples of such documents included Montaigne's own account of the history of his father's copy of Sebond, the Van Veen copy of the *Essais*, and the Anthony Bacon letters to Montaigne.

In this period, literary artefacts materialized relations and transactions between actors in historically specific ways. The actors included clerics and professors of new or reformed learning, patrons in the sense of powers (persons, institutions) that could further or hinder the writing and reading of particular texts, consumers who could both read and write for themselves, servants reading and writing for others, printers and publisher-booksellers, official and unofficial censors, contemporary and classical/patristic authors, the Books of nature and the scriptures. In an era of controversy and confessionalization, such artefacts could be as much the focus of acts of violence and hostility as of conversation and friendship.

We have therefore been concerned throughout with the relations—mediated by particular material instances of the *Essais*—between the patron-author Montaigne, individual clerics and publishers, and private or lay reader-writers of his book in various locations across Europe. The *Essais* were designed, in particular, for late Renaissance descendants of Petrucci's free literates. These were individuals who in certain circumstances could read and write books and records outside institutional contexts, out of the purview of authorities, unexercised by the demands of a public office or chair—even if they often remained bound by the more private offices or duties of a mother or a father, a daughter or a son.

For centuries in western Europe, traces of such activity had taken the material form of personal, household registers or record-books, including books first written or printed for other purposes, then adapted as personal archives. In the sixteenth century, as never before, the free literate both began to claim authority in public for his or her judgements, and became a controversial, fear-inducing figure for state and ecclesiastical authorities.

How might this approach revise, at the most general level, traditional and post-modern accounts of the historical meanings of Montaigne's work? The 'Epilogue' answers this question by beginning with Auerbach's reading of the opening of III 2—the reading invoked by Stephen Greenblatt in his highly influential account of self-fashioning (see 2.6.10). I then use concrete, paired nexuses of interactions between Montaigne's book and early seventeenth-century reader-writers—Camus and Sarpi, the Duke of Urbino and Van Veen, Charron and L'Estoile—to develop a revised description of the history of practical philosophy and self-accounting with which it is involved.

We shall see that this description tallies well with the history of Montaigne's book offered by Pierre Bayle in the early eighteenth century. Lest this seem too pat, I devote more space to the counter-example of the Duke of Urbino's copy—a copy that serves only the agenda of a grand ducal library. This is to remind us of a perspective from which 'discourses' in different cultures and times can in theory make anything they want of the *Essais*. They can construct a different 'author-function' or ignore their author altogether. I shall nevertheless argue that the design and style of the book has determined to a significant degree the agency relations to which it has given rise, relations which—in diverse situations, with diverse outcomes—focus on the situation of individuals reading and writing in non-institutional nexuses.

2.7.1 AUERBACH'S MONTAIGNE

In Istanbul, some time between May 1942 and April 1945, the great philologist Erich Auerbach began writing about Montaigne's *Essais*. Categorized as a Jew by the Nazi state, stripped of his Marburg university chair, he had arrived as an exile in the summer of 1936, to be offered a position teaching romance literatures at Istanbul State University. What he wrote on Montaigne was to become chapter 12 of one of the classics of twentieth-century literary studies: *Mimesis: The Representation of Reality in Western Literature*.[1]

Each chapter of this great book began with an extract from a key text. The authors treated ranged from Homer and the compilers of the Old Testament in the first chapter to Proust and Woolf in the last. It is not a theoretical treatise or a textbook, but a personal book of readings written by a teacher of literature, a teacher exiled from the society and the institutions that trained him.

As we heard in the last chapter (2.6.4), Auerbach was a medievalist, but the late Renaissance of Montaigne, Shakespeare, and Cervantes played a pivotal role in the highly influential story he told. In particular, the example of Montaigne served to enfranchise the modern philosophical critic of Auerbach's ilk. His analysis of the *Essais* implicitly legitimated his own enterprise as a 'late' humanist-existentialist investigating the human condition through texts.

[1] Kader Konuk, *East–West mimesis: Auerbach in Turkey* (Stanford: Stanford University Press, 2010).

For, like Auerbach himself, Montaigne proved to have discovered authentic modern representations of human reality and consciousness through a combination of reading and writing and experience. Auerbach's experiment with the *Essais* proved to be repeatable for later students encountering this great book. Nearly fifty years later, a professor in a Columbia classroom re-enacts the textual discovery using the opening of III 2: Huggins the football player 'gets' modern individuality; Denby the journalist breaks through not just by reading Montaigne, but by writing about him, in his style (2.6.6).

Auerbach's story works backwards from two, predominantly French achievements of the nineteenth and twentieth centuries: the achievement of an everyday social realism in Stendhal and Flaubert, and the achievement of the representation of interior reality as a stream of consciousness in Proust and Woolf. The desire to discover the prehistory of this latter achievement explains Auerbach's choice of text from the *Essais*. He opens his chapter with the beginning of III 2, 'Of repentance':

> Others form man; I give an account of him [*je le recite*] and portray a particular one [*un particulier*], very ill-formed, whom I should truly make very different from what he is if I had to fashion him over again. But it is done now.... I cannot keep my subject still; it staggers confusedly along with a natural drunkenness. I grasp it as it is now, just as it is at the moment I give my attention to it. I am not portraying being but becoming: not the passage from one age to another (or, as the people put it, from one seven-year period to the next), but from day to day, from minute to minute [*de jour en jour, de minute en minute*]. My history [*mon histoire*] needs to be adapted to the moment.... This is a record of varied and changeable occurrences, and of unresolved and, when it so befalls, contradictory ideas [*un contrerolle de divers et muables accidens et d'imaginations irresoluës et, quand il y eschet, contraires*]...I set forth a lowly and unillustrious life; that does not matter. You can tie up all moral philosophy with a common and private life [*toute la philosophie morale, à une vie populaire et privée*] just as well as with a life of richer stuff. Each man bears the whole form of man's estate. Authors communicate with the people by some special extrinsic mark [*quelque marque speciale et estrangere*]; I am the first to do so by my universal being, as Michel de Montaigne, not as a grammarian or a poet or a jurist [*non comme Grammarien ou Poëte, ou Jurisconsulte*].[2]

What exactly does Montaigne mean when he states that other authors form man and communicate with the people by some special extrinsic mark, while he tells of man and is the first to do so by his entire being, attaching the whole of moral philosophy to an ordinary life? How does this relate to his identification of his book as a record of various and changeable occurrences that he does not refashion or reform for the purposes of instruction or repentance?

To answer the former question, we clearly need some account of how authors in Montaigne's environment communicated via extrinsic marks, and how his own mode of communication purports to differ. We shall see that his use of the word

---

[2] III 2, NP844–5/BVH Paris 1595, bk. III, pp. 11–12/S907–8. Auerbach used Trechmann's translation and the Villey text, which in this passage contains only one significant variant from the 1595 text: 'quelque marque particuliere et estrangere' for 'quelque marque speciale et estrangere'.

'contrerolle', and elsewhere in his text of variants of the phrase 'registre et contre-rolle', is crucial in the attempt to answer the second question, for it draws upon his readership's understanding that books could be personal records which might be communicated only to family and friends.

But we heard in 2.6.4 that Auerbach was interested in different questions. He talks less of the *marques* by means of which authors communicate than of the qual-ity of Montaigne's introspective realism, which breaks through the Christian framework of the later Middle Ages. His author's emancipation from the Christian conceptual schema did not simply throw him back to the ideas and conditions of antique philosophers such as Cicero and Plutarch: 'his newly acquired freedom was much more exciting, much more of the historical moment, directly connected with the feeling of insecurity'—the same feeling, perhaps, as had grown in Auerbach himself during the 1930s and 1940s. In fact, more recent research has shown that Montaigne was working very closely with the Christian conceptual schema of his own day: the Tridentine doctrine of repentance.[3]

Auerbach subjects the whole passage to intensive close reading but neglects to make anything of the word 'contrerolle'; indeed, he paraphrases it at one point as a 'representation' ('Darstellung'), a representation produced according to a 'method'. The words he does pick up are interpreted as mirroring 'a very realistic conception of man based on experience and in particular on self-experience'. Why and how did Montaigne offer this representation? Because he was following a 'strictly experimental', and therefore 'modern', kind of 'method' (to use, he says, a 'scientific-sounding word').[4] Like so many twentieth-century critics, Auerbach draws on Pierre Villey's demonstration—to which he also had access in Istanbul—that the form of the *Essais* evolved from a miscellaneous collection of glossed exem-pla, quotations, and aphorisms into a work of positive reason.[5]

To tell his story, Auerbach had to work with what was available in the public libraries of Istanbul, which he says were not well equipped for the study of European literature. He gained special permission from the papal delegate to use a copy of Migne's nineteenth-century edition of patristic texts held in a private, attic-level room of the library in the Dominican monastery of San Pietro di Galata. But the fact was that the texts of what Auerbach thought of as the 'western' tradi-tion were available in Istanbul in one edition or another. He betrays a slight anxiety about the lack of reliable critical editions of some of his texts and the lack of refer-ence to the latest technical literature, but at the same time shows a quiet confidence that this will not have affected the core of his argument.[6]

---

[3] Auerbach, *Mimesis*, 310; George Hoffmann, 'Emond Auger et le contexte tridentin de l'essai "Du repentir"', *Bulletin de la Société des Amis de Montaigne*, 8th series, 21–22 (2001), 263–75; Smith, *Montaigne and the Roman censors*, 58–73.

[4] Auerbach, *Mimesis*, 291–2. For the German text, see Erich Auerbach, *Mimesis: dargestellte Wirklichkeit in der abendländischen Literatur* (Berne: A. Francke, 1946), 277. All short references are to the 1953, English edition, unless otherwise stated.

[5] Auerbach, *Mimesis*, 292, 295.

[6] Auerbach, *Mimesis*, 557; Erich Auerbach, *Mimesis: the representation of reality in western literature*, trans. Willard R. Trask (Princeton: Princeton University Press, 2013), 567n.15; Konuk, *East–West mimesis: Auerbach in Turkey*, 141–2. Some of the research since carried out on the circumstances of the

In the previous two centuries, Migne and other heroic editors and publishers had comprehensively constituted what he calls 'the literature of Europe'. For Montaigne, he used Villey's edition of 1930–1, published by Alcan in Paris, the ancestor of the Villey-Saulnier edition that many scholars still consider standard today. Indeed, it is arguable that the two centuries before the Second World War, not the sixteenth century, was really the period when the Gutenberg Galaxy described by Marshall McLuhan came into being in countries espousing western cultural values. It was during this time that truly modern, industrialized printing-houses naturalized and stabilized the encounter between the uniform, fixed, mass-produced 'text' and the 'general' educated reader free to read and judge it in his or her own time and way—the encounter that is the basis for *Mimesis*, and for its implicit concept of western civilization.[7]

This meant that Auerbach could read the literature of Europe as a series of widely available texts that, subjected to close reading by an educated reading public, yielded a history of the European concept of the 'real', a history in which the period of the late Renaissance was pivotal. As the Second World War and German nationalism tore Europe apart, he was of course not in a position to traverse the continent visiting rare books rooms, manuscript rooms or archives to do his work. But he did not need to, given his conception of his enterprise. He was interested in realism, not communication. He did not need to take into account the material forms, the modes and environments of composition and transmission and reception of his texts. He does not even mention that some were composed orally and only later written down, that some were composed for manuscript circulation, some—such as Montaigne's *Essais*—composed for printed circulation, but drawing on forms associated with private manuscript writing.

Nor did he need to consult the original archival documents and rare books behind the biographical and sociological contexts he adduced for those texts. Research of this kind would not have affected the readings he was giving, the history of ideas he was writing. All he needed were his texts, his philological tools, and a general sense of sociological and historical background gleaned from secondary literature. This is what we might call traditional historicism—what Auerbach calls German 'historism'—at its best. Its legacy, thankfully, continues, and it is arguable that 'new' or postmodern historicisms, including those current in comparative literature, ultimately represent less a break from than a continuation of this tradition.[8]

book's composition contests the picture Auerbach paints of a solitary scholar writing in an environment not equipped for European studies. See Konuk, *East-West mimesis: Auerbach in Turkey*; Emily S. Apter, *The translation zone: a new comparative literature* (Princeton: Princeton University Press, 2006), 41–64.

[7] Auerbach, *Mimesis*, 288, 554; Michel de Montaigne, *Les Essais*, ed. Pierre Villey, 3 vols. (Paris: F. Alcan, 1930–1); David McKitterick, *Print, manuscript, and the search for order, 1450–1830* (Cambridge: Cambridge University Press, 2003), chapters 7 and 8.

[8] Auerbach, *Mimesis*, 443–8.

2.7.2 NEXUSES IN THE HISTORY OF THE *ESSAIS*

What have been the most significant new developments in the study of early modern literature since the publication of Auerbach's book in English in 1953? As we heard in 2.6, the most widely acknowledged development between the 1960s and the early 1990s was the advent of literary theory, which challenged the epistemological and semiotic premises of an enterprise such as Auerbach's, and which gave rise to the new forms of historicism mentioned in the last paragraph of 2.7.1.

But in the three decades since D. F. McKenzie's groundbreaking 1985 lectures on 'Bibliography and the sociology of the text' an equally significant but less widely acknowledged development has become apparent. The re-cataloguing, reproduction, and re-analysis of the documentary basis of literary-historical study has been restored to the forefront of scholarship in areas that go well beyond those geared to the preparation of critical editions of canonical texts. We still study the production of discourse, à la Foucault, but in less abstract terms, and in conjunction with the material study of its writing, printing, circulation, consumption, and re-use.[9]

In the years around 1943–6, there was really only one document, one copy of the *Essais* that mattered in Montaigne studies—the famous Bordeaux copy that provided the basis for the Villey edition used by Auerbach. The only other documents of any significance were the 1580 and 1588 editions, which helped complete the picture of the compositional layers of Montaigne's text. Paris 1595 could supply readings in instances where the Bordeaux copy was illegible or cropped. Once the edition was established, if one was doing interpretative work, there was no need to go back to the copy. This remained largely true throughout the 1980s. But since then the scholarly community's sense of the place of Montaigne in the history of ideas—of the agents who placed him in the history of ideas—has been mutating due to the attention lavished on the particularities of other editions, copies, and records.

This is part of a larger trend we might describe as the history of communications. The emphasis on continuously changing and circulating texts, on their modes of production, dissemination, and collection, is changing the old game of text-and-context in ways we have not yet fully comprehended. Social and intellectual 'context' is becoming less what it was for Auerbach—a matter of a fixed set of recoverable features of the society of the initial time and place of production—and more a matter of an ongoing process—a 'dynamics of contextualisation'—that begins even before composition of a work is complete.[10]

This trend has been central to late medieval studies for decades, thanks to the work of pioneers such as Petrucci. In sixteenth- and seventeenth-century studies, scholars have more recently begun to recover the outline of a distinctive, hybrid print-and-manuscript culture, a culture awash with a whole sea of ephemeral and

---

[9] Armando Petrucci, 'Reading to read: A future for reading', in Guglielmo Cavallo and Roger Chartier (eds.), *A history of reading in the West* (Cambridge: Polity, 1999), 345–67, 349–50.

[10] Michael Lucey, 'A literary object's contextual life', in Ali Behdad and Dominic Thomas (eds.), *A companion to comparative literature* (Chichester: Wiley-Blackwell, 2011), 120–35.

polemical texts engulfing the canonical works that continue to draw much of the attention.

These texts are considered not just as mirrors of nature, or—if you are a post-modernist—as mirrors of other texts that endlessly defer the faithful mirroring of nature. They are considered as artefacts, things made and circulated and used in particular material and social conditions—the 'material text', to use the current shorthand. Text scholars in medieval and early modern studies do now feel they need to visit the archive, the rare books room, the manuscripts room, in search of alternative histories of ideas—or visit the internet to find online digital facsimiles of relevant materials.

The reorientation of literary studies towards the consideration of material and technical practices has perhaps in some instances become an end in itself, closing off questions about the social meanings of texts.[11] But once non-canonical readers and writers emerge from the early modern archive it cannot help but change our sense of the meanings-in-context of medieval and early modern literature. We read with an understanding of the ways in which production anticipated consumption, of the ways in which 'texts were written into an imagination of their contemporary reading'. The 'actual audience, the nature and practices of that audience' becomes integral to 'understanding the performativity of texts, the ways texts worked and why they were made the way they were'.[12]

Take the example of Justin Steinberg's work on Dante. Auerbach deals with Dante, as he does all his authors, as someone who is imitating earthly, historical reality more or less faithfully, in the context of a given style and genre. For Auerbach, the central point is that Dante plunges the living world of human action into the changeless existence of the afterlife for the first time. But Steinberg has found the traces of the first urban readers and copiers of Dante's poetry in the archives—the same free literates found by Petrucci.[13]

Adapting their methods of memorializing contracts and keeping accounts to the collecting of medieval Italian poetry, these urban readers and writers made copying Italian poetry a crucial aspect of how they understood and represented themselves as individuals and communities. Dante emerges from Steinberg's work as a historically specific reader and author interacting with a historically specific community of readers and authors.[14]

In the same way, we have seen in *The School of Montaigne* how Montaigne was interacting with historically specific communities. Two of these communities have been central to the study. They comprise groups of intellectuals reading and

---

[11] For an exemplary re-opening of these questions, see Narveson, *Bible readers*.

[12] Steven Zwicker, 'Habits of reading and early modern literary culture', in David Loewenstein and Janel M. Mueller (eds.), *The Cambridge history of early modern English literature* (Cambridge: Cambridge University Press, 2002), 170–98, 198; Jeroen Salman, Roeland Harms, and Joad Raymond, 'Introduction', in Jeroen Salman, Roeland Harms, and Joad Raymond (eds.), *Not dead things: the dissemination of popular print in England and Wales, Italy, and the Low Countries, 1500–1820* (Leiden: Brill, 2013), 1–29, 2.

[13] For Petrucci see, in Volume 1 of this study, the 'General Introduction: Volumes 1 and 2'.

[14] Justin Steinberg, *Accounting for Dante: urban readers and writers in late medieval Italy* (Notre Dame, Ind.: University of Notre Dame Press, 2007).

writing—for the most part—in the context of explicitly professional *personae* and public offices: the regular clergy and censors of Rome (1.7), and the learned legal professionals of the French *parlements* centred on Paris (2.1). Both cases revealed how Montaigne's book indexed an acquisition of freedom not just in literary and representational terms, but also in social and publishing terms. It did so against the background of professional forms of learning and learned *personae*.

So we have seen, on the one hand, how a book which self-consciously enfranchises a reader-writer (with increasing boldness through expanded editions) was received and used; and, on the other hand, how case studies of that book's use in others' projects of reading and writing clarify its original design, its novelty as a distinctively free and personal discourse mediated by literary technology in a public medium (print).

To achieve this, we have focused as much as possible on descriptions of the particular literary nexuses that constitute the 'circuit of communications' outlined in schematic terms by Darnton.[15] They have come from across the full early history and from a wide range of incarnations of Montaigne's work, including particular *essais* or *sentences* within the text, and particular instances of use and republication of the text and of other texts in his milieu.

For we saw in 1.4 and 1.5 that each particular *essai* of the author's judgement describes a nexus in which Montaigne engages in conversation with himself, professional interpreters, and the private reader-writers he anticipates his book will reach, whether they are named as 'patrons' or not. The clearest example is perhaps the author's role in II 37 in mediating the expert advice of the balneologists and the hydrotherapists for Madame de Duras and other court ladies in her milieu (1.4.4), though other, similar examples punctuate his text throughout.

Other nexuses discussed have come from the author's own history and have involved various participants (some *in absentia*) besides himself. In 1.1.11 we found Sebond's work of natural theology to be the focus of relations involving court *dames*, the *docteurs* who would sell them new theologies, Sebond himself, Pierre Eyquem, Pierre Bunel. In other cases it was the 1580 *Essais*, the *docteurs-moines* who censor the text, and the Master of the Sacred Palace at Rome (1.7.3); the 1580 (or perhaps the 1588) *Essais*, and Pasquier at Blois (2.1.7); Gournay, the *Essais*, and Lipsius (1.6.3–5); Gournay, the 'Love stories' of Plutarch, and Lipsius (1.6.6).

Many have involved Montaigne only in his absence, by means of his book and its individual chapters, *sentences*, or *traits*: Lancre, *Essais* I 20 and III 11, and the Jesuit demonologist Delrio (1.5.4); L'Estoile, the Montaignean *trait* on moderation (from I 29), and the duc d'Épernon (2.1.8); L'Estoile, the *trait* from *Essais* I 18, and his confessor Father des Landes (2.1.8); Goulart, Camerarius, and *Essais* I 22 and II 3 (2.2.7); Sarpi, Trevisan, *Essais* I 27, and Micanzio (2.2.9); Van Veen, the 1602 *Essais*, and his teacher Lipsius (2.4.4–8); Slingsby, the English *Essayes*, and the translator Florio (2.4.2); Lady Anne Clifford, the English *Essayes*, and her

---

[15] Robert Darnton, 'What is the history of books?', in David Finkelstein and Alistair McCleery (eds.), *The book history reader* (2nd edn., London: Routledge, 2006), 9–26.

servant Rivers (2.3.7); Tayler, Frame's version of III 2, Denby, and Huggins (2.6.6). Others have not involved the *Essais* at all (except, in the first case, as the source of the description): the court *dames*, their schoolmasters, the works of Plutarch, and Bishop Amyot (1.6.10); the 'Virtuosi' at Venice, Bacon's *Advancement of learning*, and Friar Micanzio (2.2.9).

Adapting Gell's methodology, I have argued that early modern literary nexuses were characteristically comprised of agency relations, mediated by one or other kind of literary or verbal artefact, between participants acting—or being acted-upon— as: prototypes of wisdom and learning (e.g. the Books of nature and the scriptures; *imagines ingeniorum*); writers, compilers; professional interpreters and mediators (e.g. teachers, editors, promoters, translators, bibliographers, glossators, commentators, censors, correctors); producers and disseminators whose office or trade it was to print or copy, publish, distribute, market or sell books and extracts from books; privileged recipients or patrons; particular reader-writers or collectors in the broader, unspecified public of free literates.[16] The Reformation and Counter-Reformation politicized these relations, made them controversial, even as they were commercially exploited through the book trade.

There is an important rider to this. To act in such ways in particular nexuses was not necessarily to assume a fixed social identity, but rather to perform offices in a particular *persona* in that instance. It is the argument of this study that it was Montaigne—despite his association with contingency and uncertainty—who gave the person reading and writing freely for themselves a template for the adoption of a stable *persona* and a social identity to go with this activity. The author of the *Essais* became a public example of a particular, well-born person from a landed estate in Montaigne, without any debts or obligations, who consistently read and wrote, invented and judged in this free, non-pragmatic way, without getting into trouble with ecclesiastical or civil authorities.

But Montaigne was a novelty, an exception. And, as we have seen throughout, the *Essais* themselves do not represent a pure scene of free reading and writing of the kind painted idealistically by Philip Pullman at the beginning of the 'General Introduction' to Volume 1. They bear witness to some degree to other kinds of nexus, to the author's involvement in diplomatic affairs, his performance of public offices, his relations with clerics and ecclesiastical authorities, his knowledge of Latin scholarship, his use of commonplace methods, his 'institution' in learning, his social *persona* as a client to high-ranking patrons.

And elsewhere we have seen just how much depended on the particular nexus and its description. Ginammi was in general terms a publisher-bookseller disseminating the works of others, but in some of his publications he began to assume the *persona* of a *Bibliopola insigne* who was authoring the works that appeared under his imprint (see 2.2.12). The first time Goulart read the *Essais* he was semi-officially defending the public morality of his city, and he corrected them accordingly; the

[16] One can complicate the picture further by including agents and patients within the souls of the writers and readers involved, for example the faculties of imagination, memory, reason (see 1.1.4, 1.1.12).

second time he was offering the fruits of his private reading and writing to an international Francophone public, and he extracted and vulgarized some of the very passages he had cut on the first reading—though with his Christian vocation always in mind (see 2.2.7).

Goulart's example indicates that the phrase 'public of free literates' homogenizes a very diverse phenomenon. The circumstances in each case might place an act of 'free' reading and writing, and the agents and relations involved in it, at the intersection of different points on a series of continuums from: *humeur* to *raison*, *otium* to *negotium*, private to public, lay to clerical, vernacular to Latin, miscellaneous to methodical, non-institutional to institutional, self-directed to service-directed.

Women, in particular, often read 'sotto controllo', but nevertheless with some autonomy.[17] We found in 2.3.3 and 2.3.7 that when Lady Anne Clifford is having Florio's Montaigne read to her in a leisurely context she is freer from direct, patriarchal supervision than when she is reading with the minister Ran in the Bible. Male readers were constrained in different ways. When Pasquier read the *Essais* he did so, at one and the same time, in his private *persona* as a free literate seduced by Montaigne's abundant *liberté* of discourse, and in his public *persona* as a professional lawyer-historian and semi-professional corrector who would see it conform more closely to the criteria for a national—that is, *politique*—work of literature (see 2.1.7).

Or take the case of Querenghi's reading of Naselli's *Discorsi*. He was a canon of the cathedral chapter of Padua and public reader of moral philosophy in the university. He published his official readings and lectures in Latin. At the same time, he offered the fruits of his *otium*, his more private acts of reading and writing, in speeches at the local Academy, in the *persona* of a *Ricovrato*, and in distinct, vernacular publications of free-ranging *Discorsi*—those in which he uses Naselli's Montaigne (2.2.11).

These discourses showed Querenghi fulfilling private offices of friendship for patrons, whether as an academician or not. But even in his private, self-directed studies he was still to some degree acting as a client to patrons, fulfilling the offices of a canon, and working in institutional contexts such as that of the Accademia dei Ricovrati. One of the ways in which he did the latter was to offer a secular image of the monastic, contemplative life to the Accademia's audience—the elite of Padua and Venice.

So the agency relations between participants and the *personae* adopted could vary greatly according to the particular nexus, and even within a single nexus. The patron-author and the reader-writers of the *Essais* may be characterizable in general terms as 'free literates' but their enfranchisement is always relative to specific conditions and circumstances.

And, of course, not all types of participant were involved in every nexus. Not all extracts or *sentences* have identified authors, not all books have patrons or sellers, and not all texts have commentators or teachers. When it came to the composition

---

[17] Xenia von Tippelskirch, *Sotto controllo: letture femminili in Italia nella prima età moderna* (Rome: Viella, 2011).

and publication of books there were various categories of primary and secondary authors who could relate to one another in different ways: 'authors, discoverers, retrievers (or revisers), and editors' (*auctores, inventores, recensitores, emendatores*).[18] As we have seen, even patrons and printer-publishers could be considered the 'authors' of a book, in the sense of being the primary agents behind it.

Indeed, a whole variety of actors might be considered primary or secondary agents in the history of the work, both before and after the publication of the complete edition. In the case of the *Essais* such agents range from Plutarch, Gournay, and L'Angelier, to Goulart, Charron, and Naudé. Montaigne himself moved on from the functions of a retriever and editor, to those of a translator and corrector, to that of an author who was his own *patron*. Gournay made a very similar series of moves through the literary nexuses in which she participated.[19]

Furthermore, nexuses could come in groups: books and extracts could bring relations with other books and extracts with them, and authors could bring relations with other authors. A fundamental feature of any literary nexus is the company a given book or extract is understood to be keeping on a given occasion—including antagonistic company (other books or extracts which it disputes or challenges or rivals). This is more than a matter of intertextuality. It might be a matter of intellectual or physical grouping—texts associated by paratexts or physically assembled together in one binding.[20]

In his first edition, Montaigne describes the relations of his book to La Boétie's most famous text (which he originally intended to be incorporated in a single physical book with his own texts), to his father's author Sebond, and, most significantly of all, to Amyot's Plutarch. Florio relates the English Montaigne to Sidney's *Arcadia* and the English nobleman's translations. As we shall see in 2.7.5, Rochemaillet begins the process of sealing an enduring relationship, for those selling and purchasing books in the French vernacular market, between the *Essais* and *De la sagesse*.

Sorel puts Montaigne and his *Essais* at the apex of a triangular relationship. He prefaces his section on the essayist with a consideration of Gournay's *Ouvrages* on moral and political topics. He says these show that she judged sanely of things ('elle jugeoit sainement des choses')—though he later says that her prefatory testimony to Montaigne's qualities would be received as 'interested', the testimony of a daughter over-passionate about her father. In the following section he says:

> I place the books of Pierre Charron in the company of the *Essais de Montaigne*... it is necessary to join this author to that we have just spoken of [Montaigne], in order to follow the sentiments of the majority of people, who believe that Charron is closely related to Montaigne by the liberty of his opinions.[21]

---

[18] Maclean, *Scholarship, commerce, religion*, 53 (citing Conrad Rittershausen, 1610).

[19] Maclean, *Scholarship, commerce, religion*, 77; Michel Simonin, 'Œuvres complètes or plus que complètes?: Montaigne éditeur de La Boétie', *Montaigne Studies*, 7 (1995), 5–34.

[20] Jeffrey Todd Knight, *Bound to read: compilations, collections, and the making of Renaissance literature* (Philadelphia: University of Pennsylvania Press, 2013).

[21] Charles Sorel, *La bibliotheque françoise* (Paris: Compagnie des Libraires du Palais, 1664), sigs. C10r–v, C12r, D4r.

It is arguable that for some readers in Ferrara and Geneva, the *Essais* are related more to other works by Naselli and Goulart, and by the publishers they worked with, than they are to Seneca and Plutarch.

In short, we have seen throughout this two-volume study how the agency relations surrounding the *Essais* (and extracts from/reproductions of the *Essais*) constantly change, depending on the particular nexus, and on the author and the form of the description of that nexus. It is therefore appropriate to conclude by way of some further examples.

2.7.3 BISHOP CAMUS ON THE *ESSAIS*

Over four centuries before Auerbach read the opening passage of III 2 for the student and general reader of European romance literature, a cleric singled it out for glossing in a private exchange with a young nobleman. Jean-Pierre Camus—Bishop of Belley from 1609 and a fervent disciple of the Roman Catholic Bishop of Geneva, François de Sales—introduces Montaigne's book, including Auerbach's passage, in the eighth volume of his *Diversitez* (1613), themselves miscellanies based on personal commonplace books that imitated the *Essais* throughout.[22]

Camus incorporates implicit commentary upon the III 2 passage in the context of an explanation as to why he had to stop reading the *Essais* on a daily basis. It was because of the contagiousness of Montaigne's manner of speaking of himself. For Camus the obvious comparisons are with classical authors of commentaries and lives of the great. Some of these authors had written like Montaigne of their own lives, but they were great heroes of the ilk of Caesar, who in any case did so with more *vanité*. Cicero is likewise blamed for speaking vaingloriously of himself, not with *bonne foi*. Plutarch had it easy because of the material in the lives of the great Greek and Romans.[23]

But to write of an ordinary, unexceptional life ('une vie basse, sombre, particulière, retirée, populaire, simple') in such a vein, with evident *bonne foi*—that was unique. Camus judges Montaigne to be applying, for the first time, a whole classical tradition of life-writing, of self-knowledge, and of rhetorical self-praise and self-blame, to the life of an ordinary, unexceptional gentleman: he does not form man, he tells of him ('Il ne forme pas l'homme, il le récite'). He carries out the proper office and role of man, reaches the highest stage of Socratean wisdom, which is to know oneself. In a passing but very significant remark, Bishop Camus states that Montaigne 'arrived... very close to the goal of his enterprise, if he had wanted to take one more step to reformation' ('il est... arrivé bien proche du but de son entreprise, s'il eust voulu avancer d'un pas dans la réformation').[24]

This indicates the bishop's awareness of the main point of the rest of III 2: though he shows himself to be self-knowledgeable and contrite, Montaigne knows

---

[22] On Camus, see Thomas Worcester, 'In praise of Montaigne: Bishop Jean-Pierre Camus', in Keith Cameron and Laura Lee Willett (eds.), *Le visage changeant de Montaigne/The changing face of Montaigne* (Paris: Honoré Champion, 2003), 277–86.

[23] Millet 189–90.   [24] Millet 190–1.

this does not amount to repentance in the proper theological sense. But he also knows that he does not have the desire or the capacity to reform himself.

Camus appears to accept that a noble layman can say this in the particular rhetorical context of the *Essais*. But where Montaigne says that all other authors communicate by some *marque spéciale et étrangère*, like that of a grammarian or jurist, Camus retorts that it is not possible to read the *Essais* without picking up the *marque*, the stain of Montaigne's distinctive manner of speaking of himself—just as you cannot avoid whiting up in a flour-mill: 'he wanted to write of himself; I not at all of myself; I want to form, not tell of myself [*Je désire me former, non me réciter*], and instruct myself in teaching others, not to represent myself'. The bishop does want to—his ecclesiastical office obliges him to—take the extra step into *réformation*.[25]

After Gournay's 1595 preface, Camus' letter in judgement on the *Essais* is the most important account of the school of Montaigne published in the period, as Boase acknowledged.[26] Indeed, Camus aims to displace Gournay and undermine her *suffisance* as a literary critic. He explicitly and misogynistically mocks Montaigne's *fille d'alliance*, denying her, as a weak woman, the liberty of judgement she claims with respect to the *Essais* ('quand j'entends une Dame y faire la suffisante, je m'en mocque; ce n'est pas son gibier').[27] He takes it back in the *persona* of a bishop, in a long, epideictic discourse that self-consciously overwrites her preface and that rivals Pasquier's letter, composed in the same years. It is a paradoxical *éloge*, which praises Montaigne even as it blames him, and vice versa.

The point here is that Camus, in his letter, could be characterized as delineating Montaigne's 'newly acquired freedom' (in Auerbach's words) by granting it to his noble young interlocutor, a fictional *persona* for the free literate with whom we have been concerned throughout. But the nexus of enfranchisement of his reader-writer (the fictive Achante) differs in a number of interesting ways from Auerbach's, not least because it deliberately excludes women such as Gournay.

First, it occurs in a printed letter of rhetorical praise and blame addressed by a bishop to a young sword nobleman, amongst five letters so addressed.[28] The balanced rhetoric of praise and blame in the letter is a reponse to what Camus sees as the fundamentally rhetorical character of Montaigne's discourse—itself a virtuoso example of balanced, truthful self-praise and self-blame. The context is the gentle censure of a young nobleman's manners, especially with respect to his courtly, affected way of using *lettres*. It is important to realize, however, that the bishop is not licensing irreligious behaviour on the part of Achante. The last letter of the series is a sermon on how to cooperate with God's providence, even when managing affairs at court.[29]

Second, Camus characterizes the *Essais* as a book for Achante's daily reading and writing, a book that would always be open ('Je...ne le peux manier qu'à livre

[25] Millet 191.   [26] Boase 114–15.   [27] Millet 179.

[28] Jean-Pierre Camus, *Les diversitez: tome VIII* (Paris: Cl. Chappelet, 1613), sigs. 2C3r–G4v. Millet extracts a passage from book thirty-nine, letter 106, and the whole of letter 107, and includes the corresponding page numbers for the 1613 edition.

[29] Camus, *Les diversitez: tome VIII*, sig. 2G3r–v.

ouvert'), a book he would routinely read and frequently meditate upon, like a breviary, and that would ordinarily give rise to his own writing and speech. Indeed, this is a book whose every word can generate a *sentence*, whose every line can generate a *discours*, whose every discourse can generate a whole *livre*.[30]

So, he starts by saying the *Essais* are 'le bréviaire des gentilshommes'.[31] He goes on to offer a complex meditation on the effects of his having used the *Essais* as a breviary, and the reasons why he as a clergyman cannot continue to use it as such; even if, as a gentleman who is not considering a religious vocation, Achante can and should. Montaigne's work communicates 'this liberty to speak with such fantasy' ('cette liberté de parler ainsi fantastiquement') to those who wish to trace their personal conceptions on paper. Such *liberté* is appropriate to the condition of a well-born gentleman ('gentilhomme bien né'), but not to that of a noble clergyman.

Everyday in the *Essais*, Camus had discovered, little by little, through regular perusal of the book, ever more secrets for living and for morals ('petit à petit par l'usage et la routine...tous les jours nouveaux secrets, pour la vie et les mœurs'). But he had to leave off his regular use of this book ('l'ordinaire routine et pratique de ce livre'), this breviary, precisely because—as we have seen—the distinctive *marque* of Michel de Montaigne stained his writing and speech.[32]

This brings us to the third point. Camus is fundamentally concerned not with the representation of inner reality, in Auerbach's sense, but with the representation of *personae* in terms of their effects upon others, and with the literary forms of discourse that are appropriate to the corresponding professions and offices. Camus' point throughout is that whereas Montaigne's free style of discourse is not appropriate for the professional *persona* of a bishop, whose office is to reform and teach, it is appropriate for the *persona* of a gentleman who professes arms, as well as letters when at leisure in times of peace.

There is, furthermore, an agonistic background to this last aspect. Where Auerbach claims Montaigne for an academic community of lovers of western historical realism, in the contemporary context of a war on western civilization and culture, Camus claims him for a lay community of French Roman Catholics, against the background of the ongoing controversies with French Huguenots and Genevan Calvinists.

For Camus, then, the book points not to a mode of 'scientific' representation of the inner self, the prototypical human condition, but to an extraordinary rhetorical performance, appropriate for the confessionalized literary environment of the time, on the part of an ordinary Catholic person of noble condition. Montaigne has defined a new way in which the *persona*, the private offices and the social

[30] Millet 164.
[31] He may or may not be imitating a remark elsewhere attributed to Cardinal du Perron—that the *Essais* were 'le bréviaire des courtisans'. Pierre de Lancre repeats Camus' remark in 1617 and explains that it is a breviary in the sense that the bishop always finds 'des grâces nouvelles' when going back to it on a regular basis. But Lancre is also unsure whether the description is a compliment: if Camus means that Montaigne's book 'est aussi ordinaire aus Gentilshommes que leur bréviaire' then he might mean to say that they never deign to open it. See Millet 163, 194–5.
[32] Millet 165–6, 180, 191, for this and the previous paragraph.

condition of a particular well-born but unexceptional Catholic *gentilhomme* could legitimate an informal and free style of learnedly ignorant discourse—without the 'rule' that a cleric must follow—on the subject of himself. In so doing he has incarnated the Aristotelian *persona* of the sincere or truthful man who strikes the right balance in praising and blaming himself.[33]

He has done this, furthermore, in a context of heated religious controversy that centres on the literary citation and judgement of authors. This last point is most apparent in the contrasts Camus sets up between the *persona* and literary style of Montaigne in the *Essais* and that of the Huguenot Duplessis-Mornay, and in the way he fiercely engages with a rival judgement of the *Essais* by the Genevan Calvinist Théodore de Bèze. For Camus, the nature and value of Montaigne's acquisition of freedom was obvious when one handled some of his contemporaries' books.

For Camus is clear that Montaigne's confused, disordered, unpremeditated style is a gentleman's riposte to books that use pedantic, scholastic modes of discourse ('ces partitions, divisions, et suittes méthodiquement scholaresques').[34] His mode of citing-without-citing authors and of mixing in a *diversité* of unreferenced foreign-language quotations shows his nonchalance with respect to the scholarly method of the schools ('nonchalante de l'art et de l'eschole'), which would not have been appropriate to someone of his condition.

Montaigne ostentatiously does not participate in the dominant intellectual trend of the age, as identified by Camus: exact research into textual *loci* ('exacte recherche des lieux'), for the purposes of authoritative citation in controversies and verbal contestations. Camus can understand why this scholarly practice is necessary in theological controversy, and in the professional disciplines of jurisprudence, medicine, and philosophy, but he is amazed that it has spread also to *lettres humaines*, in the form of a new science of textual and philological criticism. In fact, it seems Camus was working from an edition of the *Essais* that did have references in the margins, as he advocates striking a balance between fully incorporating quotations in the main text and satisfying the *humeur* of the professional source-hunters with some references.[35]

It is in this section of the letter that Camus contrasts Montaigne's way of making a book with that of another seigneur. If Duplessis-Mornay—that great protector of the Evangelical reformation, that foolhardy, theologian-like Captain and Captain-like theologian ('ce bravache Capitaine, comme un théologien, et théologien, comme un Capitaine')—had had the inventiveness to use his condition of *gentilhomme* in making his books (those 'rubbish-tips of falsity'), so as to neglect to embroider and burden his margins with so many citations, then he might have managed to throw dust in the eyes of a few idiots.[36]

Camus is here referring to Duplessis-Mornay's *De l'institution, usage et doctrine du saint Sacrement de l'eucharistie*, published from the Huguenot stronghold of La Rochelle in 1598, just a few months after the publication of the Edict of Nantes.

---

[33] Millet 168; Aristotle, *Nicomachean ethics*, 1127a13–b32.   [34] Millet 165–6.
[35] Millet 176–7, for this and the previous paragraph.   [36] Millet 175.

This was a sustained scholarly attack by a noble layman, at a highly sensitive political moment, on the Catholic doctrine of the Mass. It adduced thousands of passages from the Bible and from patristic authors, and caused a firestorm of protest and printed controversy. Duplessis-Mornay was accused of falsely citing patristic and other authors and confronted in debate at Fontainebleau in 1600 by Bishop Du Perron. He was adjudged to have lost the debate, and to have failed in subsequent printed apologies to recover the loss.[37]

The interesting point is that Montaigne does not avoid similarly hot topics. He himself engages—if in a completely different style—with a holy sacrament of the Roman Catholic Church. He is concerned in III 2 with contemporary applications and expressions of the Tridentine 'institution, usage and doctrine' of the sacrament of repentance, at a highly sensitive political moment in the 1580s, when confraternities of penitents, headed by the King, were taking to the streets of Paris. And he does use his own liberty of judgement as a layman; indeed, he characteristically installs his liberty of judgement as the power directing his own conscience, rather than a priest or external spiritual director.

The most prominent such director at the time was the Jesuit Emond Auger, who was driving the revival in penitential practice in the 1580s and whose written prescriptions on penitence and the agency of the priest to give repentant 'form', through absolution, to the contrite confessant are implicitly resisted and contested by Montaigne throughout the chapter.[38] But of course III 2 does not openly enter theological controversy in the manner of Duplessis-Mornay's book, which uses scholarly apparatus, names opponents, and openly advocates reform of Church doctrine and practice.

It is not, then, the contrast between the way Montaigne represents his inner reality and the way other medieval and ancient authors did that constitutes the Gascon's 'freedom' for Camus. It is, rather, the contrast between the two seigneurs and their *personae*, as manifested in the ways in which, and purposes for which, they have made their books, using their liberties of judgement as noblemen.

The contrast is at once personal, stylistic, and confessional. One of these free literates has taken the professional, scholarly route (Duplessis-Mornay). He has assumed the monstruous, hybrid *persona* of a theologian-like captain, and composed a pseudo-scholarly book full of false citations of authorities (at least, according to Camus) that aim to reform God's church. The other (Montaigne) has used his social status and *persona* as a *gentilhomme* to eschew authoritative citation and controversial discourse, to write in a free and truthful style of himself. In III 2, this means not challenging the church's doctrine of repentance but confessing that he personally—for good reason—rarely repents, in life or in his writing.

[37] USTC 3187; Mack P. Holt, 'Divisions within French Calvinism: Philippe Duplessis-Mornay and the Eucharist', in Mack P. Holt (ed.), *Adaptations of Calvinism in Reformation Europe: essays in honour of Brian G. Armstrong* (Farnham: Ashgate, 2007), 165–78.
[38] Hoffmann, 'Emond Auger'. Hoffmann's discussion represents an important revision of Malcolm Smith's in *Montaigne and the Roman censors*, which, in its brief consideration of III 2 as a continuation of the anti-Huguenot stance of the 1580 text of I 56, considers neither the new context of the 1580s (the Catholic League and the White Penitents), nor the implications of Montaigne's insistence that, for good reason, he rarely repents.

And Bishop Camus sees it as part of his office to defend this style against the liberties of judgement taken by the false prophets of Geneva. A count living in the Savoy region heard Théodore de Bèze saying that Montaigne had corrupted the French language in the same way that Lipsius (by then reconverted to Catholicism, at Louvain), had corrupted the Latin language. Camus defends 'our Montaigne' with a full-scale attack on this Genevan Babel ('ceste Babel Genevoise'), on their whole style of writing and speech, which he identifies with blasphemy and impurity.[39]

Camus' scenario is of course fictive, but it is worth pairing it momentarily with another we have encountered that is not fictive (or, at least, not self-evidently fictive). In his first letter to Achante, Camus criticizes a literary complaint the young man has sent him on the death of his great friend Pamphile. He finds it too affected and smooth, artificially derived from commonplaces in books. The true voice of grief is confused, disordered, unpremeditated ('une voix confuse, desreiglee, impremeditee'). Achante might have found—perhaps he had already found, judging by what appear to be some borrowings?—a *patron* for this voice in Montaigne's great chapter describing his perfect friendship with La Boétie (I 27, 'De l'amitié'). On this topic, says Camus, Montaigne is the master, Cicero the clerk.[40]

We saw in 2.2.9 that in Venice, in these same years, another cleric—this time a Servite friar, Paolo Sarpi, associated with anti-papal polemic—proposed attention to *De l'amitié* in the context of his informal education of another young nobleman, this time a real one (Trevisan).

The point in these two cases is that there is a related social nexus for the reading of Montaigne (a cleric informally educating a young nobleman against the background of religio-political controversy), with distinct outcomes envisaged: in one case, a realization in politically resonant social action of the proverb 'friends hold all things in common' (2.2.9); in the other case, a non-clerkish, non-controversial voice for the young Catholic nobleman who would eschew the *persona* of the reformed theologian-captain like Duplessis-Mornay, but who would retain his innate liberty of judgement and speech.

In 2.7.4, 2.7.5, and 2.7.7 we shall reconsider examples of two further ways in which we can trace the interaction of Montaigne's book with reader-writers in specific nexuses at the same moment in the early seventeenth century. In the first case, two unique copies of the 1602 *Essais* (the Urbino copy and the Van Veen copy) travel far from the author's milieu across Europe to very different locations, for very different kinds of use. In the second case, two reader-writers from Montaigne's own milieu use the *Essais* in their own book projects (Pierre de L'Estoile and Pierre Charron).

We shall see that these examples combine with Camus–Sarpi to delineate a range of contemporary nexuses that recontextualize Auerbach's passage from III 2 and the Frenchman's work as a whole. These nexuses always involve agency relations—mediated by books and extracts from books—between participants acting as free literates (Achante, Trevisan), clerical interpreters and mediators of texts

---

[39] Millet 180–2.   [40] Millet 162–3; Camus, *Les diversitez: tome VIII*, sigs. 2C3r–4v.

(Camus, Sarpi), and other entities with agency such as classical and biblical proto-types of wisdom.

In the period with which we have most particularly been concerned (1560–1640), such relations—as variously described across the confessional spectrum—more typically enfranchise subjects, through reading and writing of biblical and devotional materials, as members of particular religio-political groups or communities. The agency relations, mediated by books and book-extracts, between the cleric, the lay reader-writer, and divine and human knowledge, are central to the culture and controversies of the time.

What role should a priest or professional scholar have in the relationship between a lay person and the Books of scripture and nature? The *Essais* are described in their own time as making a particular kind of intervention in such nexuses, in order to reform the relations between the private reader-writer and the professional interpreter or mediator. They aim to enfranchise the former (with respect to human, not divine knowledge) in a non-partisan, non-controversial manner, by using the authorial *persona* of a seigneurially free literate, and by fulfilling the associated offices of liberty of judgement.[41]

The examples also show that the *Essais* interacted with their early public audience in the area of overlap between two long-established practices of self-review mediated by private reading and writing: private or 'academic' study and teaching of practical philosophy, especially 'self-knowledge' (as Camus teaches Achante, or Sarpi Trevisan); and self-accounting, or the keeping of daily accounts of everything ranging from household expenses to personal thoughts occasioned by chance events and reading (L'Estoile, Maillefer).

The public recording of private judgements in the domain of practical philosophy is thus the key liberty claimed by the book, for the practices in question correspond to learned disciplines invoked by the text in the opening to III 2: the academic discipline of *la philosophie morale*, and the extra-curricular discipline of *histoire*. Both were profoundly affected in the sixteenth and seventeenth centuries by the literary culture of the various reformations, Protestant and Catholic. We shall shortly consider the very different but related contribution made to the former in the vernacular by Charron; we have already considered de Thou's contribution to the latter, in 2.1.2, and compared it with Montaigne's.

The physical incarnation of the overlap between these practices of self-review, as I argued in 1.1.10, is the philosophical text in the margins or endleaves of which the reader inscribes knowledge or judgements particular to an individual, a family, a household. The medieval period already had a concept of a private sort of book, accessible at most to a limited circle of friends and family, in which the individual subject was both writer and reader. This concept was integral to the tradition of self-knowledge.[42]

---

[41] These points are more fully developed in 2.7.10 and 2.7.11.

[42] Sylvia Huot, 'The writer's mirror: Watriquet de Couvin and the development of the author-centred book', in Bill Bell, Philip E. Bennett, and Jonquil Bevan (eds.), *Across boundaries: the book in culture and commerce* (Winchester and New Castle, DE: St Paul's Bibliographies and Oak Knoll Press, 2000), 29–46.

The clearest examples we have encountered in this study are the Van Veen copy of Montaigne and the Montaigne copies of Caesar (extant) and Guicciardini (non-extant), along with the books into which Slingsby, Maillefer, and L'Estoile copied extracts from the *Essais*. But this is also the authorial practice one can already infer from the text of Bordeaux 1580, the practice that becomes ampler and clearer in Paris 1588 and Paris 1595. Into the margins of a book that predominantly contains miscellaneous general readings in human philosophy, Montaigne after 1580 inscribes more and more knowledge relating to a particular, noble individual and his family and friends. But he does not use this knowledge to repent, to reform himself.

2.7.4 TWO COPIES OF PARIS 1602

For Villey's generation, as we heard in 2.7.1, the crucial period in the history of Montaigne's book stretched from its earliest compositional beginnings in *c.*1572 to *c.*1592. Recent editors of Paris 1595, who have given more credence to Marie de Gournay and to the early posthumous editions, have extended the period of interest to 1598, when L'Angelier published an octavo with new·corrections made by Gournay.

But this study has argued that we should extend our sense of what counts as the crucial early history of the *Essais*, and of any early modern book. We should extend it backwards to include prior literary nexuses, such as Montaigne's letter on the death of La Boétie and his first edition of Sebond. But, more particularly, we should extend it forwards to include its early circulation within and beyond authorial circles, its early contexts of use and republication, including those outside France.

An analogy with theatre history may help. The kind of conditions in which Shakespeare's plays were first performed, and the kinds of audience expectations that were brought to them, is now held to render the playtexts themselves richer in signification. The same goes for the early 'performances', before audiences, of Montaigne's text and of selections from it—performances such as the Camus letter. They tell us as much about the history of the *Essais'* meanings as the additions and deletions in the Bordeaux copy.

Some documents we have considered from this perspective were produced as late as the early eighteenth century, but most date from the period *c.*1560 to *c.*1640, the age of confessionalization in which both the learned and the popular book boomed commercially across Europe, even as churches, states, and individual censors were attempting to control their circulation and use. And, within this period, many of the most important instances of use and republication examined in this study have dated from the quarter century *c.*1595 to *c.*1619. The snapshots of the book's force that emerge from these are related to but different from Auerbach's and other modern accounts of the 'freedom' that Montaigne acquired, and that his readers could acquire in turn, through the reading and rewriting of books and experiences.

One important notion that recurs in early modern contexts is the notion of a liberty of judgement or opinion that Montaigne has legitimately and safely assumed in his *persona* as a nobleman. Another, as we have already indicated, is the notion of a personal, daily record or *registre*, kept continuously for future review, either by just one individual (the compiler), or by a close knit circle of friends and family. We have already seen that both notions are very much in evidence in the opening to III 2, in the rest of that chapter, and in Bishop Camus' response to it.

During these crucial early years (*c.*1595–*c.*1619), Gournay and the French parliamentary intellectuals offered rival but related versions of the authorial *persona* who assumed this liberty, and the book with which it was consubstantial: on the one hand, a *sage* who is finding his place amongst a self-constituting community of *sages* comparable with the ancients; on the other hand, a man of free spirit, alien to faction, posthumously joining the community of the *politiques*.

At the same time, clerics such as Camus began to offer other versions. In the years between 1597 and 1603, the *chanoine* and *théologal* Pierre Charron conceived, composed, published, and revised *De la sagesse*, using the *Essais* as one of his principal sources. As we shall see in 2.7.5, the supposed relationship between the two authors became, in a printed *éloge* of 1606, an important part of the posthumous defence and discussion of Charron's work.

Meanwhile, Florio and Daniel promoted Montaigne's work in English in 1603 as a book that had already found secure commercement across Europe, a book by a knight-adventurer making sallies out upon custom in daring intellectual exercises. This informed Shakespeare's quasi-parodic use of the text on stage in 1610–11, when he put Florio's words in the mouth of a 'Sir Prudence'.

Readers in Italy, during these years, were still using a reduced Italian version of the *Essais* of 1580, though by 1619–21 the need for the full French version was being acknowledged. The masters of the neo-Latin republic of letters, Lipsius and Scaliger, and disciples such as Baudius, showed ambivalence during the same years in both condemning the Genevans for expurgating the work (in 1595) and doubting that such a free-thinking book could be printed in full in the Low Countries and elsewhere without correction—it was too strong for a vulgar readership (2.2.1, 2.2.3).

However, we saw in 2.2.7 that even the Genevan expurgator of the work, Simon Goulart, was using the full text by *c.*1600, and that Pyramus de Candolle and other Genevan publishers issued full editions with false imprints in 1602. We have located copies of Paris 1598 and Paris 1602 in early seventeenth century Italian collections. The acquisition of a copy of Paris 1598 for the 'Libri artium' section of the new Bodleian library was advertised to the European republic of letters via the printing of its first catalogue in 1605.[43] Thanks to Lipsius, the *Essais* had crossed over into the Latin republic of letters—if not to the degree Gournay had hoped they would.

---

[43] Thomas James, *Catalogus librorum bibliothecae publicae quam vir ornatissimus Thomas Bodleius eques auratus in Academia Oxoniensi nuper instituit* (Oxford: Joseph Barnes, 1605), sig. 2Y3v.

Indeed, from the publishing perspective, it is arguable that 1598–1604 is the crucial moment in the early history of Montaigne's book, the moment after the 1595 folio had begun to secure Montaigne's posthumous arrival on the intellectual scene of Paris. It was the breakout moment, the moment when the commercial *concurrence* between L'Angelier and Genevan publishers ensured that relatively cheap and transportable octavo editions of the full text began to reach the market all over Europe, when more copies began to travel greater distances to reach further-flung readers.

Paris 1602 is not significant for the textual bibliography of the *Essais*. It is a reproduction of Paris 1600 issued to extend the printer's privilege; what is worse, it has an index not approved by any of the author's direct agents.[44] But we have seen that copies of this edition—the Van Veen copy (1.1.7, 1.1.14, 2.4.4) and the Urbino copy (1.3.10, 2.2.8, 2.2.12)—reached consumers at different ends of Europe, giving substance to Montaigne's own claim that his book would travel afar to find new friends who can get to know him 'in three days in this record' and Daniel's claims about the recognition of the work's intellectual and commercial *franchise* across frontiers.

Paying detailed attention to the fate of such copies can switch our attention from the work as a text that encodes—or endlessly defers encoding—a representation of an author's subjectivity, to the work as a set of objects designed to travel via the networks of a publisher-bookseller such as Millanges or L'Angelier, to communicate the author's *marque* to new friends, to have an effect upon reader-writers in distant regions and times, to be used in turn by them for their own communications.

Together, the two copies in question define a geo-cultural range, from Calvinist, Francophone Holland to Roman Catholic, pro-Spanish Urbino, as well as a range of ways and spaces in which 'letters' could extend the social agency of their users and makers. One copy bears the marks, writing, and drawings of a particular individual, a free literate, while the other displays only the material traces of its acquisition for shelving in a particular subsection of a library designed to collect all scholarship—mostly Latin scholarship—in print in the Italian peninsula. One joins the family collection of a lawyer of modest social rank, while the other joins one of the grandest collections in Europe, comparable in prestige with the papal library itself. One collection is geared to the private family transmission of learning and ethos in the vernacular from father to son, the other to the dynastic transmission of scholarly learning in Latin on the regional, national, and international scales.

The first of our two copies (the Duke of Urbino's) sits, then, on the shelf of a famous library as a self-consciously rare item, with a specially tooled spine and ruled pages, ready to be noticed by Catholic clergy and university scholars looking through a section on ethics and politics—but with no sign of personal use on the part of the collector. This is a copy designed, like other copies in the collection, to

---

[44] Sayce and Maskell 41–4; Balsamo and Simonin, *Abel L'Angelier et Françoise de Louvain (1574–1620)*, 323–4.

extend the social agency of a patron and collector within a particular intellectual community centred on the duchy of Urbino and on the religious order of the Minims invited by the Duke to reside (near the library) in Casteldurante, but closely connected to Padua-Venice in one direction and Rome in another.[45]

This copy gives us an opportunity to see the company—in terms of other books—that the *Essais* might have kept in a collection such as this. It tells us that the *Essais* are held to be most closely related—as Montaigne implicitly acknowledges in Auerbach's passage—to other works of moral philosophy.

The manuscript catalogue of the Duke's library reveals more about the intellectual significance of the placement of the copy of Paris 1602 on its shelves than was indicated in 1.3.10, 2.2.8, and 2.2.12.[46] This is a library of Italian and international scholarship, and of weapons for Counter-Reformation polemic, a counterpart to the Bodleian's arsenal for the defence of English reformed doctrine. It is divided up into the widely shared categories of theological and religious literature, Platonic and Aristotelian philosophy, the liberal arts, history, geography, law, and medicine, but distributed across seventy sub-categories housed in individual *scansie*—*scansie* which are themselves further divided into sub-topics.

No less than thirty of these *scansie* are devoted to theological and religious literature, from bibles and bible commentaries to canon law, including two whole *scansie* of counter-reforming weapons against both ancient and more recent heresies ('Adversus Hereses Antiquas et Recentiores'). Besides the dominance of theology and religious controversy, the catalogue reveals at one and the same time the continued privileging of ancient and medieval *auctoritates* (especially Aristotle) and the proliferating traditions of commentary upon them, the emergence of particular topics (e.g. 'De balneis') and polemics (e.g. 'Contra Mahometanos') as axes of collection, and an overwhelming quantity of 'various' and miscellaneous texts.[47]

The collection testifies to the state of learning, and of the scholarly book trade, at the moment (*c*.1631) when the latter—especially in Italy—was collapsing, in part due to over-production and saturation. For sceptics such as Montaigne, such a library, designed to gather all scholarly knowledge in print (at least in the Italian peninsula, with many books also imported from elsewhere), for the purposes of advances in professional learning, at a moment when too much scholarship was being printed, could only reveal the vanity of the contemporary world of scholarly learning and the lack of new 'authors' and convincing systems.

[45] Massimo Moretti, 'I Padri Caracciolini del SS. Crocefisso di Casteldurante: da eredi a custodi della Biblioteca di Francesco Maria II Della Rovere', in M. Mei and F. Paoli (eds.), *La libraria di Francesco Maria II Della Rovere a Casteldurante. Da collezione ducale a biblioteca della città* (Urbino: Quattroventi, 2008), 117–28.

[46] University of Rome, 'La Sapienza', Biblioteca Alessandrina, MS 50.

[47] For this and the previous paragraph, see Alfredo Serrai, 'La Biblioteca di Francesco Maria II a Casteldurante', in M. Mei and F. Paoli (eds.), *La libraria di Francesco Maria II Della Rovere a Casteldurante. Da collezione ducale a biblioteca della città* (Urbino: Quattroventi, 2008), 15–40, 38–40; Warren Boutcher, 'Una biblioteca o due? Il rapporto fra le collezioni di libri in Urbino e in Casteldurante', in Mei and Paoli (eds.), *La libraria di Francesco Maria II Della Rovere a Casteldurante*, 95–8.

The library is an expression, in other words, not of the individual culture of the Duke, but of the late Renaissance world of professional learning and controversial scholarship, as mediated and selected by the local intellectual tradition of Urbino via its network of connections with the broader world of Italian and international scholarship and print culture.

This world had changed quite dramatically since the Duke's famous predecessor Federico da Montefeltro had formed, in the mid-fifteenth century, his predominantly manuscript library, which the last Duke was still maintaining at his death. *Scansia 2, ordine 4* of the old library held a small but choice collection of *commentationes, expositiones,* and *explicationes* centred on the texts of Aristotle's *Ethica, Politica,* and the pseudo-Aristotelian *Oeconomica.* Seven such texts by noted editors and commentators (Eustratius, Walter Burleigh, D. Acciaiuoli, Giovanni Buridano, and Leonardo Bruni Aretino) bound in red leather ('corame rosso') are accompanied by a similar number of volumes treating Aristotelian political and ethical subjects (including Egidio Romano, *De regimine principum*; Giovanni Pontano, *De principe* and *De obedientia*; L. B. Alberti, *Libri tre della famiglia*; C. Landino, *Disputationum*; Giovanni Antonio Campani, *Liber de ingratitudine*).[48]

This contained, manageable, intellectual world, centred on the authoritative Aristotelian texts, with a few prestigious commentators and a few associated treatises, had become far less manageable by the time of the last Duke's death nearly two centuries later. The Duke now had to deal, on the one hand, with published lists of prohibited and expurgated books, and with the Congregations of the Index and the Inquisition, in forming and expanding his collection. On the other hand, he had to deal with the market in learned printed books, which boomed during the period in which he was forming his collection (*c.*1570–*c.*1630).[49]

One shelf in the old library becomes three cupboards within *Scaffale* IV of the new library (*scansie* 37–9). And the expansion is not only a matter of more commented editions and translations of the *Ethica, Politica,* and *Oeconomica.* There are now approximately twenty-four of these. One or two represent printed versions of commented editions available in manuscript in the old library (Acciaiuoli, Aretino) or fifteenth-century works missing from the old library (Giovanni Argiropulo), but the majority represent new commentaries of the sixteenth century, a higher proportion of which were produced and/or published north of the Alps (e.g. P. Victorius, D. Lambinus, J. Perionius, A. Scaino [Italian paraphrase], B. Segni [Italian translation], I. G. Sepulveda, J. L. Strebaeus, Daniel Heinsius, I. Faber Stapulensis, Antonio Riccaboni, Simón Abril [Spanish translation]).[50]

[48] Maria Moranti and Luigi Moranti, *Il trasferimento dei 'Codices urbinates' alla Biblioteca Vaticana: cronistoria, documenti e inventario* (Urbino: Accademia Raffaello, 1981), 390–1.

[49] Maclean, *Scholarship, commerce, religion.*

[50] University of Rome, 'La Sapienza', Biblioteca Alessandrina MS 50 fols. 52v–59r (which lists the names of the authors of the works shelved in *scansie* 37–9), 150r–1r (which lists the titles of editions of Aristotle's individual works with a note of format and *scansia*). I identified some of these editions with the help of H. M. Adams, *Catalogue of books printed on the continent of Europe, 1501–1600, in Cambridge libraries,* 2 vols. (London: Cambridge University Press, 1967)—see A1762–1764, A1803–1842, A1910–1926. The only sure way to identify the editions held in the Duke's library is to compare the inventory entries in MS 50 with individual copies in the Biblioteca Alessandrina that can be

Many of these commentaries would have been standard items in up-to-date classes of ethics, politics, and oeconomics in libraries across Europe. A large proportion of them (including the *Essais*) are, indeed, recommended in Naudé's discriminating guide to the collection of such a class of ancient and 'new' ethics for an elite library, the *Bibliographia politica* (Venice, 1633)—a good indication of the kind of scholarly bibliographical advice that resulted in the acquisition of a French copy and its placement in the practical philosophy section of the Duke's library (see 2.2.12).

Another of Naudé's recommendations that also tallies with a feature of the Duke's library is the positioning and pairing of Seneca and Plutarch as the most important post-Aristotelian classical authorities on ethics.[51] Although they were not studied as part of the foundations of university moral philosophy, they and their commentators are listed separately at the end of *scansia* 38, 'De Principatu De Re Aulica Honore Amore et Nobilitate et Moralia Varia'. Grouped round the *Opuscula sive moralia* of Plutarch were companion texts and translations by Aulus Gellius, F. Gonz[aga?] and Hieronimus Gabrielius, and Pietro Lauro.[52] The moral works of Seneca were to be found in Latin and Spanish (no Jacques Amyot), in the editions of Justus Lipsius, of Muretus and co., with, alongside, the *castigationes* of Ferdinandus Pincianus and with 'Dionisii Gothofredi In Seneca[e] Coniectura[e] et Varia[e] lectiones' and 'Matthei Fortunati annot[ation]es in Senecae naturales quest[ion]es'.[53]

We can continue to observe continuities between Naudé's *Bibliographia* and *scansie* 37–9 when we note that the main cause of the massive bibliographical expansion in the general class of ethics is in the third category of books mentioned above. As described by Naudé, these were particular treatises placed by subject in the order assigned them in the encyclopaedia of knowledge. We should understand this to include miscellaneous collections of particular treatises—that is, *moralia varia*—as well as collections of the rhetorical elements of ethical discourse—that is, *proverbia* and *apophthegmata*.

In this ducal library, then, the *Essais*/*Discorsi* (Naselli's translation was on the same shelf) were placed as treatments of the traditional disciplines of ethics and politics (due to the political emphasis of Naselli's *Discorsi*, they were in fact placed under *Politica*). But they were surrounded by what Daniel called the 'presse of writings' on these subjects, whether these consisted of glosses upon glosses upon Aristotle or upon the newly fashionable Seneca and Plutarch, or of miscellaneous collections and treatises on the usual topics. The larger collection was dominated by theology and theological controversy.

Such a placement makes sense of Montaigne's diagnoses of the state of professional learning in his chosen field of moral or practical philosophy, as well as in

---

identified as books from the Duke's collection (usually because they have a manuscript 'Ur' in the bottom right-hand corner of the title page).

[51] Naudé, *Bibliografia politica*, 104–5, 106–7.

[52] University of Rome, 'La Sapienza', Biblioteca Alessandrina, MS 50, fols. 56v, 386r.

[53] University of Rome, 'La Sapienza', Biblioteca Alessandrina, MS 50, fols. 56v, 404v, 211v, 196v, 346r.

other fields—which is not to say that the octavo copy had much impact in the environment of the Urbino library. The Duke probably never read his text. He spent fifteen years having the entire works of Aristotle read to him by the bishop of Pesaro, Cesare Benedetti.[54]

Nevertheless, the *Essais* attempt to offer a more 'natural' and 'particular' treatment of the subject, in order to claim it back for the needs and purposes of the free literate like Van Veen, who, of much lower rank, was not bound by his position and *persona* to plough through Aristotle's works in his spare time. The *Essais*—though less so the *Discorsi*—enact what they reveal about the written record of learning in the late sixteenth century; they expand by glossing discourse and questioning their own glosses, opening up ever more doubts and uncertainties as they go. But they explicitly attempt to contain the proliferation of questions and uncertainties by stipulating that their matter is not the Aristotelian school subject of ethics or politics, but one particular noble gentleman, whose inconsistencies and self-contradictions must be faithfully reported along with all his other traits.

By the mid-seventeenth century, Sorel, in his printed library of learned, literary works that were selling in the vernacular market, could describe a very different 'cupboard' (in fact a chapter in his book) on practical philosophy from the one assembled by the Dukes of Urbino in their grand library. It consisted of a much smaller collection of printed, vernacular, French books that the free literate could acquire and study for themselves, outside the scholarly institution and exegetical discipline of moral philosophy in Greek and Latin. It was, however, similarly divided between sections on ethics ('books which treat of morals, and of the conduct of life in the world'), politics ('political books'), and miscellanies ('miscellaneous books').

Where the Duke's library was dominated by Aristotle and Plato, Sorel follows Naudé's lead in making Montaigne and Charron the touchstone authors. In the Duke's library, the *Essais* had been engulfed with Aristotelian commentaries and various treatises in the politics section of the Duke's library, and in the collection as a whole with thousands of books on theology. In Sorel's collection, the title of the whole section on practical philosophy promises a 'particular' judgement of the works of Montaigne and Charron ('Avec un jugement particulier des Oeuvres de Montagne et Charon'), as though the readership Sorel was addressing were identified by their desire and capacity to make such judgements of these two authors. Besides Sorel himself, only Balzac and Voiture (for epistles and letters) and Montaigne and Charron are given their own sections in this way.[55]

As Montaigne said in the passage with which we started in 2.7.1: 'You can tie up all moral philosophy with a common and private life'. By contrast with the first copy, this is exactly what the second copy of Paris 1602—owned by a 'general reader' with just such a life, who made a 'particular' judgement of the *Essais*—does. It has already been analysed several times in preceding chapters and need not

---

[54] Fert Sangiorgi (ed.), *Diario di Francesco Maria II della Rovere* (Urbino: QuattroVenti, 1989), 6.

[55] Sorel, *La bibliotheque françoise*, sigs. ã5v–6r ('Table des chapitres et des sections de la Bibiotheque françoise'), sig. C8r ('Des oeuvres meslees'), C10v ('Des Essais de Michel de Montaigne'), D4r ('Des oeuvres de Pierre Charron').

detain us too long here. This is a copy (Pieter van Veen's) that has been lovingly and carefully personalized with annotations, drawings, and a memoir addressed to a beloved son—a copy that extends the agency of a father down through a family posterity scarred by the religio-political conflicts of the Low Countries.

I argued in 1.1.14 and 2.4.4–8 that Montaigne's work draws on an idea of the book which is materialized most evidently in the Van Veen copy: the book as a unique, because personalized, copy shared and transmitted within the 'family', transferred from one friend to another, from one generation to the next as part of an ongoing and open conversation focused on remembrance and perpetuation of the traits and skills of particular family members.

But, again, we cannot identify this as a nexus of purely 'free' literacy, to be contrasted cleanly with the official world of scholarly learning in which the Urbino copy found itself. The *Essais* were recommended in the first instance to the family by an official professor of the humanities, Justus Lipsius. The international, scholarly republic of letters was instrumental in the transmission of Montaigne's book to both collections.

Both copies, then, act as extensions of the agency of the person who might be described as their *patron*—in the sense both of powerful consumer/collector and of 'model', though one is a Duke and one a mere lawyer. They both witness to the judgement of the owner in selecting and disposing the book. This judgement is exercised in the context of the owners' relations with professional intellectuals who recommend and direct studies in the discipline of moral philosophy in a particular confessional environment: the pre-Louvain Lipsius in the case of Van Veen, and—more indirectly—the Minim monks and the clerical professor of moral philosophy at Padua, Flavio Querenghi, in the case of the Duke of Urbino.

But where one copy testifies—on a single range from more public to more private—to a more public transmission of the professional order of moral-philosophical knowledge via a grand dynastic library designed to enhance the scholarly and religious reputation of a Duke, the other witnesses to the more private transmission of a particular individual's ethos, via traces of his personal reading and writing. If it is the latter kind of nexus that the *Essais* seek to prescribe for their own circulation, the former is representative of a wide variety of possible early modern uses (not fully explored in this study) which ignore such prescriptions and which are less readily assimilable to the lifecycle of the original work. The Urbino copy has not been part of Montaigne's literary legacy (it did not feature in any bibliography of the *Essais* until very recently); it was in the wrong place, put to the wrong kind of use.

2.7.5 L'ESTOILE AND CHARRON

The final case study pairs two reader-writers from the Parisian milieu of the early seventeenth century who compiled books based in different ways on a reading of the *Essais*. One, Pierre Charron, published in print in 1601 a vernacular treatise on wisdom that incorporated large numbers of passages from the *Essais*. Met with a hostile reception, he immediately set about correcting and reordering his own text; further corrections were mooted by the Parisian *Conseil*, after his untimely death, and a second, much changed edition was issued in Paris in 1604. The other, Pierre de L'Estoile, as we saw in 2.1.8 and 2.5.3–5, began keeping personal manuscript 'Tablettes' in 1606 that drew in various ways on the *Essais*, which were as much of a vade mecum to him as they were to Van Veen.

In his *registre-journal* for November 1603, L'Estoile recorded the sudden death of Pierre Charron, 'a learned churchman, as his writings testify' ('homme d'église et docte, comme ses écrits en font foi'). Five years later, in 1608, in the first volume of 'Tablettes', he records buying direct from the publisher Le Clerc a copy of a newly printed edition of Charron's *Traicté de sagesse*, which came in a single volume with some Christian discourses and an engraved portrait with an *éloge* of the author.[56]

In the text of this last item, by Charron's literary testator Rochemaillet, L'Estoile would have found a passage that placed the author of *De la sagesse* in a close personal relationship with the author of the *Essais*, a book which, we are told, Charron valued marvellously highly ('duquel il faisoit un merveilleux cas'). A rival to Gournay as Montaigne's literary heir had emerged on the scene. According to Rochemaillet, Montaigne left Charron the right to bear his arms as a nobleman.[57]

Whether this is actually true—there is no independent evidence to fully verify or falsify the claim—the purpose of the passage and of the *éloge* as a whole is clear: to defend Charron's works, and especially *De la sagesse*, by means of a defence of his character and conduct.[58] Montaigne's testatory act, and his friendship with Charron, implicitly legitimate the extensive, unacknowledged borrowings from the *Essais* that readers were starting to find in the writing of *De la sagesse*.

Rochemaillet's claim lies at the origins of a trend which would gather momentum in the 1620s and persist through to the end of the seventeenth century, the moment of Pierre Bayle's *Dictionaire*. For a significant proportion of the Francophone public, the principal nexus of transmission of both texts (the *Essais* and *De la sagesse*) was the relationship between them, and between their authors.[59]

This relationship could be variously described: they could be paired as equals; Charron could be the stronger author, who brought proper order and method to Montaigne's *fantasies*; sometimes he was merely a 'secretary' who copied Montaigne and other authors; sometimes both were considered dangerously 'free', with

---

[56] *Journal Henri IV*, vol. 2, 119, 364; Greffe and Lothe, *La vie, les livres*, 476. Le Clerc had issued the first edition of this collection of Charron's works in 1606.

[57] Pierre Charron, *De la sagesse livres trois* (Paris: D. Douceur, 1607), sig. ẽ3r. I have not been able to consult a copy of the 1608 collection acquired by L'Estoile, so I am quoting the 'Eloge veritable' from Douceur's 1607 edition.

[58] The only pieces of evidence beyond Rochemaillet's statement are Montaigne's gift of a copy of Ochino's *Catechismo* to Charron and the bequest made by Charron himself to Léonor de Camain, Montaigne's sister. See Alfred Soman, 'Pierre Charron: A reevaluation', *Bibliothèque d'Humanisme et Renaissance*, 32 (1970), 57–79, 64–5.

[59] One early example is Bernard de La Roche Flavin, whose work we shall briefly consider at the end of this section (2.7.5).

Charron as the focus of the scandal; sometimes—as in Garasse and Bayle—Montaigne was the free-talking layman who could say things the *chanoine* Charron could not.[60]

In other words, the breakthrough attributed to Villey's Montaigne by Auerbach would have been attributed, in different terms, to Charron–Montaigne by many readers of the later seventeenth century. For the latter, Montaigne was more usually the secondary agent, a sort of accomplice in the theologian's acquisition of secular philosophical freedom on behalf of his readers, despite the fact that the nobleman was the first to write much of the material used by Charron. From the perspective of this study, Charron–Montaigne is another instance of the shifting nexuses of relations—especially between clerical and lay reader-writers—that condition the history of the *Essais* from before their first publication through from their early to their modern reception.

Indeed, the case of Charron–Montaigne has more to tell us than is normally acknowledged. Much of the literature focuses on the question of the two authors' respective places in the tradition of philosophical scepticism, the extent to which Charron's 'Pyrrhonism' derived from Montaigne's, and so forth. The asking of this question is warranted by, for example, its appearance in Pierre Bayle's article on Charron.[61]

But there are two other aspects of a more rhetorical and social nature, also flagged by Bayle, that are equally as important. Charron was above all concerned with instituting the *persona* of the *sage* with an authoritative liberty of judgement, using elements of Montaigne's self-portrait; his concern with Pyrrhonism was a part of this. The other respect in which he was following in Montaigne's—and others'—footsteps concerned the geography of publication. His was yet another work that was published first in Bordeaux by Simon Millanges (1601), then in Paris. The story of his and his book's journey to Paris is told at the time both in private letters to Rochemaillet and in Rochemaillet's aforementioned *éloge* (the two tally closely).[62] In interesting ways, it both compares with and differs from the equivalent story of the *Essais*' and their author's arrival in the capital (which had involved Charron's rival, Gournay).

In the 'Preface' to the first edition of 1601, Charron at one point explicitly adopts and refashions the *persona* of a Montaigne-like free literate. He describes

---

[60] Jean-Pierre Cavaillé, 'Pierre Charron, "disciple" de Montaigne et "patriarche des prétendus esprits forts"', *Montaigne Studies*, 19 (2006), 29–42. See also Millet 114 (Charron as 'copiste'), 204 (Charron as producing no more than 'complications' of Montaigne; as making his 'Maistre' say what he never thought), 216 (Montaigne and Charron side-by-side), 217 (Charron as 'Secrétaire' to du Vair and Montaigne), 219 (Montaigne and Charron as equally unsuitable for 'esprits foibles'), 221 (Montaigne and Charron paired as 'Libertins'), 223 (Charron as the 'Philosophe', Montaigne as 'admirable'), 224–5 (Montaigne and Charron paired as scourges of pedagogues; Montaigne as lacking method, Charron as the new Socrates).

[61] See the end of this section.

[62] L. Auvray, 'Lettres de Pierre Charron à Gabriel Michel de la Rochemaillet', *Revue d'histoire littéraire de la France*, 1 (1894), 308–29; Soman, 'Pierre Charron: A reevaluation', 58–61. These letters were 'communicated' to Gabriel Naudé by Gassendi, who had borrowed them from Rochemaillet in order to make a copy for Peiresc. Naudé's copy is the only extant source for their content and survives in BnF MS Fr. 15536, fols. 157–63. See Bœuf, *La bibliothèque parisienne*, 10.

the work as a collection of part of his studies, given his own form and order. He has used a *grande liberté et franchise* in publishing his own opinions, even if they go against received opinion. He is not speaking in the *persona* of a *théologien* or a *cathédrant*, not subjecting himself scrupulously to their rules and style. He is, rather, claiming the liberty of the philosopher of the ancient school of Academic sceptics ('la liberté Academique et Philosophique'); so, he does not treat his subject pedantically, following the ordinary rules of the school. *Sagesse* does not discourse with such artifice.[63]

The passage in question disappeared from the second, 1604 edition, but we shall see that Charron continued formally to claim this *liberté*, and that his *persona* as a canonical theologian and doctor of laws was—despite his explicit disclaimer in 1601—perceived to be an important rhetorical context for the claim. The key point to follow later in this section (2.7.5) is that the arrival of Charron's book in Paris was eventually understood by Pierre Bayle to be a very different kind of publishing event to Paris 1588 or Paris 1595; it indexed an authoritative, public, official act of *libertas philosophandi* distinct from the unofficial, lay affirmation of liberty of judgement made by the Parisian editions of the *Essais*.[64]

After the publication of the first edition in Bordeaux in 1601, Charron becomes aware that, due to the boldness with which he says certain things, his book is 'variously taken ('diversement pris'). We can compare his situation in this respect with de Thou's after the first publication of his *Historiae* (2.1.2, 2.1.5), and with Bayle's after the first publication of his *Dictionaire* (see 2.7.6). Charron begins at the same time to prepare for a Parisian edition and for his own journey to Paris, which he is anxious should have a clear rationale (such as an invitation to preach). He begins to correct and soften a few of the bolder passages (including the one cited above), transposing and adding some chapters.

At the same time he encourages both his friend, Rochemaillet, and his new patron, Claude Dormy (the Bishop of Boulogne, who wrote to him to praise the *Sagesse*), to assist and advise him in the preparation of the new edition. He composes, like de Thou, a separate apology for his work (published posthumously by Rochemaillet as the *Petit traicté*), in this case in the form of a short treatise restating its arguments and facing down objections. Initially, he decides that it would be prudent to seek the prior approbation of two *docteurs* in the Faculty of Theology (even though, strictly speaking, this was not needed for a non-theological work), as long as this did not cause a *bruit*. He then backtracks and claims the approbation of priests would be more authentic than that of theologians.[65]

A *bruit* is exactly, in the event, what it did cause, as the Faculty of Theology, provoked by the attempts to win its approbation, attempted—unsuccessfully—to block publication of the second edition (after Charron's death). There were even

[63] Pierre Charron, *De la sagesse livres trois* (Bordeaux: S. Millanges, 1601), sigs. ẽ1v–2r; Pierre Charron, *De la sagesse*, ed. Barbara De Negroni (Paris: Fayard, 1986), 34–6.

[64] Others, of course, more straightforwardly associated the two publications in their taking of liberties. See Cavaillé, 'Pierre Charron', 31, for the same point from a different perspective.

[65] For this and the previous paragraph see Auvray, 'Lettres de Pierre Charron', 311–13, 323–9; Soman, 'Pierre Charron: A reevaluation', 72–5.

legal disputes between Millanges and the Parisian publisher Douceur. The papal nuncio's correspondence reveals that he condemned the book, alongside de Thou's *Historiae*, and the compilers of the Roman Index followed suit by prohibiting the second edition as early as 1605. But Rochemaillet, despite the official seizure of copies, managed to keep production going in Paris, while he argued his deceased friend's case in several French courts. The case was put in the hands of President Jeannin by the Chancellor and the Privy Council, and Jeannin oversaw the preparation of a further list of passages that should be corrected and 'softened'. These were not incorporated into the text, however, and Douceur was allowed to sell the 1604 edition.[66]

Montaigne and his book had arrived in Paris from Bordeaux in 1588, offering the *essais* of a lay seigneur not intent on forming man, with no Paris-based patrons or prominent censors/correctors involved in the public approbation of the book— to be, according to Gournay, largely ignored. In 1595 he was re-presented to the Parisian market as a *patron* of *sagesse*, but by an unknown woman from the provinces who could muster only a couple of passing remarks in the printed letters of a foreign humanist to back her approbation of the book.

Charron and his book arrived offering instructions on wisdom on the part of a relative unknown, but one who presented himself as a priest and theological teacher, a doctor of the laws—while eschewing the normal scholastic forms of discourse. Charron, furthermore, sought official approbation for his teachings, as well as the formal protection of ecclesiastical patrons such as Dormy and powerful aristocratic patrons such as d'Épernon (the dedicatee of the Paris 1604 edition), who is described by Charron as a *patron* of *sagesse* that will combine with his book to mould Messeigneurs his children.[67] This was exactly the kind of communication via print, the kind of authorial *marque*, from which Montaigne distinguishes his book and *persona* in III 2, but that Gournay wanted nevertheless to produce on his behalf.

We can now see that Rochemaillet's 1606 collection of texts (L'Estoile acquired the 1608 edition of the same collection) was designed to consolidate Charron's credibility and authority in Paris, especially with *robins* such as L'Estoile and Jeannin. Rochemaillet was Charron's Gournay. Both literary heirs offered refutations of ad hominem attacks on their authors' writings in the form of delineations of what they took to be their authors' philosophical *personae*. Both, in so doing, were implicitly drawing on the philosophical *persona* of the ancient *sage*. For, as we have insisted many times, to do philosophy in this period is normally to fulfil offices, consisting of responsibilities and duties, with correlative enabling rights and liberties, that are defined by one or other kind of *persona*, which draws on relations with adjacent *personae*.[68]

---

[66] Soman, 'Pierre Charron: A reevaluation', 71–2, 74–6.

[67] Pierre Charron, *De la sagesse trois livres* (Paris: David Douceur, 1604), sigs. ã2v–3r.

[68] Conal Condren, 'Specifying the subject in early modern autobiography', in Ronald Bedford, Lloyd Davis, and Philippa Kelly (eds.), *Early modern autobiography: theories, genres, practices* (Ann Arbor: University of Michigan Press, 2006), 35–48, 36–7.

The important difference, only too apparent in the divergence between Gournay's preface and Rochemaillet's life, is that both Charron's textual *sage* and his own philosophical *persona* are fashioned, on external models, in relation to the formation and authority of public, professional *personae* such as the preacher-theologian and the lawyer-jurist—what Montaigne refers to as *quelque marque spéciale et étrangère*. Whereas, again, Michel insists that his is the *persona* just of a particular noble gentleman 'of Montaigne', one not formed or fashioned on external models—even if Gournay does attempt to turn him into a contemporary *patron* of the ancient *sage*. From this perspective, he is not, as Charron arguably is, seeking publicly to enfranchise any well-born and virtuous individual—of the right religio-political credentials—with an authoritative power or liberty of judgement.

Indeed, Montaigne's book incarnates a critique of the 'false, imaginary and fantastic privileges usurped by man, by which he claims to profess, arrange and establish the truth' ('[l]es privileges fantastiques, imaginaires, et faulx, que l'homme s'est usurpé, de regenter, d'ordonner, d'establir'), and records how liberties of judgement might be taken, and philosophical offices fulfilled, in a different, more private style.[69]

In 2.1.2 we heard how de Thou claimed the formal liberty of judgement of a senior French magistrate when writing the history of the religious troubles and, in particular, when praising the qualities of some of the learned Huguenots. We heard in 2.7.3 of Camus' contempt for the publication of a work on the sacrament of the mass by a 'theologian-like captain'. We saw in 1.4.4 how the physician Joubert, with whom Montaigne engages in II 37, was described on the title page of his work, published by Millanges in Bordeaux; likewise, how Montaigne's neighbour François de Foix-Candale, with whose example Montaigne engages in II 12, was described on the title page of the *Pimandre* (as a bishop of noble family), also published at Bordeaux by Millanges.

When Charron's work was first published in the same place by the same publisher, the author was described on the title page as 'Parisien, Chanoine Theologal et Chantre en l'Eglise Cathedrale'. He offers his institution in secular wisdom in the *persona* of a canon whose office it is to teach theology and preach in a cathedral chapter—an ecclesiastical office similar to the one held by Querenghi in Padua (see 2.2.11). Indeed, especially after 1601, his work on secular wisdom is published as part of an *œuvre* which includes theological works. The ten-year privilege granted by the *Conseil* in 1600 grouped his religious and secular works: the 'Trois veritez augmentées de nouveau, les livres de la Sagesse, et autres Discours et Homelies Chrestiennes'.[70]

---

[69] II 12, NP533/BVH Paris 1595, p. 329/S563.

[70] Charron, *De la sagesse livres trois*, sig. ã7v. I side with those critics who argue that Charron, rather than arguing for irreligion per se, is arguing for a radical separation of human and divine wisdom, of the virtue of *preud'hommie* and the virtue of religion (with the latter as subordinate, not able to cause the former). See M. C. Horowitz, *Seeds of Virtue and Knowledge* (Princeton: Princeton University Press, 1998), 224–37, and Emmanuel Faye, *Philosophie et perfection de l'homme: de la Renaissance à Descartes* (Paris: Librairie philosophique J. Vrin, 1998). Charron sought ecclesiastical approval for *De la sagesse*—that is, in practice, he did not contest the Church's authority over discussions of secular morality. For the counter-argument, which finds that deliberate contradictions

On the title page of the 1604 edition, Charron became 'Parisien Docteur es Droits'. This may have been part of an attempt to facilitate approbation. L'Estoile reports the case of a minister (des Alimes) who disguised both his profession (he described himself as a medical doctor) and his name on the title page of his work, in order more easily to get a privilege signed by a *docteur* of the Sorbonne.[71]

On later title pages, Charron was described in both ways. Rochemaillet's *éloge* backs this up by describing Charron's relationship as a philosopher-priest to both of these professional vocations, while also describing how he sought to enter a religious order. The importance of these descriptions is most apparent in hostile reactions. Garasse was so outraged that a functionary could come out of the provinces, 'qualify himself' an *Ecclésiastique* and *Théologal* of several French cathedrals, and put a book full of impudent abhominations into the hands of any young law student who cared to buy it, that he seized the book from such a student and, before his very eyes, tore out particular leaves that had offended him above others.[72]

To understand how a formative philosophy could be communicated in public, in print, via a *marque*, we have, then, been able to turn to another reader-writer of the *Essais* much closer to Montaigne's milieu than L'Estoile. The transformative work Charron had to do to turn the Gascon's book into *De la sagesse*, the publication of the book and its fortunes, the conception of the *sage* it utilizes—these all throw a light back on Montaigne's project and his remarks at the beginning of III 2. For Charron systematically reduces Montaigne's work, removing all traces of the form of the private archival book, in order to produce a different kind of book, a public treatise of wisdom.

As Charles Sorel, then Pierre Bayle, were both later to say, Charron was from one perspective more radical than Montaigne; they understood that this had everything to do with the *marque* with which he published what he wrote. On the famous title page introduced for the 1604 edition, and explicated in a sonnet in the 1607 edition, 'Sagesse' stands on a small pedestal on top of the large plinth bearing Charron's title as 'Parisien Docteur es Droits'. She enjoys an empty space, signifying *liberté*; to the pedestal or cube of Justice on which she stands are enchained Passion, Opinion (held up by the *vulgaire*), Superstition, and Learning (or artificially acquired knowledge, virtue, *preud'hommie*).[73]

The *persona* of the Pedant, pictured reading an open book with 'OUI' and 'NON' on facing pages, is in the *Petit traicté* identified as the true antithesis of the

---

between Charron's prefatory remarks justify reading the treatise 'between the lines' as an argument against Christian faith, see David Wootton, 'New histories of atheism', in Michael Hunter and David Wootton (eds.), *Atheism from the Reformation to the Enlightenment* (Oxford: Clarendon, 1992), 13–53, 38–9. This argument does not, however, fully take into account the social and publishing context of what Charron was doing, including his religious works and their relationship to his secular works. My thanks to Mark Greengrass.

[71] *Journal Henri IV*, vol. 2, 233–4.

[72] François Garasse, *Apologie... pour son livre contre les atheistes et libertins de nostre siecle. Et response aux censures et calomnies de l'autheur anonyme* (Paris: S. Chappelet, 1624), sigs. M8v–9r.

[73] Charron, *De la sagesse livres trois*, 1607, sigs. ĩ1v–2v; Horowitz, *Seeds of virtue and knowledge*, 226.

persona of the *Sage*. She is enslaved to dogmatic ways of thinking derived from books. Indeed, the Pedant knows only books, precepts, and *maîtres*, where the *Sage* learns in the manner of *Essais* I 25. The Pedant fosters controversy, deals in extreme and universal judgements, by either absolutely embracing or absolutely rejecting (hence 'OUI' and 'NON') all people and all opinions, whereas the *Sage* jealously retains *verité*, *candeur*, and *intégrité* in her judgement, the basis of *preud'hommie*, conciliating opposing viewpoints as much as possible. The irony here, of course, is that in distinguishing the Pedant from the *Sage* so dogmatically, Charron caused controversy, especially amongst his mainstream readership of *robins* and literary professionals, who thought they were being identified as Pedants.[74]

In Charron, liberty of judgement is the principal authority claimed for the *Sage*.[75] Bayle would later draw the attention of the reader to a particular passage in Charron's 1604 preface, repeated in a similar form in the *Petit traicté*, that makes this clear:

> [W]isdom, which is neither common nor popular, properly has this liberty and authority, 'by her exclusive right', to judge all (it is the privilege of the sage and spiritual person, 'a spiritual person judges all things and is judged by none') and in judging, to censure and condemn (as for the most part erroneous) common and popular opinions.[76]

So, each *Sage* has an authority equivalent to that of an institution (like the Roman Catholic Church) that censors error—at least in the sphere of strictly human belief and opinion. Charron formalizes Montaigne's acquisition of freedom as an authoritative privilege of judgement owned by an official, secular, philosophical *persona*, the *Sage* (who is also *spirituel*), that is available to an anti-Jesuit French elite of professionals pursuing vocations in the church and the law—to this extent his treatise is compatible with *politique* philosophy.[77] It needs to be a formal, authoritative 'power' because it is defined in opposition to the bold judgements made by other *censeurs* on behalf of the anti-Gallican wing of the Roman Catholic Church by the Jesuits.

Charron's principal publisher, Douceur, recognizes this in relation to his readership of *parlementaires*, by means of the materials he supplies in the follow-up edition of 1607. He prints, as appendices, both the passages in the 1601 Bordeaux edition that Charron himself corrected for the Paris 1604 edition, including the original version of the chapter on the sage's liberty of judgement and will, and the

---

[74] Charron, *De la sagesse*, 850–2.

[75] Horowitz, *Seeds of virtue and knowledge*, 225: 'In fact, *Scepticism* is a misleading term, for the liberty Charron recommends affects the will as much as the judgement. In the context of *De la sagesse*, the purpose is to free the judgement from the lesser purpose of pursuing truth and to free the will from the adherence to superfluous or harmful truths in order that the *esprit* in judgment and in will might guide one in the conduct of one's individual and public life.'

[76] Pierre Bayle, *Dictionaire historique et critique*, 3 vols. (2nd edn.; Rotterdam: Reinier Leers, 1702), vol. 1, 905, note K; Charron, *De la sagesse*, ed. Negroni, 41 ('la sagesse…n'est commun ny populaire, a proprement cette liberté et authorité, *Jure suo singulari*, de juger de tout (c'est le privilege du sage et spirituel, *Spiritualis omnia dijudicat, et à nemine judicatur*) et en jugeant, de censurer et condamner (comme la plus part erronées) les opinions communes et populaires'), 821.

[77] On Charron and *politique* thought, see Horowitz, *Seeds of virtue and knowledge*, 170.

passages that President Jeannin judged should be corrected and moderated (but which in the event were not). He does this to 'content everyone, and to leave the liberty and the means to the readers to take and choose that which will seem the best [reading]'.

This is an edition for the *parlementaire* or magistrate as free literate, choosing and judging his texts in private, like L'Estoile. Douceur goes on to advertise the fact that the reader will therefore have everything that has appeared in the previous editions of Bordeaux and Paris, together with the *Eloge* of Rochemaillet, and some new paratexts.[78] In this case, Douceur's marketing, designed to attract consumers who may already have his 1604 edition or the 1601 Bordeaux edition, coincides with the intellectual principle, so appropriate in this case, that the parliamentary reader is granted the *liberté* to judge whether Charron's and Jeannin's corrections should be applied or not.

2.7.6 PIERRE BAYLE'S MONTAIGNE

Douceur's 1607 edition was the one favoured, and therefore the one (or one of its reprints) most likely used by Bayle.[79] In the second, 1702 edition of Bayle's *Dictionaire historique et critique*, both Marie de Gournay and Pierre Charron were honoured with articles (we quoted from the Charron article in 2.7.5), while Michel de Montaigne featured only in the text and footnotes to those articles, and as a cited author elsewhere.

Gournay is identified in the first line of her article as Montaigne's fille d'alliance, famous for her learning ('célèbre par son savoir'). The first footnote reveals that Bayle was much more interested than Auerbach would be in the history of books, and the paratexts they carry. It tells the story of Gournay's devotion to her father and her father's text, citing her 1635 'Preface' (recommended to all who love 'the history of books, and of editions'), the re-edited text of the praise (at the end of II 17) of Gournay for her judgement of the *Essais*, and Pasquier's narrative of her first meeting with Montaigne in Paris, and their subsequent relationship. But the core of the article is the public *raillerie* she suffered for daring to enter—on the Jesuits' side—the pamphlet war initiated by the famous attack on the Jesuit Coton (*Anti-Coton*, 1610), which accused his order of complicity in Henri IV's assassination. As a woman, she publicly claimed a liberty of judgement on a religio-political matter. Derision predictably ensued.[80]

Similarly, despite the quantity of theological and devotional works Charron published, he is identified in the first line of Bayle's article as the 'author of a book which caused a lot of scandal' ('[a]uteur d'un livre qui a fait beaucoup de bruit')— *De la sagesse*. Aside from Douceur's edition, and the paratexts it contained (including

[78] For this and the previous paragraph, see Charron, *De la sagesse livres trois*, 1607, sigs. 3A5r, 3C4v–8r, 3D3v, ã4r.
[79] Bayle, *Dictionaire historique et critique*, vol. 1, 902 (note F).
[80] Bayle, *Dictionaire historique et critique*, vol. 1, 585–6 (incl. note A); Constant Venesoen (ed.), *Marie de Gournay: Textes relatifs à la calomnie* (Tübingen: Gunter Narr Verlag, 1998).

Rochemaillet's *Eloge*), Bayle used Charles Sorel's *Bibliotheque* to tell the story of the making and publication of this book, which included the story of its companion, the *Essais*.[81]

Bayle picks up from Rochemaillet and Sorel the question of how the relationship between their texts might have indexed the conduct of the *amitié* between the two men. For Bayle it is a relationship between a *Théologien* and a *Gentilhomme*, a relationship in which—judging by the relationship between the texts—the one who should have been the instructor (the theologian) was the disciple. Bayle then infers that Charron's *docilité* towards Montaigne—evident in his text—must have been the cause of Montaigne's bequest of his arms to the theologian in his will (for which the only source is Rochemaillet).[82]

In another note he picks up Sorel's remark that some people consider Charron more dangerous because Montaigne was a 'cavalier', where the former was a doctor of theology and preacher—meaning that his book would be received as Christian instruction ('on lit son livre comme une piece recevable pour l'instruction Chestienne'). Bayle then goes on to explain the reason why the same *pyrrhonisme* is indeed more dangerous in Charron's book than in Montaigne's book. They have different *personae* as authors, and therefore different powers of persuasion.

A 'lay author with no office' ('un Auteur laïque et sans caractere')—an unofficial, free literate—should enjoy a greater *liberté* to say whatever he thinks, than a doctor of theology, a preacher, a professor. In the case of the latter, one assumes they advance nothing but by way of teaching, persuasion. One supposes they have examined their doctrinal principles, and, in view of their *caractère*, one lets oneself be carried away by their *authorité*. But, again, if it is a *laïque* with no office speaking, one is less likely to be moved; one views his particular opinions like children put on display, and as a result his *pyrrhonisme* has no consequence ('ne tire pas à consequence').[83]

In the main text of his article, Bayle tells the story, from Rochemaillet, of the publication against the odds of *De la sagesse* at Paris, and of how, in following such an enlightened philosophical path ('suivant les lumieres de la Philosophie'), in order to attack popular and superstitious beliefs, Charron could not but put forward certain maxims that seemed to shake the foundations of religion. Bayle outlines the whole scandal surrounding the book and describes the statesmen who defended it, how they represented the people of *caractère* and authority that Charron had hoped to have judge his work.

Some believe, continues Bayle, that it redounded to the glory of France to have permitted the publication of this book in these circumstances. It showed that the country did not approve the tyrannical yoke that others wanted to place on the *esprit*—by which he means principally Jesuits such as Garasse, whose declamatory

---

[81] Bayle, *Dictionaire historique et critique*, vol. 1, 901.

[82] Bayle, *Dictionaire historique et critique*, vol. 1, 901, note B.

[83] For this and the previous paragraph, see Bayle, *Dictionaire historique et critique*, vol. 1, 906, note O. In the first edition of the *Dictionnaire de l'Académie française* (1694) 'caractere' has the senses of Montaigne's own 'marque', of 'titre, dignité, qualité, puissance attachée à certains estats', and of the modern 'caractère' (i.e. 'personality'). Here the contrast is with doctor, preacher, professor, so I have translated as 'with no office'.

polemics against Charron he faces down at great length in footnotes. It showed that the country, instead, approved free philosophical thought ('la liberté de philosopher'), as long as it contained itself within certain bounds.[84]

In Bayle's description, then, the publication of *De la sagesse*—especially in Douceur's edition of 1607—enacted the official French approval of *libertas philosophandi*, against Jesuit opposition, on the part of elite *juges* with the right moral and religious *caractère*. Even though, as Sorel tells us, Montaigne and Charron were associated in the public's mind for the *liberté* of their opinions, for—we may also surmise—their *amitié* and for the verbal similarities between the two texts, Bayle reveals that he at least understood the publication of the *Essais* to be a different kind of event to the publication of *De la sagesse*.[85]

The *Essais* represented a different kind of communication, on the part of someone with no *marque*, in the sense of no official *persona* or *caractère*—as Montaigne himself had insisted at the beginning of III 2. Though public, Montaigne's acquisition of freedom was not (like *De la sagesse*) considered to be an act of official enfranchisement, facilitated by office-holding *juges* on behalf of an elite national class of such *juges*, or *sages*, facing down the Jesuits—unless, that is, by association with a methodical re-enactment in print of similar arguments by an author with a different *persona* (Charron).

When, after the publication at Rotterdam of the first edition of his *Dictionaire* (1697), Bayle met a mixed reception across France, England, and the Dutch Republic and began the process of defending and apologizing for his work, it was the *persona* of Montaigne, and the precedent set by the publishing history of his book, that he called upon. Abbé Renaudot was charged with writing a censorial report on the *Dictionaire*, which Bayle's agents were seeking permission to import into France. The report was crushing and a ban was put in place; a manuscript copy found its way to Rotterdam and into print as the 'Judgement of the public and particularly of M. L'Abbé Renaudot' on the *Dictionaire*, accompanied by an assemblage of other derogatory opinions.[86]

Bayle responds immediately in print with 'Reflections' on this judgement. He says it is hardly surprising if a learned Catholic *dévot* such as Renaudot objects to liberties which, he says, do not in fact exceed those that an *honnête homme*, a 'Laïque', can legitimately give himself. After all, could anyone say that his work comes near the *licence* of the *Essais* of Montaigne? Had Montaigne not published several editions of his book without trouble? Was it not reprinted hundreds of times? Was it not dedicated to Cardinal Richelieu? Is it not in all libraries? What confusion would there be if he, Bayle, were not afforded the liberty in Holland that Montaigne had had in France?[87]

[84] Bayle, *Dictionaire historique et critique*, vol. 1, 903, for this and the previous paragraph.
[85] Sorel, *La bibliotheque françoise*, sig. D4r.
[86] H. H. M. van Lieshout, *The making of Pierre Bayle's 'Dictionnaire historique et critique'* (Amsterdam: APA-Holland University Press, 2001), 35–44.
[87] Pierre Bayle, *Dictionaire historique et critique*, 4 vols. (Amsterdam: P. Brunel et al., 1740), vol. 4, 616. The 'Reflexions', first published as a separate pamphlet, were not incorporated in the edition of 1702, so I cite the standard, 1740 edition.

In the more substantial apology he added to the second edition of his work (1702), Bayle uses the distinction he makes in the main text between the fortunes of Montaigne's and of Charron's books to defend his own. When it is to be judged whether an *erreur* will lead to fearful consequences or not, everything depends on the circumstances of the publication or promulgation of that error. Is it taught to the people by someone in authority, who might be seeking to form a party? Someone with a venerable *caractère*, such as a *pasteur* or a professor of theology? Is it disseminated by means of sermons, lessons, systematic treatises, catechisms? Pushed by intermediaries who go door to door recommending the texts and inviting people to the meetings? If so, then yes, one must act to prevent its publication and dissemination.[88]

But if, says Bayle, it is promulgated in the *persona* of a layman like me, with no office ('un homme, tout-à-fait laïque comme moi et sans caractere'), amidst vast literary and historical 'recueils', then no trouble should be taken by the censors. Readers neither look to such miscellaneous works for the reformation of their faith, nor to such authors—who offer their own comments only in passing—as guides. Such authors' errors are without consequence. It is for this reason, he says, that the Faculties of Theology in France let by all the maxims of this author Montaigne, who piled up everything presented to him by his memory without order or system. But when the priest and theologian Charron presented some of the same thoughts in a systematic treatise on moral philosophy, the theologians awoke from their repose.[89]

We cannot pursue here the question of whether Bayle's assumption, as a man of learning who pointedly entered controversies, of the image of a layman *sans caractère*, whose miscellaneous texts related to no programme of action, is a credible one. The point we need is simple. A quarter of a century after the prohibition at Rome (1676), the history of Montaigne's book, of his *persona* as an unofficial commentator or reader-writer, could still be a precedent for the uncontroversial and successful taking of liberties in print in France and in other countries. Let us return to an earlier period in order to summarize the importance—in this history—of the form taken by the book.

2.7.7 L'ESTOILE AND THE *ESSAIS* AS *REGISTRE*

Where the doctor of laws and canon Charron removed all traces of the form of the private archival book in his rewriting of the *Essais* (together with other sources) as a public treatise in moral philosophy, one of his contemporaries chose closely to follow them in pursuing his studies as a free literate. Back in the first decade of the seventeenth century, it was not Charron and his relationship to Montaigne that shaped L'Estoile's reading of the *Essais*. It was Montaigne's description of his text, in Auerbach's selected passage and elsewhere, as a 'record' ('un contrerolle', 'un

[88] Bayle, *Dictionaire historique et critique*, 1702, vol. 3, 3136.
[89] Bayle, *Dictionaire historique et critique*, 1702, vol. 3, 3136.

registre'). Most critics who have noted Montaigne's usage of these terms describe it as metaphorical: he is continuously 'documenting', in inverted commas, the mind's activities in the way that one would normally document more mundane things such as one's revenue and expenses.[90]

In the fourth and fifth chapters of Volume 2 (2.4, 2.5) we were able to ask in more material terms what forms a personal (as opposed to a state) 'registre' of the late sixteenth or early seventeenth century might take, and what functions it might have. The answers suggested that, strictly speaking, Montaigne's usage of the term would not have been received as a metaphorical one. Encountering the manuscript books of L'Estoile—and of Slingsby and Maillefer—in the archive helps us recover an early modern perspective from which the *Essais* could have read, especially in the later editions, in some respects like a private *registre*—a *registre* which has evolved in the margins of a miscellaneous collection of commonplaces, and which has then strangely got into print. Just as L'Estoile and his friends shared their *registres* with one another, so Montaigne shared his with friends and family through the handpress.

To put it another way, Montaigne (a) more and more thinks of his book as a private *registre*, especially when he begins to enter more personal notes in the margins of existing editions; and (b) draws on his readership's relationship to a culture of written record-keeping to shape reception of his book. The scene of the *Essais'* reading and writing is not just the culture of 'various' reading notes, but of the keeping and circulating of a private record whose functions and purposes go beyond the conventional ones of domestic housekeeping, preparation for death, and shaming oneself into amendment and repentance.

For the example of L'Estoile shows that one of the things one normally does in a *registre* is go back and correct oneself. He is constantly reviewing what he has written with a view to verifying it. L'Estoile will, for example, go back to a given page to stick a slip over a judgement of a book he has bought or cross out an account of a death which he later decides is wrong.[91] This makes sense of Montaigne's insistence that he never goes back and corrects judgements he has made—a very important respect in which his *registre* claims originality in its contemporary setting.

---

[90]   Terence Cave, *How to read Montaigne* (London: Granta, 2007), 9–10: '[T]he metaphor is one of recording, of creating a continuous record which will enable the writer to review and assess his thought processes over time, rather than allowing them to evaporate into thin air. The notion of a register or inventory recurs at several points where Montaigne speaks of his attempts to pin down and record the movement of his thoughts … ; the French verb he most often uses for "to record" is "contreroller" (or its synonym "mettre en rolle"), which is related to the English word "control" but lacks its implication of constraint and dominion.' See also Richard Scholar, *Montaigne and the art of free-thinking* (Long Hanborough, Oxon.: Peter Lang, 2010), 38–41, which treats it as a metaphor—in tension with another (the painting of a self-portrait)—with specific reference to the opening passage of III 2.

[91]   See, for example, BnF MS 10300, fol. 26r/*Journal Henri IV*, vol. 2, 212–13, 215; BnF MS Fr. 10301, fol. 96v (pencil numbering)/*Journal Henri IV*, vol. 2, 501. In the first case (21 December 1606) L'Estoile corrects a judgement of a book (Leschassier's *Consultatio*) which he had declared initially to owe much to others, but which on the slip he now describes as 'bien fait' and 'à mon Iugement' owing nothing to others. The printed edition does not contain this passage. The second case, L'Estoile's correction of a *conte* about a death, was discussed in 2.5.4 (see Illus. 2.5.6).

Still more strikingly, to view the form of L'Estoile's 'Tablettes' is to see that Montaigne is transferring the openness and mutability, the liberty and authenticity, of a form of private archival book to the production of a printed book. Not just in III 2, but persistently throughout his work, Montaigne describes the writing of his book as the keeping of a *registre et contrôle*, 'from day to day, from minute to minute', a history adapted to the moment, a record of various occurrences. He is cuing his contemporary readers to see it, to receive it, as a hybridized version of a kind of archival book with which they were familiar, and that usually was 'secret', private, and authentic.

The story Montaigne is telling is that he has been remarkably assiduous in keeping this record, over a long *durée*—this is why he has, or so he tells us here, neglected other types of administratively more useful record-keeping:

> Have I wasted my time by taking stock of myself so continually, so carefully [*rendu compte de moy si continuellement, si curieusement*]? Those who merely think and talk about themselves occasionally do not examine the basics and do not go as deep as one who makes it his study, his work, and his trade, who with all good faith and with all his might binds himself to keeping a long-term account [*qui en faict son estude, son ouvrage et son mestier, qui s'engage à un registre de durée, de toute sa foy, de toute sa force*].... With the aims of teaching my mental faculty even to rave with some order and direction and so as to stop it losing its way and wandering in the wind, I need simply to give it body and to keep detailed accounts of my petty thoughts [*donner corps et mettre en registre tant de menues pensées*] as they occur to me. I listen to my reveries because I have to record them [*j'ay à les enroller*]. How often when I have been irritated by some action which politeness and prudence forbid me from openly censuring have I unburdened myself here— not without the design of giving a public reproof [*non sans dessein de publique instruction*].... And what if I now lend a more attentive ear to the books I read, being on the lookout to see whether I can thieve something with which to decorate and support my own? I have never studied so as to make a book, but I have done some study because I have made one, if studying a little means lightly touching this author or that and tweaking his head or his foot— not so as to shape my opinions but, long after they have taken shape, to help them, to back them up and to serve them.[92]

It is hoped that the reader of *The School of Montaigne* now hears this passage— along with Auerbach's passage from III 2 quoted in 2.7.1—a little differently. The so-called breakthrough, as twentieth-century scholars such as Villey and Auerbach put it, into the freedom of lived, interior experience, of being-in-process, displaced in more recent studies by deconstructive intertextuality, now returns in a different, less familiar, less modern-sounding key.

It now sounds more like a novel and artful application, in print, of the open form and shifting functions of the personal manuscript *registre* or account-book, supplemented by the fruits of reading undertaken for the purpose of decorating and supporting the writing. Montaigne draws upon this form as much as he draws upon Plutarchan *moralia*, the tradition of *leçons*, and other literary genres such as

---

[92] II 18, NP704/BVH Paris 1595, pp. 440–1/S755–6.

the letter and the legal gloss. Once again, his use of the form of a *registre* is tied to his noble *persona* as a particular, unreformed, unrepentant head-of-household— Michel of Montaigne.

So the *Essais*, especially book III, would indeed have seemed redolent to readers such as L'Estoile of a single, personal book of record into which the compiler has copied all sorts of different memoranda and extracts: words he has written on the endleaves of his printed books; notes of things that happened just recently, or in his neighbourhood; records of deaths and of the reputations of individuals; notes of his date of birth, the customs and qualities of his father, of his illnesses and cures; extracts from texts he takes or misremembers according to whim, without scholarly references; letters he has written; his election as mayor; the text of his Bull of Roman citizenship.

These *mémoires* are not of course written under dated headings, but they are the result of 'everyday', immediate, and continuous writing or dictation. 'The other day I was at Armagnac, on the estates of one of my relations', Montaigne writes, a few pages after the passage with which we began from III 2, and he goes on to register a *conte* he heard there.[93] They are also constantly checked and reviewed, added to in the margins, in the way L'Estoile's book is—but not for the purposes of correction.

The novelty lies in the fact that a private practice of continuous archival record-keeping is used to produce an 'everyday' history of one man's shifting *fantasies* in print, a history that is—yes—more secular in emphasis than L'Estoile's, and that purports not to correct or 'reform' itself, factually or morally, as it goes. A miscellaneous and mutable practice of private account-keeping used by ordinary householders for centuries becomes in the late sixteenth century a novel way of doing moral philosophy in public, without getting involved in the public transmission of authoritative knowledge or caught up in scholarly controversy and the memorialization of religious conflicts.

L'Estoile does of course get caught up in the latter enterprise, with the explicit goal of privately recording and identifying the militant, anti-monarchical Leaguer and Jesuit voices that define by opposition his own confessional identity. But it is arguable that L'Estoile follows Montaigne to a certain extent in not enacting pious self-reformation in his own *journal-registre*. Even though he declares such a goal it is unclear whether he repents of his *vanité*, or even whether he wants to.

In one meditative passage of April 1610 he describes himself as wanting to put an end to 'all vain curiosities and follies...even to this register, which is full of them' and which he would finish 'right here, willingly,' but for some other valid consideration that prevents him. Furthermore, as we heard in 2.1.8, he goes on a few months later to invoke Montaigne precisely at the moment when he resists his confessor's exhortations to repent of his errors and reform himself as a Roman Catholic.[94]

---

[93] III 2, NP852/BVH Paris 1595, bk. III, p. 17/S915.
[94] *Journal Henri IV*, vol. 3, 59.

It is in this—rather than in any strictly philosophical or epistemological innova-tion—that Montaigne goes beyond the norms of his time. He does not, like Henri III, hand over his conscience to a spiritual director, a Jesuit, or seek to amend himself by reference to some external *patron* of moral purity or *sagesse*—in the process seeking to become a secular version of a monk, like Flavio Querenghi. He uses a widespread practice of personal memorial writing to record, in print, a par-ticular individual's version of freedom of judgement and conscience. To see this one needs to follow the traces of Montaigne's book into the archive, to pay as much attention to the manuscripts composed by users of that book as one does to the text of the *Essais* themselves.

As a coda to this section, and an introduction to the theme of the rest of this final chapter, briefly consider the example of another *parlementaire*, Bernard de La Roche Flavin (1552–1627), who wrote extracts from the *Essais* into his book just a few years after L'Estoile, but who did so very much under the influence of Charron and his advertised relationship to Montaigne.

In 1617, La Roche Flavin published with Millanges at Bordeaux his *Treze livres des parlemens de France* under the *marque* of a seigneur who was a *Conseiller* and *Premier President* of the *Chambre des Requêtes* in the *Parlement* of Toulouse. John O'Brien has recently revealed that when, in book 8 of this vast and learned treatise, La Roche Flavin was defining the moral and philosophical *persona* of the *juge* or *magistrat*, he was simultaneously reading and rewriting both Montaigne and Charron, or Montaigne via Charron's and Rochemaillet's mediation of his work for learned professionals.[95] Charron–Montaigne's *sage* becomes La Roche Flavin's philosophically moderate *juge*, free of corruption and passions in making his *juge-ments* with proper *liberté*. He is turned into an 'officially' free judge.

The example of La Roche Flavin is relevant to this study for two broader reasons. He is, first, another example of a lay reader-writer who methodically collects *extraits* from the best classical and modern authors (including Montaigne and Charron), and from the *registres* of the *parlements*, in order to publish a single learned volume that would reform the morals and practice of the French magis-tracy—especially of the Toulouse *magistrats*, whose failings he revealed in detail. In so doing, of course, he himself assumed the Charronian *sage*'s liberty and authority, *jure suo singulari*, to judge all. Even though his treatise defended in the usual way the *privilèges* of the *parlementaires* against papal and other incursions, he was him-self adjudged by his co-*parlementaires* in Toulouse to have assumed this liberty and authority illegitimately.[96]

Censorship in early modern France was a patchwork of overlapping and rival jurisdictions. But since the beginning of the civil wars the *parlements* had gained more prerogatives in the religious and intellectual sphere, to the detriment of ecclesiastical and university authorities. The parliamentary court of Toulouse had

---

[95] John O'Brien, 'Le Magistrat comme philosophe: La Roche Flavin lecteur de Montaigne et de Charron', *Bulletin de la Société Internationale des Amis de Montaigne*, 55 (2012), 221–34; Bernard de La Roche Flavin, *Treze Livres des Parlemens de France* (Bordeaux: Simon Millanges, 1617).
[96] Carole Delprat, 'Savoirs et déboires d'un juriste, Bernard de La Roche Flavin (1552–1627)', *Histoire, économie et société*, 19 (2000), 163–84.

jurisdiction over the circulation of writings and used it on 12 June 1617 to suspend La Roche Flavin from his office and to tear up and rend apart his book before his very eyes. In publishing 'secret' knowledge about the *parlement* and *parlementaires*, and in pretending to instruct the reader in all they needed to know about the *palais* with just one book, he had taken too great a liberty.[97]

2.7.8 THE AGE OF LEARNING AND THE LEARNED BOOK

Can we, in the rest of this 'Epilogue', further sketch out the larger historical picture we glimpsed in the 'General Introduction' (Volume 1) and the 'Prologue' (1.1), on the basis of the case studies offered here and in other chapters? What trends in the broader European history of literacy and learning led to a situation in which a noble layman such as Montaigne came to write and publish a book of the kind he did? The power of the written word in earlier medieval Europe, especially in the Carolingian period, derived on the one hand from the reception and promotion of Christianity as a religion of the book, and, on the other hand, from the resort to writing in all aspects of governmental administration.[98]

All of the documents analysed in this study are indications of a process that stretched thereafter over the *longue durée* from the late medieval through the early modern period. In tandem with changing patterns of interaction between orality and literacy, between (in the early modern period) manuscript and print, this period sees the laicization and privatization of religious, scholarly, and bureaucratic forms of literacy.[99]

The 'laicization' of literate devotional, scholarly, and record-keeping practices does not of course entail 'secularization' in the modern sense, for it does not describe an essentially counter-religious or even counter-clerical process. A lay person could be caring for their soul, under the guidance of priests or teachers, across various, overlapping forms of devotional, humanistic, and archival reading and writing. At the same time, there was certainly a disjunction, in late medieval Italy,

---

[97] Delprat, 'Savoirs et déboires d'un juriste, Bernard de La Roche Flavin (1552-1627)', 164–5, 181–2; Soman, 'Press, Pulpit, and Censorship in France before Richelieu', 451–7; Maclean, *Scholarship, commerce, religion*, 158–61.

[98] Rosamond McKitterick, 'Text and image in the Carolingian world', in Rosamond McKitterick (ed.), *The uses of literacy in early mediaeval Europe* (Cambridge: Cambridge University Press, 1990), 297–318, 300–1, and, for the later period in England, Clanchy, *From memory to written record*. The broadest overview of this process in educational culture is now to be found in Ronald G. Witt, *The two Latin cultures and the foundation of Renaissance humanism in medieval Italy* (Cambridge: Cambridge University Press, 2012), part V. Warren Brown et al. (eds.), *Documentary culture and the laity in the early Middle Ages* (Cambridge: Cambridge University Press, 2013) warns against generalizing the case of Carolingian bureaucracy as one applicable to the entire early Middle Ages.

[99] Mark Amsler, *Affective literacies: writing and multilingualism in the late Middle Ages* (Turnhout: Brepols, 2011). There was also an equivalent process of continuity and change in the relationship between the religious houses and reading and writing over this *longue durée*. See, for example, E. A. Jones and Alexandra Walsham (eds.), *Syon Abbey and its books: reading, writing and religion, c.1400–1700* (Woodbridge: Boydell, 2010).

between urban, mercantile reader-writers of vernacular compilations, and scholastic, professional, and humanistic purveyors of official Latin culture in writing.[100]

From the perspective of the sixteenth century, however, one could describe the process as the penetration of theological and professional modes of writing, thought, and speech into all domains of lay life, as official teachers of university and church sought to civilize and confessionalize the literate public with authoritative models both of knowledge and of the *personae* that could legitimately transmit and receive it. For the core issue was the redescription and regulation of the agency relations, mediated by books and book-extracts, between the expert reader-writer, the lay reader-writer (male or female), the contemporary patrons and authorities, the producers and disseminators of printed and scribal texts, and the prototypes of divine and human knowledge.

The *Essais* all at once exemplify, describe, and reimagine this process and this issue. In so doing, at the time, they represented one intervention amongst many. For during Montaigne's century, large numbers of people reading and writing as free literates in nexuses beyond the schools and monasteries (though not beyond the reach of their teachers, disciplines, and curricula) began to constitute new *personae* and sites for the production and use of theological and philosophical knowledge. There was a proliferation of new types of students and professors of natural and divine wisdom.[101] Montaigne's unpremeditated and accidental philosopher was just one of these, in a marketplace that was generally populated with more overtly professional and scholarly types such as Duplessis-Mornay and Étienne Pasquier.

The process ebbs and flows to different rhythms in different regions, and even in different families. New elites of literate knowledge emerged in various incarnations at different times and places across Europe between the fourteenth and seventeenth centuries.[102] The office-holding *bourgeois* and *noblesse de robe* of early modern France, to which L'Estoile and La Roche Flavin belonged, was one of the most prominent and productive of these elites. They did not just use reading and writing in the course of fulfilling their professional duties; they pursued private studies which many of them then printed as authors with professional *personae*.

---

[100] Maximilian Von Habsburg, *Catholic and Protestant translations of the Imitatio Christi, 1425–1650: from late medieval classic to early modern bestseller* (Farnham: Ashgate, 2012), 244; Petrucci, *Writers and readers*, 169–235.

[101] Luce Giard, 'Remapping knowledge, reshaping institutions', in Pumfrey, Slawinski, and Rossi (eds.), *Science, culture and popular belief in Renaissance Europe*, 19–47.

[102] In the last quarter century, scholarship has moved away from the pursuit of teleological transitions in pre-modern European history from societies whose core features are determined in some way by orality or oral memory, to those determined by literacy, and later from those characterized as 'manuscript cultures' to those characterized as 'print cultures'. See M. Innes, 'Memory, orality and literacy in an early medieval society', *Past and Present*, 158 (1998), 3–36, McKitterick (ed.), *The uses of literacy in early mediaeval Europe*. On the relation in general between documentary culture and late medieval English literature, see Emily Steiner, *Documentary culture and the making of medieval English literature* (Cambridge: Cambridge University Press, 2003).

At the same time, especially in the post-Reformation age of confessionalization, the new literate technologies, their new medium (the printed book), and the new *personae* for philosophers and theologians generated widespread suspicion, resistance, and mistrust—mistrust that the *Essais* both meet head-on in the first sentence of the book ('Icy, c'est un livre de bonne foy') and foster in various ways in the course of the text.

The principal clerical authors of the sixteenth-century phase of this transformation in the spheres of divine and humane learning were Martin Luther, who rediscovered his own religious life and that of the wider lay public (who followed him) as 'a life in reading and in writing', and Desiderius Erasmus, the 'man of letters' who disseminated himself as a 'living icon throughout early modern Europe'.[103] These were clerics who used the handpress authoritatively to mediate the enfranchisement of lay reader-writers and users of divine and human knowledge. With the Reformation, and the widened social role of the individual 'protesting' reader of biblical and religious texts, the uses of written records and printed books both to buttress and to question authorities in public, and to collect and reflect upon literature in private, spread and diversified still further.

A veritable Pandora's box of public controversy and private criticism was opened over the sixteenth and seventeenth centuries, not just in religion and politics, but also across the realms of divine and humane learning. With printed bibles and other publications came critical tools for the purchaser—a trend in which historians have seen the enfranchisement of reader-writers, critics, and 'independent investigators' of various types and social background. Anyone equipped with the tools of reading and writing could exercise their private liberty of judgement to advocate or enact 'reform' of one kind or another, whether of themselves or of whole institutions, whole literatures.[104] L'Estoile and La Roche Flavin are good examples of this. La Roche Flavin went public with decades of private research geared to reform of the parliamentary *juge*—only to see his work torn asunder. L'Estoile was no public intellectual, but he formed and assessed a large collection of printed and manuscript materials, with a view to arming those who would resist the Jesuits and reform the various confessions as a reunited Church.

Such enterprises partly depended—as is very clear in the case of France and L'Estoile—on the production of ephemeral printed and scribal publications, of news, pamphlets, placards, and *libelles*. This vast literature of vituperation and conflict represented a series of attempts to solicit, create, appeal to, and empower

---

[103] Brian Cummings, *The literary culture of the Reformation: grammar and grace* (Oxford: Oxford University Press, 2002), 52; Lisa Jardine, *Erasmus, man of letters: the construction of charisma in print* (Princeton: Princeton University Press, 1993), 48.

[104] Kevin Sharpe and Steven N. Zwicker, 'Introduction: discovering the Renaissance reader', in Kevin Sharpe and Steven N. Zwicker (eds.), *Reading, society, and politics in early modern England* (Cambridge: Cambridge University Press, 2003), 1–38 (4–5). For the connection between humanistic practices of criticism and editing and the emergence of public political criticism, see Jacob Soll, *Publishing the Prince: history, reading, and the birth of political criticism* (Ann Arbor: University of Michigan Press, 2005), and for that between private reading practice and the 'development of the self as critical social observer', see Sharpe, *Reading revolutions: the politics of reading in early modern England*, 339.

groups and communities of free literates with divergent ideological, professional, and confessional identities.[105]

But at the same time they depended, in the period with which we have been centrally concerned (1560–1640), on the boom in production of learned books, and on the printer-publishers and public intellectuals—such as Millanges and La Roche Flavin, Douceur and Charron—who drove it. The learned book could be lauded as the agent of virtuous transformation and the incarnation of truth or condemned as an institution in atheism and the source of error. By the end of the sixteenth century, a hard look at the scholarly book trade would suggest that it was both a polemical object and a profit-making enterprise.[106]

This was the age of European history when scholarship, scholarly printers, and professional scholars were at their highest peak of prominence and influence in general intellectual life. The private collection of the last Duke of Urbino is one testimony to this; he saw the acquisition of all printed scholarly knowledge as crucial to the future of his dynasty.

At the very same time, however, confessionalization and commercialism combined to push the market into overdrive and saturation. On the one hand, each confessionalized society had to produce its own controversial theology, its own Holy Writ and patristic corpus, its own liturgy, and even, to a certain extent, its own versions—both in Latin and the vernacular—of classical and recent authors. On the other hand, authors and editors (such as Rochemaillet) connived with printer-publishers (such as Douceur) to market and sell more and more updated editions of existing texts, more and more learned interpretations and mediations—with the inevitable result that scepticism set in amongst purchasers and demand collapsed by the end of the period.[107]

'Learned' does not just mean international, professional, Latin scholarship. There was of course a body of publisher-booksellers who specialized in scholarly literature in Latin for transregional and transnational markets: the Latin trade. When Querenghi set about publishing his life's work he sent his public Latin lectures and philosophical treatises north for printing by such publishers in Leiden and Paris, and his private, vernacular discourses to local publishers in Padua and Vicenza.[108]

But just as these producers of scholarly literature published and sold some books in the vernaculars, and some Latin books for particular zones, so there was another, parallel body of publisher-booksellers who published more works in the vernaculars, including translations of works in foreign vernaculars, and distributed some of them transnationally, as well as offering a small proportion of their publications

---

[105] Pettegree, *The book in the Renaissance*; Szabari, *Less rightly said: scandals and readers in sixteenth-century France*, 17–18.

[106] Maclean, *Scholarship, commerce, religion*, 9–10, 46.

[107] Maclean, *Scholarship, commerce, religion*, 211–34.

[108] Luciano Stecca, 'Montaigne e Flavio Querenghi', in *Montaigne e l'Italia: atti del congresso internazionale di studi di Milano-Lecco, 26–30 ottobre 1988* (Geneva: Slatkine; Centro interuniversitario di ricerche sul 'Viaggio in Italia', 1991), 83–101, 96–7 (nn. 9–10).

in Latin.[109] They were less affected by the decline in the Latin trade in the early seventeenth century.

There were perhaps three overlapping readerships, envisaged by these two principal types of publisher-booksellers, for the full range of learned books they offered. First, there were students who would purchase textbooks, normally in Latin, in the context of attending a formal school at one level or another. Then there were specialists who would purchase scholarship—normally, again, in Latin—in the course of exercising their public functions as university scholars and learned professionals, as secular and regular clerics. Finally, there were the sixteenth-century descendants of Petrucci's free literates: inquisitive non-specialists or general readers who would purchase less technical works and more philosophical fictions, especially in the vernaculars (though they might have some Latin), for private reading.[110]

But, again, these were not fixed social identities: a student or a professional scholar or cleric might equally be in the market for books they could read freely in private, while a non-specialist general reader such as L'Estoile might be in the market for specialist scholarship for use in the exercise of private offices of judgement. Montaigne's reading encompassed the whole range of learned books in question. He is a public, but very particular example of the third type of reader-writer: the elite, educated, free literate envisaged by the Europe-wide markets in learned books in both Latin and the vernaculars.

In other words, by the mid-sixteenth century there had developed an overlap, from the point of view of consumption (and to a lesser extent from the point of view of production), between the Latin trade and the vernacular trade in the broad field of printed educative and scholarly literature, at both the national and transnational levels.[111] This is apparent in the nature of the books collected for the Bodleian in 1605. The same page of the catalogue that lists the 1598 copy of the *Essais* also registers copies of other books in the French, Italian, and Spanish vernaculars (including the works of Marot, and the *Diana* of Montemayor), alongside the expected works of Latin scholarship.[112]

The quantity of learned and philosophical books available in the vernaculars expanded rapidly after the Reformation; indeed, learned books were translated both ways. A few learned vernacular works infiltrated the Latin trade via Frankfurt and other routes; many were published and distributed in editions in more than one national market (including the *Essais*).[113]

---

[109] On the transnational vernacular trade, see Andrew Pettegree, 'North and south: cultural transmission in the sixteenth-century European book world', *Bulletin of Spanish Studies*, 89 (2012), 507–20, 515.

[110] Ian Maclean, *Learning and the market place: essays in the history of the early modern book* (Leiden: Brill, 2009), 22, 28–9, 148.

[111] Pettegree, 'North and south', 515.

[112] Maclean, *Scholarship, commerce, religion*, 54–6; James, *Catalogus*, sig. 2Y3v. Of the sixteen items listed on this page, approximately seven are in Latin, and the rest in the vernaculars (three French, three Italian, three Spanish). One item is in manuscript.

[113] Pettegree, *The book in the Renaissance*; Peter Burke, 'Translations into Latin in early modern Europe', in Peter Burke and R. Po-Chia Hsia (eds.), *Cultural translation in early modern Europe* (Cambridge: Cambridge University Press, 2007), 65–80.

And there is plenty of evidence from the time that the category of learned books was very capacious, in terms of genres. Bacon includes an extremely wide variety of types of books in his survey of the products of learning, including a range of non-scholarly genres from poetic or philosophical fictions to household journals and diaries of the kind we encountered in 2.4 and 2.5.[114]

So, for our purposes, 'the learned book' encompasses a whole range of non-popular, non-pamphlet literature from professional, discipline-bound scholarship, scholarly editions, and textbooks in Latin and other classical languages to works published in parallel Latin and vernacular editions (such as Bacon's *Advancement*), scholarly works in the vernacular (such as La Roche Flavin's), and vernacular miscellanies and fictions that betray and transmit learning, but do not make professional or pedagogical contributions to university or extra-curricular disciplines, and combine educative with other recreational or polemical purposes.[115]

Montaigne's vernacular book—recommended to Latin-literate students as private reading by humanists such as Lipsius, studded with Latin quotations, and identified consistently either as a miscellaneous work of learning or as a contribution to moral philosophy—falls towards the latter end of this range. It tended to be published and sold by publisher-booksellers who specialized more at this end (and less at the more professional, scholarly end) and whose primary commercial motivation was to cater for and expand educated publics of free literates who were exercising their own judgement in what to buy and how to read.

Of those we have seen publishing and selling Montaigne, Candolle was the most active in the scholarly Latin book market (especially once his own *Société* was formed in 1606). All of the rest—Millanges, L'Angelier, Blount, Ginammi, London—published or sold at least some books in Latin, including in most cases some scholarly books, but they were particularly invested in the market for learning in the vernaculars.[116]

This is especially clear in the case of the Newcastle bookseller William London, who specialized in learned books—more than half of those he offered were in divinity—but who offered most of his books in the vernacular. As we saw in 2.4.1, London used Montaigne in his preface as a representative 'free literate' or gentleman reader-writer, one who knew how to use learning and learned books. London refers to him in his epistle as a 'Learned Author' who, remarkably for a Frenchman, did not read romances (France was the centre of the romance trade in the 1650s).[117]

---

[114] Francis Bacon, *The advancement of learning*, ed. Michael Kiernan (Oxford: Clarendon, 2000), 69–70, 73–5.

[115] Maclean, *Scholarship, commerce, religion*, 54–6, 59–60. Maclean is concerned in this study with the market in specialist scholarly books, not with the whole market in learned books, as I am describing it here.

[116] Blount published Matthew Gwinne's neo-Latin play *Vertumnus* in 1607 (ESTC S92800, ESTC S103570), and some scholarly works in the vernacular, but his list mostly consisted of non-scholarly vernacular literature, especially history. The house of L'Angelier published about fifteen editions in Greek or Latin, including some scholarly legal treatises. See Balsamo and Simonin, *Abel L'Angelier et Françoise de Louvain (1574–1620)*, 101–2. Millanges (USTC), Candolle ('Heritage of the Printed Book' database, and WorldCat), and Ginammi (see 2.2.12) published rather more Latin and scholarly literature. For William London see the next paragraph.

[117] London, *A catalogue*, sig. C2r–v.

London's 1657 catalogue included a small selection of *c.*300 books in Greek, Latin, and Hebrew, useful for schools and scholars, but *c.*3000 books for the general gentleman reader (including clergy), with a majority consisting of learned books, largely in the vernacular (including the English *Essayes*), with some in Latin, and a minority of separately listed fictions (romances, plays, poems). He expressed an intention, never realized, to go on to produce a separate catalogue of the Latin books that were most useful and of most easy purchase (i.e. on sale in English booksellers) for this market. The catalogue he did publish included some scholarly volumes imported from the continent and some volumes in foreign vernaculars.[118]

The role of Simon Millanges in Bordeaux and Abel L'Angelier in Paris, and the commercial connections between them, in the making and marketing of the *Essais* first in the provinces, then in the capital, is now well established in Montaigne scholarship. We heard in 2.2.5 how Candolle connived with Charles Perrot of the Genevan consistory to publish an edition in Geneva in 1602 that did not follow the corrections made semi-officially in 1595. Candolle in Geneva, Blount in London, and Ginammi in Venice were kindred spirits who produced editions and translations of the *Essais*, and whose lists, like that of L'Angelier, represented whole libraries of literature for elite free literates.

But there was of course a downside to this free market in vernacular learning. Montaigne's own career as amateur editor and corrector of his friend La Boétie's works was blighted by the uncontrolled circulation and copying of *De la servitude volontaire*. Most damaging were the activities of editor Simon Goulart and the Genevan publisher-printers who printed the text without acknowledgement as part of a collection of memorial pamphlets and *libelles* designed to justify rebellion against the French king. Publishers in Ferrara and Geneva issued bowdlerized and censored editions of the *Essais*, and L'Angelier eventually relinquished his interest in the work when the Genevan competition began to flood the market.

These printer-publishers and publisher-booksellers—as I have already indicated—cannot be considered in isolation from the scholars, correctors, and translators with whom they worked, and who shaped the material, intellectual, and social conditions in which free literates used learned books. In Europe *c.*1600, clerics, university scholars, and learned professionals dominated, as never before, an intellectual world fed and led by the booming scholarly book trade. It was they who selected, promoted, and recommended books for circulation, and it was they who corrected and censored books not recommended for circulation until expurgated.

Clerics were normally charged with acting as official censors on behalf of municipal and ecclesiastical authorities that regulated licentious behaviour by, amongst other measures, expurgating and prohibiting particular texts. But we have seen that censors, and different bodies of censors (in one jurisdiction), could be in

---

[118] London (based in Newcastle) was a bookseller who, besides his printed catalogues, did finance or author at least seven editions (ESTC R37653, R36544, R209434, R207262, R230554, R27879, R209429). His catalogue may not be a personal stock list, but an indicative list of books 'vendible' to the learned laity. See 2.4.1 and Schotte, '"Books for the use of the learned and studious"', 34, 39, 46–7, and n.43; London, *A catalogue*.

tension with one another and with other authorities concerning who held the ultimate power or liberty of judgement over morals and over their expression in books. This was certainly the case in Rome, Paris, Geneva, and Venice, where different kinds of negotiated censorship were in operation. The Master of the Sacred Palace in Rome represented one of three organs of censorship jostling for position in the 1570s and 1580s.[119] He did not accept the recommendation of his *consultor* that the *Essais* be prohibited until expurgated of error.

Official censorship overlapped with another kind of textual judgement: the 'culture of correction' in Renaissance Europe. We have just explored (2.7.5) the important role this played in the publication of Charron's book. The role of corrector had a long history in classical and medieval manuscript culture and originated in the expectation that 'friends' would collaborate with authors in fashioning a text for circulation to particular audiences. We saw this culture at work in the case of Gournay, Lipsius, Brach, and the *Essais* in 1.6.8, and failing to work in the case of Pasquier's intervention in 2.1.7. Later, in relation to editions published from 1617 to 1635, Gournay was to advise the reader both that her own practical considerations and pressure from the *imprimeurs* and *libraires* had constrained her to correct aspects of the text (in ways Montaigne might not have approved), and that said *libraires* and *imprimeurs* never employed *correcteurs* of sufficient quality. Worthy readers would know how to redress the text for themselves.[120]

In the sixteenth century correctors were generally print professionals who not only expurgated errors and redacted texts in the printshop, but who also created all sorts of paratextual aids for readers in an attempt to purge a work of error and make it safe for transmission in print. They were collaborators in a broad process of authorship of labile, constantly changing texts. As played by someone like the Lutheran preacher Andreas Osiander in relation to works by both Copernicus and Cardano, or by the Jesuate Girolamo Canini in relation to Montaigne, the corrector's role was not only to amend and edit the text but also to vouch for its quality and probity. He knew how to produce a potentially dangerous book in a way that allowed it to circulate to readers without too much controversy, to make it what it had to be in order to survive.[121]

Authors, such as Erasmus, who were concerned to shape the reception of their own works also demonstrated command of the practices of correction. Readers wrote corrections in their own copies, whether following printed errata lists or making their own judgements.[122] Correction, in short, rivalled note-taking as a core link between the practice of reading and the practice of writing. Anyone who

---

[119] Fragnito, 'La censura libraria tra Congregazione dell'Indice, Congregazione dell'Inquisizione e Maestro del Sacro Palazzo (1571–1596)'.

[120] Millet 117–20.

[121] Grafton, *The culture of correction in Renaissance Europe*; Bruce Wrightsman, 'Andreas Osiander's contribution to the Copernican achievement', in Robert S. Westman (ed.), *The Copernican achievement* (Berkeley: University of California Press, 1975), 213–43.

[122] Ann Blair, 'Errata lists and the reader as corrector', in Sabrina A. Baron, Eric N. Lindquist, and Eleanor F. Shevlin (eds.), *Agent of change: print culture studies after Elizabeth L. Eisenstein* (Amherst: University of Massachusetts Press; Washington, D.C.: In association with the Center for the Book, Library of Congress, 2007), 21–41.

copied or rewrote or annotated something they read could play the role of a corrector or a censor—as we saw in different ways in the cases of Pasquier (2.1.7) and Maillefer (2.5.6).

From Erasmus and Luther on, then, university teachers, regular and secular clerics, and learned professionals, whether in their public or private offices, remained highly instrumental in determining the books read and translated, and in transmitting methods and disciplinary frameworks—despite the supposed breaking of the clerical monopoly over literate knowledge. From established Roman Catholic intellectuals to itinerant members of the international Protestant diaspora, they were key in shaping private lay encounters with the Books of scripture and nature. Through their agency, the university curriculum— and the alternative, extra-mural curricula that both complemented and opposed it—became a shared culture for an educated laity who were neither enrolled students nor specialists, but who participated in cultures of humane and divine learning.

In pursuing the history of the *Essais*, we have seen that one Roman Catholic clergyman in particular played a crucial role in the composition of the *Essais*: Jacques Amyot, bishop of Auxerre. He performed exactly the office described in the last paragraph: he chose texts for translation (Plutarch's) that shaped a whole community of reader-writers, including Montaigne himself.

Others were instrumental in the circulation and shaping of the *Essais* after publication. We have encountered Justus Lipsius, Paolo Sarpi, Martin Delrio, and Pierre Bayle—figures of different, often variable confessional hues, some anchored in one place (Sarpi, Delrio), some itinerant (Lipsius, Bayle)—performing such offices. These humanistic, scholastic, and clerical figures personified whole programmes of applied philosophical and religious study that tied texts to specific systems of instruction and interpretation, even outside the classrooms and lecture halls.

Other members of the European clergy we have met range from Charron, Baudius, Goulart, Querenghi, and Canini to the priests who recommended and supplied books to Sir Henry Slingsby and Jean Maillefer. Goulart was a major figure in the transmission of Seneca's and Plutarch's works to a general educated readership in northern Europe. Just as Goulart did for a reformed readership, Canini edited, compiled, and translated an extraordinary range of texts for a reformed Catholic readership.

But of course, as we have seen in this chapter, not only university teachers and ecclesiastical clerics were involved in this process. Learned professionals such as Rochemaillet, Pasquier, La Roche Flavin, and Bacon (see 2.7.9) also claimed prominent roles. Private tutors, secretaries, and intelligencers such as John Florio (like Bayle, a member of the international Protestant diaspora) and Girolamo Naselli had less prominent but still vital roles in teaching and translating texts outside the context of formal schooling. Florio taught modern languages via texts in aristocratic households, and went on to be secretary to a Queen, with important Italian contacts; Naselli was a secretary and intelligencer in the diplomatic world linking Ferrara and France.

Everywhere one looks in the world that first circulated copies of the *Essais*, knowledge and learning were being heavily mediated and corrected by scholars, clerics, professionals, and teachers battling over the linguistic, moral, political, and religious formation of both the educated, lay reader-writer and the vulgar consumer of knowledge. The encounter taken for granted until recently as the foundation of a literate, liberal society (to recall Philip Pullman from the 'General Introduction' to Volumes 1 and 2)—the encounter between the uniform, fixed, mass-produced, literary 'text' and the 'general' educated reader free to read and judge it in his or her own time and way—had not yet won its privileges.

In such circumstances, just how free could the elite literate person, reading and writing in private, be? Is it—to recall the question raised in the 'General Introduction'—the school genuinely *of* Montaigne, instituted by the private reader-writer's free and personal encounter with the *Essais*, or is it the school of clerics and humanists who edit, translate, and present an extravagant and unruly text for proper study? Is it the school of Lipsius, of de Thou, of Sarpi, of Goulart?

2.7.9 ENFRANCHISING THE READER-WRITER

These questions need to be considered in the context of a larger question. What was the outcome of this boom in learning and learned mediation, itself just one part of a larger explosion of printed and manuscript materials caused by the Reformation and its aftermaths? Throughout this study we have drawn on the diagnosis of Florio's brother-in-law, Samuel Daniel, published in poetic form with London 1603. He described how a 'presse of writings' threatened to overwhelm the educated nobility he served, and how the *Essayes* represented the answer. He expressed no doubt that it was the school *of* Montaigne, even if he and other humanists including Florio welcomed the author—in England—as part of the school of Philip Sidney, an analogous noble figure.

Two years later, in 1605, just such a 'presse' was listed in the printed catalogue of the Bodleian library, which we heard in 2.7.8 included a French, not an English copy of the *Essais*. In the same year, the independent investigator and career lawyer Francis Bacon reflected in disenchanted vein on the origins and fortunes of the revival of literary learning in divine and humane studies. In so doing, he conflated what are now more usually distinguished as the movements of the Reform and of humanism, and gave the revival an open-mindedly Protestant slant. As he says, 'when it pleased God', in the Reformation, 'to call the Church of Rome to account...At one and the same time, it was ordayned by the divine providence, that there should attend withall a renovation, and new spring of all other knowledges'—at which point he acknowledges the role of the Jesuits as Roman Catholic renovators of learning.[123]

Bacon identified three errors and vanities that had intervened amongst the studies of the learned professionals. One was the degeneracy of learning into which the

---

[123] Bacon, *The advancement of learning*, 37.

'Schoole-men' had fallen: 'their wits being shut up in the Cels of a few Authors (chiefely Aristotle their Dictator) as their persons were shut up in the Cells of Monasteries and Colledges'. Another was the 'facilitie of credite, and accepting or admitting thinges weakely authorized or warranted'. Just as 'choise and judgement' had not been used in (Catholic) ecclesiastical history, which too easily received and registered reports of miracles, so the same was true in natural history. Authors had been, again, accepted as 'Dictators', and Aristotle exempted from 'libertie of examination'.[124]

Like Charron, Bacon was concerned with enfranchising the judgement from professional literary enslavement to a few authors. Like Charron, but in a different way, he wanted to institutionalize the freed literate as a kind of officially (i.e. royally) sanctioned philosopher.

Bacon began with 'delicate learning, vaine Imaginations, vaine Altercations, and vaine affectations'. Martin Luther, having taken on the Roman Church all alone, and finding no aid in the opinions of his own time, had been 'enforced to awake all Antiquitie, and to call former times to his succors, to make a partie against the present time: so that the ancient Authors, both in Divinitie, and in Humanitie, which had long time slept in Libraries, began generally to be read and revolved'— 'revolved' in the sense of turned over, searched through, actively read. This led to 'more exquisite travaile in the languages originall', for the 'better understanding of those Authors, and the better advantage of pressing and applying their words'. What are now distinguished as the pragmatic and philological strands of humanism were, for Bacon, derived from the same source.[125]

According to Bacon, the religio-political opposition between the 'Schoole-men' and the reformers, the proponents of the new learning, was matched by a stylistic opposition, as the latter developed greater 'eloquence and varietie of discourse', in their efforts to win the vulgar sort over to the new religions. Bacon takes it for granted that this non-elite public was not composed of active and creative listeners, but of impressionable and volatile masses. He does not explicitly invoke the vernaculars, but his mention of the relationship between preachers and the people tells us that he has the general vulgarization of learning in mind.[126]

In Bacon's mind, then, the cleric Luther inaugurated a new era in which particular reader-writers, 'all alone', but not confined to cells in monasteries and colleges and to the *personae* that corresponded to those spaces, could read and revolve the ancient authors for their own purposes. They did so to make a party against the present time, to advocate radical reform, to win the elite public and the masses over to particular philosophical or confessional identities. This fundamental change in literary culture, which had its origins in Petrucci's late medieval period, but which arrived most emphatically with the Reformation, has been the background to the current study.

---

[124] Bacon, *The advancement of learning*, 24, 26, 27–8.
[125] Bacon, *The advancement of learning*, 21–2; Anthony Grafton and Lisa Jardine, *From humanism to the humanities: education and the liberal arts in fifteenth- and sixteenth-century Europe* (Cambridge, Mass. and London: Harvard University Press and Duckworth, 1986), 199.
[126] Bacon, *The advancement of learning*, 21–2.

Bacon was himself a product of this era—as, in different ways, were all the figures we have considered, including Montaigne, and including Gournay, who, in the context of her familiarity with ancient authors, made a remarkable judgement of the *Essais*, all alone in her remote province of France, and made a party against the Parisian literary establishment. As Cummings so helpfully insists, the Reformation and post-Reformation era did transform literary culture across the range from religious to secular studies, from acts of reading and writing such as official commentary on the Greek New Testament and Aristotle to unofficial annotation of vernacular bibles and the French Plutarch.[127]

Under the direction of learned doctors and ex-monks, some of whom were beginning personally to challenge traditional institutions of learning and to write and preach as authorities in new religious sects, words in books that had been sleeping in the libraries of universities and religious orders, or that had been monopolized by those institutions, came via print to be pressed and applied to present concerns by the educated and professional laity, the secular clergy, and—as the Roman Catholic counter-reform in turn developed—by the clerks regular of missionary orders such as the Jesuits.

Regrettably, in Bacon's eyes, this change gave rise not to a renewal of the liberal arts and philosophy and a profitable liberty of examination, but to an excessive focus on the style of speech and writing, at the expense of matter. Slavishness returned in a different guise. As in the case of the schoolmen, the reformed humanists shut their wits up in obsessive literary study of just a few authors—this time rhetoricians such as Cicero, Hermogenes, and Demosthenes. Erasmus features briefly as the excoriator of the slavish Ciceronians.[128]

A related story is told in the inverse, celebratory vein by means of the opening portrait of Jacques Lefèvre d'Étaples in the 1598 *Elogia* (Sainte-Marthe), while Montaigne in the opening to II 12 tells it in more dystopian style, with overt disapproval of Luther and the other *docteurs* who awakened the ancient authors in the context of religious controversy, and who usurped what in his mind were quite fantastic privileges to profess new truths. They were to blame for a situation in which each common individual could imagine themselves able to use their liberty of judgement to authorize their own approved versions of religious truth, just as each new church—of Geneva, of England, amongst others—established its own institutionalized truths, consisting of a sacred corpus of texts and accompanying doctrines, organs of censorship, and so forth. The freedom open to literate and even semi-literate people had got out of hand; it was dangerous and needed to be controlled, channelled.[129]

The reading and revolving, the citing and imitating, the critique and glossing of ancient and recent authors, beyond the cells of monasteries and colleges, often in the context of cross-confessional or politico-legal controversy, was indeed the intellectual hallmark of the age, especially after 1560. Not only this but, as Goulart was

---

[127] Cummings, *Literary culture*, 5–6.   [128] Bacon, *The advancement of learning*, 22.

[129] Sainte-Marthe, *Elogia*, sigs. A1r–2r; Maclean, *Scholarship, commerce, religion*, 7. See 1.4.2 in the present study. On the perception of this danger in early modern Engand, see the excellent discussion in Brayman Hackel, *Reading material*, 77–80.

aware (see 2.2.4), the way any person read and (re)wrote a particular text, whether as a private individual or as a commissioned corrector (or a mixture of both) could result in their being brought before a local or transnational tribunal of opinion, concerning the liberties they had taken in handling that particular text.

The learned, broadly Gallican culture of the French magistracy, which flourished from 1560–1630, and which shaped in different ways and to different degrees the work of de Thou, Pasquier, L'Estoile, La Roche Flavin, and Montaigne, is perhaps the best example in Europe of the link between the secularization of access to the ancient authors and the new wave of eloquent, controversial, and confessionalized learning described by Bacon in pejorative terms. The learned *parlementaire* or lawyer-scholar—often but not exclusively wedded to Gallican and *politique* positions—represented a powerful new, professional *persona* for the freed reader-writer.

However, it is implicit in Bacon's invocation of Luther as a scholastically trained monk reading and writing for his particular purposes, all alone, that in this period there was less of a hard and fast distinction between the professional scholar-commentator and what we have described throughout, following Petrucci, as the free literate—the unofficial, subjective reader-writer or private annotator. On the one hand, this was because, in the sixteenth century, the latter so often assumed, especially when appearing in print, the *persona* and authority of a professional such as the lawyer-scholar. The principal point made in this last chapter is that Montaigne was arguably unique—at least for major intellectual figures—in *not* doing this. I say 'arguably' because we saw in 2.1 that the *parlementaires* could still see the *conseiller* beneath Montaigne's seigneurially idle *persona*.

On the other hand, it was because the new kinds of 'official' interpreters such as Erasmus and Luther had themselves spoken in the first person, against the background of oppressive traditions, and encouraged their audience to react and act as particular reader-writers, while even commentators upon Aristotle read and wrote in very diverse, often personal ways.[130]

Similarly, there was no hard and fast distinction between the censors employed by an institution such as the Roman Catholic Church to read and rewrite, or expurgate literature, and the private judges such as Pasquier correcting in private as they read, on behalf of a community of legal scholars, then offering the corrections to the author for inclusion in the next edition.

At the same time, after 1560, the learned publishing boom, driven by the scholarly interpretation and mediation of texts, produced a 'presse of writings' that threatened to overwhelm the particular reader-writer using books for his or her own purposes, reducing him or her to slavish imitation or confusion.

It was, however, a positive example from the early part of this publishing boom, one that enfranchised rather than oppressed the particular reader-writer, which most immediately shaped the conception of the *Essais*. I refer to the publication

[130] Jean-Pierre Delville, *L'Europe de l'exégèse au XVIe siècle: interprétations de la parabole des ouvriers à la vigne, Matthieu 20, 1–16* (Louvain: Louvain University Press and Peeters, 2004), 594; Charles B. Schmitt, *Aristotle and the Renaissance* (Cambridge, Mass.; Harvard University Press, 1983). My thanks to David Lines for the last point.

454	*The School of Montaigne: Vol. 2*	*2.7.9*

between 1559 and 1572 of the French Plutarch, itself part of a wider boom in editions and translations in all languages of Plutarch and, to a lesser extent, the associated ancient author Seneca.[131]

As we heard in 1.6.10 and 1.7.2, the translator Amyot, Bishop of Auxerre, was—for Montaigne—the converse of Luther, the Catholic Luther of secular studies. The Gascon's description of the actions and relations to which the performance and publication of the translation of Plutarch gave rise is the most important passage in the *Essais* for this study.

In that passage, Montaigne recalls how Amyot's gift to the French nation facilitated the secular conversation of a community of non-scholarly, non-professional, elite reader-writers in the way that a breviary facilitated the religious conversation of the clergy—'sa mercy nous osons à cett'heure et parler et escrire'. For the *dames* and *gentilhommes* in this readership, to read this book was not just to hear it or see it, but to be emboldened to speak and to write, to claim intellectual sovereignty over the masters of arts in the schools. To translate, gestate, and apply Plutarch and Seneca in French was to revive antique and natural liberties of judgement, liberties exercised in a sphere of private speech and writing, along with noble values clustered around the central quality of *franchise*.[132]

Montaigne's project, in turn, depended on the reading and revolving of Amyot and the Latin Seneca, and on prior uses of Estienne's edition of Sextus Empiricus, in order to reply in non-controversial mode to Luther and other reformers. Then, in a further turn of events, Gournay—a *dame*—came across a copy of the *Essais* in Picardy, formed a remarkably prescient private judgement of the text, challenged the author's scholarly detractors, and built a literary career in the capital upon it. How one read and described the *Essais*—and wrote on the back of that reading— was to be a touchstone of one's claim to philosophical wisdom. Charron did something analogous in the very different circumstances of a provincial career as a *chanoine*.

However, we should not, with the hindsight of posterity, or with Gournay's foresight, over-estimate the prominence of the *Essais* in the literary culture of the first decades after their initial publication. As Gournay says, in many respects they met with a 'cold reception'—at least if one expected a Pantagruelian welcome. Self-avowedly dependent on classical texts, and on Amyot's Plutarch in particular, they were one amongst many projects of independent investigation, in which ancient and other authors were revolved in order to make party, in one sense or another, against the present time.

Montaigne's neighbours in the southwest, Foix-Candale and Duplessis-Mornay, were busy in their private studies building new philosophies and theologies from ancient texts (1.4.3). His contemporary Pasquier's project awakened archival documents and chronicles in the royal and other libraries to make a party against

---

[131] USTC lists 1172 editions (691 Plutarch; 481 Seneca—including Seneca the rhetorician) of the works of these authors published between 1459 and 1600. Between 1559 and 1572, 120 editions primarily containing works by Plutarch, and 34 primarily containing works by either Seneca, were published.

[132] II 4, NP382/BVH Paris 1595, p. 231/S408.

contemporary notions of the French nation and church.[133] The Genevan preacher Simon Goulart was lauded in the oration delivered at his funeral for being the most prolific polyhistor of his age, for having 'illustrated' and 'communicated' so many Greek, Latin, and French authors to his people—including, again, Seneca and Plutarch.[134]

As the revival of learning spread to the vernaculars, these were the sorts of extra-mural enterprises on the part of the educated laity and clergy that defined the post-Reformation intellectual age and that Bacon wanted to reorganize to better ends and to incorporate into a new, institutionalized structure erected by the royal state. As he was advocating this approach, the Roman Church was attempting to institutionalize—unsuccessfully—the production of a comprehensively rewritten (expurgated) literature for a Catholic readership across Europe. Geneva made a similar attempt on a smaller scale, through figures such as Goulart. States such as Venice were attempting to control the flow of information, sometimes in conjunction with the Roman Catholic Church, sometimes in opposition to it.

Across an increasingly confessionalized Europe, temporal and ecclesiastical authorities were setting up multiple, local forms of regulation to control the market in humane and divine knowledge and to produce and protect their own versions of scriptural, patristic, and philosophical, historical truth. Even as books disseminated knowledge, controls of various kinds—physical and paratextual—were placed on their circulation and use.[135]

This was going on at all levels, from towns to empires. But, as we have already heard, it was also going on at the level of the 'individual', the freed literate who in clerical (Luther, Charron) and professional (Pasquier, La Roche Flavin) incarnations was 'officially' assuming powers of judgement and censorship in reading and rewriting texts, in reforming traditional institutions and bodies of knowledge. Particular 'judges' from Montaigne's regrettably emancipated, semi-literate *vulgaire* to lawyers such as de Thou and Bacon were issuing their own privileges, instituting their own versions of truth, their own regulatory structures for sacred and profane discourse. When they entered public discourse, they did not do so in their guises as private reader-writers with no office or authority; they assumed—as the theologian-captain Duplessis-Mornay did—an authoritative *persona* (the whole force of Montaigne's 'Au lecteur' lies in this perception) and a public office of instruction.

In so doing, they were dramatically intensifying an intellectual, commercial, and cultural battle over the dissemination of literate skills and knowledge, and the accompanying capacity to exercise private and public liberties of judgement in matters of divine and secular doctrine. The battle had its roots in the twelfth

[133] Étienne Pasquier, *Les recherches de la France*, eds. Marie-Madeleine Fragonard and François Roudaut (Paris: H. Champion, 1996).

[134] Huchard, *D'encre et de sang*, 91.

[135] Maclean, *Scholarship, commerce, religion*, 134–70, for this and the previous paragraph. On the physical and paratextual attempts to control the uses of books in early modern England, see Brayman Hackel, *Reading material*, chapter 3.

century, but had originated most particularly in new developments of the late fourteenth and early fifteenth centuries.

In the rest of this final chapter I shall argue that this battle, and its distant origins, is both the contemporary European context and the deep historical background for the composition and circulation of the *Essais*, which themselves invent a new mode of philosophy based in the private liberty of judgement of a particular individual who is not a professional scholar, but a private gentleman reader-writer.[136]

The late fourteenth and early fifteenth centuries saw clerics and humanists collaborating as never before with elite lay readers to facilitate more widespread private ownership and reading of biblical and classical texts—the formation of Federico da Montefeltro's library was one highly prestigious outcome of this process. The particular event of most interest relative to the history of the *Essais* occurred in the 1430s: the composition (*c.*1434–6) of a book (*Scientia Libri creaturarum*) by a theologian in the faculty at Toulouse (Raimond Sebond), which gave the lay Latin readership a quick, private path from knowledge of the book of human nature to knowledge of God.

By the mid-sixteenth century Sebond's book had been translated by Jean Martin and printed as a private devotional manual for *gentilshommes* and *dames*. It was playing a role in the Catholic recuperation of Augustinian thought, and in the religious polemics of the period—as Bunel's gift of a copy to Pierre Eyquem and the Roman Catholic prohibition of Sebond's preface both testify. Montaigne used it, in apologetic vein, to undermine all public professions of new, dogmatic truths.[137]

For the battle to which I refer had in the meantime joined in earnest in the era of Luther, Erasmus, and the early Reformation. It would continue in other forms, including what is now called *libertinage érudit*, into the pre-Enlightenment era of John Milton and John Locke, Charles Sorel, and Pierre Bayle. From the early 1560s, which saw the beginning of Montaigne's literary career, to the 1630s, which saw his work published in Venice as the scholarly book market collapsed, it coincided with a period of militant confessionalization, institutionalized censorship, and religious war across Europe.[138]

It was a battle, in short, over the enfranchisement of the educated elite's and the semi-literate *vulgaire*'s judgement in reading the two books bequeathed by God to man: the Book of scriptures and the Book of nature. The protagonists variously sought to regulate, to facilitate, and to profit from the growing activity of private book acquisition and reading and writing, and of wider knowledge dissemination. Of course, the lion's share of the provision—depending on the particular regulatory environment—consisted of scriptural and devotional texts for private or casual use by individuals and families. But around this provision other kinds of publications aimed to shape communities of reader-writers defined by their struggles against 'other', heretical, unreformed, or otherwise antagonistic groups.

---

[136] Ian Maclean, *Montaigne philosophe* (Paris: Presses Universitaires de France, 1996).
[137] NP1554–5.   [138] Maclean, *Scholarship, commerce, religion*.

The principal weapon in the lower plain of the battle, especially from the perspective of the markets in France and the Low Countries, was the polemical *libelle* or pamphlet, the partisan memorial or collection of memorials of the conflicts. The principal weapon or commodity in the higher plane of the battle was the learned book (as very broadly defined in 2.7.8). In this more learned arena, the principal protagonists were the printers and publisher-booksellers, and the clerical and professional intellectuals who both supplied most of the content for the book trade and regulated its output on behalf of lay publics.

We have seen this battle being waged in different ways and contexts everywhere in this study. In this chapter alone we have encountered the examples of Camus' letter to Achante (2.7.3), La Roche Flavin's ill-fated one-book enfranchisement of the perfect magistrate (2.7.5), and of course Charron's audacious bid completely to separate divine and human wisdom, to separate a reading of the Book of scripture for all (*Les trois veritez*, 1593 and 1595) and a reading of the Book of nature (*De la sagesse*, 1601 and 1604) for a confined elite—both in the vernacular (2.7.5).

We have seen it being waged in institutional and commercial contexts in 1.7 (Rome) and 2.2 (Geneva), and in paratextual and epitextual contexts such as Gournay's 'Preface', Montaigne's apology for Sebond, and the bookseller William London's prefatory attempt to shape the reading and morals of his gentle clientele.

In Florio's dedication 'To the curteous Reader' it becomes a dialogue. One voice speaks for university scholars who would maintain their 'privilege of preheminence' and confine learning (including divine learning) to the ancient languages. The other voice—Florio's—speaks on behalf of translators and interpreters who would not have 'praying and preaching in an unknowne tongue', whose office it is to make learning more common by borrowing, collecting, imitating, translating—with acknowledgement, in good faith, and not by stealth. He is speaking partly on behalf of his female patronesses, who had limited access to Latin learning, and partly on behalf of a broader audience of free literates without Latin and modern foreign languages.[139]

The vocabulary used, then, was one of offices and liberties; protagonists sought to define the skills and qualities, the privileges and responsibilities, of the secular and Christian *personae* available to elite pursuers of knowledge, and commercially to consolidate and exploit the new publics of private reader-writers forming their own personal, selected libraries.[140]

It included disputes over the relationship between the spheres of divine and human knowledge. It included struggles to defeat the disputatiousness and sectarianism of opponents variously identified as controversialists, heretics, and pedants and to shape—through official mediation and persuasion—the beliefs and conduct of the credulous 'vulgar sort'. At the same time, these very categories ('pedant', 'vulgar sort', and so forth) were in the course of being distinguished from the

[139] SCETI London 1603, p. A5r.
[140] Again, William London's preface is an excellent example.

educated, judgemental elite—both official (censors) and unofficial (clerics and critics)—in various competing ways.

A significant part of the controversy concerned the distinction between types of knowledge that needed to be confined to this elite, because too strong or outspoken, and types of knowledge that were safe for broader circulation:

> Why but all would not be knowne of all. No nor can: much more we know not than we know: all know something, none know all…Why, but it is not wel Divinitie should be a childes or olde wives, a coblers, or clothiers tale or table-talke. There is use, and abuse: use none too much: abuse none too little.[141]

Charron, his supporters, and his detractors, for example, were all clear that his was a book only for 'esprits forts', and not for the *vulgaire*, who were not equipped to digest it.[142]

Pace Bacon and Florio, this was not in the higher plane a monolithic confrontation between two clearly demarcated sides (reformed humanists and schoolmen), but a matter of myriad skirmishes in different fields, with many different kinds of position taken up in particular literary nexuses. Liberties of judgement could on the one hand be held to derive legitimately from the exercise of various offices, or on the other hand redescribed as vicious licences and attributed to the passions and interests of individuals—including women such as Gournay and men such as La Roche Flavin—with no such legitimacy. This is why it is so interesting that Montaigne claims such liberties as a particular individual who—far from conquering or hiding—*publicizes* his subjection to passions.

As we have seen, the battle involved the formation of competing institutions of knowledge provision, such as the reformed churches and their ministries, the courts and courtly academies and their resident philosophers, the lawcourts and their unofficial historians and antiquarians, the households of the bourgeoisie and aristocracy, and their private tutors. The result was a series of overlapping sites and spaces for practical philosophical pursuits, as for natural philosophical pursuits: homes and households, courts and academies, legal institutions and *parlements*, lecture halls and universities, seminaries and churches. *Personae* varied accordingly, along social and gender lines; Florio's well-born women were participants in household and court pursuits, but not in formal university learning.[143]

This variety has been reflected in *The School of Montaigne*, where we have traversed spaces as varied as the cabinet of a merchant's country house outside Rheims, the private office of a lawyer in The Hague, the cabinet of a Parisian *parlementaire*, the study of a Genevan pastor, the cell of a Servite friar, the courtly

[141] SCETI London 1603, p. A5r.

[142] Cavaillé, 'Pierre Charron', 33–5. There is a longer version of this article online: Jean-Pierre Cavaillé, 'Pierre Charron, "disciple" de Montaigne et "patriarche des prétendus esprits forts"', (2009), <http://dossiersgrihl.revues.org/280>, accessed 22 January 2013.

[143] See Lorraine Daston and Katharine Park (eds.), *The Cambridge history of science volume 3: Early modern science* (Cambridge: Cambridge University Press, 2006), 'Part II: *Personae* and sites of natural knowledge'. David A. Lines, *Aristotle's 'Ethics' in the Italian Renaissance (ca. 1300–1650): the universities and the problem of moral education* (Leiden: Brill, 2002), 387–92.

households of the English nobility, the grand library of an Italian Duke, the Accademia dei Ricovrati, and the lecture halls of the university of Padua.

Montaigne himself consistently locates the writing, reading, and rewriting of his book in private cabinets, libraries, and chambers, where the offices fulfilled are not the named ones of a lawyer-historian such as Bacon or a university scholar such as Lipsius, but the unnamed ones of a well-born human being reviewing his or her fantasies and conversing with himself or herself and others. Montaigne was reading and writing the book of human nature—his own, particular nature—in a new and distinctively free way, but giving up other liberties of judgement in order to do so.

2.7.10 THE *ESSAIS* BENEATH THE BATTLE

Montaigne's book has recently been rediscovered as a kind of self-help manual that is relevant to our times.[144] This is all the more remarkable once we consider just how profoundly the kind of self-help it offered, and the literary and publishing strategies it used, were embedded in the circumstances and conditions of the late sixteenth century.

During the period 1580–1600, it became clear to many, including Montaigne, Bacon, and Charron, that the mind of the elite judge needed regulated enfranchisement from the literary culture of 'verbal contestation', from the slavish and contentious modes of reading and writing, inventing and judging, purveyed by authors and their commentators with increasing intensity since the Lutheran Reformation. All three, in different ways, contested the trend that had made theology and theological modes of thinking pervasive across the other disciplines.[145] All three contended that reading and writing needed to give rise to—index—something other than the making of literary/verbal elegancies and controversies.

Bacon wrote the *Advancement* as a civil servant who would go on to higher offices of state, and he addressed his book to important public figures with an official or professional interest in learning. His *œuvre* as a whole envisioned a state reform of learning, in which the offices of philosophers would be less like those of professional university grammarians or theologians and more like those of royal judges such as himself.[146] Only a few state officials, in other words, would be allowed to judge the invented or collected materials. At the end of his work he self-consciously acknowledges the privilege or liberty of judgement he has taken,

[144] Sarah Bakewell, *How to live: or a life of Montaigne in one question and twenty attempts at an answer* (London: Chatto & Windus, 2010); Saul Frampton, *When I am playing with my cat, how do I know she is not playing with me?: Montaigne and being in touch with life* (London: Faber and Faber, 2011). This is the case not only in Anglo-American letters but also, for example, in Belgium. See Ann Meskens, *Eindelijk buiten: filosofische stadswandelingen* (Rotterdam: Lemniscaat, 2007). My thanks to Jacomien Prins.

[145] Maclean, *Scholarship, commerce, religion*, 6–8.

[146] Bacon, *The advancement of learning*, xxxi, xxxviii; Julian Martin, 'Natural philosophy and its public concerns', in Pumfrey, Slawinski, and Rossi (eds.), *Science, culture and popular belief in Renaissance Europe*, 100–18, 103, 112–13.

in going beyond what is 'commonly received', to offer his 'opinions naked and unarmed, not seeking to preoccupate the libertie of [other] mens judgements by confutations'.[147]

It is precisely the usurpation (as Montaigne sees it)—especially through the handpress—of such privileges to profess and rearrange the truth that is contested by the *Essais* on a number of levels, and that is seen by their author as a principal source of the ills of the age. For the embattled terrain described above also shaped his book, both before and after first publication; or, rather, it was shaped as a book to survive and thrive on its own terms in such an environment.

Where Luther discovered his religious life, Montaigne discovered his leisurely, noble life as a life in reading and writing. The *Essais* provide a noble touchstone, a private philosophical *persona* and set of private unnamed offices, for the particular reader-writer we have seen incarnated in a whole series of figures from Gournay and Charron to Clifford and Van Veen. This is the person who, in the wake of the Lutheran and educational revolutions and the invention of the handpress, is, on the one hand, newly free to investigate all areas of humane and divine learning for themselves, to bring their own experience and purposes to the task, and, on the other hand, conscious of the 'presse of writings' produced by professional inter-preters and polemicists, of the risk of controversy, of the institutional constraints placed by various regulatory authorities on their liberty and internalized by their own patiency.

This was a complex and perilous situation to be in. The two principal and rival reader-writers of Montaigne's early school—Charron and Gournay—incarnate the particular reader-writer, and enact his/her troubled enfranchisement, in two very different, gendered ways. But both lead to bitter public controversies with which they are associated right up to Bayle's time.

The whole point of this study has been to insist that instead of considering them and other reader-writers in a separate sphere of more or less disappointing 'recep-tions', we consider them as participants with the author in the history of the book as an index of the exercise of liberty of judgement, participants who help to reveal how the book acted as such in the circumstances of its own time. These circum-stances centrally include the role of books and of reading and writing in the forma-tion of distinct religio-political and professional communities of 'freed' literates—as we saw on our travels with the *Essais* through Catholic Rome, *politique* Paris, and Calvinist Geneva.

The authorial *persona* to be inferred from the *Essais*, from this perspective, is one that is conscious of writing in a culture of controversy and correction, piracy and appropriation, and that aims to make the book safe for circulation across different confessional publics. The author achieves both aims by insinuating that he, his book, and potentially the readers and rewriters of his book, are free—partly by luck, partly by nature—of many of the conditions, including the *marque* of the theologian or the jurist, that threaten to confine them in servitude.

---

[147] Bacon, *The advancement of learning*, 192.

The *Essais* are above—or, better, beneath—the battle, the battle Montaigne saw going on not only around the Bible and its interpreters, the law and its interpreters, but around La Boétie's *De la servitude volontaire*, around Sebond, around manuscripts of Seneca in the Vatican library, and around applications of Senecan texts in printed works of controversy. His claim is that he and his publisher are not hard-selling 'interested' forms of scholarly knowledge to gullible publics in particular confessional markets; he is giving them something different, more 'natural'. And he is not just adding material to sell more books; he genuinely gives his public a new work with each new edition.

At the same time, Montaigne is a vernacular author (with excellent Latin) who subtly steals into the learned territories occupied by Latin scholarship and professional philosophers, lawyers, and theologians, and claims them back for the genuinely free literate, the man or woman who is reading and writing—and judging—in private, for themselves and their friends and families. As we saw in 1.4 and 1.5, and also in this chapter (2.7.3) in relation to III 2 and the Jesuit Auger, the *Essais* engage in a muted and internalized dialogue with various professional interpreters and mediators, especially the *docteurs* and the *robins*, the clerics and the censors.

But they purport to do so on behalf of an audience of particular reader-writers who interact in the private forum of an open and free *conférence* conducted in non-scholarly, non-confessional terms. The dialogue perhaps becomes most explicit in the final chapter: III 13. The opening pages mercilessly critique the increasing proliferation of scholarly mediations—glosses, commentaries, opinions, controversies—in law and theology, before offering the fruits of a different type of unmediated, unprofessional study: practical self-study.[148]

However, we should be careful not to idealize Montaigne's achievements in retrospect, to congratulate him for freedoms from ethnocentric and other prejudices that are our own most cherished liberties, to turn him into some kind of proto-liberal.[149] We should not ignore the particular cultural, religious, and political conditions of his first enfranchisement in print. His reading and his modes of reasoning do depend on the canons and the commentary of humanist teachers and scholastic philosophers. His liberty of judgement is presented as 'natural', but it is also in practice a noble privilege or immunity to be granted and renewed on specific occasions by individual and institutional authorities with whom he and his book come into contact. It cannot in the social conditions of late sixteenth century France be claimed as some kind of universal right and is not intended to be abducted by others—as La Boétie's work was—as a licence publicly to advocate 'reform' of legitimate royal and Roman Catholic authorities.[150]

---

[148] III 13, NP1111–19/BVH Paris 1595, bk. III, pp. 193–9/S1207–17.

[149] For a book that does this in a very persuasive way, see David Lewis Schaefer, *The political philosophy of Montaigne* (Ithaca: Cornell University Press, 1990). For a salutary correction of the standard liberal interpretation of one of Montaigne's most famous chapters, see David Quint, 'A reconsideration of Montaigne's *Des cannibales*', in Karen Ordahl Kupperman (ed.), *America in European consciousness, 1493–1750* (Chapel Hill: Institute of Early American History and Culture, Williamsburg, Virginia, 1995), 166–92.

[150] George Hoffmann, 'Sincérité', *Dictionnaire*, 920–2, 922.

The well-born reader-writer is privately enfranchised, but in the context of a willing servitude to the public administrations and doctrines of the sovereign church and state—*legalité et liberté*. We saw this happen in the register of Montaigne's stay in Rome in 1581 (1.7), and in III 9 we heard him describe— more resentfully—how it works in relation to the Reformed authorities in power in his own neighbourhood (1.6.1). We also see it happening in a daring chapter such as III 2, which, even as it puts on the public record the reasons why Montaigne cannot and does not desire to 'reform' himself, stops short of openly challenging the Roman Catholic doctrine of repentance. The only province over which the chapter and the *Essais* claim sovereignty is the author's own secular self-knowledge, in which his own conscience and judgement is king.

The *Essais*, in other words, are very much a product of a historical moment when states and churches across Europe were attempting to control—largely by controlling what was being read, said, and written—the public exercise of liberty of judgement in contemporary political and religious matters. From Bayle's perspective, Montaigne's enfranchisement of the individual subject of knowledge, his enactment of the acquisition of freedom, is in many ways much more private and conservative than Luther's, de Thou's, Gournay's, Charron's, Bacon's, or Spinoza's. There is no clarion call for *libertas philosophandi* (quite the opposite). Insofar as such a call was heard in the seventeenth century, it was via Montaigne's posthumous association with the more scandalous *œuvres* of Gournay and Charron.[151]

Montaigne shows the average, elite reader-writer how to exercise liberty of judgement as a matter of natural nobility, without claiming philosophical 'rights' or 'privileges' in the manner of those self-styled public intellectuals named above. He does not question the Council of Trent's re-affirmation of the Roman Catholic Church's absolute authority over the transmission of Christian doctrine, which is to be effected by priests orally in a sanctified place, and not by parishioners in their own scriptural reading and writing, or psalm-singing in random private and public spaces. This puts him at odds with Gallicans in France. He sees the need for regulation of 'everyday chroniclers and interpreters' ('interpretes et controlleurs ordinaires') of the signs of God's design in events, in the Book of nature.[152]

Montaigne's strict adherence to post-Tridentine injunctions against the Lutheran enfranchisement of the lay reader-writer of biblical texts is the flipside of his resistance to attempts to regulate non-theological, humane discourse. And if he has censored his own liberty of judgement in matters of revealed religious doctrine, he has also—much more than contemporaries such as Pasquier, de Thou, and L'Estoile—exercised self-censorship in controversial matters of contemporary politics and history, resisting his friends' exhortations that he write potentially contentious memoirs. He nowhere explicitly mentions or condemns the St Bartholomew

---

[151] On Gournay's role in shaping the *Essais* as reading for those described as 'libertins', see G. Dotoli, 'Montaigne et les libertins via Mlle de Gournay', *Journal of Medieval and Renaissance Studies*, 25 (1995), 381–405; Giovanna Devinceno, 'Marie de Gournay: une théologie libertine', *Montaigne Studies*, 19 (2007), 83–94.

[152] I 31, NP221/BVH Paris 1595, p. 127/S242.

Day's massacre. For reasons explored in 1.6.13, he suppresses the text of his great friend's treatise on *liberté*.

2.7.11 HOW CAN A BOOK BE FREE FROM SERVITUDE?

These conditions aside, how exactly does *the book* enact its freedom from servitude? We must constantly recall the fact that when we attribute agency to 'Montaigne' or 'the author' in this final chapter we are referring to an effect of a book in the hands of an early modern reader-writer such as Gournay or Florio.

A modern critic such as Philip Pullman, with whom we started in the 'General Introduction' to Volumes 1 and 2, might simply answer that it does so by being a work of literature, not an instruction manual or a textbook. But the modern category of 'literature', and the established privileges that come with it, were not available to Montaigne and his contemporaries. Let us express a similar answer in less anachronistic terms.

Montaigne's book clearly does not enact freedom from servitude in the manner of Charron's book, as a matter of a Stoic freedom from passion or vice. Nor does it work in the manner of Bacon's, as a blueprint for an institutionalized advancement of learning via intellectual enfranchisement from errors, vanities, and idols. These are more straightforwardly learned, programmatic books—books attributable to *personae* who profess learning, using art or method. Montaigne ostentatiously does not follow the order of learned knowledge or pursue its goal of moral and political reform—he is about *mélange* not *regularité*.[153]

It is precisely in this way that freedom from servitude is enacted; the text is clearly the product of a free, unregulated, not to say chaotic process of reading and writing, of invention and judgement. The book describes a distinct, natural, unmediated kind of literary nexus in which the relationship between the nobly free literate, the particular qualities of his or her person, and the book with which he or she is consubstantial purports to force other kinds of expert mediation and authoritative knowledge, the printer-publishers and patrons who promote them, and the controversies and partisanship they lead to, into the background.

The typical material index of such a nexus, as I have argued throughout, is the converse of the scholarly, Latin, printed book: the personally compiled manuscript *libro-registro*—a centuries-old form of vernacular writing—which blends various, unordered, day-by-day readings (copies of extracted texts) with records of personal experiences and family events. The *Essais* pose as a personal *registre* dressed up for public consumption with learning—which means that they do engage, in self-consciously amateur style, with the world of Latin scholarship. Each chapter (such as III 13), each individual *essai de Michel de Montaigne* is a test of the personal agency of the author using written extracts from books and written records of personal and vicarious experiences. In the context of a broad dissemination in print, rather than a familial dissemination in manuscript, the consubstantiality of book and

---

[153] As Lancre notes (Millet 201). See also Sorel, *La bibliotheque françoise*, sig. D2r.

person is a way of controlling the book's use on its travels by tightly identifying its effects with the effects of the private, non-official *persona* of their author.

The effects in question are characteristically those that divert the private reader-writer from the applied, professional, controversial uses of learning that dominated contemporary literary culture. For the *Essais* take the form of a book, as Marie de Gournay says, that is both uncorrected and naturally difficult to correct, difficult to reduce to methodical order, difficult to press pragmatically into service of the trades and offices of our public lives, of the confessional and clerical groups who dominated the production and regulation both of polemical and of learned books.[154]

It has neither been corrected through editions by the author and his friends—like Charron's and de Thou's books—nor expurgated by censors. It is neither surrounded by paratexts nor methodically partitioned (like, again, *De la sagesse*, or Venice 1633) for the lazy reader (even if it is eventually tamed somewhat by Gournay herself). It does not present itself as an official attempt systematically to 'fashion' man or his discourse, in pedagogical or philosophical terms. It is not tied to the systems of instruction and interpretation of the clerics, the *docteurs* and the humanists. Its writing is an image of the idioms and rhythms of the author's Gascon speech, not of someone else's—for example, Pasquier's—rules for proper grammar and orthography. Its quotations from ancient and modern authors are not cited as authorities but are freely incorporated.

The book has been 'authored', in fact, neither by Montaigne's patrons and friends nor by the authoritative sources served up by publishers and shelved in his library, but by the interplay between the author's fantasy and judgement, and by chance ('Fortune'). And this library, which he describes for us both as a loose catalogue of examined authors and as a space in his household, is not conceived as an arsenal of weapons for entering public controversy, for making a party against the present time. It is a casual aid to present self-study that comprises a safe retreat into antiquity in the midst of rural Périgord.

In turn, in users' hands, Montaigne's book will occupy the corner of a library, or a lady's cabinet, where it will be frequented intensively as part of daily conversation, personal reading and writing. Even when confronted with the lengthy personal discourses and extended chapters added in 1588, the reader will let the work run, and not seek to correct or abridge it.

However, this design—as I have already indicated—could look like something of a pose. It may have presented itself as a naive, unscholarly book that naturally slipped beneath the radar of the correctors, the learned doctors, the censors, and the pirates who were engaged in confessional and commercial battle. But it was clear—to Florio, for example—that the author of this book was learned, that he was canny about the book trade, and that he worked very hard to control the circulation and form of his work between *c.*1571, when he began composing his text, and 1592, when he died as he was preparing the next edition. By the time the 1588

---

[154] Millet 120.

and 1595 editions come out, it was clear that 1580 only feigned to be like 'les éditions à l'essai' that Simonin identified.[155]

The author has, in fact, assiduously corrected his text, especially its punctuation; he has included paratexts (absorbed in the main text) to ensure its safe passage; he has worked closely with a publisher-bookseller to use the privilege system to protect their joint enterprise and sell successive, amplified editions of the same work. And he has addressed a Parisian and international readership well beyond the local circles of friends and family he claimed to be addressing.

Indeed, as the book travels further afield, the author intensifies, through editions, his efforts artificially to secure the indexical relationship between this free-thinking, free-speaking book and this particular, well-born person 'Michel de Montaigne' received as someone of good faith and of 'frank' and 'free' qualities by 'honest' people in different places.

At various points from the mid-1580s until his death, surveying the *durée* of his adult life and of his book, a *durée* dominated by the violence and asperities of the religious wars, he claims in his text that he and his book have, luckily, been received in the right spirit by friend and potential foe; his and his book's *legalité et liberté* and *franchise* have been universally granted. He and his book have escaped official censure and adverse judgements, avoided capture and acts of piracy; he and his book have survived whole, retained their original integrity and freedom, without corrections or *repentirs*. He claims to have had success in this nobly hazardous action with a due and ironic sense of his own vanity, and of his debts to God, to Fortune and to his origins in a race of well-born individuals.

Of course, as we have seen, the book was in the event corrected and censored in various locations, by various reader-writers, official and unofficial. Lipsius could have promoted publication of the book in the Low Countries, but did not (2.2.1). Maillefer did not let III 5 run freely but exercised a form of private censorship (2.5.6). Neverthless, the *Essais* proved in the long-term of posterity to be the most captivating and enduring of a vast field of early modern book-indexes of the regulated enfranchisement of the reader-writer in the age of confessionalization—more so even than Charron's or Bacon's.

This was the case, as we have seen, even by the time of Bayle, who, more than modern literary critics, equated Montaigne's acquisition of freedom with the history of a book that, despite taking noteworthy intellectual and moral liberties, was published without significant problems, in an increasingly intolerant Roman Catholic world, for nearly a hundred years (1580–1676). And the *persona* of the author was ultimately more enduring in appeal—as it was for Bayle himself—than that of Charron's Stoic *sage*, or of Bacon's royal naturalist in civic office. The appeal was that of a particular well-born person with a natural privilege or liberty of judgement that is exercised below the confessional and commercial fray of the late Renaissance world of learning, in miscellaneous, non-dogmatic writing.

Let us be clear. This is to start from the premise neither that the *Essais* were the principal cause of a democratic liberation of the 'common reader' in early modern

[155] Simonin, *L'encre & la lumière*, 727–45 ('Poétiques des éditions "a l'essai" au XVIᵉ siècle').

Europe nor that all the reader-writers considered were enfranchised, or enfranchised in the same way, with the same outcomes. The category of free literates or, more accurately, of instances of advanced literate activity outside formal and professional nexuses of study and writing, covers an extraordinary diversity of situations mostly confined to the mercantile, professional, and gentle elites—though we should not forget cases such as that of Menocchio (see 2.7.2).

The divergence between the two most important early members of Montaigne's school, Gournay and Charron, is, again, a good indicator of this. From the anthropological perspective adopted here, literacy per se is a technology. All depends on the specific nexus of use and of transmission. Particular forms of literacy—including humanistic forms—may be described as emancipatory or oppressive depending on historical conditions, depending on gender, status, ideology. It may once have seemed clear that a fifteenth-century education in the liberal arts opened 'vistas of intellectual and spiritual freedom', but one classic study has influentially argued that it in fact fostered 'a properly docile attitude towards authority'.[156] It may once have seemed clear that the moment of Luther and Tyndale liberated the lay reader of the Bible, but there are historians who would tell us that the reader was in fact imprisoned.[157]

Montaigne might have agreed on both counts. For him, the most obvious outcomes of the introduction and diffusion of writing and the arts as public tools of administration and acculturation, along with learned lawyers and physicians, in both European and New World localities, was the corruption of customary liberties and natural health. But he clearly did not believe that the discerning consumer of the products of the handpress and the private keeper of writings was completely lost. Natural free-thinking was still possible.[158] Otherwise, the moment of the publication of Amyot's French Plutarch would not have assumed such great significance in his milieu.[159] Montaigne follows Amyot in claiming back the tools of writing—including the handpress—for the well-born individual concerned in private to preserve health of body-and-soul and liberty of judgement in corrupt and sick times.

If he did write the passage at the end of II 17, it is evidence he saw and publicly authorized—along with Justus Lipsius—Gournay's *jugement* of his first *Essais* as a remarkable instance of this. At the same time, as we heard in 2.7.10, his own *franchise* is privately granted to him, as a privilege or immunity fit for a gentleman of his quality, by institutional authorities such as the French crown, the Papacy, and by individual authorities like the prince of the European republic of humanistic letters, Lipsius. And when others try to claim it in different circumstances and guises—an obscure gentlewoman such as Gournay (1.6.4, 1.6.6), an unknown

---

[156] Grafton and Jardine, *From humanism to the humanities*, xii, xiv.

[157] James Simpson, *Burning to read: English fundamentalism and its Reformation opponents* (Cambridge, Mass.: Belknap Press of Harvard University Press, 2007).

[158] See Almquist, 'Examining the evidence: Montaigne in the *Registres secrets du Parlement de Bordeaux*'; Scholar, *Montaigne and the art of free-thinking*; Green, *Montaigne and the Life of Freedom*.

[159] The type of significance claimed by Montaigne for Amyot's Plutarch is analogous to that claimed for Amelot's Tacitus in Soll, *Publishing the Prince*.

théologal from the provinces such as Charron (2.7.5), a secular canon such as Flavio Querenghi (2.2.11)—their claim is disputed or disputable.

Much work had to be done in the late nineteenth and the twentieth centuries to refashion his book as an index in turn of the modern reader-writer's enfranchisement, so that a football player from California such as Huggins (2.6.6) could get modern individuality via the reading of a single text. In Villey's hands, at a moment—like our own—when the humanities were under threat, Montaigne's work enacted the schooling of a distinctively modern, self-conscious, critical reader. The 'reader' in question was at one and the same time a historical agent called Michel de Montaigne who authored the book, and a model student of idealist philosophy and literature at the contemporary École Normale Supérieure.

A majority of the influential scholars, translators, and editors who followed Villey, whether they explicitly departed from his work or not, were likewise writing *Essais* on the making of a self-critical reader, or finding such a reader by means of the *Essais*. Their work, their image of Montaigne, was likewise shaped by modern idealist philosophy and critiques of modern idealist philosophy—right up to the work of Greenblatt (see 2.6.10).

On the one hand, this tends to suggest the existence of yet another distinct artefact—Villey's *Essais*—made in the twentieth century on the model of the Bordeaux copy (or what it indicates about the genesis of the work), and multiply reproduced and utilized in various guises from Frame's translation to Greenblatt's *Renaissance Self-Fashioning*. Across the two volumes of this study we have analysed a whole series of such artefacts—editions and copies—that might appear to disperse the *Essais*' literary legacy in postmodern fashion across diverse nexuses that construct divergent images of the author and the text on particular occasions.

On the other hand, the author ('Montaigne') and the work (the *Essais* and all their derivatives) are almost always participants in these nexuses, whether as agents or patients, along with diverse publishers, readers, and patrons. And it is arguable that early modern critics, translators, and editors of the *Essais*, from Gournay to Canini, were doing something analogous to Villey and his followers, though in very different historical conditions.

There is change and continuity. The 'work' does persist across the different material forms of the text and does act to constrain the possible uses of the book in posterity. At the same time, it has never been 'purely' the author's work; others' agency—including clerics' and humanists' agency—has always been involved in the various nexuses of composition, production, and circulation.

Conclusion

In diverse material forms and historical conditions, the *Essais* have served to index the personal agency of a reader-writer: one who thinks and judges freely in their private offices as a particular individual not bound to systems of instruction or professional service. They have done so from the moment a young woman from Picardy emerged onto the literary scene as the author of a judgement of the *Essais* that miraculously matched that of a prince of the contemporary republic of letters, Lipsius himself, for prescience and insight. It is difficult not to see this as the origin of the public value placed on—the privilege granted to—the general educated reader's response to literature (in the broadest sense), and through literature to culture in general.

Villey was the first to explore this perception in depth, though very much from the perspective of his own time and place. Depending on the particular instance being described, the reader-writer in question may be Montaigne himself, a real or imagined user of his book, or both at the same time. The agency indicated may be broadly social or more strictly moral and intellectual. It may be realized, in modern terms, as the practice of a 'critical thinker' or 'cultural observer' of some kind, or in early modern terms as that of a lay participant in the conversation of self-knowledge, of what Francis Bacon calls human philosophy.

For, as Auerbach saw, the *Essais* represent the most compellingly natural paradigm there is in western European literature of a mind exercising itself freely and healthily upon randomly circulating literary and verbal artefacts. Those who pride themselves on the way they imaginatively—not routinely—consume books, from noble owners of private libraries in the seventeenth century to literary critics in the twentieth, are intrigued into making the paradigm and the natural intellectual life behind it their own, even as they marvel at the magically unattainable virtuosity of the text. This remains true whether any given critic invests in a conservative or a radical version of humanistic literacy.

And it could be argued that it remains true regardless of gender, despite the older humanism's unabashed concern with the 'inner man' and Montaigne's own condescension in relation to learned females. Female readers and critics have been equally quick to infer their own critical agency from Montaigne's book. The first person to do so at length in print was a woman (Marie de Gournay), even if has to be admitted that there is relatively little surviving evidence of other women who followed her example in the seventeenth and eighteenth centuries.[1]

---

[1] For one important exception, see Alicia C. Montoya, 'A woman translator of Montaigne. Appreciation and appropriation in Maria Heyns's *Bloemhof der dooluchtige voorbeelden* (1647)', in Paul. J. Smith and Karl A. E. Enenkel (eds.), *Montaigne and the Low Countries (1580–1700)* (Leiden: Brill, 2007), 223–45.

Nevertheless, the dedications within the *Essais* are all addressed to aristocratic patronesses. The agents of the book's transpassage in England used this fact to associate it with the education and entertainment of ladies who were privately reading works such as Sidney's *Arcadia* and who, en masse, would join the cultured court of Queen Anna. There is, in short, a strong tradition of female intellectual recipients from Marie de Gournay and Lady Anne Clifford to Virginia Woolf and Natalie Zemon Davis.[2]

There is a sense in which all books index the social agency of their readers and re-writers, and recent trends in literary historiography have heavily reinforced this. But the evidence shows that the *Essais* were performing this function in a special manner that was recognized by early consumers.

In the passage with which we started in 2.7.1, Montaigne says that he is the first to communicate himself not by some *marque spéciale et étrangère*, not as a professional reader like a grammarian or a jurist, but as himself, Michel de Montaigne, a well-born person able to relate both to servants and peasants and to courtiers and kings. In the early modern period, a whole set of official and professional *personae* were indeed available for those claiming a public stake in the pursuit of wisdom via learned books. One could pursue a philosophical way of life, produce one's moral and intellectual excellences, whilst fulfilling the offices of a rhetorician or a humanistic scholar, a university professor or a cleric, a judge or a magistrate, a courtier or a head of household (a father or a husband).[3]

But these official *personae* were the foil for Montaigne's 'natural' condition as a gentleman who exercises judgement *un*officially, not as a jurist or even as a father, in an open-form *registre* to be seen only by friends and family. When Gabriel Naudé in 1639 comes to list the *conditions* of various *bons esprits*, he describes Cardano as a medical doctor, Bodin as a lawyer, Charron as a theologian, La Noue as a soldier, Sarpi as a monk, but Montaigne as just a *gentilhomme*.[4]

The *Essais* bring the particular, idiosyncratic reader-writer out of hiding, from behind his or her professional and familial offices, and freely into print as a distinctively noble *persona* to contrast with the scholastic and professional *personae* of more methodical and official commentators. Concrete examples include Gournay (who reads and re-writes the *Essais*, however, in the *persona* of a daughter) and (the fictive) Achante (see 2.7.3). The caveat is that this act of bringing-out normally involves humanists and clerics as agents: Lipsius and Camus in the early modern period, Auerbach and Frame in the modern period.

More often than not, those so brought out were prominent actors neither in national politics nor in institutionalized intellectual life. Some were of noble condition, others were not. The public offices they did hold (in the case of the men) only very occasionally brought them into close contact with the great and with great events. As reader-writers, many were neither illustrious enough to aspire to be icons in the republic of letters, nor learned enough to be philosophers in the

[2] Jean Balsamo, 'Montaigne et ses lectrices', *Revue d'études culturelles*, 3 (2007), 71–83.
[3] See Condren, Gaukroger, and Hunter (eds.), *The philosopher in early modern Europe*.
[4] Millet 236.

schools, nor prominent enough to be official mediators of knowledge—a condition which they shared with most educated women, even high-ranking women. But they were nevertheless able to participate vicariously in both spheres by means of their skills in reading and writing, by means of the circulation of manuscript and printed materials. They have been represented in this study by figures of different ranks and genders, figures such as Gournay, Florio, L'Estoile, Van Veen, Slingsby, Maillefer, and Clifford.

The great historian of the book, Elizabeth Eisenstein, made a similar point a quarter of a century ago, when she argued that the principal condition for Montaigne's printed portrayal of a volatile state of being was the agency of print in fixing public norms and forms of behaviour.[5] Montaigne may not, as one political scientist has claimed, have been one of the earliest philosophic advocates of the modern liberal regime.[6] But his example helped embed one of the founding principles of a modern education in the liberal arts: the instrumentality of literary artefacts as indexes of the individual's liberty to think and speak freely in their own natural person, and not in the assumed social or professional *persona* of a father, a jurist, a university teacher, a Roman Catholic.

The *Essais* enacted, publicized, and ennobled the personal pursuits and qualities of a public of lay reader-writers in ways that troubled official guardians of the scholarly republic of letters from Dominicus Baudius to Pierre-Daniel Huet. They comprised an extraordinarily disordered text that cut across the methods and expertise of such guardians to forge a cult reputation as a natural source of ancient Wisdom. Here was a text that in an age of professionalized methods and intimidating scholarship helped make it possible for educated laymen and laywomen from ordinary bourgeois to noble aristocrats, alongside scholars and professional clerics in their private and informal studies, to participate actively and freely, to participate as particular persons, in the margins of their printed books or on the pages of their blank journal-registers, in the social making and transmission of philosophical Wisdom— even if only within a circle of 'friends and family' privy to their writings, even if only as a surrogate for more public and pragmatic forms of autonomy.

Like Amyot's Plutarch, it was not just a text for interpretation and appreciation, it was an instrument in this process, a breviary or vade mecum, a book which lifted 'us' ignoramuses out of the quagmire and dared 'us' to speak and write. The vexed and controversial enfranchisement of the individual Christian reader-writer of liturgical books (in the late medieval period) and of the Bible (in the wake of the

[5] Eisenstein, *The printing press as an agent of change*, vol. 1, 230–1: 'The state of being he [Montaigne] portrayed—idiosyncratic, volatile, involved with trivial concerns—contrasted in every way with the fixed norms and forms conveyed by other books. The latter dealt with the behaviour of ideal typical figures who were defined by their membership in a given group. Princes, courtiers, councillors, merchants, schoolmasters, husbandmen and the like were presented in terms which made readers ever more aware, not merely of their shortcomings in their assigned roles, but also of the existence of a solitary singular self—characterised by all the peculiar traits that were unshared by others—traits which had no redeeming social or exemplary functions and hence were deemed to be of no literary worth. By presenting himself, in all modesty, as a unique individual and by portraying with loving care every one of his peculiarities, Montaigne brought this private self out of hiding, so to speak. He displayed it for public inspection in a deliberate way for the first time.'
[6] Schaefer, *The political philosophy of Montaigne*, 375.

Reformation and Counter-Reformation) was displaced by the *Essais* to the realm of amateur philosophical conversation—which is not to say that their author avoided theological topics such as prayer and repentance.

The early modern culture of practical-philosophical conversation comprehended a broader range of practices and interests than the academic culture of modern literary and philosophical criticism. The range corresponded to Montaigne's social position as an independent 'wise man' offering opinions and judgements across the whole sphere of humane learning from administration and hydrotherapy to care of the mind and natural theology.

The aristocracy with whom he mixed had to come to terms with a new world of artists, experts, and intelligencers who brought ready-made skills, opinions, and positions in all these areas, displayed in printed and manuscript writings. Montaigne's text shows his readers how to discover their noble liberty of judgement and *franchise* in the spheres of the self, the household, the polity, how to avoid authorizing ready-made dogma and expertise, how to make their own observations and inquiries, to keep the civil conversation going, free, and open.

In other words, the text is attentive throughout to the ways in which new, literarily mediated, professionalized knowledge is credited and acted upon in the society of early modern Europe, whether in relation to balneology or repentance. Luther's attempt to recast literate culture at a stroke, in order to bring down the Roman Catholic Church, was the primary scene of this early modern intellectual revolution.

But the story of Lahontan, picked up and dramatized by Samuel Daniel for the Jacobean court, shows it at work in law and medicine too. In telling that story, Montaigne is, we might say, both an anthropological observer of the psychological and social process—indexed by verbal and literary artefacts—of cognition (involving the interplay of human faculties including imagination) and its outcomes in doctrine and action, and a critic of established explanations and judgements of that process. From the very first chapter, he is interested in the variability and irregularity of arguments from cause via *moyens* (means) to effect and back in human behavioural contexts.[7]

He observes some of these contexts directly (including Lahontan), but many are fictional, shaped by others' art, and many involve *moyens* that are themselves in one sense or another artistic artefacts. The *Journal de voyage* suggests that his interest in books is not distinct from his interest in other kinds of artefact. For a human philosopher, they all testify to 'un tour de l'humaine capacité', they are all effects of the operations of our collective mentality, of our moral and intellectual vices and virtues. In the *Essais*, he observes the ways in which the making of literary artefacts and the use of literate expertise are understood to build public reputations for virtue and authority. He critiques this type of understanding and judges differently.

But it is time to pause. Is this account of Montaigne's critical practice not rather familiar? Did the 'General preface' and 1.1 not discuss exactly such forms of

---

[7] See George Hoffmann, 'The investigation of nature', in Ullrich Langer (ed.), *The Cambridge Companion to Montaigne* (Cambridge: Cambridge University Press, 2005), 163–82. He is also interested, of course, in arguments from cause to effect and back in natural contexts, as when a natural theologian argues back from the design of the natural world to God's agency.

anthropological observation and criticism in the context of recent theory and historiography? The school of Montaigne is claiming another disciple, a disciple who is inevitably constituting and describing that school and its patron-author from the perspective of his own time, place, and community.

The point has been that humanistically trained readers encountering the *Essais* begin to infer the presence of the author, as though he were accessible beyond the covers of the book in their hands. 'Montaigne' the patron-author, or the 'school of Montaigne', is the collective product of their inference-making activity. They begin to sense him looking over their shoulder, guiding their conversation with their books, themselves, their fellow inquirers, and the experts who would tell them how and what to read and think. He becomes a guide for the particular reader-writer contemplating afresh, 'all alone', the record of human knowledge and experience. Without this particular reader-writer, inferring his presence in this way, he cannot be 'Montaigne'—as Gournay was the first to comprehend.

The author of the current study cannot, then, be excluded from the history that has been the subject matter throughout. For professional humanists, the *Essais* remain impossible to position steadily as an object of study. Montaigne's self-portrait insensibly becomes a self-portrait of the viewer, especially when that viewer is a critical thinker who is trying to free themselves of routine, professional methods and assumptions. Whatever critical viewpoint one gains on early modern culture, the text of the *Essais* somehow seems to anticipate it. This is because it was designed to act, in its earliest historical nexuses, as an instrument of freely critical thought, an instrument that is the natural person of Montaigne as he might privately have acted—even before a king—in daily conversation.

It is arguable that the battle over the enfranchisement of the unofficial reader-writer with liberty of judgement still rages, if in very different historical circumstances. Globally, it centres on the public consumption and production of written and visual information via audio-visual media and the web by private individuals or bloggers. The freedom of expression to which this phenomenon gives rise can be described in different instances as a democratic privilege or as an unacceptable abuse. Traditional clerical elites of journalists and scholars, commercial corporations such as Google, and states such as China represent some of the major protagonists both facilitating and attempting to control this trend.

Mostly, however, such consumers are creating their own materials and modes of consumption, not appropriating high literary culture, while national literacy campaigns try to force canonical books and traditional reading-as-pleasure on the young in schools. What, given these circumstances, would a contemporary version of the *Essais* and their author look like? Is it possible to imagine the emergence, in a book or a blog, of a *persona* in the guise not of a public intellectual, but of a learned amateur, a maverick who would appear to have casually mastered the canon, in private study, together with all the arts and sciences? A maverick who would provide a telling, ironic, vernacular slant on their most topical developments and their claims to knowledge, without causing offence or scandal wherever he or she is read? That would be something.

Bibliography

A. MANUSCRIPT AND ARCHIVAL SOURCES (INCLUDING UNIQUE COPIES OF PRINTED BOOKS)

BORDEAUX
Bibliothèque Municipale de Bordeaux
G. F. 495 rés. (the annotated Maillefer family copy of the Paris 1640 edition of Montaigne's *Essais*)

CAMBRIDGE
Trinity College
Wren Library
G.20.2 (copy of Lyon 1593 with annotations)

FLORENCE
Archivio di Stato di Firenze
Fondo Ducato di Urbino, classe I, divisione G, filza 219, fols. 745r–773r (letters from Flavio Querenghi to the Duke of Urbino)

GENEVA
Archives d'État de Genève
Conseil ordinaire - Petit Conseil - Conseil des XXV (vingt-cinq), Registres du Conseil, vol. 97 (references to Genevan editions of Montaigne; accessed 5 September 2011 via <https://ge.ch/arvaegconsult/>)

LONDON
British Library
Rare books
C.28.g.7 (Pieter van Veen's copy of Montaigne's *Essais*, with annotations and illustrations)

Manuscripts
Lansdowne MS 108, fol. 158 (Lady Anne Harrington to Adam Newton)

Lambeth Palace Library
Bacon MS 648, fols. 281–2, 321 (letters from Pierre de Brach to Anthony Bacon)
Bacon MS 655, fols. 185r–186r (inventory of M. Le Douz's books)

The National Archives
Public Record Office, SP 99/2 fols. 157–8, 183, 184 (Scaramelli's letters to Florio)

NOTTINGHAM
Nottingham University Library, Department of Manuscripts and Special Collections
MS Ga 12714 (Sir Henry Slingsby's 'Diary')

OXFORD
Bodleian Library
8° S 52 Art. Seld. (Mountjoy brothers' annotated copy of Sextus Empiricus, *Pyrrhoniarum hypotyposeon libri iii*, Geneva: Henri Estienne, 1562)

PADUA
Biblioteca Universitaria
Sala manoscritti e rari
11. b. 131 (copy of the 1598 *Essais de Montaigne* that was originally in the library of the German nation at the University of Padua)

PARIS
Bibliothèque nationale de France
Salle des Manuscrits
MS Dupuy 409 (letters and notes regarding de Thou's *Historiae*)
MS Dupuy 632 (letters and notes regarding de Thou's *Historiae*)
MS Dupuy 700 (letters of Charles Perrot to the Pithous)
MS Fr. 2388 (Jean de Vassan's *Secunda Scaligerana*)
MS Fr. 6678 (Pierre de L'Estoile's 'Registre journal' of the reign of Henri III)
MS Fr. (Nouvelles acquisitions françaises) 6888 (another version of L'Estoile's 'Registre journal' of the reign of Henri III)
MS Fr. 10299 (L'Estoile's 'Registre' from 1589 to 1594)
MS Fr. 10300 (L'Estoile's 'Registre' from July 1606 to January 1609)
MS Fr. 10301 (L'Estoile's 'Registre second de mes curiosités' or 'Secondes tablettes' from February 1609 to May 1610)
MS Fr. 10302 (L'Estoile's 'Continuation de mes Memoires Journaux et Curiosités tant Publiques que Particulieres' from May 1610 to May 1611)

Réserve
Rés. R-2119–R-2124 (collection of Morel imprints from the library of Claude Dupuy, including La Boétie's *Mesnagerie* and *Vers françois*)

REGGIO EMILIA
Archivio di Stato
Archivi Privati, Archivio Turri, busta n.161, fasciculo n.1 (Querenghi family papers)

RHEIMS
Bibliothèque Municipale
MS 1980 ('Mémoires de Jean Maillefer, continués par son fils (1667–1716)')

ROME
Archivio Storico Capitolino
Camera Capitolina, cred, I, tom. 1 (register of privileges of Roman citizenship)
Camera Capitolina, cred. IV, tom. 64 (memorials of Roman citizens created)

University of Rome, 'La Sapienza'
Biblioteca Alessandrina
D.e.47 (copy of Montaigne, *Essais*, Paris 1602 owned by the Duke of Urbino)
MS 50 (catalogue of Francesco Maria II della Rovere's library at Casteldurante)

VATICAN CITY
Archivio della Congregazione per la Dottrina della Fede
Indice, Protocolli C, fols. 346r–347v (Roman censors' 'animadversions' on the 1580 *Essais*)
Indice, Protocolli Y, fols. 400–405v (Milan censors' *correttione* of de Thou's *Historiae*)

Biblioteca Apostolica Vaticana
Urb. Lat. MS 860, fols. 408–444 and MS 861, fols. 1–56 (manuscript *discorsi* sent by
Flavio Querenghi to the Duke of Urbino)

VENICE
Archivio di Stato di Venezia
Senato/Dispacci/Inghilterra, filza II, fols. 113r–115r (Scaramelli's dispatch about the
Basilikon dōron)

Bibliotheca Nazionale Marciana
MS It. XI. 20–6789, fol. 39 (Lorenzo Pignoria to Domenico Molino, 19 June 1627, re
Guglielmo Sohier)

WASHINGTON DC
Folger Shakespeare Library
V. b. 327 (annotated copy of London 1603)

B. PRINTED AND OTHER SOURCES

AARONIAN, DAISY, 'La censure de Simon Goulart dans l'édition "Genevoise" des *Essais*
(1595)', *Bulletin de la Société des Amis de Montaigne*, 8th series, 27–8 (2002), 83–97.
ACHESON, KATHERINE O. (ed.), *The diary of Anne Clifford, 1616–1619: a critical edition*
(New York: Garland, 1995).
ADAMS, H. M., *Catalogue of books printed on the continent of Europe, 1501–1600, in
Cambridge libraries*, 2 vols. (London: Cambridge University Press, 1967).
AHO, JAMES ALFRED, *Confession and bookkeeping: the religious, moral, and rhetorical roots of
modern accounting* (New York: State University of New York Press, 2005).
ALLEN, JOHN WILLIAM, *A history of political thought in the sixteenth century* London:
Methuen, 1928).
ALMQUIST, KATHERINE, 'Examining the evidence: Montaigne in the *Registres secrets du
Parlement de Bordeaux*', *Montaigne Studies*, 16 (2004), 45–74.
AMELANG, JAMES S., *The flight of Icarus: artisan autobiography in early modern Europe*
(Stanford: Stanford University Press, 1998).
AMSLER, MARK, *Affective literacies: writing and multilingualism in the late Middle Ages*
(Turnhout: Brepols, 2011).
ANON., *Hæc-Vir: or, the womanish-man: Being an answere to a late booke intituled Hic-
Mulier. Exprest in a briefe dialogue betweene Hæc-Vir the womanish-man, and Hic-Mulier
the man-woman* (London: [John Trundle], [1620]).
ANON., *A pleasant comedie, called the two merry milke-maids. Or, the best words weare the
garland. As it was acted before the King, with generall approbation, by the Companie of the
Revels* (London: Bernard Alsop for Lawrence Chapman, 1620).
ANON., *Catalogus librorum altero se correctior comptiorque qui Patavii in Bibliotheca I. N. G. J.
inveniuntur sub felicissimo regimine… Caroli Nicolai a' Marpurg Nobilis Lyburni
Fluminensis* (Padua: Ex Typographia Pasquati, 1691).

APTER, EMILY S., *The translation zone: a new comparative literature* (Princeton: Princeton University Press, 2006).

ARBER, EDWARD, *A transcript of the registers of the Company of Stationers of London, 1554–1640 A.D*, 5 vols. (London: Privately printed, 1875–94).

ARMOGATHE, JEAN-ROBERT and CARRAUD, VINCENT, 'Les *Essais* de Montaigne dans les archives du Saint-Office', in Bruno Neveu, Jean-Louis Quantin, and Jean-Claude Waquet (eds.), *Papes, princes et savants dans l'Europe moderne: mélanges à la mémoire de Bruno Neveu* (Geneva: Droz, 2006), 79–96.

ASCHAM, ROGER, *The scholemaster or plaine and perfite way of teachyng children, to understand, write, and speake, the Latin tong* (London: John Day, 1570).

AUERBACH, ERICH, *Mimesis: dargestellte Wirklichkeit in der abendländischen Literatur* (Berne: A. Francke, 1946).

AUERBACH, ERICH, 'Epilegomena zu *Mimesis*', *Romanische Forschungen*, 65 (1953), 1–18.

AUERBACH, ERICH, *Mimesis: The representation of reality in western literature*, trans. Willard R. Trask (Princeton: Princeton University Press, 1953).

AUERBACH, ERICH, *Literary Language and Its Public in Late Latin Antiquity and in the Middle Ages*, trans. Ralph Manheim (New York: Pantheon Books, 1965).

AUERBACH, ERICH, *Mimesis: the representation of reality in western literature*, trans. Willard R. Trask (Princeton: Princeton University Press, 2013).

AUGER, PETER, 'The *Semaines*' dissemination in England and Scotland until 1641', *Renaissance Studies*, 26 (2011), 625–40.

AUGER, PETER, 'British responses to Du Bartas' *Semaines*, 1584–1641', unpublished doctoral dissertation (University of Oxford, 2012).

AUVRAY, L., 'Lettres de Pierre Charron à Gabriel Michel de la Rochemaillet', *Revue d'histoire littéraire de la France*, 1 (1894), 308–29.

BACON, FRANCIS, *The letters and life*, ed. James Spedding, 7 vols. (London: Longman, Green, Longman, and Roberts, 1861–74).

BACON, FRANCIS, *The advancement of learning*, ed. Michael Kiernan (Oxford: Clarendon, 2000).

BAKEWELL, SARAH, *How to live: or A life of Montaigne in one question and twenty attempts at an answer* (London: Chatto & Windus, 2010).

BALSAMO, JEAN, 'Biographie, philologie, bibliographie: Montaigne à l'*essai* d'une "nouvelle histoire" littéraire', *EMF: Studies in Early Modern France*, 9 (2004), 10–29.

BALSAMO, JEAN, 'Un gentilhomme et ses patrons: remarques sur la biographie politique de Montaigne', in Philippe Desan (ed.), *Montaigne politique, actes du colloque international tenu à University of Chicago (Paris), les 29 et 30 avril 2005* (Paris: H. Champion, 2006), 223–42.

BALSAMO, JEAN, 'Montaigne et ses lectrices', *Revue d'études culturelles*, 3 (2007), 71–83.

BALSAMO, JEAN, ' "Le plus grand bien que j'atande de cete miene charge publique": Montaigne, entre vie publique et vie privée', *Nouveau Bulletin de la Société des Amis de Montaigne*, IV/2 ('Numéro spécial: Montaigne et sa région'—also 8th series no. 48) (2008), 359–75.

BALSAMO, JEAN, 'Des *Essais* pour comprendre les guerres civiles', *Bibliothèque d'Humanisme et Renaissance*, 72 (2010), 521–40.

BALSAMO, JEAN, 'Montaigne's noble book: book history and biographical criticism', *Journal of Medieval and Early Modern Studies*, 41 (2011), 417–34.

BALSAMO, JEAN, 'Lettres de Montaigne', in Philippe Desan (ed.), *Dictionnaire de Michel de Montaigne* (2nd edn., Paris: Champion, 2007), 671–5.

BALSAMO, JEAN, 'Naselli, Girolamo (?–v. 1609)', in Philippe Desan (ed.), *Dictionnaire de Michel de Montaigne* (2nd edn., Paris: Champion, 2007), 809–10.

BALSAMO, JEAN and SIMONIN, MICHEL, *Abel L'Angelier & Françoise de Louvain (1574–1620): suivi du catalogue des ouvrages publiés par Abel L'Angelier (1574–1610) et la veuve L'Angelier (1610–1620)* (Geneva: Droz, 2002).

BANDERIER, G., 'Montaigne dans le *Thresor des Histoires Admirables* de Simon Goulart', *Bulletin de la Société des Amis de Montaigne*, 7th series, 41–2 (1995), 52–8.

BAYLE, PIERRE, *Dictionaire historique et critique*, 3 vols. (2nd edn., Rotterdam: Reinier Leers, 1702).

BAYLE, PIERRE, *Dictionaire historique et critique*, 4 vols. (Amsterdam: P. Brunel et al., 1740).

BEADLE, RICHARD and BURROW, COLIN (eds.), *Manuscript miscellanies, c. 1450–1700* (London: British Library, 2011).

BELLONI, GIOVANNI, *Discorso intorno all'Antro delle Ninfe Naiadi di Homero. Impresa de gli Academici Ricovrati di Padoua* (Padua: Francesco Bolzetta, 1601).

BENEDICT, PHILIP, *The Huguenot population of France, 1600–1685: the demographic fate and customs of a religious minority* (Philadelphia: American Philosophical Society, 1991).

BENEDICT, PHILIP, 'Shaping the memory of the French wars of religion. The first centuries', in Erika Kuijpers, et al. (eds.), *Memory before modernity: practices of memory in early modern Europe* (Leiden: Brill, 2013), 111–25.

BENOIT, ROBERT, *Vivre et mourir à Reims au Grand siècle: (1580–1720)* (2nd edn.; Arras: Artois Presses Université, 1999).

BETTINSON, CHRISTOPHER, 'The politiques and the Politique Party: a reappraisal', in Keith Cameron (ed.), *From Valois to Bourbon: dynasty, state and society in early modern France* (Exeter: University of Exeter, 1989), 35–49.

BETTONI, ANNA, 'Livres français de la bibliothèque *germanica* de Padoue à la fin de la Renaissance', *La Lecture littéraire: revue du Centre de recherche sur la lecture littéraire de l'Université de Reims*, no. 7 ('Lire à la Renaissance', ed. Jean Balsamo) (2002), 15–41.

BEUGNOT, BERNARD, 'Livre de raison, livre de retraite: interférences des points de vue chez les mémorialistes', in Noemi Hepp and Jacques Hennequin (eds.), *Les valeurs chez les mémorialistes français du XVIIe siècle avant la Fronde* ([Paris]: Éditions Klincksieck, 1979), 47–64.

BIANCHI, LORENZO, *Rinascimento e libertinismo: studi su Gabriel Naudé* (Naples: Bibliopolis, 1996).

BLAIR, ANN, 'Errata lists and the reader as corrector', in Sabrina A. Baron, Eric N. Lindquist, and Eleanor F. Shevlin (eds.), *Agent of change: print culture studies after Elizabeth L. Eisenstein* (Amherst: University of Massachusetts Press; Washington, DC: In association with the Center for the Book, Library of Congress, 2007), 21–41.

BLAIR, ANN, *Too much to know: managing scholarly information before the modern age* (New Haven: Yale University Press, 2010).

BLAND, MARK, *A guide to early printed books and manuscripts* (Chichester: Wiley-Blackwell, 2010).

BLOOM, HAROLD (ed.), *Modern Critical Interpretations: Michel de Montaigne's 'Essays'* (New York: Chelsea House Publishers, 1987).

BOASE, ALAN, 'Montaigne annoté par Florimond de Raemond', *Revue du seizième siècle*, 15 (1928), 237–78.

BOASE, ALAN, *The fortunes of Montaigne: a history of the 'Essays' in France, 1580–1669* (London: Methuen & Co., 1935).

BOASE, ALAN, 'Un lecteur hollandais de Montaigne: Pieter van Veen', *Mélanges offerts à M. Abel Lefranc par ses élèves et ses amis* (Paris: Droz, 1936), 408–17.

BODIN, JEAN, *Six livres de la republique* ([Geneva]: [Claude Juge], 1577).

BOER, WIETSE DE, *The conquest of the soul: confessions, discipline, and public order in Counter-Reformation Milan* (Leiden: Brill, 2000).

BŒUF, ESTELLE, *La bibliothèque parisienne de Gabriel Naudé en 1630: les lectures d'un libertin érudit* (Geneva: Droz, 2007).

BONNET, PIERRE, 'Une nouvelle série d'annotations de Florimond de Raemond aux *Essais* de Montaigne', *Bulletin de la Société des Amis de Montaigne*, 3rd series, 10 (1959), 10–23.

BOON, JAMES A., 'Circumscribing circumcision/uncircumcision: an essay amid the history of difficult description', in Stuart B. Schwartz (ed.), *Implicit understandings: observing, reporting, and reflecting on the encounters between Europeans and other peoples in the early modern era* (Cambridge: Cambridge University Press, 1994), 556–85.

BOTINEAU, PIERRE and DUBOIS, CLAUDE-GILBERT (eds.), *Montaigne et l'Europe: actes du colloque international de Bordeaux (21–23 mai 1992)* (Mont-de-Marsan: Éditions InterUniversitaires, 1992).

BOUTARIC, F. (ed.), *Actes du Parlement de Paris. Première série—de l'an 1254 à l'an 1328*, 2 vols. (Paris: Henri Plon, 1863).

BOUTCHER, WARREN, 'Florio's Montaigne: Translation and pragmatic humanism in the sixteenth century', unpublished doctoral dissertation (University of Cambridge, 1991).

BOUTCHER, WARREN, '"Le moyen de voir ce Senecque escrit à la main": Montaigne's *Journal de voyage* and the politics of *science* and *faveur* in the Vatican Library', *Michigan Romance Studies*, 15 (1995), 177–214.

BOUTCHER, WARREN, 'Vernacular humanism in the sixteenth century', in Jill Kraye (ed.), *The Cambridge Companion to Renaissance Humanism* (Cambridge: Cambridge University Press, 1996), 189–202.

BOUTCHER, WARREN, 'Pilgrimage to Parnassus: local intellectual traditions, humanist education and the cultural geography of sixteenth-century England', in Yun Lee Too and Niall Livingstone (eds.), *Pedagogy and Power: Rhetorics of Classical Learning* (Cambridge: Cambridge University Press, 1998), 110–47.

BOUTCHER, WARREN, 'Michel de Montaigne et Anthony Bacon: la familia et la fonction des lettres', *Montaigne Studies*, 13 (2001), 241–76.

BOUTCHER, WARREN, 'Humanism and literature in late Tudor England: translation, the continental book and the case of Montaigne's *Essais*', in J. Woolfson (ed.), *Reassessing Tudor humanism* (Basingstoke: Palgrave Macmillan, 2002), 243–68.

BOUTCHER, WARREN, '"Learning mingled with nobilitie": Directions for reading Montaigne's *Essais* in their institutional context', in Keith Cameron and Laura Lee Willett (eds.), *Le visage changeant de Montaigne/The changing face of Montaigne* (Paris: Honoré Champion, 2003), 337–62.

BOUTCHER, WARREN, 'Marginal commentaries: the cultural transmission of Montaigne's *Essais* in Shakespeare's England', in P. Kapitanak and J. M. Maguin (eds.), *Montaigne et Shakespeare: vers un nouvel humanisme* (Montpellier: Société Française Shakespeare, 2003), 13–27.

BOUTCHER, WARREN, 'Awakening the inner man: Montaigne framed for modern intellectual life', *EMF: Studies in Early Modern France*, 9 (2004), 30–57.

BOUTCHER, WARREN, 'Montaigne's legacy', in U. Langer (ed.), *The Cambridge Companion to Montaigne* (Cambridge: Cambridge University Press, 2005), 27–52.

BOUTCHER, WARREN, ' "Le pauvre patient": Montaigne agent dans l'économie du savoir', in P. Desan (ed.), *Montaigne politique: Actes du colloque international tenu à University of Chicago (Paris) les 29 et 30 avril 2005* (Paris: Honoré Champion, 2006), 243–61.

BOUTCHER, WARREN, 'From father to son: Van Veen's Montaigne and Van Ravesteyn's "Pieter van Veen, his Son Cornelis and his Clerk Hendrick Borsman" ', in P. J. Smith and K. A. E. Enenkel (eds.), *Montaigne and the Low Countries (1580–1700)* (Leiden: Brill, 2007), 263–303.

BOUTCHER, WARREN, ' "Fadaises domestiques": Montaigne marchand bourgeois bordelais lu par un marchand bourgeois rémois', *Nouveau Bulletin de la Société Internationale des Amis de Montaigne*, IV/2 ('Numéro spécial: Montaigne et sa région'—also 8th series no. 48) (2008), 401–18.

BOUTCHER, WARREN, 'Schooling America: Donald Frame, Pierre Villey, and the educational history of the *Essais*', *Montaigne Studies*, 20 (2008), 117–28.

BOUTCHER, WARREN, 'Una biblioteca o due? Il rapporto fra le collezioni di libri in Urbino e in Casteldurante', in M. Mei and F. Paoli (eds.), *La libraria di Francesco Maria II Della Rovere a Casteldurante. Da collezione ducale a biblioteca della città* (Urbino: Quattroventi, 2008), 95–8.

BOUTCHER, WARREN, 'Collecting manuscripts and printed books in the late Renaissance: Naudé and the last Duke of Urbino's library', *Italian Studies*, 66/2 (2011), 206–20.

BOUTCHER, WARREN, 'The origins of Florio's Montaigne: "Of the Institution and Education of Children, to Madame Lucy Russell, Countess of Bedford" ', *Montaigne Studies*, 24 (2012), 7–32.

BOUWSMA, WILLIAM JAMES, *The waning of the Renaissance, 1550–1640* (New Haven: Yale University Press, 2000).

BRANDEN, F. J. P. VAN DEN, *Geschiedenis der Antwerpsche Schilderschool*, 3 vols. (Antwerp: Buschmann, 1883).

BRAYMAN HACKEL, HEIDI, *Reading material in early modern England: print, gender, and literacy* (Cambridge: Cambridge University Press, 2005).

BRAYMAN HACKEL, HEIDI, 'Turning to her "Best Companion[s]": Lady Anne Clifford as reader, annotator and book collector', in Karen Hearn and Lynn Hulse (eds.), *Lady Anne Clifford: culture, patronage and gender in 17th-century Britain* (Leeds: Yorkshire Archaeological Society, 2009), 99–108.

BROWN, WARREN, et al. (eds.), *Documentary culture and the laity in the early Middle Ages* (Cambridge: Cambridge University Press, 2013).

BRUNEL, JEAN, 'Rhétorique et histoire dans les *Elogia* de Scévole de Sainte-Marthe', in Gilbert Schrenck (ed.), *Autour de l'Histoire universelle d'Agrippa d'Aubigné: mélanges à la mémoire d'André Thierry* (Geneva: Droz, 2006), 121–59.

BRUNEL, JEAN, 'Jacques-Auguste de Thou et ses amis poitevins', in Frank Lestringant (ed.), *Jacques-Auguste de Thou (1553–1617): Écriture et condition robine* (Paris: Presses de l'Université Paris-Sorbonne, 2007), 53–71.

BURKE, PETER, 'Translations into Latin in early modern Europe', in Peter Burke and R. Po-chia Hsia (eds.), *Cultural translation in early modern Europe* (Cambridge: Cambridge University Press, 2007), 65–80.

BURNS, ROBERT M. and RAYMENT-PICKARD, HUGH (eds.), *Philosophies of History: From Enlightenment to Postmodernity* (Oxford: Blackwell, 2000).

CAHIER, GABRIELLA and CAMPAGNOLO, MATTEO (eds.), *Registres de la compagnie des pasteurs de Genève: tome VIII, 1600–1603* (Geneva: Droz, 1986).

CAHIER, GABRIELLA and GRAND-JEAN, M. (eds.), *Registres de la compagnie des pasteurs de Genève tome VII: 1595–1599* (Geneva: Droz, 1984).

CALOGIERÀ, ANGELO (ed.), *Nuova raccolta d'opuscoli scientifici, e filologici: Tomo duodecimo* (Venice: Simone Occhi, 1764).

CAMERARIUS, PHILIPPUS, *Operæ horarum subcisiuarum siue meditationes historicæ… Centuria et editio correctior, atque auctior, altera* (Frankfurt: Typis Ioannis Saurii: impensis P. Kopffii, 1606).

CAMERARIUS, PHILIPPUS, *Les meditations historiques… Nouuelle édition, reueue sur le Latin augmenté par l'auteur, & enrichie d'vn tiers par le translateur; outre la nouuelle & entiere version du troisiesme volume*, ed. Simon Goulart, 3 vols. (Lyon: Widow of Antoine de Harsy, 1610).

CAMPAGNOLI, RUGGERO, 'Girolamo Naselli primo traduttore italiano di Montaigne (1590)', *Studi francesi*, 47–48 (1972), 214–31.

CAMUS, JEAN-PIERRE, *Les diversitez: tome VIII* (Paris: Cl. Chappelet, 1613).

CANINI, GIROLAMO, *Aforismi politici cavati dall'Historia d'Italia* (Venice: Antonio Pinelli, 1625).

CANO-ECHEVARRÍA, BERTA and HUTCHINGS, MARK, 'The Spanish Ambassador and Samuel Daniel's *Vision of the Twelve Goddesses*: A new document [with text]', *English Literary Renaissance*, 42 (2012), 223–57.

CARSON, ROB, 'Hearing voices in *Coriolanus* and early modern skepticism', in Graham Bradshaw, T. G. Bishop, and Peter Holbrook (eds.), *The Shakespearean international yearbook 6: special section, Shakespeare and Montaigne revisited* (Farnham: Ashgate, 2006), 140–69.

CATHCART, CHARLES, *Marston, rivalry, rapprochement, and Jonson* (Farnham: Ashgate, 2008).

CAVAILLÉ, JEAN-PIERRE, 'Pierre Charron, "disciple" de Montaigne et "patriarche des prétendus esprits forts"', *Montaigne Studies*, 19 (2006), 29–42.

CAVAILLÉ, JEAN-PIERRE, 'Pierre Charron, "disciple" de Montaigne et "patriarche des prétendus esprits forts".' (2009). 22 January 2013 <http://dossiersgrihl.revues.org/280>.

CAVE, TERENCE, *The cornucopian text: problems of writing in the French Renaissance* (Oxford: Clarendon Press, 1979).

CAVE, TERENCE, 'Problems of reading in the *Essais*', in I. D. McFarlane and Ian Maclean (eds.), *Montaigne: Essays in memory of Richard Sayce* (Oxford New York: Clarendon Press, 1982), 133–66.

CAVE, TERENCE, *How to read Montaigne* (London: Granta, 2007).

CAZALÉ BÉRARD, CLAUDE and KLAPISCH-ZUBER, CHRISTIANE, 'Mémoire de soi et des autres dans les livres de famille italiens', *Annales*, 59 (2004), 805–26.

CELLÉRIER, JACOB ELISÉE, *Notice biographique sur Charles Perrot pasteur genevois au seizième siècle* (extracted from 'Mémoires de la Société d'Histoire et d'Archéologie de Genève'; Geneva: Imprimerie Ramboz et Schuchardt, 1856).

CHAIX, PAUL, MOECKLI, GUSTAVE, and DUFOUR, ALAIN, *Les livres imprimés à Genève de 1550 à 1600* (Geneva: Droz, 1966).

CHARRON, PIERRE, *De la sagesse livres trois* (Bordeaux: S. Millanges, 1601).

CHARRON, PIERRE, *De la sagesse trois livres* (Paris: David Douceur, 1604).

CHARRON, PIERRE, *De la sagesse livres trois* (Paris: D. Douceur, 1607).

CHARRON, PIERRE, *De la sagesse*, ed. Barbara de Negroni (Paris: Fayard, 1986).

CHARTIER, ROGER, 'The practical impact of writing', in Roger Chartier (ed.), *A History of private life, volume 3: Passions of the Renaissance* (Cambridge, MA: Belknap Press of Harvard University Press, 1989), 111–59.

CHARTIER, ROGER, 'Crossing borders in early modern Europe', *Book History*, 8 (2005), 37–50.

CHATELAIN, JEAN-MARC, 'Heros togatus: culture cicéronienne et gloire de la robe dans la France d'Henri IV', *Journal des savants*, nos. 3–4 (1991), 263–87.

CHATELAIN, JEAN-MARC, 'Les recueils d'adversaria aux xvie et xviie siècles', in Henri-Jean Martin and Frédéric Barbier (eds.), *Le livre et l'historien: études offertes en l'honneur du Professeur Henri-Jean Martin* (Geneva: Droz, 1997), 169–86.

CHOPARD, MICHEL, 'En marge de la grande érudition, un amateur éclairé, Pierre de L'Estoile', *Histoire et Littérature: Les écrivains et la politique* (Paris: Presses Universitaires de France, 1977), 205–35.

CHU, P. T-D., *Im Lichte Hollands: Holländische Malerei des 17. Jahrhunderts aus den Sammlungen des Fürsten von Liechtenstein und aus Schweizer Besitz* (Zurich: VerlagsHausZürich, 1987).

CLANCHY, M. T., *From memory to written record, England 1066–1307* (2nd edn., Oxford: Blackwell, 1993).

CLARE, JANET, *Shakespeare's stage traffic: imitation, borrowing and competition in Renaissance theatre* (Cambridge: Cambridge University Press, 2014).

CLARKE, JACK ALDEN, *Gabriel Naudé, 1600–1653* (Hamden, CT: Archon Books, 1970).

CLEGG, CYNDIA SUSAN, *Press censorship in Elizabethan England* (Cambridge: Cambridge University Press, 1997).

CLELAND, JAMES, *Hērō-paideia, or, The institution of a young noble man* (Oxford: Joseph Barnes, 1607).

COCKAYNE, G. E., *The complete peerage*, ed. Vicary Gibbs et al., 13 vols. (London: St. Catherine's Press, 1910–40).

COCULA, ANNE-MARIE, 'Michel de L'Hospital, Étienne de La Boétie et Michel de Montaigne: histoire d'une filiation', in Thierry Wanegffelen (ed.), *De Michel de L'Hospital à l'édit de Nantes: politique et religion face aux églises* (Clermont-Ferrand: Presses Universitaires Blaise-Pascal, 2002), 565–73.

COLCLOUGH, DAVID, *Freedom of speech in early Stuart England* (Cambridge: Cambridge University Press, 2005).

COLDIRON, A. E. B., 'Commonplaces and metaphors', in Gordon Braden, Robert Cummings, and Stuart Gillespie (eds.), *The Oxford history of literary translation in English: Volume 2 1550–1660* (Oxford: Oxford University Press, 2010), 109–17.

CONDREN, CONAL, *Argument and authority in early modern England: the presupposition of oaths and offices* (Cambridge: Cambridge University Press, 2006).

CONDREN, CONAL, 'Specifying the subject in early modern autobiography', in Ronald Bedford, Lloyd Davis, and Philippa Kelly (eds.), *Early modern autobiography: theories, genres, practices* (Ann Arbor: University of Michigan Press, 2006), 35–48.

CONDREN, CONAL, GAUKROGER, STEPHEN, and HUNTER, IAN (eds.), *The philosopher in early modern Europe: the nature of a contested identity* (Cambridge: Cambridge University Press, 2006).

COOPER, RICHARD, 'Montaigne dans l'entourage du maréchal de Matignon', *Montaigne Studies*, 13 (2001), 99–140.

CORNEANU, SORANA, *Regimens of the mind: Boyle, Locke, and the early modern 'cultura animi' tradition* (Chicago: University of Chicago Press, 2011).

CORNWALLIS, WILLIAM, *Essayes* (London: Edmund Mattes, 1600–1).

COUZINET, MARIE-DOMINIQUE, 'Les *Essais* de Montaigne et les *Miscellanées*', in Dominique de Courcelles (ed.), *Ouvrages miscellanées et théories de la connaissance à la Renaissance: actes des journées d'études organisées par l'École nationale des chartes (Paris, 5–6 avril 2002)* (Paris: École des chartes, 2003), 153–69.

COZZI, GAETANO, *Venezia barocca: conflitti di uomini e idee nella crisi del Seicento veneziano* (Venice: Il Cardo, 1995).

CRAWFORD, JULIE, 'Lady Anne Clifford and the uses of Christian warfare', in Micheline White (ed.), *English women, religion, and textual production, 1500–1625* (Farnham: Ashgate, 2011), 101–23.

CUMMINGS, BRIAN, *The literary culture of the Reformation: grammar and grace* (Oxford: Oxford University Press, 2002).

CYPRIAN, SAINT, *Opera* (Antwerp: Apud viduam & hæredes Ioannis Stelsii, 1568).

CYPRIAN, SAINT, *Opera* (Geneva: Ioannes le Preux, 1593).

D'OSSAT, ARNAUD, *Lettere a principi di negotii politici, e di complimento, del sig. cardinal d'Ossat. Diuise in tre libri. Tradotte dal francese, messe insieme, & arricchite di alcuni discorsi*, trans. Girolamo Canini (Venice: Giacomo Sarzina, 1629).

DADSON, TREVOR J., *Libros, lectores y lecturas: estudios sobre bibliotecas particulares españolas del Siglo de Oro* (Madrid: Arco/Libros, 1998).

DANIEL, SAMUEL, *A panegyrike congratulatory delivered to the Kings most excellent maiesty at Burleigh Harrington in Rutlandshire....Also certaine epistles. With a defence of ryme, heeretofore written, and now published by the author* (London: Valentine Simmes for Edward Blount, 1603).

DANIEL, SAMUEL, *The Queenes Arcadia. A pastorall trago-comedie presented to her Majestie and her Ladies, by the Universitie of Oxford in Christs Church, in August last, 1605* (London: G. Eld for Simon Waterson, 1606).

DARNTON, ROBERT, 'What is the history of books?', in David Finkelstein and Alistair McCleery (eds.), *The book history reader* (2nd edn., London: Routledge, 2006), 9–26.

DASTON, LORRAINE and PARK, KATHARINE (eds.), *The Cambridge history of science volume 3: Early modern science* (Cambridge: Cambridge University Press, 2006).

DAUBRESSE, SYLVIE, *Le Parlement de Paris, ou, La voix de la raison: (1559–1589)* (Geneva: Droz, 2005).

DAVIS, NATALIE ZEMON, 'Beyond the market: books as gifts in sixteenth-century France', *Transactions of the Royal Historical Society*, 5th. Ser., 33 (1983), 69–88.

DAVIS, NATALIE ZEMON, 'Boundaries and the sense of self in sixteenth-century France', in T. C. Heller, M. Sosna, and D. E. Wellbery (eds.), *Reconstructing individualism: autonomy, individuality, and the self in Western thought* (Stanford: Stanford University Press, 1986), 53–63, 332–5.

DAVIS, NATALIE ZEMON, 'Fame and secrecy: Leon Modena's life as an early modern autobiography', in M. R. Cohen (ed.), *The autobiography of a seventeenth-century Venetian rabbi: Leon Modena's 'Life of Judah'* (Princeton: Princeton University Press, 1988), 51–70.

DAYBELL, JAMES, 'Gender, politics and diplomacy: women, news and intelligence networks in Elizabethan England', in Robyn Adams and Rosanna Cox (eds.), *Diplomacy and early modern culture* (Basingstoke: Palgrave Macmillan, 2011), 101–19.

DAYBELL, JAMES, 'Clifford, Anne', in Garrett A. Sullivan and Alan Stewart (eds.), *The encyclopedia of English Renaissance literature* (Chichester: Wiley-Blackwell, 2012), vol. 1, 196–200.

DE BERNARDIN, SANDRO, 'I Riformatori dello Studio: indirizzi di politica culturale nell'università di Padova', in Gianfranco Folena (ed.), *Storia della cultura veneta* (Vicenza: Neri Pozza, 1976–86), vol. 4:1, 61–91.

DE FRANCESCHI, SYLVIO Hermann, *La crise théologico-politique du premier âge baroque: antiromanisme doctrinal, pouvoir pastoral et raison du prince: le Saint-Siège face au prisme français (1607–1627)* (Rome: École française de Rome, 2009).

De Mas, Enrico, *L'attesa del secolo aureo (1603–1625): saggi di storia delle idee del secolo XVII* (Florence: Olschki, 1982).

De Renzi, Silvia, 'A career in manuscripts: genres and purposes of a physician's writing in Rome, 1600–1630', *Italian Studies*, 66/2 (2011), 234–48.

De Smet, Ingrid A. R., 'Montaigne et Jacques-Auguste de Thou', *Montaigne Studies*, 13 (2001), 223–40.

De Smet, Ingrid A. R., *Thuanus: the making of Jacques-Auguste de Thou (1553–1617)* (Geneva: Droz, 2006).

De Smet, Ingrid A. R., 'La Poésie sur le fumier. La figure de Job à l'époque des Guerres de religion', in Frank Lestringant (ed.), *Jacques-Auguste de Thou (1553–1617): Écriture et condition robine* (Paris: Presses de l'Université Paris-Sorbonne, 2007), 89–106.

de Vivo, Filippo, 'Paolo Sarpi and the uses of information', in Joad Raymond (ed.), *News networks in seventeenth-century Britain and Europe* (London: Routledge, 2006), 35–49.

de Vivo, Filippo, *Information and communication in Venice: rethinking early modern politics* (Oxford: Oxford University Press, 2007).

Dear, Peter, 'The Church and the new philosophy', in Stephen Pumfrey, Maurice Slawinski, and Paolo L. Rossi (eds.), *Science, culture and popular belief in Renaissance Europe* (Manchester: Manchester University Press, 1991), 119–39.

Dekker, R. M., *Childhood, memory and autobiography in Holland: from the Golden Age to Romanticism* (Basingstoke: Palgrave Macmillan, 2000).

Delatour, Jérôme, *Les livres de Claude Dupuy: une bibliothèque humaniste au temps des guerres de religion: d'après l'inventaire dressé par le libraire Denis Duval (1595)* (Villeurbanne: Enssib, 1998).

Delatour, Jérôme, 'Pour une édition critique des *Scaligerana*', *Bibliothèque de l'École des Chartes*, 156 (1998), 407–50.

Delprat, Carole, 'Savoirs et déboires d'un juriste, Bernard de La Roche Flavin (1552–1627)', *Histoire, économie et société*, 19 (2000), 163–84.

Delville, Jean-Pierre, *L'Europe de l'exégèse au XVIe siècle: interprétations de la parabole des ouvriers à la vigne, Matthieu 20, 1–16* (Louvain: Louvain University Press and Peeters, 2004).

Demonet, Marie-Luce, 'Le politique "nécessaire" de Montaigne', in Philippe Desan (ed.), *Montaigne politique, actes du colloque international tenu à University of Chicago (Paris), les 29 et 30 avril 2005* (Paris: H. Champion, 2006), 17–37.

Denby, David, *Great books: my adventures with Homer, Rousseau, Woolf, and other inde-structible writers of the Western world* (New York: Simon & Schuster, 1996).

Deri, C., 'Otto Vaenius ou Van Veen dit "de Brabant"', *Le folklore Brabançon*, 184 (Dec. 1969), 343–6.

Des Maizeaux, Pierre (ed.), *Scaligerana, Thuana, Perroniana, Pithoeana, et Colomesiana*, 2 vols. (Amsterdam: Cóvens and Mortier, 1740).

Desan, Philippe, 'Une édition italienne inconnue des *Essais* (Venise, 1629)', *Montaigne Studies*, 15 (2003), 169–75.

Desan, Philippe (ed.), *Montaigne politique, actes du colloque international tenu à University of Chicago (Paris), les 29 et 30 avril 2005* (Paris: H. Champion, 2006).

Desan, Philippe (ed.), *Dictionnaire de Michel de Montaigne* (2nd edn., Paris: Champion, 2007).

Desan, Philippe, 'Les éditions des *Essais* avec des adresses néerlandaises aux XVIIe et XVIIIe siècles', in Paul. J. Smith and Karl A.E. Enenkel (eds.), *Montaigne and the Low Countries (1580–1700)* (Leiden: Brill, 2007), 327–60.

DESAN, PHILIPPE, 'Montaigne: *Politicus Aquitanicus*', *Nouveau Bulletin de la Société des Amis de Montaigne*, IV/2 ('Numéro spécial: Montaigne et sa région'—also 8th series no. 48) (2008), 345–58.

DEVINCENO, GIOVANNA, 'Marie de Gournay: une théologie libertine', *Montaigne Studies*, 19 (2007), 83–94.

DIEFENDORF, BARBARA B., *Paris city councillors in the sixteenth century: the politics of patrimony* (Princeton: Princeton University Press, 1983).

DOLLIMORE, JONATHAN, *Radical Tragedy: Religion, Ideology, and Power in the Drama of Shakespeare and His Contemporaries* (Chicago: University of Chicago Press, 1984).

DOLVEN, JEFFREY ANDREW, *Scenes of instruction in Renaissance romance* (Chicago: University of Chicago Press, 2007).

DONDI DALL'OROLOGIO, FRANCESCO SCIPIONE, *Serie cronologico-istorica dei Canonici di Padova* (Padua: Stamperia del Seminario, 1805).

DOREZ, LÉON, *Catalogue de la collection Dupuy*, 2 vols. (Paris: Ernest Leroux, 1899).

DOTOLI, G., 'Montaigne et les libertins via Mlle de Gournay', *Journal of Medieval and Renaissance Studies*, 25 (1995), 381–405.

DUFFY, EAMON, *Marking the hours: English people and their prayers 1240–1570* (New Haven: Yale University Press, 2006).

DUSINBERRE, JULIET, 'Virginia Woolf and Montaigne', *Textual Practice*, 5 (1991), 219–41.

EDEN, KATHY, *Friends hold all things in common: tradition, intellectual property, and the 'Adages' of Erasmus* (New Haven: Yale University Press, 2001).

EISENSTEIN, ELIZABETH L., *The printing press as an agent of change: communications and cultural transformations in early modern Europe: Volumes I and II* (Cambridge: Cambridge University Press, 1979).

ERASMUS, DESIDERIUS, *Collected works of Erasmus Volume 31: Adages Ii1 to Iv100*, eds. Margaret Mann and Roger Aubrey Baskerville Mynors (Toronto: University of Toronto Press, 1982).

FANEGO, OTILIA LÓPEZ, 'Contribución al estudio da la influencia de Montaigne en España', *Bulletin de la Société des Amis de Montaigne*, 5th series, 22–23 (1977), 73–102.

FANEGO, OTILIA LÓPEZ, 'Quelques précisions sur Montaigne et l'Inquisition Espagnole', in Pierre Michel, et al. (eds.), *Montaigne et les 'Essais', 1580–1980: actes du Congrès de Bordeaux (Juin 1980)* (Paris: Champion-Slatkine, 1983), 368–78.

FAVARO, ANTONIO (ed.), *Atti della Nazione Germanica Artista nello Studio di Padova* 2 vols. (Venice: R. Deputazione Veneta di Storia Patria, 1911).

FAYE, EMMANUEL, *Philosophie et perfection de l'homme: de la Renaissance à Descartes* (Paris: Librairie philosophique J. Vrin, 1998).

FERGUSON, MARGARET, '1549: A new intellectual élite', in Denis Hollier (ed.), *A new history of French literature* (Cambridge, Massachusetts: Harvard University Press, 1989), 194–8.

FERNÁNDEZ, JOSÉ MARÍA PÉREZ, 'Andrés Laguna: translation and the early modern idea of Europe', *Translation & Literature*, 21 (2012), 299–318.

FINDLEN, PAULA, *Possessing nature: museums, collecting, and scientific culture in early modern Italy* (Berkeley: University of California Press, 1994).

FLORIO, JOHN, *A worlde of wordes, or, Most copious and exact dictionarie in Italian and English* (London: Arnold Hatfield for Edward Blount, 1598).

FOISIL, M., 'L'écriture du for privé', in Roger Chartier (ed.), *De la Renaissance aux Lumières* (Paris: Seuil, 1986), 333–69.

FONTANA, BIANCAMARIA, *Montaigne's politics: authority and governance in the 'Essais'* (Princeton: Princeton University Press, 2008).

FRAGNITO, GIGLIOLA, 'La censura libraria tra Congregazione dell'Indice, Congregazione dell'Inquisizione e Maestro del Sacro Palazzo (1571–1596)', in Ugo Rozzo (ed.), *La censura libraria nell'Europa del secolo XVI: convegno internazionale di studi Cividale del Friuli, 9–10 novembre 1995* (Udine: Forum, 1997), 163–75.

FRAGNITO, GIGLIOLA, 'The expurgatory policy of the church and the works of Gasparo Contarini', in Ronald K. Delph, Michelle M. Fontaine, and John Jeffries Martin (eds.), *Heresy, culture, and religion in early modern Italy: Contexts and Contestations* (Kirksville, Missouri: Truman State University Press, 2006), 193–210.

FRAME, DONALD M., *Montaigne in France, 1812–1852* (New York: Columbia University Press, 1940).

FRAME, DONALD M., *Montaigne's discovery of man: The humanization of a humanist* (New York: Columbia University Press, 1955).

FRAME, DONALD M., 'New light on Montaigne's trip to Paris in 1588', *Romanic Review*, 51 (1960), 161–81.

FRAME, DONALD M., *Montaigne: a biography* (London and New York: Hamish Hamilton and Harcourt, Brace & World, 1965).

FRAME, DONALD M., *Montaigne: a biography* (San Francisco: North Point Press, 1984).

FRAME, DONALD M., *Montaigne, une vie, une oeuvre, 1533–1592... Préface et bibliographie générale par François Rigolot*, trans. J.-C.Arnould, et al. (Paris: H. Champion, 1994).

FRAMPTON, SAUL, *When I am playing with my cat, how do I know she is not playing with me?: Montaigne and being in touch with life* (London: Faber and Faber, 2011).

FRIEDRICH, HUGO, *Montaigne*, ed. Philippe Desan, trans. Dawn Eng (Berkeley: University of California Press, 1991).

FUMAROLI, MARC, 'A spirituality for gentleman', *Times Literary Supplement*, 6 January 1984.

FUMAROLI, MARC, *L'Âge de l'Éloquence: rhétorique et 'res literaria' de la Renaissance au seuil de l'époque classique* (3rd edn., Geneva: Droz, 2002).

FURNESS, HORACE HOWARD (ed.), *A New Variorum Edition of Shakespeare: Hamlet* 2 vols. (15. edn., Philadelphia and London: J. B. Lippincott, 1918).

GABRIELI, V., 'Bacone, la Riforma e Roma nella versione hobbesiana d'un carteggio di Fulgenzio Micanzio', *English Miscellany*, 8 (1957), 195–250.

GAJDA, ALEXANDRA, *The Earl of Essex and late Elizabethan political culture* (Oxford: Oxford University Press, 2012).

GAMBA, ANTONIO and ROSSETTI, LUCIA (eds.), *Giornale della gloriosissima accademia ricovrata A: Verbali delle adunanze accademiche dal 1599 al 1694* (Padua: Accademia galileiana di scienze lettere ed arti in Padova, 1999).

GAMBA, ENRICO and MONTEBELLI, VICO, *Le scienze a Urbino nel tardo Rinascimento* (Urbino: QuattroVenti, 1988).

GARASSE, FRANÇOIS, *Les recherches des Recherches et autres œuvres de Mc Estienne Pasquier* (Paris: Sébastien Chappelet, 1622).

GARASSE, FRANÇOIS, *Apologie... pour son livre contre les atheistes et libertins de nostre siecle. Et response aux censures et calomnies de l'autheur anonyme* (Paris: S. Chappelet, 1624).

GAULLIEUR, EUSÈBE-HENRI, *Études sur la typographie genevoise du XVe au XIXe siècles et sur l'introduction de l'imprimerie en Suisse* (first published 1855; Nieuwkoop: B. de Graaf, 1971).

GELL, ALFRED, *Art and agency: an anthropological theory* (Oxford: Clarendon Press, 1998).

GERLO, A., 'Les études lipsiennes: état de la question', in A. Gerlo (ed.), *Juste Lipse (1547–1606): colloque international tenu en mars, 1987* (Brussels: VUB University Press, 1988), 9–24.

GHEYN, J. VAN DEN (ed.), *'Album Amicorum' de Otto Venius: reproduction intégrale en fac-similé* (Brussels: Société des Bibliophiles et Iconophiles de Belgique, 1911).

GIACONE, F., 'Gli *Essais* di Montaigne e la censura calvinista', *Bibliothèque d'Humanisme et Renaissance*, 48/3 (1986), 671–99.

GIARD, LUCE, 'Remapping knowledge, reshaping institutions', in Stephen Pumfrey, Maurice Slawinski, and Paolo L. Rossi (eds.), *Science, culture and popular belief in Renaissance Europe* (Manchester: Manchester University Press, 1991), 19–47.

GILMONT, JEAN FRANÇOIS, *Le livre réformé au XVIe siècle* (Paris: Bibliothèque nationale de France, 2005).

GIUSTINIANI, NICCOLO ANTONIO, *Serie cronologica dei Vescovi di Padova* (Padua: Stamperia del Seminario, 1786).

GO, KENJI, 'Montaigne's "Cannibals" and *The Tempest* Revisited', *Studies in Philology*, 109 (2012), 455–73.

GOSSMAN, LIONEL, 'Cultural history and crisis: Burckhardt's *Civilization of the Renaissance in Italy*', *Rediscovering history: Culture, politics, and the pysche* (Stanford: Stanford University Press, 1994), 404–27.

GOULART, SIMON, *Histoires admirables et memorables de nostre temps*, 3 vols. (Paris: J. Houzé, 1600–01).

GOULART, SIMON, *Thresor d'histoires admirables et memorables de nostre temps*, 4 vols. (Geneva: Samuel Crespin, 1614–20).

GRAFTON, ANTHONY, *The footnote: a curious history* (Rev. edn., Cambridge, MA: Harvard University Press, 1997).

GRAFTON, ANTHONY, 'Conflict and harmony in the *Collegium Gellianum*', in Leofranc Holford-Strevens and Amiel Vardi (eds.), *The Worlds of Aulus Gellius* (Oxford: Oxford University Press, 2004), 282–317.

GRAFTON, ANTHONY, *The Culture of Correction in Renaissance Europe* (London: British Library, 2011).

GRAFTON, ANTHONY and JARDINE, LISA, *From humanism to the humanities: education and the liberal arts in fifteenth- and sixteenth-century Europe* (Cambridge, MA and London: Harvard University Press and Duckworth, 1986).

GRAHELI, SHANTI, 'Building a library across early-modern Europe. The network of Claude Expilly', paper given at 'International Exchange in the European Book World', University of St. Andrews, 21 June 2013.

GRAVES, AMY, 'Crises d'engagement: Montaigne et la Ligue', in Philippe Desan (ed.), *Montaigne politique, actes du colloque international tenu à University of Chicago (Paris), les 29 et 30 avril 2005* (Paris: H. Champion, 2006), 329–52.

GRAVES, AMY, 'L'art du portrait chez Jacques-Auguste de Thou', in Frank Lestringant (ed.), *Jacques-Auguste de Thou (1553–1617): Écriture et condition robine* (Paris: Presses de l'Université Paris-Sorbonne, 2007), 127–42.

GREEN, FELICITY, *Montaigne and the life of freedom* (Cambridge: Cambridge University Press, 2012).

GREENBLATT, STEPHEN, *Renaissance self-fashioning: from More to Shakespeare* (Chicago: University of Chicago Press, 1980).

GREENBLATT, STEPHEN, *Marvelous possessions: the wonder of the New World* (Oxford: Oxford University Press, 1991).

GREFFE, FLORENCE and LOTHE, JOSÉ, *La vie, les livres et les lectures de Pierre de l'Estoile: nouvelles recherches* (Paris: H. Champion, 2004).

GRENDLER, PAUL F., *The Roman Inquisition and the Venetian press* (Princeton: Princeton University Press, 1977).

GRENDLER, PAUL F., *Renaissance education between religion and politics* (Farnham: Ashgate, 2006).

GROOT, JEROME DE, ' "Euery one teacheth after thyr owne fantasie": French language instruction', in Kathryn M. Moncrief and Kathryn Read McPherson (eds.), *Performing pedagogy in early modern England: gender, instruction and performance* (Farnham: Ashgate, 2011), 33–51.

GUARINI, BATTISTA, *Il pastor fido, or, The faithfull shepheard. Translated out of Italian into English* (London: [Thomas Creede] for Simon Waterson, 1602).

GULLINO, GIUSEPPE, 'I Corner e l'Accademia', in Ezio Riondato (ed.), *Dall'Accademia dei Ricovrati all'Accademia Galileiana: atti del Convegno storico per il IV centenario della fondazione (1599–1999): Padova, 11–12 aprile 2000* (Padua: Accademia Galileiana di scienze, lettere ed arti, 2001), 59–73.

GUMBRECHT, HANS ULRICH, ' "Pathos of the Earthly Progress": Erich Auerbach's everydays', in Seth Lerer (ed.), *Literary history and the challenge of philology: the legacy of Erich Auerbach* (Stanford: Stanford University Press, 1996), 13–35.

GWINNE, MATTHEW, *Orationes duæ* (London: Richard Field, 1605).

HAAK, B., *The Golden Age: Dutch Painters of the Seventeenth Century*, trans. Elizabeth Willems-Treeman (New York: Harry N. Abrams, 1984).

HAMILTON, TOM, 'Compiling histories of the French Wars of Religion: Pierre de L'Estoile's collection in context (1558–1611)', paper given at 'Transforming Information: Record Keeping in the Early Modern World', The British Academy, 9–10 April 2014.

HAMLIN, WILLIAM M., 'The Shakespeare-Montaigne-Sextus nexus: a case study in early modern reading', in Graham Bradshaw, T. G. Bishop, and Peter Holbrook (eds.), *The Shakespearean international yearbook 6: special section, Shakespeare and Montaigne revisited* (Farnham: Ashgate, 2006), 21–36.

HAMLIN, WILLIAM M., 'Florio's Montaigne and the tyranny of "Custome": appropriation, ideology, and early English readership of the *Essayes*', *Renaissance Quarterly*, 63 (2010), 491–544.

HAMLIN, WILLIAM M., 'Sexuality and censorship in Florio's Montaigne', *Montaigne Studies*, 23 (2011), 17–38.

HAMLIN, WILLIAM M., *Montaigne's English journey: reading the 'Essays' in Shakespeare's day* (Oxford: Oxford University Press, 2013).

HAMMER, PAUL E. J., 'The Earl of Essex, Fulke Greville, and the employment of scholars', *Studies in Philology*, 91 (1994), 167–80.

HAMMER, PAUL E. J., 'The uses of scholarship: the secretariat of Robert Devereux, second Earl of Essex, c.1585–1601', *English Historical Review*, 104 (1994), 26–51.

HAMMER, PAUL E. J., 'Essex and Europe: evidence from confidential instructions by the Earl of Essex, 1595–6', *English Historical Review*, 111 (1996), 357–81.

HAMMER, PAUL E. J., *The polarisation of Elizabethan politics: the political career of Robert Devereux, 2nd Earl of Essex, 1585–1597* (Cambridge: Cambridge University Press, 1999).

HAMPTON, TIMOTHY, *Literature and nation in the sixteenth century: inventing Renaissance France* (Ithaca: Cornell University Press, 2001).

HANNAY, MARGARET P., *Philip's Phoenix: Mary Sidney, Countess of Pembroke* (Oxford: Oxford University Press, 1990).

HART, THOMAS, 'Literature as language: Auerbach, Spitzer, Jakobson', in Seth Lerer (ed.), *Literary history and the challenge of philology: the legacy of Erich Auerbach* (Stanford: Stanford University Press, 1996), 227–39.

HARTLIB, SAMUEL, *The true and readie way to learne the Latine tongue* (London: R. and W. Leybourn, 1654).

HEARN, KAREN, 'Lady Anne Clifford's great triptych', in Karen Hearn and Lynn Hulse (eds.), *Lady Anne Clifford: culture, patronage and gender in 17th-century Britain* (Leeds: Yorkshire Archaeological Society, 2009), 1–24.

HEARN, KAREN and HULSE, LYNN (eds.), *Lady Anne Clifford: culture, patronage and gender in 17th-century Britain* (Leeds: Yorkshire Archaeological Society, 2009).

HEILBRON, J. L., *Galileo* (Oxford: Oxford University Press, 2010).

HENKE, ROBERT, *Pastoral transformations: Italian tragicomedy and Shakespeare's late plays* (Newark: University of Delaware Press; London: Associated University Presses, 1997).

HOFFMANN, GEORGE, *Montaigne's career* (Oxford: Clarendon Press, 1998).

HOFFMANN, GEORGE, 'Croiser le fer avec le Géographe du Roi: l'entrevue de Montaigne avec Antoine de Laval aux Etats généraux de Blois en 1588', *Montaigne Studies*, 13 (2001), 207–22.

HOFFMANN, GEORGE, 'Emond Auger et le contexte tridentin de l'essai "Du repentir"', *Bulletin de la Société des Amis de Montaigne*, 8th series, 21–22 (2001), 263–75.

HOFFMANN, GEORGE, 'Introduction', *EMF: Studies in Early Modern France,* 9 (2004), 1–9.

HOFFMANN, GEORGE, 'The investigation of nature', in Ullrich Langer (ed.), *The Cambridge Companion to Montaigne* (Cambridge: Cambridge University Press, 2005), 163–82.

HOFFMANN, GEORGE, 'Laval, Antoine Mathé de (Crémaux, 1550–Moulins, 1632)', in Philippe Desan (ed.), *Dictionnaire de Michel de Montaigne* (2nd edn., Paris: Champion, 2007), 660–2.

HOFFMANN, GEORGE, 'Millanges, Simon (Mille-Millanges, 1540–Bordeaux 1623)', in Philippe Desan (ed.), *Dictionnaire de Michel de Montaigne* (2nd edn., Paris: Champion, 2007), 764–6.

HOFFMANN, GEORGE, 'Sincérité', in Philippe Desan (ed.), *Dictionnaire de Michel de Montaigne* (2nd edn., Paris: Champion, 2007), 920–2.

HOLT, MACK P., 'L'évolution des "Politiques" face aux Églises (1560–1598)', in Thierry Wanegffelen (ed.), *De Michel de L'Hospital à l'édit de Nantes: politique et religion face aux églises* (Clermont-Ferrand: Presses Universitaires Blaise-Pascal, 2002), 591–607.

HOLT, MACK P., 'Divisions within French Calvinism: Philippe Duplessis-Mornay and the Eucharist', in Mack P. Holt (ed.), *Adaptations of Calvinism in Reformation Europe: essays in honour of Brian G. Armstrong* (Farnham: Ashgate, 2007), 165–78.

HOORN, R. J. VAN DEN, 'On course for quality: Justus Lipsius and Leiden University', in K. Enenkel and C. Heesakkers (eds.), *Lipsius in Leiden: studies in the life and works of a great humanist on the occasion of his 450th anniversary* (Voorthuizen: Florivallis, 1997), 73–92.

HOROWITZ, M. C., *Seeds of virtue and knowledge* (Princeton Princeton University Press, 1998).

HOULLEMARE, MARIE, *Politiques de la parole: le parlement de Paris au XVIe siècle* (Geneva: Droz, 2011).

HUCHARD, CÉCILE, 'Histoire et providence dans l'oeuvre de Simon Goulart', *Bulletin de la Société de l'Histoire du Protestantisme Français,* 152 (2006), 221–44.

HUCHARD, CÉCILE, *D'encre et de sang: Simon Goulart et la Saint-Barthélemy* (Paris: Champion, 2007).

HUET, PIERRE DANIEL, *Huetiana, ou, Pensées diverses de M. Huet* (Paris: J. Estienne, 1722).

HUMPHREY, LAURENCE, *Optimates, sive de nobilitate eiusque antiqua origine, natura, officiis, disciplina, et recta ac Christiana institutione libri tres* (Basel: Oporinus, 1560).

HUMPHREY, LAURENCE, *The Nobles: or, of Nobilitye: the original nature, dutyes, right, and Christian institution thereof three bookes* (London: T. Marshe, 1563).

HUNTER, IAN, 'The university philosopher in early modern Germany', in Conal Condren, Stephen Gaukroger, and Ian Hunter (eds.), *The philosopher in early modern Europe: the nature of a contested identity* (Cambridge: Cambridge University Press, 2006), 35–65.

HUOT, SYLVIA, 'The writer's mirror: Watriquet de Couvin and the development of the author-centred book', in Bill Bell, Philip E. Bennett, and Jonquil Bevan (eds.), *Across boundaries: the book in culture & commerce* (Winchester and New Castle, DE: St Paul's Bibliographies and Oak Knoll Press, 2000), 29–46.

INFELISE, MARIO, 'Masters of books: ecclesiastic and state censorship in Venice during the Counter-Reformation', paper given at 'Oxford Seminars on the History of the Book', All Souls College, University of Oxford, February 28, 2012.

INNES, M., 'Memory, orality and literacy in an early medieval society', *Past and Present*, 158 (1998), 3–36.

ISRAEL, J., *The Dutch Republic: Its rise, greatness, and fall 1477–1806* (Oxford: Oxford University Press, 1985).

JAMES, MERVYN EVANS, *Society, politics and culture: studies in early modern England* (Cambridge: Cambridge University Press, 1986).

JAMES, THOMAS, *Catalogus librorum bibliothecae publicae quam vir ornatissimus Thomas Bodleius eques auratus in Academia Oxoniensi nuper instituit* (Oxford: Joseph Barnes, 1605).

JARDINE, LISA, 'Mastering the uncouth: Gabriel Harvey, Edmund Spenser and the English experience in Ireland', in J. Henry and S. Hutton (eds.), *New perspectives on renaissance thought: essays in honour of Charles Schmitt* (London: Duckworth, 1990), 68–82.

JARDINE, LISA, *Erasmus, man of letters: the construction of charisma in print* (Princeton: Princeton University Press, 1993).

JARDINE, LISA and GRAFTON, ANTHONY, ' "Studied for action": how Gabriel Harvey read his Livy', *Past and Present*, 129 (1990), 30–78.

JARDINE, LISA and SHERMAN, WILLIAM, 'Pragmatic readers: knowledge transactions and scholarly services in late Elizabethan England', *Religion, culture and society in early modern Britain: essays in honour of Patrick Collinson* (Cambridge: Cambridge University Press, 1993), 102–24.

JARDINE, LISA and STEWART, ALAN, *Hostage to fortune: the troubled life of Francis Bacon* (London: Gollancz, 1998).

JONES, E. A. and WALSHAM, ALEXANDRA (eds.), *Syon Abbey and its books: reading, writing and religion, c.1400–1700* (Woodbridge: Boydell, 2010).

JONES, LEONARD CHESTER, *Simon Goulart, 1543–1628: étude biographique et bibliographique* (Geneva and Paris: Georg Éditeurs and Librairie Ancienne Honoré Champion, 1917).

JONSON, BEN, *Volpone or the foxe* (London: T. Thorpe, 1607).

JONSON, BEN, *Workes*, 3 vols. (London: Richard Bishop [and Robert Young] for Andrew Crooke [vol. 1]; John Beale, John Dawson, Bernard Alsop and Thomas Fawcet for Richard Meighen [Thomas Walkley and Robert Allot] [vols. 2–3], 1640–41).

JONSON, BEN, *Volpone*, ed. Philip Brockbank (London: E. Benn, 1968).

JOSTOCK, INGEBORG, *La censure négociée: le contrôle du livre à Genève, 1560–1625* (Geneva: Droz, 2007).

JOUANNA, ARLETTE, 'Les ambiguïtés des Politiques face à la Sainte Ligue', in Thierry Wanegffelen (ed.), *De Michel de L'Hospital à l'édit de Nantes: politique et religion face aux églises* (Clermont-Ferrand: Presses Universitaires Blaise-Pascal, 2002), 475–93.

KASTAN, D. SCOTT, ' "The Duke of Milan/And his brave son": dynastic politics in *The Tempest*', in V. Mason Vaughan and A. T. Vaughan (eds.), *Critical essays on Shakespeare's 'The Tempest'* (New York: G.K. Hall, 1998), 91–103.

KENNY, NEIL, 'Patrilinear transmissions of literature and learning: The example of early modern France', paper given at The Warburg Institute, 14 May 2014.

KINSER, SAMUEL, *The works of Jacques-Auguste de Thou* (The Hague: Martinus Nijhoff, 1966).

KNIGHT, JEFFREY TODD, *Bound to read: compilations, collections, and the making of Renaissance literature* (Philadelphia: University of Pennsylvania Press, 2013).

KÖHLER, ERICH (ed.), *Sprachen der Lyrik: Festschrift für Hugo Friedrich zum 70* (Frankfurt: V. Klostermann, 1975).

KOLFIN, ELMER and RIKKEN, MARRIGJE, 'A very personal copy: Pieter van Veen's illustrations to Montaigne's *Essais*', in P. J. Smith and K. A. E. Enenkel (eds.), *Montaigne and the Low Countries (1580–1700)* (Leiden: Brill, 2007), 247–61.

KONUK, KADER, *East–West mimesis: Auerbach in Turkey* (Stanford: Stanford University Press, 2010).

KOOI, C., *Liberty and religion: church and state in Leiden's Reformation* (Leiden: Brill, 2000).

KRAUSE, VIRGINIA, *Idle pursuits: literature and oisiveté in the French Renaissance* (Newark and London: University of Delaware Press and Associated University Presses, 2003).

KRAUSE, VIRGINIA, 'Confession or parrhesia? Foucault after Montaigne', in Zahi Anbra Zalloua (ed.), *Montaigne after theory, theory after Montaigne* (Seattle and Washington: University of Washington Press, in association with Whitman College, 2009), 142–60.

KRAYE, JILL, 'Conceptions of moral philosophy', in Daniel Garber and Michael Ayers (eds.), *The Cambridge history of seventeenth-century philosophy: Volume II* (Cambridge: Cambridge University Press, 1998), 1279–316.

KRISTELLER, PAUL OSKAR, *Studies in Renaissance thought and Letters III* (Rome: Edizioni di Storia e di Letteratura, 1993).

KUNIN, A. B., 'From the desk of Anne Clifford', *English Literary History*, 71 (2004), 587–608.

L'ESTOILE, PIERRE DE, *Mémoires-journaux*, eds. Gustave Brunet, et al., 12 vols. (Paris: Librairie des bibliophiles, 1875–96).

L'ESTOILE, PIERRE DE, *Journal pour le règne de Henri III (1574–1589)*, ed. Louis Raymond Lefèvre (Paris: Gallimard, 1943).

L'ESTOILE, PIERRE DE, *Journal pour le règne de Henri IV*, eds. Louis-Raymond Lefèvre and André Martin, 3 vols. (Paris: Gallimard, 1948–60).

L'ESTOILE, PIERRE DE, *Registre-journal du règne de Henri III: Tome I (1574–1575)*, eds. Madeleine Lazard and Gilbert Schrenck (Geneva: Droz, 1992).

LA BOÉTIE, ÉTIENNE DE, *La mesnagerie de Xenophon. Les regles de mariage de Plutarque. Lettre de consolation, de Plutarque à sa femme…Ensemble quelques vers latins & françois, de son invention. Item, un Discours sur la mort dudit seigneur de La Boëtie, par M. de Montaigne* (Paris: Federic Morel, 1571).

LA BOÉTIE, ÉTIENNE DE, *Mémoire sur la pacification des troubles*, ed. Malcolm Smith (Geneva: Droz, 1983).

LA BOÉTIE, ÉTIENNE DE, *De la servitude volontaire, ou, Contr'un…Avec des notes additionnelles de Michel Magnien*, eds. Malcolm Smith and Michel Magnien (2nd edn., Geneva: Droz, 2001).

LA CHARITÉ, RAYMOND C. (ed.), *O un amy!: Essays on Montaigne in honor of Donald M. Frame* (Lexington, Ky: French Forum, 1977).

LA ROCHE FLAVIN, BERNARD DE, *Treze Livres des Parlemens de France* (Bordeaux: Simon Millanges, 1617).

LAMENT, S. A., 'The Vroedschap of Leiden 1550–1600: the impact of tradition and change on the governing elite of a Dutch city', *Sixteenth Century Journal*, 12/2 (1981), 14–42.

LANCRE, PIERRE DE, *L'incredulité et mescreance du sortilege plainement conuaincue* (Paris: Nicolas Buon, 1622).

LANDAUER, CARL, 'Auerbach's performance and the American academy, or how New Haven stole the idea of *Mimesis*', in Seth Lerer (ed.), *Literary history and the challenge of philology: the legacy of Erich Auerbach* (Stanford: Stanford University Press, 1996), 179–94.

LANDTSHEER, J. DE, 'From Ultima Thule to Finisterra: surfing on the wide web of Justus Lipsius' correspondence', in K. Enenkel and C. Heesakkers (eds.), *Lipsius in Leiden: studies in the life and works of a great humanist on the occasion of his 450th anniversary* (Voorthuizen: Florivallis, 1997), 47–69.

LANDTSHEER, J. DE, 'From north to south: some new documents on Lipsius' journey from Leiden to Liège', in D. Sacré and G Tournoy (eds.), *Myricae: Essays on neo-Latin literature in memory of Jozef Ijsewijn* (Leuven: Leuven University Press, 2000), 303–31.

LANDTSHEER, J. DE, 'Justus Lipsius (1547–1606) and Publius Clodius Thraseus Paetus', *Humanismo y pervivencia del mundo clásico*, 3 (2002), 1283–8.

LANGER, ULLRICH, *Perfect friendship: studies in literature and moral philosophy from Boccaccio to Corneille* (Geneva: Droz, 1994).

LAOUTARIS, CHRIS, 'The radical pedagogies of Lady Elizabeth Russell', in Kathryn M. Moncrief and Kathryn Read McPherson (eds.), *Performing pedagogy in early modern England: gender, instruction and performance* (Farnham: Ashgate, 2011), 65–83.

LARMORE, CHARLES, 'Scepticism', in Daniel Garber and Michael Ayers (eds.), *The Cambridge history of seventeenth-century philosophy: Volume II* (Cambridge: Cambridge University Press, 1998), 1145–92.

LAS CASAS, BARTOLOMÈ DE *Istoria o breussima relatione della distruttione dell'Indie Occidentali*, trans. Giacomo Castellani (Venice: M. Ginammi, 1626).

LAVAL, ANTOINE DE, *Desseins de professions nobles et publiques* (Paris: Abel L'Angelier, 1605).

LAWRENCE, JASON, *'Who the devil taught thee so much Italian?': Italian language learning and literary imitation in early modern England* (Manchester: Manchester University Press, 2005).

LEGRAND, MARIE-DOMINIQUE, 'L'éloge de Michel de L'Hospital d'après Scévole de Sainte Marthe, Guillaume Colletet et Estienne Pasquier', in F. Argod-Dutard (ed.), *Histoire et littérature au siècle de Montaigne: mélanges offerts à Claude-Gilbert Dubois* (Geneva: Droz, 2001), 157–70.

LEGROS, ALAIN, 'Jésuites ou Jésuates? Montaigne entre science et ignorance', *Montaigne Studies*, 15 (2003), 131–46.

LEGROS, ALAIN, 'Ce qui gênait Simon Goulart dans le chapitre 'Des prières' (Montaigne, *Essais*, I, 56) ', *Bibliothèque d'Humanisme et Renaissance*, 67 (2005), 79–91.

LEGROS, ALAIN, 'Montaigne between fortune and providence', in John D. Lyons and Kathleen Wine (eds.), *Chance, literature, and culture in early modern France* (Farnham: Ashgate, 2009), 17–30.

LEGROS, ALAIN, 'Montaigne face à ses censeurs romains de 1581 (mise à jour)', *Bibliothèque d'Humanisme et Renaissance*, 71 (2009), 7–33.

LEGROS, ALAIN, 'Feuillants (monastère)', in Philippe Desan (ed.), *Dictionnaire de Michel de Montaigne* (2nd edn., Paris: Champion, 2007), 455–7.

LEMNIUS, LEVINUS, *De habitu et constitutione corporis* (Jena: Tobias Steinman, 1587).

LESTRINGANT, FRANK, *Le Brésil de Montaigne: le Nouveau Monde des 'Essais' (1580–1592)* (Paris: Chandeigne, 2005).

LEVINE, ALAN, *Sensual philosophy: toleration, skepticism, and Montaigne's politics of the self* (Lanham, MD: Lexington Books, 2001).

LEWALSKI, BARBARA KIEFER, *Writing women in Jacobean England* (Cambridge, MA: Harvard University Press, 1993).

LIESHOUT, H. H. M. VAN, *The making of Pierre Bayle's 'Dictionnaire historique et critique'* (Amsterdam: APA-Holland University Press, 2001).

LINDENBERGER, HERBERT, 'On the reception of *Mimesis*', in Seth Lerer (ed.), *Literary history and the challenge of philology: the legacy of Erich Auerbach* (Stanford: Stanford University Press, 1996), 195–213.

LINDLEY, KEITH (ed.), *The English Civil War and Revolution: A Sourcebook* (London: Routledge, 1998).

LINES, DAVID A., *Aristotle's 'Ethics' in the Italian Renaissance (ca. 1300–1650): the universities and the problem of moral education* (Leiden: Brill, 2002).

LIPSIUS, JUSTUS, *Iusti Lipsi epistolarum selectarum, centuria prima* (Antwerp [Leiden]: Plantin, 1586).

LIPSIUS, JUSTUS, *Epistolae*, eds. A. Gerlo, M. A. Nauwelaerts, and Hendrik D. L. Vervliet (Brussels: Koninklijke Academie voor Wetenschappen, Letteren en Schone Kunsten van België, 1978–).

LIPSIUS, JUSTUS, *Politica: six books of politics or political instruction*, ed. Jan Waszink (Assen: Koninklijke Van Gorcum BV, 2004).

LIPSIUS, JUSTUS, *Concerning constancy*, ed. R. V. Young (Tempe: Arizona Center for Medieval and Renaissance Studies, 2011).

LOCKE, JOHN, *De l'éducation des enfans...sur la dernière édition revue, corrigée et augmentée*, trans. Pierre Coste (Amsterdam: H. Schelte, 1708).

LOCKE, JOHN, *The educational writings*, ed. James Axtell (Cambridge: Cambridge University Press, 1968).

LOCKE, JOHN, *Some thoughts concerning education*, eds. John W. Yolton and Jean S. Yolton (Oxford: Clarendon, 1989).

LOEWENSTEIN, JOSEPH, *Ben Jonson and possessive authorship* (Cambridge: Cambridge University Press, 2002).

LOISEL, ANTOINE, *La Guyenne...qui sont huict remonstrances facites en la Chambre de Justice de Guyenne sur le subject des Edicts de Pacification* (Paris: Abel L'Angelier, 1605).

LONDON, WILLIAM, *A catalogue of the most vendible books in England (1657, 1658, 1660)* (London: Gregg Press in association with Archive Press, 1965).

LOREDANO, GIOVANNI FRANCESCO (ed.), *Discorsi academici de' signori incogniti, havuti in Venetia* (Venice: Giacomo Sarzina, 1635).

LUCEY, MICHAEL, 'A literary object's contextual life', in Ali Behdad and Dominic Thomas (eds.), *A companion to comparative literature* (Chichester: Wiley-Blackwell, 2011), 120–35.

MACDONALD, KATHERINE, 'Un exemplaire illustré des *Elogia gallorum doctrina illustrium* (1602) de Scévole de Sainte-Marthe et l'iconographie de Joachim Du Bellay: un portrait inconnu?', *Bibliothèque d'Humanisme et Renaissance*, 64 (2002), 79–95.

MACDONALD, KATHERINE, *Biography in early modern France, 1540–1630: forms and functions* (London: Legenda, 2007).

MACHARDY, K. J., 'Cultural capital, family strategies and noble identity in early modern Habsburg Austria', *Past and Present*, 163 (1999), 36–75.

MACK, MAYNARD, *Collected in himself: essays critical, biographical, and bibliographical on Pope and some of his contemporaries* (East Brunswick, London and Toronto: Associated University Presses, 1982).

MACK, PETER, 'Marston and Webster's use of Florio's Montaigne', *Montaigne Studies*, 24 (2012), 67–82.

MACLEAN, IAN, 'L'Économie du livre érudit: le cas Wechel (1572–1627)', in Pierre Aquilon, Henri-Jean Martin, and François Dupuigrenet Desroussilles (eds.), *Le livre dans l'Europe de la Renaissance: actes du XXVIIIe Colloque international d'études humanistes de Tours* ([Paris]: Promodis, Editions du Cercle de la librairie, 1988), 230–9.

MACLEAN, IAN, *Montaigne philosophe* (Paris: Presses Universitaires de France, 1996).

MACLEAN, IAN, *Learning and the market place: essays in the history of the early modern book* (Leiden: Brill, 2009).

MACLEAN, IAN, *Scholarship, commerce, religion: the learned book in the age of confessions, 1560–1630* (Cambridge, MA: Harvard University Press, 2012).

McGOWAN, MARGARET, ' "La conversation de ma vie": la voix de L'Estoile dans les *Registres/Journaux*', *Travaux de Littérature (T.L.)*, 3 (1990), 249–59.

McKITTERICK, DAVID, *Print, manuscript, and the search for order, 1450–1830* (Cambridge: Cambridge University Press, 2003).

McKITTERICK, ROSAMOND, 'Text and image in the Carolingian world', in Rosamond McKitterick (ed.), *The uses of literacy in early mediaeval Europe* (Cambridge: Cambridge University Press, 1990), 297–318.

McKITTERICK, ROSAMOND (ed.), *The uses of literacy in early mediaeval Europe* (Cambridge: Cambridge University Press, 1990).

MAGNIEN, CATHERINE, 'Étienne Pasquier "familier" de Montaigne?', *Montaigne Studies*, 13 (2001), 277–313.

MAGNIEN, CATHERINE, 'Loisel, Antoine (Beauvais, 1536–Paris, 1617)', in Philippe Desan (ed.), *Dictionnaire de Michel de Montaigne* (2nd edn., Paris: Champion, 2007), 660–2.

MAGNIEN, CATHERINE, 'Raemond, Florimond de (Agen, v. 1540–Bordeaux, 1601)', in Philippe Desan (ed.), *Dictionnaire de Michel de Montaigne* (2nd edn., Paris: Champion, 2007), 993–4.

MAGNIEN, MICHEL, 'La Boétie traducteur des anciens', in Marcel Tetel (ed.), *Étienne de La Boétie: Sage révolutionnaire et poète périgourdin: Actes du Colloque International Duke University, 26–28 mars 1999* (Paris: Honoré Champion, 2004), 15–44.

MAILLEFER, JEAN, *Mémoires de J. Maillefer, marchand bourgeois de Reims, 1611–1684, continués par son fils jusqu'en 1716*, ed. Charles Henri Jadart (Paris and Rheims: Alph. Picard and F. Michaud, 1890).

MALCOLM, NOEL, *De Dominis, 1560–1624: Venetian, Anglican, ecumenist, and relapsed heretic* (London: Strickland & Scott Academic Publications, 1984).

MANDER, K. VAN, *Lives of the illustrious Netherlandish and German painters, from the first edition of the Schilder-boeck (1603–1604): preceded by the lineage, circumstances and place of birth, life and works of Karel van Mander, painter and poet and likewise his death and burial, from the second edition of the Schilder-boeck (1616–1618)*, ed. H. Miedema, 6 vols. (Doornspijk: Davaco, 1994–1999).

MANDOSIO, JEAN-MARC, 'La miscellanée: histoire d'un genre', in Dominique de Courcelles (ed.), *Ouvrages miscellanées et théories de la connaissance à la Renaissance: actes des journées d'études organisées par l'École nationale des chartes (Paris, 5–6 avril 2002)* (Paris: École des chartes, 2003), 7–36.

MARCHI, DUDLEY M., *Montaigne among the moderns: receptions of the 'Essais'* (Providence, RI: Berghahn Books, 1994).

MARNIX, PHILIPPE DE, *Tableau des differens de la religion* (Leiden: Jean Doreau, 1602).

MARSTON, JOHN, *The Dutch Courtezan. As it was playd in the Blacke-Friars, by the Children of her Maiesties Revels* (London: T. P. for John Hodgets, 1605).

MARTIN, JULIAN, 'Natural philosophy and its public concerns', in Stephen Pumfrey, Maurice Slawinski, and Paolo L. Rossi (eds.), *Science, culture and popular belief in Renaissance Europe* (Manchester: Manchester University Press, 1991), 100–18.

MASKELL, D., 'Montaigne médiateur entre Navarre et Guise', *Bibliothèque d'Humanisme et Renaissance*, 41 (1979), 541–53.

MAYER, THOMAS F., *The Roman Inquisition: a papal bureaucracy and its laws in the age of Galileo* (Philadelphia: University of Pennsylvania Press, 2013).

MEARS, NATALIE, 'Politics in the Elizabethan Privy Chamber: Lady Mary Sidney and Kat Ashley', in James Daybell (ed.), *Women and politics in early modern England, 1450–1700* (Farnham: Ashgate, 2004), 67–82.

MEGNA, LAURA, 'Federico Cornaro e l`Accademia padovana dei Ricovrati', *Studi Veneziani*, 43 (2002), 331–48.

MELEHY, HASSAN, *The poetics of literary transfer in early modern France and England* (Farnham: Ashgate, 2010).

MESKENS, ANN, *Eindelijk buiten: filosofische stadswandelingen* (Rotterdam: Lemniscaat, 2007).

MICANZIO, FULGENZIO, *Vita del padre Paolo, dell'ordine de' Servi; e theologo della serenissima republ. di Venetia* (Leiden: Joris Abrahamsz van der Marsce, 1646).

MICHAUD, J. F. and POUJOULAT, J. J. F., *Nouvelle collection des Mémoires pour servir à l'histoire de France depuis le XIIIe siècle jusqu'à la fin du XVIIIe: . . . Registre-journal de Henri III, publié d'après le manuscrit autographe de L'Estoile*, eds. J.J. Champollion-Figeac and A.L. Champollion-Figeac (2nd ser., vol. 1; Paris: L'Éditeur du commentaire analytique du code civil, 1837).

MICHEL, E., *Catalogue raisonné des peintures du moyen-âge, de la renaissance et des temps modernes. Peintures flamandes du XVe et du XVIe siècle* (Paris: Éditions des Musées nationaux, 1953).

MILLER, PETER N., *Peiresc's Europe: learning and virtue in the seventeenth century* (New Haven: Yale University Press, 2000).

MILLET, OLIVIER, *La première réception des 'Essais' de Montaigne: (1580–1640)* (Paris: Champion, 1995).

MILLET, OLIVIER, 'Dominicus Baudius lecteur de Montaigne', in Paul. J. Smith and Karl A.E. Enenkel (eds.), *Montaigne and the Low Countries (1580–1700)* (Leiden: Brill, 2007), 119–39.

MILTON, J., 'Pierre Coste, John Locke, and the Third Earl of Shaftesbury', in Sarah Hutton, Paul Schuurman, and G. A. J. Rogers (eds.), *Studies on Locke: sources, contemporaries, and legacy: in honour of G.A.J. Rogers* (Dordrecht: Springer, 2008), 195–223.

MILTON, JOHN, *Of education. To Master Samuel Hartlib* (London: printed for Thomas Underhill and/for Thomas Johnson, 1644).

MOLHUYSEN, P. C. and BLOK, P. J. (eds.), *Nieuw Nederlandsch biografisch woordenboek* 10 vols. (Leiden: Sijthoff, 1911–37).

MONCRIEF, KATHRYN M. and MCPHERSON, KATHRYN READ (eds.), *Performing pedagogy in early modern England: gender, instruction and performance* (Farnham: Ashgate, 2011).

MONTAIGNE, MICHEL DE, *Essais*, 2 vols. (Bordeaux: Simon Millanges, 1580).

MONTAIGNE, MICHEL DE, *Essais* (Bordeaux: Simon Millanges, 1582).

MONTAIGNE, MICHEL DE, *Essais* (Paris: Abel L'Angelier, 1588).

MONTAIGNE, MICHEL DE, *Discorsi morali, politici, et militari . . . Con un discorso se il forastiero si deve admettere alla administratione della republica*, trans. Girolamo Naselli (Ferrara: Benedetto Mamarello, 1590).

MONTAIGNE, MICHEL DE, *Livre des Essais* (Lyon: Gabriel La Grange, 1593).

MONTAIGNE, MICHEL DE, *Les Essais*, ed. Marie Le Jars De Gournay (Paris: Abel L'Angelier, 1595).

MONTAIGNE, MICHEL DE, *Les Essais* (Lyon [Geneva]: François Le Febvre, 1595).

MONTAIGNE, MICHEL DE, *Les Essais* (Leiden [Geneva]: Jehan Doreau, 1602a).

MONTAIGNE, MICHEL DE, *Les Essais* (Leiden or Cologny [Geneva]: Jean Doreau, 1602b).

MONTAIGNE, MICHEL DE, *The essayes or morall, politike and millitarie discourses*, trans. John Florio (London: Valentine Simmes for Edward Blount, 1603).

MONTAIGNE, MICHEL DE, *Essayes* (London: Melch. Bradwood for Edward Blount and William Barret, 1613).

MONTAIGNE, MICHEL DE, *The essayes or morall, politike and millitarie discourses*, trans. John Florio (London: M. Flesher for R. Royston, 1632).

MONTAIGNE, MICHEL DE, *Saggi . . ., ouero Discorsi, naturali, politici, e morali*, trans. Girolamo Canini (Venice: Marco Ginammi, 1633).

MONTAIGNE, MICHEL DE, *Apologia di Raimondo di Sebonda*, trans. Anon. (Venice: Marco Ginammi, 1634).

MONTAIGNE, MICHEL DE, *Essays*, trans. Charles Cotton, 3 vols. (London: M. Gillyflower, W. Hensman and R. Wellington, 1700).

MONTAIGNE, MICHEL DE, *Essays*, trans. Charles Cotton, 3 vols. (4th edn., London: Daniel Brown et al., 1711).

MONTAIGNE, MICHEL DE, *Les Essais*, ed. Pierre Coste, 3 vols. (Paris: Par La Société, 1725).

MONTAIGNE, MICHEL DE, *'Essais' de Michel de Montaigne: texte original de 1580 avec les variantes des éditions de 1582 et 1587*, eds. Reinhold Dezeimeris and Henri Auguste Barckhausen, 2 vols. (Bordeaux: Féret & Fils, 1870–73).

MONTAIGNE, MICHEL DE, *Les Essais. . . . Publiés d'après l'exemplaire de Bordeaux, avec les variantes manuscrites & les leçons des plus anciennes impressions, des notes, des notices et un lexique*, eds. Fortunat Strowski, et al., 5 vols. (Bordeaux: Imprimerie nouvelle F. Pech & Compagnie, 1906–33).

MONTAIGNE, MICHEL DE, *Les Essais*, ed. Pierre Villey, 3 vols. (Paris: F. Alcan, 1930–31).

MONTAIGNE, MICHEL DE (ed.), *Selected Essays*, trans. Donald M. Frame (New York: W. J. Black for the Classics Club, 1943).

MONTAIGNE, MICHEL DE, *The Complete Works: Essays, Travel Journal, Letters*, trans. D. M. Frame (Stanford: Stanford University Press, 1957).

MONTAIGNE, MICHEL DE, *Complete Essays*, trans. Donald M. Frame (Stanford: Stanford University Press, 1958).

MONTAIGNE, MICHEL DE, *Œuvres complètes*, eds. Maurice Rat and Albert Thibaudet (Paris: Gallimard, 1962).

MONTAIGNE, MICHEL DE, *Essais*, eds. Pierre Villey and V.-L. Saulnier (Paris: Presses Universitaires de France, 1965).

MONTAIGNE, MICHEL DE, *The Complete Essays*, trans. M. A. Screech (London: Penguin Books, 1991).

MONTAIGNE, MICHEL DE, *Journal de voyage*, ed. François Rigolot (Paris: Presses Universitaires de France, 1992).

MONTAIGNE, MICHEL DE, *Essais*, ed. André Tournon, 3 vols. (Paris: Imprimerie nationale, 1998).

MONTAIGNE, MICHEL DE, *Les Essais*, eds. Jean Céard, et al. (Paris: Livre de Poche, 2001).

MONTAIGNE, MICHEL DE, *Les Essais*, eds. Jean Balsamo, et al. (Paris: Gallimard, 2007).

MONTOYA, ALICIA C., 'A woman translator of Montaigne. Appreciation and appropriation in Maria Heyns's *Bloemhof der dooluchtige voorbeelden* (1647)', in Paul. J. Smith and Karl

Bibliography

A. E. Enenkel (eds.), *Montaigne and the Low Countries (1580–1700)* (Leiden: Brill, 2007), 223–45.

MOORE, HELEN, 'Sir Philip Sidney and the *Arcadias*', in Mike Pincombe and Cathy Shrank (eds.), *The Oxford Handbook of Tudor Literature, 1485–1603* (Oxford: Oxford University Press, 2009), 637–51.

MORANTI, MARIA and MORANTI, LUIGI, *Il trasferimento dei 'Codices urbinates' alla Biblioteca Vaticana: cronistoria, documenti e inventario* (Urbino: Accademia Raffaello, 1981).

MORDENTI, RAUL, 'Les livres de famille en Italie', *Annales*, 59 (2004), 785–804.

MORETTI, MASSIMO, 'I Padri Caracciolini del SS. Crocefisso di Casteldurante: da eredi a custodi della Biblioteca di Francesco Maria II Della Rovere', in M. Mei and F. Paoli (eds.), *La libraria di Francesco Maria II Della Rovere a Casteldurante. Da collezione ducale a biblioteca della città* (Urbino: Quattroventi, 2008), 117–28.

MORFORD, M., '*Theatrum hodiernae vitae*: Lipsius, Vaenius, and the rebellion of Civilis', in K. Enenkel, et al. (eds.), *Recreating ancient history: episodes from the Greek and Roman past in the arts and literature of the Early Modern Period* (Leiden: Brill, 2001), 57–74.

MORFORD, M., 'Lipsius' letters of recommendation', in T. Van Houdt, et al. (eds.), *Self-presentation and social identification: the rhetoric and pragmatics of letter writing in early modern times* (Leuven: Leuven University Press, 2002), 183–98.

MORGAN, JOHN, *Godly learning* (Cambridge: Cambridge University Press, 1986).

MORGAN, V., 'Approaches to the history of the English universities in the sixteenth and seventeenth centuries', in G. Klingenstein, H. Lutz, and G. Stourzh (eds.), *Bildung, Politik und Gesellschaft: Studien zur Geschichte des europäischen Bildungswesens vom 16. bis zum 20. Jahrhundert* (Vienna: Verlag für Geschichte und Politik, 1978), 138–64.

MOSMANS, A. G. J., 'Een belanrijke maltenschap van oude schilderijen', *Oud Holland*, 54 (1937), 214–18.

MOTTA, UBERTO, *Antonio Querenghi (1546–1633): un letterato padovano nella Roma del tardo Rinascimento* (Milan: Vita e pensiero, 1997).

MOTTU-WEBER, LILIANE, PIUZ, ANNE-MARIE, and LESCAZE, BERNARD (eds.), *Vivre à Genève autour de 1600*, 2 vols. (Geneva: Slatkine, 2002–6).

MOUT, M.E.H.N., 'Justus Lipsius at Leiden University 1578–1591', in A. Gerlo (ed.), *Juste Lipse (1547–1606): colloque international tenu en mars, 1987* (Brussels: VUB University Press, 1988), 85–99.

MOUT, N., ' "Which tyrant curtails my free mind?" Lipsius and the reception of *De constantia*', in K. Enenkel and C. Heesakkers (eds.), *Lipsius in Leiden: studies in the life and works of a great humanist on the occasion of his 450th anniversary* (Voorthuizen: Florivallis, 1997), 123–40.

MÜLLER, CORINNE, 'L'édition subreptice des *Six Livres de la République* de Jean Bodin (Genève 1577). Sa génèse et son influence', *Quaerendo*, 10 (1980), 211–36.

MUNRO, LUCY, *Children of the Queen's Revels: a Jacobean theatre repertory* (Cambridge: Cambridge University Press, 2005).

NAKAM, GÉRALDE, *Montaigne et son temps: les événements et les 'Essais'* (Paris: Nizet, 1982).

NAKAM, GÉRALDE, *Les 'Essais' de Montaigne, miroir et procès de leur temps: témoignage historique et création littéraire* (Paris: Librairie A.-G. Nizet and Publications de la Sorbonne, 1984).

NAKAM, GÉRALDE, 'Estienne de La Boétie, Mémoire sur la pacification des troubles', *Bulletin de l'Association d'étude sur l'humanisme, la réforme et la renaissance*, 20 (1985), 62–6.

NAPOLI, MARIA C., *L'impresa del libro nell'Italia del Seicento: La bottega di Marco Ginammi* (Naples: Guida Editori, 1990).

NARVESON, KATE, *Bible readers and lay writers in early modern England: gender and self-definition in an emergent writing culture* (Farnham: Ashgate, 2012).

NAUDÉ, GABRIEL, *Bibliographia politica* (Venice: Apud Franciscum Baba, 1633).

NAUDÉ, GABRIEL, *Bibliografia politica*, ed. Domenico Bosco (Rome: Bulzoni, 1997).

NELLES, PAUL, 'Stocking a library: Montaigne, the market, and the diffusion of print', in Philip Ford and Neil Kenny (eds.), *La librairie de Montaigne: Proceedings of the tenth Cambridge French Renaissance Colloquium 2–4 September 2008* (Cambridge: Cambridge French Colloquia, 2012), 1–24.

NETZLOFF, MARK, 'Jonson's *Volpone* and the information economy of Anglo-Venetian travel and intelligence', in John Watkins and Kathryn Reyerson (eds.), *Mediterranean identities in the premodern era: entrepôts, islands, empires* (Farnham: Ashgate, 2014), 73–91.

NEWMAN, PETER, *The old service: Royalist regimental colonels and the Civil War, 1642–46* (Manchester: Manchester University Press, 1993).

NICHOLS, JOHN, *The progresses, processions and magnificent festivities of King James the First, his royal consort, family and court*, 4 vols. (London: J. B. Nichols, printer to the Society of Antiquaries, 1828).

NIXON, ANTHONY, *Oxfords triumph* (London: Edward Allde for John Hodgets, 1605).

NUOVO, ANGELA, 'L'Editoria veneziana del XVII secolo e il problema americano: La pubblicazione delle opere di Bartolomè de Las Casas (Venezia, Marco Ginammi, 1626–43)', in Angela Caracciolo Aricò (ed.), *L'impatto della scoperta dell'America nella cultura veneziana* (Rome: Bulzoni, 1990), 175–86.

NUOVO, ANGELA, *Il commercio librario nell'Italia del Rinascimento* (second edn.; Milan: F. Angeli, 2003).

O'BRIEN, JOHN, 'Le Magistrat comme philosophe: La Roche Flavin lecteur de Montaigne et de Charron', *Bulletin de la Société Internationale des Amis de Montaigne*, 55 (2012), 221–34.

O'BRIEN, JOHN, 'Montaigne, Sir Ralph Bankes and other English readers of the *Essais*', *Renaissance Studies*, 28 (2014), 377–91.

O'MALLEY, SUSAN GUSHEE, *Custome is an idiot: Jacobean pamphlet literature on women* (Urbana: University of Illinois Press, 2004).

O'MALLEY, SUSAN GUSHEE, 'Was Anonymous a jokester?: the anonymous pamphlet *Haec-Vir: Or The Womanish-Man*', in Janet Wright Starner and Barbara Howard Traister (eds.), *Anonymity in early modern England: 'what's in a name?'* (Farnham: Ashgate, 2011), 129–40.

OLIVIERI, ACHILLE, 'I Ricovrati e le trasformazioni dell'idea di prudenza: "l'antro e le parole"', in Ezio Riondato (ed.), *Dall'Accademia dei Ricovrati all'Accademia Galileiana: atti del Convegno storico per il IV centenario della fondazione (1599–1999): Padova, 11–12 aprile 2000* (Padua: Accademia Galileiana di scienze, lettere ed arti, 2001), 361–74.

ORRELL, JOHN, *The human stage: English theatre design, 1567–1640* (Cambridge: Cambridge University Press, 1988).

PABON, N. J., 'Iets over Mr. Pieter van Veen en zijn familie', *Oud Holland* 41 (1923–24), 241–9.

PALLIER, D., *Recherches sur l'imprimerie à Paris pendant la Ligue, 1585–1594* (Geneva: Droz, 1975).

PAPY, J., 'Lipsius's (Neo-)Stoicism: constancy between Christian faith and stoic virtue', *Grotiana*, 22–3, new series (2001–02), 47–71.

PAPY, JAN, 'Le sénéquisme dans la correspondance de Juste Lipse: Du *De Constantia* (1583) à la *Epistolarum Selectarum Centuria Prima Miscellanea* (1586)', paper given at 'Aspects du néo-stoïcisme en Europe aux XVIe et XVIIe siècles', Centre d'Études Supérieures de la Renaissance (Tours), 8–10 October 1998.

PARSONS, JOTHAM, *The church in the republic: Gallicanism & political ideology in Renaissance France* (Washington, DC: Catholic University of America Press, 2004).

PASQUIER, ÉTIENNE, *Les lettres*, 2 vols. (Paris: Laurent Sonnius, 1619).

PASQUIER, ÉTIENNE, *Choix de lettres sur la littérature, la langue et la traduction*, ed. D. Thickett (Geneva: Droz, 1956).

PASQUIER, ÉTIENNE, *Lettres familières*, ed. D. Thickett (Geneva: Droz, 1974).

PASQUIER, ÉTIENNE, *Les recherches de la France*, eds. Marie-Madeleine Fragonard and François Roudaut (Paris: H. Champion, 1996).

PERRET, JEAN-PIERRE, *Les Imprimeries d'Yverdon au XVIIᵉ et au XVIIIᵉ siècle* (Lausanne: Librairie de Droit, 1945).

PERRY, CURTIS, *The making of Jacobean culture: James I and the renegotiation of Elizabethan literary practice* (Cambridge: Cambridge University Press, 1997).

PETITMENGIN, PIERRE, 'De Théodore de Bèze à Jacques Godefroy. Travaux genevois sur Tertullien et Cyprien', in Irena Dorota Backus (ed.), *Théodore de Bèze (1519–1605): actes du colloque de Genève (septembre 2005)* (Geneva: Droz, 2007), 309–37.

PETRUCCI, ARMANDO, *Writers and readers in medieval Italy: studies in the history of written culture*, trans. Charles Radding (New Haven: Yale University Press, 1995).

PETRUCCI, ARMANDO, 'Reading to read: a future for reading', in Guglielmo Cavallo and Roger Chartier (eds.), *A history of reading in the West* (Cambridge: Polity, 1999), 345–67.

PETRUCCI, ARMANDO, *Scrivere e leggere nell'Italia medievale* (Milan: Sylvestre Bonnard, 2007).

PETTEGREE, ANDREW, *The book in the Renaissance* (New Haven: Yale University Press, 2010).

PETTEGREE, ANDREW, 'North and south: cultural transmission in the sixteenth-century European book world', *Bulletin of Spanish Studies*, 89 (2012), 507–20.

PICOT, GEORGES, *Histoire des États généraux, considérés au point de vue de leur influence sur le gouvernement de la France de 1355 à 1614*, 4 vols. (Paris: Hachette, 1872).

PINELLI, GIAN VINCENZO and DUPUY, CLAUDE, *Gian Vincenzo Pinelli et Claude Dupuy: Une correspondance entre deux humanistes*, ed. Anna Maria Raugei, 2 vols. (Florence: L. S. Olschki, 2001).

PLUTARCH, *The lives of the noble Grecians and Romanes*, trans. Thomas North (London: Thomas Vautroullier and John Wight, 1579).

PLUTARCH, *Les Œuvres morales et meslees*, ed. Simon Goulart, 2 vols. (Lyon: Paul Frelon, 1615).

POPPI, A., 'Il problema della filosofia morale nella scuola padovana del rinascimento: Platonismo e Aristotelismo nella definizione del metodo dell'etica', *Platon et Aristote à la Renaissance: XVIe Colloque international de Tours* (Paris: J. Vrin, 1976), 104–46.

PREDA, ALESSANDRA, ' "Les siècles à venir te loueront à bon droit": Montaigne et Claude Expilly', *Montaigne Studies*, 13 (2001), 187–205.

PRIOR, CHARLES W. A., *A confusion of tongues: Britain's wars of Reformation, 1625–1642* (Oxford: Oxford University Press, 2012).

PRIOR, CHARLES W. A. and BURGESS, GLENN (eds.), *England's wars of religion, revisited* (Farnham: Ashgate, 2011).

QUANTIN, JEAN-LOUIS, 'Les censures de Montaigne à l'Index romain: précisions et corrections', *Montaigne Studies*, 26 (2014), 145–62.

QUERENGHI, ANTONIO, *Hexametri carminis libri sex. Rhapsodiae variorum carminum libri V* (Rome: Apud Bartholomæum Zannettum, 1618).

QUERENGHI, FLAVIO, *Alchimia delle passioni dell'animo* ([Padua and Vicenza]: [n.p.], [1620]).

QUERENGHI, FLAVIO, *Ragionamento dello Studio di Padova nella partenza dell'illustrissimo sig. podesta Ottauiano Bon* (Padua: G.B. Martini, *c*.1622–3).

QUERENGHI, FLAVIO, *Institutionum moralium epitome; alter, de genere dicendi philosophorum, seu, de sapientiae et eloquentiae divortio* (Leiden: ex officina J. Maire, 1639).

QUERENGHI, FLAVIO, *Institutionum moralium epitome. De sapientiae & eloquentiae divortio. De consiliario. De honore. De numero virtutum moralium. Introductio in philosophiam moralem Aristotelis* (Paris: Apud Viduam Mathurini Dupuis, 1643).

QUERENGHI, FLAVIO, *Discorsi morali politici et naturali* (Padua: Giulio Crivellari, 1644).

QUINT, DAVID, *Epic and empire: politics and generic form from Virgil to Milton* (Princeton: Princeton University Press, 1993).

QUINT, DAVID, 'A reconsideration of Montaigne's *Des cannibales*', in Karen Ordahl Kupperman (ed.), *America in European consciousness, 1493–1750* (Chapel Hill: Institute of Early American History and Culture, Williamsburg, Virginia, 1995), 166–92.

QUINT, DAVID, *Montaigne and the quality of mercy: ethical and political themes in the 'Essais'* (Princeton: Princeton University Press, 1998).

RABELAIS, FRANÇOIS, *Œuvres complètes*, eds. Jacques Boulenger and Lucien Scheler (Paris: Gallimard, 1955).

RAEMOND, FLORIMOND DE, *Erreur populaire de la papesse Jane* (Bordeaux: Simon Millanges, 1587).

RAPETTI, ELENA, *Pierre-Daniel Huet: erudizione, filosofia, apologetica* (Milan: Vita e pensiero, 1999).

REDMOND, MICHAEL J., *Shakespeare, politics, and Italy: intertextuality on the Jacobean stage* (Farnham: Ashgate, 2009).

REGOSIN, RICHARD, '1595: Montaigne and His Readers', in Denis Hollier (ed.), *A new history of French literature* (Cambridge, MA: Harvard University Press, 1989), 248–53.

RENDALL, STEVEN F., 'The principle of non-correction', in Marcel Tetel and G. Mallary Masters (eds.), *Le Parcours des 'Essais': Montaigne, 1588–1988: colloque international, Duke University, Université de la Caroline du Nord-Chapel Hill, 7–9 avril 1988* (Paris: Aux Amateurs de livres, 1989), 253–62.

RIBARD, DINAH and SCHAPIRA, NICOLAS, 'À la recherche des écritures protestataires dans la France du XVIIe siècle. Du répertoire à l'action', *Genèses*, 64 (2006/3), 146–62.

RIEU, W. N. DU (ed.), *Album Studiosorum Academiæ Lugduno Batavae, 1575–1875*, 2 vols. (The Hague: Martinus Nijhoff, 1875).

RIGOLOT, FRANÇOIS, 'Montaigne et Aristote: La conversion à l'*Ethique à Nicomaque*', in Ullrich Langer (ed.), *Au-delà de la Póetique: Aristote et la littérature de la Renaissance = Beyond the Poetics: Aristotle and early modern literature* (Geneva: Droz, 2002), 43–63.

RIGOLOT, FRANÇOIS, 'Quand Montaigne emprunte à l'Ethique à Nicomaque: étude des "allongeails" sur l'" Exemplaire de Bordeaux', *Montaigne Studies*, 14 (2002), 19–35.

RINALDI, CESARE, *Lettere* (Venice: Tomaso Baglioni, 1617).

RINGER, FRITZ K., *The decline of the German Mandarins: the German academic community, 1890–1933* (2nd edn., Hanover: Wesleyan University Press, 1990).

ROBERTS, HUGH, *Dogs' tales: representations of ancient Cynicism in French Renaissance texts* (Amsterdam: Rodopi, 2006).

ROELKER, NANCY L., *One king, one faith: the Parlement of Paris and the religious reformations of the sixteenth century* (Berkeley: University of California Press, 1996).

ROSSETTI, LUCIA (ed.), *Acta nationis Germanicae artistarum, 1616–1636* (Padua: Editrice Antenore, 1967).

RUMBOLD, MARGARET E., *Traducteur huguenot: Pierre Coste* (New York: P. Lang, 1991).

RYAN, ALAN, *John Dewey and the high tide of American liberalism* (New York: W.W. Norton, 1995).

SAHLINS, PETER, *Unnaturally French: foreign citizens in the Old Regime and after* (Ithaca: Cornell University Press, 2004).

SAID, EDWARD, *The World, the Text, and the Critic* (Cambridge, MA: Harvard University Press, 1983).

SAINCT SERNIN, JONATAN DE, *Essais et observations sur les Essais du Seigneur de Montagne* (London: Edward Allde, 1626).

SAINTE-MARTHE, SCÉVOLE DE, *Virorum doctrina illustrium, qui hoc seculo in Gallia floruerunt, elogia* (Poitiers: Jean Blanchet, 1598).

SAINTE-MARTHE, SCÉVOLE DE, *Gallorum doctrina illustrium, qui nostra patrúmque memoria floruerunt, elogia* (Poitiers: Jean Blanchet, 1602).

SAINTE-MARTHE, SCÉVOLE DE, *Poemata et Elogia, collecta nunc in unum corpus, & ab auctore partim aucta, partim recognita* (Poitiers: Apud viduam Joannis Blanceti, 1606).

SAINTE-MARTHE, SCÉVOLE DE, *Opera* (Paris: P. Durand, 1616).

SALINGAR, LEO, 'King Lear, Montaigne and Harsnett', *Anglo-American Studies*, (Salamanca) 3/2 (November 1983), 145–74.

SALMAN, JEROEN, HARMS, ROELAND, and RAYMOND, JOAD, 'Introduction', in Jeroen Salman, Roeland Harms, and Joad Raymond (eds.), *Not dead things: the dissemination of popular print in England and Wales, Italy, and the Low Countries, 1500–1820* (Leiden: Brill, 2013), 1–29.

SANDERS, EVE RACHELE, *Gender and literacy on stage in early modern England* (Cambridge: Cambridge University Press, 1998).

SANGALLI, MAURIZIO, *Cultura, politica e religione nella Repubblica di Venezia tra Cinque e Seicento: Gesuiti e Somaschi a Venezia* (Venice: Istituto veneto di scienze, lettere ed arti, 1999).

SANGALLI, MAURIZIO, *Università, accademie, gesuiti: cultura e religione a Padova tra Cinque e Seicento* (Trieste: LINT, 2001).

SANGIORGI, FERT (ed.), *Diario di Francesco Maria II della Rovere* (Urbino: QuattroVenti, 1989).

SANKOVITCH, TILDE, ' "Un travail vétilleux […] fort nécessaire": The Coste Edition of 1724', *Montaigne Studies*, 7 (1995), 131–45.

SARPI, PAOLO, *Istoria del Concilio Tridentino seguita dalla 'Vita del padre Paolo' di Fulgenzio Micanzio*, ed. Corrado Vivanti, 2 vols. (Turin: Giulio Einaudi, 1974).

SAUNDERS, DAVID, 'The judicial *persona* in historical context: the case of Matthew Hale', in Conal Condren, Stephen Gaukroger, and Ian Hunter (eds.), *The philosopher in early modern Europe: the nature of a contested identity* (Cambridge: Cambridge University Press, 2006), 140–59.

SAVELLI, RODOLFO, 'The censoring of law books', in Gigliola Fragnito (ed.), *Church censorship and culture in early modern Italy* (Cambridge: Cambridge University Press, 2001), 223–53.

SCAGLIA, GIACOMO, *Breve racconto dell'amicitia, mostruosa nella perfettione, trà N. Barbarigo & M. Trivisano, gloriosi figliuoli della nobiltà Venetiana* (Venice: Francesco Baba, 1627).

SCALIGER, JULIUS CÆSAR, *Poemata in duas partes divisa* ([Geneva]: [Jacob Stoer for Gaspard de Hus], 1574).

SCALIGER, JULIUS CÆSAR, *Poemata in duas partes divisa* ([Geneva]: [Jacob Stoer] for Pierre de Saint-André, 1591).

SCALIGER, JULIUS CÆSAR, *Poemata in duas partes divisa* ([Heidelberg/Geneva]: in Bibliopolio Commeliniano, 1600).

SCHAEFER, DAVID LEWIS, *The political philosophy of Montaigne* (Ithaca: Cornell University Press, 1990).

SCHALK, FRITZ (ed.), *Ideen und Formen; Festschrift für Hugo Friedrich zum 24. XII. 1964* (Frankfurt: V. Klostermann, 1965).

SCHINO, ANNA LISA, 'Incontri italiani di Gabriel Naudé', *Rivista di Storia della Filosofia*, 44 (1989), 3–36.

SCHMITT, CHARLES B., *Aristotle and the Renaissance* (Cambridge, MA: Harvard University Press, 1983).

SCHOLAR, RICHARD, *Montaigne and the art of free-thinking* (Long Hanborough, Oxon.: Peter Lang, 2010).

SCHOTTE, MARGARET, ' "Books for the use of the learned and studious": William London's *Catalogue of Most Vendible Books*', *Book History*, 11 (2008), 33–57.

SCHURINK, FRED, 'The intimacy of manuscript and the pleasure of print: literary culture from *The Schoolmaster* to *Euphues*', in Michael Pincombe and Cathy Shrank (eds.), *The Oxford handbook of Tudor literature, 1485–1603* (Oxford: Oxford University Press, 2009), 671–86.

SCOTT-WARREN, JASON, *Sir John Harington and the book as gift* (Oxford: Oxford University Press, 2001).

SCRAGG, LEAH, 'Edward Blount and the history of Lylian criticism', *The Review of English Studies*, 46/181 (1995), 1–10.

SCREECH, M. A., *Montaigne and melancholy: the wisdom of the 'Essays'* (London: Duckworth, 1983).

SEITZ, CHARLES, *Joseph Juste Scaliger et Genève* (Geneva: Georg et Compagnie, 1895).

SELWYN, PAMELA and SELWYN, DAVID, ' "The profession of a gentleman": books for the gentry and the nobility (*c.*1560 to 1640)', in Elizabeth Leedham-Green and Teresa Webber (eds.), *The Cambridge history of libraries in Britain and Ireland: Volume I to 1650* (Cambridge: Cambridge University Press, 2006), 489–515.

SENECA, LUCIUS ANNAEUS, *Les œuvres morales et meslees*, 3 vols. ([Geneva]: J. Arnaud, 1606).

SERRAI, ALFREDO, 'La Biblioteca di Francesco Maria II a Casteldurante', in M. Mei and F. Paoli (eds.), *La libraria di Francesco Maria II Della Rovere a Casteldurante. Da collezione ducale a biblioteca della città* (Urbino: Quattroventi, 2008), 15–40.

SHAKESPEARE, WILLIAM, *The tragicall historie of Hamlet Prince of Denmarke* (London: [Valentine Simmes] for N[icholas] L[ing] and John Trundell, 1603).

SHAKESPEARE, WILLIAM, *The tragicall historie of Hamlet... Newly imprinted and enlarged to almost as much againe as it was, according to the true and perfect coppie* (London: James Roberts, 1604).

SHAKESPEARE, WILLIAM, *True chronicle history of the life and death of King Lear and his three daughters* (London: Nathaniel Butter, 1608).

SHAKESPEARE, WILLIAM, *Comedies, histories, and tragedies*, eds. Henry Condell and John Heminge (London: Isaac Jaggard and Edward Blount, 1623).

SHAKESPEARE, WILLIAM, *Hamlet*, ed. Harold Jenkins (London: Methuen, 1982).

SHAKESPEARE, WILLIAM, *The Tempest*, ed. Stephen Orgel (Oxford: Oxford University Press, 1987).

SHARPE, KEVIN, *Reading revolutions: the politics of reading in early modern England* (New Haven: Yale University Press, 2000).

SHARPE, KEVIN and ZWICKER, STEVEN N., 'Introduction: discovering the Renaissance reader', in Kevin Sharpe and Steven N. Zwicker (eds.), *Reading, society, and politics in early modern England* (Cambridge: Cambridge University Press, 2003), 1–38.

SHELFORD, APRIL, *Transforming the republic of letters: Pierre-Daniel Huet and European intellectual life, 1650–1720* (Rochester, NY: University of Rochester Press, 2007).

SHERMAN, WILLIAM H., *John Dee: the politics of reading and writing in the English Renaissance* (Amherst: University of Massachusetts Press, 1995).

SHERMAN, WILLIAM H., 'Used Books', *Shakespeare Studies*, 28 (2000), 145–8.

SIDNEY HERBERT, MARY, *The collected works Vol. 1: Poems, translations, and correspondence*, eds. Margaret P. Hannay, Noel J. Kinnamon, and Michael G. Brennan (Oxford: Clarendon, 1998).

SIDNEY, PHILIP, *The defence of poesie* (London: William Ponsonby, 1595).

SIMIZ, STEFANO, 'Jean Maillefer, dévot et honnête homme rémois au XVIIe siècle', in F. Gugelot and B. Maës (eds.), *Passion de la découverte, culture de l'échange. Mélanges offerts à Nicole Moine et Claire Prévotat* (Langres: Dominique Guéniot 2006), 223–33.

SIMONIN, MICHEL, 'Les contrefaçons lyonnaises de Montaigne et Ronsard au temps de la Ligue', in François Moureau (ed.), *Les presses grises* (Paris: Aux Amateurs de Livres, 1988), 139–59.

SIMONIN, MICHEL, 'Œuvres complètes or plus que complètes?: Montaigne éditeur de La Boétie', *Montaigne Studies*, 7 (1995), 5–34.

SIMONIN, MICHEL, *L'encre & la lumière: quarante-sept articles, 1976–2000* (Geneva: Droz, 2004).

SIMPSON, JAMES, *Burning to read: English fundamentalism and its Reformation opponents* (Cambridge, MA: Belknap Press of Harvard University Press, 2007).

SLINGSBY, HENRY, *A father's legacy.... Instructions to his sonnes. Written a little before his death* (London: J. Grismond, 1658).

SLINGSBY, HENRY, *The diary... A reprint of Sir Henry Slingsby's trial, his rare tract 'A father's legacy.' Written in the Tower immediately before his death, and extracts from family correspondence and papers, with notices, and a genealogical memoir*, ed. Daniel Parsons (London: Longman, Rees, Orme, Brown, Green, and Longman, 1836).

SMITH, GEOFFREY RIDSDILL, *Without touch of dishonour. The life and death of Sir Henry Slingsby, 1602–1658* (Kineton: Roundwood Press, 1968).

SMITH, MALCOLM, *Montaigne and the Roman censors* (Geneva: Droz, 1981).

SMITH, P. J., '"Son dire au faict de la langue françoise est admirable": Pieter van Veen, lecteur de Montaigne', paper given at 'La langue de Rabelais et de Montaigne', 'La Sapienza' University, Rome, 13–19 September 2003.

SMITH, PAUL. J., 'Introduction: Montaigne and the Low Countries—synopsis and new perspectives', in Paul. J. Smith and Karl A. E. Enenkel (eds.), *Montaigne and the Low Countries (1580–1700)* (Leiden: Brill, 2007), 1–15.

SMYTH, ADAM, *Autobiography in early modern England* (Cambridge: Cambridge University Press, 2010).

SNOOK, EDITH, *Women, reading, and the cultural politics of early modern England* (Farnham: Ashgate, 2005).

SOLL, JACOB, *Publishing the Prince: history, reading, and the birth of political criticism* (Ann Arbor: University of Michigan Press, 2005).

SOMAN, ALFRED, 'Pierre Charron: A reevaluation', *Bibliothèque d'Humanisme et Renaissance*, 32 (1970), 57–79.

SOMAN, ALFRED, 'The London edition of De Thou's history: a critique of some well-documented legends', *Renaissance Quarterly*, 24 (1971), 1–12.

SOMAN, ALFRED, *De Thou and the Index. Letters from Christophe Dupuy, (1603–1607)* (Geneva: Droz, 1972).

SOMAN, ALFRED, 'Press, pulpit, and censorship in France before Richelieu', *Proceedings of the American Philosophical Society*, 120/6 (1976), 439–63.

SOREL, CHARLES, *La bibliotheque françoise* (Paris: Compagnie des Libraires du Palais, 1664).

SOULARD, DELPHINE, 'Anglo-French cultural transmission: the case of John Locke and the Huguenots', *Historical Research*, 85 (2012), 105–32.

SPENCE, RICHARD T., *Lady Anne Clifford, Countess of Pembroke, Dorset and Montgomery (1590–1676)* (Stroud, Gloucestershire: Sutton, 1997).

SPENCER, THEODORE, 'Montaigne in America', *The Atlantic Monthly* 177/3 (1947), 91–7.

STAROBINSKI, JEAN, *Montaigne in motion*, trans. Arthur Goldhammer (Chicago: University of Chicago Press, 1985).

STECCA, LUCIANO, 'Montaigne e Flavio Querenghi', in *Montaigne e l'Italia: atti del congresso internazionale di studi di Milano-Lecco, 26–30 ottobre 1988* (Geneva: Slatkine; Centro interuniversitario di ricerche sul 'Viaggio in Italia', 1991), 83–101.

STECCA, LUCIANO, *Tradizione e innovazione: studi sulla cultura francese e italiana tra Cinque e Seicento* (Padua: CLEUP, 1996).

STEINBERG, JUSTIN, *Accounting for Dante: urban readers and writers in late medieval Italy* (Notre Dame, IN: University of Notre Dame Press, 2007).

STEINER, EMILY, *Documentary culture and the making of medieval English literature* (Cambridge: Cambridge University Press, 2003).

STEPHENS, R. C., 'John Locke and the education of the gentleman', *The University of Leeds Institute of Education: Researches and Studies*, 14 (1956), 67–75.

STEWART, ALAN, *Philip Sidney: a double life* (London: Chatto & Windus, 2000).

STEWART, J. I. M., 'Montaigne's *Essays* and *A Defence of Ryme*', *The Review of English Studies*, o.s. 9 (1933), 311–12.

STOPP, FREDERICK JOHN, *The emblems of the Altdorf Academy: medals and medal orations, 1577–1626* (London: Modern Humanities Research Association, 1974).

SZABARI, ANTONIA, *Less rightly said: scandals and readers in sixteenth-century France* (Stanford: Stanford University Press, 2010).

T., M., *The true narration of the entertainment of his Royall Majestie, from the time of his departure from Edenbrough; till his receiving at London* (London: Thomas Creede for Thomas Millington, 1603).

TACITUS, CORNELIUS, *Opere…Annali, Historie, Costumi de'Germani, e Vita di Agricola; illustrate con notabilissime aforismi del Signor D. B. A. Varienti; trasportati dalla lingua Castigliana nella Toscana*, ed. G. Canini (Venice: Appresso i Giunti, 1628).

TAYLOR, BARRY, 'Learning style from the Spaniards in sixteenth-century England', in S. K. Barker and Brenda Hosington (eds.), *Renaissance cultural crossroads: translation, print and culture in Britain, 1473–1640* (Leiden: Brill, 2013), 63–78.

THORPE, L., 'Pieter van Veen's copy of Montaigne', *Rivista di letterature moderne*, 3, second series (1952), 168–79.

THOU, JACQUES AUGUSTE DE, *Historiarum sui temporis pars I*, 2 vols. (Paris: Ambrose and Jerome Drouart, 1604).

THOU, JACQUES AUGUSTE DE, *Historiarum sui temporis tomi secundi*, 2 vols. (Paris: Ambrose and Jerome Drouart, 1606).

THOU, JACQUES AUGUSTE DE, *Historiarum sui temporis ab Anno Domini 1543 usque ad annum 1607 libri CXXXVIII*, 5 vols. ([Geneva]: de la Rovière, 1620).

THOU, JACQUES AUGUSTE DE, *Historiarum sui temporis libri CXXXVIII*, ed. Thomas Carte, 7 vols. (London: Samuel Buckley, 1733).

THOU, JACQUES AUGUSTE DE, *Choix de lettres françoises inédites*, ed. Paulin Paris (Paris: Société des Bibliophiles, 1877).

THOU, JACQUES AUGUSTE DE, *La vie de Jacques-Auguste de Thou = I. Aug. Thuani vita*, ed. Anne Teissier-Ensminger (Paris: H. Champion, 2007).

TINSLEY, BARBARA SHER, *History and polemics in the French Reformation: Florimond de Raemond, defender of the Church* (Cranbury, NJ, London and Mississuaga, Ontario: Associated University Presses, 1992).

TIPPELSKIRCH, XENIA VON, *Sotto controllo: letture femminili in Italia nella prima età moderna* (Rome: Viella, 2011).

TOMASINI, GIACOMO FILIPPO, *Petrarcha Redivivus* (Padua: Paolo Frambotto, 1635).

TOURNON, ANDRÉ, 'Le grammarien, le jurisconsulte et l'humaine condition', *Bulletin de la Société des Amis de Montaigne*, 7th series, 21–2 (1990), 107–18.

TREVOR, DOUGLAS, 'Love, anger and cruelty in "De l'affection des peres aux enfans" and *King Lear*', *Montaigne Studies*, 24 (2012), 51–66.

TUDEAU-CLAYTON, MARGARET, *Jonson, Shakespeare and early modern Virgil* (Cambridge: Cambridge University Press, 1998).

TURCHETTI, MARIO, 'Une question mal posée: L'origine et l'identité des politiques au temps des guerres de religion', in Thierry Wanegffelen (ed.), *De Michel de L'Hospital à l'édit de Nantes: politique et religion face aux églises* (Clermont-Ferrand: Presses Universitaires Blaise-Pascal, 2002), 357–90.

TURNER, JAMES GRANTHAM, *Schooling sex: libertine literature and erotic education in Italy, France, and England, 1534–1685* (Oxford: Oxford University Press, 2003).

VALDÉS, JUAN DE, *The hundred and ten considerations*, trans. Nicholas Ferrar (Oxford: Leonard Lichfield, 1638).

VALLANCE, EDWARD, *Revolutionary England and the national covenant: state oaths, Protestantism, and the political nation, 1553–1682* (Woodbridge: Boydell Press, 2005).

VAN HECK, PAUL, 'The *Essais* in Italian: the Translation of Girolamo Canini', *Montaigne Studies*, 23 (2011), 39–53.

VARCHI, BENEDETTO, *The blazon of jealousie... with speciall notes upon the same*, trans. Robert Tofte (London: T[homas] S[nodham] for John Busbie, 1615).

VENESOEN, CONSTANT (ed.), *Marie de Gournay: Textes relatifs à la calomnie* (Tübingen: Gunter Narr Verlag, 1998).

VERONESE CESERACCIU, EMILIA, 'La biblioteca di Flavio Querenghi, professore di filosofia morale (1624–1647) nello Studio di Padova', *Quaderni per la storia dell'università di Padova*, 9–10 (1976–77), 185–213.

VIDAL, GORE, 'Uncommon Sense: The charitable clarity of Montaigne's perceptions', *Times Literary Supplement*, 26 June 1992.

VIDAL, GORE, *United States: Essays, 1952–1992* (2nd edn., New York: Broadway Books, 2001).

VIGNEULLES, PHILIPPE DE, *Les cent nouvelles nouvelles*, eds. Robert H. Ivy, Charles H. Livingston, and Françoise H. Livingston (Geneva: Droz, 1972).

VILLEY, PIERRE, *Montaigne et François Bacon* (Paris: Revue de la Renaissance, 1913).

VILLEY, PIERRE, *Montaigne devant la postérité* (Paris: Ancienne librairie Furne, Boivin et Compagnie, 1935).

VON HABSBURG, MAXIMILIAN, *Catholic and Protestant translations of the Imitatio Christi, 1425–1650: from late medieval classic to early modern bestseller* (Farnham: Ashgate, 2012).

VOUGT, G., 'Primacy of individual conscience or primacy of the state? The clash between Dirck Volckertsz. Coornhert and Justus Lipsius', *Sixteenth Century Journal*, 28/4 (1997), 1231–49.

WAKE, ISAAC, *Rex Platonicus: sive, de potentissimi Principis Iacobi Britanniarum Regis, ad illustrissimam Academiam Oxoniensem, adventu, Aug. 27. Anno. 1605* (Oxford: Joseph Barnes, 1607).

WANEGFFELEN, THIERRY, *Ni Rome ni Genève: des fidèles entre deux chaires en France au XVIe siècle* (Paris: H. Champion, 1997).

WANEGFFELEN, THIERRY (ed.), *De Michel de L'Hospital à l'édit de Nantes: politique et religion face aux églises* (Clermont-Ferrand: Presses Universitaires Blaise-Pascal, 2002).

WARD, JOHN, *The lives of the professors of Gresham College* (London: John Moore for the Author and W. Innys et al., 1740).

WARNER, LYNDAN, *The ideas of man and woman in Renaissance France: print, rhetoric, and law* (Farnham: Ashgate, 2011).

WATERFIELD, GILES, *Art treasures of England: the regional collections* (London: Merrell Holberton, 1998).

WEINRICH, MARTINUS, *De ortu monstrorum commentarius* ([Leipzig]: Osthusius, 1595).

WHITE, HAYDEN, 'Auerbach's literary history: figural causation and modernist historicism', in Seth Lerer (ed.), *Literary history and the challenge of philology: the legacy of Erich Auerbach* (Stanford: Stanford University Press, 1996), 124–39.

WHITE, MICHELINE (ed.), *English women, religion, and textual production, 1500–1625* (Farnham: Ashgate, 2011).

WHITE, PAUL, 'From Commentary to Translation: Figurative Representations of the Text in the French Renaissance', in Tania Demetriou and Rowan Tomlinson (eds.), *The culture of translation in early modern England and France, 1500–1660* (Basingstoke: Palgrave Macmillan, 2015), 71–85.

WILLIAMSON, GEORGE C., *Lady Anne Clifford, Countess of Dorset, Pembroke & Montgomery, 1590–1676: her life, letters and work* (Kendal: Titus Wilson, 1922).

WITKAM, H. J., *Immatriculatie en recensie in de Leidse Universiteit van 1575 tot 1581* (Leiden: H.J. Witkam, 1975).

WITT, RONALD G., *The two Latin cultures and the foundation of Renaissance humanism in medieval Italy* (Cambridge: Cambridge University Press, 2012).

WOOLFSON, JONATHAN, *Padua and the Tudors: English students in Italy, 1485–1603* (Toronto: University of Toronto Press, 1998).

WOOTTON, DAVID, 'New histories of atheism', in Michael Hunter and David Wootton (eds.), *Atheism from the Reformation to the Enlightenment* (Oxford: Clarendon, 1992), 13–53.

WORCESTER, THOMAS, 'In praise of Montaigne: Bishop Jean-Pierre Camus', in Keith Cameron and Laura Lee Willett (eds.), *Le visage changeant de Montaigne/The changing face of Montaigne* (Paris: Honoré Champion, 2003), 277–86.

WOUDHUYSEN, H. R., *Sir Philip Sidney and the circulation of manuscripts, 1558–1640* (Oxford: Clarendon Press, 1996).

WRIGHT, NANCY E., 'Accounting for a life: the household accounts of Lady Anne Clifford', in Ronald Bedford, Lloyd Davis, and Philippa Kelly (eds.), *Early modern autobiography: theories, genres, practices* (Ann Arbor: University of Michigan Press, 2006), 234–51.

WRIGHTSMAN, BRUCE, 'Andreas Osiander's contribution to the Copernican achievement', in Robert S. Westman (ed.), *The Copernican achievement* (Berkeley: University of California Press, 1975), 213–43.

YATES, FRANCES A., *John Florio: the life of an Italian in Shakespeare's England* (Cambridge: Cambridge University Press, 1934).

YEO, RICHARD, 'John Locke and polite philosophy', in Conal Condren, Stephen Gaukroger, and Ian Hunter (eds.), *The philosopher in early modern Europe: the nature of a contested identity* (Cambridge: Cambridge University Press, 2006), 254–75.

ZEN BENETTI, FRANCESCA, 'Nuove ricerche sull'anatomico fiammingo Adriaan van den Spieghel (1578–1625)', *Quaderni per la storia dell'università di Padova*, 5 (1972), 45–71.

ZIEGLER, GEORGIANNA, 'En-Gendering the subject: florio's feminization of Montaigne's "Moy-mesmes"', *Montaigne Studies*, 8 (1996), 125–43.

ZUBER, ROGER, 'Tombeau pour des Pithou: Frontières confessionnelles et unité religieuse (1590–1600)', in Verdun L. Saulnier (ed.), *Mélanges sur la littérature de la Renaissance à la mémoire de V.-L. Saulnier* (Geneva: Droz, 1984), 331–42.

ZUCCOLO, LODOVICO, *Dialoghi... ne' quali con varietà di eruditione si scoprono nuovi, e vaghi pensieri filosofici, morali, e politici* (Venice: Marco Ginammi, 1625).

ZWICKER, STEVEN, 'Habits of reading and early modern literary culture', in David Loewenstein and Janel M. Mueller (eds.), *The Cambridge history of early modern English literature* (Cambridge: Cambridge University Press, 2002), 170–98.

Index

References to the pagination of *The School of Montaigne* include the volume number in small Roman numerals, followed by the page number (e.g. i. xliii). References to the *Essais* are to the 1595 text unless stated in parentheses.

For references to places visited by Montaigne on his 1580–1 voyage, see the entry on the *Journal de voyage*.

Bold type is used for the principal discussions of a headword or subentry. Italic type is used for references to illustrations.

Asterisks indicate the main thematic entries.

512   *Index*

Montaigne, Michel de (*cont.*)
  translation of Sebond *see* Sebond, Raymond
  as unofficial physician i. 11
  use of books i. 23, 41
  voyage see *Journal de voyage*
  see also conversation; *Essais*; friendship; *imago*
    and *imagines*; *Journal de voyage*; *liberté*
    and *franchise*; liberty of judgement; La
    Boétie, Étienne de; Lipsius, Justus (letters
    to Montaigne); offices; *persona*; practical
    and moral philosophy; school and
    schools; Sebond, Raymond; Seneca and
    Plutarch; Socrates
Montefeltro, Federico da i. 109; ii. 422
Monti, Brigitte ii. 296 n. 70
moral philosophy *see* practical and moral
  philosophy
More, Thomas i. 126
  Utopia (1516) i. lxii
Morel, Fédéric (bookseller) ii. 43
Moresini, Andrea (Venetian noble) ii. 143–4
Moulin, Charles Du
  censorship of works at Rome i. 290
Mountjoys, family and house of *see* Blount
Munro, Lucy ii. 258
Muret, Marc-Antoine i. 277, 280, 281; ii. 202
  annotated books of i. 280 and 280 n. 71
  defence of Tacitus i. 283
  lectures on Seneca i. 277
  letter to Chasteigner (1583) i. 280–1
  see also Seneca

Nakam, Géralde i. 106
Namatianus, Claudius Rutilius
  Itinerarium i. 311
Naselli, Girolamo (diplomat and translator)
  ii. 136–7
naturalia see index and indexes
naturel see Montaigne, Michel de (character and
  qualities)
Naudé, Gabriel ii. 182, 469
  Advis pour dresser une bibliotheque (1627) i.
    134, 270, 273; ii. 182–3
  Bibliographia politica (1633) ii. 183–4, 423
  copy of Querenghi's *Alchimia* ii. 174–5,
    175 n. 303, 183
Navarre, King of *see* Henri IV
Navarre (court) i. 156–7, 159
Nelles, Paul i. 19 n. 48
Neville, Sir Henry i. 140
Neville, Lady Mary ii. 198, **199**,
  238, 249–50
Nevilles, family and house of ii. 200,
  209, 249
*nexus and nexuses i. xvii–xviii, **xliii**, lix, lxxi,
  lxxiv–lxxv, 10–11, 15, 27, 62, 66–7, **91–3**,
  127, 173, 239; ii. **xxxiii**, 145, 161, 400–1,
  408–9, 466
  of Amyot's Plutarch i. 317

of the *Essais* (including all copies, editions,
  and translations except London
  1603) i. xx, lxxiv, lxxvii, 20–1, 53, 61–2,
  172, 228, 267–8, 292, **317–18**; ii. 3, 19,
  21, 75–6, 134, 136, 142, **145–8**, 150,
  152, **185–8**, 308, 316, 326–7, **389–90**,
  395, **407–11**, 412–13, 416–17, 418,
  425–7, 463, **467**, 472
of the *Essayes* i. xx; ii. 200, 209, 219, 252,
  254, 283
in French parliamentary networks ii. 25
of La Boétie's work i. 256, 317–18
of learning ii. 187, 442
of the making of books i. 61, 117, 292
of modern French scholarship i. 88
of Montaigne, Lipsius, and Gournay's works
  in 1588 i. 228
Montaigne's concept of i. 106, 107
of reading-and-writing i. 41, 175, 178, 224;
  ii. 33–4, 76, 417
of Sebond's work i. 58–9, 317
of Vasco de Quiroga's copy of *Utopia*
  i. lxxi
see also agency; Gell, Alfred; index and
  indexes
Newton, Adam (tutor and secretary) ii. 223
  n. 109, 231 n. 130, 242
nobility
  and diplomacy (women) ii. 198, 239
  in the sixteenth century i. 15
  see also *Essais*; learning; reading and writing
Norton, Grace i. 75

*offices (duties) i. **xliii–xliv**, 43–4, 66, 172,
  244; ii. **xxxiii–xxxiv**, 24, 34, 67, 272, 325
  n. 6, 368–9, 400, 413, 416, 434–6, 449,
  455, **457–9**
  of friendship in relation to writings i. 233–4;
    ii. 80
  in Montaigne (including *offices sans nom*)
    i. xx, **10–11**, 21, 53, 98–9, 139–40,
    148–51, 155, 162–3, **164–8**, 173, 179,
    187, 191, 201, 241–2, 247, 250, 314; ii.
    32–3, 60, 77, 216, 250, 408, 411,
    413–14, 417, 459, 468
  of philosophy i. liii, lx, **13–16**; ii. 142–4,
    162–3, 170–1, 177–8, 200, 409, 429–30,
    459, **469**
  see also friendship; learning (as knowledge
    services); performance; practical and moral
    philosophy
office sans nom see offices
oisiveté see idleness
Orsini, Fulvio i. 104
Ortelius, Abraham ii. 299
Ossat, Arnaud d' i. 223, 283; ii. 15–16, 39, 48,
  160–1
otium see learning (and leisure)
Oxford ii. 258–9